Fodor's 2013
COSTA RICA

Fodor's Travel Publications   New York, Toronto, London, Sydney, Auckland
www.fodors.com

FODOR'S COSTA RICA 2013

Writers: Leland Baxter-Neal, Gillian Gillers, Liz Goodwin, Dorothy MacKinnon, Holly Sonneland, Mark Sullivan, Jeffrey Van Fleet

Editor: Margaret Kelly

Production Editor: Jennifer DePrima
Maps & Illustrations: David Lindroth, Mark Stroud, *cartographers;* Rebecca Baer, *map editor;* William Wu, *information graphics*
Design: Fabrizio La Rocca, *creative director;* Tina Malaney, Chie Ushio, Jessica Ramirez, *designers;* Melanie Marin, *associate director of photography;* Jennifer Romains, *photo research*
Cover Photo: (Man on Zipline): Randy Faris/Corbis
Production Manager: Angela L. McLean

COPYRIGHT
Copyright © 2013 by Fodor's Travel, a division of Random House, Inc.

Fodor's is a registered trademark of Random House, Inc.

All rights reserved. Published in the United States by Fodor's Travel, a division of Random House, Inc., and in Canada by Random House of Canada, Limited, Toronto. Distributed by Random House, Inc., New York.

Some content provided by TripAdvisor.com®. Copyright © 2012 TripAdvisor, LLC. All rights reserved.

No maps, illustrations, or other portions of this book may be reproduced in any form without written permission from the publisher.

ISBN 978-0-307-92941-9

ISSN 1522–6131

SPECIAL SALES
This book is available at special discounts for bulk purchases for sales promotions or premiums. Special editions, including personalized covers, excerpts of existing books, and corporate imprints, can be created in large quantities for special needs. For more information, write to Special Markets/Premium Sales, 1745 Broadway, MD 3-1, New York, NY 10019, or e-mail specialmarkets@randomhouse.com.

AN IMPORTANT TIP & AN INVITATION
Although all prices, opening times, and other details in this book are based on information supplied to us at press time, changes occur all the time in the travel world, and Fodor's cannot accept responsibility for facts that become outdated or for inadvertent errors or omissions. So **always confirm information when it matters,** especially if you're making a detour to visit a specific place. Your experiences—positive and negative—matter to us. If we have missed or misstated something, **please write to us.** Share your opinion instantly through our online feedback center at fodors.com/contact-us.

PRINTED IN CHINA

10 9 8 7 6 5 4 3 2 1

CONTENTS

MAPS

ABOUT THIS GUIDE

Fodor's Ratings

Everything in this guide is worth doing—we don't cover what isn't—but exceptional sights, hotels, and restaurants are recognized with additional accolades. **Fodor's Choice** ★ indicates our top recommendations; ★ highlights places we deem **Highly Recommended**; and **Best Bets** call attention to notable hotels and restaurants in various categories. Care to nominate a new place? Visit Fodors.com/contact-us.

Trip Costs

We list prices wherever possible to help you budget well. Hotel and restaurant price categories from $ to $$$$ are noted alongside each recommendation. For hotels, we include the lowest cost of a standard double room in high season. For restaurants, we cite the average price of a main course at dinner or, if dinner isn't served, at lunch. For attractions, we always list adult admission fees; discounts are usually available for children, students, and senior citizens.

Hotels

Our local writers vet every hotel to recommend the best overnights in each price category, from budget to expensive. Unless otherwise specified, you can expect private bath, phone, and TV in your room. For expanded hotel reviews, facilities, and deals visit Fodors.com.

TripAdvisor 🕉

Our expert hotel picks are reinforced by high ratings on TripAdvisor. Look for representative quotes in this guide, and the latest TripAdvisor ratings and feedback at Fodors.com.

Ratings
★ Fodor's Choice
★ Highly recommended
☺ Family-friendly

Listings
✉ Address
✉ Branch address
✆ Mailing address
☎ Telephone
🖷 Fax
⊕ Website
✎ E-mail
✐ Admission fee
☉ Open/closed times
Ⓜ Subway
✛ Directions or Map coordinates

Hotels & Restaurants
🛏 Hotel
⌲ Number of rooms
🍽 Meal plans
✕ Restaurant
⌣ Reservations
🏛 Dress code
⊟ No credit cards
$ Price

Other
⇨ See also
☞ Take note
🏌 Golf facilities

Restaurants

Unless we state otherwise, restaurants are open for lunch and dinner daily. We mention dress code only when there's a specific requirement and reservations only when they're essential or not accepted. To make restaurant reservations, visit Fodors.com.

Credit Cards

The hotels and restaurants in this guide typically accept credit cards. If not, we'll say so.

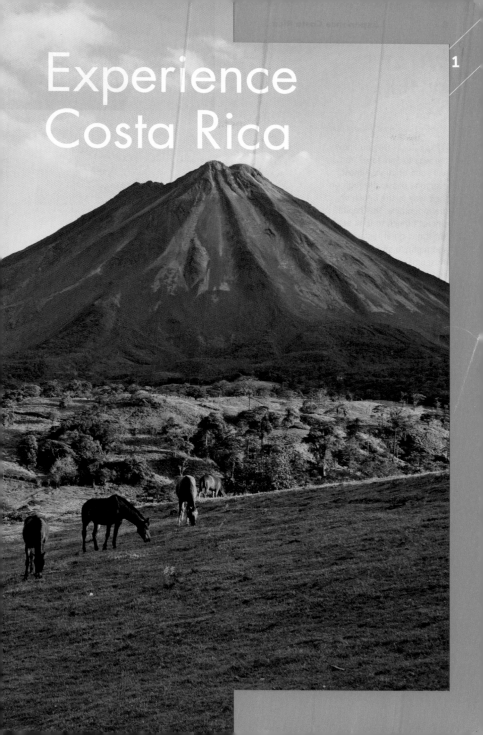

Experience
Costa Rica

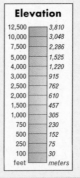

WHAT'S WHERE

Numbers correspond to chapters.

3 San José. Do you know the way to San José? You will soon enough. Almost everyone passes through on their way to the beach or the mountains. This capital city isn't much to look at, but it has great restaurants and nightlife, and fascinating museums dedicated to gold and jade.

4 The Central Valley. You won't want to linger long in the Central Valley, as it lacks any of the country's big-name attractions. But there are quite a few day-trip possibilities, including exploring mountain villages, rafting through white-water rapids, and gaping into the mouths of some of the country's most accessible active volcanoes.

5 The Northern Plains. The Northern Plains attract those who don't like sitting still. After zipping along cables through the misty jungle of Monteverde Cloud Forest, windsurfing on glittering Lake Arenal, or watching the nightly fireworks of Arenal Volcano, you can reward yourself with a dip in the bubbly waters of Tabacón Hot Springs.

6 The North Pacific. If you came for beaches, the Northern Pacific is for you. Each has a unique personality: Flamingo's endless stretch

Elevation	
12,500	3,810
10,000	3,048
7,500	2,286
5,000	1,525
4,000	1,220
3,000	915
2,500	762
2,000	610
1,500	457
1,000	305
750	230
500	152
250	75
100	30
feet	meters

of sand draws sun worshippers; Tamarindo's nightlife is legendary; Avellanas's strong swells challenge surfers; Ostional's nesting sea turtles bring nature lovers; and the Papagayo Peninsula's all-inclusive resorts provide every creature comfort.

7 The Central Pacific. The area's not just for spring breakers (although it helps in funky surf towns like Jacó). Drive down the coast to the cluster of small hotels and restaurants at Manuel Antonio. The national park, on a peninsula jutting into the ocean, has the easiest wildlife viewing on the planet.

8 The South Pacific. Also known as "the Amazon of Costa Rica," rustic lodges in the Osa Peninsula sit on the edge of the country's wildest region. Hikes reveal toucans and scarlet macaws in the treetops, and boating trips often include swimming with whales and dolphins.

9 The Caribbean. Despite its name, Costa Rica's Caribbean isn't known for white-sand beaches or crystal-blue waters. Come here for the spirited music, the tasty food, and the chance to mix with the Afro-Caribbean population. The coast also attracts turtle-watchers, as four different kinds nest at Tortuguero National Park.

COSTA RICA PLANNER

When to Go

High Season: Mid-December to April
The sunniest, driest season in most of the country occurs from mid-December through April, with Christmas and Easter bracketing the busiest tourist season. March and April get downright sweltering in lowland areas, with temperatures in the arid North Pacific, Costa Rica's hottest region, frequently exceeding 33°C (90°F).

Low Season: May to mid-December
In a stroke of marketing genius, Costa Rica promotes the rainy season as the "green season," touting lush vegetation, smaller crowds, and lower prices. Afternoon showers kick in by May and last through November most everywhere, with a brief drier season in June and July. Rain or not, North American and European summer vacations do increase the influx of visitors from June through August. Rains become more prolonged and heavy in September and October.

Shoulder Season: May, mid-November to mid-December
The transition periods between rainy and dry seasons and back again make a marvelous time to visit Costa Rica. Visitor numbers are smaller and the threat of rain does exist but is minimal.

Getting Here

San José's Aeropuerto Internacional Juan Santamaría is in the center of the country, so it's especially convenient for destinations in the Central Valley and along the Central Pacific. The closest destinations are less than an hour away. The only other international gateway is Liberia's Aeropuerto Internacional Daniel Oduber Quirós in the western part of the country. Flying here makes sense if you're planning to spend most of your time in the North Pacific region.

A relatively small number of travelers arrive in Costa Rica by road, especially with the difficulties taking rental cars between countries. Long-distance buses travel directly to San José from the larger cities in Nicaragua and Panama, but these are arduous journeys. The Managua–to–San José route takes between 8 and 10 hours.

Getting Around

To save time, many people take domestic flights to their ultimate destination. SANSA flies to various destinations from its hubs in San José's Aeropuerto Internacional Juan Santamaría and Liberia's Aeropuerto Internacional Daniel Oduber Quirós. Nature Air flies out of San José's domestic airport, tiny Aeropuerto Tobías Bolaños. Both offer flights to resort areas, especially those near the beaches. Regional airports are very small, sometimes with no terminal at all and a staff that arrives at about the same time as the plane.

Costa Rican towns are connected by regular bus service. Buses between major destinations have comfortable seats and air-conditioning. If you have to transfer along the way, you may get a converted school bus cooled only by the tropical breezes. If you're traveling a long distance, make sure to request a *directo* (express) bus. Otherwise you may stop in every small town along the way.

The country's recently improved highway system means renting a car is a great way to get around. You can travel on your own schedule, stopping where you like. San José and Liberia have rental desks; at smaller airports a representative will meet you and drive you to the nearby office.

Festivals and Celebrations

Every day is a patron saint's day somewhere in Costa Rica, so you may very well see some community's annual *festejo patronal* (patron-saint festival). Listen for the loud firecracker explosion at dawn that kicks off the festivities.

The festivals mirror Costa Rica: devoutly Catholic but increasingly secularized. The festival is a religious tradition and an important part of the day is a Mass and parade where the saint's figure is carried through the streets. That said, there's also bingo games, rickety carnival rides—a certain amount of luck and prayer is in order here—horse parades, and amateurish bullfights.

New Year's Day (*Año Nuevo*). New Year's Day is a time that most Costa Ricans spend with family and friends.

Santa Cruz Fiestas (*Fiestas de Santa Cruz*). Mid-January brings the Santa Cruz Fiestas, with bullfights, rodeos, folk dancing, and marimba music.

Holy Week. Holy Week, or *Semana Santa,* lasting from Palm Sunday through Easter Sunday, is a major observance in Costa Rica, especially on Good Friday, when there are religious processions all over the country. Little is open Thursday and Friday and the country legally goes dry. Make hotel reservations far in advance.

Día de Juan Santamaría. This public holiday, on April 11, commemorating Costa Rica's national hero.

Día del Trabajo. Costa Rica's Labor Day is celebrated on May 1.

Day of the Virgin of the Angels (*Día de la Virgen de los Angeles*). Day of the Virgin of the Angels, on August 2, celebrates Costa Rica's patron saint with religious processions from San José to the Basilica de Nuestra Señora de Los Angeles in Cartago.

Día de las Madres. Costa Rica's reverence for motherhood means that the *Día de las Madres* (Mother's Day) on August 15 is a legal holiday here.

Independence Day (*Día de la Independencia*). Independence Day is celebrated on September 15 with lantern-lighted parades the night before and marching bands throughout the country.

Immaculate Conception (*Inmaculada Concepción de la Virgen María*). Immaculate Conception, on December 8, is observed with Masses to honor the Virgin Mary.

Christmas (*Navidad*). The celebration of Christmas goes on throughout December, and extends into the last week of the month.

Money Matters

The local currency is known as the *colón*. Don't bother getting *colones* before your trip; it's difficult, and the exchange rate outside Costa Rica will be abysmal. However, there are currency exchange booths in the international arrivals terminal of San José's Aeropuerto Internacional Juan Santamaría. The baggage-claim area also has an automatic teller machine that dispenses both dollars and colones.

Most ATMs (*cajero automático*) are linked to both the Cirrus and the Plus networks, so they can be used by holders of most U.S.-issued debit and credit cards. Make sure before you leave that your PIN has four numbers, as most machines don't accept longer ones.

Credit cards are accepted by almost all businesses catering to tourists. Because businesses are charged a hefty fee for credit-card purchases, some will add a small surcharge or impose a minimum purchase amount if you use plastic. It's always a good idea to ask beforehand.

COSTA RICA
TOP ATTRACTIONS

Arenal Volcano

(A) Costa Rica has five active volcanoes, but none put on a show like the Arenal Volcano. During the day you're likely to see smoke billowing from the crater. This doesn't compare with what you'll see at night, when orangey red lava oozes down the perfectly shaped cone. If you're very lucky, the clouds will part long enough for you to spot glowing rocks shooting into the air.

Selvatura Park

(B) Soaring over the treetops on a zip line is a thrilling experience. But canopy tours aren't just for adrenaline junkies. Many rain forests have hanging bridges and elevated platforms to give you a bird's-eye view of the rain forest. Many of the best, like Selvetura, are around Monteverde Cloud Forest Biological Reserve and the Santa Elena Reserve, but others are clustered around Lake Arenal and Manuel Antonio.

Manuel Antonio National Park

(C) Some of the country's most thrilling views can be seen from the trails through Manuel Antonio National Park. As you emerge from the rain forest, don't be surprised to find yourself alone on a palm-shaded beach. Make sure to look up—sloths and three types of monkey make their home in the canopy, and on a good day you might see them all.

Corcovado National Park

(D) Bird-watchers come to this vast and pristine rain forest with hopes of catching a glimpse of the endangered harpy eagle. It's notoriously difficult to see, but other feathered friends—like the scarlet macaw, the orange-bellied trogon, and the golden-hooded tanager—practically pose for pictures. No need to head off into the rain forest with your binoculars; dozens of hummingbirds are likely to dart around you as you relax by the pool.

1

Playa Carrillo

(E) This long, picturesque beach, backed by a line of swaying palms and protective cliffs, is certainly one of the most beautiful stretches of sand in the country. Perfect for swimming, snorkeling, or just walking, the beach isn't marred by a single building. Visit on a weekday and it's possible that you may have the entire shore to yourself.

Nicoya Peninsula

(F) Popular with the sun-and-fun crowd, the peninsula still has a yet-to-be-discovered feel. Maybe that's because its sandy shores are never covered with a checkerboard of beach blankets. Drive a few miles in any direction and you can find one all to yourself. But civilization isn't far away—some of the country's best restaurants are within reach.

Turrialba

(G) Heavy rainfall, steep mountains, and rocky terrain make this region a magnet for white-water rafters, and there's a river to match anyone's level of expertise. Not far from San José, the Central Valley has outfitters who offer everything from easy day trips to challenging multiday excursions. Many of these companies congregate around Turrialba, the country's white-water capital and close to the Rio Pacuare and Rio Reventazón.

Monteverde Cloud Forest Biological Reserve

(H) The roads leading here are terrible, but you won't mind once you see the mist-covered reserve. Because of the constant moisture, this private park is unbelievably lush. It's gorgeous during the day, but many prefer night hikes, when you can see colorful birds asleep in the branches, hairy tarantulas in search of prey, and nocturnal mammals like the wide-eyed kinkajou.

FAQS

Do I need any special documents to get into the country?

Aside from a passport that's valid for at least three months after date of entry and a round-trip/outbound ticket, you don't need anything else to enter the country. You'll be given a 90-day tourist visa as you pass through immigration. You're no longer required to have your passport with you at all times during your trip, but you must carry a photocopy while you're out and about.

How difficult is it to travel around the country?

It's extremely easy. Thanks to the domestic airlines, getting to your ultimate destination takes far less time than just a few years ago; almost every worthwhile spot is within an hour of San José. Long-distance buses and vans are usually very comfortable, so don't overlook these as a way to get to far-flung destinations. Renting a car is a great way to get around, because you're not tied to somebody else's schedule. Alas, roads are not always well marked. It's good to have a detailed map if you're driving in rural areas, as it's easy to miss a turn.

Are the roads as bad as they say?

Yes and no. You'll still find potholes the size of bathtubs on the road leading to Monteverde Cloud Forest Biological Reserve, and the gravel roads on the Nicoya Peninsula are often so grooved by the rain that they feel like an endless series of speed bumps. But roads are improving. The most dramatic improvements have been made near the resort area of Lake Arenal. Repairs to the road between Nuevo Arenal and La Fortuna have cut your travel time almost in half. During and immediately after the rainy season is the worst time for driving. The constant deluge takes its toll on the pavement.

Should I rent a four-wheel-drive vehicle?

Probably. If your trip will take you mostly to the beaches, you won't necessarily need a 4WD vehicle. If you're headed to more-mountainous areas, such as any destination in the Northern Plains, you'll definitely want one. But even on the most badly maintained roads through the mountains, you'll see locals getting around just fine in their beat-up sedans. There's usually only a minor difference in the cost, so there's no reason not to go for the 4WD.

Should I get insurance on the rental car?

Even if your own insurance covers rental cars, go ahead and take full insurance. The cost is often less than $10 a day. For that you get the peace of mind of knowing that you're not going to be hassled for a scratch on the fender or a crack in the windshield. One traveler reported returning a rental car with a front bumper completely detached, and because he had full insurance the clerk just smiled and wished him a good trip home.

Should I consider a package tour?

If you're terrified of traveling on your own, sign up for a tour. But Costa Rica is such an easy place to get around that there's really no need. Part of the fun is the exploring—finding a secluded beach, hiking down to a hidden waterfall, discovering a great craft shop—and that's just not going to happen on a tour. If you're more comfortable with a package tour, pick one with a specific focus, like bird-watching or boating, so that you're less likely to get a generic tour.

Do I need a local guide?

Guides are a great idea for the first-time visitor in search of wildlife. A good guide will know where to find the animals, and will bring along a telescope so that you can

get an up-close look at that sloth high in the trees or the howler monkeys across the clearing. After the first day, however, you'll probably grab your binoculars and head out on your own. It's much more gratifying to tell the folks back home that you discovered that banded anteater all by yourself.

Will I have trouble if I don't speak Spanish?

No *problema*. Most people in businesses catering to tourists speak at least a little English. If you encounter someone who doesn't speak English, they'll probably point you to a coworker who does. Even if you're in a far-flung destination, locals will go out of their way to find somebody who speaks your language.

Can I drink the water?

Costa Rica is the only Central American country where you don't have to get stressed out about drinking the water. The water is potable in all but the most remote regions. That said, many people don't like the taste of the tap water and prefer bottled water.

Are there any worries about the food?

None whatsoever. Even the humblest roadside establishment is likely to be scrupulously clean. If you have any doubts about a place, just move on to the next one. There's no problem enjoying fruit, cheese, bread, or other local products sold from the stands set up along the roads.

Do I need to get any shots?

You probably don't have to get any vaccinations or take any special medications. The U.S. Centers for Disease Control and Prevention warn that there is some concern about malaria, especially in remote areas along the Caribbean coast. If you plan to spend any amount of time there, you may want to talk with your doctors about antimalarial medications well before your trip.

Should I bring any medications?

The only thing we recommend is using an insect repellent containing the active ingredient DEET. Ordinary repellents, even those labeled "extra strength," aren't going to do the trick against the mosquitoes of the tropics. To find a repellent with DEET, your best bet is a sporting goods store rather than your local drugstore. A formulation with 10% to 25% DEET will be fine; those with more are likely to irritate your skin.

Can I use my ATM card?

Most ATMs are on both the Cirrus and Plus networks, so they accept debit and credit cards issued by U.S. banks. Some might accept cards with just the Master-Card or just the Visa logo; if that's the case, try a machine at a different bank. Know the exchange rate before you use an ATM for the first time so that you know about how much local currency you want to withdraw.

Do most places take credit cards?

Almost all tourist-oriented businesses accept credit cards. Smaller restaurants and hotels may not accept them at all. Some businesses don't like to accept credit cards because their banks charge them exorbitant fees for credit-card transactions. They will usually relent and charge you a small fee for the privilege.

COSTA RICA TODAY

Government

Costa Rica is a democratic republic whose structure will be familiar to any citizen of the United States. The 1949 constitution divides the government into independent executive, legislative, and judicial branches. All citizens are guaranteed equality before the law, the right to own property, freedom of speech, and freedom of religion.

Costa Rica elected its first female president in 2010, the fifth of, now, six Latin American countries to take such a step. Centrist candidate Laura Chinchilla, veteran of several posts in previous administrations, won election handily and became the first person here to hold the title La Presidenta. She has continued the pro-business platform and infrastructure development of her predecessor, Oscar Arias.

The country is famous for lacking an army, which was abolished when the constitution was ratified in 1949. The country's stable government and economy have made this possible, even as its neighbors were embroiled in civil war. The country does maintain a small national guard.

Economy

By the mid-1990s, Costa Rica had diversified its economy beyond agriculture and tourism was bringing in more money than its three major cash crops: coffee, bananas, and pineapples. High-tech companies such as Intel, Hewlett-Packard, and Motorola and pharmaceutical companies like Procter & Gamble and GlaxoSmithKline opened plants and service centers in Costa Rica, providing well-paid jobs for educated professionals.

Costa Rica and its Central American neighbors have staked hopes on international free-trade agreements in recent years, most notably with United States in 2008 and the European Union in 2010.

Opponents of the treaties are wary of how much benefit they will provide for the country, however.

The economy continues to bedevil Costa Rica. Although economic growth is on the rise, it still has a $3.9 billion trade deficit and annual inflation of about 6%. Unemployment stands at just under 7%.

Tourism

Today Costa Rica faces the challenge of conserving its natural resources while still permitting modern development. The government has been unable or unwilling to control illegal logging, an industry that threatens to destroy the country's old-growth forests. Urban sprawl in the communities surrounding San José and the development of megaresorts along the Pacific coast threaten forests, wildlife, and the slow pace of life that makes Costa Rica so desirable.

Although tourism injects much-needed foreign cash into the economy, the government has not fully decided the best way to promote its natural wonders. The buzzwords now are not just ecotourism and sustainable development, but also adventure tourism and extreme sports. The two sides do not always see eye to eye.

Religion

Because it was a Spanish colony, Costa Rica continues to have a close relationship to the Catholic Church. Catholicism was made the country's official religion in the country's constitution. Because of this, priests are the only type of clergy authorized to perform civil marriages. (Others require the assistance of a legal official.)

More than 90% of Costa Ricans consider themselves Catholics. But even among this group, most people do not have a strong identification with the church or with its teachings. The live-and-let-live attitude

of most Costa Ricans does not mesh well with religious doctrine. That's also probably why the evangelical churches that have made huge inroads in neighboring countries are not as prevalent here.

Although every village has a church on its main square, it's usually hopping only once a year—when the town's patron saint is honored. These are times for food, music, and dancing in the streets. If the celebrations lack much religious fervor—well, that's Costa Rica for you.

Sports

Like everyone else on this soccer-mad isthmus, Costa Ricans take their game seriously and can get nasty when it comes to their national team; U.S. players reported being pelted with batteries and bags of urine during one game. When the national team returned after humiliating losses in the 2006 World Cup, an angry crowd met them at the airport chanting "dog" at the coach.

On the national level, the big local rivalry is between LD Alajuelense (*La Liga*, or "The League") and Deportivo Saprissa (*La Monstruo Morado*, or "The Purple Monster"). They have won the Costa Rican championship 26 and 29 times, respectively, which makes the rivalry particularly intense. You can tell how important the sport is when you fly into the country. As your plane flies across the Central Valley, you'll notice that every village, no matter how small, has a soccer field.

Cash Crops

If nearby Honduras was the original "Banana Republic," 19th-century Costa Rica was a "Coffee Republic." Coffee remains inexorably entwined with the country, with economists paying close attention to world prices and kids in rural areas still taking class time off to help with the harvest.

The irony is that it's hard to get a decent cup of the stuff here. True to economic realities of developing countries, the high-quality product gets exported, with the inferior coffee staying behind for the local market. (The same is true of bananas, Costa Rica's other signature agricultural product.) The best places to get a cup of high-quality Costa Rican coffee are upscale restaurants and hotels. Owners understand foreign tastes and have export-quality coffee on hand. Gift shops sell the superior product as well.

The Central Valley is where you'll find many of the coffee plantations. You'll recognize them immediately by the rows of brilliant green plants covered in red berries. Because many of these plants are sensitive to light, they are often shaded by tall trees or even by canopies of fabric. Tours of the plantations are a great way to get to know the local cash crop.

In recent years, the producers of coffee have focused on quality rather than quantity. That's why bananas are now the top agricultural export, followed by pineapples. Both grow in sunny lowland areas, which are abundant on both the Atlantic and Pacific coasts. These crops are treated with just as much care as coffee. You're likely to see bunches of bananas wrapped in plastic bags—while still on the tree. This prevents blemishes that make them less appealing to foreign consumers.

ECOTOURISM, COSTA RICA STYLE

Perhaps more than anyone else, the two men who wrote a field guide about tropical birds were responsible for the ecotourism movement in Costa Rica.

Environmental officials frequently identify the 1989 publication of *A Guide to the Birds of Costa Rica* by F. Gary Stiles and Alexander Skutch as drawing the first flock of bird-watchers to the country. The rest, as they say, was history.

The country's leaders, seeing so many of its primary growth forests being felled at an alarming rate by loggers and farmers, established its national park system in 1970. But it wasn't until nearly two decades later, when the birding guide was published, that they realized that the land they had set aside could help transform the tiny country's economy. (Lasting peace finally coming to neighboring countries was key to overcoming visitors' apprehensions about travel to Central America, too.)

Of the 2 million people who travel each year to Costa Rica, many are bird-watchers who come in search of the keel-billed toucan, the scarlet-rumped tanager, or any of the 850 other species of birds. Other travelers are in search of animals, such as two types of sloth, three types of anteater, and four species of monkey, all of them surprisingly easy to spot in the country's national parks and private reserves.

But other people come to Costa Rica to go white-water rafting on the rivers, soar through the treetops attached to zip lines, or take a spin in a motorboat. And many people combine a little bit of everything into their itineraries.

Which raises a couple of questions: Is the person coming to see the wildlife practicing ecotourism? Is the adventure traveler? And exactly what is the definition of ecotourism, anyway?

Defining Ecotourism

The word *ecotourism* is believed to have been coined by Mexican environmentalist Héctor Ceballos-Lascuráin in 1983. According to him, ecotourism "involves traveling to relatively undisturbed natural areas with the specific object of studying, admiring, and enjoying the scenery and its wild plants and animals."

His original definition seemed a bit too general, so in 1993 he amended it with a line that stressed that "ecotourism is environmentally responsible travel."

Ceballos-Lascuráin said he is pleased that ecotourism has gained such acceptance around the world. But he is also concerned that the term has been "variously abused and misused in many places."

The trouble, he said, is a misunderstanding about what is meant by the term *ecotourism*. In Costa Rica, for example, it has been used to describe everything from hiking through the rain forest to rumbling over the hillsides in all-terrain vehicles, and from paddling in a kayak to dancing to disco music on a diesel-powered yacht.

"I am sad to see," Ceballos-Lascuráin told a reporter for EcoClub, "that 'ecotourism' is seen mainly as adventure tourism and carrying out extreme sports in a more or less natural environment, with little concern for conservation or sustainable development issues."

That is not to say that adventure sports can't be part of a green vacation. It all depends what impact they have on the environment and the local community.

Going Green

Over the past decade, the concept of eco-tourism has made a strong impression on the average traveler. Many people now realize that mass tourism can be damaging to environmentally sensitive places like Costa Rica but that much can be done to alleviate the negative effects. At the same time, *ecotourism* has become a marketing term used to attract customers who have the best intentions. But is there really such a thing as an eco-friendly car-rental company or a green airline?

In addition to giving travelers the chance to observe and learn about wildlife, ecotourism should accomplish three things: refrain from damaging the environment, strengthen conservation efforts, and improve the lives of local people.

The last part might seem a bit beside the point, but environmentalists point out that much of the deforestation in Costa Rica and other countries is by poor people trying to eke out a living through sustenance farming. Providing them with other ways to make a living is the best way to prevent this.

What can you do? Make sure the hotel you choose is eco-friendly. A great place to start is the Costa Rican Tourism Board (⊕ *www.turismo-sostenible.co.cr*). It has a rating system for hotels and lodges called the Certification for Sustainable Tourism. The New York–based Rainforest Alliance (⊕ *www.rainforest-alliance.org*) has a convenient searchable database of sustainable lodges. The International Ecotourism Society (⊕ *www.ecotourism.org*) has a database of tour companies, hotels, and other travel services that are committed to sustainable practices.

Other Things You Can Do

What else can help? Make sure your tour company follows sustainable policies, including contributing to conservation efforts, hiring and training locals for most jobs, educating visitors about the local ecology and culture, and taking steps to mitigate negative impacts on the environment.

Here are a few other things you can do:

Use locally owned lodges, car-rental agencies, or tour companies. Eat in local restaurants, shop in local markets, and attend local events. Enrich your experience and support the community by hiring local guides.

Stray from the beaten path—by visiting areas where few tourists go, you can avoid adding to the stress on hot spots and enjoy a more authentic Costa Rican experience.

Support conservation by paying entrance fees to parks and protected sites and contributing to local environmental groups.

Don't be overly aggressive if you bargain for souvenirs, and don't shortchange local people on payments or tips for services.

The point here is that you can't assume that companies have environmentally friendly practices, even if they have pictures of animals on their website or terms like *eco-lodge* in their name. Do business only with companies that promote sustainable tourism, and you'll be helping to preserve this country's natural wonders for future generations.

WEDDINGS AND HONEYMOONS

Ever dreamed of getting married on a sandy beach shaded by palm trees? Many people who envision such a scene immediately think of the Caribbean. But Costa Rica is fast becoming a favored destination for tropical nuptials.

Compared with the complicated procedures in many other destinations, getting married in Costa Rica is easy. There are no residency restrictions or blood-test requirements. At least a month in advance, couples of the opposite sex who are over 18 should provide their local wedding planner with a copy of their birth certificates and passports so they can be submitted to the local authorities. Same-sex unions have no legal status in Costa Rica, but wedding planners here have arranged commitment ceremonies.

Any previous marriage complicates things a bit. The couple needs to provide documentation that the marriage was terminated. Divorce papers or death certificate of a previous spouse must be translated into Spanish and notarized.

The Big Day

Judges, attorneys, and Catholic priests have legal authority to certify a marriage in Costa Rica. (Most foreign couples avoid the latter because a Catholic wedding requires months of preparation.) The official ceremony is simple, but couples are free to add their own vows or anything else they would like. The officiant will register the marriage with the civil registry and the couple's embassy.

At the wedding, the couple needs to have at least two witnesses who are not family members. Many couples choose their best man and maid of honor. If necessary, the wedding planner can provide witnesses.

The license itself takes three months to issue and is sent to the couple's home address. For an extra fee, couples can ask for the process to be expedited. Virtually all Western countries recognize the legality of a Costa Rican marriage.

Beautiful Backdrops

Although Costa Rica offers no shortage of impressive backdrops for a ceremony, the Central Pacific coast sees the most tourist weddings and honeymoons. May and June are the most popular months for foreigners, but many people choose January or February because you are virtually guaranteed sunny skies. (Costa Ricans favor December weddings.) Manuel Antonio's Makanda by the Sea, La Mariposa, Si Como No, and Punta Leona's Villa Caletas are among the many lodgings here with events staffs well versed in planning ceremonies and tending to the legalities.

There are many details to attend to: flowers, music, and photography. Most large hotels have on-staff wedding planners to walk you through the process. Couples can also hire their own wedding planner, which is often less expensive. Either way, wedding planners have a wide range of services available, and couples can pick and choose.

Honeymoons

As far as honeymoons go, no place in Costa Rica is inappropriate. Although honeymoons on the beach, especially along the Northern Pacific and Central Pacific coasts, are popular, many couples opt for treks to the mountains or the rain forests. Dozens of newlyweds choose offbeat adventures, such as spotting sea turtles along the Caribbean coast or swimming with pilot whales off the Osa Peninsula.

KIDS AND FAMILIES

With so much to keep them interested and occupied, Costa Rica is a blast with kids. The activities here are things the whole family can do together: discovering a waterfall in a rain forest, snorkeling with sea turtles, or white-water rafting down a roaring river. There are also activities for kids that will allow parents time to stroll hand-in-hand down a deserted beach.

Choosing a Destination

Basing yourself in one place for several days is a great idea. Climbing into the car every day or two not only makes the kids miserable but means that the best part of the day is spent traveling. (Winding, twisting roads to a few destinations don't go well with kids who are prone to carsickness either.) The good news is that there are many destinations where you could stay for a week and still not do and see everything.

Headed to the beach? Remember that for families, not all beaches are created equal. Choose a destination with a range of activities. Manuel Antonio, on the Central Pacific coast, is your best bet. The proximity to the national park is the main selling point, but you're also close to other nature preserves. As for activities, there's everything from snorkeling and surfing lessons to kayaking excursions to zip-line adventures. And the range of kid-friendly restaurants is unmatched anywhere in the country. On the Nicoya Peninsula, Playas del Coco and Playa Tamarindo have a decent amount of activities for the small fry.

Santa Elena, the closest town to Monteverde Cloud Forest Biological Reserve, is another great base. There are several nature preserves in the area, and they offer both day and night hikes. If skies are cloudy—as they often are—there are indoor attractions like the display of slithering snakes. The town is compact and walkable, and has many eateries with children's menus. La Fortuna, the gateway to the Lake Arenal area, has activities from waterfall hikes to canopy tours. The town itself isn't attractive, so you'll want to choose a place nearby.

Believe it or not, the San José area is not a bad base. Activities like white-water rafting are nearby, and on rainy days you can visit the city's excellent museums dedicated to gold and jade. The hotels in the surrounding countryside are often a long drive from good restaurants. We prefer the hotels in the city, as dozens of restaurants line the pedestrian-only streets.

Kid-Friendly Activities

You can't beat the beach in Costa Rica. Avoid those without lifeguards, and take warning signs about rip currents very seriously. Snorkeling and surfing lessons are great for older kids, but stick with a licensed company rather than that enthusiastic young person who approaches you on the beach.

Canopy tours are good for kids of all ages. Ask the staff about how long a tour will take, because once you set out on a hike over a series of hanging bridges, you often have no choice but to continue on to the end. Zip lines are appropriate for older teens, but they should always be accompanied by an adult.

For the smallest of the small fry, the butterfly enclosures and hummingbird gardens that you find near many resort areas are wonderful diversions. Indoor activities, like the display of frogs at Santa Elena, fascinate youngsters. And don't avoid the easier hikes in the national parks. Seeing animals in the wild is likely to start a lifelong love of animals.

GREAT ITINERARIES

BEACHES, RAIN FORESTS, AND VOLCANOES

Day 1: Arrival

Arrive in San José (most arrivals are in the evening) and head straight to one of the small luxury hotels north of the city in the Central Valley. A favorite of ours is Finca Rosa Blanca, a fairy-tale retreat overlooking miles of coffee farms.

Logistics: Brace yourself for long lines at immigration if you arrive in the evening along with all the other large flights from North America. Try to get a seat near the front of the plane, and don't dawdle when disembarking.

Day 2: Poás Volcano and Tabacón Hot Springs

Volcán Poás, where you can peer over the edge of a crater, lies nearby. Fortify yourself with the fruits, jellies, and chocolates sold by vendors on the road up to the summit. A scenic drive takes you to La Fortuna area. Drop your luggage at one of many fantastic hotels (Montaña de Fuego is our pick for fabulous volcano views), and go directly to Tabacón Hot Springs & Resort. Take a zip-line or hanging-bridges tour through the forest canopy and then pamper yourself with a spa treatment. Finish the day by sinking into a volcanically heated mineral bath with a cocktail at your side as the sun sets behind fiery Volcán Arenal.

Logistics: Get an early start to get the best views of Poás. Shuttle vans can get you to Arenal and have hotel-to-hotel service.

Day 3: Caño Negro Wildlife Refuge

Spend your entire day in the Caño Negro Wildlife Refuge, a lowland forest reserve replete with waterfowl near the Nicaraguan border.

Logistics: Book your trip the night before; tour operators in La Fortuna keep evening hours for exactly that reason. All transport will be included.

Day 4: Scenic Drive to the Central Pacific

Today's a traveling day—a chance to really see the country's famous landscape and infamous roads. (Believe us, they get a lot worse than this route.) A few hours' drive from Arenal takes you to fabled Manuel Antonio on the Central Pacific coast. Beyond-beautiful hotels are the norm here, and you have your choice of seaside villas or tree-shrouded jungle lodges. We like the hillside La Mariposa, which has commanding views.

Logistics: Hotel-to-hotel shuttle-van services can get you to Manuel Antonio. If you drive instead, start out as early as possible. You'll pass through two mountainous stretches (between La Fortuna and San Ramón, and between Atenas and the coast) that fog over by midafternoon.

Day 5: Manuel Antonio National Park

Manuel Antonio is Costa Rica's most famous national park for a reason: it has beaches, lush rain forest, mangrove swamps, and rocky coves with abundant marine life. You can—and should—spend an entire day exploring the park, home to capuchin monkeys, sloths, agoutis, and 200 species of birds. It's also one of two locales in the country where you'll see squirrel monkeys.

Logistics: Almost all Manuel Antonio hotels have transport to the park. If yours doesn't, taxis are plentiful and cheap.

Day 6: Beach Yourself

Days 1 through 5 were "on the go" days. Reward yourself today with lots of relaxation. Manuel Antonio means beaches, and there are several to choose from.

Manuel Antonio and neighboring Quepos mean restaurants, too, the best selection of any beach community in the country.

Logistics: Most everything you need here is strung along the 5-km (3-mile) road between Quepos and Manuel Antonio National Park. It's practically impossible to get lost.

Day 7: San José

An easy morning drive back to San José on the new (2010) Pacific highway gives you time to spend the afternoon in the city. We like the cozy, classy Hôtel Le Bergerac. Visit the Teatro Nacional, the capital's must-see sight, and save time for late-afternoon shopping. An evening dinner caps off your trip before you turn in early to get ready for tomorrow morning's departure.

Logistics: As the number of visitors to Costa Rica grows, so does the number of passengers using Aeropuerto Internacional Juan Santamaría. We recommend that you check in three hours before your flight. Better safe than sorry.

GREAT ITINERARIES

MORE BEACHES, RAIN FORESTS, AND VOLCANOES

Day 1: Arrival

Most arrivals to Liberia, Costa Rica's second international airport, are in early afternoon. You can't go wrong with any North Pacific beach, but we like Playa Hermosa for its pivotal location, one that lets you use it as a base for visiting area attractions. Check out small, personal, breezy Hotel Playa Hermosa/Bosque del Mar, the perfect antidote to the megaresorts that lie not too far away.

Logistics: The big all-inclusives up here have their own minivans to whisk you in air-conditioned comfort from airport to resort. Smaller lodgings such as Hotel Playa Hermosa/Bosque del Mar can arrange to have transport waiting, with advance notice.

Day 2: Playa Hermosa

Morning is a great time to laze on the beach in this part of Costa Rica. The breezes are refreshingly cool and the sun hasn't started to beat down. After lunch, explore Playa Hermosa's metropolis, the small town of Playas del Coco. Quite frankly Coco is our least favorite beach up here. But we like the town for its little souvenir shops, restaurants, and local color.

Logistics: Taxis are the easiest way to travel between Playa Hermosa and Coco, about 10 minutes away. Have your hotel call one, and flag one down on the street in town when it's time to return.

Day 3: Rincón de la Vieja Volcano

The top of Rincón de la Vieja Volcano with its steaming, bubbling, oozing fumaroles lies about 90 minutes from Hermosa. Lather on the sunscreen and head for the Hacienda Guachipelín and its volcano-viewing hikes, canopy tours, rappelling, horseback riding, mountain biking, and river tubing. Cap off the day with a spa treatment, complete with thermal mud bath.

Logistics: If you don't have a rental car, book a private driver for the day, which can usually be arranged through your hotel.

Day 4: Golf or Diving

Golf is big up here. The 18-hole Reserva Conchal course at the Westin Playa Conchal resort is about 45 minutes from Hermosa. The other popular, slightly pricey, sport here is scuba diving. Dive operators are based in nearby Playas del Coco or Playa Panamá. A daylong course gives you a taste of the deep.

Logistics: The resort will arrange transport to and from the golf course, and dive operators will pick you up from and return you to your hotel.

Day 5: Palo Verde National Park

We like the morning guided tours at Palo Verde National Park, one of the last remaining dry tropical forests in Central America. The Organization for Tropical Studies, which operates the biological station here, has terrific guides. Spend the afternoon observing nature in a more relaxed fashion with a float down the nearby Río Corobicí. (These are not the screaming rapids so famed in whitewater circles.)

Logistics: This excursion is a bit roundabout, so this is the day your own vehicle would come in handiest. But you can also hire a private driver (arranged through your hotel). Bring water to drink: it gets hot here.

Gulf of Papagayo

Rincón de la Vieja Volcano

Hacienda Guachipelín

Liberia

GUANACASTE

Playa Hermosa

Playas del Coco

Bagaces

Cañas

Playa Flamingo

Filadelfia

Playa Paradisus

Brasilito

Palo Verde National Park

Day 6: Sailing

Make your final day a relaxing one with a few hours on the waves. Many sailboats operate from this section of coast. Our choice is the 52-foot *Samonique III*, which sails out of Playa Flamingo most afternoons at 2. A four-hour excursion includes sandwiches, appetizers, and an open bar. Legendary Pacific sunsets are tossed in at no extra charge.

Logistics: The *Samonique III* folks can arrange transport from hotel to boat and back again.

Day 7: Departure

Grab a last dip in the ocean this morning, because your flight departs from Liberia in the early afternoon.

Logistics: The advent of international flights to Liberia has fueled this region's meteoric rise to fame. The opening of a spiffy new airport terminal in late 2011 has eased congestion, but allow yourself plenty of time for check-in in any case.

TIPS

■ Fly into Liberia. Although it's logical to think "San José" when planning flights to Costa Rica, it makes no sense if you plan to spend your entire time in the North Pacific.

■ A car is ideal for this itinerary, yet many area attractions and tour operators provide transport to and from area lodging if you aren't too far afield (one of the reasons we like Playa Hermosa).

■ All-inclusive resorts do a good job of organizing local excursions with local operators, so if you're staying at one, take advantage of them.

■ Getting from beach to beach often requires travel back inland. There is no real (i.e., navigable) coastal road.

■ If ever there were a case for an off-season vacation, this is it. This driest, hottest part of the country gets very dry and hot from January through April. The rains green everything up, and frankly, we prefer the region during the low season after April.

FLAVORS OF COSTA RICA

A common misconception among first-time visitors to Costa Rica is that all south-of-the-U.S.-border cuisine is the same. This is absolutely not the case—people here just don't care for spicy foods, and the only place you'll dine on tacos and fajitas is in a Mexican restaurant. Costa Rican cuisine is hearty and mild, but certainly not the country's biggest draw. *Comida típica,* or typical food, consists primarily of chicken, pork, beans, and rice, although kitchens around the country serve sophisticated Thai, Indian, Italian, and Lebanese cuisine.

Start with the Staples
The cilantro-and-onion-flavored pot of black beans cooked with yesterday's rice, known as *gallo pinto* (literally "spotted rooster"), is synonymous with all things Costa Rican—As Tico as gallo pinto is common expression here. Mounds of this hearty dish—served with scrambled eggs, tortillas, and sour cream—can be had in all of the quintessential local eateries called *sodas.* (Costa Rican Spanish calls a carbonated beverage a *gaseosa.*) Gallo pinto usually serves as a breakfast staple—even McDonald's and Burger King have embraced the dish on their morning menus—but it shows up for lunch and dinner in Costa Rican homes, too.

Lunch is typically the biggest meal of the day here. *Casado* (married) is a plate that "marries" rice with cabbage salad, fried plantains, and a main entrée of beef, chicken, pork, or fish; it's always the lunchtime bargain. Hearty dishes of *olla de carne* (a beef and vegetable stew) and *sopa negra* (a black-bean soup with a poached egg) will fortify you for an afternoon of sightseeing, too. The mildly seasoned *arroz con pollo* (chicken with rice) makes a good choice if you're not feeling too adventurous. Few visitors develop of taste for the ubiquitous *chicharrones,* fried pork rinds.

Add the Bounty of the Land
You've never seen so many fruits and vegetables. The usual suspects like bananas, oranges, pineapples, lemons, mangoes, potatoes, and cabbage are all ubiquitous, but a walk through any Costa Rican market turns up new products you won't find back home. Most visitors develop a fondness for *carambola,* or star fruit, a mildly sweet treat that's perfect on a warm day.

Don't try eating plantains raw—*plátanos* should always be cooked. They end up as a side dish in casados around the country. The Caribbean coast always marches to its own drummer, of course, and cooks there mash them, fry them, and serve them as *patacones* with a touch of salt. Plátanos, along with breadfruit and yams, also get mixed in with fish or meat to make *rondón,* a hearty Caribbean stew. Coconut (*coco*) infuses Caribbean cuisine, most notably the long-simmering rice and beans—the name is always in English—that bears no resemblance to the gallo pinto you've been eating elsewhere in Costa Rica. Roadside vendors around the country will whack a coconut in half with a machete, insert a straw, and, *voilà,* a refreshing drink.

Costa Rica is one of the world's top exporters of *palmito,* the heart of palm that is a staple in salads here. The starchy palm fruit *pejibaye* is cooked and served with a dollop of mayonnaise. *Ensalada rusa,* the so-called Russian salad, mixes beets with potatoes, eggs, and mayonnaise, and is a must-have in the arsenal of any Costa Rican cook. *Elote,* or roasted corn on the cob, is a favorite at

any small-town Costa Rican celebration. The hearty, gourd-like *chayote* and the starchy cassava root *yuca* taste bland on their own, but as ingredients in other dishes, assume a variety of flavors.

Wash It Down

Café con leche mixes strongly brewed coffee with milk and lots of sugar for breakfast. (Your best bet for a decent cup of coffee is always an upscale restaurant that's attuned to foreign tastes.) Costa Rica's signature beverage takes center stage again midafternoon when seemingly the entire country takes a coffee break. Natural fruit juices, called *frescos,* also come with teeth-shattering amounts of sugar, but the variety of flavors is astounding. If you're watching your own or your child's intake, request one with only a little sugar (*con poco azúcar*); chances are it will be sweet enough, but you can always top it off if need be.

Cervecería Costa Rica, the country's sole large brewery, has a virtual monopoly on beer production, but makes some respectable lagers that pair well with beach lounging. Iconic Imperial (known by the red, black, and yellow eagle logo that adorns bar signs and tourist T-shirts) is everybody's favorite. The slightly bitter Pilsen is a close runner-up, followed by the gold, dark, and light variations of Bavaria. Feeling brave? *Guaro,* the locally distilled sugarcane firewater, really packs a punch. House wines are typically a low-end Chilean choice (this simply isn't wine-drinking country). Our advice? Go tropical! The country's abundant tropical fruit juices mix refreshingly well with local rums or, in a pinch, with a dash of guaro.

Leave Room for Dessert

You'll soon realize that Costa Ricans like things sweet; the country has one of the world's highest rates of sugar consumption. *Tres leches* mixes three milks—that's the meaning of the name—into a custardlike flan, and *Cajeta de coco* makes for a tasty coconut fudge.

THE PEOPLE OF COSTA RICA

Unlike many of its neighbors, Costa Rica never had a dominant indigenous population. When Christopher Columbus arrived in the early 16th century, he didn't encounter empires like those in present-day Mexico and Peru. Instead, a small contingent of indigenous Caribs rowed out in canoes to meet his ship. The heavy gold bands the indigenous peoples wore led to Columbus mistakenly calling the land Costa Rica, or "Rich Coast."

On the mainland, the Spanish encountered disparate peoples like the Chorotega, Bribri, Cabecar, and Boruca peoples. Archaeological evidence shows that they had lived in the region for thousands of years. But that would change with breathtaking speed. European diseases felled many of their members, and the brutality of slavery imposed by the colonial power drove most of those remaining into the mountains.

Some of these peoples still exist, although in relatively small communities. Several thousand Bribri, Kekoldi, and other peoples live in villages scattered around Talamanca, a mountainous region close to the border of Panama. Although many traditions have been lost over the years, some have managed to retain their own languages and religions. If you're interested in seeing the local culture, tour companies in the coastal communities of Limón and Puerto Viejo de Talamanca can arrange visits to these villages.

That isn't to say that there's no local culture. More than 90% of the country's residents are mestizos, or mixed-race descendants of the Spanish. But few people express any pride in their Spanish heritage. Perhaps that is because Spain had little interest in Costa Rica, the smallest and poorest of its Central

American colonies. Instead, the people here created a unique culture that mixes parts of Europe, Latin America, and the Caribbean. There's a strong emphasis on education, and the 95% literacy rate is by far the highest in the region. There's a laid-back attitude toward life, typified by the common greeting of *pura vida*, which translates literally as "pure life" but means something between "no worries" and "don't sweat the small stuff."

It sounds like a cliché, but Costa Ricans are an incredibly welcoming people. Anyone who has visited other Central American cultures will be surprised at how Ticos seem genuinely happy to greet newcomers. If you ever find yourself lost in a town or village, you may find locals more than willing to not only point you in the right direction but walk you all the way to your destination.

Others cultures have added their own spice to Costa Rica. On the Caribbean coast you'll find Afro-Caribbean peoples, descendants of Jamaicans who arrived in the late 19th century to build the railroad and remained to work on banana and cacao plantations. In the seaside town of Limón, cruise ships frequently call, and the passengers who hurry down the gangplank encounter steel-drum music, braided hair, and rickety houses painted every color of the rainbow. They may think that they have discovered the "real" Costa Rica, and they have, in a way. But they also have barely scratched the surface.

2

Biodiversity

WORD OF MOUTH

"I spotted this huge iguana measuring approximately four feet sunning along Playa Uvita; he allowed me to get within inches to take several pictures."

—Photo by Justin Hubbell, Fodors.com member

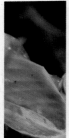

Costa Rica's forests hold an array of flora and fauna so vast and diverse that scientists haven't even named thousands of the species found here. The country covers less than 0.03% of Earth's surface, yet it contains nearly 5% of the planet's plant and animal species. Costa Rica has at least 9,000 plant species, including more than 1,200 types of orchids, some 2,000 kinds of butterflies, and 876 bird species.

Costa Rica acts as a natural land bridge between North and South America, so there is a lot of intercontinental exchange. But the country's flora and fauna add up to more than what has passed between the continents. Costa Rica's biological diversity is the result of its tropical location, its varied topography, and the many microclimates resulting from the combination of mountains, valleys, and lowlands. The isthmus also acts as a hospitable haven to many species that couldn't complete the journey from one hemisphere to the other. The rain forests of Costa Rica's Caribbean and southwestern lowlands are the most northerly home of such southern species as the crab-eating raccoon. The tropical dry forests of the northern Pacific slope are the southern limit for such North American species as the Virginia opossum. And then there are the dozens of northern bird species that spend their winter holidays here.

Research and planning go a long way in a place like Costa Rica. A short trip around the country can put you in one landscape after another, each with its own array of plants and animals. The country's renowned national park system holds examples of all of its major ecosystems, and some of its most impressive sights. In terms of activities, there's more interesting stuff to do here than could possibly ever fit into one vacation. But keep in mind that somewhere around three-fourths of the country has been urbanized or converted to agriculture, so if you want to see the spectacular nature that we describe in this book, you need to know where to go. *In addition to this section on biodiversity, you'll find regional planning information, national park highlights, and a list of our favorite ecolodges at the front of each chapter.*

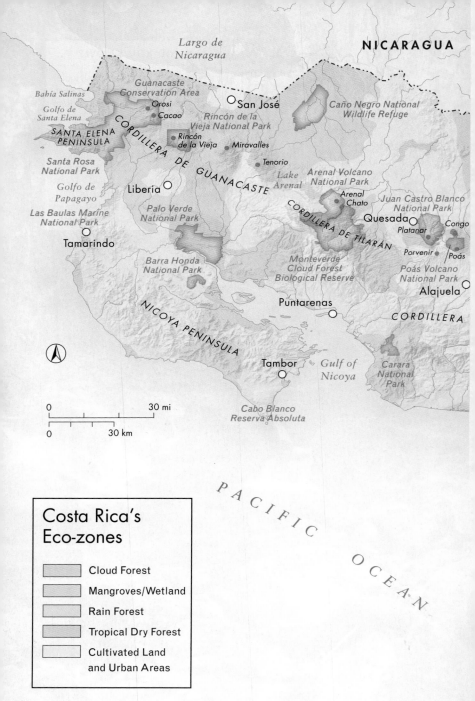

Largo de
Nicaragua

NICARAGUA

Bahía Salinas

Guanacaste
Conservation Area

Orosi
Cacao

○ San José

Caño Negro National
Wildlife Refuge

Golfo de
Santa Elena

Rincón de la
Vieja National Park

SANTA ELENA
PENINSULA

CORDILLERA

Rincón
de la Vieja

Miravalles

Santa Rosa
National Park

Tenorio

Golfo de
Papagayo

DE

GUANACASTE

Lake
Arenal

Arenal Volcano
National Park

Arenal
Chato

Juan Castro Blanco
National Park

Liberia ○

CORDILLERA

DE

TILARÁN

Quesada ○

Congo

Las Baulas Marine
National Park

Palo Verde
National Park

Platanar

Poás

Tamarindo ○

Porvenir

Barra Honda
National Park

Monteverde
Cloud Forest
Biological Reserve

Poás Volcano
National Park

Alajuela ○

NICOYA

Puntarenas ○

CORDILLERA

PENINSULA

Tambor ○

Gulf of
Nicoya

Carara
National
Park

0 ──── 30 mi

0 ──── 30 km

Cabo Blanco
Reserva Absoluta

PACIFIC

OCEAN

Costa Rica's
Eco-zones

■ Cloud Forest

■ Mangroves/Wetland

■ Rain Forest

■ Tropical Dry Forest

□ Cultivated Land
and Urban Areas

Costa Rica's Eco-zones

Barra del Colorado
Wildlife Refuge

Caribbean Sea

La Virgen
○

*Braulio Carillo
National Park*

*Tortuguero
National Park*

Cacho
Negro
●

Limón
○

Barva
●

*Turrialba Volcano
National Park*

Heredíá
○

Irazú
●

Turrialba
●

*Cahuita
National Park*

★
SAN JOSÉ

*Irazú Volcano
National Park*

Cartago
○

CENTRAL

*Chirripó
National Park*

*La Amistad
International
Biosphere*

Chirripó
(Highest point in
Costa Rica 3,810 m) ▲

CORDILLERA

Quepos
○

San de
El General
Isidro
○

Eli ▲

Utyum ▲

DE TALAMANCA

Nai ▲

PANAMA

Ena ▲

*Manuel Antonio
National Park*

Buenos Aires
○

VALLE DE EL GENERAL

Bine ▲

Río Terraba

*Ballena
National
Marine Park*

Drake
○

Golfito
○

*Piedras Blancas
National Park*

Drake Bay

OSA PENINSULA

*Golfo
Dulce*

*Corcovado
National Park*

KEY	
▲	Mountain
●	Volcano
	National Parks, Wildlife Refuges and Biological Reserves

RAIN FOREST

Warm and wet, Costa Rica's rain forest is the quintessential dripping, squawking, chirping, buzzing jungle. In this sultry landscape of green on green, birds flap and screech overhead and twigs snap under the steps of unseen creatures. All the ingredients for life—water, sunlight, and more water—drench these areas.

The amount of rain in a rain forest is stunning. The enormous swath of forest in the Caribbean lowlands averages more than 4 meters (13 feet) of rain a year. Corcovado National Park, on the Osa Peninsula, can get 5½ meters (18 feet).

The soaring canopy soaks up the lion's share of sunlight, seriously depriving the plants below. Underneath the highest trees are several distinct layers of growth. The understory is made up of smaller and younger trees, shaded but also protected from harsh winds and rainfall. Shrubby species and even younger trees stand

farther below, and small plants, fungus, dead trees, and fallen leaves cover the constantly decomposing forest floor.

Light rarely passes through these layers and layers of growth. At the forest floor, plants lie poised, in a stasis of sorts, waiting for one of the giants above to fall and open a patch of sky. When this does happen, an incredible spectacle occurs as the waiting plants unveil an arsenal of evolutionary tricks. Vines twist out, looking for other trees to pull themselves up along, shoots explode from hidden bulbs, and ferns and lianas battle for height and access to the sun.

But as competitive as the jungle sounds, it is essentially a series of ecosystems based on interdependence and cooperation. Trees depend on the animals that eat their fruit to disperse their seeds. Fungi feed off the nutrients produced by the decomposing forest floor. From death comes life—an abundance of life.

Costa Rica's rain forests have suffered from incursions by agriculture, logging, and cattle farming, but they're still home to the majority of the nation's biodiversity, with more species per square mile than anywhere else.

ADVENTURE HIGHLIGHTS

■ Novice bird-watchers can enroll in La Selva's Saturday morning bird-watching 101 class. It's taught by some of the finest naturalists in the country.

■ Join the folks at Brisas del Nara, 20 mi outside Manual Antonio, for an all-day horseback-riding excursion through the protected Cerra Nara mountain zone. It ends with a swim in a natural pool with a 350-foot (107-meter) waterfall.

■ Stray way off the beaten path on a multiday hike through Corcovado National Park with tropical biologist Mike Boston from Osa Aventura.

TOP DESTINATIONS

Most of Costa Rica's rain forest can be found across the Caribbean lowlands and on the South Pacific coast.

LA SELVA

If anybody knows anything about the rain forest, it is the researchers at La Selva biological station, situated in the midst of 3,900 acres of protected forest in the Caribbean lowlands. The station, run by the Organization for Tropical Studies, was founded by famed biologist Leslie Holdridge in 1954 and is one of the most important sites worldwide for research on tropical rain forest. The research station can sleep up to 80 people in dormitory-style rooms, two-room family cabins, and comfortable private cabins, and feed as many as 100 in the dining hall. More than 50 km (31 mi) of trails provide access to a variety of ecosystems. *(See Chapter 5.)*

MANUEL ANTONIO NATIONAL PARK

For a tame, up-close glimpse of the rain forest and some of its more photogenic inhabitants, Manuel Antonio National Park is a favorite. Located on the Central Pacific coast, Manuel Antonio is one of Costa Rica's most visited—and smallest—national parks. Capuchin monkeys are used to humans to the point of practically ignoring them, unless a snack is poking out from an unattended

A green and black poison frog, La Selva

backpack. The highly endangered squirrel monkeys are less bold, but can be seen at the park or from nearby hotels. Sloths are a common sight along the trail, as are a host of exotic birds and other creatures. But despite the apparent vibrancy of life found here, Manuel Antonio is isolated, with no biological bridges to other forests, and threatened by encroaching development. *(See Chapter 7.)*

CORCOVADO NATIONAL PARK

At the other end of the spectrum is Corcovado National Park, the remote, untamed jewel of Costa Rica's biodiversity crown. Covering one-third of the Osa Peninsula, Corcovado National Park holds about one-quarter of all tree species in Costa Rica and at least 140 identified species of mammals. Covering 172 square mi (445 square km), the park includes Central America's largest tract of lowland Pacific rain forest, including some old-growth areas. Corcovado is home to the largest concentration of jaguars left in the country, and the biggest population of scarlet macaw. There are at least 116 species of amphibians and reptiles, and about 370 bird species. Ranger stations and campsites are available for the more adventurous, and luxurious eco-lodges surround the park for those who don't like to rough it. *(See Chapter 8.)*

Squirrel Monkey; danmike, Fodors.com member

EXPERIENCING A RAIN FOREST

Photographing a spiderweb

For an ecosystem as diverse as the rain forest, it is fitting that there are a variety of ways to explore and experience it.

HIKING

Hiking or walking through any one of Costa Rica's numerous national parks is an easy way to fully experience the vibrancy of the life found there. And we can't say this too many times: guided hikes are the way to go for anyone who hopes to catch a glimpse of the more exotic and hard-to-find species or better understand the complexity of the surrounding ecosystems.

MOUNTAIN BIKING

During the dry season, some parks open up trails for mountain bikers. But once the rains begin, a bike trip can turn into a long slog through the mud. Before you rent a bike, ask about the conditions of the trails.

RAFTING

Gentle, slow-moving rivers beg to be explored by canoe or kayak. It's a wonderful way to experience the deep calm of the jungle, and stealthy enough to increase your chances of seeing wildlife. If you're more of a thrill seeker, choose from any of the white-water rafting tours that pass through rain forests.

CANOPY TOURS

Canopy tours are a wonderful way to get a bird's—or sloth's—view of the rain forest. Suspension bridges and zip lines, originally used for canopy research, offer a fantastic glimpse into the upper reaches of the forest. If you're not very mobile or don't feel like walking, go on a rain-forest tram; it's a small, slow-moving gondola that carries passengers gently through the jungle canopy.

FLORA

To enter into a Costa Rican rain forest is to be overwhelmed by the diversity and intensity of life. A single hectare (2½ acres) contains almost 100 species of trees, and many of the more than 1,000 species of orchids are nested into their branches.

GUARIA MORADA

Almost every tree here plays host to lichens, woody vines called lianas, and rootless epiphytes, including the national flower, *guaria morada* (*Guarianthe skinneri*). Because this is an orchid species, you'll find it in several different shapes and colors: the flowers can be from pure white to deep magenta, and the base of its lip can range from yellow to white. There can be anywhere from 4 to 14 flowers per stem.

SILK COTTON TREE

The silk cotton tree (*Ceiba pentandra*), known locally as ceiba, is one of the most easily recognizable of the rain-forest giants. Growing nearly 60 meters (200 feet) tall, it can be identified close to the ground by its tall, winding, and narrow roots, which act as buttresses to support the enormous trunk.

STRANGLER FIG

Aptly called *matapalo* in Spanish, meaning "tree killer," the strangler fig begins its life as an epiphyte, living high in the branches of another tree. Over several years, it slowly grows dangling roots to the forest floor that capture nutrients from the soil, thicken, and eventually meld onto the host tree. Eventually—it might take as long as 100 years—the strangler completely engulfs its host. In time the "strangled" tree decomposes and disintegrates, leaving the strangler fig—replete with branches, leaves, flowers, and fruit—standing hollow but victorious.

FALSE BIRD OF PARADISE

No avid photographer will return from Costa Rica without snapping a few shots of a heliconia, one of the most vibrant families of plants in the rain forest. This genus of flowering plant, containing between 100 and 200 species, includes the false bird of paradise (*Heliconia rostrata*), a dangling, impossibly colorful flower of alternating bulbous protrusions, colored red and tipped with green and yellow. Its vibrant colors and nectar make it a favorite for hummingbirds.

The Silk Cotton Tree

Guaria morada

Strangler Fig

False Bird of Paradise

FAUNA

Keep an eye out for three-wattled bellbirds, chestnut-mandibled toucans, or the secretive Baird's tapir. A host of wildcats, include the ocelot, jaguarundi, puma, margay, and rarely seen jaguar.

SCARLET MACAWS

Every bit the pirate's crimson parrot, these large and noisy birds mate for life, travel in pairs or large groups, and can often be found gathered in almond trees in low-elevation forests of the central and southern Pacific coast. Their cousin, the critically endangered great green macaw, travels across the Caribbean lowlands, following the ripening of the mountain almond.

Scarlet Macaw

HARPY EAGLE

The endangered harpy eagle, nearly extinct from Costa Rica, is the country's largest and most powerful raptor. It's named for the Greek spirits that carried the dead to the underworld of Hades, who are said to have the faces of humans but the bodies of eagles. Harpy eagles are huge—females are more than 0.6 meter (2 feet) in length and have a 1.8-meter (6-foot) wingspan. They hunt above the canopy, searching for large mammals or, occasionally, large birds like the macaw.

Harpy Eagle

THREE-TOED OR TWO-TOED SLOTH

Through difficult for us to spot, the barely moving three-toed sloth and two-toed sloth are principal meals for the harpy eagle. This animal's fur is a small self-sustaining ecosystem unto itself: because the forest is so wet and the sloth so inert, two species of blue-green algae thrive on its fur and provide it with needed camouflage. Nonparasitic insects also live here, feeding off the algae and keeping the growth under control.

Three-toed-sloth

MORPHO BUTTERFLY

The bright blue morpho butterfly bounces through the jungle like a small piece of sky on a string. The entire life cycle, from egg to death, is approximately 137 days, and the adult butterflies live for only about a month. Once they emerge from the cocoon, morphos have few predators, thanks to the poisonous compounds that they retain from feeding habits back in their caterpillar days. In fact, the hairy brown tufts on the morpho caterpillar have been known to irritate human skin.

■TIP➜ The vibrantly colored red-eyed tree frog, like the white tent bat, sometimes rests on the underside of large jungle leaves; gently turn a few leaves over as you're hiking and take a peek. You might get lucky.

Blue Morpho

VOLCANOES

As part of the Pacific Ring of Fire, the country has three volcanic mountain ranges: Guanacaste, Central, and Tilarán. There are around 300 volcanic points in Costa Rica, but only five have formed volcanoes that have erupted in recent memory: Turrialba, Irazú, Poás, Rincón de la Vieja, and Arenal.

Costa Rica's volcanoes are the result of friction between two enormous tectonic plates—the Cocos plate and the Caribbean plate. As these plates rub against each other, the friction partially melts rock, creating magma or lava. Magma is forced toward the surface, leaking through cracks or weak spots in the crust along with volcanic gas. In Rincón de la Vieja, lava and gas escape through craters high on the volcano, as well as seeping up through the surrounding ground, creating bubbling mud pits, hot springs, and fumaroles.

The volcanic mountain ranges divide the country's Pacific and Caribbean slopes and are responsible for the differences in climate between each side. Rain-laden trade winds blowing westward can't pass over these ranges without shedding their precipitation and rising. This creates Guanacaste's rain shadow: the dry plains and tropical dry forest that lie leeward, or west of the mountains. The mountains block the rain-producing weather system and cast a "shadow" of dryness.

Costa Rica's volcanic lakes occur when there is no natural drainage from a crater. The chemicals, minerals, and gasses from below the earth's crust infuse the water and vibrantly color it. Irazú's lake is neon green; the baby-blue lagoon in Poás is extremely acidic and gives off toxic sulfur clouds and massive amounts of carbon dioxide.

The surface ecology of a volcano varies. Rincón de la Vieja is skirted by Guanacaste's signature grasslands and tropical dry forest. Poás Volcano is blanketed with rain forest and tipped with cloud forest. Some of the country's best coffee is grown on the slopes of Poás.

ADVENTURE HIGHLIGHTS

■ A hike through lush cloud forest will take you to the five magnificent waterfalls at La Paz Waterfall Gardens near Poás Volcano National Park.

■ Anglers love the guapote, tilapia, and machaca pulled from Lake Arenal.

■ The Arenal area is the jumping-off point for Class II–IV white-water rafting trips on the Blancas, Arenal, Toro, and San Carlos rivers.

■ Take the tough hike to La Fortuna Waterfall, near Arenal. Swimming under the waterfall is a slice of paradise.

TOP DESTINATIONS

Costa Rica's volcanoes are often the centerpieces of large national parks.

ARENAL VOLCANO

At 1,680 meters (5,512 feet), Arenal Volcano, rising on the northwestern plains of San Carlos, is every bit an awesome sight. Tall and perfectly conical, its sides are scarred by a history of violent eruptions and textured by decades of flowing lava. Located at the northern end of the Tilarán Mountain Range, northwest of the capital, it is Costa Rica's best-known volcano, its most active, and one of the 10 most active volcanoes in the world. Unfortunately, Arenal's peak is often shrouded from sight because of the gasses and steam that escape from the crater. One scary bit of research concluded that Arenal has a 400-year cycle of major eruptions, and the activity since the 1968 explosion is small in comparison with what it's capable of. *(See Chapter 5.)*

RINCÓN DE LA VIEJA

A mass of slopes, craters, and biodiversity that bridges the Continental Divide, Rincón de la Vieja is in Costa Rica's arid northwest. It's not the classic conical volcano, but rather a ridge made of a series of craters that include bare, rocky bowls with brilliantly colored lakes, and velvety cones covered in rain forest. Scientists believe Rincón de la Vieja was

On the Road to Arenal; piper35w, Fodors.com member

born of simultaneous volcanic activity at nine different eruption points. The Rincón de la Vieja National Park covers nearly 35,000 acres and is a wonderland of volcanic activity that includes bubbling mud pits, hot springs, and geysers, as well as refreshing lagoons and spectacular waterfalls. *(See Chapter 6.)*

POÁS VOLCANO

Poás Volcano is Costa Rica's most visited national park, in part because it is the closest active volcano to the capital of San José and the Aeropuerto Internacional Juan Santamaría. Located in the Cordillera Volcánica Central Mountain Range, Poás is topped by three craters, the tallest reaching 2,708 meters (8,885 feet) above sea level. Only the main cone has shown any volcanic eruptions in the last 200 years. You can get a good look at the crater from the viewing deck. *(See Chapter 5.)*

Note: A 6.2 earthquake struck only 10 km (6 mi) from Poás in January 2009, destroying two nearby villages, killing 34 people, and leaving 3,000 people homeless. However, seismologists and geologists assured the public that it was not related to any volcanic activity at Poás. The most recent active volcano of note is Turrialba Volcano, which is letting off a lot of steam but poses no danger.

Gaudy Leaf Frog; Marco13, Fodors.com member.

EXPERIENCING THE VOLCANOES

2

Horseback riding in Arenal

The Guatuso people believed that the fire god lived inside the Arenal Volcano . . . and in 1968, the gods were not happy. After 500 years of dormancy, Arenal erupted savagely, burying three small villages and killing 87 people. Today, thousands live at its base in the thriving town of La Fortuna, which is literally in Arenal's shadow.

HIKING
Volcano tourism is a major draw for international visitors, but given the dangers at the active sites, activities at the top are limited. There are no zip lines across open craters, and there's no snorkeling in acidic volcano lakes. At the peak, activities are limited to viewing, hiking, and photography. But the otherworldly look and feel of these sights is reason enough to visit. On rare clear nights at Arenal, you can see lava spewing and flowing down the side of the mountain.

STANDING IN AWE
Volcanic activity is not, however, limited to a volcano's peak. The underground heat that fuels these giants also results in hot springs, bubbling mud pits, and geysers, among other geological wonders. Minerals from the dormant Tenorio Volcano create a fascinating effect in one of the rivers running down its side, the Río Celeste, giving it a baby-blue tint. Arenal's reflection can be seen in pools of water heated by the same underground lava spewing from its peak.

HORSEBACK RIDING
Many of Costa Rica's volcanoes are the centerpieces to broad national parks. Depending on the park, the infrastructure can be outstanding or nonexistent. Arenal and Poás have good horseback-riding trails and outfitters.

FLORA

The habitat and ecology of these geologic giants is influenced mostly by their surrounding ecology zones and elevation. Conditions around the crater of an active volcano are intensely harsh but some tougher species do manage to survive.

FERN

Contrary to popular stereotypes, ferns don't necessarily grow in shady, moist environments. The tongue fern (*Elaphoglossum lingua*) extends long, rubbery, tongue-shape leaves and has evolved to grow around the lava rock and hardened ash. You'll find it around the top of the Poás Volcano. Farther down, you'll find other types of ferns adapted to friendlier conditions.

Ferns

OAK

Forests in Costa Rica's higher mountain areas share some plant species with cloud forests. However, the plants here have adapted to live in cold temperatures and, if the volcano is active, in compacted ash. Surrounding the Botos Lagoon, on the south side of the principal Poás crater, is high-elevation cloud forest of oak (*Quercus costaricensis and Q. copeyensis*), small cedar (*Brunellia costaricensis*), and the flowering cypress (*Escallonia poasana*)—trees that are typically crowded with epiphytes, bromeliads, and mosses.

Great Roble Oak

MYRTLE

Myrtle (*Myrtaceae*), and other low-lying shrubs survive this environment thanks to their slow growth rate. Myrtle, poor man's umbrella (*Gunnera insignis*), papelillo (*Senecio oerstedianus*), and other shrubs and ferns cover the higher bluffs around Irazú's crater. Mistletoe (*Psittacanthus*) can be found near the major volcanoes in the Central Valley. These flowering plants are interesting because they attach to trees by haustoria, special structures that penetrate the host plant and absorb its water and nutrients. When the mistletoe dies, it leaves a mark on the tree, a woodrose or *rosa de palo*.

Wild Balsam aka Touch-me-not Balsam

WILD BALSAM

Wild balsam, oak, and poor man's umbrella carpet the inactive cones around Rincón de la Vieja. Tropical dry forest species grow farther down. Look for the guanacaste tree (*Enterolobium cyclocarpum*), Spanish cedar (*Cedrela odorata*), oak (*Q. oocarpa*), and the country's largest wild population of the guardia morada orchid, Costa Rica's national flower.

Myrtle

FAUNA

Like the flora around a volcano, the wildlife diversity of this region is dictated by the ecology around the mountain. Also, the more humans there are, the fewer animals you'll see.

Puma

PUMA

In the Barva region, pumas (also called mountain lions and cougars) and even jaguars still stalk the more remote forests, searching for the tapir or an unlucky spider monkey. The puma is an excellent climber and can jump to branches 5 meters (16 feet) off the ground, essentially giving monkeys nowhere to hide. Pumas have never been hunted for their pelts, but are suffering from habitat destruction. In Costa Rica, they are rarely found outside protected areas.

FIERY-THROATED HUMMINGBIRD

Birds are one of the most populous types of creature to live on the flanks of Poás and many more of Costa Rica's volcanoes. The fiery-throated hummingbird, the summer tanager, the sooty robin, and the emerald toucanet are among the 79 bird species that have been recorded at Poás. The fiery-throated hummingbird is recognizable by its forecrown, throat, and breast colors, as well as its bluish hump and blue-black tail.

North American Porcupine

NORTH AMERICAN PORCUPINE

The much drier region of Rincón de la Vieja has a distinctly different—and broader—set of animal inhabitants, including the North American porcupine and the agouti (a large, short-legged relative of the guinea pig). Pumas, ocelots, raccoons, and three species of monkeys (the howler, the white-faced capuchin, and the Central American spider monkey) are among the larger mammals. More than 300 bird species have been recorded there, including the collared aracari, the bare-necked umbrella bird, and the three-wattled bellbird.

Fiery-Throated Hummingbird

NINE-BANDED ARMADILLO

Irazú is home to smaller creatures such as the nine-banded armadillo, the eastern cottontail, and the little spotted cat. The nine-banded armadillo has a long snout and fantastic sense of smell. It can hold its breath for up to six minutes. This helps it keep dirt out of its nostrils while digging. Under stressful conditions, a female armadillo can prolong her pregnancy for up to three years by delaying the implantation of the fertilized egg into the uterus wall.

Nine-banded armadillo

CLOUD FOREST

The four mountain ranges that make up Costa Rica's own piece of the Continental Divide split the country into its Caribbean and Pacific regions. At these higher altitudes, temperatures cool, clouds settle, and rainfall increases. The forests found here are shrouded in mist and rich in biodiversity. Welcome to Costa Rica's famed cloud forests.

Like its lowland rain forest cousins, cloud forests are packed with plant and animal species, thanks largely to their water-drenched conditions. There's an average of 5 meters (16 feet) of rainfall a year, but that number doubles when you factor in the amount of moisture gleaned from the clouds and fog that drift through every day. Like rain forests, giant hardwoods reaching as high as almost 60 meters (200 feet) set the ceiling for this ecology zone, while a variety of smaller trees, ferns, shrubs, and other plants fill the understories. Epiphytes flourish here, as do mosses, lichens, and

liverwort. These plants cling to passing moisture and capture it like sponges. As a result, cloud forests are constantly soaking wet even when there is no rain.

Because conditions in a cloud forest can be harsh, many of the tougher and more adaptable rain-forest species make their home here. The relentless, heavy cloud cover can block sunlight even from the highest reaches of the forest, and deeper inside, light is rare. Photosynthesis and growth are slower, so the plants tend to be smaller with thicker trunks and stems. These unique conditions also produce an unusually high number of endemic and rare species.

The Monteverde Cloud Forest Preserve, one of the world's most famous protected cloud forests, shelters innumerable life-forms. There are more than 100 mammal species; 400 bird species, including at least 30 species of hummingbird; 500 plus species of butterfly; and more than 2,500 plant species, including 420 types of orchids. There are only a handful of protected cloud forests here and worldwide and this type of ecozone is increasingly threatened by human encroachment.

ADVENTURE HIGHLIGHTS

■ Leave the car at home and travel on horseback to or from the Arenal Volcano area and Monteverde Cloud Forest. Contact Desafío Adventures, the only guides we recommend for this journey.

■ Expert birder Marino Chacón of the Savegre Hotel will give you an education on one of his daylong natural history hikes around San Gerardo de Dota cloud forest.

■ Selvatura, right next to Monteverde, is the only canopy tour in the area with a zip line built entirely inside the cloud forest.

TOP DESTINATIONS

Regardless of which cloud forest you visit, bring a raincoat and go with a guide if you want to see wildlife. You'll marvel at their ability to spot a sloth at a hundred paces.

MONTEVERDE CLOUD FOREST BIOLOGICAL RESERVE

Costa Rica's most famous cloud forest reserve is packed with an astonishing variety of life: 2,500 plant species, 400 species of birds, 500 types of butterflies, and more than 100 different mammals—many of them bats—have been cataloged so far. The reserve reaches 1,535 meters (5,032 feet) above sea level, spans the Tilarán Mountain Range, and encompasses 9,885 acres of cloud forest and rain forest. There are 13 km (8 mi) of well-marked trails, zip-line tours, and suspended bridges for canopy viewing, bird tours, guided night walks, and a field research station with an amphibian aquarium. Allow a generous slice of time for leisurely hiking; longer hikes are made possible by some strategically placed overnight refuges along the way. *(See Chapter 5.)*

SAN GERARDO DE DOTA

One of Costa Rica's premier nature destinations, San Gerardo de Dota is a damp, epiphyte-laden forest of giant oak trees and an astonishing number of

Banded Anteater; maddytem, Fodors.com member

resplendent quetzals. Outdoor enthusiasts may never want to leave these parts—some of the country's best hiking is in this valley, and it's popular with bird-watchers. It's also great for horseback riding and trout fly-fishing. *(See Chapter 8.)*

BRAULIO CARRILLO NATIONAL PARK

Descending from the Cordillera Volcánica Central Mountain Range, the Braulio Carrillo National Park is an awesome, intimidating, and rugged landscape of dense cloud forest that stretches toward the rain forests of the Caribbean lowlands. The enormous park encompasses 117,580 acres of untamed jungle and is less than an hour's drive from San José. The country's principal eastbound highway cuts a path straight through it. Elusive (and endangered) jaguars and pumas are among the many animal species here, and scenic viewpoints are plentiful along the highway. A handful of trails, including the easy-to-access loop trails at the Quebrada González station, can be taken a short distance into the park's interior. *(See Chapter 5.)*

Braulio Carrillo National Park

EXPERIENCING A CLOUD FOREST

Zipline tour in Selvature just outside of Monteverde Cloud Forest

You may need to get down and dirty—well, more like wet and muddy—to experience a cloud forest's natural wonders, but then, that's half the fun.

HIKING

Well-guided hikes through this eerie landscape, draped with moss and vines, make it easier to spot the less obvious features of this complex ecosystem. Compared with the barren tropical dry forest, and colorful rain forest, cloud forests don't easily offer up their secrets. Binoculars and a good guide will go a long way toward making your hike and wildlife spotting richer experiences.

BIRD-WATCHING

Bird-watching is rewarding in the cloud forest, where some of the most vibrant and peculiar of nature's winged creatures can be found. Rise early, enjoy some locally grown coffee, and check the aguacatillo trees for quetzals. If you opt to go without a guide, bring along waterproof binoculars and a good guidebook (we recommend *The Birds of Costa Rica*, by Richard Garrigues and Robert Dean) for spotting and identifying birds.

CANOPY TOURS

Canopy tours and suspended bridges run right through the upper reaches of the cloud forest—an ecosystem in its own right. Spot birds, monkeys, and exotic orchids from a viewpoint that was once nearly impossible to reach. Get even closer to butterflies, amphibians, snakes, and insects at various exhibits in the parks' research centers.

FISHING

If freshwater fishing in spectacular surroundings is right up your alley, check out the Savegre River, in the San Gerardo de Dota Valley. It's been stocked with wild rainbow trout since the 1950s.

FLORA

A typical hectare (2½ acres) of rain forest might be home to nearly 100 species of trees. Contrast that with a mere 30 in the richest forests of North America.

ROBLE TREE

Majestic roble, or oak—principally the white oak (*Quercus copeyensis*) and black oak (*Quercus costarricensis*)—is the dominant tree of Costa Rica's cloud forests and grows to 60 meters (200 feet). The deciduous hardwood *cedro dulce*, or Spanish cedar (*Cedrela tonduzii*), is also a giant at 40 meters (147 feet). These two are joined by evergreens like the *jaúl*, or alder, and the *aguacatillo*, a name meaning "little avocado" that's given to a variety of trees from the *lauracea* family.

White Oak Tree

POOR MAN'S UMBRELLA

If you're caught in the rain, take cover under a poor man's umbrella (*Gunnera insignis* and *Gunnera talamancana*), whose broad and sturdy leaves sometimes grow large enough to shelter an entire family. These shrubby plants love the dark, moist interior of the cloud forest.

Poor Man's Umbrella

EPIPHYTES

Epiphytes thrive in cloud and rain forests, thanks to all the moisture and nutrients in the air. The *stanhopea* orchid is interesting because of its clever pollination tricks. The blossoms' sweet smell attracts bees, but the flower's waxy surface is slippery so they slide down inside. As they slowly work their way out, they brush up against the flower's column and collect pollen. This pollen is then transferred to the sticky stigma of other flowers.

Bromeliads, another family of flowering plants, compete with epiphytes for space on the branches and trunks of the forest's trees. The spiraling leaves form caches for water, falling plant material, and insect excretion. These are mineral-rich little ponds for insects and amphibians, and drinking and bathing water for birds and other animals.

Epiphyte Stanhopea

STAR ORCHID

The star orchid (*Epidendrum radicans*) is one of the few orchids that is not an epiphyte. It grows on land and mimics in color and shape other nectar-filled flowers in order to attract butterflies who unwittingly become pollinators.

Star Orchid

FAUNA

The resplendent quetzal, the blue-crowned motmot, the orange-bellied trogon, and the emerald toucanet are just some of the hundreds of species that can be logged in a cloud forest.

GLASS FROGS

One of the more bizarre amphibians is the tiny, transparent glass frog of the *Centrolenellu* genus, whose internal organs can be seen through its skin. It lives in trees and bushes and can often be heard at night near the rivers and streams. Cloud forests have fewer amphibian species than rain forests, but amphibian populations worldwide have plummeted in recent decades. No one knows the cause yet. Some blame acid rain and pesticides; others believe it is yet another sign of coming ecological disaster.

Glass Frogs

RESPLENDENT QUETZAL

Perhaps the most famed resident of Costa Rica's cloud forests is the illustrious resplendent quetzal. Every year, bird-watchers come to Costa Rica hoping to spot the green, red, and turquoise plumage of this elusive trogon. Considered a sacred creature by the Maya and the namesake of Guatemala's currency, the quetzal spends much of its time perched in its favorite tree, the *aguacatillo*.

Resplendent Quetzal

COLLARED TROGON

The collared trogon and the orange-bellied trogon are in the same family as the quetzal. They all share square black-and-white tail plumage and bright orange or yellow chest feathers. The collared trogon perches very quietly and is easy to miss. Luckily, it doesn't fly far, so its flight is easy to follow.

Collared Trogon

HOWLER MONKEYS

One of the largest New World monkeys, howlers are named for their loud, barking roar that can be heard for miles. If you want to spot a howler, be sure to scan the treetops; their diet consists mainly of canopy leaves, and they rarely leave the protection of the trees. Other cloud forest mammals include the white-faced capuchin monkey, white-nosed coatis, porcupines, red brocket deer, and Alston's singing mouse.

Howler Monkey

TROPICAL DRY FOREST

The most endangered biome in the world, these seasonal forests swing between two climate extremes—from drenching wet to bone dry. To survive, plants undergo a drastic physical transformation: forests burst into life during the rainy months, and are brown, leafless, and seemingly dead during the dry season.

For about half the year, northwestern Costa Rica is as wet as the rest of the country. The weather blows in from the Pacific, and it can rain every day. During the dry season, from January to April, weather patterns change, winds shift, and the land becomes parched.

Tall deciduous hardwoods are the giants in this ecology zone, with spindly branches creating a seasonal canopy as high as 30 meters (100 feet). A thorny and rambling understory of smaller trees and bushes thrives thanks to the plentiful light permitted once the canopy leaves fall to the forest floor. The challenges of the dry months

have forced plants to specialize. The hardwoods are solitary and diffuse, their seeds spread far and wide by animals and insects. Some even flower progressively through the dry season, depending on the plant species and the particular bees and birds that have evolved to pollinate them.

Dry season is perfect for bird- and animal watching since the lack of foliage makes wildlife spotting easy. Keep your eyes peeled for monkeys, parrots, lizards, coyotes, rabbits, snakes, and even jaguars.

There was once one great, uninterrupted swath of dry forest that began in southern Mexico, rolled across Mesoamerica, and ended in northwest Costa Rica. Today, less than 2% of the Central American tropical dry forest remains, the majority of it in Costa Rica. But even here, the forest is fractured into biologically isolated islands, thanks to decades of logging and agriculture. The Guanacaste Conservation Area has managed to corral off large chunks of land for preservation, and private and government efforts are under way to create biological corridors between isolated dry forests so that animals and plants can roam farther and deepen their gene pools, so critical to their survival.

ADVENTURE HIGHLIGHTS

■ Adrenalin-spiked tours with Hacienda Guachipelín (bordering Rincón de la Vieja National Park) include river tubing, rappelling, zip lines, and a Tarzan swing. Let the knowledgeable folks from the Organization for Tropical Studies (OTS) take you on a guided bird-watching tour through Palo Verde National Park. Boat rides float you past hundreds of waterfowl.

■ Take the kids on a bird- and monkey-watching journey down the Río Corobicí, in Palo Verde National Park.

TOP DESTINATIONS

Most of Costa Rica's remaining tropical dry forests are located in the northwest of the country, not too far from the Nicaragua border.

SANTA ROSA NATIONAL PARK

The largest piece of tropical dry forest under government protection in Central America spreads out over Santa Rosa National Park, about 35 km (22 mi) north of Guanacaste's capital, Liberia. The park, which covers 380 square km (146 square mi), also includes two beaches and coastal mangrove forest. Thanks to trails and equipped campsites, you can venture deep into the park. During the dry season, visibility is excellent and chances are good in terms of spotting some of the hundreds of bird and animal species there. Playa Nancite, Santa Rosa's northern beach, is also one of the world's most important and most protected beaches for the nesting of olive ridley sea turtles. They come ashore by the hundreds of thousands between May and October (during the rainy season when access to the beaches is difficult) in a phenomenon called the *arribada*. Access is limited to researchers. *(See Chapter 6.)*

GUANACASTE CONSERVATION AREA

Santa Rosa is part of the larger Guanacaste Conservation Area, which is composed of some tropical dry forest and

Hummingbird Nesting; reedjoella, Fodors.com member

former farmland that's being regenerated to its natural state. The park is intended to serve as a much-needed biological corridor from Santa Rosa up to the cloud forests of the Orosi and Cacao volcanoes, to the east. Park infrastructure is generally lacking, though three biological stations offer some accommodations to student groups and researchers. *(See Chapter 6.)*

RINCÓN DE LA VIEJA NATIONAL PARK

More tropical dry forest can be found inside the Rincón de la Vieja National Park, ringing the base of the two volcanoes of this protected area—Santa María and Rincón de la Vieja. *(See Chapter 6.)*

PALO VERDE NATIONAL PARK

Farther south, Palo Verde National Park skirts the northeastern side of the Río Tempisque, straddling some of the country's most spectacular wetlands and tropical dry forest. Thanks to these two very different ecology zones, Palo Verde is packed with very diverse bird, plant, and animal species—bird-watchers love this park. The Organization for Tropical Studies has a biological station at Palo Verde and offers tours and accommodations. Park guards also maintain a ranger station with rustic overnight accommodations. *(See Chapter 6.)*

Canopy Tour at Rincón de la Vieja National Park

EXPERIENCING A DRY TROPICAL FOREST

Rincón de la Vieja National Park

Many of Costa Rica's roads are rough at best, and tropical forests are often remote. We recommend hiring a 4WD for getting around.

HIKING

The absolute best way to experience these endangered woods is to strap on your hiking boots, grab a hat and lots of water, and get out and walk. Most of the dry forests are protected lands and found in Guanacaste's national parks. Some have road access, making it possible to drive through the park, but most are accessible only by hiking trails. During the rainy season, roads become mud pits and hiking trails are almost impassable, so it's best to visit during the dry season.

BIRD- AND WILDLIFE-WATCHING

Most people come to these areas for bird-watching and wildlife spotting, but it's best done during the dry season, when all the foliage drops from the trees. Bring a good bird guide or wildlife guide, binoculars, lots of water (we can't stress this enough), and plenty of patience. It's a good idea to find a watering hole and just hunker down and let the animals come to you. If you don't want to explore the forest alone, tours can be arranged through hotels, ranger stations, and private research centers inside the parks. In terms of bird and wildlife guides, we recommend *The Birds of Costa Rica* by Richard Garrigues and Robert Dean and *The Mammals of Costa Rica* by Mark Wainwright. If you'd like to know more about plants, pick up *Tropical Plants of Costa Rica* by Willow Zuchowski.

BIKING

Some parks allow biking, but again, this is certainly something you don't want to do during the rains. Contact the park that you'll be visiting ahead of time for trail and rental information.

FLORA

Among other types of flora, tropical forests are filled with deciduous hardwoods, such as mahogany (*Swietenia macrophylla*), black laurel (*Cordia gerascanthus*), ronrón (*Astronium graveolens*), and cocobolo (*Dalbergia retusa*). Much of the wood is highly prized for furniture and houses, so many of these trees are facing extinction outside national parks and protected areas.

Guanacaste

GUANACASTE
Perhaps the most striking and easy-to-spot resident of Costa Rica's tropical dry forest is the guanacaste (*Enterolobium cyclocarpum*), an imposing tree with an enormous, spherical canopy that seems straight out of the African savanna. The guanacaste is the northwest province's namesake and Costa Rica's national tree. It's most easily identified standing alone in pastures. Without the competition of the forest, a pasture guanacaste sends massive branches out low from its trunk, creating an arching crown of foliage close to the ground. The ear-shaped seedpods are also a distinct marker; the hard seeds inside are popular with local artisan jewelers.

Frangipani; plumboy,
Fodors.com member

FRANGIPANI TREE
The frangipani tree (*Plumeria rubra*) can grow up to 8 meters (26 feet) and has meaty pink, white, or yellow blossoms. The flowers are most fragrant at night to lure sphinx moths. Unfortunately for the moth, the blooms don't produce nectar. The plant simply dupes their pollinators into hopping from bloom to bloom and tree to tree in a fruitless search for food.

GUMBO-LIMBO
Costa Ricans call the gumbo-limbo tree (*Bursera simaruba*) *indio desnudo* (naked Indian) because of its red, peeling bark. This tree is also found in Florida, and the wood has historically been used for making carousel horses in the United States.

Gumbo-limbo

CORNIZUELO
The spiky, cornizuelo (*Acacia collinsii*) is an intriguing resident of the lower levels because of its symbiotic relationship with ants. This small evergreen tree puts out large thorns that serve as a home for a certain ant species. In exchange for food and shelter, the ants provide the tree protection from other leaf-munching insects or vines. Sometimes the ants will even cut down encroaching vegetation on the forest floor, allowing the tree to thrive.

Cornizuelo

FAUNA

Tropical dry forests are literally crawling with life. Bark scorpions, giant cockroaches, and tarantulas scuttle along the forest floor, and the buzz from wasps and cicadas gives the air an almost electric feel. A careful eye may be able to pick out walking sticks frozen still among the twigs. The jaguar, and one if its favorite prey, the endangered tapir, also stalk these forests.

WHITE-FACED CAPUCHIN

Monkeys are common all over Costa Rica, and the dry forests are home to three species: the howler monkeys, with their leathery black faces and deep barking call, are the loudest of the forest's mammals; the white-faced capuchin travel in playful packs; and the endangered spider monkey requires large, undisturbed tracts of forest for a healthy population to survive. This last group is in steep decline—another indicator of the overall health of this ecoregion.

White-faced capuchin

COYOTE

Nearly unique to the dry tropical forest is the coyote, which feeds on rodents, lizards, and an assortment of small mammals, as well as sea turtle eggs (when near the beach) and other improvised meals. Like the Virginia opossum and the white-tailed deer, the coyote is believed to have traveled south from North America through the once-interconnected tropical dry forest of Mesoamerica.

Coyote

NEOTROPICAL RATTLESNAKE

The venomous neotropical rattlesnake and the exquisite painted wood turtle are among the reptiles that exclusively call this region home. Salvin's spiny pocket mouse, the eastern cottontail rabbit, and both the spotted and hooded skunk are also unique to Costa Rica's dry forests.

Black-headed Trogon

BLACK-HEADED TROGON

With an open canopy for much of the year, and plentiful ground rodents and reptiles, these forests are great hunting grounds for birds of prey like the roadside hawk and the spectacled owl. The white-throated magpie jay travels in noisy mobs, while the scissor-tailed flycatcher migrates from as far north as the southern United States. The rufous-naped wren builds its nest in the spiky acacia trees. The black-headed trogon, with its bright yellow breast, and the elegant trogon both nest exclusively in Costa Rica's tropical dry forest.

Neotropical Rattlesnake

WETLANDS AND MANGROVES

Wetlands are any low-lying areas that are perpetually saturated with water. Their complex ecosystems support a variety of living things—both endemic species unique to the area and visitors who travel halfway around the hemisphere to get here. Here, land species have evolved to live much of their lives in water.

WORD OF MOUTH

"Guides take small groups out to designated "zones" along the beach [in Tortuguero]. Once the female begins laying her eggs, we get to watch the process lighted by the guides' single red light and then see her cover the nest and lumber back to the sea."
—Venturasurfwidow

One common type of wetland in Costa Rica is a floodplain, created when a river or stream regularly overflows its banks, either because of heavy rains or ocean tides. Thanks to huge deposits of sediment that are left as the floodwaters recede, the ground is extremely fertile and plants thrive, as do the animals that feed here.

Mangroves are a unique type of wetland and cover 1% of the country. They are found at the edges of tidal areas, such as ocean inlets, estuaries, and canals where saltwater mixes with fresh. Mangrove forests are made

up of a small variety of plants, principally mangrove trees, but attract a huge variety of animals.

Mangrove trees are able to survive in this stressful habitat because they have developed the ability to cope with constant flooding, tolerate a lack of oxygen, and thrive in a mix of salt- and freshwater thanks to uniquely adapted roots and leaves. The nutrient-rich sediment and mud that build up around these trees and between their prop roots create habitat for plankton, algae, crabs, oysters, and shrimp. These, in turn, attract larger and larger animals that come to feed, giving mangrove forests a remarkable level of biodiversity.

These thick coastal forests are protective barriers for inland ecosystems; they dissipate the force of storm winds and sudden surges in tides or floods triggered by coastal storms or tsunamis.

Sadly, coastal development is a big threat to mangroves. It is illegal to clear mangrove forests, but enforcement is weak, and beachfront developers have been caught doing it. The latest culprit is the huge, Spanish-owned Riú Hotel in Guanacaste. Wetlands are also threatened the diversion of water for agriculture.

ADVENTURE HIGHLIGHTS

■ Witness the spectacle of nesting turtles at Tortuguero National Park. Turtle-watching excursions require a certified guide and only take place between the February and November nesting season.

■ Anglers can hook mackerel, tarpoon, snook, calba, and snapper in the canals and along the coast of Tortuguero and Barra Colorado.

■ Take a kayaking tour through the mangrove estuary of Isla Damas, near Manuel Antonio. You'll probably see monkeys, crocodiles, and numerous birds.

TOP DESTINATIONS

The Ramsar Convention on Wetlands is an intergovernmental treaty to provide a framework for the conservation of the world's wetlands. There are 11 Ramsar wetlands in Costa Rica: all are impressive but we've listed only our top three.

PALO VERDE NATIONAL PARK

Within the Palo Verde National Park is perhaps Costa Rica's best-known wetland—a system that includes shallow, permanent freshwater lagoons, marshes, mangroves, and woodlands that are seasonally flooded by the Tempisque River. A good portion of this 45,511-acre park is covered by tropical dry forest, as mentioned earlier. In fact, this park has 12 different habitats, creating one of the most diverse collections of life in the country. At least 55 aquatic plants and 150 tree species have been identified here, and the largest number of aquatic and wading birds in all of Mesoamerica can be found at Palo Verde wetlands. A total of 279 bird species have been recorded within Palo Verde, so little surprise that it's listed by the Ramsar Convention as a wetland of international importance. The Organization of Tropical Studies maintains a research station at the park with limited accommodations but great views of the marshes, as well as extremely knowledgeable guides. *(See Chapter 6.)*

Alpha Howler Monkey; Liz Stuart, Fodors.com member

TORTUGUERO NATIONAL PARK

Ninety-nine percent of mangrove forests are found on Costa Rica's Pacific coast. But the best place to see some of the remaining 1% on the Caribbean side is Tortuguero National Park. Like Palo Verde, Tortuguero is home to a wide variety of life—11 distinct habitats in total, including extensive wetlands and mangrove forests. Beach-nesting turtles (*tortugas*) are the main attraction here, but the park is included in the Ramsar list of internationally important wetlands. Many of the species listed here can be spotted along the banks of Tortuguero's famous canals. *(See Chapter 6.)*

CAÑO NEGRO NATIONAL WILDLIFE REFUGE

A third Ramsar wetland is found in the Caño Negro National Wildlife Refuge, in the more remote northern plains close to the border with Nicaragua. Caño Negro has a seasonal lake that can cover as many as 1,975 acres and grow as deep as 3 meters (10 feet). The lake is actually a pool created by the Frio River that dries up to nearly nothing between February and May. The park also has marshes, semipermanently flooded old-growth forest, and other wetland habitats. *(See Chapter 5.)*

Tortuguero; StupFD, Fodors.com member

EXPERIENCING THE WETLANDS AND MANGROVES

Paddling through Tortuguero at dawn; Thornton Cohen, Fodors.com member

Wildlife viewing in general can be very rewarding in these areas, because a wide variety of creatures come together and share the habitat.

BIRD-WATCHING

The most populous and diverse of the creatures that live in and depend on wetlands and mangroves are birds, so bring some binoculars and your field guide and prepare to check off some species. For good photos, take a long lens and tripod, and get an early start—midday sun reflecting off the ubiquitous water can make your photos washed out or create some challenging reflections.

VIEWING PLATFORMS

Hiking can be more difficult in these areas because wetlands are by definition largely underwater. But some areas have elevated platforms that make for great up-close viewing of the interior parts of marshes and shallow lagoons.

BOATING

The best way to see Costa Rica's remaining mangrove forests is by boat—we recommend using a kayak or canoe. These vessels allow you to slip along canals and protected coastlines in near silence, increasing your chance of creeping up on many of the more impressive creatures that call this habitat home. A guided boat tour is also recommended— a good naturalist or biologist, or even a knowledgeable local, will know where creatures habitually hang out and will be able to distinguish between thick branches and a knotted boa at the top of a shoreside tree.

FISHING

Canals that are not part of protected areas can be ripe for fishing—another, tastier way to get a close-up look at some of the local fauna. Make sure to ask about what's biting, as well as local fishing regulations.

FLORA

Wetland and mangrove plants share an ability to live in soggy conditions. However, not all wetland plants are able to survive brackish water in the way coastal mangrove flora can.

Water Hyacinth

WATER HYACINTH

The succulent, floating water hyacinth (*Eichornia crassipes*) is recognizable by its lavender-pink flowers that are sometimes bundled at 8 to 15 per single stalk. The stems rise from a bed of thick, floating green leaves, whereas the plant's feathery roots hang free in the still freshwater. The water hyacinth is prolific and invasive; they've even been known to clog the canals of Tortuguero.

THORNY SENSITIVE PLANT

Aquatic grasses and herbs grow along the shallower edges of swamps and marshlands where they can take root underwater and still reach the air above. The curious dormilona, or thorny sensitive plant (*Mimosa pigra*) is another invasive wetland shrub and can be identified by the way its fernlike leaves wilt shyly to the touch, only to straighten out a little later.

Thorny sensitive plant

RED MANGROVE

Costa Rica has seven species of mangrove trees, including red mangrove (*Rhizophora mangle*), black mangrove (*Avicennia germinans*), white mangrove (*Laguncularia racemosa*), and the rarer tea mangrove (*Pelliciera rhizophorae*). Red mangrove is easily identified by its tall arching prop roots that give it a firm foothold against wind and waves. The tidal land is also unstable, so all mangroves need a lot of root just to keep upright. As a result, many have more living matter underwater than above ground. They also depend on their prop roots for extra nutrients and oxygen; the red mangrove filters salt at its roots.

Red Mangrove

BLACK MANGROVE

The black mangrove can grow as tall as 12 meters (40 feet) and has adapted to survive in its habitat by excreting salt through special glands in its leaves. It grows on the banks above the high-tide line and has evolved to breathe through small roots it sends up vertically in case of flooding.

Black Mangrove

FAUNA

Though the diversity of plant life in mangrove swamps and wetlands is small compared with other ecozones, this habitat attracts an extremely wide variety of fauna.

RAINBOW PARROT FISH

Rainbow parrot fish, in addition to many other fish species, spend time as juveniles in mangrove areas, feeding in the relative safety of the roots until they're big enough to venture out into more open water. Parrot fish have a few unusual abilities: they are hermaphroditic and can change sex in response to population density; at night they wrap themselves in a protective mucus cocoon; and they eat coral and excrete a fine white sand. One parrot fish can create a ton of sand per year, which ultimately washes ashore. Think about it the next time you're lying on the beach.

Rainbow Parrotfish

CRAB-EATING RACCOON

Bigger creatures are attracted to these mangroves precisely because of the veritable buffet of sea snacks. The crab-eating raccoon will prowl the canopy of the mangrove forests as well as the floor, feeding on crabs and mollusks. The endangered American crocodile and the spectacled caiman can be found lurking in still waters or sunning themselves on the banks of mangrove habitat.

Crab-eating Raccoon

BLACK-CROWNED NIGHT HERON

Mangroves are critical nesting habitats for a number of birds, including the endangered mangrove hummingbird, the yellow-billed continga, the Amazon kingfisher, and the black-crowned night heron. Interestingly, black-crowned night herons don't distinguish between their own young and those from other nests, so they willingly brood strange chicks.

BLACK-BELLIED WHISTLING DUCK

Bird-watchers love the wide-open wetlands and marshes, with flocks of thousands of migrating and resident species. In these tropical floodplains pink-tinged roseate spoonbills will be found stalking the shallow water alongside the majestic great egret and the bizarre and endangered jabiru stork. Keep an eye out for the black-bellied whistling duck, which actually perches and nests in trees. These migrant ducks can also be found in some southern U.S. states.

Black Crowned Night Heron

Black-Bellied Whistling Duck

SHORELINE

Costa Rica has a whopping 1,290-km-long (799-mi-long) coastline that varies from expansive beaches, tranquil bays, muddy estuaries, and rocky outcroppings. They're backed by mangrove, rain, transitional, and tropical dry forests.

Each of Costa Rica's costal environments, as well as the currents and the wind, has its own distinct impact on the ecology of the beach.

Costa Rica's sand beaches come in different shades and textures: pulverized black volcanic rock (Playa Negra), crushed white shells (Playa Conchal), finely ground white coral and quartz (Playa Carrillo), and gray rock sediment (many stretches along both coasts). These strips of sand may seem devoid of life, but they're actually ecological hotbeds, where mammals, birds, and amphibians live, feed, or reproduce. The hardiest

of creatures can be found in the tidal pools that form on rockier beaches; keep an eye out for colorful fish, starfish, and sea urchins, all of which endure pounding waves, powerful tides, broiling sun, and predator attacks from the air, land, or sea.

By law, all of Costa Rica's beaches are public, but beaches near population centers get strewn with trash quite quickly. It's one of the great ironies of Costa Rica that a country renowned for its environmental achievements litters with such laissez-faire. Limited access tends to make for more-scenic beaches. If you're worried about pollution, keep an eye out for Blue Flag beaches (marked on our maps with blue flags), an ecological rating system that evaluates water quality—both ocean and drinking water—trash cleanup, waste management, security, signage, and environmental education. Blue flags are awarded to communities, rather than to individual hotels, which feeds a sense of cooperation. In 2002, the competition was opened to inland communities. Out of 125 that applied, 84 communities—56 beaches and 28 inland towns—won flags at the 2012 ceremonies.

ADVENTURE HIGHLIGHTS

■ From October 15 to February 15, Playa Grande sees lumbering, huge leatherback turtles come ashore to nest. Sixty days later, the hatchlings will scramble toward the water.

■ Gentle, consistent waves and a couple of good surfing schools make Sámara, on the North Pacific coast, a good choice for first-timers hoping to catch a wave.

■ Snorkeling is phenomenal near Cahuita's coral reef and at Punta Uva on the Caribbean coast. Watch out for colorful blue parrot fish, angelfish, sponges, and seaweeds.

TOP DESTINATIONS

Costa Rica's beach scenes are wildly diverse, so a little planning can go a long way.

BALLENA NATIONAL MARINE PARK

This unique park is along one of the more remote stretches of coastline, on the southern end of the Central Pacific region, and encompasses several beaches. *Ballena*, which is Spanish for "whale," gets its name from the humpback whales who feed here, and for a peculiar sandbar formation at Playa Uvita that goes straight out toward the ocean before splitting and curving in two directions, much like a whale's tale. *(See Chapter 8.)*

MANUEL ANTONIO NATIONAL PARK

On the northern end of the Pacific, Manuel Antonio National Park shelters some of the country's more precious beaches. A series of half-moon bays with sparkling sands are fronted by transitional forest—a combination of flora and fauna from the tropical dry forests farther north and the tropical rain forests that stretch south. Wildlife is abundant at Manuel Antonio, and the towering jungle at the beach's edge can give the area a wild and paradisiacal feel. *(See Chapter 7.)*

Uvita Beach; Toronto Jeff, Fodors.com member

THE NICOYA PENINSULA

A succession of incredible beaches are scattered along this region of the Pacific coast, from Playa Panama in the north all the way south to Montezuma, including Avellanas, Guiones, and Sámara. Ostional, just north of Guiones, offers something none of the others can: the arribada. The beach is part of the Ostional Wildlife Refuge, granting an extra level of protection to the area. *(See Chapter 6.)*

THE CARIBBEAN

This coast has an entirely different feel from the Pacific. North of Limón, there are miles of undeveloped, protected beaches where green sea turtles come from July to October to lay eggs. There have also been sightings of the loggerhead, hawksbill, and leatherback turtles. The currents here are strong, so don't plan on swimming.

To the south of Limón, beaches are bordered by dense green vegetation all year long, and the quality of the sand can change dramatically as you wander from cove to cove. Some of the country's healthiest living coral reefs are offshore, so snorkeling is worthwhile. Beaches of note are Playa Negra, Playa Blanca, Playa Negro, and Punta Uva. *(See Chapter 9.)*

Montezuma; Justin Hubbell, Fodors.com member

EXPERIENCING THE SHORELINE

Nesting Olive Ridley Turtles at Ostional Wildlife Refuge

Costa Rica's beaches have tons of activities. If you like getting wet, the ocean is bathwater warm and there are water-sports outfitters just about everywhere. There are also plenty of hammocks and cafés.

HORSEBACK RIDING

Horseback riding on the beach is great fun, but you can't do it everywhere. Many of the most popular beaches have outlawed it for health reasons, especially if it's where a lot of people swim.

SURFING

Costa Rica is a world-class surfing destination, and the Pacific coast in particular has enough surf spots to satisfy both pros and novices. You can arrange lessons in most beach towns. Surfing is an activity that involves a lot of floating, so it allows for plenty of wildlife watching: keep a weather eye for jumping fish, sting rays, dolphins, and squads of brown pelicans.

TURTLE TOURS

Witnessing the nesting ritual of Costa Rica's visiting sea turtles is a truly unforgettable experience. Various organizations oversee the nesting beaches and arrange tours. The onslaught of mother turtles is most intense throughout the night, so setting out just before dawn is the best way to see and take pictures of the phenomenon in progress at first light.

⚠ Take great care at beaches that drop off steeply as you enter the water. This is an indicator not only of large waves that crash straight onto the shore but also of strong currents.

FLORA

The plants along the coast play an important role in maintaining the dunes and preventing erosion in the face of heavy winds and other forces.

COCONUT PALMS

Coconut palm trees are the most distinctive plants in any tropical setting. No postcard photo of a white-sand beach would be complete without at least one palm tilting precariously over the shore. Palm trees (from the *Arecaceae* family) require a lot of sunlight and will, thanks to their strong root system, often grow at nearly horizontal angles to escape the shade of beachside forests. The coconut palm is also the proud parent of the world's largest seed—the delicious coconut—which can float long distances across the ocean, washing up on a foreign shore and sprouting a new tree from the sand.

Coconut Palms

MANZANILLO DE PLAYA

Steer clear of the poisonous manchineel, or *manzanillo de playa* (*Hippomane mancinella*), the most toxic tree in Costa Rica. Its fruit and bark secrete a white latex that's highly irritable to the touch and poisonous—even fatal—if ingested. Don't burn it either, because the smoke can also cause allergic reactions. The tree can be identified by its small, yellowish apples and bright green leaves. It's found along the North Pacific coast, stretches of the Nicoya Peninsula, the Central Pacific's Manuel Antonio National Park, and on the Osa Peninsula.

Manzaniillo de playa

SEAGRAPE

Seagrape (*Coccoloba uvifera*) and similar types of shrubby, ground-hugging vegetation grow closer to the water, around the edges of the beach. These plants play a part in keeping the beach stable and preventing erosion.

MANGROVE

Mangrove swamps are rich, murky forests that thrive in brackish waters up and down Costa Rica's coasts. They grow in what's known as the intertidal zone, the part of the coast that's above sea level at low tide and submerged at high tide. Mangrove trees (*rhizophora*) are just one of the species that live in these coastal swamps—you can recognize them by their stilt roots, the long tendril-like roots that allow the tree to breathe even when it's partially submerged. These forests are vibrant and complex ecosystems in their own right *and were explained earlier in this chapter*.

Seagrape

Mangrove tree

FAUNA

Beaches are tough environments where few animals actually make their home. But as we all know, you don't have to live on the beach to enjoy it.

OLIVE RIDLEY TURTLE

At 34 to 45 kilos (75 to 100 pounds) the olive ridley (*Lepidochelys olivacea*) is the smallest of the five marine turtles that nest in Costa Rica. During mass nesting times (arribada), anywhere from tens to hundreds of thousands of females drag themselves ashore, gasping audibly, to lay their eggs. Between dusk and dawn, the prehistoric creatures crawl over the beach, sometimes even over one another, on their way between the ocean and their nests. People who are lucky enough to witness the event never forget it. Costa Rica's shores are also visited by the green turtle, the hawksbill, the loggerhead, and the leatherback turtle.

Olive Ridley Turtle

IGUANAS

A common sight on Costa Rica's sandy shores are iguanas. The green iguana (*Iguana iguana*) and the black spiny-tailed iguana, or black iguana (*Ctenosaura simi*), are often found sunning themselves on rocks or a few feet from the shade (and protection) of trees. Interestingly, green iguana has been known to lay eggs and share nests with American crocodiles and spectacled caimans.

Iguanas

PAINTED GHOST CRAB

These intriguingly named crabs are called "ghosts" because they move so quickly that they seem to disappear. They're also one of the few creatures that actually live full time on the beach. Sun beats down, wind is strong, danger lurks everywhere, and there's little to no cover, but painted ghost crabs (*Ocypode cuadrata*) survive all this by burrowing deep under the sand where the temperature and humidity is more constant and there's safe protection from surface threats, like the black iguana.

Painted Ghost Crab

BROWN PELICAN

Brown pelicans fly in tight formation, dropping low over the sea and running parallel with the swells in search of shoals of fish. Browns are unique in that they're the only pelican species that plunge from the air to catch their food. After a successful dive, they have to guard against gulls, who will actually try to pluck the freshly caught fish from their pouch.

Brown Pelican

San José

WORD OF MOUTH

"If you want to see San Jose, I believe you should stay close to downtown. Traffic can be a nightmare, and you don't want to add to the headache. Airport shuttles from downtown hotels are not common in Costa Rica. But the taxi system is efficient. You can also ask your travel agent to arrange a van and driver to meet you outside the terminal to take you to your hotel."

—Pat_Hewitt

WELCOME TO SAN JOSÉ

TOP REASONS TO GO

★ **Eating out:** After traveling around Costa Rica eating mostly rice and beans and chicken, you'll appreciate San José's varied restaurants.

★ **Gold and Jade museums:** For a sense of indigenous Costa Rica, frequently forgotten during the nation's march to modernity, the country's two best museums are must-sees.

★ **Historic Barrios Amón and Otoya:** These northern neighborhoods abutting and sometimes overlapping downtown have quiet tree-lined streets and century-old houses turned trendy hotels and restaurants.

★ **Location, location, location:** From the capital's pivotal position, you can be on a coffee tour, at the base of a giant volcano, or riding river rapids in just 30 minutes.

★ **Shopping:** San José is the best place to stock up on both essentials and souvenirs. Look for folkloric crafts, ceramics, textiles, leather-and-wood rocking chairs, and, of course, coffee.

1 Downtown. This area holds San José's historic and commercial districts and many top attractions: the Museo del Jade (Jade Museum), Museo del Oro Precolombino (Gold Museum), Mercado Central (Central Market), and Teatro Nacional (National Theater).

2 West of Downtown. The mostly residential neighborhoods here are anchored by large Parque Metropolitano La Sabana (La Sabana Park) and the Museo de Arte Costarricense (Museum of Costa Rican Art).

GETTING ORIENTED

3

The metropolitan area holds more than 1 million residents, but the city proper is small, with some 300,000 people living in its 44 square km (17 square miles). Most sights are concentrated in three downtown neighborhoods, La Soledad, La Merced, and El Carmen, named for their anchor churches. Borders are fuzzy: one barrio (neighborhood) flows into the next, districts overlap, and the city itself melts into its suburbs with nary a sign to denote where one community ends and another begins.

3 North of Downtown. Historic barrios Amón and Otoya and the Museo de los Niños (Children's Museum) are a few of the attractions to the north.

4 East of Downtown. Several good restaurants and hotels and the Universidad de Costa Rica (University of Costa Rica) are ensconced in the San Pedro suburb.

ECO-LODGES IN SAN JOSÉ

GOOD PRACTICES

Clean? Green? Pristine? San José is none of these, but even in Costa Rica's congested capital, you can count on a handful of pioneers who keep the environmental spirit alive.

The capital's few pockets of greenery are its parks, and, in this regard, the city does itself proud. The grandiose monuments so common in other Latin America countries are not very prominent. Small is the watchword in Costa Rica, so parks are places to enjoy mini eco-refuges rather than shrines to past heroes and glories. A trio of parks—Morazán, España, and Nacional—graces the area just northeast of downtown and provides a mostly contiguous several blocks of peace and quiet. Vast La Sabana Park on San José's west side once served as the country's international airport. Its lush greenery and ample space for recreation get our vote as being one of the most pleasing uses of urban space. The capital's parks have one big downside: after dark, a small cast of unsavory characters replaces the throngs of day-trippers. Make a point to vacate city parks when the sun goes down.

Use public transportation whenever possible. Buses travel everywhere in San José and suburbs, and taxis are relatively easy to find. In addition to reducing your carbon footprint, it also saves you the hassle of driving and parking in an already congested city.

Ask whether your hotel recycles glass, plastic, and aluminum. A few lodgings—and, unfortunately, "few" is the operative term here—do. Take advantage if you can.

Don't litter—the city has a burdensome trash problem—although you'll swear no one else here follows this advice. Dispose of your trash properly.

TOP ECO-LODGES IN SAN JOSÉ

To ensure that your hotel really is eco-friendly, do a bit of research or ask a few questions. Check on the property's lighting—does it use compact fluorescent bulbs? What about sensors or timers? Is any form of alternative energy, like solar or wind power, employed? Are there low-flow faucets, showers, and toilets? What sort of recycling programs are in place for guests *and* staff? Answers to such questions give you a sense of whether a property is green or not. Here are a couple of San José properties that do more than pay lip service to the environmental movement.

CLARION HOTEL AMÓN PLAZA

From its active in-hotel recycling program and its eco-friendly store that sells no products made from endangered woods, to its small garden that acquaints you with rain-forest plant species and its liaison program with the community, the Amón Plaza is greener than most countryside hotels. *(Full hotel review on page 106.)*

HOTEL PRESIDENTE

Costa Rica's first "carbon neutral" hotel has taken major steps to reduce its carbon footprint. What is left over is offset by a tree-planting project the lodging supports. The Presidente has organized a small but growing consortium of San José hotels to take up recycling. All in all, not bad for a place located smack-dab in the center of the city. *(Full hotel review on page 103.)*

HOTEL RINCÓN DE SAN JOSÉ

Your hot water in this small Barrio Otoya hotel will be solar heated, and the place makes maximum use of natural lighting during the day in its public areas. The Rincón de San José uses only biodegradable products whenever possible, it also engages in an active recycling program. Even captured rainwater finds its way into your room's toilet basin. *(Full hotel review on page 108.)*

PEDESTRIANS ONLY

The government is forever announcing some grandiose plan to make San José more livable and a bit less of an urban hell. Few, however, make it off the ground, mostly due to a chronic lack of funds. Two have come to fruition, though, and you will notice the benefit.

For years, the city government has been turning downtown streets into pedestrian-only malls. Some 34 blocks in the center city—sections of Avenidas Central and 4, and Calles 2, 3, and 17—now have *bulevar* (boulevard) status, with more on the drawing board. Thank the European Union for much of the funding. Weekday driving restrictions cover all of San José and parts of neighboring San Pedro. The last digit of your license plate dictates the day of the week when you may not bring a car into the large restricted zone from 6 am to 7 pm. The city still hosts far too many cars, but the 20% reduction in vehicles each weekday rush hour has made a noticeable difference.

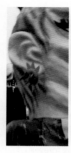

By Jeffrey Van Fleet

The center of all that is Costa Rica probably won't be the center of your trip to Costa Rica. Most visitors spend two nights in San José—tops. You'll probably head out of town the morning after you arrive, only to return the night before heading home. No, you shouldn't sacrifice precious beach or rain-forest time for a stay in San José. But the city is worth a day or two—as a way to ease into Costa Rica at the start of a visit or as a way of wrapping things up with a well-deserved dose of civilization.

Amid the noise and traffic, shady parks, well-maintained museums, lively plazas, terrific restaurants, and great hotels do exist. Further, the city makes a great base for day trips: from downtown it's a mere 30- to 40-minute drive to the tranquil countryside and myriad outdoor activities of the surrounding Central Valley.

You'd never know San José is as old as it is—given the complete absence of colonial architecture—but settlers migrating from then provincial capital Cartago founded the city in 1737. After independence in 1821, San José cemented its position as the new nation's capital after struggles and a brief civil war with fellow Central Valley cities Cartago, Alajuela, and Heredia. Revenues from the coffee and banana industries financed the construction of stately homes, theaters, and a trolley system (later abandoned and now visible only in old sepia photographs).

As recently as the mid-1900s, San José was no larger than the present-day downtown area; old-timers remember the vast coffee and cane plantations that extended beyond its borders. The city began to mushroom only after World War II, when old buildings were razed to make room for concrete monstrosities. The sprawl eventually connected the capital with nearby cities.

New York or London it is not, but for the Tico living out in Tilarán, today's San José glitters every bit as much. It has attracted people from all over Costa Rica, yet it remains, in many ways, a collection of distinct neighborhoods where residents maintain friendly small-town ways. For you, this might mean the driver you're following will decide to abruptly stop his vehicle to buy a lottery ticket or chat with a friend on the street. Or it might mean you have to navigate a maze of fruit-vendor stands on a crowded sidewalk. But this is part of what keeps San José a big small town.

PLANNING

WHEN TO GO

HIGH SEASON: MID-DECEMBER TO APRIL

San José's altitude keeps temperatures pleasant and springlike year-round. The capital's status as a business-travel destination means lodging rates rarely vary throughout the year. The dry season literally blows in with a change in wind patterns that make December and January brisk, but sunny. February warms up; by March and April, the heat and dust pick up considerably.

LOW SEASON: MAY TO MID-NOVEMBER

The wet season moves in gradually, with manageable brief afternoon showers from May through July. August becomes wetter. September and October might mean rain 24/7 for days at a time, and navigating a traffic-clogged city in a torrential rush-hour downpour is little fun.

SHOULDER SEASON: MID-NOVEMBER TO MID-DECEMBER

Rains wind down by mid-November and you'll even experience a bit of a nip in the air—it's still the tropics, though—as the city decks itself out for the holidays. The big influx of tourists won't arrive until just before Christmas itself, so this is the time to enjoy the capital at its best.

SAN JOSÉ IN A DAY

If you have only a day to spend in San José, the must-see stops are the Teatro Nacional (National Theater)—we recommend the guided tour—and the Museo del Oro Precolombino (Precolumbian Gold Museum). That's easy to accomplish because they sit on the same block.

With more time, take in the Museo del Jade (Jade Museum) and Museo Nacional (National Museum). The Museo de los Niños (Children's Museum), north of downtown, is a kid pleaser. (It's in a dicey part of the barrio El Carmen, more north of downtown than actually in downtown; take a taxi.)

Our Good Walk *(⇨ below)* gives you a taste of the city in just an hour.

BYPASS SAN JOSÉ?

OK. So San José isn't necessarily the Costa Rica you came to see. Those beaches and rain forests beckon, after all. If that is, indeed, the case, you can avoid the city altogether.

The international airport actually lies just outside the city of Alajuela, about 30 minutes northwest of the capital. Look for lodgings in Alajuela, San Antonio de Belén, Escazú, or Santa Ana—all within striking distance of the airport. Or head west. *For information about lodgings near Aeropuerto Internacional Juan Santamaría, see Chapter 4.*

Few international flights arrive in the morning, but they do exist, especially via Miami. Get here early, and you can head out of town immediately.

A third option is to join the growing number of visitors flying into Daniel Oduber International Airport in Liberia, where Costa Rica's northern and western reaches (including the North Pacific) are at your fingertips.

DAY TRIPS FROM THE CAPITAL

The capital sits smack-dab in the middle of the country and in the middle of the fertile Central Valley. Although a day trip to either coast would be grueling—despite Costa Rica's small size, it takes longer than you think to get from place to place—you can easily pop out to the Central Valley's major sights and be back in the city in time for dinner. Several of these attractions provide pickup service in San José, some for a nominal additional cost. Alternatively, tour operators include many of these attractions on their itineraries.

DESTINATION	FROM SAN JOSÉ (BY CAR)	
Basílica de Nuestra Señora de los Ángeles	30 mins southeast	⇨ p. 162
Butterfly Farm	45 mins west	⇨ p. 143
Café Britt	30 mins north	⇨ p. 152
Carara National Park	2 hrs southwest	⇨ p. 350
Doka Coffee Estate	1 hr west	⇨ p. 144
Guayabo National Monument	2 hrs southeast, 4WD necessary	⇨ p. 170
INBioparque	15 mins north	⇨ p. 150
Irazú Volcano	60 mins east	⇨ p. 162
La Paz Waterfall Gardens	2 hrs north	⇨ p. 235
Orosi Valley	60 mins southeast	⇨ p. 164
Poás Volcano	60 mins northwest	⇨ p. 184
Rain Forest Aerial Tram	45 mins north	⇨ pp. 505, 510
River Rafting	2–2½ hrs southeast or north	⇨ p. 174
Sarchí	60 mins northwest	⇨ p. 194
Tortuga Island	3 hrs west	⇨ p. 365
Tropical Bungee	60 mins west	⇨ p. 193
World of Snakes	60 mins west	⇨ p. 193
Zoo Ave	45 mins west	⇨ p. 146

GETTING HERE AND AROUND

AIR TRAVEL

Aeropuerto Internacional Juan Santamaría (16 km/10 miles northwest of downtown) receives international flights and those of domestic airline SANSA. Domestic Nature Air flights use tiny, informal Aeropuerto Internacional Tobías Bolaños (3 km/2 miles west of downtown).

BUS TRAVEL

San José's bus stations are all in sketchy neighborhoods. Always take a taxi to and from them. Better: Use air-conditioned minivan shuttles instead of buses to travel into and out of the capital.

City buses are cheap (30¢–50¢) and easy to use. For Paseo Colón and La Sabana, take buses marked "Sabana–Cementerio" from stops at Avenida 2 between Calles 5 and 7 or Avenida 3 next to the post office. For Los Yoses and San Pedro, take the "San Pedro" bus from Avenida Central between Calles 9 and 11.

CAR TRAVEL

Paved roads fan out from Paseo Colón west to Escazú and northwest to the airport and Heredia. For the Pacific coast, Guanacaste, and Nicaragua, take the Pan-American Highway (PAH) north (CA1). Calle 3 runs north into the highway to Guápiles, Limón, and the Atlantic coast through Braulio Carrillo National Park, with a turnoff to Sarapiquí. Follow Avenida Central or 2 east through San Pedro to enter the PAH south (CA2), which has a turnoff for Cartago, Volcán Irazú, and Turrialba before it heads toward Panama.

Avoid driving in the city. Streets are narrow, rush hour (7 am to 9 am and 5 pm to 7 pm) traffic is horrible, and drivers can be reckless. What's more, San José and neighboring San Pedro enforce rigid weekday driving restrictions (6 am–7 pm) for all private vehicles, including your rental car. The last digit of your license plate determines your no-driving day: Monday (1 and 2), Tuesday (3 and 4), Wednesday (5 and 6), Thursday (7 and 8), and Friday (9 and 0). Fines are $82.

TAXI

You can hail cabs on the street or call for one. All licensed cabs are red with a gold triangle on the front doors (though Taxis Unidos Aeropuerto—which go to the airport—are orange). A 3-km (2-mile) ride costs around $3; tipping isn't customary. By law cabbies must use *marías* (meters) within the metropolitan area.

HEALTH AND SAFETY

San José is safer than other Latin American capitals. Violent crime is rare; the greatest threat you're likely to face is petty theft. Standard big-city precautions apply:

Exchange money only at banks. Street money changers slip counterfeit bills into their stash, or doctor their calculators to compute unfavorable rates. In the extreme, they might grab your cash and run off.

Select ATMs in well-lighted areas. Better still, use a bank's ATM during opening hours, when a guard will likely be present. Go with a buddy, and conceal cash immediately.

Use only licensed red taxis with yellow triangles on the front doors. The license plate of an official taxi begins with TSJ ("Taxi San José").

Park in guarded, well-lighted lots (about $1 an hour). If you must park on the street, make sure informal *guachimen* (watchmen) are present. Usually this is someone with a big stick who will expect payment of about $1 per hour. Do not leave anything valuable in your parked vehicle.

MONEY MATTERS

It's a bad sign when most San José banks have televisions to watch while you pass the time in their horrendous lines. Bypass that process and get cash with your ATM card instead. Cash machines inside a bank, during the day while a guard keeps watch, are your safest bet.

RESTAURANTS

Fed up with all the chicken, rice, and beans you've been chewing on in your out-country travels? Costa Rica's capital beckons you back with the country's most varied and cosmopolitan restaurant scene. Italian, Spanish, Asian, French, Middle Eastern, Peruvian—they're all here, along with upscale, típico Costa Rican cuisine, too.

Prices in the reviews are the average cost of a main course at dinner or, if dinner is not served, at lunch.

HOTELS

San José may be the big city, but it truly shines in its selection of small to medium-size inns. They're all locally owned and their friendly, attentive staff will make you feel as if you're staying in an oasis in the middle of Costa Rica's noisy, congested capital.

Prices in the reviews are the lowest cost of a standard double room in high season.

TOURS

Grayline Tours. Grayline Tours operates sightseeing and shopping tours. ☎ 2220–2106 ⊕ www.graylinecostarica.com.

Tico Walks. Tico Walks gives 2½-hour guided walks of downtown. Show up in front of the Teatro Nacional at 10 am, Tuesday, Thursday, Saturday, or Sunday. If that doesn't fit your schedule, other times can be arranged with advance notice. ☎ 2283–8281 ▤ $25.

VISITOR INFORMATION

The ubiquitous "Tourist Information" signs you see around downtown are really private travel agencies looking to sell you tours rather than provide unbiased information. At present, the ICT, the official tourist office, operates only a booth in the arrivals area of the international airport.

ESSENTIALS

Bank/ATM BAC San José ⊠ Avda. 2, Cs. Central–1, Barrio El Carmen ☎ 2295–9797 ⊕ www.bac.net. **Banco Nacional** ⊠ Avda. 1, Cs. 2–4, Barrio La Merced ☎ 2212–2000 ⊕ www.bncr.fi.cr. **Scotiabank** ⊠ Behind Teatro Nacional, C. 5, Avdas. Ctrl.–2, Barrio La Soledad ☎ 2521–5680 ⊕ www.scotiabankcr.com.

Medical Assistance Clínica Bíblica ⊠ Avda. 14, Cs. Central–1, Barrio El Pacífico ☎ 2522–1000 ⊕ www.clinicabiblica.com. **Hospital La Católica** ⊠ Attached to San Antonio Church on C. Esquivel Bonilla, Guadalupe ☎ 2246–3000 ⊕ www.hospitallacatolica.com.

Shuttle Companies Grayline ☎ *2220–2126* ⊕ *www.graylinecostarica.com.*
Interbus ☎ *2283–5573* ⊕ *www.interbusonline.com.*

Taxis Alfaro ☎ *2223–3373.* **Coopetaxi** ☎ *2235–9966.* **San Jorge** ☎ *2221–3434.* **Taxis Unidos Aeropuerto** ☎ *2221–6865* ⊕ *www.taxiaeropuerto.com.*

Visitor Information Instituto Costarricense de Turismo (ICT). ✉ *Aeropuerto Juan Santamaría Alajuela* ☎ *2443–1535* ⊕ *www.visitcostarica.com.*

EXPLORING

3

The Irish group U-2 could have written its song "Where the Streets Have No Name" about San José. Admittedly, some of its streets have names, but no one seems to know or use them. Streets in the center of the capital are laid out in a grid, with *avenidas* (avenues) running east and west, and *calles* (streets), north and south. Odd-number avenues increase in number north of Avenida Central; even-number avenues, south. Streets east of Calle Central have odd numbers; those to the west are even.

The farther you get from downtown, the scarcer street signs become. Costa Ricans rely instead on a charming and exasperating system of designating addresses by the distance from landmarks, as in "100 meters north and 50 meters west of the school." Another quirk: "100 meters" always refers to one city block, regardless of how long it actually is. Likewise, "200 meters" is two blocks, and so on. (As you can imagine, getting a pizza delivered here is quite a challenge.)

Historically, the reference point was the church, but these days it might be a bar, Burger King, or even a long-gone landmark: the eastern suburb of San Pedro uses the *higuerón*, a fig tree that was felled long ago but lives on in the hearts of Costa Ricans. Your best bet is to follow the time-honored practice of *ir y preguntar* (keep walking and keep asking).

DOWNTOWN

It's a trend seen the world over: businesses and residents flee city centers for the space, blissful quiet, and lower-priced real estate of the burbs. Although Costa Rica's capital is experiencing this phenomenon, downtown still remains the city's historic and vibrant (if noisy and congested) heart. Government offices have largely stayed put here, as have most attractions. It's impossible to sightsee here without finding yourself downtown.

Boundaries are fuzzy. For example, the neighborhoods of El Carmen, La Merced, and La Soledad are anchored in downtown but sprawl outward from the center city. And, in an effort to seem trendier, several establishments in downtown's northern fringes prefer to say that they're in the more fashionable barrios of Amón or Otoya.

TOP ATTRACTIONS

Fodor's Choice   **Museo del Jade.** The Jade Museum has the world's largest collection of
★   American jade—that's "American" in the hemispheric sense. Nearly all the items on display were produced in pre-Columbian times, and most of the jade (pronounced *hah*-day in Spanish) dates from 300 BC

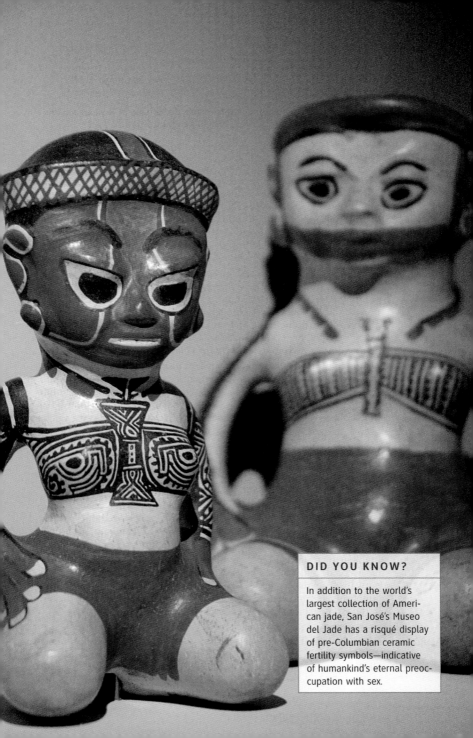

DID YOU KNOW?

In addition to the world's largest collection of American jade, San José's Museo del Jade has a risqué display of pre-Columbian ceramic fertility symbols—indicative of humankind's eternal preoccupation with sex.

to AD 700. In the spectacular Jade Room, pieces are illuminated from behind so you can appreciate their translucency. A series of drawings explains how this extremely hard stone was cut using string saws with quartz-and-sand abrasive. Jade was sometimes used in jewelry designs, but it was most often carved into oblong pendants. The museum also has other pre-Columbian artifacts, such as polychrome vases and three-legged *metates* (small stone tables for grinding corn), and a gallery of modern art. The final room on the tour has a startling display of ceramic fertility symbols. A photo-filled, glossy, English-language guide to the museum sells for $15; the Spanish version is only $3. The collection consists of 5,000-plus pieces; space constraints mean you can see only about a quarter of them. A search is underway at this writing for a larger space, but it hasn't moved much beyond the drawing-board phase. The museum's present location on the first floor of a tall office building gives it a downtown feel, even if it's at the northern edge of the city center. ⊠ *INS Bldg., Avda. 7, Cs. 9–11, Barrio Amón* ☎ *2287–6034* ⊕ *portal. ins-cr.com/Social/MuseoJade* ☜ *$8* ⊙ *Weekdays 8:30–3:30, Sat. 11–3.*

Fodor'sChoice   **Museo del Oro Precolombino.** The dazzling, modern Pre-Columbian Gold
★   Museum, in a three-story underground structure beneath the Plaza de la Cultura, contains Central America's largest collection of pre-Columbian gold jewelry—20,000 troy ounces in more than 1,600 individual pieces—all owned by the Banco Central and displayed attractively in low-lighted, bilingual exhibits. Many pieces are in the form of frogs and eagles, two animals perceived by the region's early cultures to have great spiritual significance. A spiffy new illumination system was installed in 2011 making the pieces sparkle like never before. All that glitters here is not gold: most spectacular are the varied shaman figurines, which represent the human connection to animal deities. One of the halls houses the Museo Numismática (Coin Museum; admission included with Gold Museum), a repository of historic coins and bills and other objects used as legal tender throughout the country's history. Rotating art exhibitions happen on another level of the complex. ⊠ *C. 5, Avdas. Central–2, Eastern end of Plaza de la Cultura, Barrio La Soledad* ☎ *2243–4202* ⊕ *www.museosdelbancocentral.org* ☜ *$8* ⊙ *Mid-Jan.–Mar., weekdays 9:15–6, weekends 9:15–5; Apr.–mid-Jan., daily 9:15–5.*

**NEED A
BREAK?**   A slew of unnamed *sodas*—that's the Costa Rican term for a mom-and-pop eatery—populate the heart of the Mercado Central. Grab a quick bite while you explore. It's all very informal.

★   **Teatro Nacional.** The National Theater is Costa Rica at its most enchanting. Chagrined that touring prima donna Adelina Patti bypassed San José in 1890 for lack of a suitable venue, wealthy coffee merchants raised import taxes and hired Belgian architects to design this building, lavish with cast iron and Italian marble. The theater was inaugurated in 1897 with a performance of Gounod's *Faust*, featuring an international cast. The sandstone exterior is marked by Italianate arched windows, marble columns with bronze capitals, and statues of strange bedfellows Ludwig van Beethoven (1770–1827) and 17th-century Spanish Golden Age playwright Pedro Calderón de la Barca (1600–81). The Muses of Dance, Music, and Fame are silhouetted in front of an iron cupola.

San José
Exploring

TO
GUADALUPE

SAN FRANCISCO
108

21

MIRAFLORES

TO
SAN PEDRO,
UNIVERSIDAD DE
COSTA RICA
202

OTOYA

Casa
Amarilla

6

7

5   8

ARANJUEZ

Avenida 15

Avenida 13

Avenida 11

Avenida 9

Avda. 7

Avenida 11

Avenida 9

ESCALANTE

CUESTA DE
MORAS   9

Avenida 1

LA CALIFORNIA

Avenida 5

11   10

Avenida Central

Avenida 6

Avenida 8

LOS YOSES

Avenida 8

Avenida 10

Avenida 10

MILFLOR

Avenida 12

Calle José Martí

204

Avenida 16bis

CERRITO

KEY

Rail Lines

Pedestrian Zone

The sumptuous neo-baroque interior sparkles, too. Given the provenance of the building funds, it's not surprising that frescoes on the stairway inside depict coffee and banana production. Note Italian painter Aleardo Villa's famous ceiling mural *Alegoría del Café y Banano* (*Allegory of Coffee and Bananas*), a joyful harvest scene that appeared on Costa Rica's old five-colón note. (The now-defunct

bill is prized by collectors and by visitors as a souvenir, and is often sold by vendors in the plaza between the theater and the Gran Hotel Costa Rica next door.) French designer Alain Guilhot created the building's nighttime external illumination system. (He did the same for the Eiffel Tower.) The soft coppers, golds, and whites highlight the theater's exterior nightly from 6 pm to 5 am. A project funded by the German government in 2011 restored the theater's cupola to its original red color.

You can see the theater's interior by attending one of the performances that take place several nights a week (tickets are reasonable); intermission gives you a chance to nose around. The theater prizes punctuality, one of the few institutions in this country to do so. Performances start on time. Stop at the *boletería* (box office) in the lobby and see what strikes your fancy. (Don't worry if you left your tuxedo or evening gown back home; as long as you don't show up for a performance wearing shorts, jeans, or a T-shirt, no one will care.)

For a nominal admission fee you can also move beyond the lobby for a self-guided visit during the day. (The theater is sometimes closed for rehearsals, so call before you go.) If you're downtown on a Tuesday between February and Christmas, take in one of the Teatro al Mediodía (Theater at Midday) performances that begin at noon. It might be a chamber-music recital or a one-act play (in Spanish). Admission is $2. A similar program with similar admission called Música al Atardecer (Music at Dusk) takes place each Thursday at 5 pm. Both take place in the second-floor flyer. ⊠ *Plaza de la Cultura, Barrio La Soledad* ☎ *2221–5341* ⊕ *www.teatronacional.go.cr* ✉ *$7* ⊙ *Mon.–Sat. 9–4.*

NEED A BREAK?

Café del Teatro Nacional. Duck into the Café del Teatro Nacional, off the theater lobby, to sit at a marble table and sip a hazelnut mocha beneath frescoed ceilings. The frescoes are part of an allegory of seminude figures celebrating the 1897 opening of the theater. Coffee runs from $2 to $5, depending on how much alcohol or ice cream is added. Sandwiches and cakes are $3 to $6. The café keeps the same hours as the theater but is open only until curtain time on performance nights and during intermission.

WORTH NOTING

Catedral Metropolitana. Built in 1871 and completely refurbished in the late 1990s to repair earthquake damage, the neoclassical Metropolitan Cathedral, topped by a corrugated tin dome, isn't terribly interesting outside. But inside are patterned floor tiles, stained-glass windows depicting various saints and apostles, and framed polychrome bas-reliefs illustrating the 14 Stations of the Cross. This renovation did away with one small time-honored tradition: rather than purchase and light a votive candle, the faithful now deposit a 100-colón coin illuminating a bulb in a row of tiny electric candles.

The interior of the small Capilla del Santísimo (Chapel of the Host) on the cathedral's north side evokes ornate old Catholicism, much more so than the main sanctuary itself, and is a place for reflection and prayer. A marble statue of Pope John Paul II graces the garden on the building's north side. Masses are held throughout the day on Sunday starting at 7 am, with one in English each Saturday at 3 pm. Thanks to a late-2008 restoration, the magnificent 1891 Belgian pipe organ fills the church with music once again. Although not technically part of the cathedral complex, a small statue of Holocaust victim Anne Frank graces the pedestrian mall on the building's south side. It was donated by the Embassy of the Netherlands. ⊠ *C. Central, Avdas. 2–4, Barrio La Merced* ☎ *2221–3820* ☽ *Weekdays 6:30–6, Sun. 6:30 am–9 pm.*

Centro Nacional de la Cultura. Costa Rica cherishes its state enterprises. Here the government is your light and water utility, your phone company, your Internet service provider, your bank, your insurance agent, and your hospital. It is also your distillery, and this complex served as the headquarters of the Fábrica Nacional de Licores (FANAL, or National Liquor Factory) until 1981, when it moved to a modern facility west of Alajuela. In a heartwarming exception to the usual "tear it down" mentality so prevalent in San José, the Ministry of Culture converted the sloped-surface, double-block 1853 factory into the 14,000-square-meter National Cultural Center, with ministry offices, two theaters, and a museum. The stone-block storage depot next to the water towers at the southeast side of the complex became the Museo de Arte y Diseño Contemporáneo *(⇨ below)*. A stone gate and sundial grace the entrance nearest the museum. The complex sits amid government offices, at the point where downtown's northern reaches fade into the more residential neighborhood of Barrio Otoya. ⊠ *C. 13, Avdas. 3–5, Barrio Otoya* ☎ *2257–5524* ⊕ *www.actividadescenac.com* ☽ *Weekdays 8–5, Sat. 10–5.*

Teatro FANAL. The metal Teatro FANAL, once the fermentation area, now hosts frequent theater and music performances. ☎ *2222–2974* ⊕ *www.actividadescenac.com*

Teatro 1887. The clay-brick Teatro 1887 served as the factory's personnel office, and today dedicates itself to performances by the National Dance Company. What is now the theater's lobby was once the chemical testing lab. ☎ *2222–2974* ⊕ *www.actividadescenac.com*

Correos de Costa Rica (*Central Post Office*). The handsome, carved tan exterior of the post office, dating from 1917, is hard to miss among the bland buildings surrounding it. From the balcony you can see the loading of *apartados* (post-office boxes) going on below: Costa Ricans covet these hard-to-get boxes, as the city's lack of street addresses makes mail delivery a challenge. ⊠ *C. 2, Avdas. 1–3, Barrio La Merced* ☎ *2202–2900* ⊕ *www.correos.go.cr* ☽ *Weekdays 7:30–5, Sat. 7:30–1.*

Museo Filatélico (*Philatelic Museum*). Collectors should stop at the second-floor Museo Filatélico for its display of historic stamps. Early-20th-century telegraphs and telephones are also on display. The museum is open weekdays 8 to noon and 1 to 5; admission is the purchase (downstairs at one of the post-office windows) of a prepaid postcard sufficient for mailing to North America. Also of interest to philatelists is the office to the left as you face the stamp windows; it sells first-day issues. ☎ 2223–9766.

Estatua de John Lennon. The newest installment in the capital's growing collection of public art is this whimsical statue of John Lennon on a small, slightly out-of-the-way plaza across from the La Soledad church. Sculptor José Ramón Villa's work sits on the spot where, in 1966, Costa Ricans smashed Beatles records in protest of Lennon's statement that the iconic pop group was "more popular than Jesus." The official name of the statue is *Imagine all the people living life in peace*, evoking the lyrics of Lennon's song *Imagine* and Costa Rica's love of peace. After nearly five decades, bygones are apparently bygones: Residents and tourists alike enjoy having their photos taken sitting with the casually seated figure. ⊠ *C. 9, Avda. 4, Barrio La Soledad.*

Mercado Central (*Central Market*). This block-long melting pot is a warren of dark, narrow passages flanked by stalls packed with spices (some purported to have medicinal value), fish, fruit, flowers, pets, and wood and leather crafts. But the 1880 structure is a kinder, gentler introduction to a Central American market; there are no pigs or chickens or their accompanying smells to be found here. A few stands selling tourist souvenirs congregate near the entrances, but this is primarily a place where the average Costa Rican comes to shop. There are also dozens of cheap restaurants and snack stalls, including the country's first ice-cream vendor. Be warned: the concentration of shoppers makes this a hot spot for pickpockets, purse snatchers, and backpack slitters. Enter and exit at the southeast corner of the building (Avenida Central at Calle 6). The green-and-white "salida" signs direct you to other exits, but they spill onto slightly less-safe streets. Use the image of the Sacred Heart of Jesus, the market's patron and protector, near the center of the building, as your guide; it faces that safer corner by which you should exit. (Things probably weren't planned that way.) ⊠ *Bordered by Avdas. Central–1 and Cs. 6–8, Barrio La Merced* ⊙ *Mon.–Sat. 6–6.*

Monumento al Zaguate. An estimated 1 million street dogs roam Costa Rica's cities and towns. In this newest addition to the growing selection of outdoor public art in central San José, sculptor Francisco Munguía calls attention to their plight. His steel sculpture on the pedestrian boulevard next to the Central Market is a monument to San José's *zaguates* ("mutts" in Costa Rican Spanish), and the models for the painted caricatures were 6 of the 23 dogs Munguía and his wife Deborah have rescued over the years. The artist's goal is for Bobi, Ewok, Oso, Pauleta, Shampú, and Tábata—those are the animals' names—to encourage residents to adopt a dog, too. ⊠ *Avda. Central, Cs. 6–8, Barrio La Merced.*

A GOOD WALK

This walk takes about an hour at a stroll. If you take a more leisurely approach, lingering at the parks or museums, it could take hours.

Everyone finds a way to the **Plaza de la Cultura,** a favorite meeting spot in the heart of the city, and it makes a good kick-off point for a walk. The ornate **Teatro Nacional** sits on the south side of the plaza. Pop in and buy a ticket for an evening performance, and/or grab a cup of coffee at the lobby café. The **Museo del Oro Precolombino** lies under the plaza. The gold collection could easily captivate you for an hour or two. From here, head two blocks north on Calle 5 to **Parque Morazán,** whose centerpiece Templo de Música is the symbol of the city. Traffic is particularly dangerous here, so take heed. The Edificio Metálico, a metal building that serves as a school, fronts the park's north side.

Continue just east of the park on Avenida 3 to the small **Parque España,** one of the city's most pleasant green spaces. The ornate building on the park's north side is the Andrew Carnegie–funded Casa Amarilla. At Avenida 7 is the modern Instituto Nacional Segoros (INS) building, whose ground-floor **Museo del Jade** has an extensive American jade collection. The Ministry of Culture complex, the **Centro Nacional de la Cultura,** fronts the park's east side. From Parque España, walk one long block east to the **Parque Nacional.** Two blocks south on Calle 17 is a pleasant pedestrian mall.

Pass the Asamblea Legislativa, where Costa Rica's congress meets, and come to the **Museo Nacional.** Loop around to the museum's west side to one of the higher levels on the Plaza de la Democracia, a great vantage point for sunsets. Avenida Central fronts the plaza's north side. Head back downhill, into the city center. The avenue becomes a lively pedestrian mall at Calle 9, and two blocks later you return to the Plaza de la Cultura.

NEED A BREAK?

Pop's. To sample the crème de la crème of locally made ice cream, head to Pop's. Mango is a favorite flavor. After a long walk on crowded sidewalks, it may be just what the doctor ordered. This chain is everywhere, and you'll find several outlets downtown. ⊠ *C. 3, Avda. Central, Barrio La Soledad* ☎ *2222–2336* ⊕ *www.pops.co.cr.*

Museo de Arte y Diseño Contemporáneo. This wonderfully minimalist space is perfect as the country's premier modern-art venue. The Museum of Contemporary Art and Design, or MADC as it's known around town, hosts changing exhibits by artists and designers from all over Latin America. You can arrange for a guided visit with a couple of days' notice. The museum occupies part of a government-office complex in that gray area where downtown San José transitions into residential neighborhoods. ⊠ *C. 15, Avdas. 3–5, Barrio Otoya* ☎ *2257–7202* ⊕ *www.madc.ac.cr* 🖅 *$3* ☉ *Mon.–Sat. 9:30–5.*

Museo Nacional. In the mango-color Bellavista Fortress, which dates from 1870, the National Museum gives you a quick and insightful lesson in English and Spanish on Costa Rican culture from pre-Columbian times to the present. Cases display pre-Columbian artifacts, period dress, colonial furniture, religious art, and photographs. Some of the country's foremost ethnographers and anthropologists are on the museum's staff. Outside are a veranda and a pleasant, manicured courtyard garden. A former army headquarters, this now-tranquil building saw fierce fighting during a 1931 army mutiny and the 1948 revolution, as the bullet holes pocking its turrets attest. But it was also here that three-time president José "Don Pepe" Figueres abolished the country's military in 1949.

The museum and Costa Rica are abuzz with the repatriation of nearly 1,000 pre-Columbian stone and ceramic artifacts from the Brooklyn Museum. The objects date from about AD 1000 and were taken from the country in the late 19th century by businessman Minor Keith during the construction of the Atlantic Railroad. The museum is arranging display space at this writing. ⊠ *C. 17, Avda. Central–2, Barrio La Soledad* ☎ *2257–1433* ⊕ *www.museocostarica.go.cr* ☜ *$8* ۞ *Tues.–Sat. 8:30–4:30, Sun. 9–4:30.*

Nocturbano. City walking tours are usually daytime affairs, but these folks take you on a guided, police-escorted tour of nighttime San José. Most of the participants are Costa Ricans, and tours are in Spanish, but guides will conduct tours in English with advance notice for groups of eight or more. Excursions are offered two evenings a month; check the website for dates. ☎ *No phone* ⊕ *www.chepecletas.com* ☜ *$4.*

Parque Central. At the city's nucleus, the tree-planted Central Park is more plaza than park. A life-size bronze statue of a street sweeper (*El Barrendero*) cleans up some bronze litter; look also for *Armonía* (*Harmony*), a sculpture of three street musicians. In the center of the park is a spiderlike, ocher-color gazebo donated by one-time Nicaraguan dictator Anastasio Somoza. ⊠ *Bordered by Avdas. 2–4 and Cs. 2–Central, Barrio La Merced.*

Parque España. One of our favorite spots is this shady little park. A bronze statue of Costa Rica's Spanish founder, Juan Vásquez de Coronado, overlooks an elevated fountain on its southwest corner; the opposite corner has a lovely tiled guardhouse. A bust of Queen Isabella of Castile stares at the yellow compound to the east of the park, the Centro Nacional de la Cultura. Just west of the park is a two-story, metal-sided school made in Belgium and shipped to Costa Rica in pieces more than a century ago. Local lore holds that the intended destination for the appropriately named Edificio Metálico (Metal Building) was really Chile, but that Costa Rica decided to keep the mistakenly shipped building components. The yellow colonial-style building to the east of the modern INS building is the 1912 Casa Amarilla, home of Costa Rica's Foreign Ministry (closed to the public.) The massive ceiba tree in front, planted by John F. Kennedy and the presidents of all the Central American nations in 1963, gives you an idea of how quickly things grow in the tropics. A garden around the corner on Calle 13 contains a 6-foot-wide section of the Berlin Wall donated by Germany's foreign ministry after reunification. Ask the guard to let you into the garden if you want a closer look. ⊠ *Bordered by Avdas. 7–3 and Cs. 11–17, Barrio El Carmen.*

Parque Morazán. Anchored by the 1920 Templo de Música (Temple of Music), a neoclassic bandstand that has become the symbol of the city, downtown's largest park is somewhat barren, though the pink and golden trumpet trees on its northwest corner brighten things up when they bloom in the dry months. The park is named for Honduran general Francisco Morazán, whose dream for a united Central America failed in the 1830s. Avoid the park late at night, when a rough crowd and occasional muggers appear. ⊠ *Avda. 3, Cs. 5–9, Barrio El Carmen.*

3

Parque Nacional. A bronze monument commemorating Central America's battles against American invader William Walker in 1856 forms the centerpiece of the large, leafy National Park. Five Amazons, representing the five nations of the isthmus, attack Walker, who shields his face from the onslaught. Costa Rica maintains the lead and shelters a veiled Nicaragua, the country most devastated by the war. Guatemala, Honduras, and El Salvador might dispute this version of events, but this is how Costa Rica chose to commission the work by French sculptor Louis Carrier Belleuse, a student of Rodin, in 1895. Bas-relief murals on the monument's pedestal depict key battles in the war against the Americans. ⊠ *Bordered by Avdas. 1–3 and Cs. 15–19, Barrio La Soledad.*

Plaza de la Cultura. The crowds of people, vendors, and street entertainers at the Plaza de la Cultura—it's a favored spot for marimba bands, clowns, jugglers, and colorfully dressed South Americans playing Andean music—hide the fact that the expanse is really just a mass of concrete. The ornate Teatro Nacional dominates the plaza's southern half. Pop in and buy a ticket for an evening performance. The Museo del Oro Precolombino, with its highly visited exhibits of gold, lies under the plaza. The plaza's western edge is defined by the Gran Hotel Costa Rica, with its pleasant Café 1930. ⊠ *Bordered by Avdas. Central–2 and Cs. 3–5, Barrio La Soledad.*

Plaza de la Democracia. President Oscar Arias built this terraced open space west of the Museo Nacional to mark 100 years of democracy and to receive dignitaries during the 1989 hemispheric summit. The view west toward the dark green Cerros de Escazú is nice in the morning and fabulous at sunset. Jewelry, T-shirts, and crafts from Costa Rica, Guatemala, and South America are sold in a string of stalls along the western edge. They are worth a stop. The city has been threatening to move the vendors to another location for years, but nothing happens. ⊠ *Bordered by Avdas. Central–2 and Cs. 13–15, Barrio La Soledad.*

Plaza del Banco Central. An extension of Avenida Central, this plaza is popular with hawkers, money changers, and retired men, and can be a good place to get a shoe shine and listen to street musicians. Outside the western end of Costa Rica's modern federal-reserve bank building, don't miss *Presentes,* 10 sculpted, smaller-than-life figures of bedraggled *campesinos* (peasants). *La Chola,* a bronze 500-kilogram (1,100-pound) statue of a buxom rural woman, resides at sidewalk level on the small, shady plaza south of the bank. It's public art at its best.

Museo del Oro Precolumbino has the largest collection of pre-Columbian gold jewelry in Central America.

Beware: the money changers here are notorious for circulating counterfeit bills and using doctored calculators to shortchange unwitting tourists. Instead, change money at banks or through cash machines, where you get the best rate. ⊠ *Bordered by Avdas. Central–1 and Cs. 2–4, Barrio La Merced.*

Teatro Popular Melico Salazar. Across Avenida 2 on the north side of Parque Central stands San José's second major performance hall (after the Teatro Nacional). The 1928 building is on the site of a 19th-century military barracks felled by an earthquake. The venue was later named for Costa Rican operatic tenor Manuel "Melico" Salazar (1887–1950). It was constructed specifically to provide a less highbrow alternative to the Teatro Nacional. But these days the Melico is plenty cultured and provides the capital with a steady diet of music and dance performances. ⊠ *Avda. 2 and C. 2, Barrio La Merced* ☎ *2233–5424* ⊕ *www.teatromelico.go.cr.*

NORTH AND EAST OF DOWNTOWN

Immediately northeast of downtown lie Barrio Amón and Barrio Otoya. Both neighborhoods are repositories of historic houses that have escaped the wrecking ball; many now serve as hotels, restaurants, galleries, and offices. (A few are even private residences.) Where these barrios begin and end depends on who's doing the talking. Locales on the fringes of the city center prefer to be associated with these "good neighborhoods" rather than with downtown. Barrio Escalante, to the east, isn't quite as gentrified but is fast becoming fashionable.

The sprawling suburb of San Pedro begins several blocks east of downtown San José. The town is home to the University of Costa Rica and all the intellect and cheap eats and nightlife that a student or student-wannabe could desire. But away from the heart of the university, San Pedro is awash in the consumerism of malls, fast-food restaurants, and car dealerships—although it manages to mix in stately districts such as stylish Los Yoses for good measure. To get to San Pedro, take a $3 taxi ride from downtown and get off in front of Banco Nacional, just beyond the rotunda with the fountain at its center.

RAINY-DAY TIPS
■ Do outdoor sightseeing in the morning, before the afternoon rains arrive.
■ Duck into museums—our top choices are the Gold and Jade museums.
■ Do as Costa Ricans do and *tomar café* (take a coffee break).
■ Don't wait until the evening rush hour (5–7 pm) to get a cab— empty ones are nearly nonexistent when it rains.

★ **Jardín de Mariposas Spyrogyra.** Spending an hour or two at this magical
☺ Spyrogyra Butterfly Garden is entertaining and educational for nature lovers of all ages. Self-guided tours enlighten you on butterfly ecology and let you see the winged creatures close up. After an 18-minute video introduction, you're free to wander screened-in gardens along a numbered trail. Some 30 species of colorful butterflies flutter about, accompanied by six types of hummingbirds. Try to come when it's sunny, as butterflies are most active then. A small, moderately priced café borders the garden and serves sandwiches and Tico fare. ⊠ *50 m east and 150 m south of main entrance to El Pueblo shopping center, Barrio Tournón* ☎ *2222–2937* ⊕ *www.butterflygardencr.com* 🖃 *$7* ⊙ *Daily 8–4.*

☺ **Museo de los Niños.** San José's Children's Museum is in a former prison, and big kids may want to check it out just to marvel at the castlelike architecture and the old cells that have been preserved in an exhibit about life behind bars. Three halls in the complex are filled with eye-catching seasonal exhibits for kids, ranging in subject from local ecology to outer space. The exhibits are annotated in Spanish, but most are interactive, so language shouldn't be much of a problem. The museum's most popular resident is the Egyptian exhibit's sarcophagus; the mummy draws the "oohs" and "aahs." Officially, the complex is called the Centro Costarricense de Ciencia y Cultura (Costa Rican Center of Science and Culture), and that will be the sign that greets you on the front of the building. The Galería Nacional, adjoining the main building, is more popular with adults; it usually shows fine art by Costa Rican artists free of charge. Also adjoining the museum is the classical music venue Auditorio Nacional. Though just a short distance from downtown, the walk here takes you through a dodgy neighborhood. You'll definitely feel as though you've stepped out of the hustle and bustle of the center city. Take a taxi to and from. ⊠ *North end of C. 4, Barrio El Carmen* ☎ *2258–4929* ⊕ *www.museocr.com* 🖃 *$2* ⊙ *Tues.– Fri. 8–4:30, weekends 9:30–5.*

Missing History

Blame it on the earthquakes. Costa Ricans are quick to attribute the scarcity of historic architecture in San José and around the country to a history of earth tremors. Indeed, major earthquakes have struck various locales around Costa Rica 10 times since the mid-18th century (6 times in the 20th century), felling untold numbers of historical structures.

But blame it on the wrecking ball, too, says architect Gabriela Sáenz, who works with the Ministry of Culture's Center for Research and Conservation of Cultural Patrimony. The tear-it-down approach really began to take its toll in the 1970s, an era when boxy, concrete buildings were in vogue around the world, Sáenz says. Costa Rica didn't establish its first school of architecture until 1972, staffed by faculty from Mexico, England, and Brazil. "It was hard for a real Costa Rican tradition to take hold," she explains. Mix that with a lack of government regulation and

what Sáenz calls a typical Tico do-your-own-thing penchant, and the result is a city full of squat buildings.

The tide began to turn in 1995 with the passage of the Law of Historic and Architectural Patrimony. More than 300 historic structures in the country are currently protected under the legislation, and new buildings are added to the registry each year. But legal protection is no guarantee of funding necessary to actually restore a historic landmark.

You need to look hard, but San José really does have several diamonds in the rough. The National Theater and Central Post Office remain the two most visited examples of historic architecture in the capital. But the National Museum, the National Center of Culture, and several small hostelries and restaurants around town—especially in Barrios Amón and Otoya—are all modern transformations and restorations of structures with histories.

NEED A BREAK?

Giacomín. We have to admit that Costa Rican baked goods tend toward the dry-as-dust end of the spectrum. But Italian-style bakery Giacomín, near the University of Costa Rica, is an exception—it seems that a touch of liqueur added to the batter makes all the difference. Stand, European-style, at the downstairs espresso bar, or take your goodies to the tables and chairs on the upstairs balcony. The place closes from noon to 2. You'll also find outlets in Escazú, Heredia, and Santa Ana out in the Central Valley. ☎ 2224–3463 ⊕ www.pasteleriagiacomin.com.

WEST OF DOWNTOWN

Paseo Colón, one of San José's major boulevards, heads due west from downtown and leads to vast La Sabana park, the city's largest parcel of green space. La Sabana anchors the even vaster west side of the city. A block or two off its exhaust-ridden avenues are quiet residential streets, and you'll find the U.S., Canadian, and British embassies here.

Museo de Arte Costarricense. A splendid collection of 19th- and 20th-century Costa Rican art, labeled in Spanish and English, is housed in 12 exhibition halls here. Be sure to visit the top-floor Salón Dorado to see the stucco, bronze-plate bas-relief mural depicting Costa Rican history, created by French sculptor Louis Feron. Guided tours are offered Tuesday through Friday from 10 to 3. Wander into the sculpture garden in back and take in Jorge Jiménez's 22-foot-tall *Imagen Cósmica*, which depicts pre-Columbian traditions. The museum sparkles following a two-year restoration and a 2010 reopening. ⊠ *C. 42 and Paseo Colón, Paseo Colón* ☎ *2256–1281* ⊕ *www.musarco.go.cr* ⊟ *Free* ⊙ *Tues.–Sun. 9–4.*

⟳ **Parque Metropolitano La Sabana.** Though it isn't centrally located, La Sabana (The Savannah) comes the closest of San José's green spaces to achieving the same function and spirit as New York's Central Park. A statue of 1930s president León Cortes greets you at the principal entrance at the west end of Paseo Colón. Behind the statue a 16-foot-tall menorah serves as a gathering place for San José's small Jewish community during Hanukkah. La Sabana was once San José's airport, and the whitewashed Museo de Arte Costarricense, just south of the Cortes statue, served as terminal and control tower.

The round Gimnasio Nacional (National Gymnasium) sits at the park's southeast corner and hosts sporting events and the occasional concert. A 40,000-seat stadium—a controversial gift from the government of China, which decided to use its own construction workers rather than employ local people—was completed in 18 months and opened in 2011 near the park's northwest corner. It hosts primarily soccer matches, but Shakira, Pearl Jam, and Red Hot Chili Peppers played in the stadium during its first year of operation. In between are acres of space for soccer, basketball, tennis, swimming, jogging, picnicking, and kite flying. The park hums with activity on weekend days. You're welcome to join in the early-morning outdoor aerobics classes on Saturday and Sunday. A project is under way to replace many of the park's eucalyptus trees with more bird-friendly species native to Costa Rica.

A small building boom is taking place these days, with condos and office buildings going up around the perimeter of the park, another resemblance to New York's Central Park. (Because of building codes, "skyscraper" means a maximum of about 10 floors in earthquake-prone Costa Rica.) Like most of San José's green spaces, La Sabana should be avoided at night. ⊠ *Bordered by C. 42, Avda. de las Américas, and Autopista Próspero Fernández, Paseo Colón.*

WHERE TO EAT

Wherever you eat in San José, be it a small *soda* (informal eatery) or a sophisticated restaurant, dress is casual. Meals tend to be taken earlier than in other Latin American countries; few restaurants serve past 9 or 10 pm. Local cafés usually open for breakfast at 7 am and remain open until 7 or 8 in the evening. Restaurants serving international cuisine are usually open from 11 am to 9 pm. Some cafés that serve mainly San

San José's ubiquitous red taxicabs.

José office workers limit evening hours and close entirely on Sunday. Restaurants that do open on Sunday do a brisk business: it's the traditional family day out (and the maid's day off). ⚠ Watch your things, no matter where you dine. Prowlers have been known to sneak into even the best restaurants, targeting purses slung over chair arms or placed under chairs.

DOWNTOWN

$$ ╳ **Balcón de Europa.** With old sepia photos and a strolling guitarist who
ECLECTIC seems to have been working the room forever, Balcón de Europa transports you to the year of its inception, 1909. Pasta specialties such as the *plato mixto* (mixed plate with lasagna, tortellini, and ravioli) are so popular that they haven't changed much either. (Why tamper with success?) A new owner has, however, added French and Mediterranean dishes to the menu—try the blanquette of veal or the couscous. Among the lighter fare are a scrumptious hearts-of-palm salad or a sautéed corvina. Grab a table away from the door (i.e., from the noise of the bus stop across the street). FYI: old-timers refer to the place as Balcón de Franco; the late, legendary chef Franco Piatti was the restaurant's guiding light for years. Ⓢ *Average main: $13* ⊠ *C. 9, Avda. Central-1, Barrio La Soledad* ☎ *2221–4841* ⊘ *Closed Mon.* ✛ *F3.*

$ ╳ **Café de la Posada.** The lack of alfresco dining in this tropical city is
CAFÉ disappointing, but this café's covered terrace with tables fronting the Calle 17 pedestrian mall is a pleasant exception. The owners come from Argentina, and they know how to make a great cappuccino. Salads, quiches, and empanadas are specialties. The best bargains are the four rotating *platos del día* (daily specials), with entrée, salad, beverage, and dessert for $9. If you opt for dinner, make it an early

one: the place closes at 7 on weeknights. $ *Average main: $9* ⊠ *C. 17, Avdas. 2–4, Barrio La Soledad* ☎ *2258–1027* ⊘ *Closed Sun. No dinner Sat.* ⊹ *H4.*

$

SOUTH
AMERICAN

Fodor's Choice
★

✕ **Caracas Arepas & Juice Bar.** It's a cross between a sloppy joe and a burrito, and it's the quintessential Venezuelan food, often eaten three times a day. You can make an entire lunch out of a variety of *arepas* at this fun, informal place just down the street from the Jade Museum. Try the Americano with a ham-and-cheese filling, or the Caraqueño, overflowing with shredded beef, cheese, and beans. They're just two of the many recipes the owner has gleaned from his mother and grandmother. An astounding selection of fruit smoothies—raspberry, strawberry, mango, melon, pineapple, orange, papaya—make the perfect accompaniment. Top your meal off with a sundae or a flanlike *quesillo.* If you stop by for dinner, make it an early one; the place closes at 7. $ *Average main: $5* ⊠ *Avda. 7, Cs. 7–9, Barrio Amón* ☎ *2258–6565* ⊕ *www.caracasarepas. com* ⊘ *Closed Sun.* ⊹ *F3.*

$$

CHINESE

✕ **Don Wang.** In a country where "Chinese cuisine" often means rice and vegetables bearing a suspicious resemblance to *gallo pinto* ("spotted rooster," a typical Costa Rican dish of black beans and rice), Don Wang's authenticity is a treat. Cantonese cuisine is the mainstay—the owner comes from that region of China—but these folks will Szechuan it up a bit if you ask. Don Wang is known for its immensely popular dim sum, called *desayuno chino,* literally "Chinese breakfast." You can order it all day. The dining area is built around a stone garden and small waterfall. There's no television blaring here, a refreshing change from many Costa Rican restaurants. $ *Average main: $12* ⊠ *C. 11, Avdas. 6–8, Barrio La Soledad* ☎ *2233–6484* ⊕ *www.donwangrestaurant.com* ⊹ *G4.*

$$$

ECLECTIC

Fodor's Choice
★

✕ **Kalú.** Longtime fixture on San José's restaurant scene Camille Ratton owns and manages Barrio Amón's newest, hippest dining spot, and it's a winner. The panini and pastas are the standouts here, but Kalú's menu incorporates Costa Rican, Thai, and American elements, too. For one of those Americanized touches, try the *hambuguesa* Kalú with portobello mushrooms, mozzarella cheese, and hummus. Browse in the adjoining art gallery before or after your meal, or while you wait for your food. The covered back patio offers stupendous views, especially in the evening, although long sleeves are in order if the night is brisk. $ *Average main: $17* ⊠ *C. 7 and Avda. 11, Barrio Amón* ☎ *2221–2081* ⊕ *www. kalu.co.cr* ⊘ *Closed Sun. No dinner Mon* ⊹ *F2.*

$

COSTA RICAN

✕ **La Criollita.** Kick off your day with breakfast at this emerald green restaurant. Mornings are the perfect time to snag one of the precious tables in the back garden, an unexpected refuge from noise and traffic. Breakfast platters come with eggs on the side: the *americano* has pancakes and toast; the *tico* comes with bread, fried bananas, and *natilla* (sour cream); and the huge *criollita* has ham or pork chops. Government workers from nearby offices start arriving late in the morning, and the lunchtime decibel level increases appreciably. (This is the one time of day we recommend avoiding the place.) Everyone filters out about 2 pm, and once again, you have a quiet place for coffee and dessert. $ *Average main: $8* ⊠ *Avda. 7, Cs. 7–9, Barrio Amón* ☎ *2256–6511* ⊘ *Closed Sun. No dinner Sat.* ⊹ *G3.*

$ ✕ **Mama's Place.** Mama's is a Costa Rican restaurant with a difference:
COSTA RICAN   the owners are Italian, so in addition to *corvina al ajillo* (sea bass
sautéed with garlic) and other staple Tico fare, they serve homemade
seafood chowder, traditional Italian pastas, and meat dishes with delicate wine sauces. The brightly decorated coffee shop opens onto busy
Avenida 1; the more subdued dining room upstairs accommodates the
overflow crowd. (You'll see former Chicago Bears football coach Mike
Ditka's autographed picture up there.) At lunchtime it's usually packed
with business types drawn to the delicious and inexpensive daily specials—choose from the rotating platos del día with pasta, meat, fish, or
poultry—all to the accompaniment of ample focaccia. Mama's closes
at 7 pm on weeknights. $ *Average main: $7* ⊠ *Avda. 1, Cs. Central–2,
Barrio El Carmen* ☎ *2223–2270* ⊘ *Closed Sun. No dinner Sat.* ✛ *E3.*

$ ✕ **Nuestra Tierra.** But for the traffic zipping by on one of San José's busi-
COSTA RICAN   est thoroughfares—and on that note, opt for a table on the side facing
less busy Calle 15—you might think you're out in the rural Central Valley. Bunches of onions and peppers dangle from the ceiling, recalling a
provincial Tico ranch. The generous homemade meals are delicious, and
the incredibly friendly waitstaff, who epitomize Costa Rican hospitality
and dress in folkloric clothing, prepare your coffee filtered through the
traditional cloth *chorreador.* The place is open 24 hours, just in case
gallo pinto pangs hit at 3 am. Some disparage the place as "too touristy." Perhaps it is, but it's also fun. $ *Average main: $6* ⊠ *Avda. 2 and
C. 15, Barrio La Soledad* ☎ *2258–6500* ✛ *G4.*

$ ✕ **Shakti.** The baskets of fruit and vegetables at the entrance and the
VEGETARIAN   wall of herbal teas, health-food books, and fresh herbs for sale by the
register tell you you're in a vegetarian-friendly joint. The bright and airy
macrobiotic restaurant—much homier than Vishnu, its major vegetarian competition—serves breakfast, lunch, and an early dinner, closing at
7 pm weekdays and 6 pm Saturday. Homemade bread, soy burgers, pita
sandwiches (veggie or, for carnivorous dining companions, chicken),
macrobiotic fruit shakes, and a hearty plato del día that comes with
soup, green salad, and a fruit beverage fill out the menu. The *ensalada
mixta* is a meal in itself, packed with root vegetables native to Costa
Rica. $ *Average main: $5* ⊠ *Avda. 8 and C. 13, Barrio La Soledad*
☎ *2222–4475* ⊘ *Closed Sun.* ✛ *G5.*

$$$ ✕ **Tin Jo.** The colorful dining rooms of this converted house just south-
ASIAN   east of downtown evoke Japan, India, China, Indonesia, or Thailand.
Fodor's Choice   In the Thai Room a 39-foot mural depicts a Buddhist temple. You
★   can select from all the above cuisines, with menus to match the varied
dining areas. Start with a powerful Singapore sling (brandy and fruit
juices) before trying such treats as *kaeng* (Thai shrimp and pineapple
curry in coconut milk), *mu shu* (a beef, chicken, or vegetable stir-fry
with crepes), samosas (stuffed Indian pastries), and sushi rolls. The
vegetarian menu is extensive, too. Tin Jo stands out with always-excep-
tional food, attention to detail, and attentive service that make it, hands
down, the country's top Asian restaurant. $ *Average main: $18* ⊠ *C.
11, Avdas. 6–8, Barrio La Soledad* ☎ *2257–3622* ⊕ *www.tinjo.com*
⬦ *No-smoking* ✛ *G4.*

$ VEGETARIAN 🍴 **Vishnu.** "Haciendo un nuevo mundo," proudly proclaims the sign at the door. "Making a new world" might be a bit ambitious for a restaurant goal, but Vishnu takes its vegetarian offerings seriously. The dining area looks institutional—you'll sit at a sterile booth with Formica tables and gaze at posters of fruit on the walls—but the attraction is the inexpensive macrobiotic food. A yummy, good-value bet is usually the plato del día (soup, beverage, and dessert), but the menu also includes soy burgers, salads, fresh fruit juices, and a yogurt smoothie called *morir soñando* (literally, "to die dreaming"). [$] *Average main: $5* ✉ *Avda. 1 west of C. 3, Barrio El Carmen* ☎ *2233–9976* ⏲ *No dinner weekends* ✥ *F3.*

3

NORTH AND EAST OF DOWNTOWN

$$ CAFÉ 🍴 **Café Mundo.** You could easily walk by this corner restaurant without noticing its tiny sign behind the foliage. The upstairs café serves meals on a porch, on a garden patio, or in two dining rooms. The soup of the day and fresh-baked bread start you out; main courses include shrimp in a vegetable cream sauce or *lomito en salsa de vino tinto* (tenderloin in a red-wine sauce). Save room for the best chocolate cake in town, drizzled with homemade blackberry sauce. Café Mundo is a popular, low-key gay hangout that draws a mixed gay-straight clientele. This is one of the few center-city restaurants with its own parking lot. [$] *Average main: $11* ✉ *C. 15 and Avda. 9, Barrio Otoya* ☎ *2222–6190* ⏲ *Closed Sun. No lunch Sat.* ✥ *G2.*

$$$ ECLECTIC 🍴 **Jürgen's.** Jürgen's is a common haunt for *politicos,* and San José's elites meet to eat here. Decorated in gold and terra-cotta with leather and wood accents, the dining room of this contemporary restaurant feels more like a lounge than a fine restaurant. In fact, the classy bar, with a large selection of good wine and good cigars, is a prominent feature. The inventive menu, with such delicacies as medallions of roast duck and tuna fillet encrusted with sesame seeds, sets this place apart from the city's more traditional venues. [$] *Average main: $18* ✉ *250 m north of the Subaru dealership, on Blvd. Barrio Dent, Barrio Dent* ☎ *2283–2239* ⏲ *Closed Sun. No lunch Sat.* ✥ *B5.*

$ ITALIAN 🍴 **La Trattoria.** The green and gold here might make a Green Bay Packers fan feel right at home, but it's the excellent, reasonably priced homemade pasta dishes that make this popular lunch spot worth the stop. Begin your meal with fresh bread and any number of excellent antipasti, continuing on with your favorite pasta dish. And for dessert, who can resist tiramisu? [$] *Average main: $8* ✉ *Behind Automercado, Barrio Dent, San Pedro* ☎ *2224–7065* ⏲ *No dinner Sun.* ✥ *B5.*

$$$$ FRENCH 🍴 **Le Chandelier.** San José doesn't get classier than this restaurant, where formal service and traditional sauce-heavy French dishes are part of the experience. The dining room is elegant, with wicker chairs, a tile floor, and original paintings. The Swiss chef, Claude Dubuis, might start you off with saffron ravioli stuffed with ricotta cheese and walnuts. His main courses include such unique dishes as corvina in a *pejibaye* (peach palm) sauce, hearts of palm and veal chops glazed in a sweet port-wine sauce, and the more familiar *pato a la naranja* (duck à l'orange), or, for a tropical twist on that classic dish, *pato a la maracuyá* (duck in passion

fruit). $ *Average main: $27* ✉ *50 m west and 100 m south of ICE Bldg., San Pedro* ☎ *2225–3980* ⊕ *www. lechandeliercr.com* ⊙ *Closed Sun. No lunch Sat.* ✛ *C5.*

$

ITALIAN

✕**Pane e Vino.** Look closely at the extensive menu here: there are 40 varieties of the capital's best thin-crust pizza, and no one will rush you if you spend too much time pondering what you want. This lively two-level restaurant—it's a small chain, but this was the first location—rounds out its offerings with a complete selection of pastas. You can dine until midnight daily, except on Sunday, when you'll have

to finish dinner by 10 pm. The Pizza Allessandre, topped with prosciutto, mozzarella, and olives, is the most popular dish, and for good reason. $ *Average main: $9* ✉ *50 m west and 15 m south of Más X Menos, San Pedro* ☎ *2280–2869* ⊕ *www.paneevino.co.cr* ✛ *H5.*

$

MEDITERRANEAN

✕**Olio.** Although this combination pub and restaurant serves the full contingent of Mediterranean cuisine, we like to visit the place for drinks and Spanish-style *tapas* (appetizers). The century-old redbrick house with stained-glass windows draws everybody from tie-clad businessmen to university students who have money to spend on something more upscale than run-of-the-mill campus-area bars. Groups liven up the large front room—the quieter, smaller back rooms maintain a bit more romance. The staff hauls umbrella-covered tables out to the sidewalk on warm evenings. Olio is extremely proud that it offers a copy of its menu in Braille. $ *Average main: $8* ✉ *200 m north of Bagelmen's, Barrio Escalante* ☎ *2281–0541* ⊙ *Closed Sun. No lunch Sat.* ✛ *H5.*

WEST OF DOWNTOWN

$$$

SPANISH

Fodor'sChoice

★

✕**Casa Luisa.** A big open window looking into the kitchen—where chef María Luisa Esparducer and her staff proudly show off their trade—is the first thing you encounter as you're shown to your table in this homey, upscale Catalan restaurant. The place is eclectic, with wood floors, arresting artwork, soft lighting, and flamenco music in the background. Start the meal with gazpacho or eggplant pâté, accompanied by a glass of top Spanish wine. The excellent main dishes include rosemary lamb chops, suckling pig, and rabbit in white wine sauce with truffles. Finish with a platter of nuts, dates, and figs drizzled with a wine sauce or the decadent *crema catalana* with a *brûlée* glaze. We give Casa Luisa the nod as the city's best Spanish restaurant for its combination of style and coziness. $ *Average main: $21* ✉ *400 m south and 40 m east of the Contraloría, Sabana Sur* ☎ *2296–1917* ⊙ *Closed weekends* ✛ *A4.*

$$ MIDDLE EASTERN 🍴 **Lubnan.** Negotiate the quirky wrought-iron-and-burlap revolving door at the entrance, and you've made it into one of San José's few Middle Eastern restaurants. The Lebanese owners serve a wide variety of dishes from their native region, so if you can't decide, the *mezza* serves two people and gives you a little bit of everything. For your own individual dish, try the juicy shish kebab *de cordero* (of lamb), or, if you're feeling especially adventurous, the raw ground-meat *kebbe naye* (with wheat meal) and *kafta naye* (without wheat meal). A hip bar in the back serves the same menu, but definitely eat out in the front restaurant Wednesday night for the live Middle Eastern synthesizer music and Thursday night for the 9 pm belly-dancing show. [$] *Average main: $11* ✉ *Paseo Colón, Cs. 22–24, Paseo Colón* ☎ *2257–6071* 🕒 *Closed Mon. No dinner Sun.* ✥ *B3.*

$$ PERUVIAN ★ 🍴 **Machu Picchu.** A few travel posters and a fishnet holding crab and lobster shells are the only props used to evoke Peru, but no matter: the food is anything but plain, and the seafood is excellent at both the east- and west-side branches of this mainstay. The *pique especial de mariscos* (special seafood platter), big enough for two, presents you with shrimp, conch, and squid cooked four ways. The ceviche here is quite different from and better than that served in the rest of the country. A blazing Peruvian hot sauce served on the side adds zip to any dish, but be careful—apply it by the drop. Oh, and one more warning: the pisco sours go down very easily. [$] *Average main: $12* ✉ *C. 32, 130 m north of KFC, Paseo Colón* ☎ *2222–7384* ✥ *A3* [$] *Average main: $12* ✉ *150 m south of Ferretería El Mar, San Pedro* ☎ *2283–3679.*

$$$ ECLECTIC 🍴 **Park Café.** Don't let appearances deceive you: the colonial-style house is only a decade old, but attention to architectural detail and antique furnishings make you think the building was transplanted from Antigua or Granada. An all-tapas menu makes up the fare here, with such tasty dishes as Thai-style tuna salad or red-snapper couscous. The menu varies from year to year, depending on what the owners have uncovered during their two-month European autumn buying trip. On that topic, owner Richard Neat is onetime proprietor of a two-star Michelin restaurant in London, and one of the few British chefs to achieve that distinction. Space is limited, making reservations a must. The January through April dry season takes the pressure off a bit, allowing seating to spill over from the covered veranda to the open courtyard. [$] *Average main: $16* ✉ *100 m north of Rosti Pollos, Sabana Norte* ☎ *2290–6324* 🌐 *parkcafecostarica.blogspot.com* ✍ *Reservations essential* 🕒 *No lunch* ✥ *A4.*

$ COSTA RICAN 🍴 **Soda Tapia.** One of San José's most popular restaurants fronts the east side of La Sabana Park. You can dine outdoors, but you'll have to contend with the traffic noise and the sight of the guard flagging cars in and out of the tiny parking lot. The place stays open until 2 am and around the clock on weekends. [$] *Average main: $5* ✉ *C. 42, Avdas. 2-4, Sabana Este* ☎ *2222–6734* ✥ *A4.*

WHERE TO STAY

San José has plenty of chains, including Best Western, Holiday Inn, Radisson, Quality Inn, Clarion, Meliá, and Barceló (the last two are Spanish chains). But it also has historic houses with traditional architecture that have been converted into small lodgings.

The historic houses are usually without concierge or pool and are found mainly in Barrios Amón and Otoya, and in the eastern suburb of San Pedro. The city also has a lower tier of lodgings with the simplicity (and prices) beloved of backpackers. Most smaller hotels don't have air-conditioning, but it rarely gets warm enough at this altitude to warrant it.

Many lodgings operate at near-full occupancy in high season (December through April), but the capital's status as a business-travel destination means the lodging rates remain constant year-round. Reconfirm all reservations 24 hours in advance. If you're flying out early in the morning and prefer to stay near the airport, consider booking a hotel near Alajuela or San Antonio de Belén (⇨ *See Chapter 4*).

DOWNTOWN

Staying in the downtown area allows you to travel around the city as most Ticos do: on foot. Stroll the parks, museums, and shops, and then retire to one of the many small or historic hotels with plenty of character.

For expanded hotel reviews, visit Fodors.com.

$$
HOTEL
Grand Hotel Costa Rica. You cannot get more centrally located than this longtime grande dame of San José lodgings. **Pros:** central location; great people-watching from ground-floor café. **Cons:** some street noise from the adjoining plaza; some rooms have thin walls. **TripAdvisor:** "nice historic hotel," "stay for the history," "step back in time." $ *Rooms from: $79* ⌂ *Avda. 2 and C. 3, Barrio La Soledad* ☎ *2221–4000, 800/949–0592 in U.S.* ⊕ *www.grandhotelcostarica.com* ⇨ *107 rooms, 5 suites* ❘◎❘ *Breakfast* ✛ *F3.*

$$
HOTEL
Holiday Inn San José Downtown – Aurola. All the amenities a business traveler's heart could desire and the reassuring, familiar name are yours at this conveniently located hotel on the north side of downtown. **Pros:** business facilities; central location. **Cons:** sameness of chain hotel; park across street dicey at night. **TripAdvisor:** "comfortable and clean," "excellent location," "average hotel." $ *Rooms from: $100* ⌂ *Avda. 5 and C. 5, Barrio El Carmen* ☎ *2523–1000, 800/315–2521 in North America* ⊕ *www.aurolahotels.com* ⇨ *188 rooms, 12 suites* ⚲ *No-smoking* ❘◎❘ *Breakfast* ✛ *F3.*

$$
HOTEL
Hotel Balmoral. One of the capital's landmark hotels is undergoing a major remodeling at this writing with a much-appreciated modernization of rooms. **Pros:** central location; good restaurant. **Cons:** some street noise. **TripAdvisor:** "good downtown location," "outstanding job on the remodel," "comfortable oasis." $ *Rooms from: $80* ⌂ *C. 7. Avdas. Central–1, Barrio La Soledad* ☎ *2222–5022, 800/691–4865 in North America* ⊕ *www.balmoral.co.cr* ⇨ *112 rooms, 8 suites* ❘◎❘ *Breakfast* ✛ *F4.*

CLOSE UP

Eco- or Sustainable Tourism

Ecotourism, a relatively recent addition to the English language, has been defined as travel to natural areas to observe and learn about wildlife, tourism that refrains from damaging the environment, or tourism that strengthens conservation and improves the lives of local people. The latter two definitions could also apply to sustainable tourism, which has a wider scope than ecotourism and pushes for improvements in everything from city hotels to cruise ships. Whereas proponents of ecotourism believe it has the potential to conserve nature by providing economic opportunities for the rural poor, who are responsible for much of the deforestation in the tropics, sustainable tourism advocates note that all tourism has the potential for negative impacts, and they push for improvement across the entire industry.

If you define ecotourism as tourism that contributes to conservation and community development, then ecotourism is always sustainable tourism. However, not all sustainable tourism is ecotourism, since tourism businesses located far from natural areas can and should implement sustainable practices. The list of hotels certified by the Costa Rican Tourism Board's Sustainable Tourism Certification program, for example, ranges from award-winning eco-lodges to city hotels that have made improvements such as installing sewage treatment systems and switching to energy-saving lightbulbs. For conscientious travelers who are looking for close contact with nature, sustainable may not be enough.

3

$$ B&B/INN 🏨 **Hotel Fleur de Lys.** A three-floor Victorian house with a brassy hot-pink-and-lavender exterior offers a quiet elegance that you'd never imagine lies beyond its doors. **Pros:** cozy rooms; close to sights. **Cons:** some noise from downstairs bar. **TripAdvisor:** "quirky central hotel," "excellent breakfast and very friendly staff," "oasis in San Jose." [$] *Rooms from: $96* ✉ *C. 13, Avdas. 2–6, Barrio La Soledad* ☎ *2223–1206* 🌐 *www.hotelfleurdelys.com* 🛏 *25 rooms, 6 suites* 🍴 *Breakfast* ⊕ *G4.*

$$ HOTEL 🏨 **Hotel Presidente.** You're looking at standard, medium-price, business-class accommodations here, although plenty of leisure travelers use this hotel as their San José base, too. **Pros:** central location; eco-friendly hotel. **Cons:** some street noise; some rooms have thin walls. **TripAdvisor:** "very nice rooms," "in the heart of San Jose," "heaven." [$] *Rooms from: $106* ✉ *Avda. Central and C. 7, Barrio La Soledad* ☎ *2010–0000, 877/540–1790 in North America* 🌐 *www.hotel-presidente.com* 🛏 *88 rooms, 12 suites* 🍴 *Breakfast* ⊕ *F4.*

$ B&B/INN 🏨 **Posada del Museo.** This green, wooden, Victorian-style house (circa 1928) is a great place to stay if you're bound for San José's museums; hence the name. **Pros:** cozy rooms; near museums. **Cons:** rush-hour train passes by; fronts busy street. **TripAdvisor:** "lovely rooms," "charming," "nice place and nice staff." [$] *Rooms from: $68* ✉ *Avda. 2 and C. 17, Barrio La Soledad* ☎ *2258–1027* 🌐 *www.hotelposadadelmuseo.com* 🛏 *11 rooms, 3 suites* 🍴 *Breakfast* ⊕ *H4.*

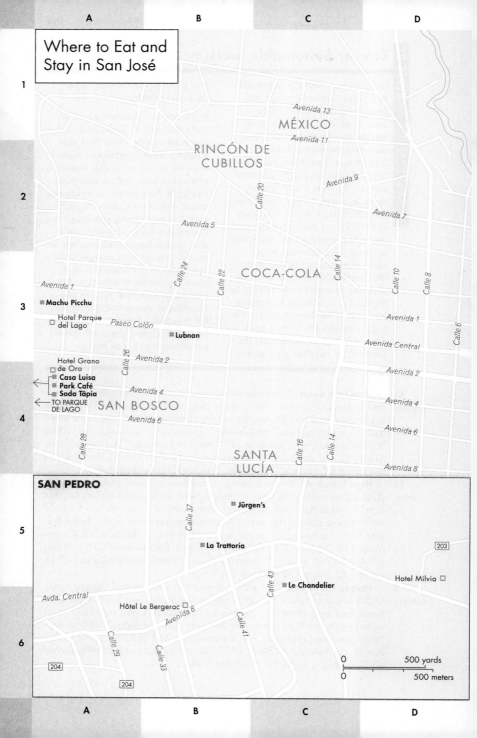

Where to Eat and Stay in San José

A   B   C   D

1

Avenida 13

MÉXICO

Avenida 11

RINCÓN DE
CUBILLOS

Avenida 9

Calle 20

Avenida 7

2

Avenida 5

COCA-COLA

Calle 24

Calle 22

Calle 14

Calle 10

Calle 8

Avenida 1

■ Machu Picchu

3

□ Hotel Parque
del Lago

Paseo Colón

■ Lubnan

Avenida 1

Avenida Central

Calle 6

Hotel Grano
□ de Oro

Calle 26

Avenida 2

Avenida 2

■ Casa Luisa
■ Park Café
■ Soda Tapia

Avenida 4

Avenida 4

← TO PARQUE
DE LAGO

SAN BOSCO

Avenida 6

Avenida 6

4

Calle 28

SANTA
LUCÍA

Calle 16

Calle 14

Avenida 8

SAN PEDRO

Calle 37

■ Jürgen's

5

■ La Trattoria

203

Calle 43

■ Le Chandelier

Hotel Milvia □

Avda. Central

Hôtel Le Bergerac □

Avenida 8

Calle 41

6

Calle 29

Calle 33

204

204

| 0 | | 500 yards |
| 0 | | 500 meters |

A   B   C   D

NORTH AND EAST OF DOWNTOWN

Just north of downtown, old homes converted into small lodgings populate Barrios Amón and Otoya, two of the capital's most historic neighborhoods. Though we generally eschew the big hotel franchises, our favorite San José chain lodging is here.

The small properties just 10 minutes by cab east of downtown, toward the university, offer personalized service and lots of peace and quiet. Plenty of restaurants and bars are within easy reach.

> ### ¿DÓNDE ESTÁ EL HO-JO?
>
> We encourage you not to play it safe at a chain hotel. Most provide you with the exact sameness you'd find in Cleveland. Smaller hotels and their Tico hospitality (although many are owned by foreigners) are quintessentially Costa Rica.

$
B&B/INN
★
Cinco Hormigas Rojas. Resident owner-slash-artist Mayra Güell has turned the 80-year-old house she inherited from her grandmother into San José's most original bed-and-breakfast–cum–art gallery. **Pros:** friendly owner; artistic decor; bird-filled patio. **Cons:** small, dark rooms. **TripAdvisor:** "personal and quaint," "great eccentric host with lots of personality," "truly one of a kind." $ *Rooms from: $40* ⊠ *C. 15, Avdas. 9–11, Barrio Otoya* ☎ *2255–3412* ⊕ *www.cincohormigasrojas. com* ⬥ *6 rooms, 4 with bath* ❑ *Breakfast* ✚ *H2.*

$$
HOTEL
Fodor's Choice
★
Clarion Hotel Amón Plaza. The cream-color Amón Plaza achieves everything we like in a business-class hotel, with all the services and amenities you could need while transcending its chain status. **Pros:** business facilities; friendly staff; eco-friendly hotel. **Cons:** lacks intimate hospitality of a smaller hotel; some rooms showing their age; sits on steep street. **TripAdvisor:** "comfortable," "convenient location," "pleasantly surprised." $ *Rooms from: $130* ⊠ *Avda. 11 and C. 3 Bis, Barrio Amón* ☎ *2523–4600, 877/424–6423 in North America* ⊕ *www. hotelamonplaza.com* ⬥ *84 rooms, 3 suites* ❑ *Breakfast* ✚ *F2.*

$
Hotel Aranjuez. Several 1940s-era houses with extensive gardens and lively common areas—where visitors swap travel advice—constitute this family-run bed-and-breakfast. **Pros:** good budget value; good place to meet other budget travelers. **Cons:** cumbersome reservations system; far from sights; very popular so difficult to procure space. **TripAdvisor:** "beautiful," "great breakfast," "friendly and helpful staff." $ *Rooms from: $56* ⊠ *C. 19, Avdas. 11–13, Barrio Aranjuez* ☎ *2256–1825, 877/898–8663 in North America* ⊕ *www.hotelaranjuez.com* ⬥ *54 rooms, 48 with bath* ❑ *Breakfast* ✚ *H2.*

$$
B&B/INN
★
Hotel Don Carlos. One of the city's first guesthouses (technically it's three houses) is that quintessential place where you'll meet fellow travelers and exchange advice and swap stories about what you've seen out-country. **Pros:** good value; good place to meet fellow travelers. **Cons:** some noise in interior rooms; some reports of long waits in restaurant. **TripAdvisor:** "beautiful interior," "old-world charm," "quirky." $ *Rooms from: $80* ⊠ *C. 9 and Avda. 9* ☎ *2221–6707, 866/675–9259 in North America* ⊕ *www.doncarloshotel.com* ⬥ *33 rooms, 31 with bath* ❑ *Breakfast* ✚ *G2.*

TEATRO NACIONAL

$ B&B/INN 🏨 **Hotel Dunn Inn.** Adjoining 1926 and 1933 houses fuse to create the cozy Barrio Amón experience at bargain prices. **Pros:** good value; friendly staff. **Cons:** difficult to get reservations; interior rooms catch noise from lobby and bar; sits at bottom of steep street. **TripAdvisor:** "a breath of fresh air," "great staff," "absolutely flawless." [$] *Rooms from: $60* ✉ *Avda. 11 and C. 5, Barrio Amón* ☎ *2222–3232, 888/545–4801 in North America* 🌐 *www.hoteldunninn.com* 🛏 *26 rooms* 🍴 *Breakfast* ✥ *F2.*

$$ B&B/INN Fodor's Choice ★ 🏨 **Hôtel Le Bergerac.** Quiet elegance doesn't often come at affordable prices, but it's yours here at San José's (we think) best inn. **Pros:** top-notch service; cozy rooms; terrific restaurant. **Cons:** rooms on the small side; not near sights, steep street if walking. **TripAdvisor:** "great customer service," "warm welcome," "quiet quality." [$] *Rooms from: $97* ✉ *C. 35, Avdas. Central–2, 1st entrance to Los Yoses, San Pedro* ☎ *2234–7850* 🌐 *www.bergerachotel.com* 🛏 *25 rooms* 🍴 *Breakfast* ✥ *B6.*

$ B&B/INN 🏨 **Hotel Milvia.** Apply the principles of feng shui to an old militia arms depository, add splashes of stunning art, and you get a charming bed-and-breakfast on a San Pedro backstreet. **Pros:** good value; artistic decor. **Cons:** can be difficult to find, far from sights. **TripAdvisor:** "spacious and comfortable," "peaceful and elegant," "convenient and eclectic." [$] *Rooms from: $69* ✉ *100 m north and 100 m east of Centro Comercial Muñoz y Nanne, San Pedro* ☎ *2225–4543* 🌐 *www.hotelmilvia.com* 🛏 *9 rooms* 🍴 *Breakfast* ✥ *D5.*

$ B&B/INN 🏨 **Hotel Rincón de San José.** This elegant little inn has comfortable guest quarters in a charming neighborhood near the Parque España, and incorporates environmentally friendly practices into its operations. **Pros:** good value; friendly management; eco-friendly hotel. **Cons:** small rooms; rooms fronting street get some noise; no on-site parking. **TripAdvisor:** "nice environment," "price and service are exceptional," "ideal for short stay." [$] *Rooms from: $72* ✉ *Avda. 9 and C. 15, Barrio Otoya* ☎ *2221–9702* 🌐 *www.hotelrincondesanjose.com* 🛏 *42 rooms* 🍴 *Breakfast* ✥ *H3.*

$ B&B/INN 🏨 **Hotel Santo Tomás.** The front of this century-old former coffee-plantation house *does* butt up against the sidewalk on a busy street, but close the front door behind you, and you'll find an oasis of quiet in the center of the city. **Pros:** good value; friendly staff; central location. **Cons:** difficult parking; borders on sketchy neighborhood; small rooms. **TripAdvisor:** "pleasant and welcoming," "best customer service," "historic property with wonderful staff." [$] *Rooms from: $58* ✉ *Avda. 7, Cs. 3–5, Barrio Amón* ☎ *2255–0448, 877/446–0658 in North America* 🌐 *www.hotelsantotomas.com* 🛏 *35 rooms* 🍴 *Breakfast* ✥ *F3.*

$ B&B/INN 🏨 **Kap's Place.** The owners of this multibuilding lodging are committed to maintaining a family atmosphere, and you'll be guaranteed peace and quiet during your stay here. **Pros:** you can pay with a credit card if you stay in the main building, but not in one of the annexes; good budget value; quiet. **Cons:** far from sights; small rooms; reception might be in another building. **TripAdvisor:** "beautiful," "welcoming," "friendly place." [$] *Rooms from: $45* ✉ *C. 19, Avdas. 11–13, 200 m west, 50 m north of Shell station, Barrio Aranjuez* ☎ *2221–1169* 🌐 *www.kapsplace.com* 🛏 *24 rooms, 17 with bath* 🚭 *No-smoking* 🍴 *Breakfast* ✥ *H2.*

WEST OF DOWNTOWN

San José's vast west side contains only a smattering of lodgings, but among them is one of the city's best.

$$ B&B/INN **Fodor's Choice** ★ 🏨 **Hotel Grano de Oro.** Two wooden houses—one dates from the turn of the 20th century, and the other from the 1950s—have been converted into one of the city's most charming inns, decorated throughout with old photos of the capital and paintings by local artists. **Pros:** friendly management; top-notch service; superb restaurant. **Cons:** remodeling took away country feel in some areas; far from sights; need taxi to get here. **TripAdvisor:** "beautiful hotel and rooms," "very good food," "gracious living." [$] *Rooms from: $135* ✉ *C. 30, Avdas. 2–4* ☎ *2255–3322* 🌐 *www.hotelgranodeoro.com* 🛏 *40 rooms, 3 suites* 🚭 *No-smoking* 🍴 *No meals* ✚ *A4.*

$$ HOTEL 🏨 **Hotel Parque del Lago.** The management that brought you the South Pacific's Lapa Ríos *(⇨ See Cabo Matapalo)*, also runs things at this eco-conscious, west-side lodging. **Pros:** good business facilities; friendly staff; eco-friendly hotel. **Cons:** far from sights; smallish rooms. **TripAdvisor:** "friendly staff," "nice hotel," "modern." [$] *Rooms from: $80* ✉ *C. 40 and Avda. 2, Paseo Colón* ☎ *2547–2000* 🌐 *www.parquedellago.com* 🛏 *33 rooms, 6 suites* 🍴 *Breakfast* ✚ *A3.*

NIGHTLIFE AND THE ARTS

THE ARTS

The best source for theater, dance, film, and arts information is the "Viva" entertainment section of the Spanish-language daily *La Nación*. The paper also publishes the "Tiempo Libre" section each Friday, highlighting what's going on over the weekend. *GAM Cultural* is a free monthly flyer found in many upscale hotels and restaurants, and publishes features about what's going on around town. Listings in both publications are in Spanish but are easy to decipher.

Unfortunately, arts offerings in the city are nearly nonexistent during the high-season weeks from mid-December through early February. That's school vacation time.

ART GALLERIES

San José's art galleries, public or private, museum or bohemian, keep daytime hours only, but all kick off a new show with an evening opening. They're free and open to the public, and they offer a chance to rub elbows with Costa Rica's art community (and to sip wine and munch on appetizers). Listings appear in *La Nación*'s "Viva" section. Your time in the capital might coincide with one of these by happenstance. (They're rarely announced in the paper more than a day or two in advance.) Look for the term *inauguración* (opening).

FILM

Dubbing of movies is rare; films are screened in their original language, usually English, and subtitled in Spanish. (Children's movies, however, *are* dubbed, although a multiplex cinema may offer some *hablada en inglés*, or screenings in English.) Plan to pay $6 for a ticket. Don't

"Our first full day in San José was full of wandering through the streets and markets. We happened upon this friendly artist who shared his paintings with us." —Photo by Liz Stuart, Fodors.com member

expect anything too avant-garde in most theaters; month-old Hollywood releases are the norm. Following trends seen elsewhere, theaters have fled downtown for the suburban malls.

Cine San Pedro. Cine San Pedro is a 10-theater multiplex a short taxi ride from downtown. ⊠ *Mall San Pedro, San Pedro* ☎ *2283–5716* ⊕ *www. ccmccinemas.com.*

Sala Garbo. The Sala Garbo theater shows arty films, often in languages other than English with Spanish subtitles. ⊠ *Avda. 2 and C. 28, Paseo Colón* ☎ *2222–1034* ⊕ *www.salagarbocr.com.*

THEATER AND MUSIC

More than a dozen theater groups (many of which perform slapstick comedies) hold forth in smaller theaters around town. If your Spanish is up to it, call for a reservation. The curtain rises at 8 pm, Friday through Sunday, with some companies staging performances on Thursday night, too. If your Spanish isn't quite theater-ready, there are plenty of dance and musical performances.

Centro Nacional de la Cultura. There are frequent dance performances and concerts in the **Teatro FANAL** and **Teatro 1887,** both in the Centro Nacional de la Cultura. ⊠ *C. 13, Avdas. 3–5, Barrio Otoya* ☎ *2257–5524* ⊕ *www.actividadescenac.com.*

Eugene O'Neill Theater. The Eugene O'Neill Theater has chamber concerts and plays most weekend evenings. The cultural center is a great place to meet expatriate North Americans. ⊠ *Centro Cultural Costarricense–Norteamericano, Avda. 1 and C. 37, Barrio Dent, San Pedro* ☎ *2207–7554* ⊕ *www.centrocultural.cr.*

Little Theatre Group. For six decades, the Little Theatre Group has presented English-language community-theater productions several times a year at the near-west-side Teatro Laurence Olivier. Check the Web site for listings. A performance may coincide with your time in town. ✉ *Avda. 2 and C. 28, Paseo Colón* ☎ *8858–1446* ⊕ *www. littletheatregroup.org.*

Teatro La Aduana. The Teatro La Aduana holds frequent dance and stage performances, and is home to the Compañía Nacional de Teatro (National Theater Company). ✉ *C. 25 and Avda. 3, Barrio La California* ☎ *2257–8305.*

Teatro Nacional. The baroque Teatro Nacional is the home of the excellent National Symphony Orchestra, which performs on several weekends (Friday evening and Sunday morning) between April and November. The theater also hosts visiting musical groups and dance companies. Tickets are $3–$40. ✉ *Plaza de la Cultura, Barrio La Soledad* ☎ *2221–1329* ⊕ *www.teatronacional.go.cr.*

Teatro Popular Melico Salazar. San José's second-most popular theater, the Teatro Popular Melico Salazar has a full calendar of music and dance shows, as well as a few offbeat productions. Something goes on several nights a week; tickets are $2–$20. ✉ *Avda. 2, Cs. Central–2, Barrio La Merced* ☎ *2233–5424* ⊕ *www.teatromelico.go.cr.*

NIGHTLIFE

The metro area's hottest nightlife has migrated to the Central Valley suburbs of Escazú and Heredia these days. (⟳ *See Chapter 4.)* Both are about 20-minute taxi rides from downtown San José. The capital isn't devoid of places to go in the evening, however. There's still plenty of bars, dance places, and restaurants and cafés where you can spend the evening. Take taxis to and from when you go; it's the safest option if you're out after dark. Most places will be happy to call you a cab—or, if there's a guard, he can hail you one—when it's time to call it a night.

AREAS

No one could accuse San José of having too few watering holes, but aside from the hotels there aren't many places to have a quiet drink, especially downtown. Barrios Amón and Otoya have little in the way of nightlife outside the occasional hotel bar.

The young and the restless hang out in the student-oriented places around the University of Costa Rica in the eastern suburb of San Pedro. The Calle de la Amargura (Street of Bitterness), named for the route Jesus took to the crucifixion, is much more secular than its name suggests and rocks loudly each night. (Nighttime robberies have occurred on "The Calle," so be wary.)

Don't write off every place around the university as rowdy. There are a few quiet bars and cafés where you can carry on a real conversation. Barrios La California and Escalante, an area anchored by the Santa Teresita church, amorphously connect central San José with San Pedro, and house some of the city's trendiest nightspots.

BARS

El Observatorio. El Observatorio strikes an unusual balance between casual and formal: it's the kind of place where folks over 30 go to watch a soccer game but wear ties, nightly except Sunday. ✉ *C. 23 across from Cine Magaly, Barrio La California* ☎ *2223–0725* ⊕ *www.elobservatorio.tv* ☉ *Mon.– Sat. 6 pm–2 am.*

★ **Jazz Café San Pedro.** Jazz Café San Pedro draws big crowds. They have live music nightly except Sunday. (Beware: the place gets very smoky.) You'll find a branch in the Central Valley suburb of Escazú. ✉ *Avda. Central next to Banco Popular, San Pedro* ☎ *2253–8933* ⊕ *www. jazzcafecostarica.com* ☉ *Mon.–Sat. 6 pm–1 am.*

BE AWARE

A few gems really do populate the downtown area, but several bars there double as prostitute pickup joints or are just boozy places where patrons go to pick fights. If you're downtown at night, drink at your hotel or one of the places we recommend, and don't wander directly south or west of Parque Central on foot.

Also avoid the Centro Comercial El Pueblo (usually known simply as El Pueblo), north of downtown. There have been problems with security at this entertainment-and-shopping complex.

Mac's American Bar. An older expat crowd hangs out at Mac's American Bar, which usually has the TV tuned to a sporting event. It gets our nod for serving the city's best burgers. ✉ *South side of La Sabana Park, next to the Costa Rica Tennis Club, Sabana Sur* ☎ *2234–3145* ⊕ *www. macsamericanbar.com* ☉ *Daily 9 am–1 am.*

Stan's Irish Pub. A refreshing change from the ubiquitous Imperial beer is what you'll find at Stan's Irish Pub, which has Guinness on tap as well as an around-the-world selection of brews. ✉ *150 m northeast of Casa Presidencial, Zapote* ☎ *2253–4360* ☉ *Wed.–Thurs. 4 pm–1 am, Fri. 4 pm–3 am, Sun. 11–11.*

CAFÉS AND RESTAURANTS

For a country so economically dependent on coffee, there's little evidence of a café culture here. Costa Ricans do observe coffee breaks religiously at home and at work, but outside of a few places we list here, making a special trip somewhere to converse with friends over coffee isn't too common.

Café 1930. The café under the arcades at the entrance to the Grand Hotel Costa Rica pulls duty as a pleasant place for an evening drink or coffee. ✉ *Avda. 2 and C. 3, Barrio La Soledad* ☎ *2221–4011* ☉ *Sun.–Thurs. 11–11, Fri.–Sat. 11 am–midnight.*

Café Mundo. The highly recommended restaurant Café Mundo is a quiet spot for a drink frequented by gay and bohemian crowds. ✉ *C. 15 and Avda. 9, Barrio Otoya* ☎ *2222–6190.*

Olio. Fill up on Spanish-style tapas at Mediterranean bar and restaurant Pub Olio. It draws a mix of professionals and older college students. ✉ *200 m north of Bagelmen's, Barrio Escalante* ☎ *2281–0541* ☉ *Mon.– Wed. noon–11, Thurs.–Fri. noon–midnight, Sat. 6 pm–midnight.*

Omar Khayyam. Smack-dab in the center of the campus nightlife, Omar Khayyam is a blissfully quiet refuge. Share a jug of wine and falafel or hummus with fried yuca on the covered patio. ☒ *C. de la Amargura, San Pedro* ☎ *2253–8455* ☺ *Mon.–Sat. 11–11.*

CASINOS

Ask about casino rules before you dive in and play: there are a few Costa Rican variations—for example, you don't get a bonus for blackjack, but you do for three of a kind or straights under local rules. (And yet some places boast that they play exactly as they do in Las Vegas.)

Be careful where you go. The casino at the pink Hotel del Rey in Barrio El Carmen—arguably the city's most famous and definitely its most notorious gambling establishment—swarms with prostitutes. Avoid it.

> **DANCE FEVER**
>
> **Merecumbé.** Step into a San José nightclub and you might think Costa Ricans are born dancing. They aren't, but most learn to merengue, rumba (bolero here), mambo, cha-cha, and swing (called *cumbia* elsewhere) as children. Play catch-up at dance school Merecumbé, which has 16 branches around Costa Rica. With a few days' notice you can arrange a private lesson with an English-speaking instructor. An hour or two is all you need to grasp the fundamentals of merengue and bolero. ☒ *100 m. south and 25 m. west of Banco Popular, San Pedro* ☎ *2224-3531* ⊕ *www.merecumbe.net.*

A few of the city's larger hotels have casinos we do recommend, including the Clarion Amón Plaza and the Gran Hotel Costa Rica. By law, casinos may open only from 6 pm to 2 am.

DANCE CLUBS

San José's discos attract a *very* young crowd. Quite frankly, you'll feel ancient if you've passed 21. Live-music halls draw dancers of all ages, but these populate rougher neighborhoods on the city's south side and are best avoided.

GAY AND LESBIAN

San José is reasonably open to gay and lesbian visitors, but given pronouncements of disapproval by city officials, you might want to temper your openness. Be discreet, and you'll be fine. The capital has a few bars, restaurants, and dance places patronized primarily by a gay and lesbian clientele, although all are welcome. The places we list have drawn crowds for years.

Club Oh!. Club Oh! is a mostly gay, techno-heavy disco with two dance floors and weekly drag shows. Take a taxi to and from here; the neighborhood's sketchy. ☒ *C. 2, Avdas. 14–16A, Barrio El Pacífico* ☎ *2248–1500* ⊕ *www.clubohcostarica.com* ☺ *Fri.–Sat. 9 pm–2 am*

El Bochinche. El Bochinche is a gay bar and dance club that doubles as a Mexican restaurant. It attracts a young crowd and keeps *very* late hours. ☒ *C. 11, Avdas. 10–12, Barrio La Soledad* ☎ *2221–0500* ⊕ *www. bochinchesanjose.com* ☺ *Wed.–Thurs. 8 pm–5 am, Fri.–Sat. 8 pm–6 am*

La Avispa. A gay and lesbian crowd frequents La Avispa, which has two dance floors with videos and karaoke as well as a quieter upstairs bar with pool tables. The last Friday of each month is ladies' night. ⊠ *C. 1, Avdas. 8–10, Barrio La Soledad* ☎ *2223–5343* ⊕ *www.laavispa.co.cr* ⊘ *Thurs.–Sun. 8 pm–1 am*

GREAT VIEWS

Several *miradores* (lookout points) dot the mountains north and south of the city.

Ram Luna. Ram Luna, in the far southern suburbs, is the most famous of these. You come here for the view—the lights of the Central Valley sparkle at your feet—and the music, more than the food. (Costa Rican fare is the staple here.) Make reservations if you plan to be here for Wednesday or Thursday evening's folklore show or Friday evening's dancing to live music. ⊠ *10 km/6 miles south of San José, near Church of San Luis Tolosa, Aserrí* ☎ *2230–3022* ⊕ *www.restauranteramluna. com* ⊘ *Tues. 4–11, Wed.–Thurs. 7–10, Fri. 4–midnight, Sat. noon–11, Sun. noon–9.*

SHOPPING

Although it might seem more "authentic" to buy your souvenirs at their out-country source, you can find everything in the city, a real bonus if you're pressed for time. If the capital has any real tourist shopping district, it's found loosely in the cluster of streets around Parque Morazán, just north of downtown, an area bounded roughly by Avenidas 1 and 7 and Calles 5 and 9. Stroll and search, because many other businesses congregate in the area as well.

The northeastern suburb of Moravia has a cluster of high-quality crafts and artisan shops—for good reason very popular with tour groups—in the three blocks heading north from the Colegio María Inmaculada school. The street is two blocks behind the city's church.

MALLS

Old-timers lament the malling over of San José. Several huge enclosed centers anchor the metro area. These are complemented by dozens of smaller strip malls. Expect all the comforts of home—food courts and movie theaters included.

Mall San Pedro. Mall San Pedro sits in its namesake suburb, a short 10-minute taxi ride from downtown San José. ⚠ **Be aware of your surroundings. There have been a few muggings in this congested area at night.** ⊠ *Rotonda de la Hispanidad, San Pedro* ☎ *2283–7540.*

Terramall. The mammoth 137-store Terramall is the far eastern suburbs' prime shopping destination. ⊠ *Autopista Florencio del Castillo, Tres Ríos* ☎ *2278–6970* ⊕ *www.terramall.co.cr.*

SPECIALTY STORES

BOOKS AND MAGAZINES

The *New York Times*, *Wall Street Journal*, *Miami Herald*, and *USA Today* arrive in San José the morning of publication, printed here and bound on bond paper. Find them at a select few outlets and shops in large hotels or at the airport.

7th Street Books. The affable owners of 7th Street Books make this store *the* place to stop in and see what's going on in the expat community. It has the city's best selection of books in English and is also strong on Latin America and tropical ecology. ⊠ *C. 7, Avdas. Central–1, Barrio La Soledad* ☎ *2256–8251.*

Casa de las Revistas. With several locations around the metro area, Casa de las Revistas has San José's best selection of magazines in English. ⊠ *C. 5, Avdas. 3–5, Barrio El Carmen* ☎ *2256–5092.*

Librería Internacional. Librería Internacional is the city's largest bookstore. It evokes that Barnes & Noble ambience, though on a much smaller scale, and stocks English translations of Latin American literature as well as myriad coffee-table books on Costa Rica. ⊠ *300 m west of Taco Bell, Barrio Dent* ☎ *2253–9553* ⊕ *www.libreriainternacional.com.*

CRAFTS

The arts-and-crafts tradition in Costa Rica isn't as strong as in, say, Guatemala or Peru. At first glance you might be disenchanted with what you see in the run-of-the-mill souvenir shops. Keep your disappointment in check until you visit two of San José's outstanding purveyors of fine artisan work.

Fodor's Choice ★ **Galería Namu.** Downtown San José's must-stop shop is Galería Namu, which sells Costa Rican folkloric art and the best indigenous crafts in town. Its inventory brims with colorful creations by the Guaymí, Boruca, Bribri, Chorotega, Huetar, and Maleku peoples—all Costa Rican indigenous groups. You can also find exquisitely carved ivory-nut Tagua figurines and baskets made by the indigenous Wounan people from Panama's Darién region and Tuno textiles from Honduras's Miskito coast. Take note of carved balsa masks, woven cotton blankets, and hand-painted ceramics.

The store looks expensive—and indeed, the sky's the limit in terms of prices—but if your budget is not so flush, say so: the good folks here can help you find something in the $10–$20 range that will make a more cherished souvenir of your trip than a *Pura Vida* T-shirt. As a bonus you'll get an information sheet describing your work's creator and art style. Namu has a reputation for fair prices for customers, and for fair pay to artists or artisans. ⊠ *Avda. 7, Cs. 5–7, behind Aurola Holiday Inn, Barrio Amón* ☎ *2256–3412* ⊕ *www.galerianamu.com* ☾ *Mon.– Sat. 9–6:30, Sun. 1–5; closed Sun., May–Nov.*

★ **Kaltak Artesanías.** The staff and selection at Kaltak Artesanías make it a real standout from all the Moravia shops. Walk in with some unformulated "I'm not sure what I want" notions, and the staff will help you find that perfect souvenir from among the selection of ceramics (Pefi and Osenbach designs, trademarks of two well-known artisans in the

Continued on page 122

LAST-MINUTE
SOUVENIR
SHOPPING

by Holly K. Sonneland

San José's markets can be crowded, but they're great fun for the savvy shopper. There are plenty of Costa Rican souvenirs for every pocketbook, and the city's bustling downtown is compact enough to make it easy to visit a few markets in a day . . . or even an afternoon. It's a great way to explore the city and take care of last-minute gift shopping.

Some markets have a mishmash of items, whereas others are more specialized. Pick up cigars or peruse antiques in the back of the sleepy La Casona building downtown, or head over to the strip of covered traveler-friendly souvenir stands by Plaza de la Democracia to browse the artsy wares. Festive fake flora in glittery, tropical blue, green, and orange hues can be found at the permanent artisan bazaars.

For a lively experience, head to the gritty and labyrinthine Mercado Central edifice right on Avenida Central where you can jostle among working-class Ticos as you pick up an Imperial beer logo–emblazoned muscle T-shirt or a homemade herbal love potion. Keep a tight hold on your bag, and have fun practicing your Spanish with the vendors.

GREAT GIFT IDEAS

Costa Rica's souvenirs pop with bright color and have that distinct *"pura vida"* (pure life) flair.

COFFEE: The authentic modern-day Costa Rica souvenir, not to mention most appreciated back home. Load up on whole bean (*grano entero*), or, if you must get ground (*molido*), buy the *"puro,"* otherwise it might have pre-added sugar. Café Britt is the country's most famous brand (₡2,500/lb).

MAYAN OCARINAS
(₡2,500–₡7,000) Calling the ocarina two-faced would be an insult, but only because you wouldn't be giving it nearly enough credit. The Mayan resonant vessel flutes depict over a half-dozen animal faces when flipped around and were often given as gifts to travelers by the Chorotega indigenous group in northwestern Guanacaste.

HAMMOCKS: Swinging in one of these is the official posture of *pura vida*. Structured hammocks with wooden dowels on the ends (₡12,000 and up) are optimal, but dowel-less, cocoon-like hammocks (₡10,000 and up) are infinitely more compactable. Get a chair hammock (₡6,000) if you have limited hanging space back home.

OXCARTS: From the Sarchí region, the oxcart has become Costa Rica's most iconic craftsman artifact. Full-size ones can run a few hundred dollars, and many dealers can arrange to have them shipped for you. There's also a coffee table-size version (₡7,000) or, better yet, an oxcart napkin holder (₡1,500).

COFFEE BREWERS: The original Costa Rican coffeemaker is called a *chorreador*. It's a simple wooden stand that's fitted with cloth sock-like filters. Finely ground coffee is dumped in the sock, and hot water is filtered into the mug beneath. Unadorned ones to sleek cherry wood cost around ₡5,000. Don't forget to buy extra sock filters (₡250).

LOCAL LIBATIONS: If you don't have room for a six-pack, be sure to take home what is probably the world's best beer label, Imperial, on a stein or T-shirt (both ₡2,500). Or, snag a bottle of Costa Rica's signature sugarcane liquor, *guaro*, most commonly sold under the Cacique brand.

JEWELRY: Go for oversized wooden hoop earrings (¢3,000), wire-wrought gold and silver baubles (¢3,500), or plaster-molded earrings adorned with toucans, frogs, and pineapples (¢1,500). Jewelry made from carved-out coco shells are popular, too.

TROPICAL WOODS AND PAPERS: Sleek mango-wood vases (¢8,250), inlaid rosewood cutting boards (¢8,000), and hand-painted rum rum wood mugs (¢3,850) are among the many elegant woodworks here. There are also scratch-and-sniff writing materials that would make Willy Wonka proud, with banana, mango, lemon, and coffee-scented (sorry, no schnozberry) stationery sets (¢3,700).

BORUCA CEREMONIAL MASKS: The Boruca people, from southern Costa Rica and one of the country's last active indigenous groups, don these masks in their annual end-of-the-year festival, Dansa de los Diablitos (Dance of the Devils). It's an animistic production that depicts the avenging of the people for the decimation wrought by the conquistadors. Cheaper imitations abound, but Galería NAMU has the best—and most authentic—selection (¢65,000 to ¢100,000).

FOLKLORIC DRESSES AND SHIRTS: While they're often only pulled out on national holidays like Independence Day, a flounced dress (¢8,000 and up) or pinafore (¢5,000) might be just the kitschy gift you're looking for. Ranchero-style shirts (¢8,000) and straw hats (¢2,000) are also an option.

MACHETES: Knives and machetes are commonly used in the country's rural jungle areas and happily sold in leather slings to travelers (¢7,000). Also, knives (¢2,000–3,000) and other items, like frogs and butterflies made out of colored resin, might not be considered traditional but represent the Rastafarian side of the country. Be aware, weapons are not welcome in carry-on luggage on planes.

* All prices listed in colons

SAN JOSÉ MARKETS

San José's navigable city center, and its proximity to the airport, make it the perfect last-minute shopping spot.

MERCADO CENTRAL

This market is geared towards locals and has some of the lowest prices anywhere. Here you can visit flower and medicinal herb (of dubious medicinal properties) shops not found in other markets. ⊠ Avenidas Central and 1, Calles 6 and 8 ⊙ Mon.–Sat. 8–6; Dec., open Sun.

LA CASONA

Souvenirs and tobacco products abound in this rambling, two-story building. At the far eastern end, go up the back stairs to the discount room, where regular items are discounted 25%–30%. Also upstairs is José "Chavo" Navarro's antique shop. ⊠ Calle Central, between Avenidas Central and 1 ☎ 2222-7999 ⊙ 9:30–6.

GALERÍA NAMU

Almost inarguably the best—and, importantly, the only free-trade—store selling indigenous artwork and handcrafts. Owner Aisling French and her staff have developed extensive ties with the Costa Rica's few remaining

Shopping for coffee at Mercado Central.

tribal peoples, bringing their top-notch artisanship to the city. In particular, NAMU sells the highest quality Bribrí ceremonial masks in the country, and has recently developed ties with the Wounan tribe in Panama, who produce museum-quality chunga palm baskets. ⊠ Avenida 7, between Calles 5 and 7 (across from Alliance Française) ☎ 2256-3412 ⊙ Mon.–Sat. 9-6:30.

PLAZA DE LA DEMOCRACIA

This strip of stands across the plaza from the National Museum is the most traveler-oriented market. Vendors also don't pay taxes here, so while some items (bulk coffee) are more expensive, others (choreadores) are actually cheaper than they are in Mercado Central. Hammocks are at the far north end, and Stand 82 has some of the best woodworks, along with Stands 25 and 66. Custom-made earrings are at Stand 40. ⊠ Calle 13, between Avenidas Central and 2 ⊙ Daily, 8 until dusk.

ARTESANÍAS DEL SOL

This is a good place to get souvenirs, especially the popular piggy banks, basic pottery, and baskets, without the crowds. Christmas decorations are sold from September through December. ⊠ 100 meters west of Plaza del Sol, Curridabat, eastern San José ☎ 2225-6800 ⊙ Daily, 8–6; Dec., daily, 8–8.

SHOPPING KNOW-HOW

Colorful clay piggy banks

MAKING A DEAL

Bargaining isn't the sport it is in other countries, and if Tico vendors do bargain, it's often only with travelers who expect it. Before you try to strike a deal, know that Ticos are not confrontational, and haggling, even if not ill-intended, will come off as rude.

Your best bet for getting a deal is to buy in bulk, or simply suggest you'll come back later and walk away. If the vendors really want to lower the price, they'll call you back. If you're buying a single item, you can ask a vendor to offer you a lower price once, at most twice, but don't push it further.

Costa Ricans are painfully polite and are particularly fond of terms of endearment, and it's worth it to indulge in the gentility when talking with market vendors. If you're comfortable enough with your Tico Spanish, or *pachuco*, use the terms in return. For example, Ticos employ a whole arsenal of royal-themed lingo: *rey* and *reina*, or king and queen, are ubiq-

uitous forms of address, especially with middle-aged Ticos, although *reina* is more common than *rey*. You can easily use a "*Gracias, mi reina,*" to the (female) vendor who's just given you a good price, but "*¿Cómo está mi rey?*" to a 20-something male vendor sounds a little strange. That being said, if you're a 20-something female shopper, be prepared to hear "*¿En cómo puedo servirle mi reina?*" literally, "How can I serve you my queen?" (said endearingly, not lecherously) from every other 50-year-old vendor whose stand you pass. *Regalar*, a verb that literally means "to gift," can be used to ask a vendor to hand you the item that you want to buy (*Puede regalarme esa bolsa verde, porfa?* I'll take that green bag, please?) or to cut you a deal (*Me la regala en tres mil?* Can you sell it to me for three thousand [colones]?)

Of course, if your Spanish is rusty, smiling always helps.

■ TIP→ While most of the shops in these markets take credit cards, vendors will be more likely to cut you a deal if you pay in cash.

PLAYING IT SAFE

Petty crime is on the rise in Costa Rica, but that shouldn't keep you from exploring the markets. It's important to note that what were once recommended precautions are now strongly advised. Keep cash in breast pockets and leave credit cards and important documents in the hotel. Also leave behind jewelry and fancy gear, especially cameras, that will make you stand out. (The lighting in the markets—all of them indoor—is very poor, and photos inevitably don't turn out anyway.) Most of the markets, like the rest of the city, are generally safe during the day but best avoided in the evening.

Ceremonial mask from Namu Gallery

capital, are well represented), wood-and-leather rocking chairs, oxcarts of all sizes, orchids, and carvings from native *cocobolo* and *guápinol* woods and ash wood. ⊠ *50 m north of Colegio María Inmaculada, Moravia* ☎ *2297–2736* ⊘ *Mon.–Sat. 9–7, Sun. 10–6.*

MUSIC

San José's music stores stock the Latin sounds of every artist from Chayanne to Shakira, but Costa Ricans take special pride in their hometown Latin-fusion group, the three-time-Grammy Award–winning Editus.

Universal. In addition to selling everything else imaginable, downtown department store Universal stocks a good selection of Latin CDs in its first-floor music department. ⊠ *Avda. Central between Cs. Central and 1, Barrio El Carmen* ☎ *2222–2222* ⊕ *www.universalcr.com.*

SOUVENIRS

Boutique Annemarie. Hotel gift shop Boutique Annemarie has a huge selection of popular souvenirs and CDs of Costa Rican musicians. ⊠ *Hotel Don Carlos, C. 9 and Avda. 9, Barrio Amón* ☎ *2233–5343* ⊘ *Daily 9–5.*

Calle Nacional de Artesanía y Pintura. Some 100 souvenir vendors congregate in the block-long covered walkway known as the Calle Nacional de Artesanía y Pintura, and offer some real bargains in hammocks, wood carvings, and clothing. In a perpetual tug-of-war, the city proposes moving the stalls to a less visible location at Avenida 4 and Calle 7. The vendors balk and the city relents, only to have dispute come up again a few months later. ⊠ *C. 13, Avdas. Central–2, Western side of Plaza de la Democracia.*

La Casona. Dozens of souvenir vendors set up shop on the two floors of La Casona, in a rickety old downtown mansion. It's much like a flea market, and it's a fun place to browse. ⊠ *C. 2, Avdas. Central–1, Barrio El Carmen* ☎ *2222–7999.*

Mercado Central. Mercado Central doesn't bill itself for souvenir shopping—the maze of passageways is where the average Costa Rican comes to stock up on day-to-day necessities—but a few stalls of interest to tourists congregate near the entrances. ⊠ *Bordered by Avdas. Central–1 and Cs. 6–8, Barrio La Merced* ⊘ *Mon.–Sat. 6–6.*

Mundo de Recuerdos. If you can't find it at Mundo de Recuerdos, it probably doesn't exist. Here's the largest of the Moravia shops with simply everything—at least of standard souvenir fare—you could ask for under one roof. ⊠ *Across from Colegio María Inmaculada, Moravia* ☎ *2240–8990* ⊘ *Daily 9–6.*

Museo del Oro Precolombino. The museum-shop concept barely exists here, but the shop at the entrance of the Museo del Oro Precolombino is the exception. Look for a terrific selection of pre-Columbian-theme jewelry, art, exclusively designed T-shirts, coin- and bill-theme key chains, notebooks, and mouse pads. ⊠ *C. 5, Avdas. Central–2, Barrio La Soledad* ☎ *2243–4202* ⊘ *Mid-Jan.–Mar., weekdays 9:15–6, weekends 9:15–5; Apr.–mid-Jan., daily 9:15–5.*

The Central Valley

WORD OF MOUTH

"We happened upon this workshop (Taller Eloy Alfaro e Hijos) by accident. It was one of the neatest experiences I've had in my visits to Costa Rica. They were constructing the world's largest oxcart for an exhibition. The family workshop runs completely on water, not electricity."

—Photo by jvcostarica, Fodors.com member

WELCOME TO
THE CENTRAL VALLEY

TOP REASONS
TO GO

★ **Avian adventures:**
Flock to Tapantí National
Park to see emerald
toucanets, resplendent
quetzals (if you're lucky),
and nearly every species of
Costa Rican hummingbird.
Rancho Naturalista is the
bird lover's hotel of choice.

★ **Coffee:** Get up close
and personal with harvesting and processing on
coffee tours at two of the
valley's many plantations:
Café Britt and Doka Estate.

★ **The Orosi Valley:**
Spectacular views and
quiet, bucolic towns make
this area a great day trip or
overnight from San José.

★ **Rafting the Pacuare
River:** Brave the rapids as
you descend through tropical forest on one of the best
rivers in Central America.

★ **The views:** Ascend
the volcanic slopes that
border the valley, meet-
ing superb views almost
anywhere you go.

**1 Areas north and west
of San José.** The areas
north and west of San José
are dominated by coffee
farms and small valley
towns whose beautiful
hotels attract lots of tourists
on their first and last nights
in the country. Café Britt
and Doka Estate are both
here, as is the international
airport, near Alajuela.

**2 Cartago and Irazú Vol-
cano.** In the eastern Central
Valley are Cartago and Irazú
Volcano. Cartago is an older
city than San José, with a
couple of historic attractions. Irazú is Costa Rica's
tallest volcano. On a clear
day you can see both the
Atlantic and Pacific oceans
from its peak.

Santa Clara

0 — 10 mi
0 — 15 km

CORDILLERA CENTRAL

Irazú Volcano
Turrialba Volcano
Guayabo National Monument
Potrero Cerrado
Turrialba
Jabillos
Pavones
La Suiza
Moravia
Cartago
Juan Viñas
Tuis
Bajo Pacuare
Paraíso
Orosi Valley
CARTAGO
Río Macho
Pacuare River
Tapantí National Park
Tres de Junio
Salsipuedes
Villa Mills

TALAMANCA

GETTING ORIENTED

The Central Valley is something of a misnomer, and its Spanish name, the *meseta central* (central plateau) isn't entirely accurate either. The two contiguous mountain ranges that run the length of the country—the Cordillera Central range (which includes Poás, Barva, Irazú, and Turrialba volcanoes) to the north and the Cordillera de Talamanca to the south—don't quite line up in the middle, leaving a trough between them. The "valley" floor is 914 to 1,524 meters (3,000 to 5,000 feet) above sea level. In the valley, your view toward the coasts is obstructed by the two mountain ranges. But from a hillside hotel, your view of San José and the valley can be spectacular.

3 Turrialba. Rafting trips on the Pacuare and Reventazón are based in Turrialba, a bustling little town. The nearby Guayabo National Monument, ruins of a city deserted in AD 1400, is Costa Rica's only significant archaeological site.

4 Orosi Valley. The Orosi Valley is an often-overlooked beauty. The drive into the valley is simply gorgeous, and a tranquil way to spend a day. Birding destination Tapantí National Park is at the southern edge of the valley.

VOLCÁN IRAZÚ

The word *Irazú* is likely a corruption of Iztaru, a long-ago indigenous community whose name translated as "hill of thunder." The name is apt.

The volcano is considered active, but the gases and steam that billow from fumaroles on the northwestern slope are rarely visible from the peak above the crater lookouts. The mountain's first recorded eruption took place in 1723; the most recent was a series of eruptions that lasted from 1963 to 1965. Boulders and mud rained down on the countryside, damming rivers and causing serious floods, and the volcano dumped up to 20 inches of ash on sections of the Central Valley.

When conditions are clear, you can see the chartreuse lake inside the Cráter Principal. The stark moonscape of the summit contrasts markedly with the lush vegetation of Irazú's lower slopes, home to porcupines, armadillos, coyotes, and mountain hares. Listen for the low-pitched, throaty song of the *yigüirro*, or clay-color thrush, Costa Rica's national bird. Its call is most pronounced just before the start of the rainy season. *(See page 162 for more information.)*

BEST TIME TO GO

Early morning, especially in the January-through-April dry season, affords the best views, both of the craters and the surrounding countryside. Clouds move in by late morning. Wear warm, waterproof clothing if you get here that early; although rare, temperatures have dropped down close to freezing around dawn.

FUN FACT

Irazú has dumped a lot of ash over the centuries. The most recent eruptive period began on the day that John F. Kennedy arrived in Costa Rica in March 1963. The "ash storm" that ensued lasted on and off for two years.

BEST WAYS TO EXPLORE

BIRD-WATCHING

The road to Irazú provides some of the best roadside birding opportunities in the country, especially on a weekday when there isn't a constant parade of cars and buses heading up to the crater. Some of the most fruitful areas are on either side of the bridges you'll pass over. Reliable bird species that inhabit these roadsides are: acorn and hairy woodpeckers, the brilliant flame-throated warbler, and, buzzing around blossoms, the fiery-throated, green violet-ear, and (aptly named) volcano hummingbirds. Once past the main entrance, there are also plenty of opportunities to stop and bird-watch roadside. Look for volcano juncos on the ground and slaty flowerpiercers visiting flowering shrubs.

HIKING

Even before you get to the main entrance, check out the park's Prusia Sector, which has hiking trails that pass through majestic oak and pine forests and picnic areas. They're popular with Tico families on weekends, so if you want the woods to yourself, come on a weekday. Trails in the park are well marked; avoid heading down any paths marked with *"paso restringido"* ("passage restricted") signs.

VOLCANIC TIPS

A paved road leads all the way to the summit, where a small coffee shop sells hot beverages, and a persistent pair of coatis cruise the picnic tables for handouts. (Please resist the urge to feed them!) The road to the top climbs past vegetable fields, pastures, and native oak forests. You pass through the villages of Potrero Cerrado and San Juan de Chicuá before reaching the summit's bleak but beautiful main crater.

TOP REASONS TO GO

EASY TO GET TO

Irazú's proximity to San José and the entire eastern Central Valley makes it an easy half-day or day trip. Public transportation from the capital, frequently a cumbersome option to most of the country's national parks, is straightforward.

THE VIEW

How many places in the world let you peer directly into the crater of an active volcano? Costa Rica offers you two: here at Irazú, and the Northern Plains' Volcán Poás. Poás's steaming cauldron is spookier, but Irazú's crater lake with colors that change according to the light is nonetheless impressive.

MORE VIEWS

"On a clear day, you can see forever," goes the old song from the musical of the same name. Irazú is one of the few places in Costa Rica that lets you glimpse both the Pacific and Atlantic (Caribbean) oceans at once. "Clear" is the key term here: clouds frequently obscure the view. Early morning gives you your best shot.

ECO-LODGES IN THE CENTRAL VALLEY

Suburbia oozes out with each passing year, eating up once-idyllic Central Valley land, but it's still surprisingly easy to find vast undeveloped stretches, even in the metro area.

You'd never know it driving the highway west from San José through the valley of shopping malls and car dealerships, but Costa Rica's Central Valley is home to an ample amount of greenery. Two of the country's five active volcanoes (Irazú and Turrialba) loom here. Suburbia gives way to farmland above Escazú and Santa Ana, and the rolling hills are perfect for tranquil day hikes. A terrific selection of country lodges populates the hills north of Alajuela and Heredia, and a stay in one of them is certain to give you that "so close (to the international airport) and yet so far" convenience. Tapantí National Park, in the far eastern sector of the valley, contains a real live cloud forest—it's not quite Monteverde, but it is far easier to get to—and Guayabo National Monument nearby is home to Costa Rica's only true archaeological ruins. The medium-size city of Turrialba has fast become the country's white-water center. And the Orosi Valley defines pastoral tranquillity.

GOOD PRACTICES

Make a point of getting out and meeting the local people here in the Central Valley. We'd argue that the tidy towns in this region are Costa Rica at its most "authentic," its most "Tico." Folks here still greet you with a hearty "Buenos días" each day. Respond in kind.

Consider taking public transportation in the Central Valley. Communities here are bunched close enough together to be well served by public buses, and taxis can fill in the gaps. Plus, as development increases in the valley, managing your own vehicle here begins to resemble city driving.

TOP ECO-LODGES IN THE CENTRAL VALLEY

FINCA ROSA BLANCA COUNTRY INN, HEREDIA

The hotel on this 8-acre working coffee plantation just outside Heredia is one of just a handful of properties in the country to have achieved the coveted "Five Leaves" status in the Certification for Sustainable Tourism (⇨ *Certificate of Sustainable Tourism in Chapter 5*). In addition to all the amenities you'd expect from one of the Central Valley's most sumptuous accommodations, you can also take Finca Rosa Blanca's unique Sustainability Tour for a behind-the-scenes look at what a hotel can do to be more eco- and community-friendly. What other tour in Costa Rica lets you take in the workings of the laundry room, the solar panels, and the compost pile? *(Full hotel review on page 159.)*

RANCHO NATURALISTA, TURRIALBA

Some 430 species of birds live on the property—few lodgings can make such a claim, let alone one so close to the metropolitan area. But the fittingly named Rancho Naturalista near Turrialba has fast become the birding center of the Central Valley. From the bird checklist in the welcome packet in your room, to the resident professional birding guide, to the delightful deck where you can continue to bird-watch even after trekking around the grounds for the day, this is one of Costa Rica's premier locales for bird-watchers of all experience levels. *(Full hotel review on page 175.)*

XANDARI RESORT HOTEL & SPA, ALAJUELA

Xandari is a favorite of honeymooners who might not be aware of its environmental stewardship. The 40-acre property in the hills above Alajuela maintains an active program of recycling and uses on-site, organically grown fruits and vegetables. The hotel is also turning back a portion of its coffee plantation to tree cover, which has been set aside as a nature reserve. Coffee is still cultivated on the remainder of the plantation and ends up in your morning cup or as part of the coffee-scrub spa treatment. *(Full hotel review on page 149.)*

COMMUNITY OUTREACH

A glance at high schools around the Central Valley reveals a growing number of outdoor eco-theme wall paintings, all part of an ever-growing annual Environmental Mural Contest. The name says it all: students from area schools compete each year to design and create original murals conveying environmental messages.

The works represent combined efforts of schools' art and biology departments, with students devoting an average of four months from the project's start to finish. Many of the murals measure 50 square meters, or around 540 square feet. The competition is designed to foster artistic skills, teamwork, and, of course, environmental awareness among students and faculty who take part.

The contest is directed by the nonprofit FUNDECOR foundation, a local non-governmental organization whose objective is to put the brakes on deforestation and promote environmental consciousness. Local businesses support the effort.

THE CENTRAL VALLEY

Updated by
Dorothy MacK-
innon and Jef-
frey Van Fleet

San José and environs sit in a mile-high mountain valley ringed by volcanoes whose ash has fertilized the soil and turned the region into Costa Rica's historic breadbasket (though other regions of Costa Rica can also make that claim these days). This will always be the land that coffee built, and the small cities of the Central Valley exhibit a tidiness and prosperity you don't see in the rest of the country.

You can't find a more ideal climate than out here in the valley. When people refer to Costa Rica's proverbial "eternal spring," they're talking about this part of the country, which lacks the oppressive seasonal heat and rain of other regions. It's no wonder the Central Valley has drawn a burgeoning number of North American and European retirees.

For you, the visitor, the valley is chock-full of activities that will keep you occupied for a couple of days. There's no shortage of terrific lodgings out here—everything from family-run boutique hotels to the big international chains are yours for the night. It used to be that everyone stayed in San José and took in the various attractions in the Central Valley on day trips. With the good selection of quality accommodation out here, why not base yourself in the Central Valley, and make San José your day trip instead?

PLANNING

WHEN TO GO
HIGH SEASON: MID-DECEMBER TO APRIL
The Central Valley's elevation keeps temperatures pleasant and spring-like year-round, slightly warmer to the west and slightly cooler to the east. Turrialba and the Orosi Valley represent a transition zone between the valley and the Caribbean slope; expect slightly higher temperatures there. December and January kick off the dry season with sunny days

and brisk nights. February, March, and April warm up considerably. Some hotels here keep rates constant throughout the year; others follow high-season/low-season fluctuations.

LOW SEASON: MAY TO MID-NOVEMBER

The rainy season moves in gradually with afternoon showers from May through July. August becomes wetter, and September and October can mean prolonged downpours. The valley's western sector—Alajuela, San Antonio de Belén, Escazú, and Santa Ana—always catches a tad less rain than their eastern counterparts do.

SHOULDER SEASON: MID-NOVEMBER TO MID-DECEMBER

Rains start to wind down by mid-November and the month before Christmas is a terrific time to enjoy the Central Valley at its most lush and green, but before the big influx of tourists arrives. (As an added bonus, the coffee harvest is underway in earnest in this part of the country, too.)

GETTING HERE AND AROUND

Although Aeropuerto Internacional Juan Santamaría is billed as San José's airport, it sits just outside the city of Alajuela. You can get taxis from the airport to any point in the Central Valley for $8 to $80. Some hotels arrange pickup.

All points in the western Central Valley can be reached by car. For San Antonio de Belén, Heredia, Alajuela, and points north of San José, turn right at the west end of Paseo Colón onto the Pan-American Highway (Autopista General Cañas). The eastern Central Valley is accessible from San José by driving east on Avenidas 2, then Central, through San Pedro, then following signs from the intersection to Cartago. To get to the Orosi Valley, head straight through Cartago, turn right at the Basílica de Los Angeles, and follow the signs to Paraíso. The road through Cartago and Paraíso continues east to Turrialba.

The best way to get around the Central Valley is by car. Most of the car-rental agencies in San José have offices at or near the airport in Alajuela. *They will deliver vehicles to many of the hotels listed in this chapter, except those in Turrialba and the Orosi Valley.*

Many visitors never consider taking a local bus to get around, but doing so puts you in close contact with locals—an experience you miss out on if you travel by taxi or tour bus. It's also cheap. Always opt for a taxi at night or when you're in a hurry.

All Central Valley towns have taxis, which usually wait for fares along their central parks.

TIMING

You could spend an entire week here without getting bored, but if you have only a week or two in Costa Rica, we recommend a maximum of two days before heading to rain forests and beaches in other parts of the country. Spending a day after you arrive, then another day or two before you fly out gives you a taste of the region, breaks up the travel time, and makes your last day interesting, rather than spent in transit back to San José. The drive between just about any two points in the Central Valley is two hours or less, so it's ideal for short trips.

RESTAURANTS

Growing Escazú has become as metropolitan as San José and has the restaurant selection to prove it. Elsewhere, as befits this cradle of the country's tradition, typical Costa Rican cuisine still reigns.

Prices in the reviews are the average cost of a main course at dinner or, if dinner is not served, at lunch.

HOTELS

Most international flights fly into Costa Rica in the evening and head out again early the next morning, meaning you likely have to stay your first and last nights in San José or nearby. Think of the Central Valley as "the nearby." For getting away from it all and still being close to the country's main airport, the lodgings around San José make splendid alternatives to staying in the city itself. It may pain you to tear yourself away from that beach villa or rain-forest lodge, but you can still come back to something distinctive here on your last night in Costa Rica. Rustic *cabinas* (cottages), sprawling coffee plantations, nature lodges, and hilltop villas with expansive views are some of your options. The large chains are here as well, but the real gems are the so-called boutique hotels, many of which are family-run places and have unique designs that take advantage of exceptional countryside locations. Subtropical gardens are the norm, rather than the exception, and air-conditioning is usually not necessary.

Prices in the reviews are the lowest cost of a standard double room in high season.

WEST OF SAN JOSÉ

As you drive north or west out of San José, the city's suburbs and industrial zones quickly give way to arable land, much of which is occupied by coffee farms. Within Costa Rica's coffee heartland are plenty of tranquil agricultural towns and two provincial capitals, Alajuela and Heredia. Both cities owe their relative prosperity to the coffee beans cultivated on the fertile lower slopes of the Poás and Barva volcanoes. The upper slopes, too cold for coffee crops, are dedicated to dairy cattle, strawberries, ferns, and flowers, making for markedly different and thoroughly enchanting landscapes along the periphery of the national parks. Because the hills above these small valley towns have some excellent restaurants and lodgings, rural overnights are a good alternative to staying in San José.

ESCAZÚ

5 km/3 miles southwest of San José.

Costa Rica's wealthiest community and the Central Valley's most prestigious address, Escazú nevertheless mixes glamour with tradition, BMWs with oxcarts, Louis Vuitton with burlap produce sacks. As you exit the highway and crest the first gentle hill, you might think you made a wrong turn and ended up in Southern California, but farther up you return to small-town Central America. Narrow roads wind their way up the steep slopes, past postage-stamp coffee fields and lengths of

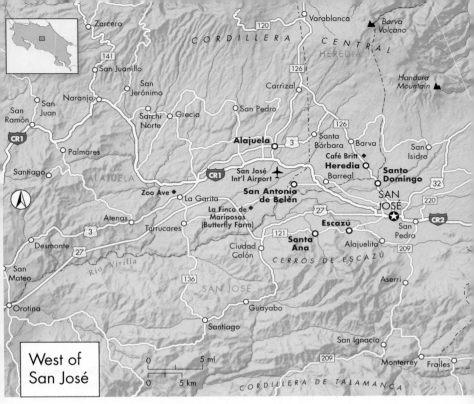

West of
San José

shoulder-to-shoulder, modest houses with tidy gardens and the occasional oxcart parked in the yard. Unfortunately, the area's stream of new developments and high-rises has steadily chipped away at the rural landscape—each year you have to climb higher to find the kind of scene that captured the attention of many a Costa Rican painter in the early 20th century. In their place are plenty of fancy homes and condos, especially in the San Antonio and San Rafael neighborhoods. Escazú's historic church faces a small plaza, surrounded in part by weathered adobe buildings. The town center is several blocks north of the busy road to Santa Ana, which is lined with a growing selection of restaurants, bars, and shops.

GETTING HERE AND AROUND

To drive to Escazú from San José, turn left at the western end of Paseo Colón, which ends at the Parque La Sabana. Take the first right, and get off the highway at the second exit. The off-ramp curves right, then sharply left; follow it about 1 km (½ mile), sticking to the main road, to El Cruce at the bottom of the hill (marked by a large Scotiabank). Continue through the traffic light for San Rafael addresses; turn right for the old road to Santa Ana. The trip takes about 15 minutes. A steady stream of buses for Escazú runs from several stops around Terminal Coca-Cola in San José (✉ Avdas. 1–3, Cs. 14–16), with service from 5 am to 11 pm.

ESSENTIALS

Bank/ATM Banco de Costa Rica ATM ✉ *North side of church.* **Banco Nacional** ✉ *Southwest side of Parque Central* ☎ *2228–0009.*

Internet Bagelmen's ✉ *San Rafael de Escazú, 500 m southwest of the Trejos Montealegre shopping center* ☎ *2228–4460* 🌐 *www.bagelmenscr.com.* **Internet CF** ✉ *Northwest corner of Parque Central, upstairs in Plaza Escazú mall* ☎ *2289–5706.*

Medical Assistance Farmacia San Miguel ✉ *North side of Parque Central* ☎ *2228–2339.* **Hospital CIMA** ✉ *Next to PriceSmart, just off the hwy. to Santa Ana, 12 km/7½ miles west of downtown San José* ☎ *2208–1000* 🌐 *www.hospitalsanjose.net.*

Post Office Correos ✉ *100 m north of church.*

Taxis Coopetico ☎ *2224–7979.*

HOCUS POCUS

During colonial days, Escazú was dubbed the City of Witches because many native healers lived in the area. Locals say that Escazú is still Costa Rica's most haunted community, home to witches who will tell your fortune or concoct a love potion for a small fee, but you'd be hard-pressed to spot them in the town's busy commercial district. Try a soccer field instead; the city's soccer team is christened Las Brujas ("the Witches"). You'll see a huge number of witch-on-a-broomstick decals affixed to vehicles here, too.

EXPLORING

High in the hills above Escazú is the tiny community of **San Antonio de Escazú,** famous for its annual oxcart festival held the second Sunday of March. The view from here—of nearby San José and distant volcanoes—is impressive by both day and night. If you head higher than San Antonio de Escazú, brace yourself for seemingly vertical roads that wind up into the mountains toward **Pico Blanco,** the highest point in the Escazú Cordillera, which is a half-day hike to ascend. Our preference is **San Miguel,** one peak east. Although you can hike these hills on your own, it is far safer to go with an outfitter.

Aventuras Pico Tours. The Tico owner of Aventuras Pico Tours has scaled some of the world's highest summits, and can lead you on a variety of hikes in the hills above town. ☎ *2289–6135* 🌐 *www.picotours.com.*

WHERE TO EAT

$$ SOUTHERN 🍴 **Barbecue Los Anonos.** For four decades, Costa Ricans have flocked to Los Anonos to enjoy its family-friendly grill fest. The original dining room, a rustic collection of deep booths with wooden benches, has been expanded upon to add a more elegant space decorated with historic photos. The crowd tends toward families on weekend nights, whereas weekdays are busier during lunch, when business executives come for the economical meals. The best bet is the grilled meat, and there is plenty to choose from, including imported U.S. beef and less expensive Tico cuts. Fresh fish, shrimp, and half a dozen salads round out the choices. [$] *Average main: $11* ✉ *400 m west of Los Anonos Bridge* ☎ *2228–0180* 🕒 *Closed Mon.*

$ ✕**Cerros.** This San Antonio hills
ITALIAN favorite combines smoky thin-crust
pizza with the essence of the Central Valley—simple and sincere. Pull
up a chair to one of the gingham-covered tables on the semienclosed
patio, and you have the perfect view
of a Costa Rican microcosm. The
valley drops down just behind the
soccer field and the green-trimmed
church across the street, revealing the shimmering panorama of
Escazú, Alajuela, and Heredia. The

pizza is the main draw, but pastas, meat dishes, and Costa Rican standbys are well represented. **$** *Average main: $9* ✉ *South side of soccer field, San Antonio de Escazú* ☎ *2228–1831* ☉ *No lunch weekdays.*

$$$$ ✕**Le Monastère.** This monastery-themed formal restaurant high in the
FRENCH San Rafael hills has a great view of the Central Valley. The dining room
is dressed up in antiques, with tables set for a five-course meal; waiters don short friar tunics over their standard black pants and white
shirts, which makes the atmosphere too theatrical for some tastes, but
the classic French dishes are outstanding. The more casual Cava Grill
dining area serves platters of grilled meat. La Cava Bar, beneath the
dining room, has tasty appetizers, and live music Thursday to Saturday, and is open into the wee hours. **$** *Average main: $26* ✉ *1½ km/1
mile southwest of the Paco Shopping Center in San Rafael de Escazú;
take old road west to Santa Ana, turn left at Paco and follow signs,
always bearing right* ☎ *2228–8515* ⊕ *www.monastere-restaurant.com*
☉ *Closed Sun. No lunch Mon.–Sat.*

$$ ✕**Plaza España.** Generous portions of Spanish tapas and entrées draw
SPANISH diners to this whitewashed adobe house up the hill near San Antonio
de Escazú. Wooden-bench tables are distributed along a wraparound
porch with views of the Central Valley; inside, settings are arranged
in small to medium-size rooms. Presentation isn't the strong suit here:
straight-up good food is, as are reasonable prices. Start with a pitcher
of sangria and begin sampling; the extensive menu includes dishes such
as Spanish omelet. **$** *Average main: $14* ✉ *Del Cruce del Barrio El Carmen, 100 m east and 50 m south, San Antonio de Escazú* ☎ *2228–1850*
☉ *Closed Mon.–Tues.*

$$$ ✕**Restaurante Cerutti.** The diva of the Central Valley's Italian eateries, this
ITALIAN little restaurant promises minimalist elegance in a lovely adobe house
built in 1817. The extensive menu, focusing on modern Italian cuisine,
ranges from roasted scallops with Spanish chorizo to ravioli stuffed
with duck and Italian ham. Core dishes are complemented by a variety
of selections that changes every month or so. No one disputes that the
quality of the food is high—with prices to match. **$** *Average main: $22*
✉ *Southeast corner of El Cruce, San Rafael de Escazú* ☎ *2228–9954*
⊕ *www.ceruttirestaurante.com* ☉ *Closed Sun.*

$$$ ✕**Taj Mahal.** This burst of northern Indian flavor is a real rarity in
INDIAN Central America. Richly swathed in warm fuchsias, red ochers, and

Costa Rica's oxcarts are folkloric symbols and a common canvas for local artisans.

golds, the mansion's dining area sprawls through a handful of small, intimate rooms and out to a gazebo in the tree-covered backyard. The price-to-portion ratio is a little high, particularly for North Americans used to good, cheap Indian food, but the sharp tandoori dishes, curries, and *biryanis* (seasoned rice dishes) are a welcome vacation from ubiquitous European and American fare. Vegetarians may swoon at the options. Helpful waiters, in black or maroon traditional Punjabi dress, are frank about recommendations. $ *Average main: $17* ✉ *1 km/½ mile west of Paco mall on old road to Santa Ana* ☎ *2228–0980* ⊕ *www.thetajmahalrestaurant.com* ⊘ *Closed Mon.*

WHERE TO STAY
For expanded hotel reviews, visit Fodors.com.

$$
B&B/INN
🏠 **Casa de las Tías.** The gamut of city services is at your doorstep, but you're blissfully apart from them at this tranquil bed-and-breakfast at the quiet end of a short road. **Pros:** tranquility without sacrificing convenience; service that goes the extra mile; excellent breakfast. **Cons:** walls could be a little thicker; slightly dated feel. **TripAdvisor:** "helpful and most welcoming," "charming," "gem." $ *Rooms from: $90* ✉ *100 m south and 150 m east of El Cruce; turn east just south of Restaurante Cerutti* ☎ *2289–5517* ⊕ *www.hotels.co.cr/casatias.html* ➷ *4 rooms, 1 junior suite* ⦿ *Breakfast.*

$
B&B/INN
🏠 **Costa Verde Inn.** When they need to make a city run, many beach-living expats head straight for this quiet B&B on the outskirts of Escazú, and you should, too. **Pros:** inviting public areas; excellent value. **Cons:** large student groups in summer; can be difficult to find; pool is for plungers, not swimmers. **TripAdvisor:** "very pleasant," "beautiful," "convenient

and friendly." $ *Rooms from: $65* ✉ *From southeast corner of second cemetery (the farthest west), 300 m south* ☎ *2228–4080* ⊕ *www. costaverdeinn.com* ⤳ *13 rooms, 3 apartments, 3 studios* ⊙| *Breakfast.*

$$
B&B/INN ⊞ **Posada El Quijote.** Perched on a hill in Escazú's Bello Horizonte neighborhood, with a great view of the city, this bed-and-breakfast strikes the right balance between a small inn and a private residence. **Pros:** peaceful, friendly place to spend first or last night; excellent staff. **Cons:** need a car to get around; can be difficult to find. **TripAdvisor:** "gorgeous view," "wonderful inn and fantastic breakfast," "outstanding service." $ *Rooms from: $95* ✉ *Bello Horizonte de Escazú, 1st street west of Anonos Bridge, 1 km/½ mile up hill* ☎ *2289–8401, 813/287–9996 in North America* ⊕ *www.quijote.cr* ⤳ *8 rooms, 2 apartments* ⊙| *Breakfast.*

$
B&B/INN ⊞ **Rainforest Dreams.** While it may not actually be in the rain forest, this small inn at the end of a residential street is a great getaway-from-it-all place that still puts you close enough to the action. **Pros:** tranquil setting; comfortable common areas; friendly owners. **Cons:** can be difficult to find. **TripAdvisor:** "very accommodating," "welcoming ambience," "cozy beds." $ *Rooms from: $70* ✉ *Los Anonos de Escazú* ☎ *2289–6087, 888/215–8710 in North America* ⊕ *www. rainforestdreamscostarica.com* ⤳ *6 rooms, 3 with bath* ⊟ *No credit cards* ⊙| *Breakfast.*

NIGHTLIFE

Escazú is the Central Valley's hot spot for nightlife—many Josefinos head here for the restaurants, bars, and dance clubs that cater to a young, cell phone–toting crowd. You can't miss the bright lights as you swing into town off the toll highway.

Cantina La Cava. The cellar tavern beneath Le Monastère restaurant is a great place to stop for a drink before dinner, or stay on and while the evening away. You can dance to live music on Friday and Saturday nights. ✉ *1½ km/1 mile southwest of Paco Shopping Center in San Rafael de Escazú; take old road west to Santa Ana, turn left at Paco, and follow signs, always bearing right* ☎ *2228–8515* ⊕ *www. monastere-restaurant.com* ☉ *Mon.–Thurs. 6:30 pm–midnight, Fri. and Sat. 6:30 pm–2 am.*

Henry's Beach Cafe. One of the more popular watering holes with the under-30 set is Henry's Beach Cafe, which features televised sports by day, varied music by night, and an island decor of beach paintings and surfboards. Costa Ricans refer to this style of bar as an "American bar," which is fairly accurate. ✉ *500 m west of El Cruce, Plaza San Rafael, 2nd fl.* ☎ *2289–6250* ⊕ *www.henrysbeachcafe.com* ☉ *Weekdays 3 pm–2 am, weekends noon–2 am.*

PICNIC TIME

Escazú's Saturday-morning farmers' market makes a terrific place to stock up on some fresh fruit and vegetables if you're preparing a do-it-yourself lunch or just want to snack. Vendors start lining the street on the south side of the church about dawn, and things begin to wind down by late morning.

4

Il Panino. A young, sophisticated crowd keeps Italian-style café Il Panino buzzing. It's a great place to start or end an evening. ⊠ *Centro Comercial Paco* ☎ *2228–3126* ⊕ *www.ilpanino.net* 🍽 *$6–$8* ⊘ *Closed Sun.*

Jazz Café Escazú. Music fans chill out at Jazz Café Escazú. The boxy club hosts an eclectic live-music lineup similar to that of its popular sister venue in San Pedro and has double the capacity. ⊠ *Next to Confort Suizo, across the hwy. from Hospital Cima; 1st exit after the toll booths* ☎ *2288–4740* ⊕ *www.jazzcafecostarica.com* 🍽 *$6–$8* ⊘ *Mon.–Sat. 6 pm–1 am.*

The high-end **Itskatzú** complex, 1 km (½ mile) east of Multiplaza, has a number of restaurants and bars ranging from the low-brow (Hooters) to places with sophisticated sushi and live Cuban music.

SHOPPING

★ If you get the shopping bug and absolutely must visit a mall while on vacation, Escazú is the place to do it. **Multiplaza,** on the south side of the toll highway, approximately 5 km (3 miles) west of San José, is a big, luxurious one.

Biesanz Woodworks. Biesanz Woodworks is where local craftsmen ply their trade and expat artist Barry Biesanz creates unique, world-class items from Costa Rican hardwoods, which are turned (a form of woodworking) on-site. It's difficult to find, so take a taxi or call for directions from your hotel. ⊠ *Bello Horizonte, 800 m south of Escuela Bello Horizonte* ☎ *2289–4337* ⊕ *www.biesanz.com* ⊘ *Weekdays 8–5, Sat. 9–3.*

SANTA ANA

17 km/10 miles southwest of San José.

Santa Ana's tranquil town center, with its rugged stone church, has changed little through the years, even if metro development, with the accompanying condos and shopping malls spreads out in all directions. The church, which was built between 1870 and 1880, has a Spanish-tile roof, carved wooden doors, and two pre-Columbian stone spheres flanking its entrance. Its rustic interior—bare wooden pillars and beams and black iron lamps—seems appropriate for an area with a tradition of ranching. Because it is warmer and drier than the towns to the east, Santa Ana is one of the few Central Valley towns that doesn't have a good climate for coffee—it is Costa Rica's onion capital, however—and is instead surrounded by pastures and patches of forest; it isn't unusual to see men on horseback here.

GETTING HERE AND AROUND

From San José, turn left at the western end of Paseo Colón, which ends at the Parque La Sabana. Take the first right, and get on the highway. Get off at the sixth exit; bear left at the flashing red lights, winding past roadside ceramics and vegetable stands before hitting the town center, about 2 km (1 mile) from the highway. The trip takes about 25 minutes if there's little traffic. Blue buses to Santa Ana leave from San José's Terminal Coca-Cola every eight minutes. To get to places along the toll highway or Piedades, take buses marked "Pista" or "Multiplaza."

CLOSE UP

Speaking Costa Rican

Spanish in Costa Rica tends to be localized. This is a land where eloquent speech and creative verbal expression are highly valued. For example, here the response to a "thank-you" is the gracious, uniquely Tico *"Con mucho gusto"* ("With much pleasure") instead of *"De nada"* ("It's nothing"), which is used in much of Latin America. In other cases, informality is preferred: the conventional *Señor* and *Señora*, for example, are eschewed in favor of the more egalitarian *Don* and *Doña*, used before a first name. Even President Laura Chinchilla is called "Doña Laura." *Exercise caution when selecting from the list below, however.* Although young Costa Rican men address everyone as *maje* (dude), you'll get a withering look if you, a visitor, follow suit.

adios good-bye; but also used as "hello" in rural areas
agarrar de maje to pull someone's leg
birra beer
brete work
cachos shoes
chunche any thingamajig
clavar el pico to fall asleep

con mucho gusto used in response to "thank you" instead of "de nada"
estar de chicha to be angry
estar de goma to have a hangover
harina money
jupa head
macho, macha a person with blond hair
maje buddy, dude, mate
mamá de Tarzán know-it-all
maría a woman's name; also a taxi meter
matar la culebra to waste time
montón a lot
muy bien, gracias a Dios very well, thank goodness
muy bien, por dicha very well, luckily
paño towel
pelo de gato cat hair; or fine, misty rain that falls in December
peso colón
pinche a tight-fisted person
ponerse hasta la mecha to get drunk
porfa please
pura vida fantastic, great
rojo red; also a 1,000-colón note
si Dios quiere God willing
soda an inexpensive local restaurant
torta a big mistake or error
tuanis cool
tucán toucan; also a 5,000-colón note
upe anyone home?

4

Those marked "Calle Vieja" leave every 15 minutes and pass through Escazú on the old road to Santa Ana. Buses run from 5 am to 11 pm.

ESSENTIALS

Bank/ATM Banco de Costa Rica ⊠ *100 m west of church* ☎ *2203–4281.* **Banco Nacional** ⊠ *Northwest corner of church* ☎ *2282–2479.* **Banco Popular** ⊠ *Southwest corner of church* ☎ *2203–7979.*

Internet Internet Café El Sol ⊠ *Southwest corner of church, across from Banco Popular* ☎ *2282–8059.*

Medical Assistance Farmacia Sucre ⊠ *25 m south of church* ☎ *2282–1296.*

Post Office Correos ⊠ *Northwest corner of church.*

WHERE TO EAT AND STAY

For expanded hotel reviews, visit Fodors.com.

$$$ ECLECTIC 🍴 **Bacchus.** Take a Peruvian chef trained in France and an Italian owner, and you get Bacchus, a welcome addition to the local dining scene. The cuisine is a mix of French and Italian dishes such as duck breast in a port sauce, baked mushroom-and-polenta ragout, and a variety of pizzas. Modern art decorates the simple but elegant interior, and outdoor seating is available. An extensive wine list and reasonable prices make it a great pick for dinner. [$] *Average main: $18* ✉ *200 m east and 100 m north of church* ☎ *2282–5441* ⏲ *No lunch, Mon.–Thurs.*

$$$ HOTEL ★ 🏨 **Alta.** The view from this colonial-style hotel perched on a hillside above Santa Ana is impressive, but so is the hotel with its Spanish-style grandeur. **Pros:** classy service; panoramic views; excellent value for price. **Cons:** lower-floor rooms lose out on the view; little to do within walking distance. **TripAdvisor:** "romantic escape," "very good restaurant," "quirky hotel with great views." [$] *Rooms from: $155* ✉ *2½ km/1½ miles west of Paco shopping center, on old road between Santa Ana and Escazú, Alto de las Palomas* ☎ *2282–4160, 888/388–2582 in North America* 🌐 *www.thealtahotel.com* 🛏 *18 rooms, 5 suites* 🍽 *Breakfast.*

$$ B&B/INN 🏨 **Hotel Posada Canal Grande.** This small Italian-owned hotel tucked into the hills to the west of Santa Ana draws an international clientele and is a great value. **Pros:** great value; international feel. **Cons:** spartan bathrooms; dining options limited. **TripAdvisor:** "an oasis," "old-style comfort and class," "great quiet relaxing place." [$] *Rooms from: $78* ✉ *On Próspero Fernández Hwy. to Ciudad Colón, 500 m north of Piedades de Santa Ana bus terminal* ☎ *2282–4089* 🌐 *www.hotelcanalgrande.com* 🛏 *12 rooms* 🍽 *Breakfast.*

SHOPPING

★ **Cerámica Las Palomas.** Large glazed pots with ornate decorations that range from traditional patterns to modern motifs are the specialties at Cerámica Las Palomas. Flowerpots and lamps are also common works, and the staff will eagerly show you the production process, from raw clay to art. ✉ *Old road to Santa Ana, opposite Alta Hotel* ☎ *2282–7001* 🌐 *www.ceramicalaspalomas.webs.com* ⏲ *Daily 7–5.*

GOLF

Valle del Sol. Although it sits inside a residential complex of the same name, Valle del Sol is the Central Valley's preeminent public golf course. Call to reserve tee times at this 7,000-yard, par 72, 18-hole course. Collared shirts and blouses are required; denim shorts and trousers are prohibited. ✉ *1,700 m west of HSBC* ☎ *2282–9222* 🌐 *www.vallesol.com* 🎟 *$94 for 18 holes with cart* ⏲ *Mon. 8–6, Tues.–Sun. 6:30–6.*

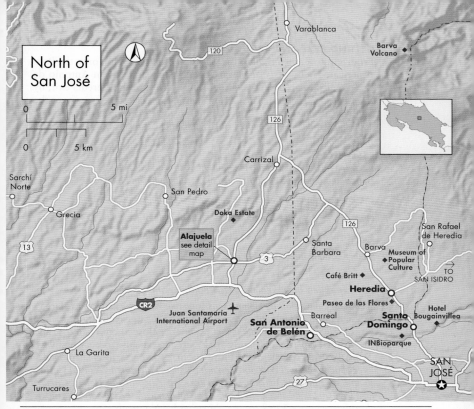

North of San José

0 — 5 mi
0 — 5 km

Varablanca

Barva Volcano

Carrizal

Sarchí Norte

Grecia

San Pedro

Doka Estate

Alajuela see detail map

Santa Barbara

San Rafael de Heredia

Museum of Popular Culture

Café Britt

Barva

Heredia

→ TO SAN ISIDRO

Paseo de las Flores

Hotel Bougainvillea

Juan Santamaría International Airport

Barreal

San Antonio de Belén

Santo Domingo

INBioparque

La Garita

SAN JOSÉ

Turrucares

CR2

13

120

126

126

3

27

NORTH OF SAN JOSÉ

As you set out from San José to explore the towns to the north, you first encounter nothing but asphalt, hotels, and malls—not especially scenic. Santo Domingo and San Antonio de Belén blend into the outskirts of San José, and it's only when you get to the heart of these small towns that you feel you've arrived in Central America. Farther north, Alajuela and Heredia are bustling provincial capitals with charismatic central parks. Throughout this area, tucked into the urban scenery and lining volcanic slopes, are fields of that quintessential Costa Rican staple, coffee.

SAN ANTONIO DE BELÉN

17 km/10 miles northwest of San José.

San Antonio de Belén has little to offer visitors but its rural charm and proximity to the international airport. The latter led developers to build several of the San José area's biggest hotels here. The town is a convenient departure point for trips to the western Central Valley, Pacific coast, and northern region. If you stay at the Marriott, you likely won't even see the town, just the busy highway between San José and Alajuela.

GETTING HERE AND AROUND

From San José, turn right at the west end of Paseo Colón onto the Pan-American Highway (Carretera General Cañas). The San Antonio de Belén exit is at an overpass 6 km (4 miles) west of the Heredia exit, by the Real Cariari Mall. Turn left at the first intersection, cross over the highway, and continue 1 km (½ mile) to the forced right turn, driving 1½ km (1 mile) to the center of town. San Antonio is only 10 minutes from the airport.

ESSENTIALS

Bank/ATM BAC San José ATM ✉ *200 m west of soccer field.*
Banco de Costa Rica ✉ *50 m north of rear of church* ☎ *2239–1149.*

Internet Belén Web Café ✉ *West end of soccer field* ☎ *2239–4181.*

Medical Assistance Farmacia Sucre ✉ *North side of church* ☎ *2239–3485.*

Post Office Correos ✉ *3 blocks west and 25 m north of church.*

Taxis Asotaxis Belén ☎ *2293–4712.*

WHERE TO STAY

For expanded hotel reviews, visit Fodors.com.

$$ RESORT 🏨 **Doubletree Cariari by Hilton.** This low-rise hotel was the metro area's original luxury hotel, and it remains popular for its excellent service and out-of-town location. **Pros:** resort experience close to both San José and the airport; kid-friendly. **Cons:** tricky car access; close to busy highway. **TripAdvisor:** "excellent staff and room," "expectations surpassed," "very nice facility." [$] *Rooms from: $139* ✉ *Autopista General Cañas, ½ km/¼ mile east of intersection for San Antonio de Belén, Cariari* ☎ *2239–0022, 800/222–8733 in North America* 🌐 *www.cariarisanjose.doubletree.com* 🛏 *198 rooms, 24 suites* 🍴 *No meals.*

$$ HOTEL 🏨 **El Rodeo.** This quiet hotel bills itself as a "country hotel," though this is more in image than fact—El Rodeo's proximity to the airport and major business parks is the real draw. **Pros:** proximity to airport; newly renovated facilities; spacious rooms. **Cons:** generic feel. **TripAdvisor:** "well maintained and comfortable," "amazingly quiet," "beautiful hotel with wonderful staff." [$] *Rooms from: $88* ✉ *Road to Santa Ana, 2 km/1 mile east of Parque Central* ☎ *2293–3909* 🌐 *www.elrodeohotel.com* 🛏 *22 rooms, 7 suites* 🍴 *Breakfast.*

$$$ HOTEL 👶 ★ 🏨 **Marriott Costa Rica Hotel.** The stately Marriott offers comprehensive luxury close to the airport, and, despite being a U.S. chain, offers many distinctively Costa Rican touches. **Pros:** excellent service; lavish grounds; close to airport. **Cons:** tendency to nickel-and-dime guests; tricky car access from highway. **TripAdvisor:** "beautiful," "spectacular location," "stunning views." [$] *Rooms from: $200* ✉ *¾ km/½ mile west of Bridgestone/Firestone, off Autopista General Cañas* ☎ *2298–0000, 800/236–2427 in North America* 🌐 *www.marriott.com* 🛏 *290 rooms, 9 suites* 🚭 *Non-smoking* 🍴 *No meals.*

ALAJUELA

20 km/13 miles northwest of San José.

Because of its proximity to the international airport (5–10 minutes away) many travelers spend their first or last night in or near Alajuela, but the beauty of the surrounding countryside persuades some to stay longer. Alajuela is Costa Rica's second-most-populated city, and a mere 30-minute bus ride from the capital, but it has a decidedly provincial air compared with San José. Architecturally, it differs little from the bulk of Costa Rican towns: it's a grid of low-rise structures painted in dull pastel colors.

GETTING HERE AND AROUND

To reach Alajuela, follow directions to San Antonio de Belén *(above)*. Continue west on the highway past the San Antonio turnoff and turn right at the airport. Buses travel between San José (⊠ *Avda. 2, Cs. 12–14, opposite north side of Parque La Merced*), the airport, and Alajuela, and run every five minutes from 4:40 am to 10:30 pm. The bus stop in Alajuela is 400 meters west, 25 meters north of the central park (⊠ *C. 3 and Avda. 1*). Buses leave San José for Zoo Ave from La Merced church (⊠ *C. 14 and Avda. 4*) daily at 8, 9, 10, 11 am, and noon, returning on the hour from 10 am to 3 pm.

ESSENTIALS

Bank/ATM Banco de Costa Rica ⊠ *Southwest corner of Parque Central* ☎ *2440–9039.* **Banco Nacional** ⊠ *West side of Parque Central* ☎ *2441–0373.*

Hospital Hospital San Rafael ⊠ *1 km/½ mile northeast of airport, on main road to Alajuela* ☎ *2436–1001.*

Internet Internet Inter@ctivo ⊠ *In front of BAC San José bank, 100 m north of Parque Central* ☎ *2431–1984.*

Medical Assistance Farmacia Chavarría ⊠ *Southwest corner of Parque Central* ☎ *2441–1231.*

Post Office Correos ⊠ *Avda. 1, C. 5.*

Taxis Cootaxa ☎ *2442–3030.*

EXPLORING

Alajuela Cathedral. The large, neoclassical Alajuela Cathedral has columns topped by interesting capitals decorated with local agricultural motifs, and a striking red metal dome. The interior is spacious but rather plain, except for the ornate cupola above the altar. ⊠ *C. Central, Avdas. 1–Central* ☎ *2443–2928* ⊙ *Daily 6-6.*

Ⓒ **Butterfly Farm** (*La Finca de Mariposas*). Observe and photograph but-
★ terflies up close at the Butterfly Farm. The farm's several microclimates keep comfortable some 40 species of tropical butterflies. Come when it's sunny if you can—they don't flutter around when it rains, although cloudy afternoons do give the best photo ops. This is Costa Rica's original butterfly farm, but there are other butterfly gardens around the country. The facility holds an annual mural contest, turning not only its own buildings but surrounding corner stores and houses into canvases for talented Costa Rican artists. You can get here via tours from San

José that depart from the capital at 7:20, 10, and 2. Regardless of your mode of transport, you can wander around the gardens on your own, or take one of the two-hour guided walks that begin at 8:30, 11, 1, or 3. If coming here by taxi or asking directions, Costa Ricans know the place as the Finca de Mariposas. ⊠ *From San José, take the Caldera Highway (Route 27) to the La Guácima exit, turn north (right), then follow the butterfly signs* ☎ *2438–0400* ⊕ *www.butterflyfarm.co.cr* ⊠ *$19, $40 with transportation from San José* ☉ *Daily 8:30–5.*

★ **Doka Estate.** Considering the amount of coffee you'll drive past in the Central Valley, you might want to devote an hour or so of your vacation to learning about the crop's production. Doka Estate, a working coffee plantation for more than 70 years, offers a comprehensive tour that takes you through the fields, shows you how the fruit is processed and the beans are dried, and lets you sample the local brew. The best time to take this tour is during the October-to-February picking season. Transportation is available from San José, Alajuela, Heredia, Escazú, or San Antonio. ⊠ *10 km/6 miles north of Alajuela's Tribunales de Justicia; turn left at San Isidro and continue 6 km/4 miles, follow signs, San Luis de Sabanilla* ☎ *2449–5152, 800/946–3652 in North America* ⊕ *www.dokaestate.com* ⊠ *$20* ☉ *Tours daily at 9, 10, 11, 1:30, 2:30, and 3:30; weekends last tour at 2:30.*

Juan Santamaría Museum. Juan Santamaría's heroic deeds are celebrated in the Juan Santamaría Museum (Museo Juan Santamaría) housed in the old jail, one block north of Parque Central. It's worth a short look if you have the time; Santamaría's story is an interesting one. Following the lead of the Teatro Nacional in San José, the museum holds a series of weekly concerts called *Música al Mediodía* ("Music at Noon") each Thursday from February to mid-December. Admission is $2. ⊠ *Avda. 3, Cs. Central-2* ☎ *2441–4775* ⊕ *www.museojuansantamaria.go.cr* ⊠ *Free* ☉ *Tues.–Sun. 10–5:30.*

Parque Central. Royal palms and massive mango trees fill the Parque Central—residents frequently refer to the park as the Parque de los Mangos—which also has a lovely fountain imported from Glasgow and concrete benches where locals gather to chat. Surrounding the plaza is an odd mix of charming old buildings and sterile concrete boxes, including a somewhat incongruous McDonald's. ⊠ *C. Central, Avdas. 1–Central.*

Parque Juan Santamaría. Alajuela was the birthplace of Juan Santamaría, the national hero who lost his life in a battle against the mercenary army of U.S. adventurer William Walker when the latter invaded Costa Rica in 1856. The Parque Juan Santamaría has a statue of the young Santamaría. After a 2005 restoration, Juan should keep his youthful good looks for years to come—which, sadly, is more than can be said for the abandoned-looking, weedy concrete lot he stands on. △ The park gets a little dicey as the sun goes down; confine your visits to daylight hours. ⊠ *C. Central and Avda. 2.*

☺ **Tortufauna.** If your vacation is confined to the Central Valley and you don't have time to trek out to the country's famed nesting sites, this conservation and protection facility is a terrific place to learn about the life and times of Costa Rica's land and freshwater turtles. New in

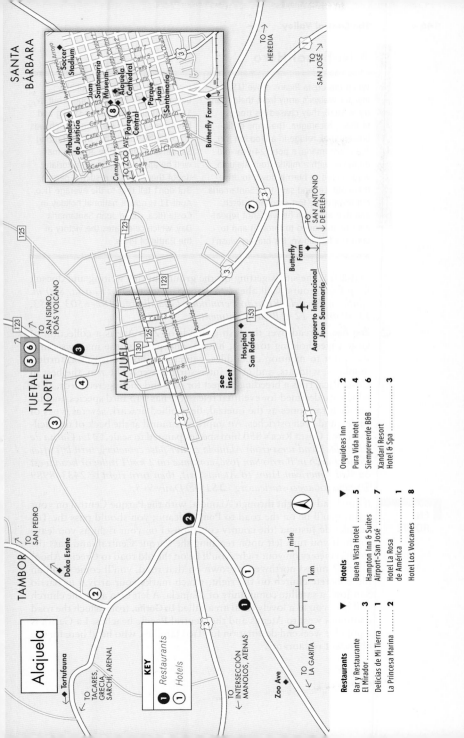

Alajuela

SANTA BÁRBARA

TUETAL NORTE

TAMBOR

Tortufauna

Doka Estate

Zoo Ave

Soccer Stadium

Juan Santamaría Museum

Tribunales de Justicia

Alajuela Cathedral

Parque Juan Santamaría

Parque Central

Butterfly Farm

TO ZOO AVE

Cemetery

ALAJUELA

see inset

Hospital San Rafael

Aeropuerto Internacional Juan Santamaría

Butterfly Farm

TO SAN ISIDRO, POÁS VOLCANO

TO SAN PEDRO

TO TACARES, GRECIA, SARCHÍ, ARENAL

TO INTERSECCIÓN MANOLOS, ATENAS

TO LA GARITA

TO SAN ANTONIO DE BELÉN

TO HEREDIA

TO SAN JOSÉ

KEY
1   Restaurants
①   Hotels

0   1 km
0   1 mile

Restaurants

▼

Bar y Restaurante El Mirador	3
Delicias de Mi Tierra	1
La Princesa Marina	2

Hotels

▼

Buena Vista Hotel	5
Hampton Inn & Suites Airport–San José	7
Hotel La Rosa de América	1
Hotel Los Volcanes	8
Orquideas Inn	2
Pura Vida Hotel	4
Siempreverde B&B	6
Xandari Resort Hotel & Spa	3

A National Hero

When the Costa Ricans drove U.S. invader Walker's army from their country in 1856, they chased his troops to Rivas, Nicaragua. The army of filibusters took refuge in a wooden fort. Juan Santamaría, a poor, 24-year-old drummer with a militia from Alajuela, volunteered to burn it down to drive them out. Legend says that Santamaría ran toward the fort carrying a torch, and that although he was shot repeatedly, he managed to throw it and to burn the fort down. His bravery wasn't recognized at the time, probably because of his modest origins, but in 1891 a statue depicting a strong and handsome soldier carrying a torch was placed in Alajuela, thus immortalizing Santamaría. The entire account may well be apocryphal; some historians doubt there ever *was* such a person. But don't tell that to the average Tico. April 11 is now a national holiday in Costa Rica, called Juan Santamaría Day, which celebrates the victory at the Battle of Rivas.

mid-2011, the site is getting off the ground at this writing and doesn't keep fixed hours. Call ahead to arrange a visit. ⊠ *La Garita, 800 m. south of Escuela Ricardo Fernández Guardia* ☎ *2487–6503* 🎫 *$3, $1.50 under 12* ☽ *By appointment.*

🄲 **Zoo Ave.** Spread over the lush grounds of Zoo Ave is a collection of large cages holding toucans, hawks, and parrots (the macaws range free), not to mention crocodiles, caimans, a boa constrictor, turtles, monkeys, wildcats, and other interesting critters. The zoo, the best in Costa Rica, runs a breeding project for rare and endangered birds, all of which are destined for eventual release. It has 115 bird species, including such rare ones as the quetzal, fiery-billed aracari, several types of eagles, and even ostriches. An impressive mural at the back of the facility shows Costa Rica's 850 bird species painted to scale. ⊠ *La Garita de Alajuela. Head west from Alajuela center past cemetery, turn left after stone church in Barrio San José, continue on 2 km/1 mile; or head west on Pan-American Hwy. to Atenas exit, then turn right* ☎ *2433–8989* ⊕ *www.zooavecostarica.org* 🎫 *$15* ☽ *Daily 9–5.*

EN ROUTE

If you head straight through Alajuela, with the Parque Central on your right, you'll be on the road to Poás Volcano; you should pass the Tribunales de Justicia (the county courthouse) on your right as you leave town. If you turn left upon reaching the Parque Central, and pass the town cemetery on your right, you'll be on the old road to Grecia. About 3 km (2 miles) northwest of town on that road, you'll come upon an old concrete church on the right, which marks your arrival in Barrio San José, a satellite community of Alajuela. A left turn after the church will take you to a lovely rural area called **La Garita,** from which the road continues west to Atenas and the Central Pacific beaches. La Garita is a popular weekend destination for Tico families, who head here for the abundant restaurants.

WHERE TO EAT

$$ ECLECTIC 🍴 **Bar y Restaurante El Mirador.** Perched on a ridge several miles north of town, El Mirador has a sweeping view of the Central Valley that is impressive by day but more beautiful at dusk and night when the basin is filled with twinkling lights. Get a window table in the dining room, or one on the adjacent porch if it isn't too cool. The menu, which includes *lomito* (tenderloin) and *corvina* (sea bass) served with various sauces, and several shrimp or chicken dishes, plays second fiddle to the view. You could just stop in around sunset for drinks and appetizers. Free transportation from most Alajuela hotels is sometimes available. There are at least two other restaurants nearby with similar names and views—this one is on the main road, close to the Buena Vista Hotel. [$] *Average main: $13* ✉ *Road to Poás, 5 km/3 miles north of Tribunales de Justicia* ☎ *2441–9347.*

4

$ COSTA RICAN 🍴 **Delicias de Mi Tierra.** A string of *típico* Costa Rican restaurants lines this road, but the "Delights of My Land" is our favorite. Tasty and traditional Tico favorites are served here: *pozol* (corn-and-pork soup), *casado campesino* (stewed beef with rice, beans, corn, potatoes, and plantains), and *chorreada con natilla* (a corn-bread pancake with sour cream). Long wooden tables and benches are surrounded by cane walls, decorative oxcart wheels, dried gourds, and tropical plants—the kind of decor trying so hard to be traditional that it's anything but. Ordering a few *entraditas* (appetizers) is a good way to sample dishes, as is the *parrillada de campo* (country barbecue), a platter with grilled chicken, beef, pork, rice, beans, fried plantains, and salad, or the larger *fiesta de gallos,* a mixed platter of corn tortillas with various fillings. There are also cheap but hearty breakfasts. Get here early for dinner, as closing time is 7 pm. [$] *Average main: $6* ✉ *1½ km/1 mile west of the Barrio San José church* ☎ *2433–8536.*

$ SEAFOOD 🍴 **La Princesa Marina.** This large open-air eatery (part of a chain) at the intersection of the old Alajuela–Grecia road and the road to La Garita is popular with Ticos, who pack it on weekends to feast on inexpensive seafood. The selection is vast, with 10 types of fish, shrimp, or octopus ceviche; fish fillets served with various sauces; three sizes of shrimp prepared a dozen ways; whole fried fish; lobster tails; and several *mariscadas* (mixed seafood plates). Pastas, rice dishes, beef, and chicken are some other choices, but the seafood is your best bet. The decor is utilitarian—bare tables, ceiling fans, and dividers of potted plants separating the sections—but you avoid that feeling of being in a contrived tourist venue. [$] *Average main: $11* ✉ *Barrio San José, north of church* ☎ *2433–7117* 🌐 *www.princesamarina.com.*

WHERE TO STAY

For expanded hotel reviews, visit Fodors.com.

$$ RESORT 🏨 **Buena Vista Hotel.** Perched high above Alajuela, this hotel's superb staff makes up for the somewhat dated, uninspired decor. **Pros:** excellent service; family-friendly. **Cons:** uninspired ambience; mediocre restaurant; farther from the airport than other options. **TripAdvisor:** "spot on," "excellent service," "friendly staff and comfortable stay." [$] *Rooms from: $95* ✉ *6 km/4 miles north of Alajuela's Tribunales de Justicia on road to Poás* ☎ *2442–8595, 800/506–2304 in North America* 🌐 *www.hotelbuenavistacr.com* 🛏 *11 rooms, 4 suites, 5 cabins* 🍽 *Breakfast.*

The Alajuela Cathedral's painted domed cupola was rebuilt after the 1991 earthquake.

$$$ HOTEL 🏨 **Hampton Inn & Suites Airport – San José.** A longtime favorite for first-night and last-night stays, this U.S. chain outlet lets you ease into and out of Costa Rica in familiar surroundings. **Pros:** airport proximity; U.S. amenities, friendly staff. **Cons:** some noise from planes in the evening; sameness of a chain hotel. **TripAdvisor:** "so easy," "comfortable accommodations," "perfect for airport." [$] *Rooms from: $170* ✉ *Blvd. del Aeropuerto* ☎ *2436–0000, 800/426–7866 in North America* 🌐 *www.hamptoninn.hilton.com* 🛏 *100 rooms* 🍴 *Breakfast.*

$$ B&B/INN 🏨 **Hotel La Rosa de América.** This small hotel tucked off the road to La Garita is a simple and relaxed place to unwind, with its Canadian owners adding a welcoming energy and a personalized touch to the place. **Pros:** great for families; helpful owners; close to a number of restaurants. **Cons:** lacks flair of other options in this price range; should have car to stay here. **TripAdvisor:** "hidden gem," "close to perfect," "great service." [$] *Rooms from: $87* ✉ *1 km/½ mile east of Zoo Ave* ☎ *2433–2741* 🌐 *www.larosadeamerica.com* 🛏 *14 rooms* 🍴 *Breakfast.*

$ B&B/INN 🏨 **Hotel Los Volcanes.** Budget travelers looking for airport proximity will find this urban oasis an excellent value. **Pros:** airport proximity; good value; historic ambience. **Cons:** some rooms are noisy; no views. **TripAdvisor:** "friendly," "attractive accommodations," "welcoming hotel with character." [$] *Rooms from: $46* ✉ *Avda. 3, Cs. 2–Central, 100 m north, 25 m east of the northwest corner of Parque Central, across from the Juan Santamaría Museum* ☎ *2441–0525* 🌐 *www.hotellosvolcanes.com* 🛏 *15 rooms, 11 with bath* 🍴 *Breakfast.*

$$ B&B/INN 🏨 **Orquídeas Inn.** A favorite with young couples and families, the friendly Orquideas proves that affordable does not have to equal generic. **Pros:** spirited environment; great for first or last night; excellent service.

Cons: rooms are ready for a face-lift; roadside rooms noisy. **TripAdvisor:** "great rooms," "surprisingly beautiful," "nice little place." ⓢ *Rooms from: $82* ✉ *2½ km/1½ miles northwest of the Princesa Marina* ☎ *2433–7128* ⊕ *www.orquideasinn.com* ⌇ *20 rooms, 6 suites, 1 dome* ⍩ *Breakfast.*

$$
★
Pura Vida Hotel. Extremely well-informed, helpful owners and proximity to the airport (15 minutes) make this a good place to begin and end a trip. **Pros:** owners active in the local community; stellar breakfast. **Cons:** large dogs may turn off those with less-than-fuzzy feelings for animals; stairs to climb. **TripAdvisor:** "great location," "amazing stay," "perfect." ⓢ *Rooms from: $90* ✉ *Tuetal, 2 km/1 mile north of Tribunales de Justicia; veer left at Y* ☎ *2430–2929* ⊕ *www.puravidahotel.com* ⌇ *2 rooms, 4 bungalows* ⍩ *Breakfast.*

$$
B&B/INN
Siempreverde B&B. A night at this isolated bed-and-breakfast in the heart of a coffee plantation might be as close as you'll ever come to feeling like a coffee farmer or to truly getting away from it all. **Pros:** off-the-beaten-path feel; plenty of tranquillity. **Cons:** isolated location; tour groups pass by for breakfast most mornings. **TripAdvisor:** "peaceful," "beautiful property," "great potential." ⓢ *Rooms from: $85* ✉ *12 km/7½ miles northwest of Tribunales de Justicia de Alajuela; turn left at high school* ☎ *2449–5562* ⊕ *www.siempreverdebandb.com* ⌇ *7 rooms* ⍩ *Breakfast.*

$$$$
Fodor'sChoice
★
Xandari Resort Hotel & Spa. The tranquil and colorful Xandari is a strikingly original inn and spa, tailor-made for honeymooners and romantic getaways. **Pros:** amazing service; ideal setting for romance; guilt-free gourmet delights. **Cons:** some noise from other rooms; should have car to stay here. **TripAdvisor:** "very stylish," "great restaurant," "a beautiful view." ⓢ *Rooms from: $265* ✉ *5 km/3 miles north of Tribunales de Justicia; turn left after small bridge, follow signs* ☏ *2443–2020, 866/363–3212 in North America* ⊕ *www.xandari.com* ⌇ *23 villas* ⍩ *Breakfast.*

SANTO DOMINGO

18 km/11 miles northeast of Escazú, 7 km/4½ miles northwest of San José.

Between Heredia and San José, the pretty town of Santo Domingo de Heredia, established in the early 19th century, has wide streets and fine examples of traditional, tile-roof houses, and a monumental church that stands out as a brilliant white landmark against the surrounding sea of green coffee farms. There's a level of tranquillity here that belies its proximity to the capital, a mere 15-minute drive away if the traffic gods smile upon you. The splendid, late-19th-century Basílica de Santo Domingo (east side of soccer field) is one of the country's only two basilicas, with two distinctive towers topped with gold domes. It's often a venue for classical music concerts throughout the year, including the July-to-August International Music Festival (masses are held from 5 to 7 pm). The older and simpler Iglesia del Rosario, built in the 1840s, faces the town's palm-shaded Parque Central (masses from 7 to 10 am).

GETTING HERE AND AROUND

For the 30-minute trip from downtown San José, head north on Calle Central 4 km (2½ miles) to the central park in Tibás; continue 100 meters and turn left. Follow this road another 2½ km (1¼ miles) to Santo Domingo. From the west end of Paseo Colón, turn right onto the Pan-American Highway (aka the Carretera General Cañas), then right off the highway just before it heads onto an overpass, after the Hotel Irazú (on the right). Keep to this road for about 2 km (1 mile) to the first intersection after it becomes one-way. Turn right at the lights, continue 3 km (2 miles), passing INBioparque, until the road Ts; a left here brings you into town. One of the Heredia bus routes leaves from Calle 1, Avenidas 7–9 every three to five minutes and passes through Santo Domingo.

ESSENTIALS

Bank/ATM Banco Nacional ⊠ *Across from south side of Iglesia del Rosario* ☎ *2244–0439.*

Post Office Correos ⊠ *Avda. Central, Cs. 2 and 4.*

EXPLORING

🅒 **INBioparque.** Santo Domingo's main attraction is INBioparque, which does an excellent job of not only explaining the country's various eco-systems, but also taking you into them. It's a useful, if slightly expensive, primer before heading out to the hinterlands. You'll wander trails through climate-controlled wetlands and out to tropical dry forest. The forests may not look much different, but your English-speaking guide will explain the subtleties. Along the way, stop at the butterfly farm, insect exhibits, and bromeliad garden. For an extra $3 (kids $2) you can visit the 15 species of snakes housed here in the National Serpentarium. The tour is packed with information—perhaps too much—but if you're visiting Costa Rica for its ecology, it's a worthwhile lesson. An open-air, upscale cafeteria serves typical Costa Rican fare, with a playground within view of terrace tables. The gift shop has a great selection of tagua-nut jewelry and natural history-themed souvenirs and books. Reservations are required for tours. Kids four to 14 years old pay $14. ⊠ *Road between Santo Domingo and Heredia, 400 m north and 250 m west of Shell gas station* ☎ *2507–8107* ⊕ *www.inbioparque.com* 💲 *$24* ⊘ *Fri. 8–5 (last admission at 3), weekends 9–5:30 (last admission at 4). Tours at 9, 11, and 2.*

WHERE TO STAY

For expanded hotel reviews, visit Fodors.com.

$$
HOTEL
🖾 **Hotel Bougainvillea.** True to its name, this modern, very comfortable, three-story hotel is awash in bougainvillea on the outside, and decorated with an impressive collection of Costa Rican art on the inside. **Pros:** lush and open spaces; of the urban hotels, one of the better bird-watching sites. **Cons:** slightly institutional smell and feel in the hallways. **TripAdvisor:** "traditional values," "glorious gardens," "absolutely beautiful." 💲 *Rooms from: $105* ⊠ *2 km/1 mile east of Santo Domingo de Heredia* ☎ *2244–1414* ⊕ *www.hb.co.cr* 🛏 *77 rooms, 4 suites* ⊘ *No meals.*

The verdant Central Valley is Costa Rica's breadbasket.

HEREDIA

4 km/3 miles north of Santo Domingo, 11 km/6 miles northwest of San José.

The lively city of Heredia, capital of the important coffee province of the same name, contains some of the country's best-preserved colonial structures along with a contrasting, youthful buzz provided by a concentration of young people attending the National University (UNA) and century-old *colegios* (high schools) scattered around the town. Heredia name is twofold: it's known as the City of Flowers, referring to a leading founding family named Flores. Flores also refers to beautiful women, of which Heredia is known for. Founded in 1706, the city bears witness to how difficult preservation can be in an earthquake-prone country; most of its colonial structures have been destroyed by the tremors and tropical climate—not to mention modernization. Still, the city and neighboring towns retain a certain historic feel, with old adobe buildings scattered amid the concrete structures. Nearby Barva is also notable for its colonial central square and venerable adobe structures. From Heredia, scenic mountain roads climb northeast, passing through the pleasant, high-altitude coffee towns of San Rafael and San Isidro, each centered by a notable, Tico-style Gothic church and a pleasant central park.

GETTING HERE AND AROUND

The narrow routes from San José to Heredia are notoriously clogged at almost all times; avoid them during rush hours if possible. Turn right at the west end of Paseo Colón. Follow Pan-American Highway 2 km (1 mile); take the second exit, just before the highway heads onto an overpass and just after the Hotel Irazú (on the right). To get to the center of

Heredia, follow that road for 5½ km (3½ miles), being careful to note which direction traffic in the alternative middle lane is traveling, then turn left at the Universidad Nacional. Buses run between San José (300 meters east of Hospital San Juan de Dios) and Heredia every 5 to 10 minutes daily (between 5 am and 10 pm), *following the above car route.* The steady stream of buses leaving from Calle 1, Avenidas 7–9 every three to five minutes passing through Santo Domingo are sometimes a better bet during rush hour, particularly the *directo* buses that start after 3:30 pm; these buses also run from midnight to 3:30 am on the hour. Better still, hop aboard the new, modern train, departing San José from the vintage Atlantic Station, on the north side of the National Park, and arriving in downtown Heredia 30 minutes later. Trains run every half hour from 5:30 to 8 am, then 3:30 to 7:30 pm, and the fare is about 75¢. If you're without a car, a taxi is the best way to get to Café Britt or Barva.

ESSENTIALS

Bank/ATM Banco de Costa Rica ATM ⊠ *North side of Parque Central, beside Casa de la Cultura.* **Banco Nacional** ⊠ *25 m south of southwest corner of Parque Central* ☎ *2277–6900.*

Internet La Floresta Internet ⊠ *South side of Parque Central, on 2nd fl* ☎ *2238–4279* ⊙ *Mon.–Fri. 8–8; Sat. 8–6.*

Pharmacy Farmacia Chavarria ⊠ *Southwest corner of Parque Central* ☎ *2263–4668* ⊙ *Mon.–Sat. 7:30–7:30, Sun. 8–5.*

Post Office Correos ⊠ *Northwest corner of Parque Central, in the stately stone building engraved with its 1915 building date, Avda. Central, C. Central-2.*

EXPLORING

★ **Café Britt.** The producer of Costa Rica's most popular export-quality coffee gives a lively Classic Coffee Tour highlighting Costa Rica's history of coffee cultivation through a theatrical presentation that is admittedly a bit hokey. Your "tour guides" are professional actors, and pretty good ones at that, so if you don't mind the song and dance, it's fun. During the 1½-hour tour, you'll take a short walk through the coffee farm and processing plant, and learn how professional coffee tasters distinguish a fine cup of java. A separate, longer Coffee Lovers Tour takes you into the world of professional coffee tasters and includes lunch and transportation. You can also stop in at their Coffee Bar and Factory Store, 8 to 5 daily. ⊠ *From Heredia, take road to Barva; follow signs* ☎ *2277–1500* ⊕ *www.coffeetour.com* ✉ *$20 Classic Coffee Tour, $37 with transportation; $60 Coffee Lovers Tour, including lunch and transportation (2-person minimum)* ⊙ *Tours: daily at 9:30 and 11 am; and at 3 pm, Dec. 15 to Apr. 30; Coffee Lovers Tour, daily at 11.*

Cathedral of the Immaculate Conception. On the east side of the park stands the impressive Cathedral of the Immaculate Conception (Catedral de la Inmaculada Concepción), built between 1797 and 1804 to replace an adobe temple dating from the early 1700s. The flat-fronted, whitewashed church has thick stone walls, small windows, and squat buttresses, which have kept it intact through two centuries of quakes and tremors. The serene, white interior has two rows of stately, gold-trimmed Ionic columns marching down a long aisle, past

Continued on page 158

Picking coffee beans from plant

COFFEE, THE GOLDEN BEAN

Tour a working coffee plantation and learn about the product that catapulted Costa Rica onto the world's economic stage, built the country's infrastructure, and created a middle class unlike any other in Central America.

Costa Rica B.C. (before coffee) was a poor, forgotten little colony with scant infrastructure and no real means of making money. Coffee production changed all of that and transformed the country into one of the wealthier and most stable in Central America. Coffee remains Costa Rica's bread and butter—the industry employs one-fourth of Costa Rica's population full- or part-time—and coffee plantations are sprinkled throughout the Central Valley and Northern Plains. All cultivate fine Arabica beans (by government decree, the inferior Robusta variety is not grown here). Visit one and learn what makes the country tick.

By Jeffrey Van Fleet

HISTORY IN A CUP

Coffee plantations near Poas Volcano, Central Valley

The country's first leaders saw this new crop as a tool with which to engineer a better life for their people. After gaining independence, new laws were created to allow average Costa Ricans to become coffee-growing landowners. These farmers formed the foundation of a middle-class majority that has long distinguished the country from the rest of Latin America. Costa Rica's infrastructure, institutional organizations, and means of production quickly blossomed—young entrepreneurs established small import-export houses, growers banded together to promote a better infrastructure, and everyone plowed their profits into improving the country's primitive road system.

SOCIAL TRANSFORMATION

As the coffee business became more profitable, prominent families were sending their children abroad to study, and doctors, lawyers and other skilled professionals in search of jobs began arriving by the

DRINKING THE GOOD STUFF

Here's the kicker for you, dear coffee-loving visitor: It's tough to find a decent cup in Costa Rica. True to the realities of developing-country economics, the good stuff goes for export, leaving a poorer quality bean behind for the local market. Add to that that the typical household here makes coffee with heaps of sugar. Your best bet for a good cup is an upscale hotel or restaurant, which is attuned to foreign tastes and does use export-quality product. The decorative foil bags you see in souvenir shops and supermarkets are also export-quality and make terrific souvenirs.

COFFEE TIMELINE

Local workers harvesting coffee beans in 1800s

1720	Coffee arrives in New World.
1791	Coffee plants introduced to Costa Rica.
1820	First coffee exports go to Panama.
1830	Legislation paves way for coffee profits to finance government projects.
1860	Costa Rican coffee first exported to United States.
1890	Atlantic Railroad opens, allowing for easier port access.

Enjoying a cup of coffee in Montezuma, Nicoya Peninsula

4

IN FOCUS COFFEE, THE GOLDEN BEAN

boatload. Returning students and well-educated immigrants brought a new world view that contributed to the formation of Costa Rica's liberal ideology.

MODERN TIMES

Development gobbled up land in the Central Valley by the last half of the 20th century, and coffee production began to spread to other areas of the country. A worldwide slump in coffee prices in the 1990s forced many producers out of the business. Prices have risen since 2002, and the government looks to smooth out any fluctuations with added-value eco-certification standards and innovative marketing.

Today, some 70% of the country's *número uno* agricultural crop comes from small family properties of under 25 acres owned by 250,000 farmers. They seasonally employ over four times that number of people, and kids in rural areas still take class time off to help with the harvest.

CAFÉ CHEAT SHEET

café solo: black
con azúcar: with sugar
con crema: with cream
con leche: with milk
descafeinado: decaffeinated (not easy to find here)

■

grano entero: whole beans
grano molido: ground
tostado claro or *tueste claro:* light roast
tostado oscuro or *tueste oscuro:* dark roast

Oxcarts built in the early 1900s to transport coffee

1897	Coffee barons construct San José's ornate Teatro Nacional.
1992	Costa Rica adopts new environmental laws for coffee industry.
1997	Tourism displaces coffee as Costa Rica's top industry.
Today	Costa Rica turns to eco-certification and fair-trade marketing of coffee.

COSTA RICA'S BEAN COUNTRY

Coffee plantations from Cervantes to Orosi Central Valley

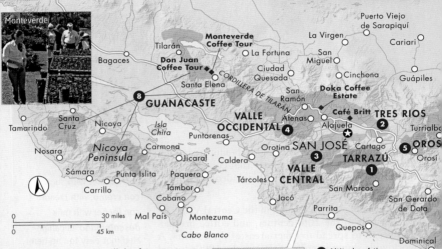
Monteverde

Puerto Viejo de Sarapiquí
La Virgen
Cariari
Tilarán
Monteverde Coffee Tour
La Fortuna
San Miguel
Bagaces
Don Juan Coffee Tour
Ciudad Quesada
Cinchona
Guápiles
Santa Elena
San Ramón
Doka Coffee Estate
8 GUANACASTE
VALLE OCCIDENTAL 4
Atenas
Café Britt TRES RIOS 2
Alajuela
Turrialba
Santa Cruz
Nicoya
Isla Chira
Puntarenas
Orotina SAN JOSÉ Cartago 5 OROS
Tamarindo
Nicoya Peninsula
Carmona
Caldera
3
TARRAZÚ 1
Orosi
Nosara
Jicaral
Tárcoles
VALLE CENTRAL
San Marcos
Sámara
Punta Islita
Paquera
Tambor
Jacó
San Gerardo de Dota
Carrillo
Cobano
Parrita
30 miles
Mal País
Montezuma
Quepos
45 km
Cabo Blanco
Dominical

Costa Rica possesses all the factors necessary—moderately high altitude, mineral-rich volcanic soil, adequate rainfall but distinct rainy and dry seasons—to be a major coffee player. Costa Rican growers cultivate only Arabica coffee beans. The industry eliminated the inferior Robusta variety in 1989 and hasn't looked back. The Costa Rican Coffee Institute certifies eight regional coffee varieties.

The coffee-growing cycle begins in April or May, when rains make the dark-green bushes explode in a flurry of white blossoms. By November, the fruit starts to ripen, turning from green to red. The busy harvest begins as farmers race to get picked "cherries" to *beneficios* (processing mills), where beans are removed, washed, machine-dried, and packed in burlap sacks either for export or to be roasted for local consumption.

Coffee plantations, Central Valley

❶ Aficionados wax poetic about the bean that come from **Tarrazú**, the high-altitude Los Santos Region in the Southern Pacific. It has good body, high acidity, and a chocolaty flavor.

❷ Coffee grown in **Tres Ríos**, east of San José, has high acidity, good body, and a nice aroma.

❸ Altitude of the **Valle Central** (around San José, Heredia and Alajuela) affects the size and hardness of the coffee bean and can influence certain components, particularly the acidity. This is an important characteristic of Arabica coffee.

❹ **Valle Occidental**, in the prosperous western Central Valley, gives you hints of apricots and peaches.

Arabica coffee beans

Coffee beans | Coffee bean pickers | Hand picking coffee beans

Coffee plant

Siquirres
Moín
6 TURRIALBA
Puerto Viejo de Talamanca
Cahuita
Bribri
Sixaola
PANAMA
CORDILLERA DE TALAMANCA
an Isidro
Buenos Aires
Salitre
7
BRUNCA
Palmar Norte
Paso Real
Ciudad Cortés
Palmar Sur
Pan-American Hwy
San Vito
Ciudad Neily
Drake
Rincón
Golfito
Río Claro
Osa Peninsula
Puerto Jiménez
Paso Canoas
Carate
Zancudo
Pavones
Matapalo

5 Tasters describe **Orosi** coffee, from the southeastern Central Valley, as "floral."

6 The lower altitudes of nearby **Turrialba** give its product a medium body.

7 The high-altitude **Brunca** region, near San Vito in southern Costa Rica, produces

coffee with excellent aroma, good body, and moderate acidity.

8 Guanacaste is a diverse region that includes Monteverde and the central Nicoya Peninsula. Here they produce a medium-body coffee.

PLANTATIONS WITH TOURS

Wonder where your cup of morning coffee originates? The following purveyors give informative tours of their facilities and acquaint you with the life and times of the country's favorite beverage.

CAFÉ BRITT Barva, Heredia *(see the Central Valley chapter)* Café Britt incorporates a small theater production into its tour, presenting the history of Costa Rican coffee in song and dance. Britt also presents a separate, more academic tour giving you a participatory glimpse into the world of professional coffee tasters.

DOKA COFFEE ESTATE San Luis de Sabanilla, Alajuela *(see the Central Valley)* Doka Coffee Estate offers a comprehensive tour through the entire growing and drying process and lets you sample the local brew. The best time to take this tour is during the October-to-February picking season.

DON JUAN COFFEE TOUR Monteverde *(see the Northern Plains)* A personalized excursion with a small group is the hallmark of this tour to a coffee plantation a few miles outside the town of Santa Elena.

MONTEVERDE COFFEE TOUR Monteverde *(see the Northern Plains)* Monteverde Coffee offers you some hands-on experience. Depending on the time of year, you can help with picking, drying, roasting or packing.

All of the above tours guide you through the plant-to-cup process in English or Spanish, taking you from picking to drying to roasting to packing to brewing.

Reservations are essential and you should plan on spending a half-day for any of these outings. The whole package will set you back about $30 per person.

lovely stained-glass windows. The church is flanked by tidy side gardens, where you can stroll among sculpted trees along concrete paths incised with a floral pattern. Daily masses are held at 6 am and 6 pm. ⊠ *Eastern end of Parque Central* ☎ *2237–0779* ۞ *Daily 5 am–7 pm.*

Feria (*farmers' market*). On Saturday mornings starting at 5, Heredia's open-air *feria* stretches for almost a kilometer (½ mile) along Avenida 14. An explosion of trendy, new shops is changing the local shopping scene downtown.

Little Fort (*Fortín*). On the north side of the Parque Central in its own little park stands a strange tower called the Little Fort. Built as a military post in the 1870s, it never did see action and now serves as a symbol of the province, one of the few military monuments in this army-less country. The tower is closed to the public. The old brick building next to the Fortín is the Town Hall (Palacio Municipal). To the east of the fort, the tile-roof building with the handsome wood veranda is the recently restored Casa de la Cultura, which almost always has a free exhibition by local artists. Inside, there's a very small museum of town history, as well as a handsome inner atrium, with wooden galleries, where concerts are often held. ⊠ *C. Central and Avda. Central.*

Museum of Popular Culture. At the edge of a middle-class neighborhood between Heredia and Barva, the Museo de Cultura Popular is housed in a farmhouse with a large veranda built in 1885 with an adobe-like technique called *bahareque*. Run by the National University, the museum is furnished with antiques and surrounded by a garden and a small coffee farm. Just walking around the museum is instructive, but calling ahead to reserve a hands-on cultural tour (such as one on tortilla making) really makes it worth the trip. An open-air restaurant serves bread baked in a clay oven, and fresh tortillas and tamales. The museum is open only on Sundays 10 to 5, but groups of 10 or more can reserve a tour during the week. ⊠ *Between Heredia and Barva; from Musmanni bakery in Santa Lucia de Barva, 100 m north, then turn right 1 km/½ mile east; follow signs* ☎ *2260–1619* ⊕ *www.museo. una.ac.cr* ▣ *$2* ۞ *Sun. 10–5.*

New Market (*Mercado Nuevo*). Three blocks southeast of the Parque Central is Heredia's covered New Market, which holds dozens of *sodas* (simple restaurants) along with the usual food stands. ⊠ *C. Central and Avda. 6* ۞ *Mon.–Sat. 7–6.*

Parque Central. Heredia is centered on tree-studded Parque Central, one of the country's loveliest and liveliest central parks, surrounded by some notable buildings spanning more than 250 years of history. The park has a large, round, cast-iron fountain imported from England in 1879 and a Victorian bandstand where the municipal band plays Sunday-morning and Thursday-night concerts. Families, couples, and old-timers sit on park benches, shaded by fig and towering palm trees, often inhabited by noisy and colorful flocks of crimson-fronted parakeets. Drop into Pops, a national ice-cream chain at the south side of the park and pick up an ice-cream cone, then take a seat on a park bench and watch the passing parade. Tap your foot but don't start dancing—for some arcane reason, dancing in this park is *prohibido*! ⊠ *C. Central and Avda. Central.*

Paseo de Las Flores. This airy, pleasant, and huge shopping mall is on the main road south of town. It has a branch of almost every international fashion boutique, as well as a multiplex cinema and a wide choice of cafés and restaurants. 🕒 *Mon.–Sat. 10:30–9, Sun. 11–8.*

Sibú Chocolate. Get to know a bean of another kind during a private tasting at the workshop of the country's best artisanal chocolate-makers ($24, minimum of two) that starts with an informative talk about the historical and cultural significance of the cacao bean, includes a demonstration of tempering chocolate by hand and ends, of course, with a sampling of exquisite chocolates made from 100% organic cacao. Tasters can also stay for an elegant lunch on Sibú's pretty terrace ($16). Reserve 24 hours in advance. ✉ *Turnoff for San Isidro de Heredia, off highway to Braulio Carrillo National Park* ☎ *2268–1335* 🌐 *www.sibuchocolate.com* 🕒 *Tues.–Sat. 11–3.*

4

WHERE TO EAT

$ COSTA RICAN

🍴 **Barco de los Mariscos.** For an authentic Heredia experience, head to this antique hacienda in San Rafael de Heredia for lunch or dinner on the veranda, with a view of the town's imposing, cream-color Gothic church. The 100-year-old wooden house, painted sea blue, was actually moved by oxcart years ago from a nearby coffee *finca* (farmhouse), and now sits in a rose garden on a busy corner of the town. Ceviche and seafood are the main attractions—marinated sea bass with avocado is the most popular dish—along with daily *casados* (rice, beans, plantains, and salad) and excellent *patacones* (fried, squashed plantain slices) served with *molida,* a smooth, refried bean dip. [$] *Average main: $7* ✉ *Across from Banco Nacional, San Rafael de Heredia, 3 km (2 miles) northeast of the National University* ☎ *2263–3909.*

$ ITALIAN

🍴 **L'Antica Roma.** More than 40 versions of pizza baked in a wood-burning oven are the main event at this very popular, upscale Italian eatery. Every pizza comes with a trio of condiments to spice it up to your taste: homemade hot chili or a garlicky sauce, and grated cheese. Framed black-and-white photos of famous Italians eating spaghetti may inspire you to try one of the decent homemade pastas. There's also an exhaustive menu of meat and chicken cooked Italian style—juicy beef tenderloin substitutes for veal in all the classic Italian veal dishes. Italian wine can be ordered by the glass, carafe, or bottle. Two large-screen TVs with sports add to the happy buzz indoors on busy nights; the tables out on the wrought-iron-enclosed patio lend themselves better to conversation, once rush-hour traffic has subsided. It's open for lunch and dinner daily. [$] *Average main: $10* ✉ *C. 7 and Avda. 7, across from the Hotel Valladolid* ☎ *2262–9073.*

WHERE TO STAY

For expanded hotel reviews, visit Fodors.com.

$$$$ B&B/INN Fodor's Choice ★

🏨 **Finca Rosa Blanca Country Inn.** Set amid fields of green coffee, this exclusive, hilltop bed-and-breakfast hideaway has a much-deserved reputation as one of the country's top sumptuous splurges. **Pros:** eco-consciousness; indulgence with style; service par excellence. **Cons:** some units short on closet and drawer space; overpriced restaurant; hard to find if you are driving your own car. **TripAdvisor:** "a total delight," "haven of peace," "a bit of paradise." [$] *Rooms from: $300* ⊠ *800 m north of Café Britt Distribution Center in Santa Barbara de Heredia, Barrio Jesús* ☎ *2269–9392* ⊕ *www.fincarosablanca.com* ⟿ *11 junior suites, 2 master suites* ⦿| *Breakfast.*

$$ **Hotel Valladolid.** The classiest hotel in downtown Heredia, this four-
HOTEL   story narrow building has 12 modern rooms that first attracted busi-
ness travelers and visiting professors at the nearby National University,
although guests now are just as likely to be vacationers. **Pros:** central
location; friendly staff; extensive buffet breakfast with homemade torti-
llas. **Cons:** limited parking; a few rooms show their age. [$] *Rooms from:
$87* ⊠ *C. 7 and Avda. 7, 400 m north and 100 m west of main entrance
of La Universidad Nacional* ☎ *2260–2905* ⊕ *www.hotelvalladolid.net*
⟿ *11 rooms, 1 suite* ⦿| *Breakfast.*

Barva de Heredia. About 3 km (2 miles) due north of Heredia, this colo-
nial town is famous for making masks and for its **Parque Central,** still
surrounded by the original adobe buildings with Spanish-tile roofs on
three sides, and a white-stucco church to the east. The park is filled
with whimsical sculptures, including a park bench shaped like an entire
seated family, and bizarre masks and clown's heads decorating garbage
receptacles. A new amphitheater and stage stand ready for the annual
mask-making festival held every August. The stout, handsome church
with terra-cotta bas-relief flourishes dates from the late 18th century
and has a lovely grotto shrine to the Virgin Mary in the church garden.

**EN
ROUTE**

On a clear day you can see verdant Volcán Barva towering to the north,
and if you follow the road that runs in front of the church and veer left
at the Y, you will wind your way up the slopes of that volcano to Vara
Blanca, where you can either drive north to La Paz Waterfall Gardens
or continue straight to Volcán Poás National Park. If instead you veer
right at the Y and drive up the steep, narrow road, you'll pass through
San José de la Montaña and Paso Llano to reach Sacramento, where the
road turns into a rough dirt track leading to the Barva sector of Braulio
Carrillo National Park. If you turn left when you reach Barva's central
plaza, you'll head to San Pedro and Santa Barbara, where roads head
south to Alajuela and also north to Vara Blanca.

CARTAGO AND IRAZÚ VOLCANO

Cartago, due east of San José, is Costa Rica's oldest city, home to some
beautiful old churches, including the country's national shrine, plus
other notable historical structures. To the north of Cartago towers
massive Irazú Volcano, which is covered with fertile farmland enriched
by the volcano's many eruptions, and topped by an impressive crater.

CARTAGO

22 km/14 miles southeast of San José.

Although earthquakes have destroyed most of its structures from the
colonial era, Cartago still has some attractive restored buildings, most
of them erected after the devastating 1910 earthquake. The city served
as the country's first capital until 1823, when the seat of government

was moved to the emerging economic center of San José. Today, Cartago is a bustling market town, shopping center, and vibrant student hub. Most visitors see Cartago on their way to or from the Orosi Valley or Turrialba, and there is little reason (or place) to stay the night. The Orosi Valley, a short drive away, has better choices.

GETTING HERE AND AROUND

For the 25-minute drive from San José, drive east on Avenida 2 through San Pedro and Curridabat to the highway entrance, where you have three road options—take the middle one marked Cartago. Shortly before Cartago, a Y intersection marks the beginning of the route up Irazú, with traffic to Cartago veering right. Buses between San José and Cartago leave every 10 minutes daily (Avenida 10 and Calle 5, 400 meters south of the Teatro Nacional) from 5 am to 6 pm; after 6 the buses leave from Avenida 2 between Calle 1/3, in front of the National Theater. Cartago buses to San José pick up 300 meters west of the Municipal Museum of Cartago (formerly called the Comandancia), from 4:35 am to 11 pm. Buses to Orosi leave Cartago every 15 minutes from 5:15 am to 7:30, then every 30 minutes until 7 pm, with a bus at 8 and 9 pm, 100 meters east, 25 meters (82 feet) south of the southeast corner of Las Ruinas.

ESSENTIALS

Bank/ATM ATH ⊠ *Beside Papa John's on south side of central park.*
Banco Popular ⊠ *Southeast corner of Las Ruinas* ☎ *2591–4484* ⊙ *Weekdays 8:45–4:30, Sat. 8:15 am–11:30 am.*

Hospital Hospital Dr. Max Peralta ⊠ *200 m south, 150 m east of Las Ruinas* ☎ *2550–1999.*

Pharmacy Farmacia Central ⊠ *South side of Las Ruinas* ☎ *2551–0698* ⊙ *Daily 8–8.*

Post Office Correos ⊠ *Avda. 2, Cs. 15–17.*

Taxis Taxis El Carmen ☎ *2551–0836.*

EXPLORING

Cartago Cemetery. A little farther west, at the entrance to town, lies this sculpture-filled *campo santo*, founded in 1813 and declared a national monument in 1994. It's worth a stroll through the San Francisco section, overflowing with ornate mausoleums and lovely tomb sculptures, backed by views of distant mountains. ⊠ *Av. 2, entrance to city, on west side.*

La Iglesia de María Auxiliadora. At the opposite end of town, don't miss this recently restored, neo-Gothic masterpiece: a metallic church painted brick red, with a stunning all-white wooden interior in the Victorian gingerbread style. It sits in a huge public garden, which is also home to the town's brand-new, modernistic cultural center. ⊠ *Av. 1 and C. 13, west side of Cartago.*

Las Ruinas. Churches in some form or another stood at the site of the present-day Parque Central from 1575 to 1841; they kept being knocked down by earthquakes and reconstructed again and again. After the major earthquake in 1841, the citizens of Cartago began work on a new, Romanesque cathedral. But the devastating earthquake of 1910 put an end to the last attempt at building a structure on the site.

Las Ruinas, or "the Ruins," of this unfinished house of worship now stand in a pleasant park, and the interior has been transformed into a lush garden with fountains, a small pond, and flowers planted in the original stone pillar bases. Among the many legends attributed to the ruins is the gruesome story of the priest who, after falling in love with his sister-in-law, was murdered by his brother. His headless ghost still haunts the grounds. Although the park is billed as a Wi-Fi hotspot, we recommend not pulling out your laptop in such a public place—and this has nothing to do with alleged hauntings. ⊠ *Avda. 2, Cs. 1–2* 🔲 *Free* ⊙ *Weekends 8–4, Tues. and Thurs. 10–noon and 1–4.*

Our Lady of the Angels Basilica (*Basílica de Nuestra Señora de los Angeles*). Our Lady of the Angels Basilica is a hodgepodge of architectural styles from Byzantine to baroque, with a dash of Gothic. The interior is even more striking, with a colorful tile floor, intricately painted, *faux*-finish wood columns, and lots of stained glass. The church is open daily 6 am to 7 pm. The basilica is the focus of an annual pilgrimage to celebrate the appearance of La Negrita, or the Black Virgin, Costa Rica's patron saint. ⊠ *C. 16, Avdas. 2–4, 7 blocks east of central square* ☎ *2551–0465.*

WHERE TO EAT

Although you can find decent pasta and pizza, haute cuisine just doesn't exist here. Cartago does give you a fine opportunity to eat some *comida típica* (typical food). On just about any street downtown you'll find a soda (simple café), and the women in the kitchen will serve you the same style of food they cook at home for their own families. One rule of thumb: the busier, the better—the locals know where to eat well.

$ ✕ **La Puerta del Sol.** A cut above the usual soda, this large, long-established
COSTA RICAN   restaurant across from the basilica has been feeding pilgrims since 1957. Along with hearty portions of seafood, grilled meats, and typical casados, the restaurant has a popular bar and terrace. 💲 *Average main: $9* ⊠ *North side of basilica plaza* ☎ *2551–0615.*

VOLCÁN IRAZÚ

Volcán Irazú. Costa Rica's highest volcano, at 3,422 meters (11,260 feet), is one of the most popular with visitors since you can walk right down into the crater. Its presence is a mixed blessing: The ash fertilizes the Central Valley soil, but the volcano has caused considerable destruction through the centuries. ⚠ **Do not leave anything of value in your car. There have been a lot of thefts in the parking lot here, even though it is supposed to be guarded.** ☎ *2200–5025 for ranger station* 🔲 *$10* ⊙ *Daily 8–3:30.*

GETTING HERE AND AROUND

Follow directions to Cartago (⇨ *above*), but shortly before the city a Y intersection marks the beginning of the road up Irazú; traffic to Cartago veers right, then left immediately past the first lights. From downtown Cartago, a 45-minute trip, take the road to Irazú at the northeast corner of the basilica. Signs from Cartago lead you to the park. Buses head to Volcán Irazú from San José (⊠ *Avda. 2, Cs. 1–3*) daily at 8 and 8:45 am and return at 12:30 pm.

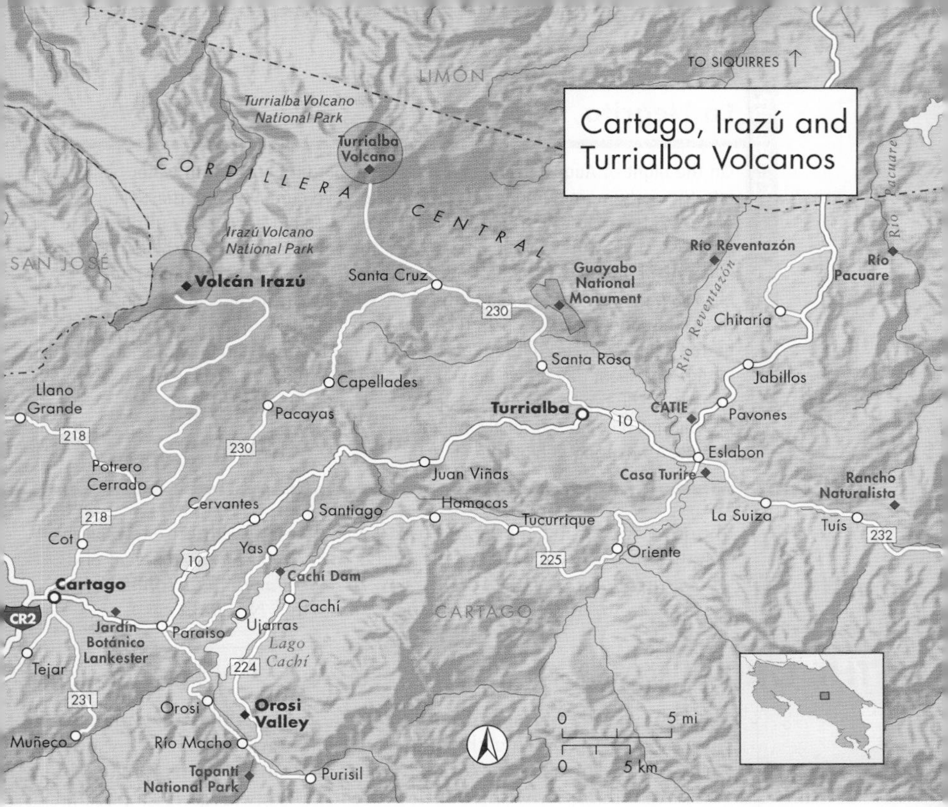

Cartago, Irazú and Turrialba Volcanos
TO SIQUIRRES ↑
LIMÓN
Turrialba Volcano National Park
Turrialba Volcano
CORDILLERA CENTRAL
Irazú Volcano National Park
SAN JOSÉ
Volcán Irazú
Santa Cruz
230
Guayabo National Monument
Río Reventazón
Río Pacuare
Chitaría
Santa Rosa
Capellades
Jabillos
Llano Grande
Pacayas
Turrialba
10
CATIE
Pavones
218
230
Eslabon
Potrero Cerrado
Juan Viñas
Casa Turire
Rancho Naturalista
Cervantes
Hamacas
La Suiza
218
Santiago
Tucurrique
Tuís
232
Cot
Yas
Oriente
10
225
Cachí Dam
Cartago
CARTAGO
Cachí
CR2
Jardín Botánico Lankester
Paraiso
Ujarras
Lago Cachí
Tejar
224
231
Orosi
Orosi Valley
0 5 mi
0 5 km
Muñeco
Río Macho
Purisil
Tapantí National Park

WHERE TO EAT

$ COSTA RICAN 🍴 **Restaurant 1910.** Decorated with vintage photos of early-20th-century buildings and landscapes, this upscale restaurant also documents the disastrous 1910 earthquake that rocked this area and all but destroyed the colonial capital of Cartago. The menu is predominantly Costa Rican, with such traditional specialties as *trucha* (trout) and rice with chicken, along with some more-sophisticated dishes, like *corvina* (sea bass) fillet with a coconut liqueur sauce. The Sunday típico buffet is a great introduction to Costa Rican cooking (served 11:30 to 4, $22). [$] *Average main: $9* ✉ *Road to Parque Nacional Volcán Irazú, 300 m north of Cot–Pacayas turnoff* ☎ *2536–6063* ⏲ *No dinner Sun.*

$ COSTA RICAN 🍴 **Restaurante Noche Buena.** If you've raced up Irazú to catch the clear early-morning views, a late breakfast or early lunch at this bright roadside stop is a great excuse to linger in the area. Hearty soups and a side of excellent fried yuca will warm you up, along with hot drinks, including *agua dulce*, a traditional drink made with brown sugar. There's also a changing selection of fancy desserts. Main dishes are decent but overpriced. The cozy interior has a cast-iron stove, but the glassed-in patio, especially on a sunny day, is a fresher option; neither has particularly impressive views. The Costa Rican owner, Federico Gutiérrez, has built a 3-km (2-mile) nature trail ($3) to waterfalls, and there's an interactive volcano museum ($4) that tells you everything you ever wanted to know

CLOSE UP

La Negrita

On the night of August 1 and well into the early-morning hours of August 2, the road to Cartago from San José clogs with worshippers, some of whom have traveled from as far away as Nicaragua to celebrate the 1635 appearance of Costa Rica's patron saint, *La Negrita* (the Black Virgin). The feast day draws an estimated 1 million pilgrims each year, not bad for a country of just 4 million people. At a spring behind the church, people fill bottles with water believed to have curative properties. Miraculous healing powers are attributed to the saint, and devotees have placed thousands of tiny symbolic crutches, ears, eyes, and legs in a room to the left of the altar. Tour buses and school groups, along with shops selling the saint's likeness, make the scene a bit of a circus.

about volcanoes in general and Irazú in particular. Get here early, as the restaurant closes at 3:30 on weekdays and 4:30 on busier weekends. *[$] Average main: $10 ✉ At Km 24.5, road to Parque Nacional Volcán Irazú ☎ 2530–8013 🌐 www.nochebuena.org 🕑 No dinner.*

THE OROSI VALLEY

If you have a day to spend near San José, this idyllic valley makes a classic day trip, passing through coffee plantations shaded by poró trees, oceans of chayote-squash vines, and small towns backed by verdant landscapes, with countless breathtaking views. It's a popular weekend drive for Costa Ricans, but still relatively off the beaten tourist path. The region is one of the few areas in Costa Rica that has remnants (ruins and churches) of the 17th-century Spanish colonial era. A good road makes a loop around the valley, easy to do if you have your own vehicle, or if you go on a guided tour—it's a staple of most San José tour operators' offerings. Public transportation is trickier here: Buses travel clockwise and counterclockwise, but neither route completes the loop.

ESSENTIALS

Bank/ATM Banco Nacional *✉ 200 m south of soccer field ☎ 2533–1390 ✉ West side of central park, Paraíso ☎ 2574–7274.*

Internet PC Orosi *✉ 200 m south of church.*

Pharmacy Farmacia Candelaria *✉ North side of Retaurante Coto, across from soccer field ☎ 2533–1919.* **Farmacia Sucre** *✉ 200 m west of central park, Paraíso ☎ 2574–7286.*

Post Office Correos *✉ 125 m east of central park, Paraíso.*

EXPLORING

Iglesia de San José de Orosi. The town of Orosi, in the heart of the valley, has but one major attraction: this beautifully restored 1743 church, the country's oldest house of worship still in use, and one of the few

Cartago's Basilica de Nuestra Señora de los Angeles is the focus of the annual pilgrimage to celebrate the appearance of the Black Virgin.

structures remaining from the colonial era. Set in a garden, against a green mountainside, it has a classic Spanish-colonial whitewashed facade and bell tower, with a roof made of cane overlaid with terra-cotta barrel tiles. Inside are an antique wooden altar and ancient paintings of the Stations of the Cross and the Virgin of Guadalupe, all brought to Costa Rica from Guatemala. The religious-art museum next door has a small but exquisite collection of furniture and artifacts from the original Franciscan monastery here. A huge, modern new church is being built beside the historic one, but happily it's just far enough away not to spoil photos of the picturesque church. ⊠ *Across from soccer field* ☎ *2533–3051* ☒ *Museum $1* ⊙ *Church Tues.–Fri. 9–noon and 1–5, weekends 9–noon and 1–7; museum Tues.–Sun. 9–noon and 1–5.*

Iglesia de Ujarrás. Continue past the dam into the small hamlet of Ujarrás, then follow the signs to the site of the romantic ruins of Costa Rica's first church. Built between 1681 and 1693 in honor of the Virgin of Ujarrás, the church, together with the surrounding village, was abandoned in 1833 after a series of earthquakes and floods wreaked havoc here, at the lowest point of the Orosi Valley. An unlikely Spanish victory in 1666 over a superior force of invading British pirates was attributed to a prayer stop here. Today the impressive, often-photographed ruins sit in a beautifully maintained park with lawns, flower gardens, and a pretty picnic area. A final, scenic 6-km (4-mile) winding drive to Paraíso from Ujarrás completes the road that loops the valley. ⊠ *In a small park, 1 km/½ mile from Restaurante Típico Ujarrás* ☎ *2574–8366* ☒ *Free* ⊙ *Daily 6–6.*

Bulls dressed in their finest for an oxcart parade in Cartago.

Jardín Botánico Lankester. At the basílica in the center of Cartago, turn right, and then left onto the busy road to Paraíso and Orosi. After 6 km (4 miles), a blue sign on the right marks the short road (500 meters/1,640 feet) to the lush gardens of Lankester Botanical Garden, one of the world's foremost orchid collections, with more than 1,100 native and introduced species of orchids. Bromeliads, heliconias, and aroids also abound in the 7-acre garden, along with 80 species of trees, including rare palms. A new Japanese garden has a graceful bridge and a teahouse. The best time to come is February through April, when the most orchids are in bloom. The garden's gift shop is one of the few places in Costa Rica to buy orchids that you can take home legally. (They come in small bottles and don't flower for four years, so you'll need some serious patience.) The garden is wheelchair-accessible and has excellent restrooms. ⊠ *West entrance to Paraíso, Cartago* ☎ *2552–3247* ⊕ *www.jbl.ucr.ac.cr* 💳 *$7.50* ☾ *Daily 8:30–4:30.*

Sanchiri Mirador. Head east toward Paraíso and then into the town itself. Hang a right at the central park. Some 2 km (1 mile) beyond is the Sanchiri Mirador, a restaurant/bar with excellent food and one of the valley's best *miradores* (lookout points). But our favorite vantage point is at a point on the road just beyond Sanchiri where the earth appears to drop away and the valley comes into view as you make the steep descent to the town of Orosi. Here's a case for letting someone else do the driving. A little farther along, there's free parking at the **Orosi Mirador**, a public park with spectacular views, sheltered picnic tables and grills, and a children's playground. There are some steep steps to climb but the views—and the clean restrooms—at the top are worth it.

Tapantí National Park. South of Orosi, the road becomes a rugged track following the Río Grande de Orosi past coffee plantations, elegant fincas (farmhouses), and seasonal barracks for coffee pickers before it's hemmed in by the steep slopes of thick jungle. At the bottom of the loop road, follow signs for Tapantí National Park. Though it's worth the trip for just an hour or two of exploring, you could easily fill a day in the park. Stretching all the way to the Talamanca Mountains, the reserve encompasses 47 square km (18 square miles) of largely pristine, remote cloud forest, refuge for more than 400 bird species, including the emerald toucanet, violaceous trogon, and many of the country's hummingbirds. The rangers' office and visitor center are on the right just after the park entrance. You can leave your vehicle at a parking area 1½ km (1 mile) up the road. From here loop trails head off into the woods on both sides. The Oropendola trail passes a picnic area and several swimming holes with (cold) emerald waters. The other trail is up a steep forested hillside. About 1½ km (1 mile) up from the parking area is an entrance to La Pava trail on the right, leading down a steep hill to the riverbank. If you continue ½ km (¼ mile) past the trailhead, you arrive at a 91-meter (300-foot) stair trail leading to a lookout. Get an early start—you can enter on foot before 8 am, as long as you pay as you leave. The park clouds over markedly by afternoon and is renowned as the country's wettest national park, so be prepared with a poncho or umbrella. ⊠ *14 km/8 miles south of Orosi* ☎ *2206–5615* 💵 *$10* 🕙 *Daily 8–4.*

WHERE TO EAT

$$ | COSTA RICAN
✕ **Bar y Restaurante Coto.** A local institution since 1952, this large rancho restaurant and bar is famous for its huge meat platters—we're talking 1 to 1½ kilos (2.2 to 3.3 pounds!) of meat with all the típico side dishes. Or you can dine more daintily on sautéed trout. The dining area is actually quite smart, with fresh white tablecloths overlaid with colored cloths, and a view of the lovely Orosi church. 💲 *Average main: $12* ⊠ *Northwest corner of soccer field* ☎ *2533–3032.*

$ | ECLECTIC
✕ **Gekko's.** This textbook backpacker hangout is affiliated with OTIAC, a Dutch-Canadian–owned Spanish school and hostel in Orosi. The café is bright and open, with groovy music and lots of T-shirts and sarongs for sale. The casual and cheap menu ranges from traditional Costa Rican food to *Kroketa* (a Dutch-style, deep-fried meat roll on a bun) and burritos. Helpful staff run a tourist information desk inside. 💲 *Average main: $5* ⊠ *400 m south of church* ☎ *2533–3640* 🌐 *www.montanalinda.com* 🚫 *No credit cards.*

$$ | COSTA RICAN | ★
✕ **La Casona del Cafetal.** The valley's most scenic and elegant lunch stop is on a coffee plantation overlooking the Cachí Reservoir. It's firmly on the beaten path, which means frequent visits from tour groups. The spacious indoor dining area has a high barrel-tile roof, but the most sought-after tables are out on the tiled, lakeside portico, draped with flowering vines framing gorgeous lake views. The menu has both Costa Rican staples and sophisticated dishes such as *corvina guarumos* (bass stuffed with mushrooms). Expect a wait on weekends, when diners come from miles around for the gargantuan $25 lunch buffet that ends with delicious, coffee-flavored desserts and Cafetal's own coffee, made

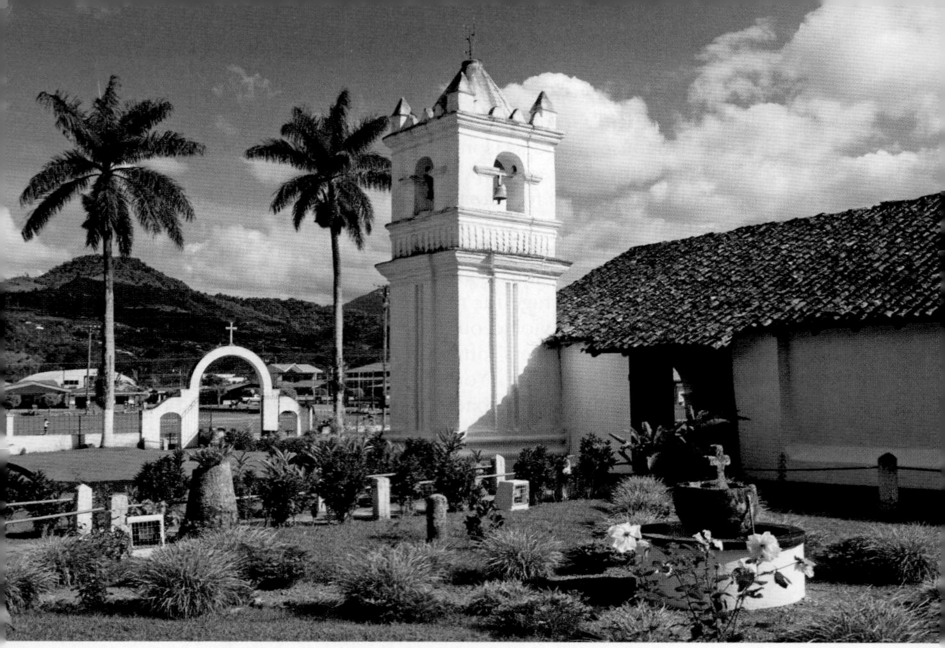

Iglesia de San José de Orosi is the county's oldest church that is still in use.

cup-by-cup in the old-fashioned Costa Rican way. After lunch, take a stroll down the garden path to the lake or check out the souvenir stalls in the parking lot. $ *Average main: $11* ✉ *2 km/1 mile south of Cachí Dam* ☎ *2577–1414* 🌐 *www.lacasonadelcafetal.com* ⏲ *No dinner.*

$ COSTA RICAN
🍴 **Soda El Guayabo.** For a quick, cheap breakfast or lunch, take a seat with the locals at the counter or at a picnic table, at this main street, open-air diner. The chicken fajitas are spicy and flavorful and the ladies behind the counter make the crispiest french fries around. Wash it all down with a large, fresh-fruit smoothie. It's open 6 to 4. $ *Average main: $5* ✉ *Main St., 300 m south of soccer field* ☎ *No phone* 💳 *No credit cards* ⏲ *Closed Sun. No dinner.*

WHERE TO STAY

For expanded hotel reviews, visit Fodors.com.

$$ B&B/INN
🏨 **Hotel Río Perlas Spa & Resort.** Thermal springs fill one of the pools at this Mediterranean-style spa hotel squeezed into a small, lush valley beside a rushing river. **Pros:** springs nice to bask in after a day of sightseeing; gorgeous river setting; trout fishing. **Cons:** basic rooms; not a lot of peace and quiet if there is a special event underway. **TripAdvisor:** "very nice quiet place," "nice place to chill," "beautiful setting." $ *Rooms from: $111* ✉ *6 km/3 miles south of Paraíso, turn right at bridge, then 2½ km/1½ miles; look for large sign* ☎ *2533–3341, 800/286–2922 in North America* 🌐 *www.rioperlasspaandresort.com* 🛏 *60 rooms* 🍽 *Breakfast.*

$ B&B/INN
🏨 **Kiri Mountain Lodge.** Small and very affordable, this family-run hotel has easy access to Tapantí park and its own 175-acre private reserve with waterfalls. **Pros:** secluded location; friendly owners; great birding.

Cons: basic rooms; need a car to stay here. **TripAdvisor:** "great for bird watching," "remote spot," "very cheerful reception." [$] *Rooms from: $45 ⊠ Turnoff 2 km/1 mile before Tapantí park entrance ☎ 2533–2272 ⊕ www.kirilodge.net ⤳ 6 rooms* ⃝❘ *Breakfast.*

$

B&B/INN

🏠 **Orosi Lodge.** Run by a young German couple who have built a warm rapport with the community, the little lodge blends in with Orosi's pretty, old-town architecture: whitewashed walls are trimmed in blue, ceilings are high, and natural wood is used throughout. **Pros:** affordable, pleasant. **Cons:** no restaurant, café only. **TripAdvisor:** "highly professional and well run," "special in many ways," "gorgeous lodge in an amazing valley." [$] *Rooms from: $55 ⊠ 350 m south, 100 m west of soccer field ☎ 2533–3578 ⊕ www.orosilodge.com ⤳ 6 rooms, 1 chalet* ⃝❘ *No meals.*

SHOPPING

Casa del Soñador (*House of the Dreamer*). Stop in at this unique artisan shop, a picturesque wood cottage embellished with monumental carvings by local wood sculptor Macedonio Quesada, the creator of the House of the Dreamer. Though Macedonio died years ago, his sons Miguel and Hermes and a former apprentice are still here, carving interesting, often comical little statues out of coffee roots, which they sell for only $10. It's open 8 to 6 daily. ⊠ *2 km/1 mile south of Cachí Dam ☎ 2577–1186, 2577–1533.*

THE TURRIALBA REGION

The main attractions near the bustling market town of Turrialba are its namesake volcano, an internationally famous agricultural research center and the pre-Columbian archaeological ruins of Guayabo. The town lies considerably lower than the Central Valley, so it enjoys a more moderate climate, a transition between the cooler Central Valley and the sweltering Caribbean coast. There are two ways to reach this area from San José, both of which pass spectacular scenery. The more direct route, accessible by heading east through both Cartago and Paraíso, winds through coffee and sugar plantations before descending abruptly to Turrialba. For the second route, turn off the road between Cartago and the summit of Irazú near the town of Cot, heading toward Pacayas. That narrow route twists along the slopes of Irazú and Turrialba volcanoes past some stunning scenery—stately pollarded trees lining the road, riotous patches of tropical flowers, and metal-girder bridges across crashing streams. As you begin the descent to Turrialba town, the temperature rises and sugarcane alternates with fields of neat rows of coffee bushes.

TURRIALBA

58 km/36 miles east of San José.

The relatively well-to-do agricultural center of Turrialba is a bustling town, with a youthful vibe from the nearby university, a colorful open-air market, and a tree-shaded central park filled with an intriguing collection of large-scale animal sculptures. Turrialba also has two major factories: Firestone, which you'll see on the road to Siquirres, and a

Rawlings factory, which makes all the baseballs used in the major leagues. (Rawlings, unfortunately, does not offer tours.) Thanks to some spectacular scenery, patches of rain forest in the surrounding countryside, and a handful of upscale nature lodges, ecotourism is increasingly the focus of the town's efforts. Significant numbers of kayakers and rafters also flock here to run the Pacuare and Reventazón rivers. And, of course, looming above the town is Volcán Turrialba. Recent eruptions of ash, along with a heavily damaged road, prevent visitors from going to the top.

CORRUPTION CRACKDOWN

Long a proponent of do-as-I-say, not-as-I-do anticorruption policies, Costa Rica got tough on bigwigs in 2004. Two former presidents were taken into custody for allegedly accepting bribes in a telecommunications deal. A third—José María Figueres—hid out in Switzerland until it was safe to return to Costa Rica, in 2011. The sight of former leaders being led away in handcuffs has shaken many Costa Ricans' faith in their democracy, but others see it as a positive sign that no one is above the law.

GETTING HERE AND AROUND

The road through Cartago continues east through Paraíso, where you turn left at the northeast corner of the central park to pick up the road to Turrialba. Marked by signs, this road leads north to Guayabo National Monument. Direct buses between San José and Turrialba leave hourly (8 am to 8 pm; slower buses run as early as 5:15 am and as late as 10 pm) from Calle 13, Avenida 6, just west of the downtown court buildings. Direct buses depart from the Turrialba terminal (at the entrance to Turrialba) for San José on the hour from 5 am to 5 pm; on the half hour to Cartago, and every two hours to Siquirres.

ESSENTIALS

Bank/ATM Banco de Costa Rica ⊠ *Avda. 0 and C. 1* ☎ *2556–0472.* **Banco Nacional** ⊠ *C. 1 and Avda. Central* ☎ *2556–1211.*

Hospital Hospital Dr. William Allen ⊠ *Avda. 2, 100 m west of C. 4* ☎ *2558–1300.*

Internet ECA Internet ⊠ *Southeast corner of central park, upstairs* ☉ *Weekdays 8–10, weekends 9–9.*

Pharmacy Farmacia San Buenaventura ⊠ *50 m south of east side of central park* ☎ *2556–0379* ☉ *Mon. to Sat. 8–8; Sun. 8–1.*

Post Office Correos ⊠ *Avda. 6 and C. Central, 200 m north of central park.*

Taxis Transgalo ☎ *2556–9393.*

EXPLORING

Guayabo National Monument. On the slopes of Turrialba Volcano lies Costa Rica's most significant archaeological site, recently recognized by the American Society of Civil Engineers as a feat of Latin American civil engineering second only to Machu Picchu. Records mentioning the ruins go back to the mid-1800s, but systematic investigations didn't begin until 1968, when a local landowner out walking her dogs discovered what she thought was a tomb. Archaeologists began excavating

"For a fun ride, try rafting the Pacuare River in October or November when the water is high." —Photo by Linda137, Fodors.com member

the site and unearthed the base wall of a chief's house in what eventually turned out to be the ruins of a large community (around 10,000 inhabitants) covering 49 acres, 10 of which have been excavated. The city was abandoned in AD 1400, probably because of disease or war. Guided tours (about two hours) in Spanish or English make the stones come alive, with knowledgeable guides from the U-Suré Guide Association (the name is the indigenous word for house). Starting from the new, round, thatch-roof reception center, they'll take you through the rain forest to a *mirador* (lookout) from which you can see the layout of the excavated circular buildings. Only the raised foundations survive, since the conical houses themselves were built of wood. As you descend into the ruins, notice the well-engineered surface and covered aqueducts leading to a trough of drinking water, which still functions today. Next you'll pass the end of an impressive 8-km (5-mile) paved walkway used to transport the massive building stones; the abstract patterns carved on the stones continue to baffle archaeologists, but some clearly depict jaguars, which were revered as deities. The hillside jungle is captivating, and the trip is further enhanced by bird-watching possibilities: 200 species have been recorded. There's a souvenir hut opposite the entrance, a pleasant picnic area, and brand-new, modern restrooms in a replica of a thatched indigenous hut. The access route from the east via the Santa Teresita (Lajas) has some rough spots, but you can make it in any car. The alternative Santa Cruz route is a little rougher, but you can still make it in a regular car, unless the road is wet—in which case you may need a 4WD vehicle to get here. ✛ *Drive through the center of Turrialba to a girdered bridge; take road signed Guayabo National Monument northeast for a total of 16 km/10 miles (about 25–30 mins' driving); watch for a signed left turnoff, which will take you the final 3 km/2 miles to the monument. If you've taken the scenic Irazú foothills route to Turrialba, the Santa Cruz route—11 km/7 miles (about 35 mins' driving)—is an option. Turn left on rough road from Santa Cruz; climb 5 km/3 miles, past the Escuela de Guayabo; turn right at the sign for the monument; the road descends 6 km/4 miles to the site* ☎ 2559–1220, 2559–0117, 8798–8669 *to reserve a guide* ⊕ www.accvc.org ✉ *$6 entrance fee plus $15 guide fee for 1–3 people, $30 for 4–9 people* ☉ *Daily 8–3:30.*

Volcán Turrialba. Although you can't drive up to its summit as you can at Poás and Irazú, Volcán Turrialba is worth visiting, albeit with some precautions these days. The volcano has been increasingly active since early 2010 it spewed out enough steam and ashes to close off the surrounding area, both to farmers and visitors. In late 2011 another burst of activity closed the surrounding National Park. Since the road up to the summit has not been repaired, visitors cannot visit the summit at this writing. If and when the road is serviceable, volcanologists suggest visits be limited to a 20-minute max because of the heavy content of sulfur dioxide in fumes emanating from the volcano, a phenomenon that has taken its toll on plant and animal life here. The reward for the steep climb is an eerie lunarscape with unique plants that have adapted to this challenging environment. Check to be sure the road and the park is open before you make the climb. ⚠ **If you suffer from any type of heart or respiratory condition or are pregnant, stay away.** On the road that runs from Pacayas to Turrialba through Santa Cruz, there is a signed turnoff at La Pastora, west of Santa Cruz, that leads up the mountain. The drive up is 14 km (8¾ miles) and starts paved, but the road gets worse the higher you go. In most cases you'll need a 4WD to make the last section before the trailhead, which is in a very small community called La Central de Turrialba. The road veers left toward the Volcán Turrialba Lodge, and a washed-out road leads right, toward the summit. If you want to take the latter route, you can park on the left just after the school; usually someone is around to charge you a few dollars for the privilege, but, as elsewhere in the country, this in no way guarantees your car's safety. We recommend parking at Volcán Turrialba Lodge—they don't charge, they'll point you in the direction of some safe hikes on the lower slopes of the volcano, and you can rest up with some snacks and hot chocolate at the restaurant when you're finished. Get an early start and dress for the weather—it can get chilly up here even during the day.

Volcán Turrialba Lodge. The easiest way to arrange the excursion is to call the Volcán Turrialba Lodge and request a guide. You can ascend the 6 km (4 miles) from the lodge on foot or horseback in one to two hours (allow up to four hours for the round-trip, plus exploring time) and, at 3,340 meters (10,958 feet), with luck you'll see clear down to the Caribbean coast. ☎ 2273–4335.

OFF THE BEATEN PATH

Tropical Agricultural Research and Higher Education Center. A good place for bird-watchers and garden enthusiasts, the Centro Agronómico Tropical de Investigación y Enseñanza, better known by its Spanish acronym, CATIE, is one of the leading tropical research centers in Latin America.

Costa Rica's first church, Iglesia de Ujarrás, was abandoned in 1833 after a series of earthquakes and floods, along with pirate attacks, wreaked havoc.

You might catch sight of the yellow-winged northern jacana or the purple gallinule in the lagoon near the main building. The 10-square-km (4-square-mile) property includes landscaped grounds, seed-conservation chambers, greenhouses, orchards, experimental agricultural projects, a large swath of rain forest, labs and offices, and lodging for students and teachers. Behind the administration building lies the lake that once was rapids on the Reventazón River. The most popular attraction is the **Botanical Garden Tour,** a two-hour guided walk to taste, smell, and touch tropical fruits, along with cacao, coffee, and other medicinal and stimulant plants. A favorite stop is the "miracle fruit" tree, whose berries magically make anything sour taste sweet. ⊠ *3 km/2 miles outside Turrialba, on road to Siquirres* ☎ *2556–2700* ⊕ *www.catie.ac.cr* ✉ *$25 with guide, $10 on your own; $35 for half day tour, $50 for full-day tour, including lunch* ☯ *Botanical Garden Mon.–Fri. 7–4; 8–4 weekends; reservations recommended for guided tours, especially on weekends.*

OUTDOOR ACTIVITIES

Ecoaventuras. Based in Turrialba, this adventure company covers all the stops—horseback riding and mountain biking at the top of the volcano, kayaking and rafting, and a three-in-one day tour to Guayabo, CATIE, and a serpentarium, with pickup from San José hotels. ⊠ *600 m south of bus terminal, next door to Maderas Amoto* ☎ *2556–7171* ⊕ *www. ecoaventuras.co.cr.*

Explornatura. Located in downtown Turrialba, this company organizes kayaking, horseback riding, mountain biking, and rafting tours, including a teen adventure camp and a family-friendly rafting trip with lots

CLOSE UP

White-Water Thrills

You're struggling to hang on and paddle, you can't hear a thing over the roar, and you were just slammed with a mighty wall of water. Sound like fun? Then you're in the right place. The **Río Pacuare** and the **Río Reventazón** draw rafters and kayakers from all over the world to Turrialba. Right next to Turrialba, the Reventazón has Class II, III, and IV rapids. The Pacuare, farther from Turrialba, has a spectacular 29-km (18-mile) run with a series of Class III and IV rapids. The scenery includes lush canyons where waterfalls plummet into the river and expanses of rain forest.

Nearly every outfitter has day trips, but some also have multiday trips that include jungle hikes. Costa Rica Nature Adventures and Ríos Tropicales even have their own lodges on the river. Age requirements for children vary by outfitter; Explornatura in Turrialba runs a family trip on the gentler Pejibaye River that kids as young as five can enjoy. The typical trip starts with a van ride to the put-in; including a breakfast stop, it usually takes about 2½ hours from hotel to river. After the first half of the run, guides flip one of the rafts over to form a crude lunch table. Then you continue up the river to

Siquirres, and pile back in the van for the ride home.

It would be unwise to choose your company based merely on price: Those with bargain rates are probably skimping somewhere. Good outfitters require you to wear life vests and helmets, have CPR-certified river guides with near-fluent English skills, and have kayakers accompany the rafts in case of emergencies. A 5:1 guest-to-guide ratio is good; 10:1 is not. Local Turrialba companies have better prices and allow you to book a trip at the last minute. Hotels and travel agencies book trips with larger outfitters, who can pick you up from nearly anywhere in the Central Valley. Prices range from about $75 to $100.

People fall out of the raft all the time, and it is usually no big deal. The worst-case scenario is getting trapped underwater in an eddy, or under the raft, but surprisingly, most fatalities are heart-attack victims, so don't participate if you're high-risk. You should also be able to swim. Almost every long-standing company has had a death—it is an unfortunate reality of the business. Don't hesitate to ask about safety records. The vast majority of trips, however, are pure exhilarating fun.

of thrills but fewer chances of spills. ⊠ *40 m west of Hotel Wageliaz* ☎ *2556–2070, 866/571–2443 toll-free from U.S. and Canada* ⊕ *www. explornaturacr.com.*

WHITE-WATER OUTFITTERS

Loco's Tropical Tours. Most outfitters are based in San José, and many offer both rafting and kayaking. Loco's is in Turrialba. ☎ *2556–6035* ⊕ *www.whiteh2o.com.*

WHERE TO EAT

$
COSTA RICAN

✕ **La Garza Bar y Restaurante.** With weathered, blond-wood tables and chairs, and big windows with a view out onto the central park, La Garza is a popular meeting spot with a little more atmosphere than most of the eateries in town. The menu runs the gamut from hamburgers to chicken and has a good seafood selection. (Sorry, vegetarians, "beetsteak" is a misprint.) This is a good place for a late dinner, as it's open from 10:30 am until 11 pm. There's a pleasant bar here, too, backed by a Latin sound track. $ *Average main: $8* ✉ *Northwest corner of park* ☎ *2556–1073.*

$$
COSTA RICAN

✕ **Restaurante La Feria.** A permanent exhibition of art by a nationally renowned artist and the Turrialba expertise of owner Don Roberto (if you speak Spanish) make this a worthwhile stop. This pleasant, family-style restaurant has the usual midscale Costa Rican fare, ranging from fast food to filet mignon; the house specialty is beef tenderloin topped with a Spanish-inspired red-wine-and-mushroom sauce. Casados and gallo pinto compete with more-familiar chicken and seafood dishes. Even paella is on the menu (with three hours' notice), and there's home-baked apple pie for dessert. $ *Average main: $12* ✉ *Across from Enersol gas station at western entrance to town* ☎ *2556–5550* ⊙ *Daily 11:30–10* ⊙ *No dinner Tues.*

WHERE TO STAY

For expanded hotel reviews, visit Fodors.com.

$$$
B&B/INN
Fodor'sChoice
★

⊡ **Casa Turire.** Lush gardens and manicured lawns surround this gorgeous, hacienda-style, luxury hotel overlooking a scenic lake. **Pros:** excellent value; beautiful grounds; four-leaf sustainability rating. **Cons:** small, one-room spa; standard-room bathrooms could use a little upgrading. **TripAdvisor:** "most charming place to stay," "quaint and lovely," "a quiet Swiss-like retreat." $ *Rooms from: $160* ✉ *8 km/ 5 miles south on Carretera a la Suiza from Turrialba* ☎ *2531–1111, 877/750–6855 toll-free in U.S. and Canada* ⊕ *www.hotelcasaturire.com* ⤴ *12 standard rooms, 3 suites, 1 master suite* ⦿*Breakfast.*

$$
B&B/INN

⊡ **Guayabo Lodge.** If fresh mountain air appeals to you, this upscale mountain retreat has comfortable rooms, a first-class restaurant, and spacious, glassed-in sitting areas to enjoy unbeatable volcano and valley views by day and blazing fireplaces by night. **Pros:** cozy and comfortable; 100% smoke-free; high sustainability consciousness. **Cons:** weather can be wet and cool; clouds can obscure the view. **TripAdvisor:** "fantastic views and accommodating staff," "excellent service and lodgings," "delightful proprietors." $ *Rooms from: $90* ✉ *2 km (1¼ miles) west of Santa Cruz de Turrialba* ☎ *2538–8492* ⊕ *www.guayabolodge. com* ⤴ *22 rooms, 4 junior suites* ⦿*Breakfast.*

$$$
B&B/INN

⊡ **Rancho Naturalista.** Unparalleled bird-watching within a 160-acre private nature reserve with more than 400 recorded species, plus first-class food, and comfortable cabins and rooms are the reasons bird-watchers and nature lovers from all over the world stay here. **Pros:** birder's paradise; hiking trails for guests; warm atmosphere. **Cons:** some rooms are a little dated; not a convenient base for adventure day trips. **TripAdvisor:** "comfortable place for birding," "great people," "wonderful hospitality." $ *Rooms from: $165* ✉ *20 km/12 miles southeast of Turrialba, 1½*

4

km/1 mile south of Tuís, then up a rough road ☎ *2433–8278 for reservations, 888/246–8513 in North America, 2554–8100 for directions* 🌐 *www.ranchonaturalista.net* 🛏 *16 rooms* 💳 *No credit cards* 🍴 *All meals.*

> **KEEPING COOL**
>
> The Central Valley's climate is often a great surprise to first-time visitors—it's not at all the steamy tropics you've imagined. It's usually cool enough at night to go without air-conditioning, so don't be surprised if many hotels don't have it.

$ B&B/INN 🏨 **Turrialtico.** Dramatically positioned on a hill overlooking the valley east of Turrialba, this Costa Rican–owned rustic, wood lodge is the best budget option in the area. **Pros:** rich views at budget prices; coffeemakers in rooms; good opportunity to mingle with Ticos. **Cons:** thin walls in main lodge; less service-oriented than other options. **TripAdvisor:** "great food," "friendly staff," "comfortable rooms." [$] *Rooms from: $64* ✉ *8 km/5 miles east of Turrialba on road to Siquirres* ☎ *2538–1111* 🌐 *www.turrialtico.com* 🛏 *12 rooms, 7 cabins* 🍴 *Breakfast.*

$ B&B/INN 🏨 **Volcán Turrialba Lodge.** On the upper slope of the volcano, this affordable, rustic lodge is as close as you can get to an active volcano. **Pros:** good value; proximity to volcano; friendly staff. **Cons:** gets chilly and rooms smell of wood smoke; options limited on rainy days; need a car to stay here. **TripAdvisor:** "magical place," "casual relaxation," "great views and great service." [$] *Rooms from: $50* ✣ *20 km/12 miles east of Cot, turn right at Pacayas on road to Volcán Turrialba, 4 km/2½ miles on dirt road; or from the Turrialba side, follow signs in La Pastora for national park, 14 km/7 miles along a patchily paved road; 4WD advised for last 3 km/2 miles on rough road* ☎ *2273–4335* 🌐 *www.volcanturrialbalodge.com* 🛏 *14 rooms* 🍴 *No meals.*

5

The Northern Plains

WORD OF MOUTH

"Here is a beautiful view of the Arenal Volcano, the most active volcano in Costa Rica. We stayed at a nearby hotel and had a room with a volcano view, as well as skies so clear we could see the summit."

—Photo by Msoberma, Fodors.com member

WELCOME TO THE NORTHERN PLAINS

TOP REASONS TO GO

★ **Arenal Volcano:** You can hear the rumblings of the world's third-most-active volcano for miles around, and, on clear nights, watch crimson rock and gas ooze down its flanks.

★ **Walk down to the waterfall:** The reward for a tough hike down to Cataratas de la Fortuna is a magnificent series of waterfalls.

★ **Walk in a cloud:** Explore Monteverde's misty world on treetop walkways up to 41 meters (138 feet) off the ground.

★ **Watching wildlife:** Waterbirds, monkeys, turtles, crocodiles, jaguars, and sloths abound in the 25,000-acre Caño Negro National Wildlife Refuge.

★ **Windsurfing:** Lake Arenal is one of the top windsurfing spots on earth; winds can reach 50 to 60 mph December through April.

1 Monteverde Cloud Forest Area. Home to the rainiest of cloud forests, the Monteverde Cloud Forest Area is also the canopy-tour capital of Costa Rica. Hanging bridges, treetop tram tours, and zip lines: it's got it all. As if that's not enough, horseback riding, rappelling, and nature hikes are also available.

2 The Far North. Caño Negro National Wildlife Refuge, in the Far North, is great for fishing, bird-watching, and communing with nature.

3 The Sarapiquí Loop. The Sarapiquí Loop circles Braulio Carrillo National Park, rare for its easy-to-access primary rain forest. The loop's highlight is Poás Volcano; its turquoise crater lake and steaming main crater make it the favorite volcano of many visitors.

```
0          10 mi
0        10 km
```

Río San Juan

35 Acapulco
Pangola
Santa Domingo
Boca Arenal
Altamira
Puerto Víejo de Sarapiquí
4
Angeles
La Fortuna
Platanar
Chiles
3
Braulio Carrillo National Park
Puerto Viejo Loop
35
San Isidro
Ciudad Quesada
San Miguel Angeles
4
Poás Volcano
Naranjo
Grecia
CR2
Alajuela
SAN JOSÉ

GETTING ORIENTED

Geographically, the Zona Norte (Northern Zone), as it is known locally, separates neatly into two alluvial plains. The rich, lush terrain runs from the base of the Cordillera Central in the south to the Río San Juan, on the border with Nicaragua in the north. Most visitors begin their visit to Costa Rica in San José, many then heading north to La Fortuna, using it as a base for exploring the volcano, waterfall, and Caño Negro, and participating in activities like sportfishing, windsurfing, and kitesurfing at Lake Arenal, and rafting on the Sarapiquí River.

5

5 Arenal Volcano.
The Arenal Volcano area is one of the hottest tourist destinations in Costa Rica. La Fortuna is the closest town to the volcano; among many nearby diversions are the Tabacón Hot Springs. Tilarán, west of Lake Arenal, is the place to be if you're a windsurfer.

4 Northwest of San José.
Northwest of San José is one of the country's best crafts communities, Sarchí, and some luxurious countryside lodges.

CAÑO NEGRO

Think a smaller version of Florida's Everglades and you'll have a good picture of the Refugio Nacional de Vida Silvestre Caño Negro.

This lowland rain-forest reserve in the far northern reaches of Costa Rica near the Nicaraguan border covers 98 square km (38 square miles). It looks remote on the map, but is easily visited on an organized day tour, especially from La Fortuna. In 2007 Caño Negro was designated the core of a new UNESCO biosphere called *Agua y Paz* (Water and Peace), which encompasses more than 2 million acres of wildlife habitat in Costa Rica and Nicaragua.

Caño Negro has suffered severe deforestation over the years, but most of the length of the Río Frío, its principal river, is still lined with trees. The park's vast lake, which floods according to seasonal rains, is an excellent place to watch waterfowl. On land, pumas, tapirs, ocelots, cougars, and the always-elusive jaguar make up the mammal life found here—consider yourself fortunate if you spot that last one. Caimans snap everywhere in the knee-deep marshy waters, too. *(See page 232 for more information.)*

BEST TIME TO GO

It gets *hot* here, with March and April brutally so, but the January-through-March dry season is the best time to spot the reserve's migratory bird population. Opportunities abound the rest of the year, too, though. No matter what the season, bring sunscreen, water, insect repellant, and a brimmed hat.

FUN FACT

In addition to other bird species, the reserve is the best place to spot the Nicaraguan grackle. This New World blackbird is only found in Nicaragua and northern Costa Rica. It's medium size, with a long, graduated tail and fairly long bill and legs.

BEST WAYS TO EXPLORE

BIRD-WATCHING

This is the best place in the country to see waterbirds. Just sit back in your tour boat and survey the passing parade. You're sure to see anhingas spreading their wings to dry; both glossy and white ibis recognizable by their long curved beaks; rose-ate spoonbills often mistaken for flamingos; and the jabiru, king of the storks. Herons and kingfishers lurk on the banks, ready to spear fish; while jacanas, with their huge feet, forage in the water lettuce, looking as though they are actually walking on water. Above the water, watch for gray-color snail kites, which, true to their name, are hunting for snails.

BOAT TOURS

In the dry season you can ride horses, but a visit here chiefly entails a wildlife-spotting boat tour. You could drive up here on your own—roads to the area are in good shape—but once here, you'd need to arrange for boat transportation. Visiting with a tour company out of La Fortuna—it's a 90-minute ride one way—is the easiest way to see the park.

CAIMAN LAND

Famous for its caimans, Caño Negro still boasts a sizable population. They're smaller than crocodiles, though—at most 2½ meters (8 feet) long—and they are relatively unthreatening because they're too small to eat large mammals (this includes humans). It's a thrill to see them sunning on a bank or to see their spectacled eyes floating just above the water line. Unfortunately, the caimans here are under serious threat from hunters who sneak across the Nicaraguan border and slaughter them by the hundreds for their skins. The proof is sadly on display in the souvenir shops in Nicaragua, where you will see purses and belts made from caiman hides.

TOP REASONS TO GO

BIRD-WATCHING

The reserve is one of Costa Rica's lesser-sung bird-watching and wildlife-viewing destinations. Caño Negro is growing in popularity, but, for now, a visit here still gives you that "I'm in on a secret the rest of the world doesn't know about" satisfaction.

FISHING

It's not all about wildlife viewing here: Caño Negro is also one of Costa Rica's prime freshwater fishing destinations, with snook and marlin yours for the catching and the bragging rights during the July through March season. (There's barely enough water in the lake the other months of the year, so fishing is prohibited then.) The two lodges inside the reserve can hook you up.

GREAT TOURS

It's easy to get here from the Arenal area, with top-notch operators and their teams of knowledgeable guides organizing day tours from La Fortuna and so-called "evening" tours that actually get you here by the very warm midafternoon and depart around dusk.

ARENAL VOLCANO

The 2-km-high (1-mile-high) Arenal Volcano, Costa Rica's youngest and most active volcano, dominates the region's landscape.

Volcanologists estimate Arenal's age at around 4,000 years, and it was dormant for at least 400 years until 1968. It may be local folklore, but residents before then referred to Arenal as simply "the mountain" and apparently, despite its conical shape, did not realize it was a volcano. On July 29, 1968, an earthquake shook the area, and 12 hours later Arenal blew.

Since then, Arenal has been in a constant state of activity—thunderous, rumbling eruptions are sometimes as frequent as one per hour. These earthshaking events remind everyone what it really means to coexist with the world's third-most-active volcano. Night is the best time to view the action: on a clear evening you can see rocks spewing skyward. Although everyone refers to "lava," "pyroclastic flow," a mix of incandescent rock and gas, is a more apt description of what the volcano churns out. Call it what you will: the spectacle rarely fails to impress. *(See page 197 for more information.)*

BEST TIME TO GO

To be honest, viewing Arenal can be hit or miss any time of year. January through April, especially in the early morning, usually means fewer clouds to obscure daytime views. The dry season's clear evenings give the best spectacle of the volcano's flows. Patience is a virtue here.

FUN FACT

Researchers at INBio, the National Biological Institute in Santo Domingo, north of San José have been hard at work around the volcano. They see promise in the lichens growing on Arenal's slopes as a source of new antibiotics.

BEST WAYS TO EXPLORE

BIRD-WATCHING

If you decide to hike the park's Los Tucanes trail, chances are you'll see at least one of the five species of toucan that have been recorded here: chestnut-billed and keel-billed toucans, the yellow-eared and emerald toucanet, and the collared aracari. You'll never look at a box of Froot Loops the same after seeing the real thing. Hummingbirds also abound on the volcano's slope. Look for anything tiny and purple.

HIKING

For intrepid hikers who want to get a little closer to the action, Las Heliconias trail, which starts at the park reception center, wends through secondary forest and passes by the cooled lava flow from the 1968 eruption. Los Tucanes trail also leads to the lava fields, but it's more of an uphill hike, beginning near the entrance to the Arenal Observatory Lodge. There's also a hiking trail up to Cerro Chatto, a lopsided, extinct crater, partially filled with water, creating a pretty lake. Volcano activity and lava flow can change suddenly, so check with the park rangers to see which trails are currently safe to hike.

VOLCANIC TIPS

Two words: "from afar." Under no circumstances should you hike even the volcano's lower slopes on your own. Lava rocks and volcanic gas have killed trekkers who got too close, most recently in 2000. The tour operators we recommend know where the danger lies and take appropriate precautions. Wait until around 2 pm to see if the weather will cooperate, and then book your afternoon volcano hike.

Beyond that, take a liberal interpretation of "exploring" the volcano, and gaze at its majesty from the distance and safety of several area hotels, restaurants, and hot springs that afford postcard views.

TOP REASONS TO GO

ALL BUDGETS WELCOME

We lament that budget and even moderate travelers are being priced out of the market in certain regions of Costa Rica. Not so here. Choose from everything from backpackers' digs to luxury hotels in the area around Arenal. Feel free to stay for days, no matter what your budget.

A PERFECT VOLCANO

Look up *volcano* in the dictionary. You half expect to see a picture of Arenal. Its perfect cone, red-hot flow, plumes of ash, and menacing location close to the tourist town of La Fortuna practically define the term.

SPORTS AND ADVENTURE

No other attraction in Costa Rica has given rise to a list of accompanying entertainment offerings quite so extensive. Come here to pay your respects to Arenal, and you'll find enough other area activities to keep you occupied for days. (You'll also appreciate the backup on those occasions when clouds obscure your view of the volcano.)

5

POÁS VOLCANO

Towering north of Alajuela, the verdant Poás Volcano is covered with a quilt of farms and topped by a dark green shawl of cloud forest.

That pastoral scene disappears once you get to the summit, and you gaze into the steaming, bubbling crater with smoking fumaroles and a gurgling, gray-turquoise sulfurous lake. You'll swear you're peering over the edge of a giant witches' cauldron. That basin, 2 km (1 mile) in diameter and nearly 305 meters (1,000 feet) deep, is thought to be the largest active volcanic crater in the world.

Poás is one of Costa Rica's five active volcanoes—it has erupted 40 times since the early 1800s—and is one of those rare places that permit you to see volcanic energy this close with minimal risk to your safety. Authorities closely monitor Poás's activity following several eruptions in March 2006, the first significant increase in activity since 1994. Access is normally open at this writing, but park officials close the route up here on those occasions of any activity they deem "irregular." *(See page 235 for more information.)*

BEST TIME TO GO

The peak is frequently shrouded in mist, and you might see little beyond the lip of the crater. Be patient and wait awhile, especially if some wind is blowing—the clouds can disappear quickly. Aim to get here before 10 am. The earlier in the day you go, the better.

FUN FACT

Forgot your umbrella? (It gets wet up here.) Duck under a *sombrilla de pobre* (poor man's umbrella) plant. These giant leaves can grow to diameters of 1 to 1½ meters (4 to 5 feet)— plenty big enough to shelter a few hikers caught out in the rain.

BEST WAYS TO EXPLORE

BIRD-WATCHING

Although birding can be a little frustrating here because of cloud and mist, more than 330 bird species call Poás home. One of the most comical birds you'll see in Costa Rica is usually spotted foraging in plain sight on the ground: the big-footed finch whose oversize feet give it a clownish walk. Its cousin, the yellow-thighed finch, is easy to recognize by its bright yellow, er . . . thighs. Arrive early and bird around the gate before the park opens, and stop along the road to the visitor center wherever you see a likely birding area. In the underbrush you may find spotted wood-quail or the elusive, buffy-crowned wood-partridge. The trees along the road are a favorite haunt of both black-and-yellow and long-tailed silky flycatchers.

HIKING

From the summit, two trails head into the forest. The second trail, on the right just before the crater, winds through a thick mesh of shrubs and dwarf trees to the eerie but beautiful Botos Lake (**Laguna Botos**), which occupies an extinct crater. It takes 30 minutes to walk here and back, but you'll be huffing and puffing if you're not used to this altitude, almost 2,743 meters (9,000 feet) above sea level.

VOLCANIC TIPS

A paved road leads all the way from Alajuela to Poás's 2,682-meter (8,800-foot) summit. The 2009 earthquake wrecked the eastern-approach road from Varablanca, so check before you try that route. No one is allowed to venture into the crater or walk along its edge. ■TIP→ **Take periodic breaks from viewing: Step back at least every 10 minutes, so that the sulfur fumes don't overcome you. Be sure to bring a sweater or a jacket—it can be surprisingly chilly up here.**

TOP REASONS TO GO

A+ FACILITIES

You're on your own in many Costa Rican national parks, which have little by way of facilities. This park is a pleasant exception, with an attractive visitor center containing exhibits, cafeteria, gift shop, and restrooms.

LAVA AND ASH

"Up close and personal with nature" takes on a whole new meaning here. Costa Rica forms part of the Pacific Rim's so-called "Ring of Fire," and a visit to the volcano's summit gives you a close-up view of a region of the earth that is still in formation.

LOCATION, LOCATION, LOCATION

Poás's proximity to San José, the western Central Valley, and many destinations in this chapter makes it an easy half-day trip. Mix and match a volcano visit with several other area attractions.

MORE THAN A VOLCANO

The park is not just about its namesake volcano. A few kilometers of hiking trails wind around the summit and let you take in the cloud forest's lichens, ferns, and bromeliads.

ECO-LODGES IN THE NORTHERN PLAINS

This territory as a whole doesn't garner the attention in eco-circles that other parts of Costa Rica do, but the country has a no more diverse region than the Northern Plains.

Cloud forests, rain forests, volcanoes, thermal springs, white-water rivers, waterfalls, coffee and banana plantations, and rolling farmland combine to create the vast landscape that stretches across the northern third of Costa Rica. That translates into a variety of environmentally themed pursuits unmatched anywhere else in the country. The mists of Monteverde define *cloud forest*, and the original Quaker settlers stamped their environmental consciousness on the area. La Fortuna and environs have parlayed the presence of the nearby Arenal Volcano into myriad activities. The Sarapiquí region is one of the lesser-known (but no less impressive) rainforest regions with a growing selection of small lodges. (And don't forget that this region gave Costa Rica the zip-line canopy tour, one of its best-known and most popular tourist activities.) The tourist industry up here knows what the region has to offer and is keen to preserve what is green. Hotel owners and tour operators are just as eager to show it off to you.

GOOD PRACTICES

Consider public or semi-public transportation for negotiating the Northern Plains. No question: distances are vast, and your own wheels *do* offer you the greatest convenience. It's surprisingly easy, though, to take shuttle transport, base yourself in Arenal or Monteverde, and use occasional taxis to get around once you arrive. Many tour operators in both places are happy to pick you up at your hotel, too.

Also, ask if your hotel recycles. In Monteverde, the answer will usually be yes, but it'll be less likely in other places. If enough guests keep requesting it, more lodgings just might hop on the eco-bandwagon.

TOP ECO-LODGES IN THE NORTHERN PLAINS

ARCO IRIS LODGE, MONTEVERDE

The German management here eschews the overused word "ecotourism," insisting that many in Costa Rica view the concept as simply e¢otouri$m. But if any lodging were entitled to use the term in its marketing, it would be this one. Comfortable cabins are scattered around the grounds here, and though you're right in the center of town, Arco Iris has managed to create a country feel. That, along with the organic foods, active recycling program, biodegradable materials, and involvement in the community, makes this one of our favorite Costa Rican eco-lodges—even if it doesn't call itself that. *(Full hotel review on page 229.)*

LAGUNA DEL LAGARTO LODGE, CIUDAD QUESADA

It doesn't get mentioned in the pantheon of better-known Costa Rican eco-lodges, but this smallish property near the Nicaraguan border offers a variety of nature-theme activities to rival any of the big guys. Accommodation is rustic in this remote locale, but impact on the environment has been minimal. The 1,250-acre rain forest here makes for terrific bird-watching, hiking, and canoeing. Laguna del Lagarto gives back to its community, and has succeeded in bringing employment to a poorer, often forgotten corner of Costa Rica. *(Full hotel review on page 198.)*

LA SELVA, PUERTO VIEJO DE SARAPIQUÍ

You would expect any lodging that functions as a working biological station and where research biologists make up the primary clientele to be eco-friendly. La Selva does not disappoint. The Durham, North Carolina–based Organization for Tropical Studies operates the facility along with two other similar stations in Costa Rica, and offers a fascinating program of nature-theme activities for you, the nonprofessional guest. Keep one caveat in mind, though: scientists take priority in procuring space in the rustic but comfortable cabins. *(Full hotel review on page 246.)*

PLANTING TREES

"Costa Rica" equals "forest" in the minds of most visitors. Truth be told, about half the country has been deforested, much of it occurring in this region. The reasons are mostly understandable: coffee, bananas, and dairy cattle make the Northern Plains the country's breadbasket; for decades, trees have been cleared for farmland. Enter the *A Que Sembrás un Árbol* program. Loosely translated, that means "May you plant a tree." It forms part of the United Nations' international Planting for the Planet program, whose goal is to plant 3.5 billion trees worldwide each year. Costa Rica's contribution to the agenda aims for an annual figure of 7 million trees, around one-third of which are targeted for this region.

Like most environmental initiatives here, the program began at the grassroots level, with area students kicking off the tree planting, soliciting support from area businesses, and petitioning the government to become officially involved.

THE NORTHERN PLAINS

By Jeffrey Van Fleet

The vast expanse that locals call the Zona Norte (Northern Zone) packs in more variety of activities than any other part of the country. You'll find almost everything in this region that Costa Rica has to offer, except beaches, of course.

Spend any amount of time here and you can partake of—take a deep breath—volcano viewing, horseback riding, canoeing, kayaking, rafting, rappelling, windsurfing, kitesurfing, wildlife-viewing, bird-watching, bungee jumping, shopping, cloud and rain-forest hiking, swimming, and hot-springs soaking. The zip-line canopy tour deserves special mention. The activity was invented in Costa Rica and has spread to all corners of the planet. Zipping along cables from platform to platform high in the trees has become Costa Rica's signature adventure activity.

We'd argue that those myriad activities make the Northern Plains Costa Rica's most kid-friendly region. Young children especially will "ooh" (and "eeewwww") at various area animal exhibits devoted to bats (Monteverde, La Virgen de Sarapiquí), frogs (Monteverde, Braulio Carrillo National Park, La Virgen de Sarapiquí, La Paz Waterfall Gardens), butterflies (Monteverde, La Fortuna, La Paz Waterfall Gardens), hummingbirds (Monteverde, La Paz Waterfall Gardens), felines (La Paz Waterfall Gardens), and snakes (Grecia, Monteverde, La Virgen de Sarapiquí, La Paz Waterfall Gardens). Guided nature hikes abound; shorter treks can be entertaining and cater to younger ones' shorter attention spans. Most sure-footed and confident teenagers can participate in adult activities. We recommend white-water rafting and canopy tours.

A few operators around here will tell you that kids older than eight can participate in canopy tours. We're skeptical of such claims, even if their brochures show children happily zipping from platform to platform. The gondolalike trams (Braulio Carrillo National Park, Monteverde) are far safer ways to see the rain-forest canopy.

Most of those activities do go on rain or shine, so don't feel you have to avoid a rainy-season visit here. During the wet months, it's almost a given that you'll get a bit damp on your canopy tour, hike, or horse-back ride, and most tour operators provide ponchos. But to avoid a thorough soaking, plan activities for the morning. Rains usually begin around 2 pm, like clockwork, from July through December, although they can be more prolonged in September and October. The clearest time of day is normally before 8 am.

We frequently overhear comments such as "I didn't know it would be so rainy in the rain forest." You heard it here first: that's why they call it the rain forest! During the rainy season it's not unusual for it to rain for several days straight, and even during the dry season, brief showers will come up without notice. Be sure to bring a poncho or rain jacket and waterproof footwear.

PLANNING

WHEN TO GO
HIGH SEASON: MID-DECEMBER TO APRIL

Climate is difficult to pinpoint in this vast region. The Northern Plains links the rainier Caribbean in the east to drier Guanacaste in the west. Precipitation generally decreases from east to west. Grecia, Sarchí, and San Ramón enjoy a climate similar to Costa Rica's higher-elevation Central Valley, with a well-defined dry season. Monteverde has a significantly different climate: it's cool, damp, and breezy much of the time, with high winds in January and February. Elsewhere, rain can occur outside the official wet season since the area's low elevation frequently hosts battles between competing weather fronts. Visibility changes daily (and hourly), so your chances of seeing the Arenal and Poás volcano craters are more or less the same year-round, though you may have more luck from February to April, the hottest and driest time of the year.

LOW SEASON: JUNE TO MID-NOVEMBER

Throughout the entire region, the warm and humid rainy season normally lasts from June to December. Many places in Arenal and Monteverde are beginning to impose high-season rates in July and August to correspond with prime North American and European vacation times.

SHOULDER SEASON: MAY TO JUNE

The wet season just starts to kick in by May, but rarely to a degree that will interfere with your travels. A little precipitation provides a welcome clearing and freshness of the air in the countryside.

GETTING HERE AND AROUND

Nature Air has daily flights from its own airport in San José to La Fortuna (FTN). Most travelers to this region fly into San José's Aeropuerto Internacional Juan Santamaría or Liberia's Daniel Oduber Airport. Monteverde and Arenal are equidistant from both. Base your choice of airport on which other areas in Costa Rica you plan to visit in addition to this one.

Buses in this region are typically large, clean, and fairly comfortable, but often crowded Friday through Sunday. Don't expect air-conditioning. Service tends toward the agonizingly slow: even supposedly express buses marked *directo* (direct) often make numerous stops.

Road access to the northwest is by way of the paved two-lane Pan-American Highway, which starts from the west end of Paseo Colón in San José and runs northwest to Peñas Blancas at the Nicaraguan border. Turn north at Naranjo or San Ramón for La Fortuna; at Lagarto for Monteverde; and at Cañas for Tilarán. Calle 3 heading north from downtown San José becomes the Braulio Carrillo Highway and provides the best access to Puerto Viejo de Sarapiquí and environs.

GETTING AROUND

This region manages to mix some of the country's smoothest highways with some of its most horrendous roads. (The various roads to Monteverde are legendary in the latter regard, but the final destination makes it worth the trip.) Four-wheel-drive vehicles are best on the frequently potholed roads. If you don't want to pay for 4WD, at least rent a car with high clearance. (Many rental agencies insist you take a 4WD vehicle if you mention Monteverde as part of your itinerary.) You'll encounter frequent one-lane bridges; if the triangular "CEDA EL PASO" faces you, yield to oncoming traffic. Driving in this region can be slow going if you get behind a large truck transporting sugarcane. As the north is prime sugar country, they ply the highways up here.

It is possible to rent a car in La Fortuna, but for a far better selection, most visitors pick up their rental vehicles in San José or Liberia.

HEALTH AND SAFETY

This region is Costa Rica's capital of adventure tourism—it gave birth to the canopy tour—so any risks up here are far more likely to be natural than criminal. Before you set out rafting, zip-lining, rappelling, or bungee jumping, be brutally frank with yourself about your abilities, your physical condition, and your fear levels. (It's almost impossible to turn back on many excursions once you've started.) Even an activity as innocuous as hiking or horseback riding poses a certain amount of risk, and you should never go alone. Nature here is not an amusement park. As Dorothy says in *The Wizard of Oz,* "Toto, I don't think we're in Kansas anymore."

Remember also that little government oversight over adventure tourism exists here. Pay close attention during any safety briefings and orientation. Don't be afraid to ask questions, and don't be afraid to walk away if something seems off to you.

MONEY MATTERS

The days of nonexistent ATMs out here are, fortunately, over. Yet outside the centers of Monteverde, La Fortuna, Tilarán, San Ramón, and Puerto Viejo de Sarapquí, machines are still few and far between. Stock up on cash when you get a chance.

RESTAURANTS

You'll never go hungry in this region. The north is the country's bread-basket, and the hotels and restaurants out here make use of the bounty to whip up the best in *típico* Costa Rican cuisine.

Prices in the reviews are the average cost of a main course at dinner or, if dinner is not served, at lunch.

HOTELS

A few sumptuous resorts hold court in northern Costa Rica, but this region is largely the province of smaller, nature-themed lodgings that invite you to partake of all their eco-activities, and offer good value for the money.

Prices in the reviews are the lowest cost of a standard double room in high season.

TIMING

Although not centrally located, the Northern Plains can be easily tacked onto stays in other regions of Costa Rica. Fairly decent—decent for Costa Rica, that is—transportation links the region to San José, the Central Valley, and the North Pacific. (Always the exception, Monteverde sits isolated, approached only by rugged roads from all directions.)

If your stay here is limited to two or three days, make La Fortuna your base. Don't miss the volcano, the Tabacón Hot Springs, or a day trip to the Caño Negro Wildlife Refuge.

Most tour operators who have volcano hikes end the day at one of the various thermal springs in the area. "Half-day" tours to Caño Negro actually take most of a day, from around 7:30 am to 4 pm.

A week in the Northern Plains is more than enough time to experience a great deal of this area—especially if you're longing to get out and get moving. Give yourself four days in La Fortuna/Arenal, a great base for exploring the region. Devote the rest of your week to Monteverde Cloud Forest.

Driving yourself between Monteverde and Arenal means negotiating some pretty horrendous roads. Tour operators can arrange for boat or even horse transfers.

NORTHWEST OF SAN JOSÉ

The rolling countryside northwest of San José and west of Alajuela holds a mix of coffee, sugarcane, and pasture, with tropical forest filling steep river valleys and ravines. The Pan-American Highway makes a steady descent to the Pacific coast through this region, which is also traversed by older roads that wind their way between simple agricultural towns and past small farms and pastoral scenery. West of San Ramón the valley becomes narrow and precipitous as the topography slopes down to the Pacific lowlands. An even narrower valley snakes northward from San Ramón to the northern lowlands beyond.

GRECIA

26 km/16 miles (45 mins) northwest of Alajuela, 46 km/29 miles (1 hr) northwest of San José.

The quiet farming community of Grecia is reputed to be Costa Rica's cleanest town—some enthusiastic civic boosters extend that superlative to all Latin America—but the reason most people stop here is to admire its unusual church.

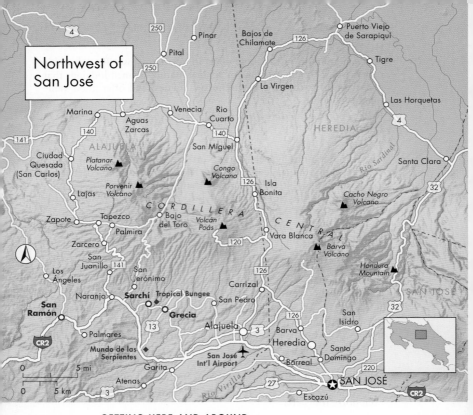

GETTING HERE AND AROUND

From San José continue west on the highway past the airport—the turnoff is on the right—or head into Alajuela and turn left just before the Alajuela cemetery. Buses leave Calle 20 in San José for Grecia every 30 minutes from 5:30 am to 10 pm. From Alajuela, buses to Grecia/Ciudad Quesada pick up on the southern edge of town (Calle 4 and Avenida 10).

ESSENTIALS

Bank/ATM BAC San José ⊠ *100 m north of central park.*
Banco Nacional ⊠ *Northwest corner of Central Plaza* ☎ *2494-3600.*

EXPLORING

Church of Our Lady of Mercy. The brick red, prefabricated iron Church of Our Lady of Mercy (Iglesia de las Mercedes) was one of two buildings in the country made from steel frames imported from Belgium in the 1890s (the other is the metal schoolhouse next to San José's Parque Morazán), when some prominent Costa Ricans decided that metal structures would better withstand the periodic earthquakes that had taken their toll on so much of the country's architecture. The frames were shipped from Antwerp to Limón, then transported by train to Alajuela—from which the walls of the church were carried by oxcarts. Although the park fronting the church is a Wi-Fi hotspot, we advise against pulling out your laptop in such a public setting (though your Wi-Fi-equipped smartphone should be okay to use here.) ✉ *Avda. 1, Cs. 1–3* ☎ *2494–1616* ⏲ *Daily 8–4.*

World of Snakes. On a small farm outside Grecia, the World of Snakes (Mundo de las Serpientes) is a good place to see some of the snakes that you are unlikely—and probably don't want—to spot in the wild. Sequestered in the safety of cages here are some 50 varieties of serpents, as well as crocodiles, iguanas, poison dart frogs, and various other cold-blooded creatures. Admission includes a 90-minute tour. ✉ *Poro, 2 km/1 mile east of Grecia, on road to Alajuela* ☎ *2494–3700* 🌐 *www.theworldofsnakes.com* 🎟 *$11* ⏲ *Daily 8–4.*

PAINTED OXCARTS

Coffee has come to symbolize the prosperity of the Central Valley and the nation. Nineteenth-century coffee farmers needed a way to transport this all-important cash crop to the port of Puntarenas on the Pacific coast. Enter the oxcart. Artisans began painting the carts in the early 1900s. Debate continues as to why: the kaleidoscopic designs may have symbolized the points of the compass, or may have echoed the landscape's tropical colors. In any case, the oxcart has become the national symbol. Give way when you see one out on a country road, and marvel at the sight.

OUTDOOR ACTIVITIES

BUNGEE JUMPING

A 79-meter-tall (265-foot-tall) bridge that spans a forested gorge over the Río Colorado is the perfect place to get a rush of adrenaline in a tranquil, tropical setting. Even if you aren't up for the plunge, it's worth stopping to watch a few mad souls do it.

Tropical Bungee. Tropical Bungee organizes trips to the bridge. The first jump is $75 and the second is $35. Transportation is free if you jump; $10 if you don't. Reservations are essential. If this is your last hurrah in Costa Rica, a van can take you and your bags straight to the San José airport after your jump. ✉ *Pan-American Hwy., 2 km/1 mile west of turnoff for Grecia, down a dirt road on the right* ☎ *2248–2212 in San José, 8980–5757* 🌐 *www.bungee.co.cr* ⏲ *Daily 8–11:30 and 1–4.*

WHERE TO STAY

For expanded hotel reviews, visit Fodors.com.

$$ B&B/INN Fodor's Choice ★ **Vista del Valle Plantation Inn.** Honeymooners (and many posters to Fodors.com) frequent this bed-and-breakfast on an orange and coffee plantation outside Grecia overlooking the canyon of the Río Grande. **Pros:** attentive staff; secluded cabins; healthful food served. **Cons:** a car is necessary for staying here. **TripAdvisor:** "a great place to wind down," "so beautiful," "hidden gem." [$] *Rooms from: $100* ✉ *On hwy. 1 km/½ mile west of Rafael Iglesia Bridge; follow signs* ☎ *2451–1165* 🌐 *www.vistadelvalle.com* 🛏 *17 cottages* 🍴 *Breakfast.*

SARCHÍ

8 km/5 miles west of Grecia, 53 km/33 miles (1½ hrs) northwest of San José.

Tranquil Sarchí is Costa Rica's premier center for crafts and carpentry. People drive here from all over the country to shop for furniture, and tour buses regularly descend upon the souvenir shops outside town. The area's most famous products are its brightly painted oxcarts—replicas of those traditionally used to transport coffee.

GETTING HERE AND AROUND

To get to Sarchí from San José, take the highway well past the airport to the turnoff for Naranjo; then veer right just as you enter Naranjo. Direct buses to Sarchí depart from Alajuela (⊠ *C. 8 between Avdas. 1 and 3*) every 30 minutes 6 am to 9 pm; the ride takes 90 minutes.

ESSENTIALS

Bank/ATM Banco Nacional ⊠ *South side of soccer field* ☎ *2454-3044.*

Post Office Correos ⊠ *50 m west of central plaza.*

EXPLORING

Eloy Alfaro and Sons Workshop (*Taller Eloy Alfaro e Hijos*). Costa Rica's only real oxcart factory left, Eloy Alfaro and Sons Workshop, was founded in 1920, and its carpentry methods have changed little since then, although the "e Hijos" portion of the family (the sons and grandchildren) run the operation these days. The two-story wooden building housing the wood shop is surrounded by trees and flowers—mostly orchids—and all the machinery on the ground floor is powered by a waterwheel at the back of the shop. Carts are painted in the back, and although the factory's main product is a genuine oxcart—which sells for about $2,000—there are also some smaller mementos that can easily be shipped home. ⊠ *200 m north of soccer field* ☎ *2454-4131* ⊕ *www. fabricadecarretaseloyalfaro.com* ☉ *Weekdays 8–4.*

Else Kientzler Botanical Garden (*Jardín Botánico Else Kientzler*). If you enjoy plants, the Else Kientzler Botanical Garden is well worth a break from your shopping. The site exhibits some 2,000 plant species, tropical and subtropical, over its sprawling 17 acres. The German owner named the facility, affiliated with an ornamental-plant exporter, after his late plant-loving mother. About half of the garden's pathways are wheelchair accessible. The services of a guide cost an extra $25 for groups up to 15 people. ⊠ *800 m north of soccer field* ☎ *2454-2070* ☜ *$13* ☉ *Daily 8–4.*

Parque Central. Sarchí's Parque Central resembles the central park of any other Costa Rican small town—the facade of its church is frequently compared to a wedding cake—but the park's real attraction is the world's largest oxcart, constructed and brightly painted by longtime local factory Taller Eloy Alfaro e Hijos and enshrined in the *Guinness Book of World Records*. The work logs in at 18 meters (45 feet) and weighs 2 tons. Since no other country is attached to oxcarts quite the way Costa Rica is, we don't look for that record to be broken anytime soon. ⊠ *Center of Sarchí.*

SHOPPING

Sarchí is the best place in Costa Rica to buy miniature oxcarts, the larger of which are designed to serve as patio bars or end tables and can be broken down for easy transport or shipped to your home. Another popular item is a locally produced rocking chair with a leather seat and back.

Fodor's Choice ★ **Chaverrí Oxcart Factory** (*Fábrica de Carretas*). The nicest of the many stores south of town is the Chaverrí Oxcart Factory, and you can wander through the workshops in back to see the artisans in action. (Despite the name, much more is for sale here than oxcarts.) Chaverri is a good place to buy wooden crafts; nonwood products are cheaper in San José. ⊠ *Main road, 2 km/1 mile south of Sarchí* ☎ *2454–4411* ⊕ *www. sarchicostarica.net.*

Las Carretas. Chaverri also runs a restaurant next door, Las Carretas, which serves a variety of local food all day until 6 pm and has a good lunch buffet. ☎ *2454–4411* ⊕ *www.sarchicostarica.net.*

Plaza de la Artesanía. Sarchí's answer to a shopping mall, the Plaza de la Artesanía gathers 34 artisan and souvenir shops under one roof. If you can't find it here, it probably doesn't exist. ⊠ *2 km/1 mile south of Sarchí* ☎ *2454–3430.*

SAN RAMÓN

23 km/14 miles west of Sarchí, 59 km/37 miles (1½ hrs) northwest of San José.

San Ramón hides its real attractions in the countryside to the north, on the road to La Fortuna, where comfortable lodges offer access to private nature preserves. There's not much to see in San Ramón other than its church.

GETTING HERE AND AROUND

San Ramón is on the Pan-American Highway west of Grecia. To reach the hotel we list north of town, head straight through San Ramón and follow the signs. Buses leave hourly for San Ramón from San José's Terminal de Puntarenas. From Alajuela, buses to San Ramón/Ciudad Quesada pick up on the southern edge of town (⊠ *C. 4 and Avda. 10*).

ESSENTIALS

Bank/ATM HSBC ⊠ *150 m north of Palí supermarket* ☎ *2445–3602.*
Scotiabank ⊠ *Pan-American Hwy., entrance to San Ramón* ☎ *2447–9190.*

Internet Cybercafé San Ramón ⊠ *100 m east of Banco Central* ☎ *2447–9007.*

EXPLORING

Church of San Ramón. Aside from its poets, the massive Church of San Ramón (Iglesia de San Ramón), built in a mixture of the Romanesque and Gothic styles, is the city's claim to fame. In 1924 an earthquake destroyed the smaller adobe church that once stood here, and the city lost no time in creating a replacement—this great gray concrete structure took a quarter of a century to complete, from 1925 to 1954. To ensure that the second church would be earthquake-proof, workers poured the concrete around a steel frame that was designed and forged

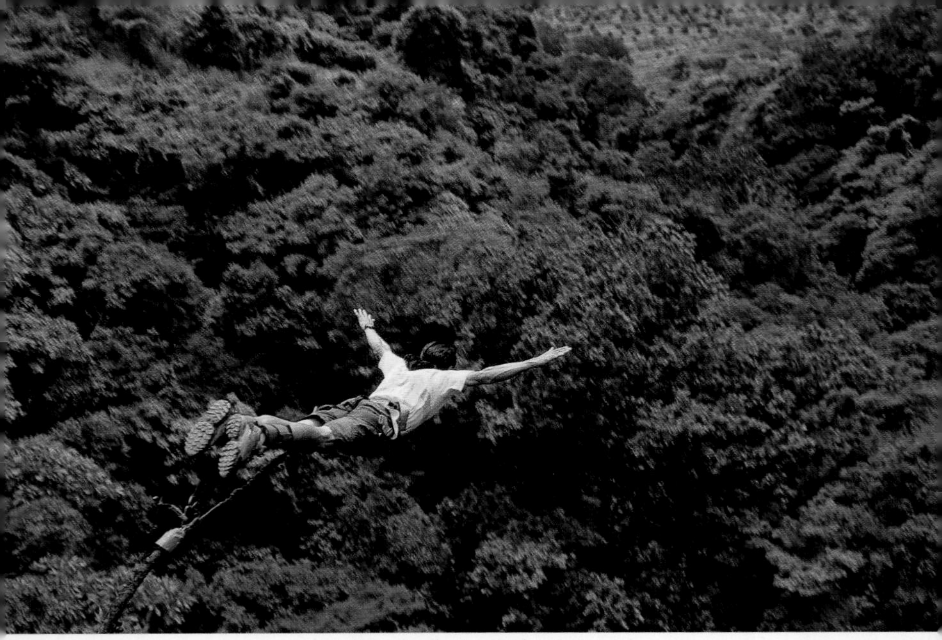

Taking the plunge. Bungee jumping at the Colorado River Bridge, Grecia.

in Germany (by Krupp). Step past the formidable facade and you'll discover a bright, elegant interior. ✉ *Across from Parque Central* ☎ *2445–5592* ⏲ *Daily 6–11:30 am and 1:30–7 pm.*

WHERE TO EAT AND STAY

For expanded hotel reviews, visit Fodors.com.

$$$ ★ 🏨 **Villa Blanca.** This charming country hotel is on a working dairy and coffee farm constructed and once owned by former Costa Rican president Rodrigo Carazo. **Pros:** attentive service; many activities; secluded location. **Cons:** far from sights; need a car to stay here. **TripAdvisor:** "great place for relaxation," "rustic and remote," "excellent meals." [$] *Rooms from: $189* ✉ *20 km/12 miles north of San Ramón on road to La Fortuna* ☎ *2461–0300, 877/256–8399 in North America* 🌐 *www.villablancacr.com* 🛏 *34 casitas* 🍴 *Breakfast.*

EN ROUTE

Zarcero. The small town of Zarcero, 15 km (9 miles) north of Sarchí on the road to Ciudad Quesada, looks as if it was designed by Dr. Seuss. Evangelisto Blanco, a local landscape artist, modeled cypress topiaries in fanciful animal shapes—motorcycle-riding monkeys, a lightbulb-eyed elephant—that enliven the park in front of the town church. The church interior is covered with elaborate pastel stencil work and detailed religious paintings by the late Misael Solís, a well-known local artist. Sample some cheese if you're in town, too; Zarcero-made cheese is one of Costa Rica's favorites. The town is frequently included as a short stop on many organized tours heading to this region of the country. ✉ *Zarcero.*

THE ARENAL VOLCANO

Whether you come here from San José or Liberia, prepare yourself for some spectacular scenery—and a bumpy ride. As you bounce along on your way to Arenal, you may discover that "paved" means different things in different places, and that potholes are numerous. Any discomfort you experience is more than made up for by the swaths of misty rain forest and dramatic expanses of the Cordillera Central. Schedule at least 3½ hours for the trip.

CIUDAD QUESADA (SAN CARLOS)

55 km/33 miles (1 hr) northwest of Zarcero.

Highway signs point you to "Ciudad Quesada," but this friendly hub city is simply "San Carlos" in local parlance. Like so many other places in Costa Rica, the landscape is splendid, but what passes for architecture varies from ordinary to downright hideous. San Carlos is where everyone in the region comes to shop, take in a movie, get medical care, and generally take care of the necessities. There's also an enormous bus terminal (with shopping center and multiplex movie theater) where you can make connections to almost anywhere in the northern half of the country. If you're traveling from San José to points north, your bus will stop here even if it's a so-called express. This lively mountain market town–provincial capital serves a fertile dairy region and is worth a stop for a soak in the soothing thermal waters in the area.

GETTING HERE AND AROUND

Ciudad Quesada lies 55 km (33 miles) off the Pan-American Highway north of Zarcero. Buses from San José leave Terminal Atlántico Norte on the hour, from 5 am to 7 pm. The trip takes around three hours. The Ciudad Quesada bus terminal is a couple of kilometers from the center of town; taxis wait at the terminal to take you into town. Driving is straightforward in this part of the country, as long as you don't get stuck behind a slow-moving truck transporting sugarcane to the Central Valley. Try to get an early start if you're driving yourself; the road between Zarcero and Ciudad Quesada begins to fog over by early afternoon.

ESSENTIALS

Bank/ATM BAC San José ✉ *100 m north and 125 m west of cathedral.*
Banco Nacional ✉ *Across from north side of cathedral* ☎ *2401–2000.*
Scotiabank ✉ *Across from Mercado de Artesanía* ☎ *2461–9660.*

Internet Internet Café ✉ *150 m north of park* ☎ *2460–3653.*

Medical Assistance Hospital de San Carlos ✉ *2 km/1 mile north of park* ☎ *2460–1176.*

Post Office Correos ✉ *Across from Escuela Chávez.*

Tourism Information Instituto Costarricense de Turismo
✉ *75 m north of Universidad Católica* ☎ *2461–9102* ⊕ *www.ict.go.cr*
⊙ *Weekdays 8–noon and 1–4.*

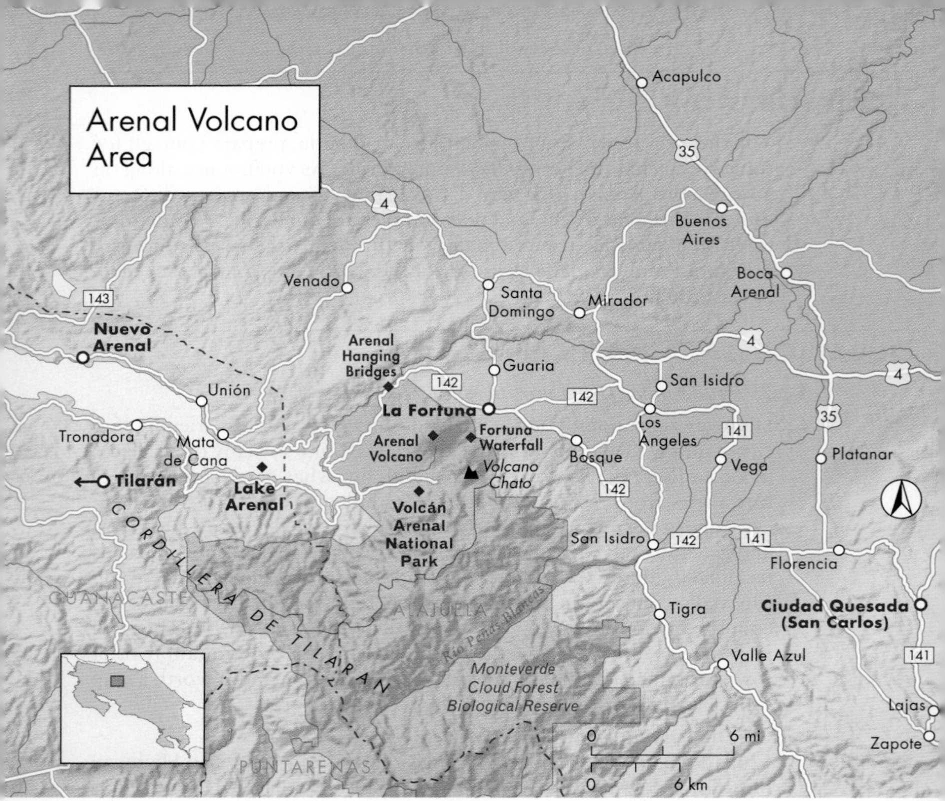
Arenal Volcano Area
Acapulco
35
4
Buenos Aires
Boca Arenal
Venado
Santa Domingo
Mirador
143
Nuevo Arenal
Arenal Hanging Bridges
Guaria
San Isidro
142
Unión
La Fortuna
Los Ángeles
141
Tronadora
Mata de Cana
Arenal Volcano
Fortuna Waterfall
Bosque
Vega
Platanar
Tilarán
Volcano Chato
Lake Arenal
Volcán Arenal National Park
San Isidro
Florencia
CORDILLERA DE TILARAN
GUANACASTE
ALAJUELA
Tigra
Ciudad Quesada (San Carlos)
Río Peñas Blancas
Valle Azul
Monteverde Cloud Forest Biological Reserve
Lajas
Zapote
0
6 mi
0
6 km
PUNTARENAS

EXPLORING

Termales del Bosque. Termales del Bosque lets you soak those tired muscles, as you watch the birds, for a more reasonable price than most of the other hot springs in the region. The Day Pass admission price includes breakfast and/or lunch. ✉ *Hwy. 140, 7 km/4½ miles east of Ciudad Quesada* ☎ *2460–4740* 🌐 *www.termalesdelbosque.com* 🎟 *Day pass $21–$33, hot springs only $12* 🕒 *Daily 8 am–10 pm.*

WHERE TO STAY

For expanded hotel reviews, visit Fodors.com.

$ ★ 🏨 **Laguna del Lagarto Lodge.** One of Costa Rica's smaller and more remote eco-lodges sits in a 1,250-acre rain forest near the Nicaraguan border and gives shelter to 380 bird species and counting. **Pros:** small size; attentive service; great excursions. **Cons:** rough road to get here; spartan rooms. **TripAdvisor:** "a nice place in the rainforest," "birds all over the place," "a naturalist's fantasy come true." [$] *Rooms from: $62* ✉ *7 km/4 miles north of Boca Tapada, 135 km/78 miles northeast of Ciudad Quesada* ☎ *2289–8163 in San José* 🌐 *www.lagarto-lodge-costa-rica.com* 🛏 *20 rooms, 18 with bath* 🍴 *No meals.*

LA FORTUNA

50 km/30 miles (45 mins) northwest of Ciudad Quesada, 75 km/45 miles (90 mins) north of San Ramón, 17 km/11 miles east of Arenal Volcano, 190 km/118 miles (3 hrs by car; 25 mins by plane) northwest of San José.

As they say, "Location, location, location." Who would think that a small town sitting at the foot of massive Arenal Volcano would attract visitors from around the world? Nobody comes to La Fortuna—an ever-expanding mass of hotels, tour operators, souvenir shops, and *sodas* (small, family-run restaurants)—to see the town itself.

> **CAUTION**
>
> The ubiquitous "Official Tourist Information" signs around La Fortuna and Monteverde aren't "official" at all, but are merely storefront travel agencies and tour operators hoping to sell you tours.

Instead, thousands of tourists flock here each year to use it as a hub for visiting the natural wonders that surround it. The volcano, as well as waterfalls, vast nature preserves, great rafting rivers, and an astonishing array of birds, are to be found within an hour or less of your hotel. La Fortuna is also the best place to arrange trips to the Caño Negro National Wildlife Refuge (⇨ *below*).

After the 1968 eruption of Arenal Volcano, La Fortuna was transformed from a tiny, dusty farm town to one of Costa Rica's tourism powerhouses, where visitors converge to see the volcano in action. Volcano viewing can be hit or miss, though, especially during the rainy season (May through November). One minute Arenal looms menacingly over the village; the next minute clouds shroud its cone. Early morning, especially in the dry season, is always the best time to catch a longer gaze.

NAVIGATING LA FORTUNA
Taxis in and around La Fortuna are relatively cheap, and will take you anywhere; a taxi to the Tabacón resort should run about $15. Get a cab at the stand on the east side of Parque Central.

GETTING HERE AND AROUND

Choose from two routes from San José: for a slightly longer, but better road, leave the Pan-American Highway at Naranjo, continuing north to Zarcero and Ciudad Quesada. Head northwest at Ciudad Quesada to La Fortuna; or for a curvier but shorter route, continue beyond Naranjo on the Pan-American Highway, turning north at San Ramón, arriving at La Fortuna about 90 minutes after the turnoff. Either route passes through a mountainous section that begins to fog over by afternoon. Get as early a start as possible. Nature Air flies daily to La Fortuna (FTN); flights land at an airstrip at the hamlet of El Tanque, 7 km (4 miles) east of town. Van transport ($5 one-way) meets each flight to take you into La Fortuna.

Gray Line has daily shuttle bus service between San José, La Fortuna, and Arenal ($44), and Monteverde ($35). Interbus also connects San José with La Fortuna and Monteverde (each $45) daily, with connections from here to a few of the North Pacific beaches. Public buses depart five times daily from San José's Terminal Atlántico Norte. Travel time is four hours. Although billed as an express route, the bus makes many stops.

"Our best day in Costa Rica—canyoneering and waterfall rappelling near the active Arenal Volcano." —Photo by sportster, Fodors.com member

Desafío Adventures provides a fast, popular three-hour transfer between Monteverde and La Fortuna via taxi, boat, then another taxi, for $29 each way.

ESSENTIALS

Bank/ATM BAC San José ✉ *75 m north of gas station.*
Banco de Costa Rica ✉ *Money exchange booth; across from south side of church.* **Banco Nacional** ✉ *Central Plaza* ☎ *2479–9355.*

Bus Contacts Gray Line Tourist Bus ☎ *2220–2126.*
Interbus ☎ *2283–5573* ⊕ *www.interbusonline.com.*

Internet Expediciones Fortuna ✉ *Across the street from Central Plaza* ☎ *2479–9104.*

Medical Clinic Seguro Social ✉ *300 m east of Parque Central* ☎ *2479–9643.*

Pharmacy FarmaTodo ✉ *50 m north of La Fortuna's gas station* ☎ *2479–8155.*

Post Office Correos ✉ *Across from north side of church.*

Rental Cars Alamo ✉ *100 m west of church* ☎ *2479–9090*
⊕ *www.alamocostarica.com.* **Mapache** ✉ *800 m west of church* ☎ *2479–0010*
⊕ *www.mapache.com.*

EXPLORING
TOP ATTRACTIONS

Arenal Hanging Bridges. Arenal Hanging Bridges is actually a series of trails and bridges that form a loop through the primary rain forest of a 250-acre private reserve, with great bird-watching and volcano viewing. Fixed and hanging bridges allow you to see the forest at different

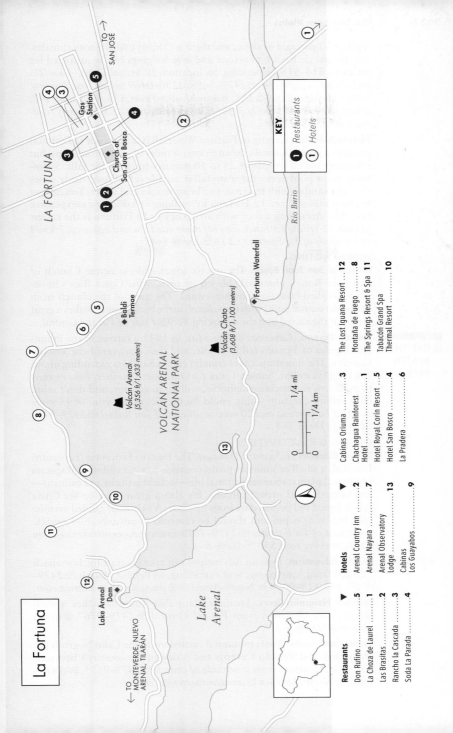

La Fortuna

KEY

● 1 Restaurants

● 1 Hotels

TO SAN JOSÉ →

LA FORTUNA

Gas Station

Church of San Juan Bosco

Río Burio

♦ Fortuna Waterfall

♦ Baldi Termae

VOLCÁN ARENAL NATIONAL PARK

▲ Volcán Arenal (5,356 ft/1,633 meters)

Volcán Chato (3,608 ft/1,100 meters)

♦ Lake Arenal Dam

Lake Arenal

← TO MONTEVERDE, NUEVO ARENAL, TILARÁN

1/4 mi

1/4 km

0

0

Restaurants ▼

Don Rufino 5
La Choza de Laurel 1
Las Brasitas 2
Rancho la Cascada 3
Soda La Parada 4

Hotels ▼

Arenal Country Inn 2
Arenal Nayara 7
Arenal Observatory
  Lodge 13
Cabinas
  Los Guayabos 9

Cabinas Oriuma 3
Chachagua Rainforest
  Hotel 1
Hotel Royal Corin Resort . 5
Hotel San Bosco 4
La Pradera 6

The Lost Iguana Resort .. 12
Montaña de Fuego 8
The Springs Resort & Spa . 11
Tabacón Grand Spa
  Thermal Resort 10

levels. It's open rain or shine, and there are things to do in both climates. Shuttle service from La Fortuna and area lodgings can be arranged for an extra $14–$18, depending on location. ⊠ *Arenal Dam, 4 km/2½ miles west of Tabacón* ☎ *2479–9686, 2290–0469 in San José* ⊕ *www. hangingbridges.com* ≊ *$24, natural history tour $36, bird tour $47, shuttle $14–$18* ☉ *Daily 7:30–4:30; evening tour at 5:30, early birding tour at 6 am.*

Fodor's Choice
★

Fortuna Waterfall. Getting to Fortuna Waterfall (Cataratas de la Fortuna) requires a strenuous walk down ½ km (¼ mile) of precipitous steps, but it's worth the effort. Allow 25 to 50 minutes to reach the falls. Swimming in the pool under the waterfall is usually safe. Wear sturdy shoes or water sandals with traction, and bring snacks and water. You can get to the trailhead from La Fortuna by walking or taking an inexpensive taxi ride. Arranging a tour with an agency in La Fortuna is the easiest option. ⊠ *Yellow entrance sign off main road toward volcano, 7 km/4 miles south of La Fortuna* ≊ *$6* ☉ *Daily 8–4.*

WORTH NOTING

Church of San Juan Bosco. The town's squat, pale, concrete Church of San Juan Bosco, unremarkable on its own, wins Costa Rica's most-photographed-house-of-worship award. The view of the church from across the central park, with the volcano in the background, makes a great photo of the sacred and the menacing. ⊠ *West side of Parque Central.*

OFF THE BEATEN PATH

Venado Caverns (*Cavernas de Venado*). In 1945 a farmer in the mountain hamlet of Venado fell in a hole, and thus discovered the Venado Caverns. The limestone caves contain eight chambers extending about 2½ km (1½ miles). Sunset Tours (⇨ *Outdoor Activities, below*) runs trips. If you're nonclaustrophobic, willing to get wet, and don't mind bats—think carefully—this could be the ticket for you. ⊠ *45 mins north of La Fortuna and 20 mins southeast of San Rafael* ☎ *2479–9415* ≊ *$65* ☉ *Daily 7–8.*

OUTDOOR ACTIVITIES

Ⓒ **Danaus Ecocenter** (*Ecocentro Danaus*). The Danaus Ecocenter (Ecocentro Danaus), a small ecotourism project outside town, exhibits 500 species of tropical plants, abundant animal life—including sloths and caimans—and butterfly and orchid gardens. It's also a great place to see Costa Rica's famed red poison dart frogs up close. A two-hour guided evening tour begins at 6 pm and should be reserved in advance. ⊠ *4 km/2½ miles east of La Fortuna* ☎ *2479–7019* ⊕ *www.ecocentrodanaus.com* ≊ *$6, evening tour $30* ☉ *Daily 8–4.*

Fodor's Choice
★

Desafío Adventures. Desafío Adventures can take you rafting, horseback riding, hiking, canyoning, and rappelling. ⊠ *Behind church* ☎ *2479–0020, 855/818–0020 in North America* ⊕ *www.desafiocostarica.com.*

Jacamar Naturalist Tours. Jacamar Naturalist Tours launches a variety of tours. ⊠ *Across from Parque Central* ☎ *2479–9767* ⊕ *www. arenaltours.com.*

Sunset Tours. Sunset Tours pioneered excursions to the Caño Negro Wildlife Refuge and Venado Caverns and is one of the country's best tour operators. ⊠ *Across from south side of church* ☎ *2479–9585, 866/417–7352 in North America* ⊕ *www.sunsettourcr.com.*

CANOPY TOURS

Ecoglide Arenal Park. Ecoglide Arenal Park offers a slight variation on the standard canopy tour by replacing one of the zip lines—15 in all—with a so-called "Tarzan swing." Yes, you swing between two of the platforms, but far more securely than Johnny Weismuller ever did on his vine in the old *Tarzan* movies. As with all zip-line tours in Costa Rica, reservations should be made in advance, but you don't have to adhere to fixed tour starting times. You decide when you'd like to begin. ⊠ *3 km/2 miles west of La Fortuna* ☎ *2479–7120* ⊕ *www.arenalecoglide.com* ✉ *$45* ⊙ *Daily 8–4.*

ADVENTURE ALTERNATIVE

Desafío Adventures. If you're feeling more community-minded than adventurous, Desafío Adventures has a daylong tour ($75) that takes you to an area animal-rescue center, women's arts-and-crafts cooperative, organic medicinal-plant farm, and recycling center. Lunch is included. ⊠ *Behind church* ☎ *2479–0020, 855/818-0020 in North America* ⊕ *www.desafiocostarica.com.*

5

Arenal Volcano Park. This canopy tour–bridge walk–tram complex near La Fortuna, is operated by the Sky Trek–Sky Walk folks in Monteverde. Alpine-style gondolas transport you to the site, from which you can descend via 3 km/2 miles of zip lines, hike through the cloud forest along a series of suspended bridges, or go back the way the came, on the tram. Butterfly and orchid gardens round out the offerings. ⊠ *12 km/7 miles west of La Fortuna, El Castillo* ☎ *2479–9944* ⊕ *www.skyadventures.travel* ✉ *$89 all offerings, $73 tram and zip lines, $61 tram and walk, $42 tram only, $33 walk only, shuttle $10* ⊙ *Daily 7–4.*

FISHING

Lake Arenal is enormous and stocked with game fish, including tilapia, *guapote* (Central American rainbow bass), and *machaca* (Central American shad). Most tour operators and hotels can set you up with guides. Rates begin at $150.

Jacamar Naturalist Tours. Jacamar Naturalist Tours (⇨ *above*) has morning and afternoon sportfishing trips to Lake Arenal and Caño Negro Lagoon.

HORSEBACK RIDING

★ **Desafío Adventures.** If you're interested in getting up to Monteverde from the Arenal–La Fortuna area without taking the grinding four-hour drive, there's an alternative: Desafío Adventures has a five-hour guided horseback trip ($85). The trip involves taxi or van service from La Fortuna to the southern shore of Lake Arenal, and from that trail's end you ride to Monteverde, circumventing poorly maintained trails. A boat ride across Lake Arenal is included. You leave La Fortuna at 8:30 am and arrive in Monteverde around 2:30 pm. You can also take the trip in reverse. Desafío will provide a driver to transport your rental vehicle, but you must arrange to include that driver in your rental agreement. ■TIP➔ Many other agencies—many of them nothing more than a guy and a horse—lead riding tours between La Fortuna and Monteverde, but along treacherous trails, and some riders have returned with stories of terrified horses barely able to navigate the way. Stick with Desafío. ⊠ *Behind church* ☎ *2479–0020, 855/818–0020 in North America* ⊕ *www.desafiocostarica.com.*

Chaves Tours. The ride from La Fortuna to the Fortuna Waterfall is appropriate for both novice and experienced riders. Chaves Tours is one of the most established operators in the area. Its three-hour excursions to the waterfall leaves daily at 8 am and 1 pm. ☎ *8354–9159, 2479–9023* ⊕ *www.horsebackridingarenal.com.*

Desafío. Desafío (⇨ *above*) leads guided horseback tours to the falls and Monteverde.

RAFTING AND KAYAKING

Several La Fortuna operators offer Class III and IV white-water trips on the Río Toro. The narrow river requires the use of special, streamlined boats that seat just four and go very fast. The easier Balsa, Peñas Blancas, Arenal, and San Carlos rivers have Class II and III rapids and are close enough to town that they can be worked into half-day excursions.

Canoa Aventura. Canoa Aventura can design a canoeing trip with ample wildlife viewing on the Río Peñas Blancas and also has daylong canoe tours of the Caño Blanco Wildlife Refuge. Tours are appropriate for beginners, with a selection of easy floats if you're not feeling too adventurous, and instruction is provided, but the folks here can tailor excursions if you're more experienced. ☎ *2479–8200* ⊕ *www.canoa-aventura.com.*

★ **Desafío Adventures.** Desafío Adventures pioneered rafting trips in this region, and has day trips on the Toro and Sarapiquí rivers (both Class III–IV) for experienced rafters ($85) and half-day rafting on the Balsa river (Class II–III) for less-experienced paddlers ($65). Kayaking outings on Lake Arenal ($53) are ideal for beginners, as is a leisurely wildlife-viewing float on the Peñas Blancas ($45). If you're in the mood for something new, Desafío has begun half-day stand-up-paddling excursions on the lake ($65). ⊠ *Behind church* ☎ *2479–0020, 855/818–0020 in North America* ⊕ *www.desafiocostarica.com.*

Flow Trips. Local operator Flow Trips does the standard rafting excursions on the Sarapiquí river (Classes II, III, and IV), as well as kayaking trips on Lake Arenal and the Peñas Blancas river. ⊠ *1 km/½ mile west of La Fortuna* ☎ *2479–0075* ⊕ *www.flowtrips.com.*

RAPPELLING

EN ROUTE

Increased development on the highway between La Fortuna and the Tabacón resort has led to a noticeable increase in traffic. It is hardly the proverbial urban jungle, and it is one of the country's prettiest stretches of road, but you should drive with caution. Cars dart in and out of driveways. Visitors congregate along the side of the road (likely a sloth-

---

CAUTION

What's the newest craze in Monteverde and Arenal? Four-wheel all-terrain vehicles. Seemingly everybody rents them out these days, but we've heard too many reports of rollover accidents and don't recommend them. (They're also noisy, and we object to them on that principle.)

spotting). Drivers gaze up at the volcano that looms over the highway. Keep your eyes on the road.

WHERE TO EAT

$$ | ECLECTIC ✕ **Don Rufino.** The town's most elegant-looking restaurant is really quite informal. The L-shaped bar fronting the main street has become a popular expat and tourist hangout and lends a relaxed air to the place. No need to dress up here: this is La Fortuna, after all. The friendly waitstaff might suggest tilapia in bacon-and-tomato sauce or spinach ricotta to the accompaniment of coconut rice. $ *Average main: $14* ⊠ *Across from gas station* ☎ *2479–9997* ⊕ *www.donrufino.com.*

$ | COSTA RICAN ✕ **La Choza de Laurel.** Tantalizing rotisserie chicken, and pretty cloves of garlic and bunches of onions dangling from the roof draw in passersby to this old favorite, open-air Costa Rican–style restaurant a short walk from the center of town. The place opens early, perfect for a hearty breakfast on your way to the volcano. $ *Average main: $8* ⊠ *300 m northwest of church* ☎ *2479–7063* ⊕ *www.lachozadelaurel.com.*

$ | COSTA RICAN ✕ **Las Brasitas.** Chicken turns over wood on a rotisserie in a brick oven at this pleasant restaurant on the road heading out of town toward the volcano. Try the succulent chicken when it ends up in the tasty fajitas or any of the other ample-size Mexican dishes. Service is good, and you have your choice of three open-air dining areas arranged around a garden. Two are secluded and intimate; the third is less so, being closer to the road. $ *Average main: $8* ⊠ *200 m west of church* ☎ *2479–9819* ⊕ *www.lasbrasitas.com.*

$ | COSTA RICAN ✕ **Rancho la Cascada.** You can't miss its tall, palm-thatch roof in the center of town. The festive upstairs contains a bar, with large TV, neon signs, and flashing lights. Downstairs the spacious dining room—decorated with foreign flags—serves basic, midprice Costa Rican fare. Its location right in the center of town makes it a favorite for tour groups. $ *Average main: $8* ⊠ *Across from northeast corner of Parque Central* ☎ *2479–9145.*

$ | COSTA RICAN ✕ **Soda La Parada.** La Fortuna's only 24-hour eatery does a brisk business day and night, and it's a convenient place to grab a quick, cheap meal, and to stock up on snacks for long bus rides. ("La Parada" refers to the bus stop.) $ *Average main: $5* ⊠ *Across from Parque Central and regional bus stop* ☎ *2479–9547* ⊕ *www.restaurantelaparada.com.*

RICE AND BEANS

"More tico than *gallo pinto*" is an old saying here, but just how Costa Rican is the country's signature dish? Nicaraguans also claim it and the rivalry has led to five *Guinness Book of World Records* bids for the largest batch. Costa Rica captured the first title in 2003, only to have Nicaragua top it a mere 12 days later. Costa Rica recaptured the prize in 2005. In 2008 Nicaragua snatched the title back with a 22,000-dish batch of rice and beans. Costa Rica more than doubled that amount at a March 2009 event with a whopping 50,000 servings, a record that stands at this writing. Nicaragua, it's your serve.

5

WHERE TO STAY

For expanded hotel reviews, visit Fodors.com.

$$
B&B/INN
▦ **Arenal Country Inn.** It doesn't quite approximate an English country inn, although this place on the south end of town is still charming. **Pros:** good value; friendly staff. **Cons:** several blocks from center of town; removed from sights. **TripAdvisor:** "very quaint," "old-fashioned hotel in beautiful setting," "super-friendly staff." $ *Rooms from: $103* ✉ *1 km/½ mile south of church of La Fortuna, south end of town* ☎ *2479–9670, 2283–0101 in San José* ⊕ *www.arenalcountryinn.com* ↪ *20 rooms* ⦿ *Breakfast.*

$$$
RESORT
▦ **Arenal Nayara.** This upscale lodge has expansive grounds scattered with cabins, all strategically aligned to provide balcony views of the volcano. **Pros:** luxurious rooms; great volcano views; good restaurant. **Cons:** massive grounds navigable only by golf-cart shuttles; can be difficult to find. **TripAdvisor:** "romantic," "absolute paradise," "extremely comfortable." $ *Rooms from: $230* ✉ *5 km/3 miles west of La Fortuna* ☎ *2479–1600, 866/311–1197 in North America* ⊕ *www.arenalnayara. com* ↪ *44 rooms* ⦿ *Breakfast.*

$$
HOTEL
▦ **Arenal Observatory Lodge.** This isolated lodge is as close as anyone should be to an active volcano—a mere 1¾ km (1 mile) away, down a winding road that leads to the lodge. **Pros:** best volcano views; secluded location; numerous activities. **Cons:** rough road to get here; isolated location. **TripAdvisor:** "unique," "a beautiful lodge," "stunning views and lovely hotel." $ *Rooms from: $82* ✉ *3 km/2 miles east of dam on Laguna de Arenal; from La Fortuna, drive to Tabacón resort and continue 4 km/2½ miles past resort to turnoff at base of volcano; turn and continue for 9 km/5½ miles* ☎ *2479–1070, 2290–7011 in San José* ⊕ *www.arenalobservatorylodge.com* ↪ *51 rooms, 46 with bath; 2 suites* ⦿ *Breakfast.*

$
HOTEL
▦ **Cabinas Los Guayabos.** A great budget alternative to the more-expensive lodgings lining the road to the volcano is this group of basic but spotlessly clean cabins managed by a friendly family. **Pros:** good budget value; friendly owners; great volcano views. **Cons:** rustic rooms; best to have a car to stay here. **TripAdvisor:** "quaint and clean," "great view," "great rooms and hospitality." $ *Rooms from: $55* ✉ *9 km/5½ miles west of La Fortuna* ☎ *2479–1444* ⊕ *www.hotellosguayabos.com* ⦿ *No meals.*

$
HOTEL
▦ **Cabinas Oriuma.** Right in the center of town, Oriuma is a popular choice for budget travelers and tour groups. **Pros:** good budget value; close to center of town. **Cons:** some rooms get street noise; boxy design. **TripAdvisor:** "left as friends," "nice hotel," "incredible." $ *Rooms from: $45* ✉ *15 m north of Parque Central* ☎ *2479–9111* ⊕ *cabinas-oriuma.blogspot.com* ↪ *22 rooms* ▭ *No credit cards* ⦿ *Breakfast.*

$$
HOTEL
▦ **Chachagua Rainforest Hotel.** At this working ranch, intersected by a brook, you can see *caballeros* (cowboys) at work, take a horseback ride into the rain forest, and look for toucans from the open-air restaurant, which serves local meat and dairy products. **Pros:** secluded location; many activities. **Cons:** rustic rooms; far from sights. **TripAdvisor:** "amazing," "paradise in rainforest," "nice quiet getaway."

A leisurely stroll across a suspension bridge in Monteverde.

$ *Rooms from: $135* ✉ *12 km/7 miles south of La Fortuna* ☎ *2468–1011* ⊕ *www.chachaguarainforesthotel.com* ⇱ *9 rooms, 19 cabinas* ❍❙ *Breakfast.*

$$$
RESORT

☷ **Hotel Royal Corín Resort.** One of the newest entries into the Arenal-area lodging stakes is a big hit thanks to its friendly service and on-site hot springs and spa. **Pros:** small but nice on-site hot springs; pleasant surroundings, friendly service. **Cons:** sits close to the road so a few rooms get traffic noise. **TripAdvisor:** "fantastic property in paradise," "prepare to be pampered," "great hotel with nice ameni-ties." $ *Rooms from: $230* ✉ *4 km (2½ miles) west of La Fortuna* ☎ *2479–2200, 877/642–6746 in North America* ⊕ *www.royalcorin. com* ⇱ *42 rooms, 12 suites.*

$$
HOTEL

☷ **Hotel San Bosco.** Covered in blue-tile mosaics, this two-story hotel is certainly the most attractive and comfortable in the main part of town. **Pros:** good value; close to center of town. **Cons:** some rooms get street noise; boxy design. **TripAdvisor:** "pleasant," "quiet," "just right." $ *Rooms from: $75* ✉ *220 m north of La Fortuna's gas station* ☎ *2479–9050, 800/393–0902 in North America* ⊕ *www.hotelsanboscocr.com* ⇱ *34 rooms* ❍❙ *Breakfast.*

$$
HOTEL

☷ **La Pradera.** "The Prairie" is a simple roadside hotel with comfortable guest rooms that have high ceilings, spacious bathrooms, and verandas. **Pros:** good value; good restaurant. **Cons:** spartan rooms; lackadaisical staff. **TripAdvisor:** "beautiful setting," "comfortable," "great food." $ *Rooms from: $76* ✉ *2 km/1 mile west of La Fortuna* ☎ *2479–9597* ⊕ *www.lapraderadelarenal.com* ⇱ *28 rooms* ❍❙ *Breakfast.*

$$$
HOTEL

⬚ **The Lost Iguana Resort.** Despite its relative isolation—you're several kilometers beyond Tabacón—the Lost Iguana hums with activity, and is a favorite among Fodors.com posters. **Pros:** secluded location; great volcano views; many activities. **Cons:** removed from sights; ideally need car to stay here. **TripAdvisor:** "amazing views and wildlife," "idyllic setting," "hard to complain." $ *Rooms from: $245* ✉ *31 km/19 miles west of La Fortuna on hwy. toward Nuevo Arenal* ☎ *2479–1557, 2267–6148 in San José* ⊕ *www.lostiguanaresort.com* ⟳ *42 rooms* ⦿ *No meals.*

$$
RESORT
Fodor's Choice
★

⬚ **Montaña de Fuego.** On a manicured grassy roadside knoll, this highly recommended collection of cabins affords utterly spectacular views of Arenal Volcano. **Pros:** great volcano views; many activities for guests only; good restaurant. **Cons:** some cabins face highway noise; sometimes difficult to find space. **TripAdvisor:** "great views," "excellent stay," "lovely hotel." $ *Rooms from: $110* ✉ *8 km/5 miles west of La Fortuna* ☎ *2479–1220, 877/383–4612 in North America* ⊕ *www.montanadefuego.com* ⟳ *66 cabinas* ⦿ *Breakfast.*

$$$
RESORT

⬚ **The Springs Resort & Spa.** You've seen this lodge with its hot springs and forested surroundings if you followed the 2011 season of the ABC television series *The Bachelor*. **Pros:** stupendous volcano views from rooms and restaurant; beautiful springs complex; friendly service. **Cons:** rough final road to get here. **TripAdvisor:** "absolutely stunning luxury property," "awesome views," "just breathtaking." $ *Rooms from: $415* ✉ *9 km (5½ miles) west of La Fortuna, then 4 km (2½ miles) north* ☎ *2401–3313, 954/727–8333 in North America* ⊕ *www.springscostarica.com* ⟳ *42 rooms, 2 villas.*

$$$
RESORT
Fodor's Choice
★

⬚ **Tabacón Grand Spa Thermal Resort.** Without question, Tabacón, with its impeccably landscaped gardens and hot-spring rivers at the base of Arenal Volcano, is one of Central America's most famous and compelling resorts, and a 2008 remodeling of all units here cemented that status. **Pros:** luxurious hot springs; great volcano views; good restaurant. **Cons:** crowded with tour groups; chain-hotel design; music sometimes too loud. **TripAdvisor:** "paradise," "mesmerizing spa and tranquil location," "really worth it." $ *Rooms from: $230* ✉ *13 km/8 miles northwest of La Fortuna on hwy. toward Nuevo Arenal* ☎ *2479–2000, 2519–1999 in San José, 877/277–8291 in North America* ⊕ *www.tabacon.com* ⟳ *100 rooms, 14 suites* ⬿ *No smoking* ⦿ *Breakfast.*

NIGHTLIFE

People in La Fortuna tend to turn in early, though there's a place or two for night owls.

Vagabundo. Pizzeria Vagabundo turns into a lively bar in the evening, with foosball and billiards in the back room. ✉ *3 km/2 miles west of La Fortuna* ☎ *2479–9565* ⊘ *Daily noon–10.*

VOLCÁN ARENAL NATIONAL PARK

Fodor's Choice
★

Costa Rica's largest inland body of water, shimmering Lake Arenal, all 125 square km (48 square miles) of it, lies between rolling green hills and a rumbling volcano. Many visitors are surprised to learn it's a man-made lake, created in 1973 when a giant dam was built. A natural depression was flooded, and a 32-km-long by 14.4-km-wide (20-mile-long by 9-mile-wide) lake was born. The almost constant winds from the Caribbean make this area a windsurfing mecca. Outfitters in La Fortuna, Nuevo Arenal, and Tilarán run fishing, windsurfing, and kitesurfing trips on the lake. Desafío, an operator based in La Fortuna and Monteverde, has a half-day horseback trip between the two towns, with great views of the lake (⤳ *see Outdoor Activities in La Fortuna, above*). The best places to stay when visiting this area are La Fortuna amd Neuvo Arenal.

> **IN MEMORIAM**
>
> Those yellow hearts with halos painted on the pavement mark spots where people have died in car accidents or vehicles that have struck and killed pedestrians. An alarming number of them dot streets and roads around the country. Drive (and walk) with utmost caution.

NUEVO ARENAL

40 km/25 miles (1 hr) west of La Fortuna.

Much of the original town of Arenal, at one of the lowest points near Lake Arenal, was destroyed by the volcano's 1968 eruption, and the rest was destroyed in 1973, when Lake Arenal flooded the region. The *nuevo* (new) town was created about 30 km (19 miles) away from the site of the old. It doesn't have much to interest tourists, but is about halfway between La Fortuna and Tilarán, making it a good stop for a break, and an even better base with a couple of truly lovely lodgings nearby.

GETTING HERE AND AROUND

The route from La Fortuna to Nuevo Arenal around the north shore of Lake Arenal is in better shape than it has been in years, with only a couple of short atrocious sections to negotiate. Expect smooth sailing west of the Tabacón resort as far as the Arenal Dam, beyond which you should stick to daylight travel only. Watch out for the raccoonlike coatimundis (*pizotes* in Spanish) that scurry along the road. Longtime human feeding has diminished their ability to search for food on their own, and the cookies and potato chips they frequently get make matters worse. Public buses run twice daily from La Fortuna to Nuevo Arenal and beyond to Tilarán.

ESSENTIALS

Bank/ATM Banco Nacional ⊠ *West side of church* ☎ *2694–4122.*

Internet Tom's Pan ⊠ *300 m south of gas station* ☎ *2694–4547.*

Post Office Correos ⊠ *Next to Guardia Rural.*

The perfect way to end the day: a nice soak in the hot springs in Arenal Volcano National Park.

WHERE TO STAY

For expanded hotel reviews, visit Fodors.com.

$ B&B/INN Fodor's Choice ★ 🏨 **Chalet Nicholas.** John and Cathy Nicholas (and their five resident Great Danes) have converted their hillside home into a charming bed-and-breakfast with stunning views of the lake and volcano. **Pros:** attentive owners; great breakfasts; terrific value. **Cons:** best for dog lovers; need a car to stay here. **TripAdvisor:** "beyond our expectations," "a nature park on its own," "a beautiful slice of paradise." [$] *Rooms from: $68* ✉ *3 km/2 miles west of Nuevo Arenal* ☎ *2694–4041* 🌐 *www.chaletnicholas.com* 🛏 *3 rooms* 💳 *No credit cards* 🚭 *Non-smoking* 🍴 *Breakfast.*

$$$ HOTEL 🏨 **La Mansión Inn Lake Arenal.** Halfway between La Fortuna and Nuevo Arenal, elegant La Mansión Inn sits at the point where the volcano begins to disappear from sight, but the lake views (and the sunsets) remain as spectacular as ever. **Pros:** luxurious furnishings; stupendous lake views. **Cons:** far from sights; need a car to stay here. **TripAdvisor:** "comfortable and friendly," "beautifully situated," "serenity away from the crowds." [$] *Rooms from: $195* ✉ *Road between Nuevo Arenal and La Fortuna* ☎ *2692–8018, 877/660–3830 in North America* 🌐 *www.lamansionarenal.com* 🛏 *17 cottages, 3 suites* 🍴 *Breakfast.*

$$ B&B/INN Fodor's Choice ★ 🏨 **Villa Decary.** There's everything to recommend at this hillside lodging overlooking Lake Arenal, but it all goes back to the owners and their attentive service. **Pros:** attentive owners; great breakfasts; good value. **Cons:** need a car to stay here. **TripAdvisor:** "wonderful bed and breakfast," "amazing staff," "so much beauty." [$] *Rooms from:*

$109 ⊠ 2 km/1 miles east of Nuevo Arenal ☎ 800/556–0505 in North America ☎ 2694–4330 ⊕ www.villadecary.com ⤳ 5 rooms, 3 bungalows ⦿| Breakfast.

TILARÁN

22 km/14 miles (45 mins) southwest of Nuevo Arenal, 62 km/38 miles (1½ hrs) west of La Fortuna.

A windmill farm in the hills high above Tilarán attests to its being the windiest place in the country, and this lakeside town is used as a base by bronzed windsurfers. For those days when you get "skunked" (the wind fails to blow), horseback riding and mountain biking can keep you busy. A lakeside stroll is a pleasant way to while away a few hours.

GETTING HERE AND AROUND
The road from La Fortuna via Nuevo Arenal is in reasonable shape these days, with a few short potholed stretches. Give yourself sufficient time—say, two hours—for the trip, and make the trip during daylight hours. Public buses travel to and from La Fortuna twice daily, and from a small terminal at Calle 20 and Avenida 3 in San José five times daily.

ESSENTIALS
Bank/ATM Banco Nacional ⊠ *Central Plaza* ☎ *2695–5610.*

Hospital Clínica Tilarán ⊠ *200 m west of Banco Nacional* ☎ *2695–5093.*

Post Office Correos ⊠ *115 m west of municipal stadium.*

OUTDOOR ACTIVITIES
WINDSURFING AND KITESURFING
Tico Wind. Rent wind- and kitesurfing equipment at Tico Wind during the December-to-April season. It offers one-hour beginner's lessons starting at $50, or enroll in a multiday course for $200. ⊠ *30 km/18 miles west of Nuevo Arenal* ☎ *2692–2002* ⊕ *www.ticowind.com.*

Tilawa Windsurf Center. The best selection of wind- and kitesurfing equipment for rent or purchase can be found at Tilawa Windsurf. It's the only outfitter here open year-round. Half-day beginner's lessons start at $100. ⊠ *Hotel Tilawa, 8 km/5 miles north of Tilarán* ☎ *2695–5050* ⊕ *www.windsurfcostarica.com.*

WHERE TO STAY
For expanded hotel reviews, visit Fodors.com.

$$
HOTEL
⛰ **Lakeview Hotel.** How many Costa Rican hotels have an on-site microbrewery? **Pros:** many activities; stupendous lake views; great beers. **Cons:** isolated location. **TripAdvisor:** "relaxing restaurant," "great hidden gem," "a breathtaking view." ⓢ *Rooms from: $60* ⊠ *8 km/5 miles north of Tilarán* ☎ *2695–5050, 888/318–7873* ⊕ *www.volcanobrewingcompany.com* ⤳ *20 rooms* ⦿| *No meals.*

5

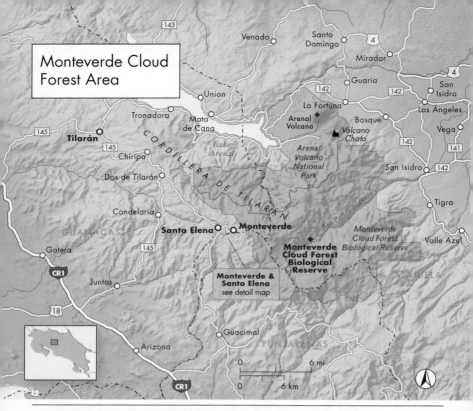

Monteverde Cloud
Forest Area

143
Venado
Santo
Domingo
4
Mirador
Guaria
4
Union
142
142
San
Isidro
La Fortuna
Los Ángeles
Tronadora
Mata
de Cana
Arenal
Volcano
Bosque
Volcano
Chato
Vega
145
Tilarán
Lake
Arenal
142
141
Chiripa
Arenal
Volcano
National
Park
San Isidro
142
Dos de Tilarán
Río Peñas Blancas
Tigra
CORDILLERA DE TILARÁN
Candelaria
GUANACASTE
Santa Elena
Monteverde
Monteverde
Cloud Forest
Biological Reserve
Valle Azul
145
Gotera
Monteverde
Cloud Forest
Biological
Reserve
ALAJUELA
CR1
Monteverde &
Santa Elena
see detail map
Juntas
18
Guacimal
PUNTARENAS
0   6 mi
Arizona
0   6 km
CR1

MONTEVERDE CLOUD FOREST

Monteverde is a rain forest, but you won't be in the tropics, rather in the cool, gray, misty world of the cloud forest. Almost 900 species of epiphytes, including 450 orchids, are found here; most tree trunks are covered with mosses, bromeliads, ferns, and other plants. Monteverde spans the Continental Divide, extending from about 1,500 meters (4,920 feet) on the Pacific slope and 1,350 meters (4,430 feet) on the Atlantic slope up to the highest peaks of the Tilarán Mountains at around 1,850 meters (6,070 feet). Make Santa Elena your base of operations when visiting this area.

MONTEVERDE CLOUD FOREST BIOLOGICAL RESERVE

Fodor'sChoice **Monteverde Cloud Forest Biological Reserve.** Close to several fine hotels, the
★ private Reserva Biológica Bosque Nuboso Monteverde is one of Costa
Rica's best-kept reserves, with well-marked trails, lush vegetation, and
a cool, damp climate. The collision of moist winds with the Continental
Divide here creates a constant mist whose particles provide nutrients
for plants growing at the upper layers of the forest. Giant trees are
enshrouded in a cascade of orchids, bromeliads, mosses, and ferns, and
in those patches where sunlight penetrates, brilliantly colored flowers

What Is a Cloud Forest?

Cloud forests are a type of rain forest, but are different from the hot, humid lowland forests with which most people are familiar. First of all, they're cooler. Temperatures in Monteverde Cloud Forest, for example, are in the 18°C (65°F) range year-round, and feel colder because of the near-constant cool rain. Cloud forests—also known as montane forests—occur at elevations of around 1,950 to 3,450 meters (6,500 to 11,500 feet). At this altitude, clouds accumulate around mountains and volcanoes, providing regular precipitation as well as shade, which in turn slows evaporation. Moisture is deposited directly onto vegetation, keeping it lush and green.

The trees here, on top of high ridges and near the summits of volcanoes, are transformed by strong, steady winds that sometimes topple them and regularly break off branches. The resulting collection of small, twisted trees and bushes is known as an elfin forest. The conditions in cloud forests create unique habitats that shelter an unusually high proportion of rare species, making conservation vital. Monteverde is Costa Rica's most touristed cloud forest, but not its only one. Other cloud forests are in nearby Santa Elena Reserve, Los Angeles Cloud Forest Reserve near San Ramón (⇨ above), and around San Gerardo de Dota (⇨ Chapter 8).

flourish. The sheer size of everything, especially the leaves of the trees, is striking. No less astounding is the variety: 2,500 plant species, 400 species of birds, 500 types of butterflies, and more than 100 different mammals have so far been cataloged at Monteverde. A damp and exotic mixture of shades, smells, and sounds, the cloud forest is also famous for its population of resplendent quetzals, which can be spotted feeding on the *aguacatillo* (similar to avocado) trees; best viewing times are early mornings from January until September, and especially during the mating season of April and May. Other forest-dwelling inhabitants include hummingbirds and multicolor frogs.

For those who don't have a lucky eye, a short-stay aquarium is in the field station; captive amphibians stay here just a week before being released back into the wild. Although the reserve limits visitors to 160 people at a time, Monteverde is one of the country's most popular destinations. We do hear complaints (and agree with them) that the reserve gets too crowded with visitors at times. As they say, the early bird catches the worm, and the early visitor has the best chance at spotting wildlife. Allow a generous slice of time for leisurely hiking to see the forest's flora and fauna; longer hikes are made possible by some strategically placed overnight refuges along the way. At the reserve entrance you can buy self-guide pamphlets and rent rubber boots; a map is provided when you pay the entrance fee. You can navigate the reserve on your own, but a 2½-hour guided tour (7:30 and 11:30 am and 1 pm) is invaluable for getting the most out of your visit. There's also another option: Take advantage of their two-hour guided night tours starting each evening at 6:15 (reservations required). The reserve provides transport from area hotels for an extra $3. If you're a morning person, a guided walking bird-watching tour up to the reserve leaves from Stella's Bakery each morning at 6 for groups of two to six people. Advance reservations are required. ⊠ *10 km/6 miles south of Santa Elena* ☎ *2645–5122, 2253–3267 in San José* ⊕ *www.cct.or.cr* ⊠ *$17, plus $10 with guide services; $17 night tour; $64 morning bird-watching tour* ☉ *Daily 7–4.*

| DID YOU KNOW?

Monteverde's Quakers, or more officially, the Society of Friends, no longer constitute the majority here these days, but their imprint on the community remains strong. (Don't expect to see anyone dressed like the man on the Quaker Oats box.) The Friends' meetinghouse, just south of the Cheese Factory on the road to the reserve, welcomes visitors at meetings of worship, 10:30 am Sunday and 9 am Wednesday. Most of the time is spent in quiet reflection.

GETTING HERE AND AROUND

Buses from San José leave twice daily from the Terminal Atlántico Norte (⊠ *C. 12 and Avda. 9*), at 6:30 am and 2:30 pm, stopping in the center of Santa Elena and at various locations on the way up the mountain as far as the Cheese Factory. Buses from Santa Elena leave for San José at 6:30 am and 2:30 pm daily. Taxis from Santa Elena are $7. Buses from Tilarán to Santa Elena leave once a day, at 12:30 pm. The roads to the area are some of the worst in the country.

MONTEVERDE AND SANTA ELENA

Monteverde is 167 km/104 miles (5 hrs) northwest of San José; Santa Elena is 6 km/4 miles (30 mins) north of Monteverde and 35 km/22 miles (2 hrs) southeast of Tilarán.

The area's first residents were a handful of Costa Rican families fleeing the rough-and-ready life of nearby gold-mining fields during the 1940s. They were joined in the early 1950s by Quakers, conscientious objectors from Alabama fleeing conscription into the Korean War. A number of things drew them to Costa Rica: just a few years earlier it had abolished its military, and the Monteverde area offered good grazing. But it was the cloud forest that lay above their dairy farms that soon attracted the attention of ecologists. Educators and artisans followed, giving Monteverde and its "metropolis," the village of Santa Elena, a mystique all their own. In any case, Monteverde looks quite a bit different than it did when the first wave of Quakers arrived. New hotels have sprouted up everywhere, traffic grips the center of town, and a small shopping mall has gone up just outside of town on the way up the mountain. A glut of rented all-terrain vehicles contributes to the increasing din that disrupts Monteverde's legendary peace and quiet. Some define this as progress. Others lament the gradual chipping away at what makes one of Costa Rica's most special areas so, well, special. We side with them. You can still get away from it all up here, but you'll have to work harder at it than you used to. In any case, you'll not lack for things to do if seeing nature is a primary reason for your visit.

Note that a casual reference to "Monteverde" generally refers to this entire area, but officially the term applies only to the original Quaker settlement, which is by the dairy-processing plant just down the mountain from the reserve entrance. If you follow road signs exclusively, you'll end up a bit outside the town of Santa Elena.

The only way to see the area's reserves, including the Monteverde Cloud Forest, is to hike them.

NAVIGATING
MONTEVERDE
AND SANTA
ELENA

There will be times you wish you had your own vehicle, but it's surprisingly easy to get around the Monteverde area without a car. Given the state of the roads, you'll be happy to let someone else do the driving. However, if you do arrive by rental car, the road up the mountain from Santa Elena is paved as far as the gas station near the entrance to the Hotel Belmar. Taxis are plentiful; it's easy to call one from your hotel, and restaurants are happy to summon a cab to take you back to your hotel after dinner. Taxis also congregate in front of the church on the main street in Santa Elena. Many tour companies will pick you up from your hotel and bring you back at the end of the day, either free or for a small fee.

GETTING HERE AND AROUND

Getting here means negotiating some of the country's legendarily rough roads, but don't let that deter you from a visit. Years of promises to pave the way up here have collided with politics and scarce funds, but many residents remain just as happy to keep Monteverde out of the reach of tour buses and day-trippers. ("Do we really want this to be a shore excursion for cruise ships?" some residents ask.) Your own vehicle gives you the greatest flexibility, but a burgeoning number of shuttle-van services connect Monteverde with San José and other tourist destinations throughout the country.

If your bones can take it, a very rough track leads from Tilarán via Cabeceras to Santa Elena, near the Monteverde Cloud Forest Biological Reserve, doing away with the need to cut across to the Pan-American Highway. You need a 4WD vehicle, and you should inquire locally about the current condition of the road. The views of Nicoya Peninsula, Lake Arenal, and Arenal Volcano reward those willing to bump around a bit. Note, too, that you don't really save much time—on a good day it takes about 2½ hours as opposed to the 3 required via Cañas and Río Lagarto on the highway.

Gray Line has daily shuttle bus service between San José, La Fortuna, and Arenal ($44), and Monteverde ($44). Interbus also connects San José with La Fortuna and Monteverde (each $45) daily, with connections from here to a few of the North Pacific beaches.

Desafío Adventures provides a fast, popular three-hour transfer between Monteverde and La Fortuna. The taxi-boat-taxi service costs $29 one-way.

ESSENTIALS

Bank/ATM Banco Nacional ⊠ *50 m north and 50 m west of bus station, Santa Elena* ☎ *2645–5027.*

Bus Information Gray Line Tourist Bus ☎ *2220–2126* ⊕ *www. graylinecostarica.com.* **Interbus** ☎ *2283–5573* ⊕ *www.interbusonline.com.*

Internet Historias Internet Café ⊠ *Road to Jardín de Mariposas, 75 m down from Pizzería de Johnny, Cerro Plano* ☎ *2645–6914.*

Medical Clinic Seguro Social ⊠ *150 m south of soccer field, Santa Elena* ☎ *2645–5076.*

Pharmacy Farmacia Vitosi ⊠ *Across from Super Compro supermarket, Santa Elena* ☎ *2645–5004.*

Post Office Correos ⊠ *50 m south of Serpentario, Santa Elena.*

Tourist Information Centro de Visitantes Monteverde ⊠ *Across from Super Compro supermarket, Santa Elena* ☎ *2645–6565* ⊙ *Daily 9–4.*

OUTDOOR ACTIVITIES

ZIP-LINE TOURS

(S) **Original Canopy Tour.** The Original Canopy Tour near Santa Elena was the first zip-line tour in Costa Rica, with 10 platforms in the canopy, and lasting 2½ hours. You arrive at most of the platforms using a cable-and-harness traversing system and climb 12½ meters (42 feet) inside a strangler fig tree to reach one. ⊠ *Cerro Plano* ☎ *2291–4465 in San José for reservations* ⊕ *www.canopytour.com* 🖃 *$45.*

Fodor'sChoice **Selvatura.** Selvatura, a cloud forest park outside Monteverde Reserve, ★ has the only zip-line tour built entirely inside the cloud forest. It has 15 lines and 18 platforms, with an optional Tarzan swing at the end to round out the excursion. Mix and match packages to include the complex's hanging bridges, hummingbird and butterfly gardens, and reptile exhibition. (See more on Selvatura, below.) ⊠ *Office across from church, Santa Elena* ☎ *2645–5929* ⊕ *www. selvatura.com* 🖃 *$45.*

HANGING BRIDGES AND TRAMS

(S) **Monteverde Park.** Here's a tram/zip-line/hanging-bridges entertainment complex all in one. A tram, similar to that found at the Arenal Volcano Park near La Fortuna, takes you on a mile-long gondola ride through the rain-forest canopy. You can descend via the tram, or along a series of five hanging bridges, at heights of up to 41 meters (138 feet), connected from tree to tree. Your third descent option is 3 km/2 miles of zip lines through the cloud-forest canopy. Imposing towers, used as support, mar the landscape somewhat. A hummingbird garden rounds out the offerings. ⊠ *Office across from Banco Nacional, Santa Elena* ☎ *2645–5238* ⊕ *www.skyadventures.travel* 🖃 *$83 all offerings, $66 tram and zip lines, tram and bridges $55, tram only $42, bridges only $33* ⊙ *Daily 7–4.*

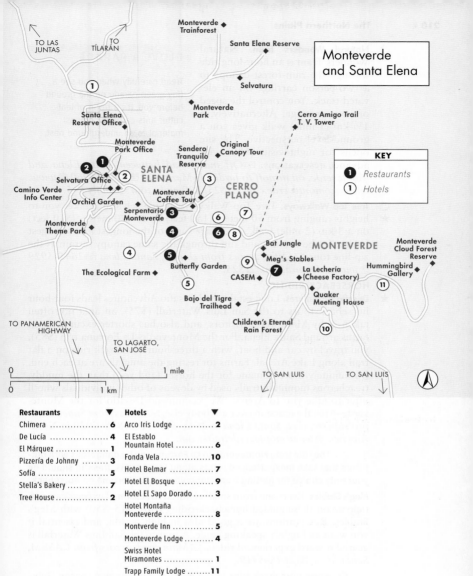

Monteverde and Santa Elena

KEY

1 *Restaurants*

① *Hotels*

TO LAS JUNTAS

TO TÍLARÁN

Monteverde Trainforest

Santa Elena Reserve

Selvatura

Monteverde Park

Cerro Amigo Trail T. V. Tower

Santa Elena Reserve Office

Monteverde Park Office

Sendero Tranquilo Reserve

Original Canopy Tour

SANTA ELENA

Selvatura Office

Camino Verde Info Center

Orchid Garden

CERRO PLANO

Monteverde Coffee Tour

Serpentario Monteverde

Monteverde Theme Park

Bat Jungle

Meg's Stables

MONTEVERDE

Monteverde Cloud Forest Reserve

Hummingbird Gallery

The Ecological Farm

Butterfly Garden

CASEM

La Lechería (Cheese Factory)

Bajo del Tigre Trailhead

Quaker Meeting House

TO PANAMERICAN HIGHWAY

TO LAGARTO, SAN JOSÉ

Children's Eternal Rain Forest

0 — 1 mile

0 — 1 km

TO SAN LUIS

TO SAN LUIS

Restaurants ▼

Chimera **6**
De Lucía **4**
El Márquez **1**
Pizzería de Johnny **3**
Sofía **5**
Stella's Bakery **7**
Tree House **2**

Hotels ▼

Arco Iris Lodge **2**
El Establo
Mountain Hotel **6**
Fonda Vela **10**
Hotel Belmar **7**
Hotel El Bosque **9**
Hotel El Sapo Dorado **3**
Hotel Montaña
Monteverde **8**
Montverde Inn **5**
Monteverde Lodge **4**
Swiss Hotel
Miramontes **1**
Trapp Family Lodge **11**

☾ **Natural Wonders Tram.** Natural
Wonders Tram is an hour-long ride
through the rain-forest canopy in
a two-person carriage on an elevated track. You control the speed
of your carriage. Alternatively, a
1½-km (1-mile) walk gives you a
ground-level perspective. The site
opens for night visits ($30) with

advance reservations. ⊠ *Off main road between Santa Elena and
Monteverde, on turnoff to Jardín de Mariposas* ☎ *2645–5960* ⊕ *www.
telefericomonteverde.com* ⊟ *$25; $30 night tour* ☉ *Daily 8–5.*

☾ **Tree Top Walkways.** Tree Top Walkways, inside Selvatura, takes you to
★ heights ranging from 50 meters (150 feet) up to 170 meters (510 feet)
on a 3-km (2-mile) walk. These are some of the longest and strongest
bridges in the country and run through the same canopy terrain as the
zip-line tour. ⊠ *Office across from church, Santa Elena* ☎ *2645–5929*
⊕ *www.selvatura.com* ⊟ *$25.*

HORSEBACK RIDING

★ **Desafío Adventures.** Long-established Desafío Adventures leads four-hour
horseback tours to the San Luis Waterfall ($75), an area not often
taken in by Monteverde visitors, and also has shorter excursions on
farms around Santa Elena. For the Monteverde–La Fortuna trip ($85),
you travel by car and boat, with a three-hour horseback ride on a flat
trail along Lake Arenal. Farms for resting the animals are at each end.
It's infinitely more humane for the horses (and you) than the muddy,
treacherous mountain trails used by dozens of other individuals who'll
offer to take you to Arenal. We recommend Desafío for the Monteverde–Arenal excursion over anybody else. ⊠ *Across from Super Compro supermarket, Santa Elena* ☎ *2645–5874, 855/818–0020 in North
America* ⊕ *www.monteverdetours.com.*

■TIP→ The ride from Monteverde to La Fortuna can be dangerous with outfitters that take inexperienced riders along steep trails. Desafío should be
your only choice for getting from Monteverde to La Fortuna on horseback.

Meg's Stables. Everyone from small children to seasoned experts can participate on these guided horseback-riding trips ($15–$50) with Meg's
Stables. Reservations are a good idea in high season, and essential if
you want an English-speaking guide. A tour to the San Luis Waterfall is
geared toward experienced riders. ⊠ *Main road, across from CASEM,
Santa Elena* ☎ *2645–5419.*

■TIP→ Book horseback trips in the morning during rainy season (July–
December). Rains usually begin around 2 pm.

EXPLORING
TOP ATTRACTIONS

☾ **Butterfly Garden.** Forty species of butterflies flit about in four enclosed
botanical gardens at the Butterfly Garden (Jardín de Mariposas). Morning visits are best, since the butterflies are most active early in the day.
Your entrance ticket includes an hour-long guided tour and, if you
like, a 20-minute video introduction to the subject matter. ⊠ *Near*

Continued on page 224

"This is our 5 year old on his first zipline through the rainforest of Manuel Antonio."
—Jill Chapple, Fodors.com member

CANOPY TOURS

Costa Rica invented the concept of the canopy tour, and the idea has spread across the globe. Zip lining through the treetops is a once-in-a-lifetime experience, and exploring the jungle canopy is the best way to see the most eye-catching animals.

A canopy tour is an umbrella term describing excursions that take you to the jungle's ceiling. The experience is distinctly Costa Rican and is one of the country's signature activities for visitors. There are two types of tour: one gives you a chance to see animals (from bridges and platforms), and the other lets you swing through the trees like them (on zip lines). We know of around 80 tours nationwide but recommend only about a third of that number. You'll find tour information in most chapters of this book.

By Jeffrey Van Fleet

WHAT EXACTLY IS A CANOPY TOUR?

Canopy cable ride at Monteverde cloud forest

WHAT TO EXPECT

Plan on a half-day for your canopy tour, including transportation to and from your hotel and a safety briefing for zip line excursions. Most zipline tours begin at fixed times and reservations are always required, or at least advised. Hanging-bridges tours are far more leisurely and can be done at your own pace. The occasional mega-complex, such as Monteverde's Selvatura, offers both types of tours. For most, it's one or the other.

BRIDGES AND TRAMS

These are canopy tours in a literal sense, where you walk along suspension bridges, ride along in a tram, or are hoisted up to a platform to get a closer look at birds, monkeys, and sloths. They're also called hanging-bridges tours, sky walks, or platform tours. If seeing nature at a more leisurely pace is your goal, opt for these, especially the bridge excursions. They're peaceful and unobtrusive. Early mornings are the best time for animal sightings—at 50–250 feet above ground, the views are stupendous—and the weather is usually better.

ZIP LINES

This type of tour is a fast-paced, thrilling experience. You're attached to a zip line with a safety harness, and then you "fly" at about 30 miles per hour from one tree platform to the next. (You may be anywhere from 60–300 feet above the forest floor.) Tree-to-tree zip lines date from the 19th century and have been a bona fide activity for visitors to Costa Rica since the mid-1990s when the first tour opened in Monteverde. When most people say "canopy tour" they're referring this type of excursion. These tours are tremendous fun, but don't plan on seeing the resplendent quetzal as you zip from platform to platform. (Your shouts of exhilaration will probably scare them all away.) An average fitness level—and above-average level of intrepidness—are all you need.

TOP CANOPY TOURS BY REGION

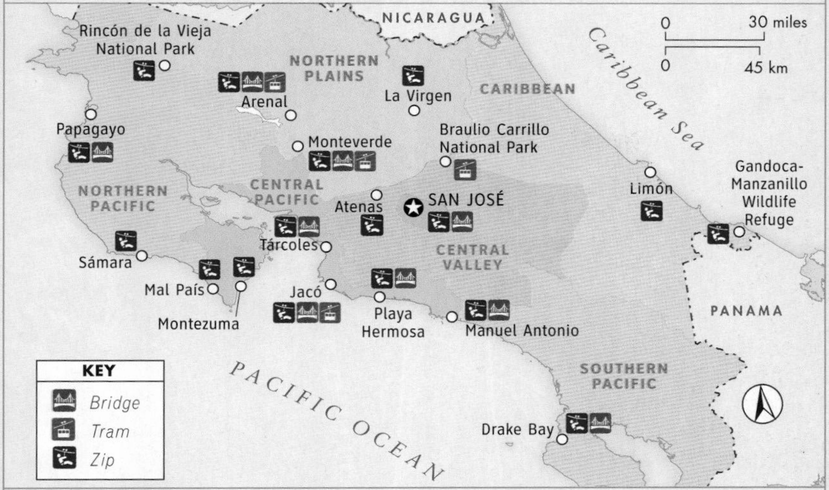

KEY
- Bridge
- Tram
- Zip

TOUR OPERATOR	LOCATION	TYPE		
Arenal Hanging Bridges	Arenal		Bridge	
Arenal Volcano Park	Arenal	Zip	Bridge	Tram
Canopy Safari	Manuel Antonio	Zip	Bridge	
Canopy del Pacífico	Malpaís	Zip		
Cocozuma	Montezuma	Zip		
Crazy Monkey Canopy	Gandoco-Manzanillo	Zip		
Ecoglide Arenal Park	Arenal	Zip		
Hacienda Poco Azul	La Virgen, Sarapiquí	Zip		
Hotel Villa Lapas	Tárcoles	Zip	Bridge	
Natural Wonders Tram	Monteverde			Tram
Original Canopy Tour	Monteverde	Zip		
Original Canopy Tour	Drake Bay	Zip	Bridge	
Original Canopy Tour	Veragua, Limón	Zip		
Rain Forest Adventures	Braulio Carrillo National Park	Zip		Tram
Rain Forest Adventures	Jacó	Zip		Tram
Rincón de la Vieja Canopy	Rincón de la Vieja National Park	Zip		
Selvatura	Monteverde	Zip	Bridge	
Tití Canopy Tour	Manuel Antonio	Zip		
Monteverde Park	Monteverde	Zip	Bridge	Tram
Waterfall Canopy Tour	Jacó	Zip	Bridge	
Wing Nuts Canopy Tour	Sámara	Zip		
Witch's Rock Canopy Tour	Papagayo	Zip	Bridge	

SAFETY FIRST

(top left) Zip lining Aventuras del Sarapiqui. (bottom right) Brown-Throated Three-Toed Sloth. (right) Sky Tram, Rainforest Canopy Tour, Arenal

PLAYING IT SAFE

Flying through the air, while undeniably cool, is also inherently dangerous. Before you strap into a harness, be certain that the safety standards are first rate. There's virtually no government oversight of the activity in Costa Rica. Here is a list of questions you should ask before you book:

1. How long has the company been in business?

2. Are they insured?

3. Are cables, harnesses, and other equipment manufacturer-certified?

4. Is there a second safety line that connects you to the zip line in case the main pulley gives way?

5. What's the price? Plan on paying $50 to $80—a low price could indicate a second-rate operation.

6. Are participants clipped to the zip line while on the platform? (They should be.)

KEEP IN MIND

■ Listen closely to the guides' pre-tour safety briefing and obey their instructions.

■ Never argue with the guide when s/he is making a decision to preserve your safety.

■ Don't attempt to take photos in flight.

■ Gauge your abilities frankly. Remember, once you start, there's no turning back.

■ If anything seems "off" or makes you uncomfortable, walk away.

Monteverde Inn; take right-hand turnoff 4 km/2½ miles past Santa Elena on road to Monteverde, continue for 2 km/1 mile ☎ 2645–5512 ⊕ www.monteverdebutterflygarden.com ⊠ $9, $3 kids 12 and under ⊙ Daily 9:30–4.

↺ **Monteverde Cloudforest Train.** Rain forest . . . "train forest." The concept is a bit cheesy, but riders enjoy the 90-minute excursion in one of three rail cars pulled by an old-fashioned locomotive high above Monteverde. After 3 km (2 miles), the train stops for a photo/snack/coffee/hot chocolate break and then returns to the starting station. Tours depart hourly. ⊠ *6 km/4 miles north of Santa Elena ☎ 2645–5700 ⊕ www.trainforest. com ⊠ $50, free for kids 6 and under ⊙ Daily 8–4.*

↺ **Monteverde Theme Park** (*Ranario de Monteverde*). Only in Monteverde would visitors groove to the nightlife at an exhibition of 20 species of frogs, toads, and other amphibians. Bilingual biologist-guides take you through a 45-minute tour of the terrariums in the Frog Pond of Monteverde (Ranario de Monteverde), just outside Santa Elena. For the best show, come around dusk and stay well into the evening, when the critters become more active and much more vocal. (Your ticket entitles you to a second visit the same day, as well as a guided tour.) The complex added a butterfly garden with 40 different species in 2011. There's a small cafeteria and a frog-and-toad-and-butterfly theme gift shop. ⊠ *½ km/¼ mile southeast of Super Compro supermarket, Santa Elena ☎ 2645–6320 ⊕ www.monteverdethemepark.com ⊠ Frog pond: $12, children 6–12 $10; butterfly garden: $12, children 6–12 $10; both $20, children 6–12 $16; children under 6 free ⊙ Frog pond: daily 9–8:30; butterfly garden: daily 9–4.*

Santa Elena Reserve. Several conservation areas that have sprung up near Monteverde make attractive day trips, particularly if the Monteverde Reserve is too busy. The 765-acre Santa Elena Reserve just west of Monteverde is a project of the Santa Elena high school, and has a series of trails of varying lengths and difficulties that can be walked alone or with a guide on tours that depart each morning at 7:30 and 11:30. The 1.4-km (¾-mile) Youth Challenge trail takes about 45 minutes to negotiate and contains an observation platform with views as far away as the Arenal Volcano—that is, if the clouds clear. If you're feeling hardy, try the 5-km (3-mile) Caño Negro trail, clocking in at around four hours. There's a shuttle service to the reserve with fixed departures and returns. Reservations are required, and the cost is $2 each way. ⊠ *6 km/4 miles north of Santa Elena ☎ 2645–5390 ⊕ www. reservasantaelena.org ⊠ $14, plus $15 with guide services ⊙ Daily 7–4.*

↺ **Selvatura.** If your time in Monteverde is limited, consider spending it
Fodor's Choice at Selvatura, a kind of nature theme park—complete with canopy tour
★ and bridge walks—just outside the Santa Elena Reserve. A 100-bird hummingbird garden, an enormous enclosed 50-species *mariposario* (butterfly garden), a *herpetario* (frog and reptile house), and an insect exhibition sit near the visitor center. Transportation from area hotels is included in the price. You can choose from numerous mix-and-match packages, depending on which activities interest you, or take it all in, with lunch and guide included, for $138. Most visitors get by for

much less, given that you couldn't take in all there is to do here in one day. ⊠ *Office across from church, Santa Elena* ☎ *2645–5929* ⊕ *www. selvatura.com* 🖾 *Prices vary, depending on package* ⊙ *Daily 8:30–4:30.*

WORTH NOTING

ↄ **Bat Jungle.** Butterflies, frogs, and snakes already have their own Monteverde-area exhibits. The Bat Jungle gives its namesake animal equal time with guided tours into the life of one of the planet's most misunderstood mammals. Admission includes a 45-minute guided tour. An adjoining museum documents the history of the region, in particular, its early settlement by the Quakers. ⊠ *Across from El Bosque Lodge* ☎ *2645–7701* ⊕ *www.batjungle.com* 🖾 *$10* ⊙ *Daily 9–7:30.*

ↄ **Children's Eternal Rain Forest.** The 54,000-acre Children's Eternal Rain Forest (Bosque Eterno de los Niños) dwarfs the Monteverde and Santa Elena reserves. It began life as a school project in Sweden among children interested in saving a piece of the rain forest, and blossomed into a fund-raising effort among students from 44 countries. The reserve's **Bajo del Tigre trail** makes for a gentle, self-guided 1½-km (1-mile) hike through secondary forest. Along the trail are 27 stations at which to stop and learn about the reserve, many lessons geared toward kids. A separate guided twilight walk ($20) begins at 5:30 pm and lasts two hours, affording the chance to see the nocturnal side of the cloud forest; reservations are required. Much of the rest of the reserve is not open to the public, but the Monteverde Conservation League offers stays at San Gerardo and Poco Sol, two remote field stations within the forest. The $50 packages include dormitory accommodation and meals. ⊠ *100 m south of CASEM* ☎ *2645–5003* ⊕ *www.acmcr.org* 🖾 *Forest $20; transportation from area hotels $2, $12 children 7–12, free for children under 7* ⊙ *Daily 8–4:30.*

Don Juan Coffee Tour. Small groups are the hallmark of the Don Juan Coffee Tour, lasting about two hours and letting you see the coffee process from start to finish at the plantation of Don Juan Cruz, one of the original settlers in the area. Transportation to the farm on the road to Tilarán can be arranged from all Monteverde-area lodgings. ☎ *2645–7100* ⊕ *www.donjuancoffeetour.com* 🖾 *$30* ⊙ *Tours at 8, 10 am and 1, 3 pm.*

Ecological Farm. The Ecological Farm (Finca Ecológica) is a private wild-life refuge with four trails on its 75 acres, plus birds, sloths, agoutis, coatimundis, two waterfalls, and a coffee plantation. If you can't make it all the way up to the Monteverde Reserve for the evening hike, there's a top-notch guided, two-hour twilight walk that begins each evening at 5:30. Reservations are required. ⊠ *Turnoff to Jardín de Mariposas, off main road between Santa Elena and Monteverde* ☎ *2645–5869* 🖾 *$10, twilight walk $25* ⊙ *Daily 7–5.*

★ **Monteverde Coffee Tour.** Bite your tongue before requesting Costa Rica's ubiquitous Café Britt up here. Export-quality Café Monteverde is the locally grown product. The Monteverde Coffee Tour lets you see the process up close from start to finish, from shade growing on the area's Turín plantation, 7 km (4 miles) north of Santa Elena; transport to the *beneficio,* the processing mill where the beans are washed and dried; and finally to the roaster. Reservations are required, and pickup is from area hotels. ☎ 2645–5901 ⊕ *www.cafemonteverde.com* 🖃 $30 ⊙ *Tours at 7:30 am and 1:30 pm.*

Orchid Garden (*Jardín de Orquídeas*). The Orchid Garden (Jardín de Orquídeas) showcases more than 450 species of orchids, one of which is the world's smallest. The Monteverde Orchid Investigation Project manages the gardens. Admission includes a 30-minute tour. ✉ *150 m south of Banco Nacional* ☎ 2645–5308 ⊕ *www.monteverdeorchidgarden. net* 🖃 $7 ⊙ *Daily 8–5.*

Sendero Tranquilo Reserve. The 200-acre Sendero Tranquilo Reserve is managed by the Hotel Sapo Dorado and bordered by the Monteverde Cloud Forest Biological Reserve and the Guacimal River. Five kilometers (3 miles) of narrow trails are designed to have as little impact on the forest as possible (only groups of two to six are allowed). A guide leads you through primary and secondary forest and an area that illustrates the effects of deforestation. Because of the emphasis on minimal environmental impact, animals here tend to be more timid than at some other reserves. ✉ *3 km/2 miles north of Monteverde Reserve entrance, Cerro Plano* ☎ 2645–5010 ⊕ *www.sapodorado.com* 🖃 $35 ⊙ *Tours depart daily at 7:30 am and 1 pm; reservations required.*

Ⓒ **Serpentarium of Monteverde** (*Serpentario de Monteverde*). At the Serpentarium of Monteverde, greet 40 species of live Costa Rican reptiles and amphibians with glass safely between you and them. Guided tours in English or Spanish are included in your admission price. ✉ *Just outside Santa Elena on road to Monteverde* ☎ 2645–6002 ⊕ *www.snaketour. com* 🖃 $9 ⊙ *Daily 11–7.*

NEED A BREAK?

La Lechería. Long before tourists flocked up here, dairy farming was the foundation of Monteverde's economy. Quakers still operate what is locally referred to as the Cheese Factory, or La Lechería. The factory store sells local cheeses and ice cream. Stop in for a cone. It's open Monday through Saturday 7:30 to 5 and Sunday 7:30 to 4. If you have more time, take a two-hour tour of the operation Monday through Saturday at 9 or 2. Tours are $10 and wind up with a cheese-sampling session. Reserve in advance. If you're not heading up the mountain, these folks also operate a stand across from the Tree House restaurant on the main street in Santa Elena. ✉ *½ km/¼ mile south of CASEM, halfway between Santa Elena and Monteverde Reserve* ☎ 2645–2850, 2645–7090 tours.

WHERE TO EAT

$

ECLECTIC

✕ **Chimera.** Karen Nielsen, owner of nearby Sofía, also operates this all-tapas (appetizers) offering, where you can mix and match small plates from the à la carte menu. Prices do add up quickly, but two or three menu items will make a filling meal out of such diverse minidishes as sea bass with passion-fruit cream, or coconut shrimp in mango-ginger sauce. Excellent dessert choices include a chocolate mousse or vanilla ice cream with pineapple-ginger-rum syrup, and a terrific selection of tropical-style cocktails and European and South American wines. A scant nine tables dot the place. Arrive before 7 if you want a guaranteed table, although the wait is never too long. $ *Average main: $9* ✉ *Cerro Plano* ☎ 2645–6081.

CLOSE UP

Bird Country

Nearly 850 bird species have been identified in Costa Rica, more than in the United States and Canada combined. Consequently, bird-watchers flock here by the thousands. The big attractions tend to be eye-catching species like the keel-billed toucan, but it is the diversity of shape, size, coloration, and behavior that makes bird-watching in Costa Rica so fascinating.

Tropical superstars: Parrots, parakeets, and macaws; toucans and toucanets; and the elusive but legendary resplendent quetzal are a thrill for those of us who don't see them every day.

In supporting roles: Lesser-known but equally impressive species include motmots, with their distinctive racket tails; oropéndolas, which build hanging nests; and an array of hawks, kites, and falcons.

Color me red, blue, yellow . . . : Two of the most striking species are the showy scarlet macaw and the quirky purple gallinule; tanagers, euphonias, manakins, cotingas, and trogons are some of the country's loveliest plumed creatures, but none of them matches the iridescence of the hummingbirds (⇨ *below*).

Singing in the rain: The relatively inconspicuous clay-color robin is Costa Rica's national bird. It may look plain, but its song is melodious, and because the males sing almost constantly toward the end of the dry season—the beginning of their mating season—local legend has it that they call the rains.

The big and the small of it: The hummingbird is a mere 6¼ cm (2½ inches) tall and weighs just over 2 grams, whereas the jabiru, a long-legged stork, can grow to more than 1.2 meters (4 feet) tall and weigh up to 14 pounds. Costa Rica hosts 51 members of the hummingbird family, compared with just one species for all of the United States east of the Rocky Mountains.

"Snow birds": If you're here between October and April, don't be surprised if you see some feathered friends from home. When northern birds fly south for the winter, they don't all head to Miami. Seasonal visitors like the Kentucky warbler make up about a quarter of the amazing avian panorama in Costa Rica.

Bird-watching can be done everywhere in the country. And don't let the rainy season deter you: seasonal *lagunas* (lagoons) such as Caño Negro and the swamps of Palo Verde National Park, which disappear during the dry months, are excellent places to see birds.

5

$$$
ECLECTIC

✕ **De Lucía.** Cordial Chilean owner José Belmar is the walking, talking (in five languages) menu at this elegant restaurant, always on hand to chat with guests. Entrées include sea bass with garlic sauce, and orange chicken, and are served with grilled vegetables and fried plantains. The handsome wooden restaurant with red mahogany tables is given a distinct South American flavor by an array of Andean tapestries and ceramics. An excellent dessert choice is *tres leches* (three milks), a richer-than-rich cake made with condensed, whole, and evaporated milk. $ *Average main: $19* ✉ *Turnoff to Jardín de Mariposas, off main road between Santa Elena and Monteverde, Cerro Plano* ☎ *2645–5337* ⊕ *www.deluciamonteverde.com.*

$ ✕ **El Márquez.** Seafood is an unexpected treat up here in the mountains,
SEAFOOD and it's fresh: the owner gets shipments from Puntarenas several times
weekly. The place is nothing fancy—expect plastic tables and chairs, with
lots of local flavor—but when area residents want a special restaurant
meal, this is where they come. Portions are big, but prices aren't. You could
have trouble finishing the generous mixed seafood platter with shrimp,
crab, and octopus in a white-wine sauce, or the jumbo shrimp with a sauce
of mushrooms and hearts of palm. $ *Average main: $9* ⊠ *Next to Suárez*
veterinary clinic, Santa Elena ☎ *2645–5918* ⊘ *Closed Sun.*

$$ ✕ **Pizzería de Johnny.** Everyone makes it to this stylish but informal place
ITALIAN with candles and white tablecloths. The Monteverde pizza, with the
works, is the most popular dish, and pastas, sandwiches, and a decent
wine selection round out the menu. $ *Average main: $14* ⊠ *Road to*
Monteverde Reserve, 1½ km/1 mile southeast of Santa Elena ☎ *2645–*
5066 ⊕ *www.pizzeriadejohnny.com.*

$$$ ✕ **Sofía.** Here's one of the area's most stylish restaurants, but this is still
ECLECTIC Monteverde, so you can leave your fancy clothes at home. Waiters in
Fodor's Choice crisp black aprons scurry attentively around the three dining rooms with
★ ample window space. We like Sofía for its variety of about a dozen main
courses: a mix of chicken, beef, pork, seafood, and vegetarian entrées.
Try the chimichanga with corvina and shrimp and a side of coconut
rice. There's an extensive wine and cocktail selection, too. $ *Average*
main: $21 ⊠ *Turnoff to Jardín de Mariposas, off main road between*
Santa Elena and Monteverde, Cerro Plano ☎ *2645–7017.*

$ ✕ **Stella's Bakery.** This local institution is one of the few spots that open
CAFÉ at 6 am. It's a good place to get an early-morning fix before heading
to the Monteverde Reserve. Pastries, rolls, muffins, natural juices, and
coffee are standard breakfast fare. Take them with you if you're running short of time. Lunch and dinner consist of light sandwiches, soups,
and pastas. $ *Average main: $7* ⊠ *Across from CASEM* ☎ *2645–5560*
⊕ *stellasbakery.webs.com.*

$$ ✕ **Tree House.** The name describes the place: this two-story restaurant
ECLECTIC on Santa Elena's main street is built around a 60-year-old fig tree. Tree
branches shelter first-floor tables from the afternoon mist, but not
entirely. If that's a problem, grab a table on the covered upper floor. The
menu mixes pastas and seafood with Costa Rican cuisine. For a taste
of everything, try the típico platter. The service here is "leisurely" or
"slow," depending on your perspective. $ *Average main: $12* ⊠ *Across*
from AyA, Santa Elena ☎ *2645–5751* ⊕ *www.treehouse.cr.*

WHERE TO STAY
For expanded hotel reviews, visit Fodors.com.

$$ ⌂ **Arco Iris Lodge.** You're almost right in the center of town, but you'd
B&B/INN never know it at this tranquil spot with cozy cabins set on 4 acres of
★ birding trails. **Pros:** attentive owner and staff; terrific breakfasts; ecology-minded place. **Cons:** back of bank blocks views; steep walk if on
foot. **TripAdvisor:** "gorgeous," "best accommodation in Costa Rica,"
"extremely helpful staff." $ *Rooms from: $85* ⊠ *50 m south of Banco*
Nacional, Santa Elena ☎ *2645–5067* ⊕ *www.arcoirislodge.com* ⇌ *20*
cabins, 1 suite ⦿ *No meals.*

5

$$$
HOTEL

El Establo Mountain Hotel. The area's largest, grandest hotel complex gets high marks for its huge suites and many activities. **Pros:** luxurious furnishings; many activities. **Cons:** massive grounds; lacks intimacy of other Monteverde lodgings. **TripAdvisor:** "beautiful," "great service," "fantastic views." $ *Rooms from: $216 ⊠ 3½ km/2 miles northwest of Monteverd* ☎ *2645–5110, 877/553–7822 in North America* ⊕ *www.hotelelestablo.com* ⤴ *155 rooms* ⦿*| Breakfast.*

$$
B&B/INN
Fodor'sChoice
★

Fonda Vela. Owned by the Smith brothers, whose family was among the first American arrivals in the 1950s—their father's paintings grace the lodging's public areas— these steep-roof chalets have large

> ## THE UBIQUITOUS SODA
>
> In Costa Rica the word *soda* has nothing to do with a carbonated beverage. (That's a *gaseosa* here.) Instead, a soda is a small, often family-run restaurant frequented by locals that you'll find in every town and city. Don't expect anything as fancy as a menu. A board usually lists specials of the day. The lunchtime *casado* (literally, "married")—a "marriage" of chicken, pork, or beef with rice, beans, cabbage salad, and natural fruit drink—sets you back about $3. No one will bring you a bill; just pay the cashier when you're finished.

bedrooms with white-stucco walls, wood floors, and huge windows. **Pros:** rustic luxury; secluded location; terrific restaurants. **Cons:** far from town; rough road to get here. **TripAdvisor:** "excellent amenities," "very comfortable," "huge room and good food." $ *Rooms from: $120 ⊠ 1½ km/1 mile northwest of Monteverde Reserve entrance* ☎ *2645–5125   800/270–8091* ⊕ *www.fondavela.com* ⤴ *40 rooms* ⦿*| Multiple meal plans.*

$$
B&B/INN

Hotel Belmar. Built into the hillside, the friendly Hotel Belmar resembles two tall Swiss chalets and commands extensive views of the Golfo de Nicoya and the hilly peninsula. **Pros:** good value; friendly staff. **Cons:** far from town; steep walk if on foot. **TripAdvisor:** "very helpful staff," "stunning," "wonderful food." $ *Rooms from: $102 ⊠ 4 km/2½ miles north of Monteverde* ☎ *2645–5201, 866/978–6424 in North America* ⊕ *www.hotelbelmar.net* ⤴ *28 rooms* ⦿*| Breakfast.*

$
HOTEL

Hotel El Bosque. Convenient to the Bajo del Tigre nature trail and Meg's Stables, El Bosque's quiet, simple rooms are grouped around a central camping area. **Pros:** good budget value; seclusion, especially in rooms away from road. **Cons:** basic rooms; lackluster staff. **TripAdvisor:** "nature lover's paradise," "exceptional care," "lovely location." $ *Rooms from: $53 ⊠ 2½ km/1½ miles southeast of Santa Elena on road to Monteverde Reserve* ☎ *2645–5158* ⊕ *www.bosquelodgecr.com* ⤴ *27 rooms* ⦿*| Breakfast.*

$$
B&B/INN

Hotel El Sapo Dorado. The "Golden Toad" has grown through the years to become a very pleasant hotel with a terrific restaurant and lots of on-site nature activities. **Pros:** rustic luxury; attentive service; excellent value. **Cons:** trails between cabins get muddy in rainy season; no screens on some windows; steep walk if on foot. **TripAdvisor:** "excellent restaurant," "lovely grounds," "rustic but great views." $ *Rooms from: $107 ⊠ 6 km/4 miles northwest of Monteverde Reserve entrance*

☎ *2645–5010, 800/407–3903 in North America* 🌐 *www.sapodorado.com* 🛏 *30 rooms* 🍴 *Breakfast.*

$$ HOTEL 🏨 **Hotel Montaña Monteverde.** The area's first hostelry—it dates from 1979—underwent a sparkling 2007 makeover worthy of a reality TV show and the updated furnishings make the place one of the area's premier lodgings once again. **Pros:** luxurious furnishings; stupendous views. **Cons:** a little farther outside Santa Elena than some might want; a few front rooms get noise from road. **TripAdvisor:** "breathtaking view," "fairly good facilities," "very enjoyable." [$] *Rooms from: $85* ✉ *Cerro Plano* ☎ *2645–5046* 🌐 *www.monteverdemountainhotel.com* 🛏 *42 rooms* 🍴 *No meals.*

$ B&B/INN 🏨 **Monteverde Inn.** One of the cheapest inns in the area has bargain prices and friendly owners as its selling points. **Pros:** good rock-bottom budget value; friendly owners; good views. **Cons:** spartan rooms. **TripAdvisor:** "lovely hosts," "cozy and peaceful," "quaint and charming with beautiful views." [$] *Rooms from: $45* ✉ *50 m past Butterfly Garden on turnoff road, Cerro Plano* ☎ *2645–5156* 🌐 *www.monteverdeinncr.com* 🛏 *10 rooms* 💳 *No credit cards* 🍴 *Multiple meal plans.*

$$$ HOTEL Fodor's Choice ★ 🏨 **Monteverde Lodge.** The well-established Costa Rica Expeditions operates this longtime favorite and can put together a plethora of mix-and-match packages that include lodging, nature activities, and transportation from San José. **Pros:** rustic luxury; attentive service; many activities. **Cons:** ground-floor rooms can be noisy; not centrally located relative to Santa Elena or reserve. **TripAdvisor:** "comfortable," "clean rooms," "accommodating staff." [$] *Rooms from: $178* ✉ *200 m south of Monteverde Theme Park, Santa Elena* ☎ *2645–5057, 2257–0766 in San José, 800/866–2609 in North America* 🌐 *www.costaricaexpeditions.com* 🛏 *27 rooms* 🍴 *Multiple meal plans.*

$ B&B/INN 🏨 **Swiss Hotel Miramontes.** Switzerland meets the cloud forest at this Swiss-owned and -operated small inn at the edge of town on the road to Tilarán. **Pros:** pleasant, small operation; friendly owners. **Cons:** not many frills; far from sights. **TripAdvisor:** "oasis of Europe in Central America," "charming," "pleasant stay with a welcoming staff." [$] *Rooms from: $50* ✉ *1 km/½ mile south of Santa Elena* ☎ *2645–5152* 🌐 *www.swisshotelmiramontes.com* 🛏 *8 rooms* 🍴 *Breakfast.*

$$ B&B/INN 🏨 **Trapp Family Lodge.** The closest lodge to the Monteverde reserve has enormous rooms, with wood paneling and ceilings, have lovely furniture marvelously crafted from—you guessed it—wood. **Pros:** rustic luxury; good value; closest lodging to reserve entrance. **Cons:** far from town; rough road to get here. **TripAdvisor:** "cozy cabin in the woods," "pleasant mountain experience," "great staff." [$] *Rooms from: $85* ✉ *Main road from Monteverde Reserve* ☎ *2645–5858, 305/712–5634 in North America* 🌐 *www.trappfamilylodgecr.com* 🛏 *26 rooms* 🚭 *No smoking* 🍴 *No meals.*

SHOPPING

Librería Chunches. Librería Chunches has new and used books in English, as well as a good selection of Spanish-language literature and CDs from Costa Rican artists. ✉ *25 m south of Banco Nacional, Santa Elena* ☎ *2645–5147* 🕓 *Mon.–Sat. 8–6.*

ARTS AND CRAFTS

Cooperativa de Artesanía de Santa Elena y Monteverde (*CASEM*). The Cooperativa de Artesanía de Santa Elena y Monteverde, an artisans' cooperative made up of 89 women and three men, sells locally made crafts. The prices are higher than at most other places, but the high quality here and the knowledge that you are contributing to the livelihood of the community make them worth it. ⊠ *Next to El Bosque Lodge* ☏ *2645–5190* ⊕ *www.casemcoop.org.*

Coopesanta Elena. Coopesanta Elena is the distributor for packages of the area's gourmet Café Monteverde coffee and accoutrements. ⊠ *Next to CASEM* ☏ *2645–5901* ❂ *Daily 7–7.*

Hummingbird Gallery. The Hummingbird Gallery sells books, gifts, T-shirts, great Costa Rican coffee, prints, and slides by nature specialists Michael and Patricia Fogden, as well as watercolors by nature artist Sarah Dowell. ⊠ *Outside entrance to Monteverde Reserve* ☏ *2645–5030* ❂ *Daily 8–5.*

NIGHTLIFE

"Wild nightlife" takes on its own peculiar meaning here. You can still get up close with nature after the sun has gone down. Several of the reserves have guided evening walks—advance reservations and separate admission are required—and the Frog Pond at Monteverde Theme Park, Serpentario, and Bat Jungle keep evening hours.

Sounds and Scenes of the Cloud Forest. Noted area biologist Richard LaVal presents a slide show called *Sounds and Scenes of the Cloud Forest* at the Monteverde Lodge nightly at 6:15 ($5). Advance reservations are required.

Beyond that, you'll probably while away the evening in a restaurant or your hotel dining room chatting with fellow travelers. Monteverde is an early-to-bed, early-to-rise kind of place.

CAÑO NEGRO REFUGE

Long a favorite among fishing enthusiasts and bird-watchers, this remote area is off the beaten track and may be difficult to get to if your time in Costa Rica is short. You can cross into Nicaragua, via Los Chiles, but there are almost no roads in this part of southern Nicaragua, making access to the rest of the country nearly impossible. The border crossing at Peñas Blancas, near the north Pacific coast, is far more user-friendly (⇨ *Crossing into Nicaragua at Peñas Blancas, in Chapter 6).*

CAÑO NEGRO NATIONAL WILDLIFE REFUGE

Caño Negro National Wildlife Refuge. It's a shame that Caño Negro doesn't grab the same amount of attention in wildlife-viewing circles as other destinations in Costa Rica. The reserve is a splendid place to watch waterfowl and resident exotic animals. If you're not staying at one of the two lodges up here, the refuge is most easily visited as a day trip from La Fortuna. Sunset Tours pioneered the Caño Negro excursions, but most every Arenal-area tour operator can set you up. ⊠ *180 km/108 miles north of La Fortuna* ☏ *$10* ❂ *Daily 7–4.*

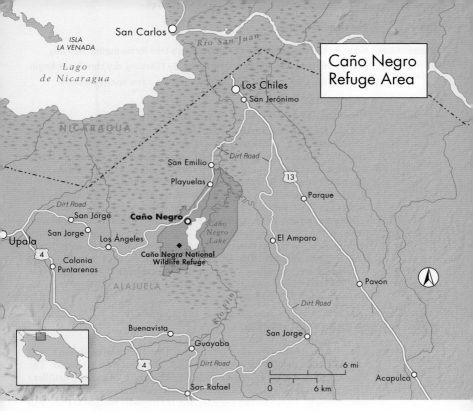

Caño Negro
Refuge Area

GETTING HERE AND AROUND

The highway from La Fortuna to Los Chiles is one of the best main-tained in the northern lowlands. You can catch public buses in San José at Terminal Atlántico Norte twice a day, a trip of about five hours, with many stops. Public buses also operate between La Fortuna and Los Chiles. If they have room, many tour companies (Sunset Tours included) will allow you to ride along with them on their shuttles, for a cost of around $10. If you're not staying way up here, an organized tour of the reserve from La Fortuna is the way most visitors get to and from.

OUTDOOR ACTIVITIES

Several La Fortuna–area tour companies have trips to Caño Negro.

Jacamar Naturalist Tours. Jacamar Naturalist Tours is a well-established tour operator with half-day trips ($72) to the Río Frío in the Caño Negro reserve. ☎ 2479–9767 ⊕ *www.arenaltours.com*.

Sunset Tours. Sunset Tours pioneered tours to the reserve, and runs top-notch, informative daylong or half-day tours, among the best in the country, to Caño Negro for $63 to $98, with higher rates in effect if you stay at one of the more far-flung Arenal lodgings. Bring your jungle juice: the mosquitoes are voracious. ☎ 2479–9585, 866/417–7352 in North America ⊕ *www.sunsettourcr.com*.

DID YOU KNOW?

Now you see it, now you don't: Caño Negro's lake forms during the rainy season when the Río Frío floods its banks. By February, dry conditions begin to shrink the lake, and by April, all that's left are a few spotty lagoons.

WHERE TO STAY

For expanded hotel reviews, visit Fodors.com.

$$ HOTEL **Caño Negro Natural Lodge.** That such an upscale property exists in this remote place might amaze you, but this Italian-designed, family-operated resort on the east side of the reserve is never pretentious. **Pros:** secluded location; close to reserve. **Cons:** need a car to get here. **TripAdvisor:** "hospitable and friendly," "lovely grounds," "special place." [$] *Rooms from: $105* ✉ *Caño Negro village* ☎ *2471–1426, 2265–3302 in San José* 🌐 *www.canonegrolodge.com* 🛏 *42 rooms* 🍴 *Breakfast.*

$$ HOTEL **Hotel de Campo.** All are welcome here, though this lodge is best known for its fishing tours, equipment and boat rental, and nearby lake filled with tarpon and bass. **Pros:** secluded location; close to reserve. **Cons:** need a car to get here. **TripAdvisor:** "great service and friendly staff," "a bird lover's paradise," "remote and wonderful." [$] *Rooms from: $95* ✉ *Caño Negro village* ☎ *2471–1012* 🌐 *www.hoteldecampo.com* 🛏 *15 rooms* 🍴 *Breakfast.*

THE SARAPIQUÍ LOOP

The area immediately north of the San José metro area doesn't leap to mind when discussing ecotourism in Costa Rica, but it should. The Sarapiquí River gave its name to this region at the foot of the Cordillera Central mountain range. To the west is the rain forest of Braulio Carrillo National Park, and to the east are Tortuguero National Park and Barra del Colorado National Wildlife Refuge. These splendid national parks share the region with thousands of acres of farmland, including palm, banana, and pineapple plantations, as well as cattle ranching. Cheap land and rich soil brought a wave of Ticos to this area a half century ago. Until the construction of Highway 126 in 1957, which connects the area to San José, this was one of the most isolated parts of Costa Rica, with little or no tourism. Government homesteading projects brought many residents, who cleared massive swaths of the rain forest for cattle grazing and agriculture. Now, ironically, old-growth lowland rain forest, montane cloud forest, and wetlands exist only within the borders of the national parks and several adjoining private reserves. A growing selection of nature lodges has set up shop here, and you can enjoy their offerings 60 to 90 minutes after you leave the capital. (Just try getting to the Osa Peninsula on the southern Pacific coast in that same time.)

POÁS VOLCANO NATIONAL PARK

Fodor'sChoice
★ *37 km/23 miles (45 mins) north of Alajuela, 57 km/35 miles (1 hr) north of San José.*

Arenal may be Costa Rica's most famous volcano, but you can walk right up to the crater here at Poás. That gives it an edge in the "cool volcano visit" department.

GETTING HERE AND AROUND

Taxis from San José are around $100 (and around $50 from Alajuela). From the Pan-American Highway north of Alajuela, follow the signs for Poás. The road is in relatively good condition. One public bus departs daily at 8 am from San José (⊠ *Avda. 2, Cs. 12–14*) and returns at 2 pm. A slew of tours from San José take in the volcano and combine the morning excursion with an afternoon at La Paz Waterfall Gardens, or tours of Café Britt near Heredia or the Doka Estate near Alajuela (⇨ *Chapter 4*). (⊠ *From Alajuela, drive north through town and follow signs* ☎ *2482–2424, 192 national parks hotline in Costa Rica* 🖬 *$10* ☉ *Daily 8:30–3:30*).

EXPLORING

★ **La Paz Waterfall Gardens.** Five magnificent waterfalls are the main attractions at La Paz Waterfall Gardens, on the eastern edge of Volcán Poás National Park, but they are complemented by the beauty of the surrounding cloud forest, an abundance of hummingbirds and other avian species, and the country's biggest butterfly garden. A concrete trail leads down from the visitor center to the multilevel, screened butterfly observatory and continues to gardens where hummingbird feeders attract swarms of these multicolor creatures. The trail then enters the cloud forest, where it leads to a series of metal stairways that let you descend into a steep gorge to viewing platforms near each of the waterfalls. A free shuttle will transport you from the trail exit back to the main building if you prefer to avoid the hike uphill. Several alternative paths lead from the main trail through the cloud forest and along the river's quieter upper stretch, providing options for hours of exploration—it takes about two hours to hike the entire complex. (Enter by 3 pm to give yourself adequate time.) The complex's new Jungle Cat exhibit serves as a rescue center for 35 felines (jaguars, ocelots, and pumas). The visitor center has a gift shop and open-air cafeteria with a great view. The gardens are 20 km (12 miles) northeast of Alajuela, and are a stop on many daylong tours from San José that take in the Poás Volcano or area coffee tours. ⊠ *6 km/4 miles north of Vara Blanca* ☎ *2482–2720, 954/727–3997 in North Ameirca* ⊕ *www.waterfallgardens.com* 🖬 *$35, $47 with lunch, $75 with round-trip transportation from San José* ☉ *Daily 8–5.*

VOLCANO-VIEWING ON AN EMPTY STOMACH

No question: the earlier you get to Poás, the better the views you'll be afforded. If that means skipping breakfast, a number of roadside stands on the way up the volcano sell strawberry jam, *cajeta* (a pale fudge), and rather bland corn crackers called *biscochos* to tide you over until you can have a hearty típico breakfast in the park visitor center's cafeteria.

5

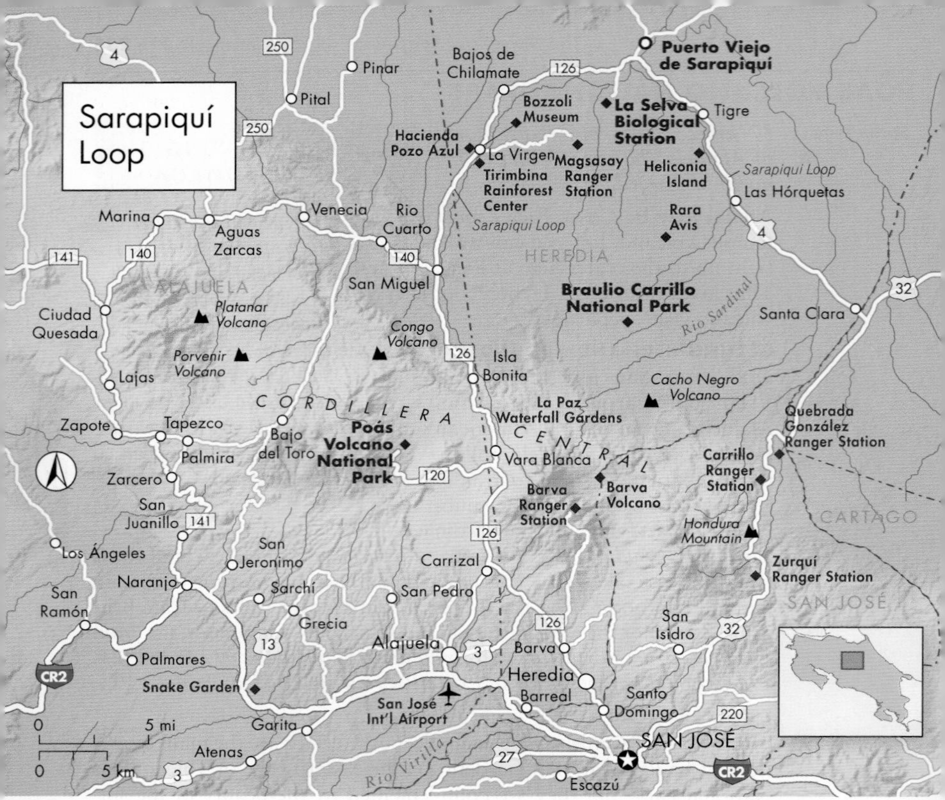
Sarapiquí Loop
Puerto Viejo de Sarapiquí
Bajos de Chilamate
Pinar
Pital
Bozzoli Museum
La Selva Biological Station
Tigre
Hacienda Pozo Azul
La Virgen
Tirimbina Rainforest Center
Magsasay Ranger Station
Heliconia Island
Sarapiquí Loop
Las Hórquetas
Rara Avis
Marina
Aguas Zarcas
Venecia
Rio Cuarto
HEREDIA
ALAJUELA
San Miguel
Braulio Carrillo National Park
Río Sardinal
Santa Clara
Ciudad Quesada
Platanar Volcano
Congo Volcano
Porvenir Volcano
Isla Bonita
Cacho Negro Volcano
Lajas
CORDILLERA CENTRAL
La Paz Waterfall Gardens
Quebrada González Ranger Station
Zapote
Tapezco
Bajo del Toro
Poás Volcano National Park
Palmira
Vara Blanca
Carrillo Ranger Station
Zarcero
Barva Ranger Station
Barva Volcano
San Juanillo
CARTAGO
Honduras Mountain
Los Ángeles
San Jeronimo
Carrizal
Zurquí Ranger Station
Naranjo
Sarchí
San Pedro
San Ramón
SAN JOSÉ
Grecia
San Isidro
Alajuela
Barva
Palmares
Heredia
Snake Garden
San José Int'l Airport
Barreal
Santo Domingo
Garita
SAN JOSÉ
Atenas
Río Virilla
Escazú
0 5 mi
0 5 km
4
250
126
141
140
120
32
13
3
27
220
CR2

WHERE TO EAT AND STAY

For expanded hotel reviews, visit Fodors.com.

$ 🍴 **Chubascos.** Amid tall pines and colorful flowers on the upper slopes of Poás Volcano, this popular restaurant has a small menu of traditional Tico dishes and delicious daily specials. Choose from the full selection of casados and platters of *gallos* (homemade tortillas with meat, cheese, or potato fillings). The *refrescos* (fresh fruit drinks) are top-drawer, especially the ones made from locally grown *fresas* (strawberries) and *moras* (blackberries) blended with milk. [$] *Average main: $8* ✉ *1 km/½ mile north of Laguna de Fraijanes* ☎ *2482–2280* ⏰ *No dinner.*

COSTA RICAN

Fodor's Choice ★

$ 🍴 **Jaulares.** Named after the *jaul*, a tree common in the nearby cloud forest, this spacious restaurant specializes in grilled meat, though there are also several fish dishes and *chicharrones* (deep-fried meaty pork rinds). All the cooking is done with wood, which adds to the rustic ambience of terra-cotta floors, bare wooden beams, and sylvan surroundings. The house specialty, *lomito Jaulares* (Jaulares tenderloin), is a strip of grilled meat served with *gallo pinto* (rice and beans) and a mild *salsa criollo* (creole sauce). Though primarily a lunch spot, Jaulares stays open until midnight on weekends for live music—Latin rhythms on Friday night and rock on Saturday night. Four basic cabinas in back are an inexpensive overnight option, though you'll need to reserve them early for

COSTA RICAN

concert nights. $ *Average main: $8 ⊠ 2 km/1 mile north of Laguna de Fraijanes* ☎ *2482–2155* ⊕ *www.jaulares.com.*

$$$
HOTEL
★

▦ **Peace Lodge.** These rooms overlooking the misty forest of La Paz Waterfall Gardens seem like something out of the *Lord of the Rings,* with their curved, clay-stucco walls, hardwood floors (note that all but the top floors can be noisy because of creaky stairs), stone fireplaces (gas), and four-poster beds made of varnished logs, complete with mosquito-net canopy. **Pros:** many activities included in rates; whimsical furnishings; rates include admission to the Waterfall Gardens. **Cons:** popular with tour groups; sometimes difficult to find space. **TripAdvisor:** "escape to a beautiful place," "the luxury of peace," "absolutely amazing." $ *Rooms from: $315 ⊠ 6 km/4 miles north of Vara Blanca* ☎ *2482–2720, 2225–0643 in San José, 954/727–3997 in North America* ⊕ *www.waterfallgardens.com* ⇥ *17 rooms, 1 villa* ⍥ *No meals.*

$$
B&B/INN

▦ **Poás Volcano Lodge.** Like a phoenix rising from the ashes, this country lodge, which suffered severe damage in the Poás earthquake of January 2009, has reinvented itself with luxurious suites in an entirely new modern main lodge and elegantly refurbished original rooms. **Pros:** close to volcano; coffeemakers and electric teakettles in rooms. **Cons:** difficult walking on pasture parts of trails; weather can be wet and foggy. **TripAdvisor:** "very tranquil and serene," "excellent food," "cozy lodge with tasteful rustic elegance." $ *Rooms from: $100 ⊠ 6 km/4 miles east of Chubascos restaurant, on road to Vara Blanca* ☎ *2482–2194* ⊕ *www. poasvolcanolodge.com* ⇥ *7 rooms, 5 suites* ⍥ *Breakfast.*

SHOPPING

Neotrópica Foundation. The Neotrópica Foundation sells nature-themed T-shirts, cards, and posters in the national park's visitor center and devotes a portion of the profits to conservation projects.

BRAULIO CARRILLO NATIONAL PARK

30 km/19 miles (45 mins) north of San José.

Barva Volcano. The 2,896-meter (9,500-foot) summit of Barva Volcano is the highest point in Braulio Carrillo National Park. Dormant for 300 years now, Barva is massive: its lower slopes are almost completely planted with coffee fields and hold more than a dozen small towns, nearly all of which are named after saints. On the upper slopes are pastures lined with exotic pines and the occasional native oak or cedar, giving way to the botanical diversity of the cloud forest near the top. The air is usually cool near the summit, which combines with the pines and pastures to evoke the European or North American countryside.

Barva's misty, luxuriant summit is the only part of Braulio Carrillo where camping is allowed, and it's a good place to see the rare resplendent quetzal early in the morning. Because it's somewhat hard to reach, Barva receives a mere fraction of the crowds that flock to the summits of Poás and Irazú. A two- to four-hour hike in from the Barva ranger station takes you to the main crater, which is about 162 meters (540 feet) in diameter. Its almost vertical sides are covered in *sombrillas de pobre,* a plant that thrives in the highlands, and oak trees laden with epiphytes (nonparasitic plants that grow on other plants). The crater is filled with an otherworldly black lake. Farther down the track into the forest lies a smaller crater lake. ■TIP→ Bring rain gear, boots, and a warm shirt. Stay on the trail when hiking anywhere in Braulio Carrillo; even experienced hikers who know the area have lost their way up here, and the rugged terrain makes wandering through the woods very dangerous. In addition, muggings of hikers have been reported in the park. (This is the closest national park to San José and its attendant urban problems.) Go with a ranger if possible.

For access to the volcano, start from Sacramento, north of Heredia. North of Barva de Heredia the road grows narrow and steep. At Sacramento the paved road turns to dirt, growing worse as it nears the Barva ranger station. We recommend a 4WD vehicle, especially during the rainy season. From the ranger station you can take a 4WD vehicle over the extremely rocky road to the park entrance (dry season only), or hike up on foot. The walk through the cloud forest to the crater's two lakes takes two to four hours, but your efforts should be rewarded by great views (as long as you start before 8 am, to avoid the mist). ⊠ *Access via the park's Barva ranger station* ☏ *2283–5906, 192 national parks hotline in Costa Rica* 🖾 *$10 (in addition to $6 Braulio Carrillo Park entrance)* 🕙 *Tues.–Sun. 7–4.*

Braulio Carrillo National Park. In a country where deforestation is still rife, hiking through Parque Nacional Braulio Carrillo is a rare opportunity to witness dense, primary tropical cloud forest. The park owes its foundation to the public outcry provoked by the construction of the highway of the same name through this region in the late 1970s—the government bowed to pressure from environmentalists, and somewhat ironically, the park is the most accessible one from the capital thanks to the highway. Covering 443 square km (171 square miles), Braulio Carrillo's extremely diverse terrain ranges from 55 meters (108 feet) to about 2,896 meters (9,500 feet) above sea level and extends from the central volcanic range down the Caribbean slope to La Selva research station near Puerto Viejo de Sarapiquí. The park protects a series of ecosystems ranging from the cloud forests on the upper slopes to the tropical wet forest of the Magsasay sector; it is home to 6,000 tree species, 500 bird species, and 135 mammal species.

For all its immense size and proximity to the capital, visitor facilities in the park are limited. Your exposure will most likely take place when you pass through on the way to the Caribbean, or when you stay at any of the lodgings that fringe Braulio Carrillo. Penetrating the park's depths is a project only for the truly intrepid:

The **Zurquí ranger station** is to the right of the highway, ½ km (¼ mile) before the Zurquí Tunnel. Here a short trail loops through the cloud forest. Hikes are steep; wear hiking boots to protect yourself from mud, slippage, and snakes. The main trail through primary forest, 1½ km (1 mile) long, culminates in a *mirador* (lookout point), but alas, the highway mars the view. Monkeys, tapirs, jaguars, kinkajous, sloths, raccoons, margays, and porcupines all live in this forest, and resident birds include the resplendent quetzal and the eagle. Orchids, bromeliads, heliconias, fungi, and mushrooms live closer to the floor. Another

La Paz Waterfall Gardens attracts 24 different species of hummingbirds and has a huge butterfly garden.

trail leads into the forest to the right, beginning about 17 km (11 miles) after the tunnel, where it follows the Quebrada González, a stream with a cascade and swimming hole. There are no campsites in this part of the park. The **Carrillo ranger station,** 22 km (14 miles) northeast along the highway from Zurquí, marks the beginning of trails that are less steep. Farther north on this highway, near the park entrance/exit toward Guápiles, is the **Quebrada González** ranger station. To the east of Heredia, a road climbs **Barva Volcano** *(⇨ below)* from San Rafael. ☎ *2290–8202 Sistemas de Areas de Conservación, 192 national parks hotline in Costa Rica* ✉ *$10* ⏲ *Daily 7–4.*

San Rafael de Heredia. San Rafael de Heredia, 2 km (1 mile) northeast of Heredia, is a quiet, tidy, coffee town with a large church notable for its stained-glass windows and bright interior. The road north from the church winds its way up Barva Volcano to the Hotel La Condesa, ending atop the Monte de la Cruz lookout point.

GETTING HERE AND AROUND
From San José, travel northeast on Calle 3, which becomes the Guápiles Highway (Highway 32), toward Limón. This highway winds through the park, entering at the main ranger station, Zurquí, and exiting at the Quebrada González ranger station. The Barva station is on the west side of the park, north of Zurquí, and is the easiest to access. From Heredia, drive north to Sacramento on Highway 114. The station is 4 km (2½ miles) northeast of Sacramento on a trail that's accessible on foot or by 4WD (except during heavy rains). If you're doing the driving, try to make this a morning trip. The highway through the park begins to fog over in the afternoon.

Any bus going to Guapiles, Siquirres, and Puerto Viejo de Sarapiquí can drop you off at the Zurquí ranger station. Buses ($2) depart from San José Monday through Saturday from the Atlántico Norte bus station (for Guápiles) or the Gran Terminal del Caribe (for Siquirres or Puerto Viejo de Sarapiquí) several times daily. A cab from San José costs $40 to $50. A number of tour companies offer one-day tours from San José.

OUTDOOR ACTIVITIES

HIKING

Barva Volcano. The upper slopes of Barva Volcano have excellent hiking conditions: cool air, vistas, and plentiful birds. The crater lakes topping the volcano can be reached only on foot, and if you haven't got a 4WD vehicle, you'll also have to trek from Sacramento up to the entrance of Braulio Carrillo National Park. The trails are frequently muddy; ask about their condition at the ranger station.

Sendero Botello. The Sendero Botello trail, on the east side of the park (entrance near the Quebrada González ranger station off the Guápiles Highway), is a better choice for casual hikers.

WHERE TO STAY

For expanded hotel reviews, visit Fodors.com.

$$
HOTEL

Hotel & Villas La Condesa Monte de la Cruz. The stone fireplace surrounded by armchairs and a small bar in La Condesa lobby is one of the many facets of the hotel that suggest a lodge you'd expect to find in a more northern latitude. **Pros:** rustic luxury; easily reached from San José. **Cons:** isolated; not much within walking distance. **TripAdvisor:** "beautiful facility," "wonderful accommodation," "great staff." *Rooms from: $145 ⊠ Next to Castillo Country Club, 10 km/6 miles north of San Rafael de Heredia ☎ 2267–6000 ⊕ www.hotellacondesa.com ⬦ 70 rooms, 25 suites ⦿ Breakfast.*

$$
HOTEL

Hotel Chalet Tirol. The Austrian design here doesn't seem out of place amid the pines, pastures, and cool air of Volcán Barva's upper slopes. **Pros:** cozy surroundings; good restaurant. **Cons:** need a car to stay here. **TripAdvisor:** "beautiful décor and landscaping," "spacious rooms," "the most amazing genuine service." *Rooms from: $93 ⊠ Main road, 10 km/6 miles north of San Rafael de Heredia ☎ 2267–6222, 800/720–1167 in North America ⊕ www.hotelchaleteltirol.com ⬦ 13 suites, 10 chalets ⦿ Breakfast.*

$$
HOTEL

Las Ardillas. Surrounded by old pines on a country road, these unpretentious log cabins are inviting retreats for those looking to lock themselves up in front of a fireplace and tune out the world. **Pros:** secluded location; good restaurant; easily reached from San José. **Cons:** rustic rooms; chilly here at night. **TripAdvisor:** "a place to breathe peace," "unforgettable," "heavenly." $\boxed{S}$ *Rooms from: $80* ⊠ *Main road, Guacalillo de San José de la Montaña* ☎ *2266–1003, 2266–0211* ⊕ *www. grupoardillas.com* ⇌ *8 cabins* ⦿l *Breakfast.*

PUERTO VIEJO DE SARAPIQUÍ

6½ km/4 miles north of La Selva.

One of Costa Rica's lesser-known eco-destinations has been developing a growing selection of nature-theme activities in recent years. In the 19th century, Puerto Viejo de Sarapiquí was a thriving river port and the only link with the coastal lands straight east. Fortunes nose-dived with the construction of a full-fledged port in the town of Moín near Limón, and today Puerto Viejo has a slightly run-down air. The activities of the Nicaraguan Contras made this a danger zone in the 1980s, but now that the political situation has improved, boats once again ply the old route up the Sarapiquí River to the San Juan River on the Nicaraguan frontier, from where you can travel downstream to Barra del Colorado or Tortuguero. (Wars of words still occasionally flare up between Costa Rica and Nicaragua, but they need not concern you as a visitor.) A few tour companies have Sarapiquí River tours with up to Class III rapids in the section between Chilamate and La Virgen, with plenty of wildlife to see. If you prefer to leave the driving to them, many of the lodges operate boat tours on the tamer sections of the river.

GETTING HERE AND AROUND

The Braulio Carrillo Highway runs from Calle 3 in San José and passes the Zurquí and Quebrada González sectors of Braulio Carrillo National Park. It branches at Santa Clara, north of the park, with the paved Highway 4 continuing north to Puerto Viejo de Sarapiquí. Alternatively, an older winding road connects San José with Puerto Viejo de Sarapiquí, passing through Heredia and Vara Blanca. The former route is easier, with less traffic; the latter route is more scenic but heavily trafficked. (If you are at all prone to motion sickness, take the newer road.) The roads are mostly paved, with the usual rained-out dirt and rock sections; road quality depends on the time of year, the length of time since the last visit by a road crew, and/or the amount of rain dumped by the latest tropical storm. Heavy rains sometimes cause landslides that block the highway near the Zurquí Tunnel inside the park, in which case you have to go via Vara Blanca. Check conditions before you set out. Get an early start; fog begins to settle in on both routes by midafternoon. ■ TIP → There are gas stations on the Braulio Carrillo Highway at the turn-off to Puerto Viejo de Sarapiquí, as well as just outside town. Fill the tank when you get the chance.

Buses travel several times daily via both routes and leave from San José's Gran Terminal del Caribe.

ESSENTIALS

Bank/ATM Banco Nacional ⊠ *Across from post office* ☎ *2766–6012.*

Internet Internet Sarapiquí ⊠ *Next to Joyería Mary* ☎ *2766–6223.*

Medical Clinic Red Cross ⊠ *West end of town* ☎ *2766–6901.*

Post Office Correos ⊠ *50 m north of soccer field.*

EXPLORING

Hacienda Pozo Azul. A working dairy farm and horse ranch, the Hacienda Pozo Azul runs guided tours of the ecologically sound 2,000-acre, 360-cattle dairy operation. It also has many adventure tours that you can mix and match into various packages (⇨ *Outdoor Activities, below*). ⊠ *La Virgen de Sarapiquí, 17 km/11 miles southwest of Puerto Viejo* ☎ *2438–2616, 877/810–6903 in North America* ⊕ *www.pozoazul. com* 🖃 *$10* ☉ *By reservation.*

CAUTION

Don't confuse Puerto Viejo de Sarapiquí with Puerto Viejo de Talamanca on the south Caribbean coast (⇨ *Puerto Viejo de Talamanca, in Chapter 9*). Locals refer to both as simply "Puerto Viejo." Buses for both towns depart from San José's Gran Terminal del Caribe with nothing more than a *"puerto viejo"* sign in the station to designate either. Point to the map and ask for clarification before boarding.

Heliconia Island. Heliconias abound at the aptly named Heliconia Island in the Sarapiquí River. Some 70 species of the flowering plant, a relative of the banana, are among the collections that populate 5 acres of botanical gardens here. Expect to see ample bird and butterfly life, too. ⊠ *La Chaves, 8 km/5 miles south of Puerto Viejo de Sarapiquí* ☎ *2764–5220* ⊕ *www.heliconiaisland.com* 🖃 *$10, $15 with guide* ☉ *Daily 8–5.*

★ **Dr. María Eugenia Bozzoli Museum of Indigenous Cultures.** Costa Rica's indigenous peoples don't get the visibility of those in Guatemala or Mexico, probably because they number only 40,000 out of a population of 4 million. The Dr. María Eugenia Bozzoli Museum of Indigenous Cultures (Museo de Culturas Indígenas Doctora María Eugenia Bozzoli), part of the Centro Neotrópico Sarapiquís, provides a well-rounded all-under-one-roof introduction to the subject. Nearly 400 artifacts of the Boruca, Bribri, Cabécar, Guaymí, and Maleku peoples are displayed, including masks, musical instruments, and shamanic healing sticks. Start by watching a 17-minute video introduction, *Man and Nature in Pre-Columbian Costa Rica*. A botanical garden next door cultivates medicinal plants still used by many traditional groups. In 1999 researchers discovered an archaeological site on the grounds that contains pre-Columbian tombs and petroglyphs dating from the 15th century. The site is still under study. ⊠ *La Virgen de Sarapiquí, 17 km/11 miles southwest of Puerto Viejo* ☎ *2761–1004* ⊕ *www.sarapiquis.org* 🖃 *$12 (includes guide)* ☉ *Daily 9–5.*

Ⓒ **Snake Garden.** The newest of Costa Rica's serpentaria is the aptly named Snake Garden, with some 50 species of reptiles on display, including all the poisonous snakes (and most of the nonpoisonous ones) found here in Costa Rica, as well as pythons, anacondas, and rattlesnakes from elsewhere in North and South America. You can handle a few specimens (the nonvenomous varieties, at least) upon request and under supervision. ⊠ *La Virgen de Sarapiquí, 400 m south of Centro Neotrópico Sarapiquís* ☎ *2761–1059* 🖃 *$8* ☉ *Daily 9–5.*

Insanely steep hills and heavy rainfall make this country a mecca for white-water sports.

Standard Fruit Company. Curious about the life and times of Costa Rica's most famous yellow fruit? The Standard Fruit Company, known as Dole in North America, has two-hour Banana Tours to guide you through the process from plantation to processing to packing. Visits are best arranged through several San José travel agencies, who will transport you to any of the three sites. Options include a longer tour at a plantation here in Sarapiquí or a shorter tour south of the Caribbean port of Limón, which is primarily geared toward cruise-ship passengers. ☎ 2768–8683, 8383–4596 ⊕ *www.bananatourcostarica.com* ✉ *$15* ⊘ *Tours daily at 10 am.*

Tirimbina Rainforest Center. Bats are not blind, contrary to popular belief, and most have no interest in sucking your blood. These are just a couple of things you learn on the **Bat Tour** at the nonprofit Tirimbina Rainforest Center. Also in the "did you know?" category, touching frogs will not give you warts. You'll learn that on Tirimbina's evening Frog Tour. An informative three-hour guided tour during the day is a terrific value. The center encompasses 750 acres of primary forest and 8 km (5 miles) of trails, some of them traversing hanging bridges at canopy level. Reservations are required for some tours but recommended for all. ⊠ *La Virgen de Sarapiquí, 17 km/11 miles southwest of Puerto Viejo* ☎ 2761–0333 ⊕ *www.tirimbina.org* ✉ *$15, $22 guided nature walk, $20 night walk, $20 bat tour, $20 frog tour, $24 bird-watching tour, $22 chocolate tour* ⊘ *Daily 7–5. Guided nature walks daily 8 and 10 am and 1:30 and 3 pm; bird-watching tour daily 6 am; bat tour daily 7:30 pm with reservation; frog tour daily 7:30 pm with reservation; chocolate tour daily 8 and 10 am and 1:30 and 3 pm; night walk at 7:30 pm with reservation.*

OUTDOOR ACTIVITIES

Hotel Gavilán Río Sarapiquí. Hotel Gavilán Río Sarapiquí runs wildlife- and bird-watching tours from its site on the river near Puerto Viejo de Sarapiquí. ✉ *700 m north of Comando Atlántico (naval command)* ☎ *2766–6743, 2234–9507 in San José* 🌐 *www.gavilanlodge.com.*

CANOPY TOUR

Hacienda Pozo Azul. The canopy tour ($50) at Hacienda Pozo Azul *(⇨ above)* has 12 zip lines, ranging in height from 18 to 27 meters (60 to 90 feet). ✉ *La Virgen de Sarapiquí, 17 km/11 miles southwest of Puerto Viejo* ☎ *2438–2616, 877/810–6903 in North America* 🌐 *www.pozoazul.com.*

HORSEBACK RIDING

Hacienda Pozo Azul. Dairy farm Hacienda Pozo Azul *(⇨ above)* is also a horse ranch and has riding excursions for all experience levels through the region around La Virgen. A two-hour tour is $42, a half day is $50. Check out the multiday tours, too, if you're an experienced rider. ✉ *La Virgen de Sarapiquí, 17 km/11 miles southwest of Puerto Viejo* ☎ *2438–2616, 877/810–6903 in North America* 🌐 *www.pozoazul.com.*

MOUNTAIN BIKING

Hacienda Pozo Azul. Hacienda Pozo Azul *(⇨ above)* has half-day, full-day, and two-day rough-and-tumble back-roads bike tours ($45–$75). ✉ *La Virgen de Sarapiquí, 17 km/11 miles southwest of Puerto Viejo* ☎ *2438–2616, 877/810–6903 in North America* 🌐 *www.pozoazul.com.*

RAFTING

The Virgen del Socorro area is one of the most popular "put-in points" for white-water rafters, and offers both Class II and III rapids. Trips leaving from the Chilamate put-in are more tranquil, with mostly Class I rapids. The put-in point depends on the weather and season.

Several operators lead tours on the Sarapiquí River.

Ríos Tropicales. Ríos Tropicales takes in the Sarapiquí on day excursions from San José ($80). ☎ *2233–6455, 866/722–8273 in North America* 🌐 *www.riostropicales.com.*

RAPPELLING

Hacienda Pozo Azul. Hacienda Pozo Azul *(⇨ above)* guides you on a 27-meter (90-foot) river canyon descent ($38). ✉ *La Virgen de Sarapiquí, 17 km/11 miles southwest of Puerto Viejo* ☎ *2438–2616, 877/810–6903 in North America* 🌐 *www.pozoazul.com.*

WHERE TO STAY

For expanded hotel reviews, visit Fodors.com.

$$ HOTEL 🏨 **Centro Neotrópico Sarapiquís.** Overlooking the Sarapiquí River, the CNS is an environmental educational center, museum, garden, and hotel all rolled into one, and you'll never be at a loss for something to do here. **Pros:** good value; many activities; whimsical furnishings. **Cons:** no air-conditioning; sometimes difficult to find space. **TripAdvisor:** "unique lodging," "charming," "beautiful surroundings." [$] *Rooms from: $120* ✉ *La Virgen de Sarapiquí, 17 km/11 miles southwest of Puerto Viejo* ☎ *2761–1004, 866/581–0782 in North America* 🌐 *www.sarapiquis.org* 🛏 *36 rooms* 🍴 *No meals.*

$ ⊞ **Hotel Gavilán Río Sarapiquí.** Beautiful gardens run down to the river,
HOTEL   and colorful tanagers and three types of toucan feast in the citrus trees
on the grounds of this two-story lodge with comfortable rooms, white
walls, terra-cotta floors, and decorative crafts. **Pros:** lovely gardens;
many activities. **Cons:** rustic rooms; need a car to stay here. **TripAdvisor:** "great hotel for relaxation," "good birding," "quality time with
family." $ *Rooms from: $60* ✉ *700 m north of Comando Atlántico
(naval command)* ☎ *2766–6743, 2234–9507 in San José* ⊕ *www.
gavilanlodge.com* ⇋ *20 rooms* ¶○¶ *Multiple meal plans.*

$$ ⊞ **La Quinta Sarapiquí.** This small, family-owned and -operated inn has
HOTEL   rooms set among tropical gardens rich in heliconias, gingers, palms, and
flowering trees. **Pros:** friendly staff, beautiful gardens. **Cons:** smallish
rooms. **TripAdvisor:** "a place of endless discovery," "good base for
wildlife stuff," "rustic and comfortable retreat." $ *Rooms from: $110*
✉ *5 km/3 miles east of La Virgen* ☎ *2761–1052, 2222–3344 in San José*
⊕ *www.laquintasarapiqui.com* ⇋ *28 rooms* ¶○¶ *No meals.*

$ ⊞ **Posada Andrea Cristina.** The Martínez family owns and operates this
HOTEL   basic, but friendly and comfortable, bed-and-breakfast. **Pros:** good
value; secluded location; attentive owners. **Cons:** rustic rooms; need a
car to stay here. **TripAdvisor:** "a place with soul," "first-class accommo-
dations and hosts," "good hospitality." $ *Rooms from: $52* ✉ *½ km/
¼ mile west of town* ☎ *2766–6265* ⊕ *www.andreacristina.com* ⇋ *6
cabins* ▭ *No credit cards* ¶○¶ *Breakfast.*

$$ ⊞ **Selva Verde Lodge.** Built on stilts over the Sarapiquí River, this expan-
HOTEL   sive complex stands on the edge of a 2-square-km (1-square-mile) pri-
★   vate reserve of tropical rain forest and caters primarily to natural-history
tours. **Pros:** ecology-minded staff; many activities. **Cons:** popular with
tour groups; sometimes difficult to find space; steep walk to reach a few
bungalows. **TripAdvisor:** "deep in the rainforest," "relaxing," "really
enjoyable." $ *Rooms from: $131* ✉ *7 km/4 miles west of Puerto Viejo
de Sarapiquí* ☎ *2761–1800, 800/451–7111 in North America* ⊕ *www.
selvaverde.com* ⇋ *40 rooms, 5 bungalows* ¶○¶ *Multiple meal plans.*

LA SELVA BIOLOGICAL STATION

☾   **La Selva Biological Station.** At the confluence of the Puerto Viejo and
Sarapiquí rivers, La Selva packs about 420 bird species, 460 tree species, and 500 butterfly species into just 15 square km (6 square miles).
Spottings might include the spider monkey, poison dart frog, agouti,
collared peccary, and dozens of other rare creatures. Extensive, well-
marked trails and swing bridges, many of which are wheelchair accessible, connect habitats as varied as tropical wet forest, swamps, creeks,
rivers, secondary regenerating forest, and pasture. The site is a project of the Organization for Tropical Studies, a research consortium
of 63 U.S., Australian, Latin American, and African universities, and
is one of three biological stations OTS operates in Costa Rica. To see
the place, take an informative three-hour morning or afternoon nature
walk with one of La Selva's bilingual guides, who are some of the country's best. Walks start every day at 8 am and 1:30 pm. You can add
a noontime lunch to your walk for $12; schedule it in advance. For a
completely different view of the forest, set off on a guided two-hour

walk at 5:45 am or the night tour at 7 pm. If you get a group of at least five together, you can enroll in the daylong Bird-Watching 101 course or one of the nature-photo workshops, which can be arranged anytime—either is $40 per person. Or get a group of at least six together and tag along with one of the resident research scientists for a half day. Young children won't feel left out either, with a very basic nature-identification course geared to them. Even with all the offerings, La Selva can custom-design excursions to suit your own special interests, too. Advance reservations are required for the dawn and night walks as well as for any of the courses. ✉ *6 km/4 miles south of Puerto Viejo de Sarapiquí* ☎ *2766–6565, 2524–0607 in San José, 919/684–5774 in North America* 🌐 *www.threepaths.co.cr* 🎫 *Nature walk $30, morning plus afternoon walks $38, dawn or night walk $40* 🕓 *Walks daily at 8 am and 1:30 pm.*

GETTING HERE AND AROUND

To get here, drive south from Puerto Viejo, and look for signs on the west side of the road. For those without wheels, La Selva is a $4 taxi ride from Puerto Viejo de Sarapiquí.

WHERE TO STAY

$$$ B&B/INN 🏨 **La Selva.** Other lodges provide more luxury for the money, but none can match the tropical nature experience at La Selva, a working biological-research station. **Pros:** many activities, ecology-minded staff. **Cons:** rustic room; no air-conditioning; sometimes difficult to procure overnight space. [$] *Rooms from: $168* ✉ *6 km/4 miles south of Puerto Viejo de Sarapiquí, Puerto Viejo de Sarapiquí* ☎ *2766–6565, 2524–0607 in San José* 🌐 *www.threepaths.co.cr* 🛏 *60 bunk beds share 12 baths, 18 cabins* 🍴 *All meals.*

OFF THE BEATEN PATH

South of Puerto Viejo de Sarapiquí, the tiny hamlet of Las Horquetas is a jumping-off point for two lodges, at different ends of the comfort scale:

$$ RESORT 🏨 **Rara Avis.** Toucans, sloths, great green macaws, howler and spider monkeys, vested anteaters, and tapirs may be on hand to greet you when you arrive at remote Rara Avis, one of Costa Rica's most popular private reserves, open only to overnight guests. **Pros:** many activities. **Cons:** rough trip to get here; expensive for amenities provided. **TripAdvisor:** "true rainforest experience," "unique place," "an adventure to remember." [$] *Rooms from: $120* ☎ *2764–1111* 🌐 *www.rara-avis.com* 🛏 *16 rooms, 10 with bath* 🍴 *All-inclusive.*

$$ HOTEL 🏨 **Sueño Azul Resort.** This nature lodge and wellness retreat is the most luxurious property in the Sarapiquí area, and a favorite for honeymooners and those attracted by the wide variety of yoga and other "wellness" disciplines. **Pros:** lovely furnishings. **Cons:** no air-conditioning. **TripAdvisor:** "a piece of paradise," "beautiful walks," "a hotel with a personal touch." [$] *Rooms from: $119* ✉ *Just west of Horquetas, off Hwy. 4* ☎ *2764–1000, 2253–2020 in San José* 🌐 *www.suenoazulresort.com* 🛏 *65 rooms* 🍴 *No meals.*

The North Pacific

WORD OF MOUTH

"Samara also has restaurants and accommodations on the beach, but the 'town' also stretches 3 or 4 blocks inland. The beach is very pretty and very safe for swimming, not so great for surfing, although a good place to learn as waves can be much smaller."

—Allylam

WELCOME TO
THE NORTH PACIFIC

TOP REASONS
TO GO

★ **Beaches:** White sand, black sand; palm-fringed strands; beaches for swimming, partying, surfing, and sunbathing—you can't beat Guanacaste's beaches for sheer variety.

★ **Big wind:** From December to May, the trade winds whip across northern Guanacaste with a velocity and consistency that make the Bahía Salinas a world-class sailboarding and kitesurfing destination.

★ **Endangered nature:** Guanacaste's varied national parks protect some of Central America's last remaining patches of tropical dry forest, an unusual ecosystem where you might spot magpie jays or howler monkeys in the branches of a gumbo-limbo tree.

★ **Scuba diving:** Forget the pretty tropical fish. Sharks, rays, sea turtles, and moray eels are the large-scale attractions for divers on the Guanacaste coast.

★ **Surfing:** The waves are usually excellent at more than a dozen North Pacific beaches.

GETTING ORIENTED

1 Far Northern Guanacaste. Dry, hot Far Northern Guanacaste is traditionally ranching country, but it does include the impressive wildernesses of Santa Rosa and Rincón de la Vieja national parks, the latter of which holds one of Costa Rica's five active volcanoes. Farther to the north is Bahía Salinas, second only to Lake Arenal for wind- and kitesurfing.

2 Nicoya Peninsula Coast and Interior. The number and variety of beaches along the Nicoya Coast make it a top tourist destination. Each beach has its specialty, be it surfing, fishing, diving, or just plain relaxing. Hotels and restaurants are in generous supply. National parks Palo Verde and Barra Honda are the main attractions in the interior. The former is a prime bird-watching park; the latter has caves and waterfalls to explore.

Guanacaste Province—a vast swath of land in northwestern Costa Rica—is bordered by the Pacific Ocean to the west and the looming Cordillera de Guanacaste volcanic mountain range to the east. To the south is the Nicoya Peninsula, with almost continuous beaches along more than 100 km (62 miles) of Pacific coastline, as the crow flies. Many roads are unpaved, especially those to the national parks and those connecting less-developed beaches, so the best way to get around is in a 4WD vehicle. Take a plane, bus, or shuttle van to Liberia and pick up your rental car there.

6

PALO VERDE NATIONAL PARK

One of the best wildlife and bird-watching parks in the country, Palo Verde extends over 198 square km (76 square miles) of dry deciduous forest, bordered on the west by the wide Tempisque River.

With fairly flat terrain and less-dense forest than a rain forest, wildlife is often easier to spot here. Frequent sightings include monkeys, coatis, peccaries, lizards, and snakes. (Keep an eye out for the harlequin snake. It's non-poisonous but mimics the deadly coral snake coloring.)

The park contains seasonal wetlands at the end of the rainy season that provide a temporary home for thousands of migratory and resident aquatic birds, including herons, wood storks, jabirus, and flamingolike roseate spoonbills. Crocodiles ply the slow waters of the Tempisque River year-round, and storks nest on islands at the mouth of the river where it empties into the Gulf of Nicoya. Trails are well marked, but the weather here can be very hot and windy. Mosquitoes, especially in the marshy areas, are rampant. *(See page 340 for more information.)*

BEST TIME TO GO

The best time of year to go is at the beginning of the dry season, especially in January and February, when the seasonal wetlands are shrinking and birds and wildlife are concentrated around smaller ponds. Set off early in the morning or after 3 in the afternoon, when the sun is lower and the heat is less intense.

FUN FACT

The park is named after the lacy, light green Palo Verde bush, also known as the Jerusalem thorn. Even when it loses its leaflets, this tree can still photosynthesize through its trunk, so it can withstand the droughts common to this area.

BEST WAYS TO EXPLORE

BIRD-WATCHING

The greatest number of creatures you're likely to see here are birds, close to 300 recorded species. Many of them are aquatic birds drawn to the park's vast marshes and seasonal wetlands. The most sought-after aquatic bird is the jabiru stork, a huge white bird with a red neck and long black bill. You'll most likely see it soaring overhead—it's hard to miss. Other birds endemic to the northwest, which you may find in the park's dry-forest habitat, are streaked-back orioles, banded wrens, and black-headed trogons.

There's a raised platform near the OTS station with a panoramic view over a bird-filled marsh. Be prepared to climb a narrow metal ladder.

PARK STRATEGIES

Unlike many of the other national parks, you can drive 7 km (4½ miles) of fairly rough road from the park entrance to the Organization for Tropical Studies (OTS) research station, where most of the trailheads begin. From that point, the best way to see the park is on foot. Plan to spend a couple of nights in the dormitory-style park lodge so that you can get an early-morning start. You'll want to start early because this is a very, very hot area. Hike open areas in the cooler mornings and then choose shaded forest trails for hikes later in the day. Make sure you have a good sun hat, too.

RIVER CRUISE

A river does run through the park, so a delightful and less-strenuous wildlife-viewing option is to cruise down the Tempisque River on a chartered boat with a guide who'll do the spotting for you. Without a boat, you are limited to observing the marshy areas and riverbanks from a long distance. Be sure the boat you choose has a bilingual naturalist on board who knows the English names of birds and animals.

TOP REASON TO GO

BIRDS, BIRDS, BIRDS

Even if you're not used to looking at birds, you'll be impressed by the waves of migratory waterbirds that use this park as a way station on their migratory routes. Think of the 2001 documentary *Winged Migration*, and you'll have an idea of the numbers of birds that flock here.

LOTS OF WILD ANIMALS

Hiking the forest trails is hot work, especially in the dry season. But the wildlife viewing here makes it worthwhile. Watch for monkeys, peccaries, large lizards, and coatis. Take plenty of water with you wherever you walk, and use repellent or wear long sleeves and pants.

OUTDOOR ADVENTURES

The Organization for Tropical Studies has a number of activities that are good for just about any type of group. Choose from guided nature walks, mountain biking, boat tours, and even an occasional night-time tour. Accommodations can be a little rugged here, but that's half the fun.

6

RINCÓN DE LA VIEJA NATIONAL PARK

Rincón de la Vieja National Park is Costa Rica's mini-Yellowstone, with volcanic hot springs and bubbling mud pools, refreshing waterfalls, and cool forest trails. Often shrouded in clouds, the volcano dominates the landscape northwest of Liberia, rising above the sunbaked plains.

It has two windswept peaks, Santa María, 1,916 meters (6,323 feet) high on the east slope, and Rincón de la Vieja at 1,895 meters (6,254 feet) on the west. The latter slope has an active crater that hardy hikers can climb up to, and easily accessible fumaroles on its lower slope that constantly let off steam. The park protects more than 177 square km (54 square miles) of the volcano's forested slopes. The wildlife list includes more than 250 species of birds, plus mammals such as white-tailed deer, coyotes, howler and capuchin monkeys, armadillos, and the occasional harlequin snake (not poisonous). Las Pailas entrance has the most accessible trails, including an easy loop trail that wends past all the interesting volcanic features. *(See page 261 for more information.)*

BEST TIME TO GO

Good times to visit are January through May, during the dry season. January can be very windy, but that means temperatures stay cooler for hiking. May to November—the green season—is when the fumaroles and boiling mud pots are most active, but the crater is often covered in clouds so it's not the best time to hike to the top. Trails can get crowded during school break (mid-December through February). Get here early, well before 9 am, if you plan a long hike or a climb to the crater, since the park officially closes at 3 pm but you can still exit up until 5 pm. The park is closed Monday all year.

BEST WAYS TO EXPLORE

BIRD-WATCHING

Wherever you walk in this park, you are bound to hear the three-note song of the long-tailed manakin. It sounds something like "Toledo," and that's what the locals call this bird. Along with their lavish, long tail feathers, the males are famous for their cooperative courting dance: two pals leap back and forth over each other, but only the senior male gets any girl who falls for this act. The hard-to-spot rock wren lives closer to the top of the volcano. Birding is excellent most of the year here except for January when the weather is dry but often too windy to distinguish between a fluttering leaf or a flittering bird.

HIKING

The only way to explore the park trails is on foot, along well-marked paths that range from easy loops to longer, more-demanding climbs. The ranger station at Las Pailas entrance provides maps of the park trails and washrooms before you set off. The easiest hike is Las Pailas loop, which starts just past the ranger station; it takes about two hours to hike. If you want to venture farther afield, follow the signs for La Cangreja trail. After passing through dense, cool forest, you'll emerge through an avenue of giant agave plants into an open, windy, meadow. Your reward is the cool waterfall and swimming hole at the end of the trail. There are also warm springs in the rocks surrounding the pool, so you can alternate between warm and cool water in this natural spa.

ON HORSEBACK

Saddle up to explore the lower slopes of the volcano, just outside the park borders. Local ranches and lodges organize daylong trail rides to waterfalls and sulfur springs. Your nose will tell you when you are approaching the springs—it's not the picnic lunch gone bad, it's the distinctive rotten-egg smell of sulfur.

TOP REASON TO GO

BIRDING

The park's forest, alive with the haunting songs of the long-tailed manakin and the loud whinnies of the ivory-billed woodcreeper, is prime bird-watching territory. For intrepid birders, the winding trail leading to the crater is home to the rock wren, which can only be found on these slopes.

CLIMBING TO THE CRATER

The hike to the crater summit is the most demanding, but also the most dramatic. The trail climbs 8 km (5 miles) through shaded forest, then up a sunbaked, treeless slope to the windswept crater, where temperatures plummet. Be sure to check wind and weather conditions at the ranger station before attempting this hike.

GEOLOGICAL WONDERS

Three-kilometer (2-mile) Las Pailas loop trail showcases the park's famous geothermal features. Along the trail you'll see fumaroles with steam hissing out of ground vents, a *volcancito* (baby volcano), and boiling mud fields named after pots (*pailas*) used for boiling down sugarcane.

SANTA ROSA NATIONAL PARK

Renowned for its wildlife, Santa Rosa National Park protects the largest swath of extant lowland dry forest in Central America, about 91,000 acres. *Dry* is the operative word here, with less than 1,500 cm (59 inches) of rainfall a year in some parts of the park.

If you station yourself near watering holes in the dry season—January to April—you may spot deer, coyotes, coatis, and armadillos. The park also has the world's only fully protected nesting beach for olive ridley sea turtles. Treetop inhabitants include spider, capuchin, and howler monkeys, as well as hundreds of bird species. The deciduous forest here includes giant kapok, Guanacaste, and mahogany trees, as well as calabash, acacia, and gumbolimbo trees with their distinctive peeling bark. The park is also of historical significance to Costa Rica because it was here, in 1856, that an army of Costa Rican volunteers decisively defeated an invading force of mercenaries led by an American adventurer named William Walker. *(See page 267 for more information.)*

BEST TIME TO GO

Dry season is the best time to visit if you want to see wildlife. The vegetation is sparse, making for easy observation. It's also the best time to drive to the park's beaches. Be aware: it can get very hot and very dry, so take plenty of water if you plan on hiking. In the rainy season, trails can become mud baths.

FUN FACT

Moving from sparse, sunlit secondary forest into the park's shady primary forest areas, you can experience an instant temperature drop of as much as 5C° (9F°). It's a little like walking into a fridge, so wear layers.

BEST WAYS TO EXPLORE

GETTING AROUND

Only the first 12 km (7 miles) of the park's roads are accessible by vehicles. The rest of the park's 20 km (12 miles) of trails are for hiking only. It's easy to drive to La Casona headquarters along a paved road and pick up a loop hiking trail, but beyond that point you need a four-wheel-drive vehicle. During the rainy season, the roads beyond La Casona are often impassable even to four-wheel-drive vehicles. Get an early start for any hikes to take advantage of cooler temperatures.

A HISTORICAL TOUR

Costa Rica doesn't have many historical sites—relics of its colonial past have mostly been destroyed by earthquakes and volcanic eruptions. So La Casona, the symbolic birthplace of Costa Rica's nationhood, is a particularly revered site. Most Costa Ricans come to Santa Rosa on a historical pilgrimage. Imagine the nation's horror when the place was burned to the ground in a fire purposely set in 2001 by disgruntled poachers, who had been fined by park rangers. The government, schoolchildren, and private businesses came to the rescue, raising the money to restore the historic hacienda and replace the exhibits of antique farm tools and historical photos.

TURTLE-WATCHING

Thousands of olive ridley sea turtles emerge from the sea every year, from July to December, to dig nests and deposit eggs on the park's protected beaches at Playa Nancite and Playa Naranjo. Green sea turtles and the huge leatherbacks also clamber ashore, but in much smaller numbers. If you're a hardy outdoors type, you can hike the 12 km (8 miles) to Playa Naranjo and pitch your tent near the beach. Unlike most other turtle-nesting beaches with organized tours, this is a natural spectacle you'll get to witness far from any crowds. Playa Nancite is a totally protected beach and thus off-limits to tourists.

TOP REASONS TO GO

EXPLORE THE FOREST

The short (about 1 km/ ½ miles) La Casona nature-trail loop, which starts from the park headquarters, is a great way to get a sampling of dry tropical forest and to spot wildlife. Look for signs leading to the *Indio Desnudo* (Naked Indian) path, named after the local word for gumbo-limbo trees.

SERIOUS SURFING

Off Playa Naranjo lies the famous Witch's Rock, a towering rock formation famous for its surfing breaks. If you're interested in checking it out but don't feel like walking for miles, take a boat from Playas del Coco, Playa Hermosa, or Playa Tamarindo.

WILDLIFE WATCHING

Wildlife is easy to spot here thanks to the low-density foliage of this tropical dry forest. Scan the treetops and keep an eye out for spider, white-faced capuchin, and howler monkeys. If you're lucky you might even spot an ocelot.

6

ECO-LODGES IN THE NORTH PACIFIC

On the mainland, sweeping plains bordered by volcanoes hold remnants of Central America's tropical dry forest. On the Pacific-edged Nicoya Peninsula, conservationists try to protect turtle-nesting beaches from the encroachments of ever-grander resort hotels and vacation houses.

These tropical dry forests change from relatively lush landscapes during the rainy season to desertlike panoramas in the dry months. The national parks of Santa Rosa, Rincón de la Vieja, Palo Verde, and Barra Honda all protect vestiges of dry forest, as do the private reserves of Hacienda Guachipelín and Rincón de la Vieja Mountain Lodge, where guests can explore on horseback. Visitors can experience the region's wetlands and waterways by riverboat tours and raft. The Nicoya Peninsula is also the site of Las Baulas National Marine Park, where massive leatherback sea turtles lay their eggs on Playa Grande from October to March; and Ostional National Wildlife Refuge, where thousands of olive ridley turtles clamber ashore to nest on moonlit nights, mostly from July to January.

GOOD PRACTICES

After a decade of uncontrolled development in the North Pacific province of Guanacaste, *Guanacastecation* became a pejorative watchword in Costa Rica for unsustainable development.

Playas Junquillal, Negra, Nosara, and Punta Islita are some of the notable exceptions to overdevelopment, managing to maintain a balance between nature and commercial development. Eco-minded tourists who are planning a beach vacation may want to visit these less-developed areas and reward lodge owners who have worked hard to keep their pieces of paradise as sustainable as possible.

TOP ECO-LODGES IN THE NORTH PACIFIC

BORINQUEN MOUNTAIN RESORT & SPA

This luxury resort of stylish villas on the western slope of Rincón de la Vieja doesn't fit the typical eco-lodge profile. But the hotel's eco-conscious policies have won it three leaves in the Green Leaf sustainability program. As well as putting sustainable practices to work, staff members teach the local community about the importance of recycling, waste separation, and organic gardening. The hotel uses earth-friendly, biodegradable products; conserves energy consumption and water use; and helps support community schools with proceeds from recycling refunds. *(Full hotel review on page 265.)*

HARMONY HOTEL

Steps from Playa Guiones in Nosara, this former surfer hotel has been transformed into a luxury resort with a sustainable mind-set. From permaculture-inspired landscaping with native plants and the use of biodegradable cleaning products and toiletries, to solar-heated hot water and conscientious recycling and waste-management policies, the hotel owners cover all the eco-stops, garnering the country's top five-leaf Sustainability Certificate. Hotel employees, most of them local hires, also volunteer in the town schools, mentoring and teaching English classes and computer literacy. *(Full hotel review on page 331.)*

HOTEL LAGARTA LODGE

Perched high on a hill, Hotel Lagarta Lodge has a wonderful view of distant Ostional National Wildlife Refuge. With only 12 guest rooms, the hotel minimizes its environmental impact by keeping a sharp eye on its consumption of water and energy, as well as on waste management and recycling. Its eco-friendly hospitality and gardening practices have earned it three leaves in the national Green Leaf sustainability program. By far the most salient eco-aspect of the lodge, though, is its 90-acre private Nosara Biological Reserve. *(Full hotel review on page 331.)*

NESTING LEATHERBACK TURTLES

You simply cannot believe how big a leatherback turtle is. Weighing in at 550 kilos (more than 1,200 pounds), females come ashore under cover of night to lay clutches of up to 100 golf ball–size eggs in nests they dig out of the sand with their flippers. People will go to great lengths in the hopes of catching this incredible sight. Your best chance is at Playa Grande in Las Baulas National Marine Park. As night falls, groups of visitors, each shepherded by a local guide, hunker down at the park entrance, waiting for the summons to sprint down the beach to take their turn, standing silently and witnessing the monumental egg laying. A decade ago, it was almost a sure thing to find at least one laying turtle on the beach during the nesting season. But today, some groups will come away disappointed, a sad reminder of how in the past 25 years, shore development and commercial fishing have reduced sea turtle populations by 99%.

NORTH PACIFIC

Updated
by Dorothy
MacKinnon

Reliably sunny, dry weather brings planeloads of sun-starved northerners to the North Pacific area of Costa Rica every winter, and a windswept coastline makes Guanacaste popular with surfers eager to relive the legendary "Endless Summer" of the sport's early years.

An abundance of marine life and stellar diving spots also lure fishers and underwater aficionados. Add in some stunningly scenic national parks and a range of thrilling outdoor adventures, and you have all the ingredients that make Guanacaste an all-around top spot to experience Costa Rica's charms. Although most tourists head here for the dry, "high" season, it's even more beautiful—and cheaper and cooler and less crowded—in the "green" or low season, April to December.

PLANNING

WHEN TO GO
HIGH SEASON: MID-DECEMBER TO APRIL
This is the driest region of the country, with only 165 cm (65 in) of average annual rainfall. It's also the hottest region, with average temperatures around 30°C to 35°C (86°F to 95°F) in high season. It's no wonder that planeloads of sun-starved northerners come here for guaranteed sunshine and heat. The beaches and trails can get packed during these drier months, especially mid-December to February, when school is out in Costa Rica. January can be quite breezy, especially along the coast, thanks to the annual Papagayo winds. February through April are the driest months: skies are clear, but the heat is intense and the landscape is brown and parched. Fishing and scuba diving are at their best during this period, though.

LOW SEASON: MAY THROUGH OCTOBER
Major downpours are pretty much guaranteed every afternoon during the rainy season, which bring lower prices, fewer crowds, and a lush green landscape. But mornings are usually fresh and clear. Roads can become quite muddy, though, making travel difficult.

SHOULDER SEASON: NOVEMBER TO MID-DECEMBER

This is the best time to visit, when the rains have abated, the landscape is lush, and the evening air is cool. Hotels and restaurants are prepped for the impending tourist influx, and staff are fresh and eager to please. High-season rates begin mid-November; except for the popular U.S. Thanksgiving week, you can usually make a deal.

GETTING HERE AND AROUND

Most unpaved roads here alternate between being extremely muddy and treacherous during the rainy season, and being extremely dusty and treacherous during the dry season. That said, it can be a real adventure exploring the coastline if you have a 4WD or a hired driver with a good, sturdy car. The major artery in this region is the Pan-American Highway (CA 1), which heads northwest from San José to Liberia, then due north to the Nicaraguan border. It's fairly well maintained, but the convoys of trucks and buses often create heavy traffic and there are few passing opportunities. To skip the hours of frustrating driving, consider flying into Liberia, whose airport provides easy access to the region. Local hotels and tour companies can help you arrange for ground transportation in many cases. In Guanacaste, it's usually safe to take *pirata* (pirate, or unofficial) taxis, but always negotiate the price before getting into the cab, or ask your hotel to call a reputable driver.

AIR TRAVEL

Aeropuerto Internacional Daniel Oduber Quirós (LIR) in Liberia is an international gateway to the coast and recent expansion has almost doubled its size and comfort, with a new air-conditioned terminal. Tamarindo, Nosara, Playa Sámara, Playa Carrillo, and Punta Islita also have airstrips. Flying in from San José to these airports is the best way to get here if you are already in the country. If your primary destination lies in Guanacaste or Nicoya, make sure you or your travel agent investigates the possibility of flying directly into Liberia instead of San José, which saves some serious hours on the road.

SANSA and Nature Air have scheduled flights between San José and destinations on the Nicoya Peninsula.

BUS TRAVEL

You can ride in a comfortable, air-conditioned minibus with Gray Line Tourist Bus, connecting San José, Liberia, Playa Flamingo, Playa Conchal, Playa Potrero, Playa Brasilito, Playa Hermosa, Playas del Coco, Ocotal, Tamarindo, Rincón de la Vieja, and Playa Langosta. Fares are $45 to $49 to most beach destinations. The Gray Line Tourist Bus from San José to Liberia and Tamarindo begins picking up passengers from hotels daily around 8:45 am. The return bus leaves the Tamarindo and Flamingo areas around 8:40 am and 4 pm. Interbus has door-to-door minivan shuttle service from San José to all the major beach hotels (in Papagayo, Flamingo, Tamarindo, Cocos, Ocotal, Nicoya, and Sámara), for $45 per person. Reserve at least one day in advance.

CAR TRAVEL

The northwest is accessed via the paved two-lane Pan-American Highway (CA 1), which begins at the top of Paseo Colón in San José. Take the Friendship Bridge (aka Río Tempisque Bridge) across the Tempisque

River to get to the Pacific beaches south of Liberia. Once you get off the main highway, dust, mud, potholes, and other factors come into play, depending on which beach you visit. The roads to Playa Flamingo, Playa Conchal, Playa Brasilito, Tamarindo, Playa Grande, Playa Sámara, Playas del Coco, Hermosa, and Ocotal are paved all the way; every other destination requires some dirt-road maneuvering.

RESTAURANTS

Seafood and fresh fish are tops here, followed by fast food—pizza, tacos, BBQ—to satisfy the hordes of hungry surfers and beachgoers. But there are many sophisticated restaurants, too, offering Asian-fusion, Italian, French and international cuisine, especially in the tourist-heavy beach towns of Hermosa, Flamingo, Tamarindo, Nosara, and Sámara.

■TIP→ **Many restaurants, especially tourist-oriented ones with dollar-denominated menus, do not include the 13% tax plus mandatory 10% service. By law, menus are required to show the total price including tax, but many owners flout this law. Be sure to ask if taxes are included; otherwise you may be surprised by a bill that's 23% higher than you expected.**

Prices in the reviews are the average cost of a main course at dinner or, if dinner is not served, at lunch.

HOTELS

A wide range of lodging options awaits you in the North Pacific, so choose wisely. If your goal is to take leisurely swims and lounge quietly on the beach with a cocktail in hand, then avoid the beaches that are renowned for surfing waves. Superexpensive resorts like the Four Seasons are generally well balanced with budget hotels that charge less than $75 per night. As in all of Costa Rica, the places we recommend most highly are the small owner-operated hotels and bed-and-breakfasts that blend in with unspoiled nature and offer one-on-one attention from the staff and owners. Most hotels will be able to connect you with local tour operators and knowledgeable staff members who can help show you the best aspects of each destination, whether it's a local park with howler monkeys, a great family-run restaurant on the beach, or a thrilling canopy tour.

Prices in the reviews are the lowest cost of a standard double room in high season.

TIMING

Visiting this region for 10 days to two weeks will introduce you to its wonders and give you with a real taste of the North Pacific. Schedule plenty of beach time for lounging, sunbathing, surfing, diving, and snorkeling. Logistically, you also need to take into consideration slow travel over bumpy roads. A beach with lots of restaurants and nightlife can keep you entertained for a week or more, whereas a more solitary beach might merit only a couple of days. Also plan to visit some protected areas to enjoy canopy tours, wildlife viewing, and hiking. Outdoorsy types should consider spending a few days around Rincón de la Vieja National Park for its amazing hiking, bird-watching, and horseback riding. Other parks to consider are Palo Verde National Park, Santa Rosa National Park, and Barra Honda National Park. Most North Pacific beaches are just a few hours' drive from the Arenal Volcano area (⇨ *Chapter 5*), so the region can be combined with the Northern Plains.

TOUR OPERATORS

The excellent **Horizontes Nature Tours** (☎ 2222–2022 ⊕ *www.horizontes. com*) has independent, private tours with your own guide/driver and small-group tours.

Swiss Travel Service (☎ 2282–4898 ⊕ *www.swisstravelcr.com*) specializes in Guanacaste and has a new office near the Liberia airport. Despite the name, it's operated by Costa Ricans with lots of local experience. Custom-design a guided private or small-group tour.

ESSENTIALS

Bus Contacts Gray Line Tourist Bus ☎ 2220–2126 ⊕ www.graylinecostarica. com. **Interbus** ☎ 2283–5573 ⊕ www.interbusonline.com.

FAR NORTHERN GUANACASTE

North from Liberia, all the way to the Nicaragua border, a towering volcanic mountain range looms over vast plains that end at a windy coastline dotted with pristine beaches. This is Far Northern Guanacaste, one of the lesser-traveled but vastly rewarding parts of Costa Rica. Liberia, the capital of Guanacaste province, is the closest town to Costa Rica's second-largest airport. You'll most likely pass through it on your way to the beaches southwest of the city or to the nearby national parks of Guanacaste, Santa Rosa, or Rincón de la Vieja. This last park is home to Volcán Rincón de la Vieja, an active volcano that last erupted in 1991.

Northwest of Rincón de la Vieja, on the coast, Parque Nacional Santa Rosa (Santa Rosa National Park) is a former cattle ranch where Costa Ricans defeated the invading mercenary army of American William Walker in 1856. As part of the larger Guanacaste Conservation Area, Santa Rosa protects the country's largest remnant of tropical dry forest, as well as an important nesting beach for olive ridley sea turtles, which lay their eggs in the sand between July and November. Closer still to the Nicaraguan border is the town of La Cruz, overlooking the lovely Golfo de Santa Elena, and the remote, windswept beaches of Bahía Salinas.

RINCÓN DE LA VIEJA NATIONAL PARK

25 km (15 miles) northeast of Liberia.

★ **Rincón de la Vieja National Park.** Rincón de la Vieja National Park is Costa Rica's mini-Yellowstone, with steaming volcanic hot springs and boiling, bubbling mud ponds. The park protects more than 140 square km (54 square miles) of the volcano's upper slopes, which are covered with forest. Often enveloped in clouds, the volcano dominates the scenery to the east of the Pan-American Highway. It has two peaks: Santa María (1,916 meters/6,323 feet) and the barren Rincón de la Vieja (1,895 meters/6,254 feet). The latter has an active crater and fumaroles on its lower slope that constantly let off steam, making an eruption unlikely anytime soon. The wildlife here is diverse: more than 250 species of birds, including long-tailed manakins and blue-crowned motmots;

plus mammals such as white-tailed deer, coyotes, howler and capuchin monkeys, and armadillos. There are two main entrances: Santa María and Las Pailas; the latter is the most common place to enter the park because it has the most accessible trails and there are several hotels along the road leading up to it. ■ TIP→ If you want to explore the slopes of the volcano, go with a guide—the abundant hot springs and geysers have given unsuspecting visitors some very nasty burns. In addition, the upper slopes often receive fierce and potentially dangerous winds—before ascending, check at either ranger station for conditions. The park does not have guides; we recommend the guides at Hacienda Guachipelín and Rincón de la Vieja Mountain Lodge (⇨ below). You must sign in and pay at the ranger station. Many of the attractions people visit in Rincón de la Vieja are accessible without actually entering the park, since the ranches that border it also hold significant forest and geothermal sites. Unfortunately that same geothermic energy has now been harnessed by a huge electricity-generating plant, evidence of which you will see on your way to Las Pailas entrance: a huge pipeline now snakes around the scrubby pastureland on the approach to the park. It's unsightly but one of the unavoidable costs of "clean" energy. ☎ 2666–5051 ⤳ $10 ☉ Tues.–Sun. 7–5; last entry at 3 pm.

GETTING HERE AND AROUND

There are two park entrances on the volcano's southern slope: the less-traveled one at Hacienda Santa María on the road leading northeast from Liberia (one hour), where there is camping available; and the one at Las Pailas, past Curubandé off the Pan-American Highway. To get to Las Pailas entrance from Liberia, take the first entrance road 5 km (3 miles) northwest of Liberia off the Pan-American Highway. The turnoff is easy to miss—follow signs for Hacienda Guachipelín or the town of Curubandé. It's a very rough 23-km (14-mile) dirt road, enveloped in white dust, and you have to pay a small toll (about $1.50). The Santa María entrance is 25 km (15 miles) northeast of Liberia along the Colonia Blanca route, which follows the course of the Río Liberia. The turnoff from the Pan-American Highway to the hotels on the western slope of the volcano is 12 km (7 miles) northwest of Liberia, turning right at the road signed for Cañas Dulces. A 4WD vehicle is recommended, though not essential, for all these slow and bone-rattling rides.

La Posada del Tope Tours. There is no bus service to Rincon de la Vieja, but La Posada del Tope Tours arranges shuttle van transportation to the park entrance for $20 round-trip per person, leaving Liberia at 7 am and returning from the park at 4 pm. ⊠ *C. Real between Avdas. 2 and 4, 150 m south of cathedral entrance, Downtown, Liberia* ☎ *2666–3876.*

OUTDOOR ACTIVITIES

Borinquen Mountain Resort & Spa. Borinquen Mountain Resort & Spa offers a day package ($80) that begins with a horseback ride and a 90-minute canopy tour, followed by lunch and free time in the hotel's hot springs and natural steam bath. ⊠ *12 km/7½ miles northwest of Liberia on the Pan-American Hwy., then 23 km/14 miles north on the dirt road that passes Cañas Dulces* ☎ *2690–1900* ⊕ *www.borinquenresort.com.*

Buena Vista Lodge & Adventure Center. Buena Vista Lodge & Adventure Center, west of the park, lies on a large ranch contiguous with the park where visitors enjoy horseback riding, waterfall hikes, a canopy tour, hanging bridges, a 425-meter (1,394-foot) (long, not steep) waterslide through the forest, and hot springs. Tours are $30 to $45 per person; a combination tour that lasts six to seven hours costs $80, including lunch. ⊠ *Western slope of volcano, 10 km/6 miles north of Cañas Dulces* ☎ *2665–7759 in Liberia* ⊕ *www.buenavistalodgecr.com.*

Fodor's Choice ★ **Hacienda Guachipelín Adventure Tours.** This experienced outfitter has the most exciting tours in the area, including horseback riding, river tubing, hot springs and mud baths, and guided waterfall and hikes on the slopes of the national park volcano (from $25 to $50, special rates for children under 10 and students under 18). The popular canyon tour includes rock climbing, rappelling, zip lines, suspension bridges, and a Tarzan swing. A one-day, all-you-can-do adventure pass is $85, including lunch. ⊠ *Road to Rincón de la Vieja National Park* ☎ *2666–8075* ⊕ *www.guachipelin.com.*

Tours Your Way. Playa Hermosa–based Mainor Lara Bustos guides tours to Rincón de la Vieja or Palo Verde for $95 to $115, depending on pickup location, including transportation, entrance fees, lunch, and snacks. ☎ *8820–1829* ⊕ *www.tours-your-way.com.*

CANOPY TOURS

Buena Vista Lodge & Adventure Center. The zip-line canopy tour ($40) with Buena Vista Lodge & Adventure Center (⇨ *above*) has cables that are up to 27 meters (90 feet) off the ground and up to 135 meters (450 feet) long.

Rincón de la Vieja Canopy. This combined horseback and canopy tour ($45) includes a 16-platform zip line, a ride to Los Azufrales sulfur springs, or a forest hike to a waterfall with a box lunch. The tours take about 3½ hours. ⊠ *Rincón de la Vieja Mountain Lodge* ☎ *2200–0238* ⊕ *www.hotelrincondelavieja.com.*

HIKING

Nearly all the lodges and outfitters in the area offer guided hikes through the park to the fumaroles, hot springs, waterfalls, summit, or the edge of the active crater.

If you're doing a self-guided hike, stop for trail maps and hiking information at the park stations at both entrance gates. To give yourself enough time to complete the longer hikes, make sure you start out between 7 and 9 am.

Trail to the summit. The 8-km (5-mile) trail to the summit heads up into the forest from Las Pailas park entrance, then emerges onto a windy, exposed shale slope that's slippery and hard going, and has poor visibility owing to clouds and mist. It's a trip for serious hikers, best done in dry season with preparation for cold weather at the top.

loop through the park. A less-strenuous option is the fascinating 3-km (2-mile) loop through the park, which takes about two hours to complete, starting at Las Pailas entrance. Along the well-marked trail you'll see fumaroles exuding steam, a *volcáncito* (little volcano), and Las Pailas, the boiling mud fields named after pots used for boiling down sugarcane. If you tread softly in the nearby forest, you may spot animals such as howler, capuchin, and spider monkeys, as well as raccoonlike coatis looking for handouts. ■TIP➔ Remember the cardinal rule of wildlife encounters: don't feed the animals.

La Cangreja Waterfall loop. Another popular hike out of Las Pailas is a four-hour, 10-km (6-mile) La Cangreja Waterfall loop, passing through beautiful primary forests and windswept savannas. The *catarata* (waterfall) has a cool swimming hole below; the surrounding rocks have pockets of hot springs.

HORSEBACK RIDING

Borinquen Mountain Resort & Spa. Horseback tours ($80) on this lodge's 494-acre ranch pass through patches of forest and along ridges with views of nearby Rincón de la Vieja. The horseback tours can be combined with a hike to waterfalls, or a canopy tour. The tour combos include lunch and use of hot springs, and range in price from $80 to $95.

Buena Vista Lodge & Adventure Center. This lodge and tour operator (⇨ *above*) has horseback trips to hot springs and to Borinquen Waterfall ($45). If not everyone in your party is a horse lover, tractor transport ($35) is available to the hot springs as well.

Hacienda Guachipelín. This is the premier working ranch in the area, with more than 100 well-bred and well-trained horses, and miles of trails to three waterfalls, tropical dry forest, and hot springs. Horseback tours range from $25 to $40. The Hacienda also offers a weekly bull-riding demonstration and a cowboy-for-a-day tour ($50, kids $40) that includes harnessing your horse, rounding up cattle, and milking a cow. ✉ *Hacienda Guachipelín.*

Rincón de la Vieja Mountain Lodge. This lodge, closest to the national park, *(⇨ below)* also has guides for hiking in the park, or horseback riding near the park. ✉ *Rincón de la Vieja Lodge.*

WHERE TO STAY

For expanded hotel reviews, visit Fodors.com.

$$$ RESORT **Borinquen Mountain Resort & Spa.** The spacious villas on this 12,000-acre ranch are the most upscale—and expensive—accommodations in the area, but the room rate includes access to their hot springs and mud baths. **Pros:** attractive, well-equipped bungalows; peaceful environment; lots of outdoor activities. **Cons:** far from park entrance; pricey; restaurant a notch below accommodations. **TripAdvisor:** "tranquil," "lovely European-style resort," "beautiful rooms." [$] *Rooms from: $194* ✉ *13 km/8 miles northwest of Liberia on Pan-American Hwy., then 29 km/18 miles north on the dirt road toward Cañas Dulces* ☎ *2690–1900* 🌐 *www.borinquenresort.com* 🛏 *22 villas, 17 bungalows* 🍴 *Breakfast.*

$$ B&B/INN Fodor's Choice ★ **Hacienda Guachipelín.** One of the best values in the Rincón area for hair-raising adventure and nature tours *(⇨ Outdoor Activities, above)*, this hotel also gets top billing for its comfortable rooms, excellent restaurant, and friendly service. **Pros:** near park entrance; lots of activities; excellent value. **Cons:** caters to lots of large groups and day visitors; no air-conditioning in some rooms; vegetarians may have trouble finding meat-free dishes. **TripAdvisor:** "outstanding in all categories," "great place," "tours were good." [$] *Rooms from: $96* ✉ *17 km/10 miles northeast of the Pan-American Hwy., on road to Las Pailas park entrance* ☎ *2666–8075* 🌐 *www.guachipelin.com* 🛏 *52 rooms, 2 suites* 🍴 *Breakfast.*

$ B&B/INN **Rancho Curubandé Lodge.** Convenient to both Rincón de la Vieja and Santa Rosa National Park, these very affordable, equipped bungalows and modern rooms are part of a working farm owned by a Costa Rican family. **Pros:** easy access to highway to Santa Rosa National Park; very affordable, family-friendly bungalows **Cons:** some highway noise; half-hour uphill climb to Rincón de la Vieja National Park. **TripAdvisor:** "wonderful accommodation," "very nice," "great place for nature." [$] *Rooms from: $65* ✉ *Off Pan-American Hwy. on road to Las Pailas* ☎ *2665–0375* 🌐 *www.rancho-curubande.com* 🛏 *16 rooms, 2 villas* 🍴 *No meals.*

$ B&B/INN **Rincón de la Vieja Mountain Lodge.** This is the closest you can stay to Las Pailas park entrance, which makes it a good spot for hikers and nature lovers who care more about the natural setting than fancy rooms. **Pros:** close to park; lots of tour options; reasonably priced. **Cons:** rustic rooms; mediocre food. **TripAdvisor:** "wonderful staff," "quiet," "beautiful natural atmosphere." [$] *Rooms from: $70* ✉ *21 km/12 miles northeast of Pan-American Hwy.; 5 km/3 miles north of Hacienda Guachipelín; 2 km/1 mile south of Las Pailas park entrance* ☎ *8708–0238* 🌐 *www.hotelrincondelavieja.com* 🛏 *42 rooms* 🍴 *Breakfast.*

6

SANTA ROSA NATIONAL PARK

35 km/22 miles northwest of Liberia.

Santa Rosa National Park. Renowned for its wildlife, which is easy to spot in the dry season, thanks to sparser foliage, Santa Rosa protects the largest swath of tropical dry forest in Central America. It is officially known now as the Santa Rosa sector of the even larger Guanacaste Conservation Area. Camping expeditions serving bird-watchers, naturalists, and backpackers often venture deep into the interior, but it's possible to experience a good bit of its impressive flora and fauna on a full-day or half-day visit. Treetop inhabitants include spider, capuchin, and howler monkeys, as well as hundreds of bird species. If you station yourself next to water holes during the dry season, you may also spot deer, coyotes, coatis, or armadillos. Typical dry-forest vegetation includes kapok, Guanacaste, mahogany, calabash, acacia thorn, and gumbo-limbo trees.

Santa Rosa's wealth of flora and fauna is due in part to its remoteness, since much of it is still inaccessible to the common tourist. To get anywhere in the park, you must have a vehicle—preferably 4WD. The park headquarters, a historic ranch house and museum called La Casona, and a nearby camping area are 7 km (4½ miles) from the Pan-American Highway via a paved road. Within this dense, shady forest, temperatures drop by as much as 5°C (9°F).

In rainy season the park's rough road to the beach cannot be accessed by even 4WD vehicles, but several short trails head into the forest from its first, flat stretch, and day hikers can easily explore the first stretch of the steep part on foot. Park off the road just before it descends into the forest. From the park headquarters it's 11 km (7 miles) to **Playa Naranjo**, where the famed Witch's Rock surf break is located (surfers often get there by boat). **Playa Nancite**—the site of one of the world's few completely protected olive ridley turtle *arribada,* or mass nesting (accessible primarily to biologists and students; permit required)—is an additional 5 km (3 miles) by footpath north of Playa Naranjo. For more information, visit the park's website. ✉ *Km 269, Pan-American Hwy. 35 km/22 miles north of Liberia* ☎ *2666–5051* ⊕ *www.acguanacaste. ac.cr* 🎟 *$10* ⊙ *Daily 8–4.*

GETTING HERE AND AROUND

The turnoff for Santa Rosa National Park from the Pan-American Highway is well marked, about 30 minutes out from Liberia. From Liberia you can hop on a bus heading north to La Cruz and get off at the park entrance, but you'll have to hitchhike or hike 8 km (5 miles) in the hot sun to La Casona from here. La Posada del Tope *(⇨ above)* arranges shuttle vans from Liberia to the park entrance for $20 per person round-trip.

OUTDOOR ACTIVITIES

HIKING

Casona nature-trail loop. The short (about 1-km/½-mile) Casona nature-trail loop from the park headquarters is worth taking to get a brief sampling of the woods. Look for the "Indio Desnudo," or "Naked

Indian," path, named after the local word for gumbo-limbo trees. ■TIP→ Carry plenty of water and insect repellent.

Several other short trails lead off the road **to the beaches** before it becomes impassable to vehicles. The hike to Playa Naranjo (11 km/7 miles west of La Casona) requires good physical condition and lots of water. You can get a map of the trails at the park entrance.

SURFING

★ **Witch's Rock.** Witch's Rock towers offshore over a near-perfect beach break off Playa Naranjo in Santa Rosa National Park. If you are interested in surfing Witch's Rock, take a boat tour from Playas del Coco, Playa Hermosa, or Playa Tamarindo, to the south.

> **WALKER'S LAST STAND**
>
> Santa Rosa Park was the site of the 1856 triumph over American invader William Walker in the famous Battle of Santa Rosa— one of the few historic military sites in this army-less country. The rambling colonial-style ranch house called **La Casona** was the last stand of a ragged force of ill-equipped Costa Ricans who routed the superior mercenary army of the notorious Walker. Disgruntled poachers burned La Casona to the ground in 2001, but it has since been rebuilt.

WHERE TO STAY

For expanded hotel reviews, visit Fodors.com.

There are basic, dormitory-style lodgings and a camping area near the park's administrative center; you can also camp within Santa Rosa National Park at the very basic and remote campsites at the beaches of Naranjo and Murcielego. Call the park headquarters (☎2666–5051) for information. Most people visit the park on day trips from Liberia, or nearby Cuajiniquil.

PLAYA BAHÍA JUNQUILLAL

26 km/16 miles northwest of Santa Rosa National Park entrance.

Playa Bahía Junquillal. This 2½-km (1½-mile), tree-fringed, Blue Flag beach is as close as you can get to a white-sand beach in this part of Guanacaste. The warm, calm water makes it one of the best swimming beaches on the Golfo de Santa Elena. Not to be confused with the Playa Junquillal on the western coast of the Nicoya Peninsula farther south, this beach is part of the Guanacaste Conservation Area, and is a wildlife refuge, to the north of Santa Rosa. Stay for the day or camp out in the well-kept, shaded camping area with cold-water showers, bathrooms, grills, and picnic tables ($1 park entrance, plus 75¢ per person per night to camp). You can snorkel if you've got your own gear. ✉ *18 km/11 miles west of Pan-American Hwy., Cuajiniquil turnoff.*

GETTING HERE AND AROUND

From the Pan-American Highway, take the road signed for Cuajiniquil, 43 km (26 miles) northwest of Liberia and 8 km (5 miles) north of Santa Rosa National Park. Follow the paved road 14 km (8 miles) to the beach turnoff, along a dirt road for another 4 km (2½ miles). From the Bahía Salinas area, take the scenic dirt road (4WD recommended);

CLOSE UP

Guanacaste National Park

The 325-square-km (125-square-miles) Parque Nacional Guanacaste, bordering the east side of the Pan-American Highway 30 km (18 miles) north of Liberia, was created to preserve rain forests around Cacao Volcano (1,633 meters/5,443 feet) and Orosi Volcano (1,464 meters/4,879 feet), which are seasonally inhabited by migrant wildlife from Santa Rosa. The park isn't quite ready for tourism yet. There are very few facilities and no well-marked trails; if you want to hike, it's best to hire a professional guide. In rainy season, roads are impassable; a 4WD vehicle is required year-round. The park is part of the Guanacaste Conservation Area, a mosaic of interdependent protected areas, parks, and refuges; the goal is to accommodate the migratory patterns of animals, from jaguars to tapirs. Much of the park's territory is cattle pasture, which, it is hoped, will regenerate into forest. Today the park has more than 300 different birds and more than 5,000 species of butterflies and moths.

Park headquarters. To really explore the park, you must stay in the heart of it, at one of three biological stations. They are mostly reserved for students and researchers, but you can request accommodations from the park headquarters. ☎ *2666–5051.*

6

then follow the road near Puerto Soley (signed for Cuajiniquil) 7 km (4½ miles) to the beach entrance. It's about 30 minutes from the Pan-American turnoff and one hour from Bahía Salinas.

WHERE TO STAY

For expanded hotel reviews, visit Fodors.com.

$ 🏨 **Santa Elena Lodge.** This simple family-run lodge on the outskirts of
B&B/INN Cuajiniquil provides the closest accommodations to both Playa Bahía Junquillal and Santa Rosa National Park, making it a good option for nature lovers and anyone who wants to stray from the vacationing crowds. **Pros:** friendly; near beach and park; lots of outdoor options. **Cons:** little English spoken; basic accommodations; close to road. [$] *Rooms from: $70* ✉ *10 km/6 miles west of Pan-American Hwy., 8 km/5 miles east of Junquillal, Cuajiniquil* ☎ *2679–1038* ✉ *santaelenahotel@gmail.com* 🛏 *8 rooms* 🍴 *Breakfast.*

LA CRUZ

40 km/25 miles northwest of Liberia.

North of Santa Rosa National Park on the west side of the highway is the turnoff to La Cruz, a scruffy, bustling little town, noteworthy only for the stunning views of Bahía Salinas from its bluff and its proximity to the nearby windswept beaches on the south shore of Bahía Salinas, in the hamlet of Jobo, and in the Golfo de Santa Elena. The Nicaraguan border lies just north of La Cruz at Peñas Blancas. ■ **TIP→ All travelers are stopped at two checkpoints south of La Cruz for passport and cursory vehicle inspection. Police vigilance is heightened in the region.**

GETTING HERE AND AROUND

La Cruz is a straight-shot, one hour's trip north of Liberia on the Pan-American Highway. Buses leave Liberia for La Cruz, or you can flag down a bus that says "La Cruz" on its windshield anywhere along the highway north of Liberia.

ESSENTIALS

Bank Banco Nacional ⊠ *Pan-American Hwy. across from police station* ☎ *2679–9389.* **Banco Popular** ⊠ *50 m east of northeast corner of central park* ☎ *2679–9352.*

Hospital Clinica de La Cruz ⊠ *Main hwy. across from police station* ☎ *2679–9116.*

Internet Internet Moroni ⊠ *Beside Banco Popular.*

Pharmacy Farmacia La Cruz ⊠ *1 block north of central park* ☎ *2679–8048* ⊙ *Daily 8–8.*

Post Office Correo ⊠ *Behind police station on west side of central park.*

CROSSING INTO NICARAGUA AT PEÑAS BLANCAS

Costa Rica and Nicaragua share a busy border crossing at Peñas Blancas, 18 km (11 miles) north of La Cruz along a paved highway. ■TIP➡ Rental vehicles may not leave Costa Rica. Tica Bus and Transnica bus companies (⇨ *Bus Travel in Travel Smart Costa Rica*) travel direct between San José and Managua via this route. You can also take a Tralapa bus to the border from other points in Costa Rica. You'll make your crossing, then catch a Nicaraguan bus or taxi to Rivas, 35 km (22 miles) farther, which is the regional hub for buses departing to other parts of Nicaragua. The fee to cross the border is $7 (paid on the Nicaraguan side), plus a $2 surcharge if you cross from noon to 2 pm or on weekends. Nicaraguan shuttle taxis transport people between the border posts. Returning to Costa Rica is basically the same process in reverse; you are charged a $1 municipal tax and $2 exit tax to leave Nicaragua by land. The crossing is open daily 6 am to 10 pm, but only until 8 pm on Sunday; get there with time to spare or you *will* be stranded. Banks on both sides of the border change their own currency and U.S. dollars. Colones are not accepted or exchanged in Nicaragua; likewise for Nicaraguan córdobas in Costa Rica. Overland border-crossing procedures can be confusing if you don't speak Spanish, but attendants on the cross-border buses can help shepherd you through the formalities. The colonial city of Granada, the twin volcanoes of the island of Ometepe, and the lively beach town of San Juan del Sur—site of two consecutive seasons (2010 and 2011) of the television series *Survivor*—are the draws in southern Nicaragua.

BAHÍA SALINAS

15 km/9 miles west of La Cruz.

The large windswept bay at the very top of Costa Rica's Pacific coast is the second-windiest area in the country, after Lake Arenal, making it a mecca for windsurfers and kite-surfers, as well as beachgoers looking for breezy, uncrowded, pristine beaches. Strong breezes blow from November to May, when only experienced surfers are out on the water and the water grows steadily cooler. The south (bay) side has the strongest winds, and choppy, colder water from January to May.

In July and August the wind is more appropriate for beginners, whereas any time of year you can enjoy the area's diving and beaches. On the sheltered Golfo de Santa Elena, to the west, are two beaches that rank among the most beautiful in all of Costa Rica: Playa Rajada and Playa Jobo, a far cry from the overdeveloped beaches of Guanacaste's gold coast farther to the south.

THIEVES ON THE BEACHES

The North Pacific's idyllic land-scapes and friendly people belie an ever-present threat of theft. Though there aren't too many, Costa Rica's thieves manage to ruin a lot of vacations by absconding with backpacks, cameras, wallets, and passports, the last of which necessitates a trip to San José. Keep your valuables in your hotel safe—preferably the safe in the hotel office—and don't ever leave anything in an unattended car, even while checking into your hotel. Hotel parking lots are popular spots for local klepto-maniacs, as are beaches.

GETTING HERE AND AROUND

From a high point in La Cruz, the road to Salinas descends both in altitude and condition. It's only 15 km (9 miles) southwest to Hotel Ecoplaya Beach Resort, but after the first 2 km (1 miles) of paved road, the rest of the road varies from bad to worse, so it may take up to 45 minutes or an hour. Signs direct you to Puerto Soley and El Jobo, an end-of-the-road hamlet, about 2 km (1 mile) past the turnoff for Ecoplaya. Playa Copal is about 13 km (8 miles) along the same road from La Cruz.

EXPLORING

Playa Copal. Playa Copal is a narrow, dark-beige beach that wouldn't be worth visiting except for the fact that it is one of the main venues for kitesurfing. There are villas and rooms for rent. A couple of kilometers to the east, Playa Papaturro also has kitesurfing and simple accommodations. ⊠ *About 2 km/1 mile east of the branch road that leads to Ecoplaya.*

★ **Playa Jobo.** Playa Jobo is a gem with fine sand and calm water. It's fringed with acacia trees that have sharp thorns, so keep your distance. There's a shady parking area about 150 meters (500 feet) off the beach where you have to leave your car. ⊠ *3 km/2 miles walk or drive, west from Ecoplaya Beach Resort.*

Playa Rajada. Gorgeous, horseshoe-shaped Playa Rajada is a wide sweep of almost-white, fine-grain sand. Shallow, warm waters make it

Semana Santa

Don't underestimate how completely Costa Rica shuts down for Holy Week, the week preceding Easter. Cities become ghost towns—San José turns beguilingly peaceful—save for religious processions. Many businesses close the entire week; little opens on Thursday or Friday. Tourists, local and international, flock to the beaches. Make reservations months in advance if you plan to be here during that week, and expect greatly inflated room rates. Know that Holy Thursday and Good Friday are, by law, dry days. Bars and liquor stores must close, and no one, including restaurants or your hotel dining room, is permitted to sell alcohol.

perfect for swimming, and an interesting rock formation at the north end invites snorkelers. It's also a favorite beach for watching sunsets. ⊠ *5 km/3 miles west of Ecoplaya Beach Resort or 3 km/2 miles north of the town of El Jobo.*

OUTDOOR ACTIVITIES

Inshore fishing is quite good in the bay during windy months, when snapper, roosterfish, wahoo, and other fighters abound. Scuba divers also encounter plenty of big fish from December to May, though visibility can be poor then. From May to December the snorkeling is good around the rocky points and Isla Bolaños.

Ecoplaya Beach Resort. Local adventure tours organized by this resort hotel include kayaking to Isla Bolaños (a tiny island that is a refuge for such seabirds as the brown pelican), inshore fishing, horseback riding, hiking, and snorkeling and windsurfing, as well as farther-afield adventure tours to Santa Rosa National Park, Palo Verde National Park Hacienda Guachipelín, and the historic city of Granada, in nearby Nicaragua. ⊠ *La Coyotera Beach, 15 km/10 miles west of La Cruz on a rough dirt road* ☎ *2676–1010* ⊕ *www.ecoplaya.com.*

KITESURFING AND WINDSURFING

Cometa Copal Kite Surfing Centre and School. Cometa Copal Kite Surfing Centre and School, on Playa Copal (10 km/6 miles west of La Cruz), is run by American Bob Selfridge, who provides kitesurfing lessons and rents equipment. ⊠ *Playa Cometa* ☎ *2676–1192.*

Kite Surfing School. Ideally situated on windy Playa Papaturro (11 km/7 miles west of La Cruz, turn left at sign for Papaturro), this kitesurfing school is run by Nicola Bertoldi, a multilingual instructor with lots of experience; nine hours of beginner's kitesurfing private lessons cost $319, including equipment. But the best deals are all-inclusive packages that include lessons, lodging, and meals at the school's Blue Dream Hotel, on a ridge with ocean views. The hotel also has a wood-oven pizzeria. ☎ *8826–5221, 2676–1042* ⊕ *www.bluedreamhotel.com.*

WHERE TO STAY

For expanded hotel reviews, visit Fodors.com.

$$ RESORT 🏨 **Ecoplaya Beach Resort.** Set between La Coyotera Beach and a mangrove estuary, this Best Western–affiliated small resort has a sprawling collection of equipped villas and two-story concrete buildings (with several types of spacious rooms) that dot ample, landscaped grounds. **Pros:** friendly; quiet; lots of activities. **Cons:** timeworn; service inconsistent; pool gets packed during holidays. **TripAdvisor:** "remote but wonderful place," "nice beaches," "excellent for families." [$] *Rooms from: $120* ✉ *La Coyotera Beach, 15 km/10 miles west of La Cruz on a rough dirt road* ☎ *2676–1010, 2228–7146 in San José* 🌐 *www.ecoplaya.com* *26 villas, 18 rooms.*

LIBERIA

214 km/133 miles (4–5 hrs) northwest of San José.

Once a dusty cattle-market town, Liberia has galloped toward modernization, becoming the commercial, as well as the administrative capital, of Guanacaste. There are still a few vestiges of its colonial past on quieter side streets and the occasional *sabanero* (cowboy) on horseback still ambles into town. But Liberia has virtually become one big shopping mall, complete with fast-food restaurants—dueling McDonald's and Burger King face off at the entrance to town—and a multiplex theater. Walk a couple of blocks south of the main street along Calle Real, though, and you can still find some whitewashed adobe houses for which Liberia was nicknamed the "White City," as well as some grand town houses that recall the city's glory days. A few have been restored and are now hotels and cafés. Liberia today is essentially a good place to have a meal and make a bank stop at any one of a dozen banks, including Scotiabank, Citibank, and HSBC. Liberia can also serve as a base for day trips to Santa Rosa and Rincón de la Vieja national parks. The drive from San José takes between four and five hours, so it makes sense to fly directly into Liberia if you're going only to the North Pacific. It's easy to rent a car near the airport.

NAVIGATING LIBERIA The *avenidas* (avenues) officially run east–west, whereas the *calles* (streets) run north–south. Liberia is not too big to walk easily, but there are always taxis lined up around the pleasant central park.

GETTING HERE AND AROUND

From San José, follow the Pan-American Highway west past the Puntarenas exit, then north past Cañas to Liberia. The road is paved but is poorly maintained in places. It's a heavily traveled truck and bus route, and there are miles and miles where it is impossible to pass, but many drivers try, making this a dangerous road. Hourly direct buses leave San José for Liberia each day, and there are half a dozen daily flights, so it might be worth busing or flying to Liberia and renting a car from here.

ESSENTIALS

Bank/ATM **Banco de Costa Rica** ✉ *C. Central at Avda. 1, diagonally across from central park* ☎ *2666–9002.*

Hospital **Liberia Hospital** ✉ *North end of town* ☎ *2666–0011.*

Liberia

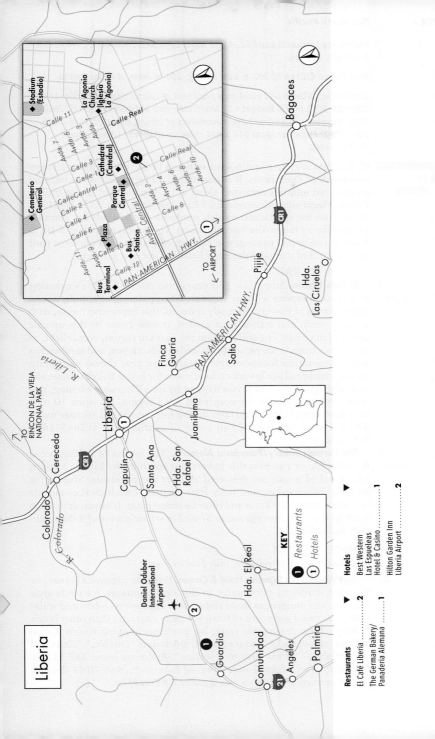

Restaurants ▸

El Café Liberia **2**

The German Bakery/
Panadería Alemana **1**

Hotels ▸

Best Western
Las Espueleas
Hotel & Casino **1**

Hilton Garden Inn
Liberia Airport **2**

KEY

1 Restaurants

① Hotels

Map Labels

TO RINCON DE LA VIEJA NATIONAL PARK

R. Colorado

Colorado

Cereceda

R. Liberia

Liberia

Capulin

Santa Ana

Hda. San Rafael

Juanilama

Finca Guaria

Salto

PAN-AMERICAN HWY.

Piijie

Hda. Las Ciruelas

Bagaces

CR1

Daniel Oduber International Airport

Hda. El Real

Guardia

Comunidad

Angeles

Palmira

Liberia (inset)

Cemeterio General

Stadium (Estadio)

Calle 11

Avda. 7
Avda. 5
Avda. 3
Avda. 1

La Agonia Church
Iglesia La Agonía

Calle Real

Cathedral (Catedral)

Calle 3
Calle 1
Calle Central
Calle 2
Calle 4
Calle 6

Avda. Central

Parque Central

Calle Real

Avda. 2
Avda. 4
Avda. 6
Avda. 8
Avda. 10

Calle 8

Avda. 9
Avda. 11

Calle 10
Calle 12

Plaza

Bus Station

Bus Terminal

PAN-AMERICAN HWY.

TO AIRPORT

CR1

Pharmacy Farmacia Lux ✉ *C. 4 and Avda. Central* ☎ *2666–0061* 🕒 *Mon.–Sat. 8–10; Sun. 8–4 pm.*

Post Office Correo ✉ *300 m west of hwy., 200 m north of Avda. Central.*

Rental Cars Alamo ✉ *2 km/1 mile northeast of Liberia airport* ☎ *2668–1111, 800/522–9696 in U.S.* **Budget** ✉ *1 km/½ mile east of Liberia airport* ☎ *2668–1118.* **Economy** ✉ *3½ km/2 miles southwest of Liberia airport* ☎ *2666–2816, 2666–7560.* **Hola Rentacar** ✉ *6 km/4 miles southwest of Liberia airport* ☎ *2667–4040.*

EN ROUTE 👶 Yes, that is a life-size dinosaur standing beside the highway 20 minutes north of Puntarenas. It is one of 26 lifelike models of extinct and endangered animals arranged along a 1½-km (1-mile) forest trail at Parque MegaFauna Monteverde (✉ *Pan-American Hwy.* ☎ *2638–8193*). Along with the spectacular models outdoors, the $5 (kids $3) entrance fee includes an impressive insect museum. The park is open daily 8 am to 5 pm. If you're just passing, you can still stop and take a photo of your kids in front of the baby dinosaur hatching out of a giant egg.

WHERE TO EAT

$ ECLECTIC

🍴 **El Café Liberia.** Step back 150 years into one of Liberia's grandest mansions, complete with an original ceiling painting of cupids, doves, and garlands of flowers. Recently restored, this impressive house, with a music room and a courtyard garden, is now home to this upscale café and juice bar. The coffee, from the Tarrazú region, is excellent, as are the homemade soups, sophisticated salads, crepes, and sandwiches with a vegetarian focus—veggie burgers and goat cheese with pesto on ciabatta bread are favorites. Save room for home-baked cheesecake and other goodies. And if you happen by on a Thursday evening, you may catch a movie in the courtyard Art Cinema. It's open 10 to 8 Monday through Saturday; later during high season. [$] *Average main: $7* ✉ *C. Real Antigua, 125 m south of central park* ☎ *2665–1660* 🕒 *Closed Sun.*

$ GERMAN

🍴 **The German Bakery/Panaderia Alemana.** The aroma of baking bread is irresistible as you pass this bakery just south of the Liberia airport, whose baked goods are delivered all over the peninsula. Stop in for strudels, Bundt cakes, and flaky fruit pastries. Lunch choices include bratwurst with sauerkraut and (non-German) pizza. It's open daily from 6 am to 6 pm. [$] *Average main: $6* ✉ *2 km/1 mile west of Liberia airport* ☎ *2668–1081.*

WHERE TO STAY

For expanded hotel reviews, visit Fodors.com.

$$ HOTEL 👶

🏨 **Best Western Las Espuelas Hotel & Casino.** From the gigantic Guanacaste tree that shades its parking lot to the local paintings, hacienda-style benches, and indigenous stone statues that decorate its lobby and walkways, this motel just south of town has more character than other hotels in town. **Pros:** reasonable rates; big pool; no-smoking rooms. **Cons:** highway noise; tacky casino room. **TripAdvisor:** "reliable," "clean and comfortable," "great customer service." [$] *Rooms from: $87* ✉ *Pan-American Hwy., 2 km/1 mile south of Liberia* ☎ *2666–0144* 🌐 *www.bestwestern.co.cr* 🛏 *44 rooms, 2 suites* 🍽 *Breakfast.*

CLOSE UP

Making a Difference

National park or reserve entrance fees help support the preservation of Costa Rica's wildlife and places. You can also make your visit beneficial to the people living nearby by hiring local guides, horses, or boats; eating in local restaurants; and buying things (excluding wild-animal products) in local shops. You can go a few steps further by making donations to local conservation groups or to such international organizations as Conservation International, the Rainforest Alliance, and the World Wide Fund for Nature, all of which support important conservation efforts in Costa Rica. It's also helpful to explore private preserves off the beaten path and to stay at lodges that contribute to environmental efforts and to nearby communities. By planning your visit with an eye toward grassroots conservation efforts, you join the global effort to save Costa Rica's tropical ecosystems and help ensure that the treasures you traveled so far to see remain intact for future generations.

$$
HOTEL

⬚ **Hilton Garden Inn Liberia Airport.** Comfortable and convenient, especially if you're catching an early-morning flight or you need a break from driving before heading south to the beach, this brand-new, five-story contemporary Hilton has all the mod cons, including high-speed Internet, high-definition TVs, MP3 players, microwaves, and fridges. **Pros:** cool; convenient; very comfortable; free shuttle to and from airport. **Cons:** no shaded parking area; impersonal cookie-cutter rooms could be anywhere in the world; pricey. **TripAdvisor:** "service above and beyond," "beautiful but isolated," "comfortable and convenient." ⬚ *Rooms from: $149* ✉ *Across from Liberia International Airport on main hwy.* ☎ *2690–8888* ⊕ *www.liberiaairport.hgi.com* ⬚ *169 rooms, including 8 handicapped-access rooms, 8 suites* ⬚ *No meals.*

NICOYA PENINSULA COAST AND INTERIOR

Strung along the coast of the Nicoya Peninsula are sparkling sand beaches lined with hotels and resorts in every price category. As recently as the 1970s, fishing and cattle ranching were the area's mainstays. Development has barreled ahead full speed, though, turning laid-back fishing villages into beach towns with sophisticated restaurants, hotels, shops, and nightlife. Development has also brought congestion, noise, construction chaos, water pollution, and higher prices. If resort life and the party scene are not your style, there are still some blissfully tranquil beaches just beyond the paved roads. South of Tamarindo, you'll find the interesting anomaly of a trendy restaurant or upscale hotel plunked at the end of a tortuous dirt road. The key to enjoying Nicoya is to pick your spot—happening beach town or off-the-beaten-path seclusion.

The parks and wildlife refuges in and around the Río Tempisque are prime places to hike, explore caves, and spot birds and other wildlife, and there's a smattering of culture, too, in the town of Nicoya with its colonial-era church and in Guaitil, with pottery made in the pre-Colombian Chorotega tradition. The town of Nicoya is the commercial and political hub of the northern Nicoya Peninsula. By road, Nicoya provides the best access to Sámara, Nosara, and points south and north and is linked by a smooth, well-paved road to the artisan community of Guaitil and the northern Nicoya beach towns.

PAPAGAYO PENINSULA

The Papagayo Peninsula, a crooked finger of land cradling the west side of Bahía Culebra (Snake Bay), has guaranteed sun from January to April, making it a prime site for all-inclusive hotels catering to snowbirds escaping northern winters. Five large hotels are already situated around Papagayo Bay, and many others are slated to be built here, all part of a government-sponsored development program modeled after Cancún. Although the hotels are modeled on their Caribbean counterparts, the beaches are distinctly Costa Rican, with brown sand and aquamarine water that grows cool from January to April. Isolation is the name of the game here, which means that getting out of man-made "paradise" to explore anything off-property often entails a pricey tour.

High season here coincides with dry season, when the heat is intense and the landscape becomes brown and brittle. In the rainy season (August to December), the landscape is greener and lusher. Sparkling water and spectacular sunsets are beautiful year-round.

GETTING HERE AND AROUND

All hotels here have airport pickup. To get to the Four Seasons from the Liberia airport (the hotel refuses to put up directional signs in order to "protect its privacy"), drive 10 km (6 miles) south of Guardia, over the Río Tempisque Bridge, then take the turn on the right signed for Papagayo Allegro Resort. Follow this road about 20 km (12 miles) to its end at the entrance to the resort.

OUTDOOR ACTIVITIES

CANOPY TOUR

Witch's Rock Canopy Tour. Taking advantage of one of the few remaining patches of dry tropical forest on the Papagayo Peninsula, Witch's Rock Canopy Tour gives you your money's worth: 23 platforms, with a thrilling 450-meter (1,485-foot) cable zip between two of them; four hanging bridges; a waterfall in rainy season; and hiking trails. The 1½-hour tour is $75 per person; transportation is extra. ☎ *2696–7101, 2696–7103* 🌐 *www.witchsrockcanopytourl.com.*

WHERE TO STAY

For expanded hotel reviews, visit Fodors.com.

$$$ B&B/INN ★ 🏨 **Casa Conde del Mar.** Spread over verdant grounds just behind relatively pristine Playa Panama, Casa Conde has an excellent location with bay views, balmy breezes, and a huge swimming pool. **Pros:** spacious rooms; immaculate grounds; close to beach. **Cons:** unsightly, unfinished construction right next to hotel; loud sound track playing at pool. **TripAdvisor:** "pleasant grounds and rooms," "nice and quiet," "beautiful setting." [$] *Rooms from: $185* ✉ *Playa Panama, 3 km/2 miles north of Playa Hermosa* ☎ *2226–0808 San José office, 2672–1001*

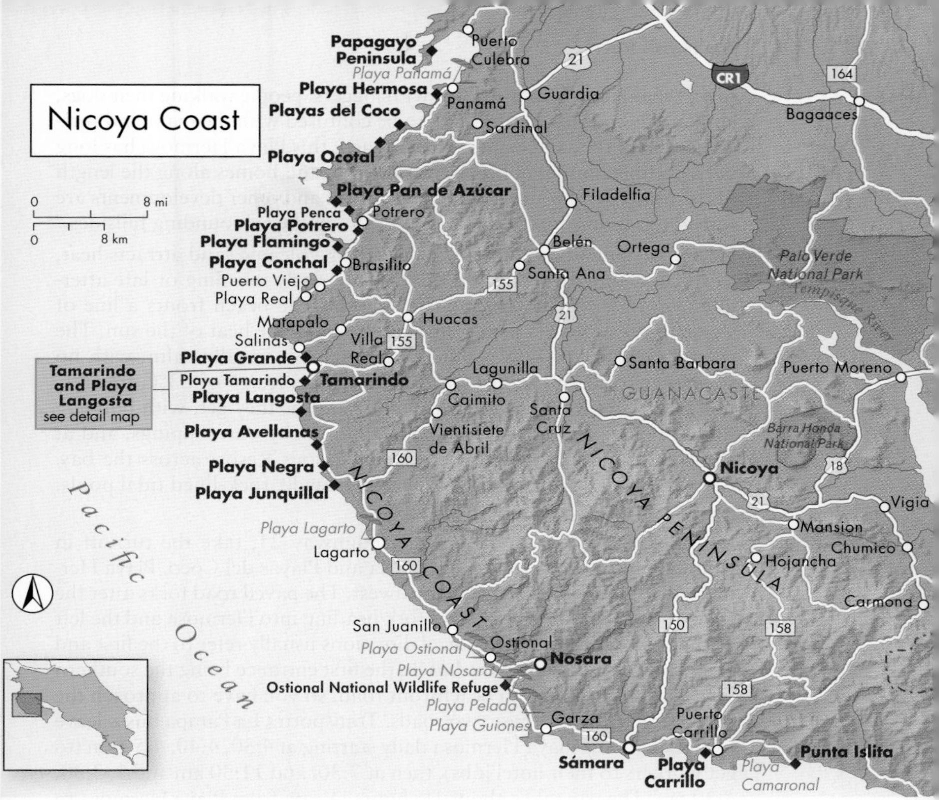

🌐 *www.grupocasaconde.com* 🛏 *20 rooms, 4 suites, 2 master suites, 2 handicapped-accessible suites* 🍴 *Breakfast.*

$$$$ RESORT 🏨 **Four Seasons Resort Costa Rica.** By far one of the most luxurious hotels in Costa Rica, the Four Seasons is extremely secluded (it's nearly 30 minutes from the main road). **Pros:** impeccable service; lovely beach; no-smoking rooms. **Cons:** isolated; expensive. **TripAdvisor:** "excellent resort for families," "paradise in the middle of nowhere," "fantastic." [$] *Rooms from: $625* ✉ *25 km/15 miles west of Guardia; follow signs to Papagayo Allegro Resort and continue to end of road* ☎ *2696–0000* 🌐 *www.fourseasons.com/costarica* 🛏 *123 rooms, 36 suites, 21 villas* 🍴 *No meals.*

PLAYA HERMOSA

27 km/17 miles southwest of Liberia airport.

Playa Hermosa. Beautiful Playa Hermosa, once a laid-back, fishing community, has grown like Topsy, with condominiums and villas covering the scrubby hills overlooking the wide, curved beach with its warm, swimmable water, prime dive sites, choice fishing grounds, and sunset views of the Papagayo Peninsula—all reasons why Canadian and American expatriates are buying up those condos. In the early morning, though, Playa Hermosa is still the kind of place where the beach is the town's main thoroughfare, filled with joggers, people walking their dogs, and families out for a stroll. Not to be confused with the mainland surfers' beach of the same name south of Jacó, this Playa Hermosa has long been occupied by small hotels, restaurants, and homes along the length of the beach, so the newer hotel behemoths and other developments are forced to set up shop off the beach or up on the surrounding hillsides.

Hermosa's mile-long crescent of dark gray volcanic sand attracts heat, so the best time to be out on the beach is early morning or late afternoon, in time for the spectacular sunsets. The beach fronts a line of shade trees, so there's a welcome respite from the heat of the sun. The crystal clear water—it's a Blue Flag beach—is usually calm, with no strong currents and with comfortable temperatures of 23°C to 27°C (74°F to 80°F). Sea views are as picturesque as they get, with bobbing fishing boats, jagged profiles of coastline, rocky outcroppings, and at night the twinkling lights of the Four Seasons Resort across the bay. At the beach's north end, low tide creates wide, rock-lined tidal pools.

GETTING HERE AND AROUND
Heading south from Liberia along Highway 21, take the turnoff in Comunidad signed for Playa Hermosa and Playas del Coco. Playa Hermosa is about 15 km (9 miles) northwest. The paved road forks after the small town of Sardinal, the right fork heading into Hermosa and the left leading to Playas del Coco. Local directions usually refer to the first and second entrance roads to the beach, the first entrance being the southern one. There is no through beachfront road, so you have to approach the beach from either of these two roads. Transportes La Pampa buses leave from Liberia for Playa Hermosa daily starting at 4:30, 4:40, 4:50 am (to get workers to their hotel jobs), then at 7:30, and 11:30 am and 1, 3:30, 5:30 pm. The trip takes about 1½ hours. A taxi from Playa Hermosa to Playas del Coco costs about $15 and takes about 15 minutes.

ESSENTIALS
Playa Hermosa has a large supermarket, Luperón, on the main road, between the first and second beach entrances, open daily 7 am to 8:30 pm—where you can stock up on just about everything you need—food, wine, liquor, toiletries, even fresh-baked French and ciabatta bread.

OUTDOOR ACTIVITIES
Aqua Sport. Aqua Sport organizes fishing, surfing, and snorkeling trips and rents every kind of boat and board from a kiosk right on the beach. ⊠ *Beach road; heading south, take 2nd entrance to Playa Hermosa and follow signs* ☎ *2672–0050.*

Charlie's Adventure. Operating out of the Hotel Condovac, this tour company organizes ATV tours ($85) and horseback riding ($55), as well as the seven-hour Aqua Combo boat tours of Hermosa Bay, including snorkeling, bottom fishing, and a beach barbecue lunch ($75, including drinks). ⊠ *Hotel Condovac, north end of beach* ☎ *2672–1041, 2672–0275.*

Hotel El Velero. This beachfront hotel has a 38-foot sailing yacht for five-hour sunset cruises ($60 per person). Daytime tours include snorkeling and a gourmet lunch with drinks ($80 per person). ⊠ *100 m north of Aqua Sport* ☎ *2672–1017* ⊕ *www.costaricahotel.net.*

Velas de Papagayo. Operating out of Hotel Playa Hermosa Bosque del Mar at the south end of the beach, this outfit runs morning and sunset cruises of Papagayo Bay that include snorkeling, drinks, and snacks ($110). ⊠ *Hotel Playa Hermosa Bosque del Mar* ☎ *2223–2508* ⊕ *www. velasdepapagayo.com.*

DIVING AND SNORKELING

Average water temperature of 23°C (75°F), and average visibility of 6 meters (20 feet), and frequent sightings of sea turtles, sharks, manta rays, moray eels, and very big fish make Hermosa a great place to dive. There is little coral in the area, but rock reefs attract large schools of fish, and countless critters lurk in their caves and crannies.

Charlie's Adventure. Snorkeling trips are organized by Charlie's Adventure and by Hotel el Velero.

Diving Safaris. This is the most experienced dive operation in the area, with a full range of scuba activities, from beginner training to open-water PADI certification courses. Multitank dives are organized at more than 20 sites. Guides and trainers are very good, and their safety standards have the DAN (Divers Alert Network) seal of approval. This dive shop has also earned the coveted five-star, gold-palm status from PADI. Prices range from $80 for two-tank morning dives to $425 and up for the PADI open-water certification course. ⊠ *2nd entrance road to Playa Hermosa, almost at beach on right side* ☎ *2672–1259* ⊕ *www. costaricadiving.net.*

FISHING

The fishing at Playa Hermosa is mostly close to the shores, and yields edible fish like *dorado* (mahimahi), snapper, amberjack, tuna, and wahoo. Roosterfish, marlin, and sailfish are all catch-and-release. Local restaurants are happy to cook your catch for you. You can rent a boat with **Aqua Sport** *(⇨ above)*. **Charlie's Adventure** *(⇨ above)* runs fishing trips. **Papagayo Gulf Sport Fishing** (☎ *2670–1564* ⊕ *www. papagayofishing.typepad.com*) also runs various fishing tours in the area, as well as snorkeling and surfing tours and water taxis around the bay.

WHERE TO EAT

A few of Playa Hermosa's best restaurants are at hotels *(⇨ Where to Stay, below)*.

$$
ECLECTIC
★

✕ **Ginger Restaurant Bar.** This tapas restaurant, featuring Asian and Mediterranean flavors in a modernistic glass-and-steel tree house that's cantilevered on the side of a hill, is such a big hit that a new, large deck has doubled the dining space. Delectable appetizer-size offerings include seared pepper-crusted tuna atop pickled ginger slaw, or panfried sea bass fillets with a divine ginger–and–mandarin orange butter sauce. Not to be missed are Ginger's crispy shoestring fries, served with roasted garlic mayo. Portions are small, but layers of condiments and garnishes make them surprisingly satisfying. The fun thing to do is order several dishes and share. The varied wine list includes Old and New World wines by the glass, and specialty martinis and tropical cocktails go well with the tapas. For dessert, warm chocolate lava cake is rich enough to share, but only with someone you truly love. Be aware that the menu prices do not include tax and service (another 23 percent). It's open 5 to 10 pm. $ *Average main: $14* ✉ *Main hwy., south of Hotel Condovac* ☎ *2672–0041* ⊕ *www.gingercostarica.com* ☉ *Closed Mon.*

WHERE TO STAY
For expanded hotel reviews, visit Fodors.com.

$$
B&B/INN
☺

⌂ **Hotel El Velero.** This laid-back hotel is right on the beach, and, though nothing fancy, it has attractive, comfortable rooms and it's an excellent option if you're watching your expenses. **Pros:** on the beach; affordable; friendly; informal. **Cons:** tiny pool; most rooms have no views; can be noisy. **TripAdvisor:** "very friendly staff," "right on the beach," "a quiet retreat." $ *Rooms from: $79* ✉ *2nd entrance to Playa Hermosa, on beach road* ☎ *2672–0036* ⊕ *www.costaricahotel.net* ⇌ *22 rooms* ⦿ *No meals.*

$$
B&B/INN
★

⌂ **Hotel La Finisterra.** From its perch high above the southern end of Playa Hermosa, this classy, small hotel commands the best view of the beach and bay, along with the best terrace for watching sunsets. **Pros:** good food; very friendly staff; great views. **Cons:** steep climb up from beach; small pool. **TripAdvisor:** "great food," "very helpful staff," "beautiful view." $ *Rooms from: $120* ✉ *1st entrance to Playa Hermosa, left before Hotel Playa Hermosa, 250 m up hill* ☎ *2672–0227* ⊕ *www. lafinisterra.com* ⇌ *10 rooms* ⦿ *Breakfast.*

$$$
B&B/INN
★

⌂ **Hotel Playa Hermosa Bosque del Mar.** Vastly expanded and expensively upgraded, this beachfront hotel has replaced its vintage bungalows with luxury rooms and suites, but thankfully, the century-old, vine-draped trees that shade the property on the southern end of Playa Hermosa have been saved. **Pros:** superb garden and beachfront location; beautiful restaurant. **Cons:** some rooms are dark and gloomy; food doesn't match up to restaurant decor; expensive for the area. **TripAdvisor:** "relaxation in paradise," "lovely for monkey gawkers," "beautiful beach hotel." $ *Rooms from: $175* ✉ *End of 1st entrance to Playa Hermosa* ☎ *2672–0046* ⊕ *www.hotelplayahermosa.com* ⇌ *20 junior suites, 12 deluxe suites, 1 penthouse suite* ⦿ *No meals.*

$
B&B/INN

⌂ **Villa del Sueño.** Although the handsome garden restaurant ($16) is the main attraction at this elegant hotel, the spacious rooms and well-equipped villas are quite comfortable, too, though the hotel is about a block from the beach. **Pros:** excellent restaurant; good value. **Cons:** not on the beach; can be noisy when there's live music; breakfast not included in high season. **TripAdvisor:** "a shady oasis," "well-groomed property," "charming." $ *Rooms from: $75* ✉ *1st entrance to Playa Hermosa, 350 m west of main hwy.* ☎ *2672–0026* ⊕ *www.villadelsueno. com* ⇌ *14 rooms, 27 villas, 3 two-bedroom villas* ⦿ *No meals.*

NIGHTLIFE
Hotel El Velero. This lively beachfront hotel hosts beach barbecues on Wednesday and Saturday nights in high season. The crowd is thirtyish and up. ✉ *2nd entrance to Playa Hermosa, then 100 m north of Aqua Sport on beach road.*

Villa del Sueño. In high season, Villa del Sueño hosts live music (jazz and rock) on Tuesday, Friday, and Sunday nights, as well as occasional concerts featuring top national bands and performers. ✉ *1st entrance to Playa Hermosa, 350 m west of main hwy.*

SHOPPING

Kaltak Art and Craft Market. This souvenir emporium has five rooms of high-quality crafts and gifts, including organic-cotton blouses and dresses and traditional leather-and-wood rocking chairs, which they will ship for you. Look for the gigantic toucan sculptures perched by the roadside. ⊠ *South of airport on road to Santa Cruz.*

Villa del Sueño. The small but upscale gift shop at Villa del Sueño has brilliantly colored paintings by local artist Barbara Braman, classy beach bags, and locally designed and made beach cover-ups that will flatter any woman. ⊠ *1st entrance to Playa Hermosa, 350 m west of main hwy.*

PLAYAS DEL COCO

25 km/16 miles southwest of Liberia airport.

Messy, noisy, colorful, and interesting, Playas del Coco has the best shopping, most dive shops, and liveliest nightlife and barhopping on this part of the coast. It's still a working fishing port, with a port captain's office, a fish market, and an ice factory for keeping the catch of the day fresh—not for cooling margaritas, although many are enjoyed here. The dark-sand beach is still a workplace, and it hasn't yet met the Blue Flag standards of cleanliness, but a beautiful new boardwalk has made the beach much more attractive. An explosion of condominium and villa projects has brought new money to the community, along with new commercial development, including an upscale shopping center at the entrance to town with a flagship AutoMercado, the country's top grocery chain. Although fresh seafood, myriad souvenir shops, and plenty of bars have always drawn tourists here, Playas del Coco also has a high concentration of tour operators, including diving, fishing, and surfing at remote breaks such as Ollie's Point and Witch's Rock. Because Coco is mere minutes from Playa Hermosa, however, you can just as easily enjoy those sports while staying at that more pleasant beach. If you like to shop and party, and want some local color, Coco's slightly down-at-the-heels ambience can be appealing.

GETTING HERE AND AROUND

The easy drive from the Liberia airport to Playas del Coco takes about 30 minutes. The paved highway turns into a grand, divided boulevard as you enter town; it ends at the beach. If you don't have a car, the best way to get here from Playa Hermosa is in a taxi, for about $15 each way.

ESSENTIALS

Bank/ATM Banco Nacional ⊠ *Main street, at entrance to town.*

Hospital Public Health Clinic ⊠ *Next to La Puerta del Sol hotel* ☎ *2670–0987.*

Post Office Correo ⊠ *At entrance to town on main road.*

Continued on page 289

Choosing a Beach

From pulverized volcanic rock and steady waves to soft white sand and idyllic settings, all of the beaches along Nicoya's coast have their own distinct merits. Playa Brasilito has a restaurant so close to the ocean the surf spray salts your food; Playas Hermosa and Sámara are family-friendly spots with swimmable waters; and Playas Langosta and Pelada are made for contemplative walks.

NORTHERN NICOYA PENINSULA

Playa Tamarindo

1 Popular all-inclusive resorts line the beaches of the **Papagayo Peninsula**.

2 **Playa Hermosa** is one of the few Costa Rican beaches with calm, crystal-clear waters.

3 Diving and fishing are the name of the game at **Playas del Coco** and its lively beach town.

4 **Playa Ocotal** is a quiet black-sand beach with great views, diving, and good snorkeling.

5 **Playa Pan de Azúcar** is difficult to access, but practically deserted once you get there.

6 **Playa Potrero** is the jumping-off point for diving trips to the Catalina Islands.

7 Busy white-sand **Playa Flamingo** is ideal for swimming and sunning.

8 Shells sprinkle the sand at chilled-out **Playa Conchal**, near a small fishing village.

9 Lively **Tamarindo** is a hyped-up surfing and water-sports beach with wild nightlife.

BEACHES KEY

Diving	
Snorkeling	
Fishing	
Surfing	
Kayaking	
Sailing	
Swimming	
	Blue Flag Ecological Award

CENTRAL NICOYA PENINSULA

(top) Playa Avellanas (bottom) Sunset at Sámara

❶ **Playa Langosta** is great for walks up its estuary and watching dramatic sunsets.

❷ **Playa Avellanas** is a no-frills backwater surf spot.

❸ **Playa Negra** has some of Costa Rica's best surfing waves.

❹ Peaceful and pretty, **Playa Junquillal** is all about relaxation.

❺ Hemmed in by rocks, **Playa Pelada** is a calm beach staked out by territorial Tico surfers.

❻ Long, clean **Playa Guiones** is backed by dense jungle.

❼ **Sámara's** gentle waters make it perfect for kayaking and swimming.

❽ Perhaps the most beautiful beach in the country, **Playa Carrillo** fronts an idyllic half-moon bay.

❾ Rocky **Punta Islita** has interesting tidal pools to explore.

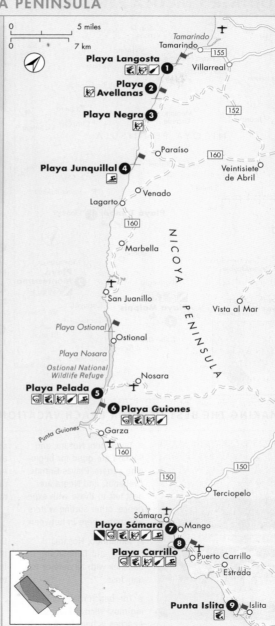

6

IN FOCUS CHOOSING A BEACH

SOUTHERN NICOYA PENINSULA

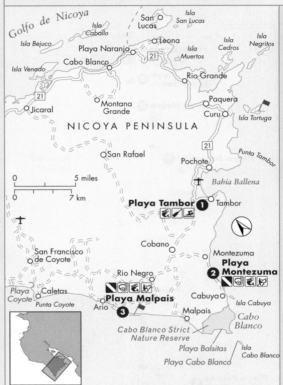

(top) Montezuma (bottom) Surfing at Malpaís

❶ Crescent-shaped **Tambor** is flanked by all-inclusive resorts.

❷ **Montezuma's** off-beat town is as much a draw as its bayside beach.

❸ Some of the largest surfing waves in Costa Rica are at **Malpaís**.

MAKING THE BEST OF YOUR BEACH VACATION

■ Tamarindo, Nosara, and Sámara are good for beginning surfers. Playas Grande, Avellanas, and Negra are best left to those with experience; other surfing waters are somewhere in between.

■ Tamarindo, Nosara, Sámara, and Tambor are beaches with air service to San José.

■ The beach road connecting most Nicoya Peninsula beaches is hard to stomach any time of year, and virtually impassable during the August through December rains. Take easier inland routes instead.

■ Riptides are seriously dangerous and hardly any Costa Rican beaches have lifeguards; get information from your hotel about where to swim safely.

OUTDOOR ACTIVITIES
DIVING AND SNORKELING
Half a dozen dive shops populate this small town. The standard price for a two-tank dive is $80; Catalina Island dives are $110. This coast doesn't have the coral reefs or the clear visibility of the Caribbean coast, but it does have a lot of plankton (hence the lower visibility) that feeds legions of fish, some of them really, really big. Manta rays and sharks (white-tipped, nurse, and bull varieties) are among the stars of the undersea show. It takes about 20 to 45 minutes to reach most dive sites.

Deep Blue Diving Adventures. This organization is a reliable option. ⊠ *Main street, in Hotel Coco Verde parking lot* ☎ *2670–1004* ⊕ *www. deepblue-diving.com.*

Rich Coast Diving. This long-time operator has enthusiastic guides and instructors and limits tours to five divers per instructor and 15 divers per boat. ⊠ *Main street, near intersection with road to Playa Ocotal* ☎ *2670–0176* ⊕ *www.richcoastdiving.com.*

Summer Salt Dive Center. Most of the dive shops have instruction, including this Main Street dive center. ⊠ *Main street* ☎ *2670–0308* ⊕ *www. summer-salt.com.*

FISHING
Fishing charter boats go out 24 to 64 km (15 to 40 miles) seeking yellowfin tuna, mahimahi, grouper, and red snapper close in, and sailfish, marlin, and roosterfish offshore (beyond 64 km/40 miles). Boats, moored here and in nearby Ocotal, can pick you up from a beach near your hotel.

Blue Marlin Service Sportfishing. This downtown fishing charter office has 11 boats to choose from, ranging from a 25-foot boat for close-in fishing ($325 half day) to larger boats that go out to sea for a full day offshore ($850). Prices are for four to five fishers. ⊠ *Main street* ☎ *2670–0707* ⊕ *www.sportfishingbluemarlin.com.*

TranquilaMar. With three 28-foot Cummins diesel-power boats moored in nearby Ocotal, this outfit can pick you up at any local beach. Just bring sunscreen and your hat, says the captain. Trips are $500 for a half day and $700 for a full day. With fewer sportfishing boats going out in this area, the fishing is getting better, says the owner. ☎ *2670–0833* ⊕ *www.tranquilamar.com.*

GOLF
Papagayo Golf & Country Club. This 18-hole, par-72 course is very affordable; you can play the whole course for $95, including golf cart and a cooler with ice and water, or play 9 holes for $55. There's a restaurant and bar, and a tournament every Sunday morning. ⊠ *10 km/6 miles southeast of Playas del Coco* ☎ *2697–0169* ⊕ *www.papagayo-golf.com.*

SURFING
★ **Witch's Rock and Ollie's Point.** These legendary surfing spots are a one-hour boat ride away from Playas del Coco off the coast of Santa Rosa National Park. You can surf as long as you pay the $10 park entrance fee.

You can sign up for a surfing trip with any beach-town tour operator, but local authorities allow excursions to Witch's Rock and Ollie's Point to originate only from the main dock at Playas del Coco, in boats owned by local boat owners, in order to curb overcrowding and undue environmental stress.

WHERE TO EAT AND STAY

For expanded hotel reviews, visit Fodors.com.

$$ SPANISH 🍴 **At Claudio & Gloria Restaurant.** The coolest dining in Coco is this breezy, sophisticated patio restaurant, just steps from the beach, specializing in Spanish and Peruvian seafood dishes. The same family has had a beachfront restaurant here since 1955, but the old place was demolished to make room for the new beach boardwalk. This new incarnation is stylish and romantic, with white tablecloths and candlelight, and a view of fishing boats bobbing in the bay. The menu has been updated, too. Try the Catalan-style fish with almonds or the Peruvian chaufa, rice, and shrimp spiced with Japanese flavors. Desserts include crepes, flans, and grilled pineapple. The wine list is notable for a wide range of Spanish and Italian wines, some available by the glass. It's now open from 8 to 9 daily, serving breakfast, lunch, and dinner. You can also order pizza to pick up in the evenings. [$] *Average main: $12* ✉ *75 m east of Lizard Lounge, or just walk east along the beach* ☎ *2670–1514, 2670–0756 Pizza orders* 🌐 *www.dondeclaudioygloria.com.*

$$ SEAFOOD 🍴 **Restaurante Papagayo Seafood.** The food here is straightforward, reliably fresh, and flavorful. Start with fish ceviche, or seafood soup generously packed with shrimp, squid, fish, and crab. Then sink your teeth into the catch of the day (including lobster, most notably), prepared any one of a dozen ways, or Papagayo seafood au gratin, which is a mix of sautéed seafood in a tarragon cream sauce. Seating is available downstairs, between the stuffed fish and potted plants, or on the cooler, quieter second floor. The restaurant also sells fresh fish to take home. And for those who like their fish raw, there's a new Papagayo Sushi Boat downstairs. It's open daily starting at noon. Meat lovers can order from the menu of the contiguous Papagayo Steakhouse, which has local and USDA beef, as well as a kids' menu. [$] *Average main: $12* ✉ *Main street, across from Hotel Coco Beach* ☎ *2670–0298.*

$$ B&B/INN 🏨 **La Puerta del Sol.** Facing a formal garden with sculpted shrubs and a lovely, small pool just two blocks from the beach, this tranquil enclosure of stylish suites has modern, airy Mediterranean-style guest rooms shot through with hot, tropical colors. **Pros:** intimate; comfortable. **Cons:** a walk to the beach; small; breakfast but no restaurant. **TripAdvisor:** "charming grounds," "very cute," "cozy and comfortable." [$] *Rooms from: $100* ✉ *180 m to right (north) off main road to town* ☎ *2670–0195* 🌐 *www.lapuertadelsolcostarica.com* 🛏 *9 rooms, 1 suite* 🍽 *Breakfast.*

NIGHTLIFE

Coconutz. Most local expats meet and greet here. It's usually packed around happy hour (3 to 7), when they often have live music. They also have pool tables; lots of big TVs for games, including Monday Night Football; the full range of bar food; and live concerts on weekends. ✉ *Main road, across from Hotel Coco Beach* ☎ *2670–1982* 🌐 *www.coconutz–costarica.com.*

THE ECOLOGICAL BLUE FLAG

The tourist industry here estimates that three-quarters of visitors to Costa Rica make a beach excursion. With that in mind, the national water utility, Acueductos y Alcantarillados (AyA), in conjunction with the Instituto Costarricense de Turismo, began evaluating and ranking water and environmental quality in coastal communities in 1996. Those that achieved at least a 90% score were awarded a Bandera Azul Ecológica (ecological Blue Flag) to fly as a symbol of excellence. The program, modeled on one begun in Spain in 1986, awards flags as prizes for communities. Participants are required to form a Blue Flag committee, a move that brings together diverse sectors of an area's population, many of which otherwise fiercely compete for tourist dollars. The program has prompted communities to put resources into improving environmental quality of life for themselves and for their guests.

Blue Flag locales receive year-round inspections of water quality—both ocean and drinking water—trash cleanup, waste management, security, signage, and environmental education. (Winners dare not rest on their laurels: a few know the shame of having their flags yanked.) In 2002, the competition was opened to inland communities; 2006 saw schools recognized; eco-friendly businesses and institutions were added in 2008. (Even an exceptionally green auto mechanic shop in San José was awarded a flag at the 2012 ceremony.)

Blue flags fly proudly in the following locations covered in this book:

CENTRAL VALLEY
Carrizal (Alajuela), Heredia.

NORTHERN PLAINS
La Fortuna, La Selva Biological Station, Las Horquetas, Monteverde Cloud Forest Reserve, San Rafael de Heredia, Vara Blanca.

NORTH PACIFIC
Bahía Junquillal, Nosara (Playa Guiones, Playa Pelada), Ostional, Playa Avellanas, Playa Carrillo, Playa Conchal, Playa Flamingo, Playa Hermosa, Playa Junquillal, Playa Langosta, Playa Pan de Azúcar, Playa Panamá, Playa Potrero, Punta Islita, Sámara.

CENTRAL PACIFIC
Curú National Wildlife Refuge, Isla Tortuga, Malpaís, Manuel Antonio (Playa Manuel Antonio, Playa Espadilla Norte, Playa Espadilla Sur, Playa Gemelas), Playa El Carmen, Playa Hermosa, Puntarenas, Punta Leona (Playa Blanca, Playa Limoncito, Playa Mantas), Rain Forest Adventures, Santa Teresa.

SOUTH PACIFIC
Ballena National Marine Park, Barú, Cabo Matapalo, Las Cruces Biological Station, Playa Nicuesa, Playa Pavones, Puerto Jiménez (Playa Blanca), San Gerardo de Rivas, San Marcos de Tarrazú.

CARIBBEAN
Cahuita (Puerto Vargas, Playa Blanca, Playa Negra), EARTH, Gandoca-Manzanillo Wildlife Refuge, Puerto Viejo de Talamanca (Playa Chiquita, Playa Cocles, Punta Uva), Rain Forest Adventures.

6

Lizard Lounge. At this popular lounge there's Mexican food and dancing every night on a big thatch-roofed dance floor. The reggae, techno, and rap beats appeal to a very young crowd. Happy hour is 4 to 8 and there's free Wi-Fi. ⊠ *Main road, west of Hotel Coco Beach.*

Zouk Santana. This split-level lounge has a hip, quieter ambience that combines bars, couches, and small dance floors for moving to the eclectic, international mix of music. There's also a Zouk Café serving espresso and brioche from 7 am and a sophisticated, light menu in the evenings. ⊠ *Main road, west of Hotel Coco Beach* ⊕ *www.zouksantana.com.*

SHOPPING

Souvenir stalls and shops line the main drag near the entrance to the beach.

Galería & Souvenirs Sussy. If you're looking for something in particular and you can't find it at this cluttered emporium, chances are they don't make it in Costa Rica. Along with a huge selection of interesting notebooks and albums made of botanical materials, the place also sells locally made shell belts. ⊠ *Main street, next to Coco Beach Hotel.*

PLAYA OCOTAL

3 km/2 miles north of Playas del Coco.

Playa Ocotal. One of the most dramatic beaches in the country, this serene crescent of black sand beach contrasts nicely with the sparkling, clean turquoise water. The beach is ringed by rocky cliffs. It's only ½ km (¼ mile) long, but the views stretch for miles and include nearby offshore islands and the jagged profile of the Santa Elena Peninsula 34 km (21 miles) away. This is prime fishing, diving, and relaxing territory. Right at the entrance to the Gulf of Papagayo, it's a good place for sportfishing enthusiasts to hole up between excursions. There's good diving at Las Corridas, just 1 km (½ mile) away, and excellent snorkeling in nearby coves and islands, as well as right off the beach around the rocks at the east end of the beach.

GETTING HERE AND AROUND

The drive is 10 minutes from Playas del Coco on a paved road to the gated entrance of Playa Ocotal. The road winds through a heavily populated Tico residential area, so be on the lookout, especially at night, for bicyclists without lights, children, dogs, cows, and horses on the road. There are no buses from Playas del Coco to Ocotal, but it's about $10 by taxi.

OUTDOOR ACTIVITIES

DIVING AND SNORKELING

The rocky outcrop at the north end of the beach near Los Almendros is good for close-to-shore snorkeling.

Ocotal Beach Resort. The dive shop at this beachfront resort is one of the few PADI Instruction Development Centers in Costa Rica, offering the highest-level diving courses and five diving boats. The shop has excellent equipment, safety standards, and instruction. A regular dive costs $78; equipment rental is $26. The shop also rents snorkeling equipment for $12 per day. Or you can take a snorkeling boat tour for $50,

DID YOU KNOW?

Magnificent beaches and a dramatically sculpted shoreline are the Nicoya Peninsula's trademarks. Here you'll find no shortage of wildlife-watching opportunities. Be sure to check out the tide pools that form on the rocky headlands at each end of Playa Ocotal.

including gear. ⊠ *3 km/2 miles south of Playas del Coco* ☎ *2670–0321* ⊕ *www.ocotaldiving.com.*

FISHING

Ocotal Beach Resort. This resort has a sportfishing operation with three 32-foot Morgan hulls powered by twin 260-horsepower Cummins engines ($650 half day; $935 full day for up to four fishers). Marlins are catch-and-release, but you can keep—and eat—the mahimahi, yellowfin tuna, grouper, and amberjack you catch.

WHERE TO EAT AND STAY

For expanded hotel reviews, visit Fodors.com.

$$$
COSTA RICAN

✗ **Picante.** It's hot and it's tropical, and, as the name warns (*picante* means "spicy"), some of the dishes here make your taste buds tingle. The menu spices up (literally) local fish and tropical fruits in dishes like grilled mahimahi with a picante mango sauce. Smoked pork chops come with a spicy mora (blackberry sauce). If you can't face a whole red snapper, try the excellent fish tacos made with fresh snapper. (There's also a milder kids' menu.) The large terrace restaurant, recently painted a nautical blue and white, is poolside, facing the gorgeous beach backed by a cookie-cutter condominium development at Bahía Pez Vela. The cheap dinette furniture is out of sync with the innovative food, but you may forgive the furniture faux pas when you taste the homemade brownies and cheesecake. It's open from noon to 8 pm. Ⓢ *Average main: $16* ⊠ *At the beach, Bahía Pez Vela, 1½ km/1 mile south of Ocotal* ☎ *2670–0321.*

$$$
B&B/INN
★

▦ **Hotel Villa Casa Blanca.** For romance, you can't beat this Victorian-style, all-suites bed-and-breakfast on a hillside buried in a bower of tropical plantings. **Pros:** romantic; fabulous breakfasts. **Cons:** smallish rooms; noisy parrots. **TripAdvisor:** "charming and unique," "great cozy place," "wonderful hospitality." Ⓢ *Rooms from: $105* ⊠ *Inside gated entrance to El Ocotal Beach Resort* ☎ *2670–0448* ⊕ *www.hotelvillacasablanca.com* ⤴ *17 suites* ⏐◯⏐ *Breakfast.*

$$$
RESORT

▦ **Ocotal Beach Resort.** This large resort spread across a ridge has the best sea views hereabouts and is also one of the best dive and sportfishing resorts in the country. **Pros:** lots of excursions; great infrastructure; lovely views. **Cons:** resort-y; spotty service; steep hill to climb. **TripAdvisor:** "premises were dated," "the place with the view," "tired." Ⓢ *Rooms from: $160* ⊠ *3 km/2 miles south of Playas del Coco, along paved road* ☎ *2670–0321* ⊕ *www.ocotalresort.com* ⤴ *42 rooms, 5 suites, 12 bungalow suites* ⏐◯⏐ *Breakfast.*

NIGHTLIFE

Father Rooster Sports Bar & Grill. The best place to enjoy a quiet sunset margarita with an ocean view is at this laid-back bar and restaurant right on the beach. There's big-screen TV, music, pool, and beach volleyball for energetic visitors. Or you can relax on the wooden deck and enjoy a romantic dinner, featuring fresh fish and Tex-Mex favorites. It's open 11:30 to 9:30, except when it's booked for private parties. ⊠ *Next door to El Ocotal Beach Resort, 3 km/2 miles south of Playas del Coco* ☎ *2670–1246* ⊕ *www.fatherrooster.com.*

PLAYA PAN DE AZÚCAR

8 km/5 miles north of Flamingo Beach.

Playa Pan de Azúcar. Playa Pan de Azúcar (literally "Sugar Bread Beach," though most people call it simply Sugar Beach) has a quality that can be hard to come by in this area—with only one built-up property, the entire stretch of soft, light-color sand feels practically deserted and very private. The north end of the beach has some good snorkeling when the sea is calm—usually around low tide—and the swimming out from the middle of the beach is relatively safe. But if the swell is big, children and weak swimmers shouldn't go in past their waist. Playa Penca, a short walk south along the beach, can be a good swimming beach as well. A large part of the attraction here is the forest that hems the beach, where you may see howler monkeys, black iguanas, magpie jays, trogons, and dozens of other bird species.

GETTING HERE AND AROUND

Getting to this beach is an adventure in itself. It's still a very bumpy road 20 minutes from Flamingo Beach. If you have a 4WD vehicle and an excellent sense of direction, you can attempt to drive (dry season only) the 16-km (11-miles) Monkey Trail, which cuts through the mountains from Sardinal to Flamingo. But even some Ticos get lost on this route, so keep asking for directions along the way. There are no buses to Playa Pan de Azúcar; a taxi from Playa Flamingo costs about $20.

6

OUTDOOR ACTIVITIES

Most of the operators who work out of Flamingo *(⇨ below)* can pick up guests at the Hotel Sugar Beach for skin diving, sportfishing, sailing, horseback riding, and other excursions.

WHERE TO STAY

For expanded hotel reviews, visit Fodors.com.

$$ RESORT Fodor's Choice ★ **Hotel Sugar Beach.** The theme of this secluded, ultracomfortable hotel with a shimmering infinity pool and thin, curving beach is harmony with nature. **Pros:** friendly; natural setting; practically private beach; kids under 12 stay free with parents. **Cons:** waves and rocks can make the ocean dangerous for kids; bumpy road to get to off-site restaurants. **TripAdvisor:** "pretty setting," "peaceful relaxation," "a glimpse of paradise." [$] *Rooms from: $132* ✉ *8 km/5 miles north of Playa Flamingo* ☎ *2654–4242* 🌐 *www.sugar-beach.com* *22 rooms, 6 suites, 2 houses* 🍴 *Breakfast.*

PLAYA POTRERO

4 km/2½ miles north of Flamingo.

Playa Potrero. Stretching 4 km (2½ miles), this relatively undeveloped wide, brown-sand beach, across Potrero Bay from built-up Flamingo, catches ocean breezes and spectacular sunsets, which you can watch while bobbing in the warm, swimmable water. The pelican-patrolled beach is anchored at one end by the small Tico community of Potrero with a church, school, and supermarket arranged around a soccer field, and at the other end by the Flamingo skyline. Although large houses and condominium developments have sprung up on any hill with a view, at beach level there is only one unimposing hotel and some low-lying private houses set well back from the beach; beachgoers never feel hemmed in or crowded. The best area for swimming is midway between Flamingo and Potrero town, near the hotel Bahía del Sol. The best beach view and best breeze are from a bar stool at Bar Las Brisas. About 10 km (6 miles) offshore lie the Catalina Islands, a barrier-island paradise for divers and snorkelers; dive boats based in Flamingo can get there in 10 minutes.

GETTING HERE AND AROUND

Just before crossing the bridge at the entrance to Flamingo, take the right fork signed for Playa Potrero. The road, which is alternately muddy or dusty, is rough and follows the shoreline. Local buses run from Flamingo to Potrero, but it's so close that you're better off taking a taxi.

OUTDOOR ACTIVITIES

DIVING

Catalina Islands. Marked as Santa Catarina on some maps, the Catalina Islands, as they are known locally, are a major destination for dive operations based all along the coast. These barrier islands are remarkable for their diversity, and appeal to different levels of divers. On one side, the islands have 6- to 9-meter (20- to 30-foot) drops, great for beginners. The other side has deeper drops of 18 to 24 meters (60 to 80 feet), better suited to more-experienced divers. The top dive sites around the Catalina Islands are **The Point** and **The Wall**. From January to May, when the water is colder, you are almost guaranteed manta-ray sightings at these spots. Cow-nosed and devil rays are also spotted here in large schools, as well as bull and white-tipped sharks, several types of eels, and an array of reef fish. Dive operators from Playa Hermosa south to Tamarindo offer trips to these islands. Reserve through your hotel.

Costa Rica Diving. This well established dive shop has been specializing in Catalina Islands dives for more than 16 years, with two-tank, two-location trips limited to four divers and costing $85 per person. The German owners also offer courses and are noted for their precision and high safety standards. ✉ *1 km/½ mile south of Flamingo on the main hwy., next door to Banco de Costa Rica* ☎ *2654–4148* ⊕ *www. costarica-diving.com.*

WHERE TO EAT

$ ✕ **Bar Las Brisas.** This quintessential beach bar is a shack with a cov-
MEXICAN   ered deck and a view of the entire sweep of Playa Potrero. From a nearby souvenir stand, wind chimes tinkle in the constant breeze. The kitchen serves up fairly basic bar fare and some fresh seafood such as rice with shrimp, and a grilled mahimahi sandwich. The fish tacos are outstanding—breaded strips of fish smothered in lettuce, tomato, and refried beans and encased in both a crisp taco and a soft tortilla shell. Wednesday is ladies' night, when the joint really jumps and a DJ plays dance music. The place is decorated with old surfboards, rusty U.S. license plates, and wall murals. It's open noon to 9 or 10 daily. $ *Average main: $7* ✉ *100 m west of soccer field, across from supermarket* ☎ *2654–4047.*

WHERE TO STAY

For expanded hotel reviews, visit Fodors.com.

$$$
RESORT
Fodor'sChoice
★

Bahía del Sol. Located on the best spot on the beach, Bahía del Sol has a gorgeous, beachfront pool and comfortable rooms built around a mini–rain forest of tropical shrubs and towering trees. **Pros:** on the beach; lovely grounds; excellent restaurant; friendly, first-rate service. **Cons:** front terraces are not very private. **TripAdvisor:** "little gem," "awesome for everyone," "comfortable accommodations." $ *Rooms from: $165* ⊠ *South end of Potrero Beach, across from El Castillo* ☎ *2654–4671* ⊕ *www.potrerobay.com* ⤴ *10 standard rooms, 3 deluxe rooms, 4 one-bedroom suites, 10 two-bedroom suites.* ⟨○⟩ *Breakfast.*

$$
B&B/INN

Bahía Esmeralda Hotel & Restaurant. Although it's not on the beach, this Italian-owned hotel has style at an affordable price, with ocher-color villas spread out around a pretty pool, gardens, and lawn. **Pros:** friendly service; economical villas and suites. **Cons:** not on the beach; could use some updating; Continental breakfast included in rate only for the 4 rooms. **TripAdvisor:** "very comfortable," "perfect place to explore hidden beaches," "lovely." $ *Rooms from: $77* ⊠ *1 block east of Potrero village* ☎ *2654–4480* ⊕ *www.hotelbahiaesmeralda.com* ⤴ *4 rooms, 8 apartments, 2 suites, 2 villas* ⟨○⟩ *Breakfast.*

PLAYA FLAMINGO

80 km/50 miles southwest of Liberia.

Playa Flamingo. One of the first northern Nicoya beaches to experience the wonders of overdevelopment—a fact immortalized in the concrete towers that straggle up the hill above the bay—Flamingo still has some hidden charms, including one of the loveliest Blue Flag beaches and one of the best restaurants in Costa Rica. The place is still abuzz with real-estate activity, and any ledge of land with a view is a building site. But Flamingo Beach, hidden away to the southwest of the town, is picture-perfect, with almost-white sand sloping into a relatively calm sea and buttonwood trees separating it from the road. This beach is great for swimming, with a fine-sand bottom and no strong currents, though there are a few submerged rocks in front of the Flamingo Beach Resort, so you should swim a bit farther south. There's sometimes a bit of surf, so if the waves are big, keep your eye on little paddlers. There is little shade along the beach's 1-km-long (½-mile-long) stretch, and no services, though there are restaurants in the beach resort and the adjacent town. To find the beach, go straight as you enter town, and instead of going up the hill, turn left after the Flamingo Beach Resort.

Flamingo is perhaps most famous for its large sportfishing fleet, though they've been moored out in the bay for more than seven years now waiting for the government to grant a new concession to update and operate the marina here. Working girls are lured to Flamingo by the boatloads of single-for-the-week fishermen. This adds a faintly salacious whiff to some local nightspots.

6

GETTING HERE AND AROUND

To get to Playa Flamingo from Liberia, drive 45 km (28 miles) south to Belén and then 35 km (22 miles) west on a good, paved road. The trip takes about three hours. If you're coming from the Playas del Coco and Ocotal area, you can take a 16-km (10-miles) shortcut, called the Monkey Trail, starting near Sardinal and emerging at Potrero. It's then 4 km (2½ miles) south to Flamingo. Attempt this only in dry season and in a 4WD. You can also take a bus from Liberia (⇨ *Bus Travel in Travel Smart Costa Rica*).

ESSENTIALS

Bank/ATM Banco de Costa Rica ⊠ *Main road leading to Playa Flamingo, at the intersection of the road to Playa Potrero* ☎ 2654–4984.

Pharmacy Farmacia Playa Flamingo ⊠ *Plaza beside Marie's Restaurant at entrance to town* ☎ 2654–5524 ⊘ *Weekdays 8:30–7, Sat. 9–7, Sun. 9–5.*

OUTDOOR ACTIVITIES

Catalina Islands. Flamingo offers the quickest access to the Catalina Islands, visible from its beach, where big schools of fish, manta rays, and other sea creatures gather. Coastal reefs to the north are visited on day trips that combine snorkeling with time on undeveloped beaches.

BOATING

Lazy Lizard Catamaran Sailing Adventures. Laze away a morning or afternoon, sailing or sunbathing on this 34-foot catamaran. Or jump in the water for a swim or snorkel. The four-hour tours start at 8:30 am (minimum of eight people) and 2 pm and cost $75, with snorkeling equipment, kayaks, drinks, and food included. ☎ 2654–5900 ⊕ *www.lazylizardsailing.com.*

Samonique III. Sail off for an afternoon of snorkeling, snacking, and sunset drinks on *Samonique III*, a *trés jolie* 52-foot French ketch ($75 per person, minimum of 10 passengers). The ship sails daily at 2 and returns at 6:30 pm. ☎ 2654–5280, 8706–3723 ⊕ *www.costarica-sailing.com.*

DIVING AND SNORKELING

Aquacenter Diving. Based in the Flamingo Marina Resort, this dive shop runs two-tank dives at the Catalina Islands ($85 plus $16 gear rental) and snorkeling trips ($55, including equipment), as well as offering a full range of PADI certification courses. ⊠ *In Flamingo Marina Resort* ☎ 2654–4141 ⊕ *www.aquacenterdiving.com.*

Costa Rica Diving (⇨ *See Playa Potrero, above).*

FISHING

Although the marina is still closed while officials consider bids to rebuild it, there are plenty of sportfishing boats bobbing in Flamingo Bay. Larger boats have moved to moorings in the new Papagayo Marina near the Four Seasons Hotel. In December the wind picks up and many of the smaller, 31-foot-and-under boats head to calmer water farther south. But the wind brings cold water and abundant baitfish, which attract marlin (blue, black, and striped), Pacific sailfish, yellowfin tuna, wahoo, mahimahi, grouper, and red snapper. January to April is consequently prime catch-and-release season for billfish.

The reclusive zebra moray eel likes to hide its entire body in rock or coral holes.

WHERE TO EAT

$$$
FRENCH
Fodor's Choice
★

✕ **Mar y Sol.** Linger over a fine French-accented dinner at this chic but casual terrace restaurant—it's truly one of the best dining experiences in Costa Rica. Come early to catch the spectacular sunset view over the ocean from the popular second-floor cocktail lounge. It's perched on a breezy hillside where you can munch on pizza studded with lobster and brie cheese, or fried shrimp with a starfruit habañera dipping sauce. Chef/owners Alain and Jean-Luc Taulere represent the sixth and seventh generations of a family of French restaurateurs, so of course there is traditional French onion soup and chateaubriand for two on the menu. Even more interesting are young Jean-Luc's creative fusions of French tradition with tropical flavors, such as duck confit served with a polenta cake and fresh plum sauce. For smaller appetites there's a new menu of medium-size dishes, such as yuca-encrusted yellowfin tuna with a citrus reduction sauce. Popular starters include the restaurant's signature dish: *coco del mar*, a not-to-be-missed *mélange* of local seafood, flavored with ginger and lemongrass and cooked in lobster stock and fresh coconut milk. Instead of classic crème brûlée, there's a guava flan, along with cool and luscious homemade coconut ice cream. Chocolate lovers will swoon over the molten chocolate volcano cake. There's an extensive wine cellar to match the sophisticated menu, and you can sample 20 or so wines by the glass. Service is faultless and smoothly professional. Open for lunch and dinner; closed Tuesday. $ *Average main: $18* ⌧ *150 m uphill (west) from Flamingo Marina Resort* ☎ *2654-4151* ⊘ *Closed Tues. and Sept. and Oct.*

$$
SEAFOOD
★

✕ **Marie's Restaurant.** A Flamingo institution, serving beachgoers and locals for more than two decades, this popular restaurant serves an array of sandwiches and salads, as well as reliably fresh seafood in large portions at reasonable prices. Settle in at one of the wooden tables beneath the ceiling fans and massive thatched roof for a traditional Costa Rican ceviche, avocado stuffed with shrimp, or heart of palm and *pejivalle* (palm fruit). The main fare includes whole-fried red snapper, shrimp and fish kebabs, and a delicious *plato de mariscos*

> **THE GUANACASTE TREE**
>
> Massive and wide spreading, with tiny leaflets and dark brown, earlike seedpods, the Guanacaste tree is common through this region, and is Costa Rica's national tree.

(shrimp, lobster, and fish served with garlic butter, potatoes, and salad). Save room for Marie's signature banana-chocolate bread pudding. At breakfast, try unusual papaya pancakes, French toast made with cream cheese and jam, or eggs Benedict. There's free Wi-Fi for customers. $ *Average main: $10* ⊠ *Main road in the new plaza commercial center, near north end of beach* ☎ *2654–4136.*

WHERE TO STAY

For expanded hotel reviews, visit Fodors.com.

$$$
RESORT
☾

Flamingo Beach Resort. Remodeled, expanded, and upgraded, this three-story hotel has the prime location overlooking beautiful Flamingo Beach, along with a huge swimming pool and every water sport that kids of any age could want. **Pros:** beachfront; big pool; excellent value; all-inclusive meal plans available. **Cons:** noisy with kids during vacation times; more than 100 rooms. **TripAdvisor:** "pretty looking," "beautiful sunsets," "adventure paradise." $ *Rooms from: $180* ⊠ *Hotel entrance on left past Marie's Restaurant* ☎ *2654–4444, 2283–8063 in San José, 877/856–5519 toll-free in U.S.* ⊕ *www.resortflamingobeach. com* ➷ *109 rooms, 11 suites* ❏ *Multiple meal plans.*

$$
RESORT
☾

Flamingo Marina Resort. Though a short walk from Flamingo Beach, there's still plenty to do at this collection of hillside rooms and villas, with four pools, tennis courts, a beach, a dive shop, a tour desk, a sport-fishing operation, and a small beach. **Pros:** spacious rooms; sea views; ample grounds. **Cons:** not on main beach, which is down a very steep hill; lots of kids, which may or may not be what you want. **TripAdvisor:** "amazing getaway," "quaint," "great view and food." $ *Rooms from: $119* ⊠ *Halfway up hill above Flamingo Bay* ☎ *2654–4141, 2290–1858 San José office* ⊕ *www.flamingomarina.com* ➷ *22 rooms, 6 suites, 80 condos* ❏ *Multiple meal plans.*

$
B&B/INN

Hotel Guanacaste Lodge. On the outskirts of Flamingo, a short drive from the beach, this Tico-run lodge offers basic accommodations for a fraction of what the town's big hotels charge. **Pros:** affordable; better-than-average rooms; friendly. **Cons:** no in-room phones; simple furnishings. $ *Rooms from: $60* ⊠ *200 m south of the Potrero-Flamingo crossroads* ☎ *2654–4494* ⊕ *www.guanacastelodge.com* ➷ *9 rooms* ▭ *No credit cards* ❏ *Breakfast.*

NIGHTLIFE

Mariner Inn Bar. This often boisterous bar, thick with testosterone, is the place to be if you enjoy socializing with fishermen trading fish tales. ⊠ *Bottom of hill, entering Flamingo.*

PLAYA CONCHAL

8 km/5 miles south of Flamingo.

Playa Conchal. Lovely, secluded Playa Conchal is an idyllic strand of sugary sand sloping steeply into aquamarine water and lined with trees and dominated by the sprawling Paradisus Playa Conchal resort, but you don't need to stay at that all-inclusive resort to enjoy Conchal, since it's a short beach walk south from Brasilito. Named for the bits of broken shells that cover its base of fine white sand (the Spanish word for shell is *concha*), the southern part of the beach is often deserted. The point that defines Conchal's northern end is hemmed by a lava-rock reef that is a popular snorkeling area—locals rent equipment on the beach.

GETTING HERE AND AROUND

The drive south from Flamingo is 10 minutes on a paved highway. Both town and beach are just 1 km (½ mile) north of the entrance to Paradisus Playa Conchal. To reach Playa Conchal, turn left at the end of the town square and follow the dirt road across a stretch of beach and over a steep hill; the beach stretch is impassable at high tide. Buses run from Flamingo to Conchal three times daily, at 7:30 and 11:30 am and 2:30 pm. A taxi from Flamingo is about $6.

ESSENTIALS

The closest bank and ATM are in Flamingo.

Hospital Costa de Emergencias ⊠ *300 m northwest of crossroads at Huacas* ☎ *2653–6440.*

Pharmacy Farmacia El Cruce ⊠ *Crossroads at Huacas* ☎ *2653–8787* ⊘ *Daily 8 am–8 pm.*

EXPLORING

Brasilito. A small, scruffy fishing village just 1 km (½ mile) north of Conchal, Brasilito has ramshackle houses huddled around its main square, which doubles as the soccer field. It's cluttered, noisy, and totally Tico—a lively contrast to the controlled sophistication of the Playa Conchal resort and residential development. Fishing boats moor just off a wide beach, about 3 km (2 miles) long, with golden sand flecked with pebbles and a few rocks. The surf is a little stronger here than at Flamingo Beach, but the shallow, sandy bottom keeps it swimmable. The sea is cleaner off nearby Playa Conchal, which is also a more attractive beach. A few casual *marisquerias* (seafood eateries) and one notable restaurant line Brasilito's beach.

OUTDOOR ACTIVITIES

GOLF

Reserva Conchal Golf Club. One of the best golf courses in the country, the Reserva Conchal Golf Club is an 18-hole, par-71 course designed by Robert Trent Jones Jr. The perfectly maintained course is reserved for guests of The Westin Resort & Spa, who can try out their swing on 18 holes for $150, cart included. ⊠ *The Westin Resort & Spa, Playa Conchal, entrance, less than 1 km/½ mile south of Brasilito* ☎ *2654–3500.*

WHERE TO EAT AND STAY

For expanded hotel reviews, visit Fodors.com.

$$ SEAFOOD 🍴 **El Camarón Dorado.** Much of the appeal of this open-air bar-restaurant whose name translates as "The Golden Shrimp" is its bougainvillea-shaded location on Brasilito's beautiful beach. Some tables are practically on the beach, with the surf lapping just yards away, making it the perfect spot for sunset drinks. The white-plastic tables and chairs are not up to the standards of the food, which is mostly locally caught fish and seafood served in bountiful portions. The house specialties include mahimahi prepared various ways, *arroz a la marinera* (rice with seafood), grilled lobster, and either jumbo or the smaller pinky shrimp *al ajillo* (sautéed with garlic). If you have a reservation, a van can pick you up from Flamingo; or if you are a party of six or more, from Tamarindo hotels. [$] *Average main: $12* ✉ *On Brasilito Beach, 200 m north of Brasilito Plaza* ☎ *2654–4028.*

$ ITALIAN 🍴 **Il Forno.** For a break from seafood, try lunch or dinner at this romantic Italian garden restaurant. There are 17 versions of thin-crust pizzas, plus fine homemade pastas and risotto. Vegetarians have lots of choices (if you can get past the thought that veal is on the menu), including an eggplant lasagna and interesting salads. They also serve some tasty seafood and meat dishes. At dinner, candles glimmer all through the garden and on tables grouped under thatched roofs. Spanish and Italian wines are available by the glass or bottle. It's open Tuesday through Sunday 12:30 pm to 9:30 pm. [$] *Average main: $10* ✉ *Main road, 200 m east of the bridge in Brasilito* ☎ *2654–4125* 💳 *No credit cards* ⏲ *Closed Mon. and Oct.*

$ B&B/INN 🏨 **Hotel Brasilito.** Backpackers and travelers who don't need amenities will love this vintage, two-story, wooden hotel's affordable price and seafront location, if not its no-frills but adequate rooms. **Pros:** inexpensive; across the street from beach; knowledgeable manager. **Cons:** very basic rooms; can be noisy and hot. **TripAdvisor:** "right on the beach," "paradise," "very basic." [$] *Rooms from: $44* ✉ *Between soccer field and beach, Brasilito* ☎ *2654–4237* 🌐 *www.brasilito.com* 🛏 *13 rooms* 🍽 *No meals.*

$$$$ RESORT ALL-INCLUSIVE 🏨 **The Westin Resort & Spa, Playa Conchal.** So vast that guests ride around in trucks covered with awnings and the staff gets around on bicycles, this all-inclusive resort has been taken over by the Starwood hotel group and upgraded, redecorated, and rebranded as a Westin resort. **Pros:** lovely, upgraded rooms; beach access; abundant activities. **Cons:** expensive; massive; most rooms are far from beach. **TripAdvisor:** "almost perfection," "beautiful," "Costa Rican paradise." [$] *Rooms from: $325* ✉ *Entrance less than 1 km/½ mile south of Brasilito* ☎ *2654–3500* 🌐 *www.starwoodhotels.com/westin* 🛏 *292 suites, 122 Royal Service suites* 🍽 *All-inclusive.*

NIGHTLIFE

Happy Snapper. Live music, both acoustic guitar and rowdier dance bands, keeps the Happy Snapper hopping most weekends during high season. Owner Mike Osborne often mans the bar and spikes the drinks with his own brand of wry humor. And if you come hungry, there's always fresh whole snapper to sink your teeth into and apple pie à la mode. During the day, there's a small pool that will keep children occupied. ⊠ *On main street, across from beach in Brasilito.*

EN ROUTE Gas stations are few and far between in these hinterlands. If you're heading down to Tamarindo from the Flamingo/Conchal area, fill up first. Your best bet is the 24-hour Oasis Exxon, 3 km (2 miles) east of Huacas.

TAMARINDO

82 km/51 miles southwest of Liberia.

Once a funky beach town full of spacey surfers and local fishermen, Tamarindo is now a pricey, hyped-up hive of commercial development and real estate speculation, happily accompanied by a dizzying variety of shops, bars, and hotels, and probably the best selection of restaurants of any beach town on the Pacific coast. There's a tony shopping center at the entrance to town with an upscale AutoMercado supermarket and a Scotiabank branch and ATM. On the down side, still-unpaved roads kick up dust and mud alternately, depending on the season; and strip malls and high-rise condominiums clutter the rest of the main street and obscure views of the still-magnificent beach. Some low-life elements are also making security an issue. But once you're on the beach, almost all the negatives disappear (just keep your eyes on your belongings). Wide and flat, the sand is packed hard enough for easy walking and jogging. How good it is for swimming and surfing, however, is questionable, since the town has twice lost its Blue Flag clean-beach status (because of overdevelopment and the total absence of water treatment). The water quality is especially poor during the rainy months, when you'll want to do your swimming and surfing at nearby Playa Langosta, or Playa Grande. ■ TIP→ Strong currents at the north end of the beach get a lot of swimmers into trouble, especially when they try to cross the estuary without a surfboard.

Surfing is the main attraction here, and there's a young crowd that parties hard after a day riding the waves. Tamarindo serves as a popular base for surfing at the nearby Playas Grande, Langosta, Avellanas, and Negra. There are plenty of outdoor options in addition to surfing, though, among them diving, sportfishing, wildlife watching, and canopy tours. You can play 18 rounds at the nearby Hacienda Pinilla golf course, or simply stroll the beach and sunbathe.

GETTING HERE AND AROUND

Both Nature Air and SANSA fly to Tamarindo from San José. By car from Liberia, travel south on the highway to the turnoff for Belén, then head west and turn left at the Huacas crossroads to Tamarindo. Stretches of the paved road from Belén are often in deplorable states of disrepair. There are no direct bus connections between Playa Grande or Playa Avellanas and Tamarindo. A taxi or a shuttle van is the way to go from nearby towns if you don't have wheels.

Tamarindo Shuttle. The Tamarindo Shuttle ferries passengers between the various beaches in a comfortable van and will also pick you up at the Liberia airport, $20 per person, minimum of two. ☎ *2653–4444, 2653–2626* ⊕ *www.tamarindoshuttle.com.*

ESSENTIALS

Bank/ATM Banco Nacional ⊠ *Across from Tamarindo El Diriá Hotel.*

Medical Assistance Coast Medical Services ⊠ *At the crossroads in Villa Real, inland from Tamarindo.* **Farmacia Tamarindo** ⊠ *Main road into town, diagonally across from Best Western Tamarindo Villas* ☎ *2653–0210.*

Post Office Correo ⊠ *Across from airport on main road into town.*

Rental Cars Alamo ⊠ *Diagonal to Hotel El Diriá main road* ☎ *2653–0727.* **Budget** ⊠ *Hotel Zullymar, main road* ☎ *2653–0756.* **Economy** ⊠ *Main road entering Tamarindo, across from Witch's Rock Surf Camp* ☎ *2653–0728.*

Taxis Olman Taxi ☎ *8347–8553 cell.*

A taxi from the airport to the center of Tamarindo costs about $12 for two people with luggage.

OUTDOOR ACTIVITIES

BOATING

Rocky Isla El Capitán, just offshore, is a close-in kayaking destination, full of sand-dollar shells. Exploring the tidal estuaries north and south of town is best done in a kayak at high tide, when you can travel farther up the temporary rivers. Arrange kayaking trips through your hotel.

Blue Dolphin. Set sail on a 40-foot catamaran for an afternoon of sunning, snorkeling, and kayaking aboard the *Blue Dolphin*. The boat departs at 1 pm from the beach, in front of El Pescador Restaurant, and returns around sunset. It's $75 per person, including food and open bar. During high season there's also a morning tour, from 8 am to noon, $65 (kids under 12 half price) including snorkel gear and fishing poles. ☎ *8842–3204* ⊕ *www.bluedolphinsailing.com.*

Iguana Surf. This long-time surf shop has an office with information on guided two-hour kayaking tours of the San Francisco Estuary ($35 per person) and a full roster of local tours, including snorkeling. ⊠ *On beach, 100 m north of El Diriá Hotel* ☎ *2653–0148* ⊕ *www. iguanasurf.net.*

FISHING

Tamarindo Sportfishing. A number of fishing charters in Tamarindo cater to saltwater anglers. The most experienced among them is Tamarindo Sportfishing, run by Randy Wilson, who has led the way in developing catch-and-release techniques that are easy on the fish. Wilson has roamed these waters since the 1970s, and he knows where the big ones lurk. His 38-foot *Talking Fish* is equipped with a marlin chair and a cabin with a shower, and costs $1,500 for a full day, $850 for a half. A fishing trip for up to four anglers on one of two 27-foot boats costs $825 to $975 for a full day; $550 to $695 for a half. ☎ *2653–0090* ⊕ *www.tamarindosportfishing.com.*

GOLF

Hacienda Pinilla. Mike Young, who has designed some of the best golf courses in the southern United States, designed the par-72 championship course at Hacienda Pinilla. It has ocean views and breezes, and

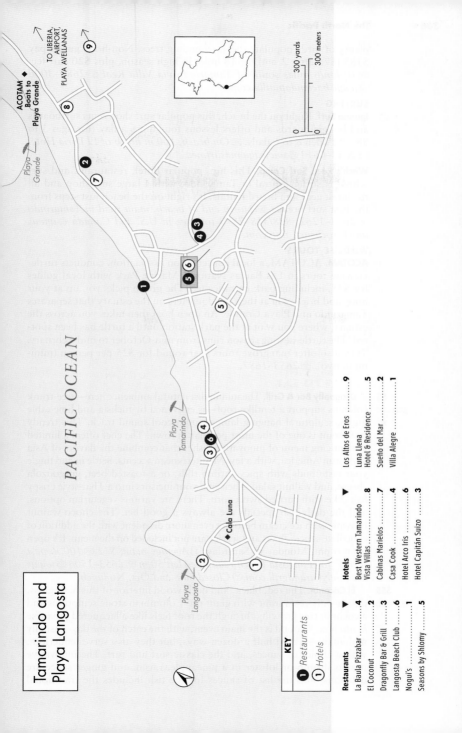

Tamarindo and Playa Langosta

PACIFIC OCEAN

ACOTAM ◆ Boats to Playa Grande

TO LIBERIA, AIRPORT, PLAYA AVELLANAS

Playa Grande

Playa Tamarindo

Playa Langosta

◆ Cala Luna

KEY
1 *Restaurants*
1 *Hotels*

0 ——— 300 yards
0 ——— 300 meters

Restaurants ▶
La Baula Pizzabar 4
El Coconut 2
Dragonfly Bar & Grill 3
Langosta Beach Club 6
Nogui's 1
Seasons by Shlomy 5

Hotels ▶
Best Western Tamarindo ....
Vista Villas 8
Cabinas Marielos 7
Casa Cook 4
Hotel Arco Iris 6
Hotel Capitán Suizo 3

Los Altos de Eros 9
Luna Llena ....
Hotel & Residence 5
Sueño del Mar 2
Villa Alegre 1

plenty of birds populate the surrounding trees. Non-hotel guests pay $185 ($75 after 2 pm) for 18 holes in high season, plus $20 cart fee. ✉ *10 km/6 miles south of Tamarindo via Villa Real* ☎ *2680–3000* 🌐 *www.haciendapinilla.com.*

SURFING

👶 **Iguana Surf.** Right on the beach, this popular surf shop rents surfboards and boogie boards and offers lessons four times a day (for ages 3 to 88). It's open 8 to 6 daily. ✉ *On beach, 100 m north of El Diriá Hotel* ☎ *2653–0613* 🌐 *www.iguanasurf.net.*

Witch's Rock Surf Camp. This hip, popular hotel, restaurant, and surf school is surfer central in Tamarindo, with a large surf shop and all the latest gear and board rentals. It's right on the beach just steps from the best surf breaks. ✉ *North end of beach, main road in Tamarindo* ☎ *2653–1262, 888/318–7873 toll-free in U.S. and Canada* 🌐 *www.witchsrocksurfcamp.com.*

WILDLIFE TOURS

ACOTAM. ACOTAM, a local conservation association, conducts turtle-viewing tours in Las Baulas National Marine Park with local guides for $35, including park entrance fee. The group picks you up at your hotel and briefs you at their headquarters on the estuary that separates Tamarindo and Playa Grande. An open boat then takes you across the estuary, where you wait at the park station until a turtle has been spotted. The turtle-nesting season runs from mid-October to mid-February. They also offer mangrove tours year-round for $25 per person (minimum two). ☎ *2653–1687.*

WHERE TO EAT

$$ ECLECTIC ★ 🍴 **Dragonfly Bar & Grill.** The minimalist natural ambience here—tree-trunk columns support a tentlike roof—is enlivened by fuchsia and lime table linens, sculptural hanging lamps, and a cool sound track. This trendy restaurant is one of the most popular in town. The chef offers a limited but enticing menu of innovative dishes that combine the flavors of Asia and Latin America, with a few Mediterranean accents. Settle in and tingle your taste buds with spicy shrimp rolls, or a roasted beet, gorgonzola cheese, and walnut salad. Then sink your incisors into a Thai-style crispy fish cake with curried sweet corn. There are various vegetarian options, and the daily fish specials are always a good bet. The choco-walnut brownie with ice cream becomes even more decadent with the addition of chocolate sauce. Taxes and service are not included on the menu. It's open from 6 pm, Monday to Saturday. [$] *Average main: $12* ✉ *100 m past turnoff for Langosta Beach road, then left 50 m* ☎ *2653–1506* 🌐 *www.dragonflybarandgrill.com* 🕒 *Closed Sun. and Oct. No lunch.*

$$$ SEAFOOD 🍴 **El Coconut.** The red, black, and dark-wood interior of this high-gloss, dinner-only restaurant with giant pre-Colombian stone sculptures and a coconut tree growing through the roof feels like a lacquered Japanese *bento* box. Seafood is the main event, with the catch of the day—usually mahimahi—served half a dozen ways, but they also serve tenderloin, with a choice of sauces, and the classic surf and turf. The innovative jumbo shrimp or lobster in a pineapple, raisin, and ginger sauce are delicious, and the list of sauces for the fish includes the traditional

Norwegian *sandefjords smor* (a creamy butter sauce with lime)—the owner, Katharina, is from Norway. Service is smooth and more formal than at most beach restaurants, and they have a good wine list, but the food and drink are much more expensive here than at the competition and tax and service are not included on the menu. $ *Average main: $20* ⊠ *Main street, 150 m south of Tamarindo Vista Villas* ☎ *2653–0086* ⊕ *www.elcoconut-tamarindo.com* ⊘ *Closed Mon. No lunch.*

$$
PIZZA
☾

✕ **La Baula Pizzabar.** Wildly popular, this casually chic, alfresco pizzeria on a quiet side street has plenty of cars parked outside most nights, particularly Sunday when all the Tamarindo locals seem to meet and greet here. Families are especially fond of La Baula—the Costa Rican name for the leatherback turtle—because of its reasonable prices, noisy buzz, and adjacent playground and picniclike dining area. There's also a softly lighted dining area for more-romantic dinners. Everyone enjoys the consistently delicious thin-crust pizzas. The prosciutto, arugula, and Parmesan pizza is perfect. If you're not a fan of pizza, there's little other choice on the menu, which consists of two-dozen pies and a mixed salad. They also serve Italian wine by the glass and a tasty little tiramisu, followed by a glass of Limoncello or Sambuca. It's open daily from 5 pm. $ *Average main: $12* ⊠ *Next door to Dragonfly Bar & Grill* ☎ *2653–1450* ⊘ *No lunch.*

$$
SEAFOOD

✕ **Nogui's.** Pleasing a loyal legion of local fans since 1974, Nogui's offers a hearty Costa Rican menu and an ocean view. It is one of Tamarindo's best options for lunch, with a good selection of sandwiches and huge salads. At dinner they offer a full seafood menu and various meat dishes. The recipes and presentation are nothing fancy, but the seafood is fresh and instead of the ubiquitous rice and beans on the side, Nogui's has a puree of *tiquisque,* a potatolike tuber. Prices are a little high, but they do include service and tax as required by law, unlike so many other restaurants in town. The homemade pies are legendary, notably the coconut cream and apple pie à la mode. Their signature margarita is made with tamarind fruit. After 5 pm the restaurant on Nogui's second floor offers the same menu with a higher ocean view and balmy breezes. On the down side, the waitresses here often seem sullen and put out. $ *Average main: $15* ⊠ *South side of Tamarindo Circle, on beach* ☎ *2653–0029* ⊘ *Closed Wed. and first 2 wks in Oct.*

$$$
MEDITERRANEAN

✕ **Seasons by Shlomy.** Innovative chef Shlomy Koren, Israeli-born and Cordon Bleu–trained, is making a lot of diners happy in Tamarindo again. After closing his heralded Pachanga restaurant, Koren resurfaced at an intimate poolside terrace in the Hotel Arco Iris and is once again transforming fresh local ingredients into sophisticated Mediterranean-fusion dishes you would pay a small fortune for on the Riviera. Portobello mushrooms and caramelized onions accompany pan-seared snapper with a balsamic reduction; sashimi comes doused in ginger-flavored, sizzling sesame oil; and masala chicken is cooked with almonds and sage. Chocolate lovers will long remember Seasons' version of Toblerone—dense chocolate with almond nougat combined with a rich chocolate ganache. $ *Average main: $17* ⊠ *Hotel Arco Iris, uphill from turnoff to Langosta beach road* ☎ *8368–6983* ⊕ *www.seasonstamarindo.com* ▭ *No credit cards* ⊘ *Closed Sun. and mid-Sept. to mid-Oct.*

6

A group of local musicians rocking out in Tamarindo.

WHERE TO STAY

For expanded hotel reviews, visit Fodors.com.

$ HOTEL **Best Western Tamarindo Vista Villas.** This is traditionally the surfer's hangout in Tamarindo, where the talk around the pool bar is all about surfing. **Pros:** near beach break; ocean views from villas; affordable. **Cons:** not right on the beach; spotty service; a little down at the heel. **TripAdvisor:** "unsurpassed hospitality," "great views," "excellent value and location." [$] *Rooms from: $69* ✉ *Main road entering Tamarindo, on left* ☎ *2653–0114* 🌐 *www.tamarindovistavillas.com* 🛏 *12 rooms, 17 villas* 🍴 *Breakfast.*

$ B&B/INN **Cabinas Marielos.** The rooms at this centrally situated, locally owned hotel are among the best of the budget category in Tamarindo. **Pros:** cheap; near beach; pretty garden; relatively quiet. **Cons:** basic rooms; no air-conditioning or hot showers in some rooms. **TripAdvisor:** "lovely garden and room," "simple but close to the beach," "nice people." [$] *Rooms from: $60* ✉ *Across main dirt road from beach, on left after Best Western* ☎ *2653–0141* 🌐 *www.cabinasmarieloscr.com* 🛏 *24 rooms* 🍴 *No meals.*

$$ B&B/INN **Hotel Arco Iris.** Beautifully remodeled bungalows dot the grounds of this newly smartened-up small inn half a block off one of Tarmarindo's main drags. **Pros:** recently remodeled with air-conditioning; boutique feel; great restaurant. **Cons:** not a lot of privacy in bungalows; dusty walk to beach. **TripAdvisor:** "best hospitality," "a perfect retreat," "beautiful hotel with accommodating staff." [$] *Rooms from: $119* ✉ *Follow signs past turnoff to Playa Langosta and go up hill to right* ☎ *2653–0330* 🌐 *www.hotelarcoiris.com* 🛏 *5 bungalows, 7 rooms* 🍴 *Breakfast.*

$$$
RENTAL
★

🏠 **Casa Cook.** With just a few rooms on the quiet, southern end of the beach, this friendly, family-run beachfront place is one of Tamarindo's most secluded lodging options. **Pros:** small; secluded, beachfront; friendly. **Cons:** often full; not a lot of privacy in casita. **TripAdvisor:** "wonderful staff," "relaxing in the sun," "paradise found." $ *Rooms from: $210* ✉ *Road to Playa Langosta, 100 m before Hotel Capitán Suizo* ☎ *2653–0125* ⊕ *www.casacook.net* ⤳ *2 cabinas, 1 casita, 1 apartment, 1 house* ⦿ *No meals.*

$$$
B&B/INN
Fodor's Choice
★

🏠 **Hotel Capitán Suizo.** For folks who value nature, tranquillity, and a beautiful beach setting, along with luxurious rooms and an idyllic swimming pool, this is the best choice in town. **Pros:** beachfront; secluded; friendly; lovely gardens and pool. **Cons:** not a lot of privacy in garden bungalows; some rooms lack air-conditioning; pricey. **TripAdvisor:** "beautiful beach," "luxury small hotel," "the best place to relax." $ *Rooms from: $205* ✉ *Right side of Playa Langosta road, halfway between Tamarindo and Langosta* ☎ *2653–0075* ⊕ *www.hotelcapitansuizo.com* ⤳ *22 rooms, 8 bungalows, 1 apartment* ⦿ *Breakfast.*

$$$$
B&B/INN

🏠 **Los Altos de Eros Luxury Inn & Spa.** This intimate adults-only inn is the place to be for honeymooning couples with enough money left over after the wedding to pamper themselves, or for stressed-out high-achievers in need of some relaxation therapy. **Pros:** secluded; excellent service; romantic. **Cons:** scheduled mealtimes; remote; not a lot of privacy in rooms; very pricey. **TripAdvisor:** "excellent staff," "Costa Rica paradise," "luxury and class." $ *Rooms from: $395* ✉ *Cañasfistula, 14 km/8½ miles southeast of Tamarindo* ☎ *8850–4203* ⊕ *www.losaltosdeeros.com* ⤳ *4 rooms, 1 suite* ⦿ *Some meals.*

$$
B&B/INN

🏠 **Luna Llena Hotel & Residence.** Looking a little like a Fellini film set of a fantasy tropical village, this collection of bright yellow, conical thatch-roof huts is fun and affordable. **Pros:** secluded; lush grounds; cheerful decor. **Cons:** several blocks away from beach; small pool. **TripAdvisor:** "charming," "comfortable and convenient," "beautiful perfect hotel." $ *Rooms from: $90* ✉ *From road to Playa Langosta, 1st left (uphill)* ☎ *2653–0082* ⊕ *www.hotellunallena.com* ⤳ *7 rooms, 7 bungalows* ⦿ *Breakfast.*

NIGHTLIFE

Tamarindo is one of the few places outside San José where the nightlife really jumps. In fact, it has the dubious distinction of being featured on Entertainment Television's explicit *Wild On* series, which spotlights the rowdiest party scenes around the world.

Although party-hearty hot spots come and go with the tides, Tamarindo does have some perennially popular nightspots, along with a couple of low-key options.

Aqua Discoteque. With a waterfall in the middle of the dance floor and an oceanfront patio, this trendy disco is open Monday, Wednesday, Friday, and Saturday nights, from about 10 pm, with changing DJs and live bands. There's a $4 cover charge. ✉ *75 m north of Hotel El Diriá* ⊕ *www.aquadiscoteque.com.*

Crazy Monkey Bar. Friday night at Crazy Monkey Bar is ladies' night. The live salsa music attracts locals who really know how to move and a crowd of appreciative onlookers. ✉ *Tamarindo Vista Villas, main road entering Tamarindo.*

Hotel Capitán Suizo. For a pleasantly sedate Friday evening, try barbecue on the beach at the Hotel Capitán Suizo, starting at 6:30 with a cocktail, then on to a lavish barbecue buffet and live folk music ($34 plus tax, reserve in advance). ✉ *Right side of road toward Playa Langosta; veer left before circle.*

Jazz at Playa Langosta Beach Club. Sink into a comfortable chair at this chic pool-side lounge on Playa Langosta, to watch the sunset over the Pacific, and stay for jazz under the stars, Fridays 7 to 9 pm.

SHOPPING

Most stores in the strip malls lining the main road sell the same souvenirs. It's hard to leave town without at least one sarong or T-shirt in your suitcase. There are a few upscale clothing and jewelry shops worth a visit.

Amo La Vida. One of the most beautiful and intriguing shops in town, this eclectic emporium has exquisite local jewelry, plus exotic home-decorating items from Morocco and Egypt, including atmospheric wall sconces and accent lamps. ✉ *Main street, beside El Diriá Hotel* ☎ *2653–1507.*

Calypso. Owner Anne Loriot, a Parisian, has raised the bar on beach fashion with fabulous Indonesian- and Mexican-style cover-ups and elegant, cool dresses, all available in real women's sizes, plus exotic jewelry. ✉ *Main street, at Tamarindo El Diriá Hotel* ☎ *2653–1436.*

PLAYA LANGOSTA

2 km/1 mile south of Tamarindo.

Playa Langosta. Playa Langosta is actually two beaches: To the north is an upscale, residential area where every foot of beachfront has been built up; to the south is a pristine protected annex of Las Baulas National Marine Park, where the occasional leatherback turtle nests at night and beachcombers and surfers roam by day. The dividing point is the San Francisco Estuary, the mouth of which is a knee-high wade at low tide, and a deep river with dangerous currents around high tide. If you walk a ways up the river at low tide, you may see snowy egrets, baby blue herons, tail-bobbing spotted sandpipers, and, if your eyes are sharp, tiny white-lored gnatcatchers, endemic to these parts. Sort of a chic bedroom community of Tamarindo, just five minutes away by car, most of the low-rise development on the northern half is tucked behind the mangrove trees, so you can enjoy an unsullied dramatic beachscape, with surf crashing against rocky outcroppings. A few high-rise condominiums have invaded the area, but they are mostly set back. The beach here is rather narrow, since the coast is lined with rocks, and the light gray sand is rather coarse. There's a wider, less rocky stretch in front of the Barceló Resort, where you can walk across the San Francisco Estuary at low tide to stroll and swim on the beach's southern half.

GETTING HERE AND AROUND

The dirt road from Tamarindo is alternately dusty or muddy, but reliably rough. To keep down the dust, the road is periodically spread with an industrial mixture of molasses, which accounts for the stickiness and the lovely sweet smell. You can walk along the beach, at low tide, all the way from Tamarindo Beach, but be careful not to get caught on the headland rocks as the tide comes in. Most car-free visitors get picked up from Tamarindo by their hotels. Or you can take a taxi.

OUTDOOR ACTIVITIES

Tour operators in Tamarindo, just a few miles north, offer activities in the Playa Langosta area.

WHERE TO EAT

$$$ FRENCH ★ 🍴 **Playa Langosta Beach Club.** Looking for romance with spectacular food that matches the ambience? This brand new beach club/restaurant/lounge/jazz club is the most romantic and the most sophisticated dining spot on the beach. At dinner, tables set with white linens and candles are arranged around two glowing pools, under palms festooned with fairy lights. The sound of waves breaking on the beach blends with the very cool, soft-jazz sound track. Once you have drunk in the ambience, the best is yet to come: delectable fish, shellfish, and beef tenderloin cooked and sauced to French-accented perfection. Start with a tuna carpaccio or a flaky pastry nest filled with goat cheese and spinach. Move on to a divine fillet of sole bathed in a velvety, peppery champagne cream sauce. Or sink your teeth into a grilled, tender beef fillet smothered in a mushroomy Normande sauce. There's a good wine list and light, refreshing Spanish wines by the glass. For dessert there are scrumptious caramelized apple crepes with honey and ice cream. On Friday there's live sunset jazz starting at 7. At lunch, the menu features fish carpaccios, panini, fresh tuna salad, lobster, and mussels with french fries. [$] *Average main: $18* ✉ *Langosta Beach road, 200 m north of Capitan Suizo, Tamarindo* ☎ *2653–1127.*

WHERE TO STAY

For expanded hotel reviews, visit Fodors.com.

$$$ B&B/INN ★ 🏨 **Sueño del Mar.** The name of this place means "Dream of the Sea," and the front gate opens into a dreamy world of intimate gardens, patios, and hand-painted tiles. **Pros:** intimate; well appointed; great beachfront. **Cons:** tiny pool; lack of privacy in small rooms; pricey. **TripAdvisor:** "perfect spot to relax," "quiet," "impeccable." [$] *Rooms from: $195* ✉ *130 m south of Capitán Suizo, veer right for 45 m, then right again for about 90 m to entrance gate, across from back of Cala Luna Hotel* ☎ *2653–0284* 🌐 *www.sueno-del-mar.com* 🛏 *3 rooms, 1 suite, 2 casitas* 🍽 *Breakfast.*

$$$ B&B/INN ★ 🏨 **Villa Alegre.** A visit here is like coming to stay with dear friends who just happen to have a really terrific house on one of the most scenic beaches in Costa Rica. **Pros:** lovely grounds; friendly; good value; no-smoking rooms. **Cons:** some dark rooms; no kids under 12 (but this could be considered a pro, too!). **TripAdvisor:** "wonderful hosts," "nice refuge," "charming." [$] *Rooms from: $170* ✉ *300 m south of Hotel Capitán Suizo* ☎ *2653–0270* 🌐 *www.villaalegrecostarica.com* 🛏 *4 rooms, 2 villas, 1 casita* 🍽 *Breakfast.*

6

PLAYA GRANDE

21 km/13 miles north of Tamarindo.

Playa Grande. Down the (long, paved) road from Tamarindo, but only five minutes by boat across a tidal estuary, lies beautiful, pristine Playa Grande, by day one of the best surfing beaches in the country and, by night, one of the world's most important nesting beaches for the giant leatherback sea turtle. The beach has thus far escaped the overdevelopment of nearby Tamarindo, and is consequently lined with thick vegetation instead of hotels and strip malls. In addition to being a paradise for surfers and sunbathers, the forest that lines this long Blue Flag beach holds howler monkeys and an array of birds, and the mangrove estuary on the north end of the beach has crocodiles. The only problem with Playa Grande is the abundance of mosquitoes during the rainy months, especially near the estuary, so bring plenty of repellent. Its shores and waters here are protected within Las Baulas Marine National Park. Admission is free during daylight hours but off-limits at night during the turtle-nesting season (October 20 to February 20), when hundreds of tourists come on guided turtle tours, hoping to catch sight of a leatherback turtle building a nest and depositing eggs. The beach's protected status is in part because a surfer who arrived here more than 30 years ago was so upset by the widespread turtle-egg poaching that he adopted a conservationist's agenda. Louis Wilson, owner of Las Tortugas Hotel, spearheaded a campaign to protect the nesting *baulas* (leatherback turtles) that eventually resulted in the creation of Las Baulas Marine National Park.

Playa Grande isn't immune to development, though; developers have sold hundreds of lots, and there are at least 100 finished houses. The ongoing battle to protect the beach continues. The good thing is that the homes are well back from the beach, thanks to a legislated buffer zone and a decree that no lights can be visible from the beach, to avoid disturbing the turtles. A few hotels and restaurants make this a pleasant, tranquil alternative to Tamarindo. And if you want to go shopping or bar-hopping, Tamarindo is only a boat ride away. ■TIP➔ **Recent trip reports suggest that crime in the Playa Grande area has increased of late. Take reasonable precautions, choose a hotel with room safes, bring very few valuables, and stay alert.**

GETTING HERE AND AROUND

The road from Tamarindo is paved for the duration of the 30-minute drive. Palm Beach Estates, where most hotels are, is about 3 km (2 miles) south of the main Playa Grande entrance on a dirt road. Alternatively, you can take a small boat across the Tamarindo Estuary for about $2 per person and walk 30 minutes along the beach to the surf break; boats travel between the guide kiosk at the north end of Tamarindo and either Villa Baulas or Hotel Bula Bula in Playa Grande.

EXPLORING

TURTLE-WATCHING

Nesting giant leatherback turtles. Playa Grande hosts the world's largest visitation of nesting giant leatherback turtles. From October 20 to February 20, during the peak nesting season, the beach is strictly off-limits from 6 pm to 6 am. You can visit only as part of a guided tour, waiting

Continued on page 318

BIRD-WATCHING

by Dorothy
MacKinnon

Even if you've never seen yourself as a bird-watcher, Costa Rica will get you hooked. Waking you before dawn, calling to you throughout the day, and serenading you through tropical nights, birds are impossible to ignore here.

Luckily, Costa Rica has a wealth of world-class ornithologists and local bird guides who can answer all your questions. Every licensed naturalist guide also has some birding expertise, so virtually every tour you take in the country will include some bird-watching.

The sheer variety and abundance of birds here make bird-watching a daily pastime—with less than 0.03% of the planet's surface, Costa Rica counts some 875 bird species, more than the United States and Canada combined. You don't have to stray far from your hotel or even need binoculars to spot, for instance, a kaleidoscopic-colored Keel-billed Toucan, the bird of Fruit Loops cereal fame. But armed with a pair of binoculars and a birding guide, the sky is literally the limit for the numbers of birds you can see.

Part of the thrill of walking along a jungle trail is the element of surprise: What is waiting around the path's next curve? Catching sight of a brilliantly colored bird is exciting, but being able to identify it after a couple of encounters is even more thrilling. For kids, spotting birds makes a great game. With their sharp, young eyes, they're usually very good at it—plus it's wildly educational.

About 10% of Costa Rica's birds are endemic, so this is a mecca for bird-watchers intent on compiling an impressive life list.

BEST BIRDING DESTINATIONS

The most sought-after bird is the aptly named Resplendent Quetzal, sporting brilliant blue, green, and red plumage and long tail feathers. The best places to spot it are the new **Los Quetzales National Park** in the Cerro de la Muerte highlands, the **San Gerardo de Dota valley,** and the **Monteverde Cloud Forest Reserve.**

Another bird high on many bird-watchers' lists is the Scarlet Macaw, the largest of the parrot family here. You'll see pairs performing aerial ballets and munching in beach almond trees in **Corcovado National Park,** along the **Osa Peninsula's coastline,** and around **Carara National Park** in the Central Pacific region.

The **Tempisque River delta's** salty waters, at the north end of the Gulf of Nicoya, are famous for a wealth of water birds, notably Wood Storks, Glossy Ibis, and Roseate Spoonbills. A little farther north, in **Palo Verde and Caño Negro National Parks,** look for the rarest and largest of wading birds, the Jabiru.

The network of jungle-edged natural canals in **Tortuguero National Park,** in the northern Caribbean, is home to a host of herons, including the spectacular Rufescent Tiger-Heron and the multi-hued Agami Heron.

More than 50 species of hummingbirds hover around every part of the country. Look for them around feeders at lodges in the **Cerro de la Muerte area, Monteverde,** and the **Turrialba region.**

WHEN TO GO: The best time to bird is November to May, when local species are joined by winter migrants. Breeding season, which varies by species throughout the year, is the easiest time to spot birds, as males put on displays for females, followed by frequent flights to gather nesting material and then food for the chicks. Also keep your eye on fruit-bearing trees that attract hungry birds.

Quetzal in Río Savegre Valley;
Krasinsky, Fodors.com member

Binoculars are the most important piece of equipment. They don't have to be a very expensive pair, but they should have good light-gathering lenses and be waterproof. A magnification of 7 to 8 is ideal; any higher and your range of vision becomes very limited.

A good guidebook is essential. The standard "bible" has been a comprehensive tome written by Dr. Alexander Skutch, but beginners (and experienced birders) will probably find the new field guide, written by Richard Garrigues and illustrated by Robert Dean, much more useful—and lighter to carry. It has range maps for every bird and lists the most obvious field marks to help you identify each species. Gift shops and hotels also sell plastic-laminated, one-page guides for local birds that can get you started.

The most important advice for new birders is to find the bird with your naked eye and then bring your binoculars to your eyes, without losing your focus on the bird. Look for beak shape; characteristic rings around the eye; bars, stripes, spots, and mottling on plumage; and, of course, colors on feathers, eyes, beaks, legs, and feet.

10 EASY-TO-IDENTIFY BIRDS FOR BEGINNERS

❶ Blue-Crowned Motmot

Unmistakable with those long tail feathers that look like tennis racquets, this gorgeous turquoise and green bird perches low in trees often close to a stream. They're usually silent but their call is easy to identify: a repeated, low "whoop."

❷ Keel-Billed Toucan

Half a dozen of these rainbow-colored, huge-billed birds often travel together, hunting for berries and fruits. Look for them in Cecropia trees, and listen for the loud, rapid beat of their wings.

❸ Great Kiskadee

You can tell the kiskadee from the similar-looking flycatchers by its *pecho amarillo* (yellow breast), black-and-white-striped head, reddish tinted wings, and its call—it really does say *Kiss-kah-deeee*!

❹ Orange-fronted Parakeet

Found in forest canopy on the Pacific side of the country, these highly social and noisy little birds feed in flocks of up to 100. The adults are mainly green, and have shorter tails than their crimson-fronted cousins. The head is distinctive, with a blue crown, and orange forehead. Sadly, the population has been decreasing for a number of years thanks to the pet trade.

❺ Rufous-tailed Hummingbird

Stake out hibiscus hedges or any flowering shrub for the country's most common hummingbird. An iridescent green color, with a long red beak and reddish-brown tail, it makes a loud "tse, tse" chipping sound as it goes about its business.

❻ Scarlet Macaw

Look for this huge scarlet, yellow, and blue parrot in the beach almond trees that edge South Pacific beaches. They usually travel in pairs and you'll probably hear their raucous squawks before you see them.

❼ Blue-Gray Tanager

Abundant everywhere—cities, towns, gardens, and countryside—this bluish-gray bird, always seen in pairs, loves fruit. You'll often find them at feeding platforms and in fruiting fig trees.

❽ Black Vulture

Almost every large black bird you see circling high in the sky will be a vulture; these have white-tipped wings. You'll also see them hopping along the roadside feasting on roadkill.

❾ Roadside Hawk

This raptor sits quietly on low perches in trees alongside fields and roads, waiting to pounce on lizards, large insects, and small mammals. It has a gray head, a yellow beak and legs, and a brown and white striped chest.

❿ Cherrie's Tanager (on Pacific slope), aka Passerini's Tanager (on Carribean slope)

The unmistakable scarlet-rumped, velvety-black male travels with a harem of olive-and orange-colored females, making a lot of scratchy noises as they hunt insects in dense shrubbery.

your turn at the park entrance, beside Hotel Las Tortugas, until spotters find a nesting turtle. At their signal, you'll walk down the beach as silently as you can, where in the darkness you'll witness the remarkable sight of a 500-pound creature digging a hole in the sand large enough to deposit up to 100 golf ball–size eggs. About 60 days later, the sight of hundreds of hatchlings scrambling toward open water in the early morning is equally impressive. Turtle-watching takes place around high tide, which can be shortly after sunset, or in the early morning. From December to mid-February, try to reserve your tour a week ahead of time, or stop by the ranger station early the morning of the day you want to do the tour, since they allow only 40 people on the beach per night, half of which can register that day. Plan on spending one to four hours at the ranger station waiting for a turtle to come up, during which you can watch a video on the turtles in English (the guides speak mostly Spanish). ⚠ **The number of turtles in recent years has, sadly, diminished, owing to long-line commercial fishing boats that trap turtles in their nets, causing the turtles to drown.** ⊠ *Playa Grande, 100 m east of main beach entrance* ☎ *2653–0470* ⊠ *$20, includes guided tour* ☼ *Oct. 20–Feb. 20 by reservation made between 8 am and 5 pm.*

OUTDOOR ACTIVITIES

■ TIP➔ Unless you are a strong swimmer attached to a surfboard, don't go in any deeper than your waist here. There is calmer water for snorkeling about a 20-minute walk north of Las Tortugas, at a black-sand beach called Playa Carbón.

All the hotels can arrange boat tours of the estuary, where you may see crocodiles, monkeys, herons, kingfishers, and an array of other bird-life; go either early in the morning or late in the afternoon, and bring insect repellent.

Hotel Las Tortugas. This turtle-theme hotel right on the turtle-nesting beach has a full menu of nature tours, including guided nature walks, and canoeing with a bilingual nature guide on the estuary; they can also tell you how to get to Playa Carbón, the nearest snorkeling spot. ⊠ *Las Baulas Marine National Park* ☎ *2653–0423* ⊕ *www.lastortugashotel.com.*

SURFING

Playa Grande is renowned for having one of the most consistent surf breaks in the country. Only experienced surfers should attempt riding this beach break, which often features big barrels and offshore winds. The waves are best at high tide, especially around a full moon.

Hotel Bula Bula. You can rent both long- and shortboards for $25 a day at this surfer-friendly hotel. ⊠ *Palm Beach Estates, 2 km/1 mile east of Playa Grande* ☎ *2653–0975* ⊕ *www.hotelbulabula.com.*

Hotel Las Tortugas. Hotel Las Tortugas (⇨ *above*) rents boards for $5 to $20 a day and offers surfing lessons at their beachfront Caribbean-style snack bar.

WHERE TO EAT

$$$
MEDITERRANEAN

✕ **Hotel Cantarana.** Chefs come and go at this upscale restaurant/hotel but you can always count on creative, *au courant,* interesting dinners here. The current chef is a young woman from Germany, trained in

Michelin-starred restaurants in Europe. The menu changes depending on availability of local ingredients at this airy, elegant second-story restaurant. Think lots of seafood, such as huge shrimp served with a papaya chutney and bathed in vanilla-flavored foam. Meat dishes might include a baked saddle of lamb with olive gnocchi and braised fennel on the side. For dessert, there's a semi-liquid chocolate cake accompanied by a dollop of mango mousse. Presentation is always beautiful and the service is efficient and friendly. [$] *Average main: $18* ✉ *Palm Beach Estates, 2 km/1 mile east of park headquarters* ☎ *2653–0486* 🌐 *www.hotel-cantarana.com* 🕓 *Closed Sun.*

$$ SEAFOOD 🍴 **Upstairs@the Ripjack.** A block from the beach, this casual place usually has an ocean breeze to complement the ceiling fans, which are best enjoyed from the hammock in the corner. There are rooms for rent downstairs, but most people who head here come to eat, or party at the long bar, which occupies about a third of the restaurant. Sushi is the star of the show here, with a dedicated sushi chef. On the seafood side, you can also count on ceviche, calamari, and fish fillets spiced, Asian-style, with wasabi and ginger. Meat and potatoes are represented by flank steak served with mashed potatoes, The lunch menu has a good selection of salads and sandwiches. Save room brownies and ice cream. There's free Wi-Fi, too. [$] *Average main: $16* ✉ *100 m south of park headquarters* ☎ *2653–0480* 🌐 *www.ripjackinn.com.*

6

WHERE TO STAY

For expanded hotel reviews, visit Fodors.com.

$$ B&B/INN 🏨 **Hotel Bula Bula.** At the eastern edge of the estuary near Palm Beach Estates, Bula Bula has its own landing for ferrying guests and restaurant patrons the short distance to and from Tamarindo. **Pros:** friendly; good food; lots of amenities. **Cons:** rooms small for price; 10-minute walk from beach; restaurant is overpriced. **TripAdvisor:** "the greatest," "nice location," "great place to chill." [$] *Rooms from: $95* ✉ *Palm Beach Estates, 3 km/2 miles east of Playa Grande* ☎ *2653–0975, 877/658–2880 in U.S.* 🌐 *www.hotelbulabula.com* 🛏 *10 rooms* 🍽 *Breakfast.*

$$ B&B/INN ★ 🏨 **Hotel Las Tortugas.** With a prime location on the beach, steps away from Playa Grande's famous surf break, this place is perfect for surfers, nature lovers, and sun worshippers. **Pros:** on the beach; friendly owners; good value. **Cons:** busy spot; spotty service at times. **TripAdvisor:** "surrounded by nature," "authentic unique beachfront hotel," "easygoing atmosphere." [$] *Rooms from: $90* ✉ *Entrance to Las Baulas Marine National Park, 33 km/20 miles north of Tamarindo* ☎ *2653–0423* 🌐 *www.lastortugashotel.com* 🛏 *11 rooms, 1 suite, 8 dorms, 17 apartments* 🍽 *No meals.*

$ B&B/INN 🏨 **Mi Casa Hostel El Manglar.** If you like cooking for yourself, consider the villas at this pleasant hotel-cum-hostel. **Pros:** quiet; near beach; affordable. **Cons:** foam mattresses; no restaurant (but breakfast included); long walk from surf break. **TripAdvisor:** "awesome visit," "simplistic luxury," "tranquil." [$] *Rooms from: $40* ✉ *Palm Beach Estates, 2 km/1 mile south of Playa Grande, south of Hotel La Cantarana* ☎ *2653–0952* 🌐 *www.micasahostel.com* 🛏 *2 dorms, 4 double rooms, 4 one-bedroom villas, 1 two-bedroom villa.*

PLAYA AVELLANAS

17 km/11 miles south of Tamarindo.

Playa Avellanas. Traditionally a far cry from Tamarindo's boom of real-estate development, this 1-km-long (½-mile-long), golden sand beach's main claims to fame are surfing and hanging out at Lola's, a very cool beach restaurant/bar. As you bump along the dusty, rough beach road, most of the cars you pass have surfboards on top. Nevertheless, Avellanas (pronounced ah-vey-*ya*-nas) is a lovely spot for anyone who likes sea and sand, though you shouldn't go in deeper than your waist when the waves are big, because of rip currents. Tamarindo escapees have been slowly encroaching on Avellanas for years, building private houses and a smattering of small hotels, but the inauguration of a massive Marriott here in 2008 marked the beginning of major development. The beach itself is beautiful, with rocky outcroppings at its southern end, a small river mouth, and a mangrove swamp behind its northern half. Unfortunately, security is an issue here, as at most Costa Rican beaches; posted signs warn visitors not to leave anything of value in parked cars or unattended on the beach. There is guarded parking at the beach entrance.

GETTING HERE AND AROUND

You have to drive inland from Tamarindo to Villa Real, where you turn right for the 13-km (8-miles) trip down a very bumpy road to reach Playa Avellanas. It takes about half an hour. There are rivers to cross in rainy season, when you may want to drive via Paraíso and Playa Negra.

Tamarindo Shuttle. If you're without a car, take the Tamarindo Shuttle van; call for current rates. ☎ 2653–2626.

OUTDOOR ACTIVITIES

SURFING

Locals claim there are eight breaks here when the swell is big, which means Avellanas doesn't suffer the kind of overcrowding the breaks at Playas Negra and Langosta often do. Tamarindo-based surf schools can arrange day trips here.

Cabinas Las Olas. You can rent boards at Cabinas Las Olas for $15 a day. ⊠ *Main road, on right* ☎ 2652–9315.

WHERE TO EAT AND STAY

For expanded hotel reviews, visit Fodors.com.

$
VEGETARIAN
★

✕ **Lola's.** In deference to Lolita, the owners' new pet pig (the original Lola used to freely roam the beach and enjoy the surf), the menu at this hip beach café is heavily vegetarian. It has exactly the kind of ambience one comes to Costa Rica for, with tables scattered along the beach amid palm and almond trees, hammocks swinging in the wind, palm fronds rustling, and surfers riding the glistening waves in front. Seating, or more precisely, lolling, is all on the sand at low hardwood tables and reclining chairs, or on colorful cushions on rattan mats. A second-floor lounge specializes in Asian appetizers. Along with the fresh-fruit smoothies and ultrathin vegetarian pizzas, the menu includes organic chicken and "responsible fish" (fish caught in nets that don't also trap turtles). Seared ahi tuna with sun-dried tomato and olive

Costa Rica's shores are visited by the green turtle, the olive ridley (above), the hawksbill, the loggerhead, and the leatherback turtle.

tapenade served on ciabatta bread is a winner, as are the ceviche, fish-and-chips, and assorted salads. You can arrange in advance for private beach dinners by candlelight. They're open from 8 am to sunset and they have very clean, pleasant restrooms. $\boxed{\$}$ *Average main: $10* ✉ *At main entrance to Playa Avellanas* ☎ *2652–9097* ▭ *No credit cards* ⊘ *Closed Mon. No dinner.*

$$
B&B/INN
🏨 **Cabinas Las Olas.** Frequented mainly by surfers, this is a good option for anyone seeking easy beach access, relative solitude, and comfortable, if not fancy, lodging. **Pros:** near beach; in forest; secluded. **Cons:** mosquitoes a problem in rainy season; simple rooms. **TripAdvisor:** "charming," "our Costa Rican home," "comfortable." $\boxed{\$}$ *Rooms from: $90* ✉ *1 km/½ mile before Avellanas, on right* ☎ *2652–9315* ⊕ *www.cabinaslasolas.co.cr* ⇄ *10 rooms* ⊘ *Closed Oct.* ⦿ *No meals.*

PLAYA NEGRA

3 km/2 miles south of Playa Avellanas.

Playa Negra. Surfer culture is apparent here in the wave of beach-shack surfer camps along the road that leads to this rocky strand, but there are also some interesting cafés and restaurants catering to beachgoers and residents of an upscale residential development called Rancho Playa Negra. Contrary to the name, the beach is not black, but rather beige with dark streaks. It's not great for swimming because it tends to have big waves and is lined with rocks, though there is one short stretch of clear sand to the south of the one hotel and at low tide a large tidal pool forms there. The spindly buttonwood trees that edge the beach provide sparse shade.

GETTING HERE AND AROUND

From Playa Avellanas, continue south 10 minutes on the rough beach road to Playa Negra. If it's rainy season and the road is too rough, you can approach along a slightly more civilized route from Santa Cruz. Drive 27 km (16½ miles) west, via Veintisiete de Abril, to Paraíso, then follow signs for Playa Negra for 4 km (2½ miles). Taxis are the easiest way to get around if you don't have a car.

> **A SURF CLASSIC**
>
> Americans—surfer Americans, at least—got their first look at Playa Negra in 1994's *The Endless Summer II,* a film by legendary surf documentarian Bruce Brown.

OUTDOOR ACTIVITIES

SURFING

Surfing cognoscenti dig the waves here, which are almost all rights, with beautifully shaped barrels. It's a spectacular, but treacherous, rock-reef break for experienced surfers only. There's also a small beach break to the south of the rocks where neophytes can cut their teeth. Both breaks can be ridden from mid- to high tide.

Hotel Playa Negra. The point break is right in front of the only beachfront hotel, which can arrange surfing classes ($35 per hour for a private lesson), and rents boards ($20 per day). ✉ *4 km/2½ miles northwest of Paraíso on dirt road, then follow signs carefully at forks in road* ☎ *2652–9298* 🌐 *www.playanegra.com.*

WHERE TO STAY

For expanded hotel reviews, visit Fodors.com.

$$ RESORT ★ 🏨 **Hotel Playa Negra.** Pastel-color, round cabinas are sprinkled across sunny lawns strewn with tropical plants at this gorgeous oceanfront place with a huge round pool. **Pros:** in front of reef break; friendly; comfortable accommodation. **Cons:** not a great swimming beach; rocky road to hotel. **TripAdvisor:** "great food and restaurant," "authentic," "relax and enjoy." [$] *Rooms from: $100* ✉ *4 km/2½ miles northwest of Paraíso on dirt road (watch signs for Playa Negra), then follow signs carefully at forks in road* ☎ *2652–9134* 🌐 *www.playanegra.com* 🛏 *10 bungalows; 7 bungalow suites* 🕒 *Restaurant closed Sept. 15–Nov. 1* 🍴 *No meals.*

PLAYA JUNQUILLAL

4 km/2½ miles south of Paraíso, 34 km/22 miles southwest of Santa Cruz.

👶 **Playa Junquillal.** Seekers of oceanfront tranquillity need look no further than Junquillal (pronounced hoon-key-*yall*), a wide swath of light-brown sand that stretches over 3 km (2 miles), with coconut palms lining much of it and hardly a building in sight. Two species of sea turtle nest here, and a group of young people collect and protect their eggs, releasing the baby turtles after sunset. Although it qualifies as a Blue Flag beach, the surf here is a little strong, so watch children carefully. There's a kids' playground right at the beach, and a funky little restaurant with concrete tables amid the palms. It's also a perfect beach for taking long, romantic strolls. Surfers head here to ride the beach break near Junquillal's northern end, since it rarely gets crowded. A surprisingly cosmopolitan mélange of expats has settled in this area, and there's a new supermarket at the entrance to an upscale housing development. But Junquillal is still barely on the tourist map. Its handful of hotels consequently offers some of the best deals on the North Pacific coast.

DID YOU KNOW?

Guanacaste was a political monkey-in-the-middle for centuries, bouncing between Spain, Nicaragua, and independence. In 1858 Guanacastecans finally voted to annex themselves to Costa Rica, an event celebrated every July 25 with a national holiday.

GETTING HERE AND AROUND

In rainy season, the 4-km-long (2½-miles-long) beach road from Playa Negra to Playa Junquillal is sometimes not passable. The alternative is driving down from Santa Cruz one hour on a road that's paved most of the way. The Castillos bus company runs a bus to Junquillal from the central market in Santa Cruz four times a day (at 5 and 10 am, and 2:30 and 5:30 pm); the trip takes about 40 minutes. A taxi from Santa Cruz or Tamarindo costs about $40; from the Liberia airport, $90 to $100.

ESSENTIALS

The closest town for most services is Santa Cruz, 34 km (22 miles) northeast.

Hospital Clínica ✉ *16 km/10 miles northeast of Playa Junquillal, Veintisiete de Abril.*

OUTDOOR ACTIVITIES

HORSEBACK RIDING

Paradise Riding. At this German-run stable, the 16 horses are in tip-top shape, as is the impressive tack room, with top-quality saddles lined up in a neat row. There are two- or three-hour trail rides ($55–$59, minimum of four riders), or you can set off for a whole day of riding. The moonlight rides are popular and have been the scene of a few marriage proposals. The maximum number of riders they can handle is eight. Week-long riding and lodging packages are available, too. You'll saddle up at the friendly owner's house, across from the entrance to Guacamaya Lodge. ✉ *Main road to beach* ☎ *2658–8162* 🌐 *www.paradiseriding.com.*

WHERE TO EAT

$ COSTA RICAN 🍴 **Restaurante Playa Junquillal.** This funky, open-air restaurant's seating is a jumble of wooden and concrete tables with a scattering of coconut palms—a classic Costa Rican beach bar. It regularly fills up in the evening, when local expats gather to watch the sunset. The lunch options include a small selection of appetizers, a fish sandwich, and the typical Costa Rican *casado* (fish fillet, or barbecued steak with rice and beans). At dinner, you can also get a fish fillet, or shrimp sautéed with garlic, barbecued chicken, or beef, and a few vegetarian options. It's basically just a good spot for a drink and snack on the beach, cooled by the constant sea breeze. [$] *Average main: $7* ✉ *Main entrance to Playa Junquillal* ☎ *2658–8432.*

WHERE TO STAY

For expanded hotel reviews, visit Fodors.com.

$ ⬚ **Guacamaya Lodge.** Spread across a breezy hill with expansive views
B&B/INN   above the treetops of the surrounding forest and the sea, the Guaca-
♺   maya is a real find, with affordable, spacious cabinas surrounding a
Fodor'sChoice   generous-size pool, lawn, and tropical plants. **Pros:** excellent value;
★   clean; friendly. **Cons:** hilly 10-minute walk to the beach. **TripAdvisor:** "great pool," "good food," "Swiss efficiency meets Costa Rican
beauty." $ *Rooms from: $60* ✉ *275 m east of Playa Junquillal* ☎ *2658–
8431* ⊕ *www.guacamayalodge.com* ⬎ *6 bungalows, 4 studios, 1 two-
bedroom villa* ⊘ *Closed Sept. and Oct.* ⦿ *No meals.*

$ ⬚ **Hotel TaTanka.** This modest, Italian-run hotel has tasty food and very
B&B/INN   comfortable rates. **Pros:** inexpensive; near beach. **Cons:** rooms a bit
dark; musty. $ *Rooms from: $75* ✉ *Main Junquillal road, just south
of Guacamaya Lodge* ☎ *2658–8426, 866/498–0824 toll-free* ⊕ *www.
hoteltatanka.com* ⬎ *10 rooms, 2 apartments* ⊘ *Closed last 2 wks of
Oct.; restaurant closed Mon.* ⦿ *Breakfast.*

$$ ⬚ **Hotel Villa Serena.** Serenely spread across verdant grounds a short
B&B/INN   walk from the beach, this hotel is certainly aptly named. **Pros:** closest
rooms to beach; quiet. **Cons:** only TV is at the bar; mosquitoes; hard to
contact by phone. $ *Rooms from: $87* ✉ *Main Junquillal road, south
of main beach access* ☎ *2658–8430* ⊕ *www.land-ho.com* ⬎ *12 rooms*
⦿ *No meals.*

PLAYA NOSARA

28 km/17 miles southwest of Nicoya.

One of the last beach communities for people who want to get away
from it all, Playa Nosara's attractions are the wild stretches of side-by-
side beaches called Pelada and Guiones, with surfing waves and miles
of sand on which to stroll, and the tropical dry forest that covers much
of the hinterland. Regulations here limit development to low-rise build-
ings 180 meters (600 feet) from the beach, where they are, thankfully,
screened by trees. Americans and Europeans, with a large Swiss con-
tingent, are building at a fairly rapid pace, but there appears to be an
aesthetic sense here that is totally lacking in Tamarindo and Sámara.
The town itself is inland and not very interesting, but the surrounding
flora and fauna keep nature lovers entertained.

For years, most travelers headed here for the surf. The wide range of surf
schools and waves varying from beginner to expert levels makes Nosara
one of the best place to learn to surf. Along with surfing, the Nosara
Yoga Institute, which offers instructor training, and daily classes for
all levels, is increasingly a draw for health-conscious visitors. Healthy-
food options, spas, and exercise classes abound plus there's an organic
market Saturday mornings from 7 to noon on the main road near the
Giardino Tropicale Hotel, selling organic produce plus fish, meat, eggs,
dairy products, fresh juices, and baked goods.

Bird-watchers and other nature enthusiasts can explore the tropical
dry forest on hiking trails, on horseback, or by boating up the tree-
lined Nosara River. The access roads to Nosara are abysmal, and the

labyrinth of woodsy roads around the beaches and hard-to-read signs make it easy to get lost, which is why most hotels here provide local maps for their guests.

GETTING HERE AND AROUND

From Nicoya, drive south, almost to Sámara, but take the very first road signed for Nosara, 1 km (½ mile) south of the big gas station before Sámara. This high road is rough for about 8 km (5 miles), but there are bridges over all the river crossings. When you join up with the beach road near Garza, you still have a very bumpy 10 km (6 miles) to go. The roads into Nosara are in

CAUTION

To approach Playa Nosara along the coast from Junquillal to the north used to involve fording many rivers, some of them impassable during the wet season. The good news is that two new bridges now span the Río Rosario and the Río Juanillo, the widest and deepest rivers. But this beach road still requires 4WD. If you have a compact car, or it has been raining a lot, you are better off driving via Nicoya on the paved road.

really bad shape, so a 4WD vehicle is definitely recommended. Budget about one hour for the trip. You can also fly directly to the town of Nosara on daily scheduled SANSA and Nature Air flights, or take an air-conditioned shuttle van from San José. A couple of major rent-a-car companies have offices in Playa Guiones.

ESSENTIALS

Bank/ATM Banco de Costa Rica ✉ *Next to Servicentro Nosara gas station, main road* ⊙ *Weekdays 9–4.*

Hospital Centro Médico Nosara ✉ *In front of strip mall next to Café de Paris, on road to Playa Guiones* ☎ *2682–1212.*

Internet Café de Paris ✉ *At entrance to Playa Guiones* ☎ *2682–0087.*

Pharmacy Farmacia Nosara ✉ *In town, on right side of air strip* ☎ *2682–5149* ⊙ *Mon.–Sat. 8–noon and 1–7.*

Post Office Correo ✉ *Next to soccer field in town.*

Rental Cars Alamo ✉ *Café de Paris shopping center, Playa Guiones road* ☎ *2242–7733.* **Economy** ✉ *Below Marlin Bill's Restaurant, Playa Guiones main road* ☎ *2682–1146.*

Taxis Abel's Taxi. Independent drivers provide taxi service. Abel's Taxi is reliable. A taxi ride from Nosara to Samara will set you back $50, a measure of how punishing the road is. ☎ *8812–8470.*

EXPLORING

★ **Nosara Biological Reserve.** This 90-acre private reserve is a natural treasure, with trails through a huge mangrove wetland and old-growth forest along the Nosara River. A concrete walkway passes over an eerily beautiful mangrove swamp, with fantastical stilt roots and snap-crackling sound effects from respiring mollusks. More than 270 bird species have been spotted here. There are always crabs, lizards, snakes, and other creatures rustling in the grass and howler monkeys and iguanas in the trees. Pick up a self-guided trail map from the Hotel Lagarta

Beginning surfers love Sámara's almost placid water and its undeveloped palm-fringed beach.

Lodge when you pay your admission fee, or better yet, hire Gabriele, the resident nature guide; call ahead if you want to hire a guide. The best times to do the hike, which takes about two hours, are early in the morning or late in the afternoon, which means you can follow your trek with breakfast, or sunset cocktails at the Hotel Lagarta Lodge. ✉ *Trailhead 168 steps down from Hotel Lagarta Lodge, top of hill at the north end of Nosara* ☎ *2682–0035* ✉ *$6 with guide (reserve 1 day in advance).*

Ostional National Wildlife Refuge (*Refugio Nacional de Fauna Silvestre Ostional*). This wildlife refuge protects one of Costa Rica's major nesting beaches for olive ridley turtles. Locals have formed an association to run the reserve on a cooperative basis, and during the first 36 hours of the *arribadas* (mass nesting) they are allowed to harvest the eggs, on the premise that eggs laid during this time would likely be destroyed by subsequent waves of mother turtles. Though turtles nest here year-round, the largest arribadas, with thousands of turtles nesting over the courses of several nights, occur from July to December, though smaller arribadas take place between January and May. They usually occur around high tide, the week of a new moon. People in Nosara usually know when an arribada has begun. The mandatory guide-led tours of the nesting and hatching areas cost $10 per person. Stop at the kiosk at the entrance to the beach to arrange a tour, or at the Association of Guides office, 25 meters south of the beach entrance on the main road, next to Cabinas Ostional. ✉ *7 km/4½ miles north of Nosara* ☎ *2682–0428* ✉ *$10 for tour.*

Playa Guiones. With some of the most consistent surf on the Pacific coast, Playa Guiones attracts a lot of surfboard-toting visitors but the breezy beach, with vegetation rising up from the high-tide mark for its length, is also a haven for sun lovers, beachcombers, and anyone who wants to connect with nature. The only building in sight is the bizarre Hotel Nosara, which was originally the only choice for lodging in town, but which is now a rambling private residence complete with an eccentric observation tower. Otherwise, this glorious beach has 7 km (4½ mile) of

> **HELP ON THE ROAD**
>
> The more remote the area, the more likely that someone will stop to help you change a tire or tow you out of a river. Usually, Good Samaritans won't accept any payment and are more trustworthy than those who offer to "help" in the States. Near Ostional, there's a farmer named Valentin who regularly pulls cars out of the flooded river with his tractor. So he is known as Valentin *con chapulin* (with a tractor).

hard-packed sand, great for jogging, riding bikes, and saluting the sun. Because there's a 3-meter (9-foot) tide, the beach is expansive at low tide but rather narrow at high tide, when waves usually create strong currents that can make the sea deadly for nonsurfers. Most hotels post tide charts. Guiones is at the south end of the Nosara agglomeration, with three public accesses. The easiest one to find is about 300 meters (1,000 feet) past the Harmony Hotel, heading straight at the intersection.

Playa Pelada. North along the shore, Playa Guiones segues seamlessly into crescent-shaped Playa Pelada, where the water is a little calmer. There are tide pools to explore and a blowhole that sends water shooting up when the surf is big. Lots of trees provide shade. This is the locals' favorite vantage point for watching sunsets—great photo ops, with beached fishing boats adding color and interest to the foreground. Olga's Bar, a ramshackle Tico beach bar, is an atmospheric place for a cool beer.

MASSAGE AND YOGA

Harmony Hotel. Closer to Playa Guiones, the Harmony Hotel (⇨ *below*) holds yoga and Pilates classes daily, for $12 a session. They also have a wide selection of therapeutic massages and a full range of herbal spa services. Visit the aptly, if poetically, named Healing Center of Radiant Awakening.

The Nosara Yoga Institute. This reputable, internationally known institute focuses on teacher certification, but also offers several daily 90-minute yoga classes to the public ($10), as well as weeklong workshops and retreats. ⊠ *Southeast end of town, on main road to Sámara* ☎ *2682–0071, 866/439–4704 in U.S.* ⊕ *www.nosarayoga.com.*

Tica Massage. Relaxing massages in a jungle setting ($60 per hour) are available by appointment here, plus spa services such as facials and salt glows. There are also Pilates and yoga classes in a specially designed exercise studio on the property. ⊠ *Across from Casa Tucán, Playa Guiones* ☎ *2682–0096* ⊕ *www.ticamassage.com.*

OUTDOOR ACTIVITIES

Experience Nosara. For in-depth insights into the natural world, join bilingual naturalist/ecologist Felipe Lopez on a three-hour kayak tour along the Río Nosara ($60 per person), or on a leisurely hike to a hidden waterfall with swimming holes ($50). On clear nights around the full moon, there's also a Moonlight Kayak tour ($65). Out on the ocean, the company offers surfing and stand-up paddle lessons and tours. ☎ *2682–1435* ⊕ *www.experience-nosara.com.*

Fishing Nosara. This outfit can hook you up with English-speaking, local captains to take you fishing for 2½ hours, a half day or full day, on boats ranging from 6 to 10 meters (20 to 32 feet). Rates start at $200 for 2½ hours and top out at $900 for a full day on the largest, best-equipped boat. ✉ *In Paradise Rentals office on main road to Playa Guiones, Playa Guiones* ☎ *2682–0606* ⊕ *www.fishingnosara.com.*

Harbor Reef Surf Resort. This long-established hotel has an excellent tour desk that can arrange fishing, surfing, nature tours, and river expeditions. ✉ *Follow signs from Café de Paris turnoff, Playa Guiones* ☎ *2682–0059, 2682–1000* ⊕ *www.harborreef.com.*

Safari Surf School. Run by Tim and Tyler Marsh, surfing brothers from Hawaii, this popular school is certified by the International Surfing Association. There are special packages for women, as well as a kids' surf camp. Most students come on package deals that include transportation and a choice of lodging. You can also pay as you learn, $45 per hour, including surfboard. ✉ *Casa Tucán Hotel, Playa Guiones* ☎ *2682–0113* ⊕ *www.safarisurfschool.com.*

BIRD-WATCHING

Experience Nosara. Experience Nosara *(⇨ above)* bilingual naturalist Felipe Lopez leads serious bird-watchers on a two-session bird-watching tour, with an early-morning expedition on foot, followed by an afternoon kayak paddle up river to catch sight of some of the 270 species recorded here ($125, including transportation). Guests can also opt for a brunch between the sessions ($10 extra).

☾ **River Safari.** Glide up the Nosara and Montaña rivers in a flat-bottom catamaran with an almost noiseless electric motor. Wading herons, egrets, roseate spoonbills, ospreys, and kingfishers are common sights. The German-born naturalist guide also knows where crocodiles hunker down in mud caves along the riverbank. Trips are $35 per person. ✉ *Boat moored at bottom of hill leading to Hotel Lagarta Lodge, follow signs to the boca [mouth] of Nosara River* ☎ *2682–0610* ⊕ *www.nosaraboattours.com.*

HORSEBACK RIDING

☾ **Boca Nosara Tours.** German equestrienne Beate Klossek and husband Hans Werner take small groups of up to six people on 2½-hour horseback nature tours through the jungle and along the beach ($50 to $70 per person, according to group size). They can also take a group of up to 12, with one guide for every four riders. Horses are well mannered and well treated. There are smaller saddles for kids, from six years old and up. ✉ *150 m below Hotel Lagarta Lodge, at mouth of Nosara River* ☎ *2682–0280* ⊕ *www.bocanosaratours.com.*

SURFING

If you ever wanted to learn to surf, Nosara is the place. Guiones is the perfect beginners' beach, with no rocks to worry about. Local surf instructors say that the waves here are so consistent that there's no week throughout the year when you won't be able to surf. In March and April, the Costa Rican National Surf Circuit comes here for surf trials.

> ### CAUTION
>
> Many restaurants do not include the legally required 13% tax and 10% service charge in their menu prices, but tack them onto the bill at the end. It might be indicated somewhere on the menu that tax and tip are not included, but that's not always the case. If you're not sure, ask.

Coconut Harry's Surf Shop. This Nosara surfing institution on the main road has boards ($15 to $20 per day), gear, and lessons ($45 for 1½ hours, board included, for a group of three; a private lesson is $65). The shop also has a beach location 100 meters (328 feet) from the main Playa Guiones beach entrance. ✉ *Main road, across from Café de Paris* ☎ *2682–0574* ⊕ *www.coconutharrys.com.*

Corky Carroll's Surf School. Run by a renowned, veteran American surfer, this school has its own hotel for surfing students, with prebooked lodging and lessons packages only; no walk-ins. ✉ *Near Casa Romántica, on Playa Guiones road* ☎ *2682–0384, 888/454–7873 toll-free in U.S.* ⊕ *www.surfschool.net.*

Nosara Surf Shop. This large surf shop offers group lessons ($40 per hour), rents boards by the day ($15–$20), and has lots of gear for sale, too. Have a credit card handy to pay a deposit on the rental board. ✉ *500 meters west of Café de Paris, on road to Playa Guiones* ☎ *2682–0186* ⊕ *www.nosarasurfshop.com.*

WHERE TO EAT

$$
ECLECTIC
✕ **Café de Paris.** The Swiss-French owners have turned this corner restaurant into a chic, alfresco eatery. In addition to the tried-and-true wood-oven pizzas and hearty sandwiches, they have such Continental treats as fish and vegetables baked in papillote, plus jumbo shrimp spiced with chipotle peppers. The pastry shop is great for take-out beach picnics, with classic French baguettes, savory croissants and quiches, chocolate bread, and a mouthwatering array of pastries and tarts and rum-flavored truffles. The rich chocolate mousse is ready to go in a plastic cup. $ *Average main: $12* ✉ *Main road, at Playa Guiones entrance* ☎ *2682–1036.*

$$
ITALIAN
★
✕ **Giardino Tropicale.** Famous for its crispy-crust, wood-oven pizzas loaded with toppings, as well as the bowls of homemade chili-pepper sauce that grace every table, this thatch-roof, multilevel restaurant casts a wide net to include daily fresh seafood and fish specials, such as ravioli stuffed with snook. The tuna carpaccio is delicious and usually available. Sit on one of the upper decks by day, and you'll dine amid the treetops. Recently renovated and upgraded, the restaurant is a little more sophisticated and romantic in the evening, with elegant white tablecloths. The owners are also working to make the restaurant

ecologically sustainable. Service is always fast and very friendly. $ *Average main: $13* ⊠ *Giardino Tropicale Hotel, main street, north of entrance to Playa Guiones* ☎ *2682–0258* ⊘ *Closed Mon.*

$$
AMERICAN

✗**Marlin Bill's.** Sink your teeth into classic New York strip steak, pork chops, and lobster in American-size portions at this open-air restaurant with a great sunset view. Lighter choices include eggplant parmigiana and delicious "dorado fingers"—battered fish fillet strips served with tartar sauce. Homemade desserts here are delicious, including key lime pie. The decor is decidedly fishy, with fish-themed art on the walls. Fishing and real estate talk over beer and chicken wings keeps the U-shaped bar abuzz. The kitchen is closed from 3 pm to 6 pm, and on Sunday, unless there is a play-off NFL football game on the big-screen TV. There's free Wi-Fi, too. $ *Average main: $12* ⊠ *Hilltop above main road, near Coconut Harry's Surf Shop* ☎ *2682–0458* ⊘ *Closed Sun.*

$
VEGETARIAN

✗**Robin's Wholesome Foods Cafe.** Famous for homemade ice creams and tropical-fruit sorbets, this casual patio café also serves breakfasts and lunches with a focus on wholesome foods, including vegetarian and raw-food dishes. Over-stuffed veggie quesadillas will appeal to all tastes, along with pad thai rolls and yummy vegan veggie burger. Locals line up to buy the dense, fudgy brownies when they come out of the oven. $ *Average main: $8* ⊠ *Road to Playa Guiones, 25 m west of Banco Popular* ☎ *2682–0617* ▭ *No credit cards* ⊘ *Mon.–Sat. 8–6; Sun. until 4:30.*

WHERE TO STAY
For expanded hotel reviews, visit Fodors.com.

$$
B&B/INN
★

Casa Romántica Hotel. The name ("Romantic House") says it all: the Spanish Colonial–style house has a balustraded veranda upstairs and below, a graceful arcade with views of a crystal-blue kidney-shaped pool surrounded by a glorious tropical garden. **Pros:** very close to beach; good restaurant; good value. **Cons:** rooms not spectacular; can be noisy. **TripAdvisor:** "private paradise," "great restaurant," "beautiful simplicity." $ *Rooms from: $98* ⊠ *200 m west of Giardino Tropicale, on left.* ☎ *2682–0272* ⊕ *www.casa-romantica.net* ⟿ *12 rooms, 1 house* ⦿❙ *Breakfast.*

$$
B&B/INN

Giardino Tropicale Hotel. In the lush gardens downhill from the popular restaurant *(⇨ above)*, shaded by large trees, are comfortable suites and cabinas, and a sparkling 17-meter (56-foot) swimming pool—the only good lap pool in town. **Pros:** good value; environmentally friendly; laptop-size safety boxes. **Cons:** road noise; extra charge for air-conditioning; short walk to beach. **TripAdvisor:** "tranquility in the jungle," "great find," "wonderful and relaxing." $ *Rooms from: $85* ⊠ *Main street, past entrance to Playa Guiones* ☎ *2682–4000* ⊕ *www.giardinotropicale.com* ⟿ *5 standard rooms, 4 deluxe suites, 1 apartment* ⦿❙ *No meals.*

$
B&B/INN

The Gilded Iguana. This lively hotel/bar/restaurant has been a Nosara fixture for more than 25 years. **Pros:** economical; laid-back; lively bar. **Cons:** spotty service; can be noisy. **TripAdvisor:** "an orchid in a field of dandelions," "a fun stay," "great atmosphere." $ *Rooms from: $75* ⊠ *Playa Guiones* ☎ *2682–0259* ⊕ *www.thegildediguana.com* ⟿ *10 rooms, 2 suites* ⦿❙ *No meals.*

$$
B&B/INN
🏨 **Harbor Reef Lodge.** It's easy to lose yourself at this comfortable surfer hotel, with its junglelike garden grounds centered around two small pools, one presided over by a concrete crocodile, the other by a tiny waterfall. **Pros:** attractive grounds; near beach; good restaurant. **Cons:** bland rooms; very small pools. **TripAdvisor:** "unbeatable location," "lovely atmosphere," "great service and hospitality." [$] *Rooms from: $85* ✉ *Follow signs from Café de Paris turnoff toward Playa Guiones* ☎ *2682–1000* 🌐 *www.harborreef.com* 🛏 *9 standard rooms, 4 deluxe rooms, 10 suites, 5 houses* 🍴 *No meals.*

$$$$
B&B/INN
Fodor's Choice ★
🏨 **The Harmony Hotel.** Surf's up, *upscale*, that is; this formerly frayed surfer's haunt has been transformed into an ultracool, holistic retreat that gets top marks for both comfort and sustainability. **Pros:** near beach; excellent food; loaner laptops and laptop-size safe boxes; one free yoga class. **Cons:** pricey; not overly kid-friendly but babies welcomed; standard rooms don't have much privacy. **TripAdvisor:** "favorite hotel in Costa Rica," "absolutely amazing," "truly relaxing." [$] *Rooms from: $280* ✉ *From Café de Paris, take road almost all the way to Playa Guiones, look for sign leading to tree-shaded parking lot on right* ☎ *2682–4114, 2682–1073* 🌐 *www.harmonynosara.com* 🛏 *10 rooms, 13 one-bedroom bungalow suites, 1 two-bedroom suite* 🍴 *Breakfast.*

6

$$
B&B/INN
Fodor's Choice ★
🏨 **Hotel Lagarta Lodge.** A birders' and nature lovers' Valhalla, this magnificent property on a promontory has amazing views of the forest, river, and coast north of Nosara from both its comfortable rooms and terrace restaurant. **Pros:** amazing views and grounds; close to nature; sustainable; good value. **Cons:** not on the beach; some steps to rooms; steep, rough road to get here. **TripAdvisor:** "Costa Rican beauty and Swiss precision," "great sunset and meal," "luxury wildlife lodge." [$] *Rooms from: $80* ✉ *Top of hill at north end of Nosara* ☎ *2682–0035* 🌐 *www.lagarta.com* 🛏 *12 rooms.*

$$
B&B/INN
★
🏨 **Luna Azul.** Sequestered in the green hills above Playa Ostional, several miles north of Nosara, Luna Azul is a tranquil, tasteful spot full of clever design and healthful attributes; there are abundant birds and wildlife, thanks to the surrounding private nature reserve. **Pros:** isolated in a picturesque environment; good restaurant; luxurious rooms; excellent breakfast. **Cons:** off the beaten path; restaurant prices do not include tax and service. **TripAdvisor:** "best in class," "a fantastic experience," "exceptional hospitality." [$] *Rooms from: $145* ✉ *1 km (½ mile) north of Ostional, 5 km (3 miles) north of Nosara* ☎ *8821–0075, 2682–1400* 🌐 *www.hotellunaazul.com* 🛏 *3 bungalows, 2 duplex bungalows with 2 rooms each* 🍴 *Breakfast.*

NIGHTLIFE

The Gilded Iguana. Live acoustic music on Tuesday and Friday nights draws a big crowd. ✉ *Playa Guiones* ☎ *2682–0259.*

Olga's Bar. Sunset is the main event in the evening, and both locals and tourists gather to watch it here at this ramshackle beach shack with the best view. ✉ *Playa Pelada* ☎ *No phone.*

Soft music and cocktails on the beach at La Vela Latina in Sámara.

Tropicana. The popular Tropicana is where the action is on Friday and Saturday nights for locals who love to dance and visitors who want to join in. ⊠ *Downtown Nosara, beside the soccer field* ☎ *No phone.*

SHOPPING

Arte Guay. This is the place to find local crafts and every imaginable souvenir, plus beachwear and sun hats. ⊠ *Just past Café de Paris on road to Playa Guiones, right-hand side* ☎ *2682–0757.*

Arteinti Glass. This Italian-owned shop sells lovely, handmade glass-bead jewelry and enchanting wind chimes, plus unique hangings, lampshades, and mobiles made from handmade paper. ⊠ *Road to Playa Guiones, across from Centro Medico* ☎ *2682–1406.*

Coconut Harry's Surf Shop. Along with surfing wear and gear, this funky, jam-packed shop has an interesting selection of jewelry and bottled hot sauces that will spice up the local *comida tica* (typical fare). ⊠ *Main road, across from Café de Paris.*

SÁMARA

36 km/23 miles southwest of Nicoya, 26 km/16 miles south of Nosara.

This is the perfect hangout beach, with plenty of shade, bars, and seafront restaurants to take refuge in from the sun. Playa Sámara has miles of palm-shaded beach, safe swimming water, and an abundance of budget accommodations and seafront restaurants. This makes it especially popular with budget travelers, both Tico and foreign.

Sámara's wide sweep of light gray sand is framed by two forest-covered hills jutting out on either side. The waves break out on a reef that lines the entrance of the cove, several hundred yards offshore, which keeps the water calm enough for safe swimming but leaves enough surf to have fun in. The reef holds plenty of marine attractions for diving and snorkeling excursions. Isla Chora, at the south end of the bay, provides a sheltered area that is especially popular for kayakers and snorkelers—it even has a tiny beach at lower tides. This can be a lively place on weekends, with bars on the beaches and handicraft vendors set up on the main drag. Take care on a sandy roadway running through the coconut palms and Indian almond trees that line the beach, so be sure to look both ways when you move between the surf and Margaritaville.

Sámara isn't the cleanest of beaches (no Blue Flag), and those seeking solitude should head to the beach's western or eastern ends. Though it lacks the rip currents that make many Costa Rican beaches dangerous, Sámara is not the best beach for swimming from September to December, when daily rains flush plenty of things you wouldn't want to swim with into the sea.

GETTING HERE AND AROUND

The drive from Nicoya to Sámara is one of the most scenic in Costa Rica, passing through rolling hills and green vistas before descending to the wide, south-facing bay hemmed by palm-lined sand. The road is paved all the way and takes about an hour. ■ TIP→ Potholes are spreading, so drivers need to keep their eyes on the road instead of the beautiful views. A rough beach road from Nosara is passable in dry season (it's more direct, but takes just as long); do not attempt this road when it rains. To get from Nosara to Sámara via the paved road, drive south, 5 km (3 miles) past Garza. At the T in the road, ignore the road toward Sámara (the beach road) and take the road to the left, toward Nicoya. This will take you uphill to merge with the main Nicoya–Sámara highway. Sámara-bound buses leave Nicoya from a stop 300 meters (1,000 feet) east of the central park. They depart almost hourly from 5 am to 3 pm (there's no bus at 7 am) and then at 4:30, 6:30, 8, and 9:45 pm. Carrillo Tours (next door to Palí supermarket , 2656–0606) runs a daily shuttle van from the Liberia airport or Tamarindo to Sámara for $45 per person, two-person minimum.

ESSENTIALS

Bank/ATM Banco Nacional ✉ *50 m west of catholic church* ☎ *2656–0089.*

Hospital Clinica ✉ *1 km/½ mile west of Sámara in Cangreja* ☎ *2656–0166.*

Pharmacy Farmacia Sámara ✉ *North end of soccer field* ☎ *2656–0123.*

Post Office Correo ✉ *Beside church, across from soccer field.*

Rental Cars Alamo ✉ *Main road into town* ☎ *2656–0958.*

OUTDOOR ACTIVITIES

Sámara is known more for gentle water sports such as snorkeling and kayaking than for surfing, although there are a couple of surf schools in town. There are also two high-flying adventures here: zip-line tours and ultralight flights and flying lessons. ATV tours, tearing along dirt roads, are popular with travelers who are particularly fond of dust, or mud, according to the season. For information on area activities, visit the town's official website at ⊕ *www.samarabeach.com.*

Carrillo Adventures. Carrillo Adventures organizes horseback riding, river kayaking, dolphin-watching, fishing, snorkeling, and trips to Palo Verde National Park. This long-established, local tour company also provides daily shuttle service to the Liberia airport ($45 per person, minimum two people) and to Tamarindo for the same price. ⊠ *Miniplaza next door to Palí supermarket in downtown Sámara* ☎ 2656–0606 ⊕ *www. carrilloadventures.com.*

SkyNet Travel Center. This tour operator offers an array of local tours and bus and plane tickets to other parts of the country, and also rents bikes and motorcycles. ⊠ *Main street, beside Hotel Giada* ☎ 2656–0920 ⊕ *www.samara-tours.com.*

CANOPY TOURS

Wing Nuts Canopy Tour. Named after a famous surfer, this three-hour, 10-platform zip-line tour flies through a patch of tropical forest just south of town, with ocean views from some of the platforms ($60). It's small but just right for younger or timid kids, and they have special kid-size harnesses for kids as young as two years old ($40 for kids 12 and under). ⊠ *In hills above Sámara* ☎ 2656–0153.

DIVING AND SNORKELING

The reef offshore is the best place to snorkel. Kayakers also paddle out to Isla Chora to snorkel on the leeward side of the island.

KAYAKING

Plastic sit-on-top kayaks can be rented at Villas Playa Sámara *(⇨ below),* which is quite close to Isla Chora and the reef.

C&C Surf Shop. This established surf shop runs three-hour kayak snorkeling tours to Isla Chora and the nearby reef ($30). You can also rent kayaks for $8 per hour or $35 per day. ⊠ *On beach next to Tree House Inn* ☎ 2656–0590.

SURFING

The surf is relatively gentle at Sámara, so it's a good place for beginners. The challenging waves for more-experienced surfers are farther south, at Playa Camaronal, which has both left and right breaks.

C&C Surf Shop. This surf shop has a beachfront surf school ($40 per private lesson, including board rental) and rents boards ($4 for the first hour, $2 per hour thereafter).

ULTRALIGHT FLIGHTS

Flying Crocodile Lodge. This German-run lodge on a beach north of Sámara gives ultralight flights and flying lessons ($100 cash for 20-minute tour). ⊠ *Playa Buena Vista, 6 km/4 miles northwest of Sámara* ☎ 2656–8048 ⊕ *www.autogyroamerica.com.*

WHERE TO EAT

$$
ITALIAN
★

✕ **Al Manglar.** Hidden on a rutted side street, this informal Italian eatery beneath a large thatch roof doesn't look like much at first, but there are usually plenty of cars parked in front, since it's been a favorite of local expatriates for more than 15 years. Italian cooks—two ladies of Verona—are in the kitchen, preparing fresh pasta, fish, and meat dishes to order, or sliding thin, crispy pizzas out of the oven. They make the best pizza in town, with more than two dozen varieties to choose from. The ricotta-and-spinach ravioli with a sauce of porcini mushrooms have made many a mouth water, as have the homemade gnocchi—but ask for the salmon ravioli, which isn't on the menu but is often available, smothered in creamy shrimp sauce. Nearly everything is fresh, which means you have to wait a little longer here than at the competition. Tablecloths and candlelight add a romantic glow later in the evening. It's open from 5 pm. [$] *Average main: $12* ✉ *200 m west and 150 m south of Banco Nacional* ☎ *2656–0096* 🕓 *No lunch.*

$$$ STEAKHOUSE ★ 🍴 **El Lagarto.** With varnished wooden tables scattered across the sand amid ficus and Indian almond trees, close enough to the sea to hear the surf above the mix of Latin music on the stereo, El Lagarto has Sámara's best buzz by far. But its big draw is the food—fresh local seafood and high-quality meat grilled to perfection on a massive, open-air barbecue. The name means "The Crocodile," but you won't find croc steaks on the menu. You can, however, sink your teeth into juicy tenderloin, lamb chops, mahimahi, prawns, tuna, mussels, chicken breast stuffed with mushrooms and cheese, portobello mushrooms, or a whole grilled lobster. You won't find any barbecue sauce here; everything is simply brushed with extra-virgin olive oil seasoned with a bit of garlic, salt, and pepper to complement the flavor of the wood. Dinners include grilled vegetables and potatoes; a salad is à la carte. Vegetarians can order the grilled mixed mushrooms. They have a kids' menu, an ample wine list, and an extensive cocktail selection, not to mention banana splits. It's open from 5 pm. [$] *Average main: $18* ✉ *200 m west and 200 m south of Banco Nacional or just walk west along the beach past Las Olasl* ☎ *2656–0750* 🌐 *www.ellagartobbq.com* 🕓 *Closed Oct. No lunch.*

$$ ITALIAN 🍴 **Pizza & Pasta a Go-Go.** An ample selection of good Italian food, including 14 versions of crispy pizzas, 19 pastas, generous salads, and a lengthy Italian wine list (available by the glass, too), is just one reason to drop in at this sidewalk trattoria. Tuna carpaccio is a lighter option or try their insalata caprese with fresh basil. Unlike the checkered tablecloths you'd find elsewhere, here you have glass tabletops showcasing shells, or plain wooden tables by the pool. Save room for a delicious Tico-Italian version of tiramisu or a mint-chocolate panna cotta. [$] *Average main: $12* ✉ *Hotel Giada lobby, main strip, 150 m north of beach* ☎ *2656–0132.*

$$ COSTA RICAN 🍴 **Tabanuco Beachfront Restaurante & Bar.** Right on the beach, this lively nightspot also has an elegant terrace restaurant that's romantically torch-lighted at night. Come for fresh ceviche, and grilled fish and seafood, Tico-style, as well as chicken and meat dishes. It's open for lunch, too, with lots of shade under tall trees and breezes off the ocean. [$] *Average main: $12* ✉ *On the beach, 30 m west of main beach entrance* ☎ *2656–1056* 🕓 *Closed Sun.*

WHERE TO STAY

For expanded hotel reviews, visit Fodors.com.

$ B&B/INN 🏨 **Hotel Casa del Mar.** Less than a block from the beach, this pleasant, well-tended hotel is one of Sámara's best values. **Pros:** helpful staff; easy on the wallet. **Cons:** close, but not right on the beach; no swimming pool; noise from road. **TripAdvisor:** "excellent lodging," "great staff," "quaint hotel with perfect location." $ *Rooms from: $45* ✉ *Main beach strip, 45 m east of school* ☎ *2656–0264* ⊕ *www.casadelmarsamara.net* ↘ *17 rooms, 6 with shared bathroom.*

$ ⌗ **Hotel Giada.** Giada means "jade" in Italian, and this small hotel in the
B&B/INN heart of town, with two small swimming pools surrounded by greenery and brilliant bougainvillea, has been decorated with the artistic Italian owners' precious, polished creations. **Pros:** affordable; friendly; hair dryers in rooms. **Cons:** not right on the beach; smallish rooms. **TripAdvisor:** "what a fun place," "great option," "comfy rooms and good restaurant." $ *Rooms from: $70* ✉ *Main strip, 250 m from beach* ☎ *2656–0132* ⊕ *www.hotelgiada.net* ↘ *26 rooms* ⦀ *Breakfast.*

$$ ⌗ **Tree House Inn.** One of the few hotels right on the beach, this small
B&B/INN inn has lofty, breezy bungalows up at palm-tree level, perfect for folks who love the open air and looking down on the beach action. **Pros:** right on the beach; small and cozy. **Cons:** neighboring bars and restaurants can be noisy; very small pool. **TripAdvisor:** "highlight of our trip," "beachfront excellence," "paradise in Samara." $ *Rooms from: $135* ✉ *Beach road, across from supermarket* ☎ *2656–0733* ⊕ *www. samaratreehouseinn.com* ↘ *5 cabinas, 1 room* ⦀ *Breakfast.*

$$ ⌗ **Villas Kalimba.** You may never want to leave this tranquil oasis of
RENTAL luxury villas hidden behind scrolled white-and-orange walls, where the
★ architecture is Mexican, but the style is all Italian. **Pros:** spacious villas; all the comforts of home; lovely garden. **Cons:** not right on beach; some noise from beach road. **TripAdvisor:** "relax and enjoy," "perfect choice," "great location." $ *Rooms from: $135* ✉ *200 m east of Sámara Police Station, along beach road* ☎ *2656–0929* ⊕ *www.villaskalimba. com* ↘ *6 villas, 3 casas* ⦀ *No meals.*

$$ ⌗ **Villas Playa Sámara.** Families come back to this property year after
RESORT year for good reason: there's lots to do, the villas are spacious and prac-
ↂ tical, and the beach setting is fabulous. **Pros:** great location; spacious villas; ample grounds. **Cons:** villas a little timeworn; cleaning inconsistent. **TripAdvisor:** "best sunsets in Costa Rica," "incredibly lovely," "real paradise." $ *Rooms from: $135* ✉ *Off main road, 2 km/1¼ miles south of town* ☎ *2656–1111* ⊕ *www.villasplayasamara.com* ↘ *59 villas, 16 deluxe rooms* ⦀ *No meals.*

NIGHTLIFE

Las Olas. The liveliest, noisiest beach bar is at Cabinas Las Olas. Three pool tables, bright lights, and a pulsing Latin sound track attract a mix of locals and young backpackers. Tabanuco *(⇨ above)*, also on the beach, is a little more upscale and attracts a slightly older crowd. The action heats up at the huge bar and on the dance floor after 10 pm, with a high-tech sound system and live reggae bands some nights. ✉ *On beach, 200 m west and 200 m south of Banco Nacional* ☎ *No phone.*

★ **La Vela Latina Beach Bar.** This is the coolest place for grown-up soft music and cocktails on the beach. They also serve sushi. ✉ *Across from Villas Kalimba, on beach* ☎ *No phone.*

Sporting Club Gusto Beach. This is Nosara's latest incarnation of a hopping beach hangout, with tables and chairs spread out across the sand.

Idyllic Playa Carrillo is perfect for swimming, snorkeling, or just sunning.

Fruit shakes, drinks, and a creative Italian-flavored menu feed the mostly 25-and-unders who come here for the music, music, music all day and much of the night. ✉ *On beach, center of town* ☎ *2656–0252.*

Tutifruti. This local dance club, right on the beach, swings on Friday and Saturday nights when it gets packed with young Costa Ricans. ✉ *50 m west of police station* ☎ *No phone.*

SHOPPING

Souvenir stands are set up along the main street and the entrance to the beach, along with the inevitable handmade jewelry stalls. Most shops here have pretty much the same beachwear and souvenirs for sale.

Dragonfly Galería. Weird and wonderful, this arts-and-crafts gallery sells local art and carvings, plus shell, feather, and bead jewelry. The owner also paints temporary henna tattoos. Just follow the trail off the main road through the trees decorated with fantastical glowing lamps. ✉ *Across the street from Century 21 office, Main road leading to beach* ☎ *No phone.*

PLAYA CARRILLO

7 km/4½ miles southeast of Sámara.

Fodor's Choice
★
Playa Carrillo. With its long, reef-protected, crescent beach backed by an elegant line of swaying coconut palms and sheltering cliffs, Playa Carrillo (interchangeably called Puerto Carrillo) is a candidate for the most picturesque beach in Costa Rica. A smooth, paved boulevard runs along the beach, with sparkling turquoise waters on the sea side and a continuous hedge of scarlet bougainvillea on the land side. Unmarred

by a single building, it's ideal for swimming, snorkeling, walking, and lounging—just remember not to sit under a loaded coconut palm. Signs posted by the municipality cleverly announce that the only entry "fee" is: Make no fires, and take your garbage away with you. There are some concrete tables and benches, but they get snapped up quickly. This is a popular beach with locals, and it gets quite busy on weekends. The only commercial activity is a hand-wheeled cart selling fruit ices. The main landmark here is the Hotel Guanamar, high above the south end of the beach. Unfortunately the former private fishing club and previously grand hotel has been bought and sold so often that its charm has faded. But its bar still has the best view.

GETTING HERE AND AROUND
You can fly into Playa Carrillo on SANSA or Nature Air and land at the airstrip, or head south 15 minutes on the smooth, paved road from Sámara. If you're not staying at a hotel in Carrillo, you'll have to park your car either in a sunbaked concrete lot halfway along the beach or on the grassy median at the south end of the beach. You can also leave the driving to Interbus (⇨ *Planning, at start of chapter*) and get here in an air-conditioned van.

ESSENTIALS
Sámara is the closest town for banks and other services.

EXPLORING

☁ **La Selva Wildlife Refuge & Zoo.** Most nature lovers are no fans of zoos, but this modest collection of mostly rescued small animals offers a great chance to see them up close in chest-high corrals under the shade of trees. The Italian owners are a little eccentric, and the place is not terribly well kept. There are plenty of usually hard-to-see nocturnal animals, so the best time to visit is at sunset when the roly-poly armadillos and big-eyed kinkajous are starting to stir. There are also skunks, spotted pacas, raccoons, and scarier species like bats, boas, poison dart frogs, caimans, and crocodiles. A bromeliad and orchid collection is artistically arranged around the zoo. If you come early in the day, your ticket is also good for a return evening visit. It's pricey, but the ticket price helps to buy food for the animals. Kids under six years are free. ⊠ *Look for signed road on left, just after crossing bridge at south end of beach* ☎ *2656–2236* 🎟 *$15* ⊘ *Daily 8 am–7 pm.*

OUTDOOR ACTIVITIES

FISHING
Kingfisher. From January to April, the boats moored off the beach take anglers on fishing expeditions for catch-and-release marlin and sail fishing, as well as good-eating dorado, yellowfin tuna, and wahoo.

Captain Rick Ruhlow, a U.S. Coast Guard–licensed skipper with 21 years' experience fishing Costa Rican waters, takes up to four to five anglers out on *Kingfisher,* a fully equipped 31-foot Palm Beach fishing boat, for a full day offshore ($1,100) or inshore ($700). ☎ *8834–7125, 2656–0091* ⊕ *www.costaricabillfishing.com.*

WHERE TO EAT

$$ ARGENTINE **El Colibrí Steakhouse.** Tired of fish? Sink your chops into steak—rib eye, New York, or T-bone—grilled on an open fire and served Argentine-style with garlicky chimichurri sauce at this family-run, pleasant rancho restaurant. Other specialties include grilled chorizo sausages or Milanesa, the classic Argentine breaded steak, served with french fries. Wash it down with a glass or bottle of South American *vino tinto*. There's salad, chicken, and, yes, fish when available on the menu, but people come here mainly because of the meat. Six air-conditioned cabinas, some with kitchens, face a small pool next to the restaurant. There's free transportation from Sámara for a party of four or more. *Average main: $15 From main beach road, turn left at soccer field, then left again 2656–0656 www.cabinaselcolibri.com Closed Mon.*

PUNTA ISLITA

16 km/11 miles south of Playa Carrillo in dry season, 30 km/21 miles south of Carrillo by alternative mountain route in rainy season.

Punta Islita. Punta Islita is named for a tiny tuft of land that becomes an island at high tide. It's synonymous in Costa Rica with Hotel Punta Islita, one of the country's most exclusive, luxurious, and gorgeous resorts, popular with honeymooners and romantics of any age. The curved beach is rocky but good for walking, especially at low tide when tidal pools form in the volcanic rock. Not to be missed is a stroll through the small village, which has become an artistic work in progress, thanks to a community art project led by a few renowned Costa Rican artists who have turned almost all the buildings into galleries, workshops, or works of art in themselves. Just about everything—from outdoor activities to food—revolves around, and is available through, the resort.

GETTING HERE AND AROUND

During the dry season, it's a quick trip south of Playa Carrillo in a 4WD vehicle with high-enough clearance to get across the soft-bottom river, but in the rainy season, it's often impossible to cross the Río Ora, so you have to make a longer detour along a winding, mostly paved road with spectacular mountain views. Most well-heeled guests consequently fly into the hotel's private airstrip.

WHERE TO STAY

For expanded hotel reviews, visit Fodors.com.

$$$$ RESORT Fodor's Choice ★ **Hotel Punta Islita.** Overlooking the ocean from a forested ridge, this secluded and sublime hotel is luxury incarnate, with villas, casitas, suites, and spacious rooms sprinkled around the bougainvillea-bedecked hillside. **Pros:** gorgeous views; ultraluxurious rooms; top-notch service. **Cons:** isolated; distant beach; very pricey; steep paths to and from restaurant and beach club but there is a shuttle van. **TripAdvisor:** "subdued luxury," "Costa Rica at its best," "secluded sophistication with stunning views." *Rooms from: $330 16 km/11 miles south of Playa Carrillo 2231–6122 in San José, 2656–2020 hotel, 866/446–4053 toll-free U.S. www.hotelpuntaislita.com 14 rooms, 8 suites, 8 casitas, 25 villas Breakfast.*

6

PALO VERDE NATIONAL PARK

52 km/32 miles south of Liberia.

Palo Verde National Park. One of the best wildlife and bird-watching parks in Costa Rica, Palo Verde protects a significant amount of deciduous dry forest and its denizens, along with seasonal wetlands that provide a temporary home for thousands of migratory birds toward the end of the rainy season. The park is bordered on the west by the Río Tempisque and encompasses more than 198 square km (76 square miles). The terrain is fairly flat—the maximum elevation in the park is 268 meters (879 feet)—and the forest is less dense than a rain forest, which makes it easier to spot the fauna. While crocodiles ply the Tempisque's waters year-round, from September through March you can see dozens of species of migratory and resident aquatic birds, including herons, wood storks, jabirus, and elegant, flamingo-like roseate spoonbills. It's almost always hot and humid in these lowlands, so be prepared with water, hat, and insect repellent. ■TIP➔ A raised platform near the ranger station, about 8 km (5 miles) past the park entrance, gives you a vantage point over a marsh filled with ducks and jacanas. But be prepared to climb a narrow metal ladder. Hostel-type lodging in rustic dormitory facilities with bunk beds and shared bathrooms ($13) and family-style meals ($7 breakfast; $9 for lunch or dinner) can be arranged through the park headquarters. There are also camping facilities. ⊠ *29 km/18 miles southwest of Bagaces* ☎ *2206–5965* 🖼 *$10* ⏱ *Daily 8–dusk; entrance gates open 8–noon and 1–4.*

GETTING HERE AND AROUND

To get to Palo Verde from Liberia, drive south along the Pan-American Highway to Bagaces, then turn right at the small, easy-to-miss sign for Palo Verde, along a rough dirt road for 28 km (17 miles). Count on an hour to drive the distance from the main highway to the park entrance; it's a very bumpy road. You'll have to pay the $10 park entrance fee to get to the Organization for Tropical Studies station. The OTS station is about 7 km (4½ miles) beyond the park entrance; the park headquarters is less than 1 km (½ mile) farther. The gatekeeper takes lunch from noon to 1 pm. The drive from Liberia should take a total of about 1½ hours.

EXPLORING

Llanos de Cortés. Just 3 km (2 miles) north of the Palo Verde road at Bagaces, take the dirt road signed for Llanos de Cortés to get to this hidden waterfall less than 2 km (1 mile) off the highway. About ½ km (¼ mile) along the dirt road you'll see on your right a large rock with "Cataratas" scrawled on it. Follow this bumpy road about 1.3 km (0.8 mile) to its end and then clamber down a steep path to the pool at the bottom of a spectacular, wide, 15-meter (50-foot) waterfall. This is a great place for a picnic; avoid weekends if you can when it's often crowded and noisy. ■TIP➔ Don't leave anything of value in your car. ⊠ *Off Inter-American Highway, Bagaces.*

Las Pumas Rescue Shelter. Sad but sobering, one of the few places left in the country where you are guaranteed to see large wild cats, including a

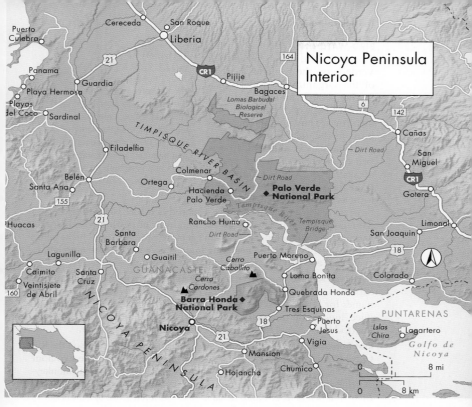

jaguar, is this animal rescue center (Centro de Rescate Las Pumas). The small enclosures also hold jaguarundis, pumas, margays, ocelots, and oncillas. Some small animals and birds are rehabilitated and released into the wild. The larger cats are probably here for life, as it's dangerous for them to be released. There's also a nature trail guests can hike, along the Corobici River. Admission is $10 and donations to the nonprofit foundation are welcomed. It's open daily 8 to 4. ⊠ *4½ km/3 miles north of Cañas on main highway* ☎ *2669–6044, 2669–6019 for reservations* ⊕ *www.laspumas.net.*

OUTDOOR ACTIVITIES

Organization for Tropical Studies. This nonprofit, scientific consortium offers overnight packages with a guided walk, family-style meals, and lodging in rustic, bunk-bedded double rooms with fans and private bath ($92 per person, double occupancy). Their biological research station overlooks the Palo Verde wetlands, and they also offer a boat tour plus longer hikes with expert naturalist guides and a rain-forest photography workshop as affordable add-ons to the package. Guests still have to pay the $10 entrance fee to the national park. ☎ *2524–0607* ⊕ *www.ots.ac.cr.*

BIRD-WATCHING

The best bird-watching in Palo Verde is on the wetlands in front of the Organization for Tropical Studies' (OTS) biological station. The OTS has expert guides who can help you see and identify the varied birds in the area, but if you have good binoculars and a bird book, you can identify plenty of species on your own. A boat excursion to Isla Pájaros south of the Río Tempisque is particularly interesting for birders. Toward the end of rainy season this 6-acre island near Puerto Moreno is an exciting place to see hundreds of nesting wood storks, cormorants, and anhingas. You can get close enough to see chicks being fed in nests. ■ **TIP→ The best time to go is very early in the morning, to avoid heat and to guarantee the most bird sightings.**

> **THE FIRST GUANACASTECOS**
>
> The Chorotega tribe first settled the Guanacaste area and grew corn and fished. Chief Nicoya was the Chorotegan leader who greeted the conquistadors in 1523 and bequeathed his name to the town and peninsula.

Aventuras Arenal. This adventure tour company specializes in ecological tours and has guides with good eyes who usually know the English names for birds. Their boat tours up the Río Tempisque ($45, include juice, lunch, and transportation) depart from the dock at Bebedero or Puerto Humo. ☎ *2479–9133* 🌐 *www.arenaladventures.com.*

Ríos Tropicales. Paddle down the easy Class I and II rafting route on the Río Corobicí with this experienced, national rafting company. The two-hour trips ($55 excluding ground transportation) are great for bird- and monkey-watching and are safe enough for kids ages seven and older. ✉ *Km 193, Inter-American Hwy., Cañas* ☎ *2233–6455* 🌐 *www.riostropicales.com.*

👶 **Safaris Corobici.** This small, local company specializes in two-hour Class I and II floats down the Río Corobicí ($40) that put in (and end at) the Restaurante Rincón Corobicí, at Km 193 on the Pan-American Highway 5 km (3 miles) north of Cañas. They also offer an early-morning bird-watching float tour ($48 including a snack) and a day-long float trip on the Tenorio River ($90 including lunch). Their office is right at the entrance to Las Pumas Rescue Shelter. ✉ *Main highway to Liberia, 4½ km/3 miles north of Cañas, Cañas* ☎ *2669–6191* 🌐 *www.safaricorobici.com.*

WHERE TO STAY

For expanded hotel reviews, visit Fodors.com.

$ B&B/INN 🏨 **La Ensenada Lodge.** Part of a national wildlife refuge, this is the most comfortable and affordable base for bird-watching, crocodile spotting, and nature appreciation on this side of the Río Tempisque. **Pros:** wildlife; interesting setting; good value. **Cons:** very simple rooms; large tour groups at times; no air-conditioning. **TripAdvisor:** "rustic lodging in beautiful location," "relaxed atmosphere," "quiet oasis." [$] *Rooms from: $60* ✉ *Take the signed turnoff at Km 155 of the Pan-America Hwy. and drive along a gravel road, about 13 km/8 miles southwest to the lodge* ☎ *2289–6655* 🌐 *www.laensenada.net* 🛏 *25 cabin rooms* 💳 *No credit cards* 🍴 *No meals.*

Rafting on the Corobicí River, North Guanacaste.

BARRA HONDA NATIONAL PARK

100 km/62 miles south of Liberia, 13 km/8 miles west of Río Temp-isque Bridge.

GETTING HERE AND AROUND

From the Río Tempisque Bridge, drive west along a paved highway. Then follow a dirt road (signed off the highway) for 10 km (6 miles) to the park entrance. There are buses that come here from the town of Nicoya, but they don't leave until 12:30 and 4 pm, a little late to start a hike. You can also take a taxi from Nicoya to the park entrance or go with one of many tour companies in beach towns on the Nicoya Peninsula.

EXPLORING

Barra Honda National Park. Once thought to be a volcano, 390-meter (1,184-foot) **Barra Honda Peak** actually contains an intricate network of caves you can explore on a guided tour to see geological features and catch sight of some of the abundant underground animal life, including bats, birds, blindfish, salamanders, and snails. Created by erosion after the ridge emerged from the sea aeons ago, the caves are spread around almost 23 square km (14 square miles), but many of them remain unexplored.

Every day from 8 am to 1 pm, local guides take groups rappelling 18 meters (58 feet) down into **Terciopelo Cave,** which shelters unusual formations shaped (they say) like fried eggs, popcorn, and shark's teeth. You must wear a harness with a rope attached for safety. The tour costs $36 (minimum of two) including equipment rental, guide, and entrance fee. Kids under 10 are not allowed into this cave, but they can visit the kid-size La Cuevita cavern ($10), which also has interesting stalagmites. Both cave visits include interpretive nature hikes.

If you suffer a fear of heights, or claustrophobia, the cave tour is not for you, but Barra Honda still has plenty to offer, thanks to its extensive forests and abundant wildlife. You can climb the 3-km (2-mile) Los Laureles trail (the same trail that leads to the Terciopelo cave) to Barra Honda's summit, where you'll have sweeping views over the surrounding countryside and islet-filled Gulf of Nicoya. Wildlife you may spot on Barra Honda's trails includes howler monkeys, white-faced monkeys, skunks, coatis, deer, parakeets, hawks, dozens of other bird species, and iguanas. It's a good idea to hire a local guide from the **Asociación de Guias Ecologistas**. The park has camping facilities. ⊠ *13 km/8 miles west of Río Tempisque Bridge* ☎ *2659–1551* ☒ *$10* ⊙ *Daily 7:30–4.*

Park office. An off-site park office provides information and maps of the park. It's open weekdays 8 am to 4 pm. ⊠ *Across from colonial church, Nicoya* ☎ *2686–6760*

NICOYA

27 km/15 miles west of the Río Tempisque Bridge.

Once a quaint provincial town, Guanacaste's former colonial capital is now bustling shopping center, thanks to the new bridge bringing tourists headed for the nearby coast, but there are still a few historical remnants around the central park. A noticeable Chinese population, descendants of 19th-century railroad workers, has given Nicoya numerous Chinese restaurants. The town has Internet cafés, supermarkets, 24-hour service stations, and ATMs that take international cards.

GETTING HERE AND AROUND
The town of Nicoya is 40 minutes west of the Río Tempisque Bridge on a paved road. If you're running out of gas, oil, or tire pressure, the Servicentro Nicoyano on the north side of Nicoya, on the main road, is open 24 hours.

ESSENTIALS
Bank/ATM Banco de Costa Rica ⊠ *West side of central park* ☎ *2685-5110.* **Coopmani ATH** ⊠ *Main street, beside Fuji Film store.*

Hospital Hospital de L'Anexion ⊠ *Main road into town from hwy.* ☎ *2685-8400.*

Pharmacy Farmacia y Clinica Medica Nicoyana ⊠ *Main street, near Restaurante Nicoya* ☎ *2685-5138* ⊙ *Weekdays and Sat. 8 am-10 pm, Sun. 9-5.*

Post Office Correo ⊠ *Southwest corner of park.*

EXPLORING
Church of San Blas. Nicoya's last remaining colonial landmark is the impressive, whitewashed, mission-style Church of San Blas. Originally built in 1644, the church was reconstructed after the first church was leveled by an 1831 earthquake. The spare interior is made grand

by seven pairs of soaring carved-wood columns. Inside are folk-art wood carvings of the Stations of the Cross arrayed around the stark white walls, a small collection of 18th-century bronze mission bells, and some antique wooden saints. Arched doorways frame verdant views of park greenery and distant mountains. ✉ *North side of central park* ☎ *No phone* 🎟 *By donation* ⏲ *Erratic hrs.*

CHOROTEGAN POTTERY

In the country village of Guaitil 24 km (15 miles) north of Nicoya, artists—most of them women—have revived a vanishing tradition by producing clay pottery handmade in the manner of pre-Columbian Chorotegans. The town square is a soccer field, and almost every house facing it has a pottery shop out front and a round, wood-fired kiln in back. Pottery designs range from imitation Mexican to inspired Cubist abstractions. Prices range from $12 to $300, depending on size; most are around $30. Pieces do crack easily, so pack them carefully.

OUTDOOR ACTIVITIES

Hiking and cave exploring in Barra Honda are the main outdoor adventures here.

BIRD-WATCHING

Fodor's Choice ★ **Rancho Humo Private Ecological Reserve.** To experience a watery wonderland amid all the dry grasslands hereabouts, visit Rancho Humo Private Ecological Reserve. The highlight of the five-hour tour ($95, four-person minimum) is a guided ride in an electric "safari" cart along earthern dikes within a spectacular wetland, teeming with a who's who of Costa Rican aquatic birds and wildlife. The tour also includes a boat trip on the Río Tempisque to a close-by island where thousands of birds nest, plus an inside look at cattle ranching, including milking a cow and riding in an oxcart. You can also take only the boat tour ($75, three-person minimum) or only the wetlands tour ($65, four-person minimum). All tours include a fresh-fruit feast and lunch. Make reservations at least 24 hours in advance. ✉ *Pozo de Agua, 28 km (17 miles) north of Quebrada Honda, just east of Tempisque River Bridge* ☎ *2233–2233, 8301–5930* 🌐 *www.ranchohumo.com.*

WHERE TO EAT AND STAY

For expanded hotel reviews, visit Fodors.com.

$ CHINESE 🍴 **Restaurante Nicoya.** There are many Chinese restaurants from which to choose in Nicoya. This one is the most atmospheric, with hanging lanterns, a colorful collection of international flags, and an enormous menu with 85 Asian dishes, such as stir-fried beef with vegetables. The fresh sea bass sautéed with fresh pineapple, chayote, and red peppers is excellent. It's open from 10:30 am to 3 pm; then 5 to 10:30 for dinner. [$] *Average main: $9* ✉ *Main road, 70 m south of Coopmani Bldg.* ☎ *2685–5113* ⏲ *Closed daily 3–5.*

$ HOTEL 🏨 **Hotel de Lujo Río Tempisque.** There aren't many reasons to stay overnight in Nicoya, but if you get stuck here, this large "luxury" lodge is the best option. **Pros:** quiet; convenient; affordable. **Cons:** simple; not memorable; not quiet in January. [$] *Rooms from: $70* ✉ *Hwy. north to Santa Cruz, outside Nicoya* ☎ *2686–6650* 🛏 *108 rooms* 🍽 *No meals.*

$ HOTEL 🏨 **Hotel Mundiplaza.** If you just need a bed for the night, this affordable hotel is the town's most modern. **Pros:** near hospital and service stations; air-conditioning; inexpensive. **Cons:** nothing special about rooms; no meals. [$] *Rooms from: $46* ✉ *Main road into Nicoya, near hospital* ☎ *2685–3535* 🛏 *25 rooms* 🍴 *No meals.*

Central Pacific

WORD OF MOUTH

"At the end of a hike through Manuel Antonio, we finally reached a beach where a troop of white-faced capuchins had gathered. They entranced everyone as they ran along low-hanging branches, tantalizingly close."

—Photo by Gwen Morris, Fodors.com member

WELCOME TO CENTRAL PACIFIC

TOP REASONS TO GO

★ **Adventure sports:** Snorkel among colorful fish, get muddy on ATV mountain rides, and zip through treetops near Jacó, Manuel Antonio, or Montezuma.

★ **Fishing:** Deep-sea fishing at Quepos, Tambor, Jacó, or Herradura gives a chance to hook a sailfish, marlin, wahoo, or yellowfin tuna.

★ **Nature and wildlife:** Explore seaside flora and fauna at Manuel Antonio National Park, Curú National Wildlife Refuge, and Cabo Blanco Absolute Nature Reserve.

★ **Sunsets:** Whether you view it from the beach in Malpaís or while sipping hilltop cocktails in Manuel Antonio, this region has some of the country's best venues for watching the sunset.

★ **Surfing:** This is Costa Rica's surf central. Jacó, Malpaís, and Playa Hermosa swarm with surfers, from beginners to pros.

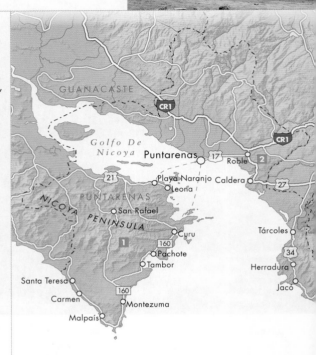

1 Southern Nicoya Tip. On the Southern Nicoya Tip, across the gulf from the "mainland," towns are more tranquil and more spread out. Beaches and surfing dominate.

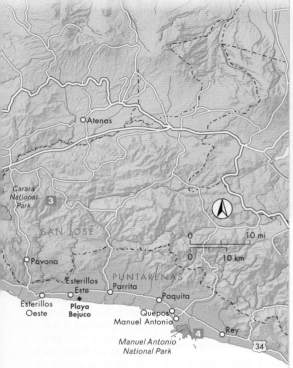

GETTING ORIENTED

Most of the Central Pacific is mountainous, and beach towns are backed by forested peaks. Humid evergreen forests, oil-palm plantations, and cattle pastures blanket the land. The coastal highway connects all towns from Tárcoles to the southern Pacific. The hub town of Jacó makes a good base for visiting surrounding beaches and wildlife areas. Farther south are neighboring Quepos and Manuel Antonio, one of Costa Rica's most popular destinations, followed by smaller towns barely touched by tourism. Across the Gulf of Nicoya, the more tranquil southern tip of the Nicoya Peninsula is also surrounded by impressive mountains, but with dry tropical forests that change radically from the rainy to the dry season.

7

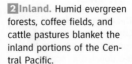

2 Inland. Humid evergreen forests, coffee fields, and cattle pastures blanket the inland portions of the Central Pacific.

3 Carara National Park. Carara National Park is home to an impressive collection of plants and animals.

4 Coast. From Tárcoles, the highway along the coast connects lively tourist hubs Jacó, Quepos, and Manuel Antonio, and on down to the South Pacific. This is the place to surf, do a multitude of active tours, laze on the beach, and explore Manuel Antonio National Park.

CARARA NATIONAL PARK

One of the last remnants of an ecological transition zone between Costa Rica's drier northwest and more humid southwest, Carara National Park holds a tremendous collection of plants and animals.

Squeezed into its 47 square km (18 square miles) is a mixed habitat of evergreen and deciduous forest, river, lagoon, and marshland. Much of the park's terrain is blanketed with dramatic primary forest, massive trees laden with vines and epiphytes. This is a birder's and plant-lover's haven. The sparse undergrowth makes terrestrial wildlife and ground birds easier to see, but of course nothing is guaranteed. Your chances of seeing wildlife increase dramatically the earlier you get here. The most famous denizens—apart from the crocodiles in the adjoining Río Tárcoles—are the park's colorful and noisy scarlet macaws, which always travel in pairs. An oxbow lake (a U-shaped body of water that was once part of a river) adds an extra wildlife dimension, attracting turtles and waterfowl—and the crocodiles that dine on them. Bring lots of drinking water; this park can get very hot and humid.

BEST TIME TO GO

Dry season, January to April, is the best time to visit. The trails get very muddy during the rainy season and may even close in the wettest months. This small park can feel crowded at the trailheads, so arrive early and walk far. Bird-watchers can call the day before to arrange early admission.

FUN FACT

The crowning glory of Carara is the successful conservation program that has doubled its scarlet macaw population. You can't miss these long-tailed, noisy parrots—look for streaks of brilliant blue and red in the sky.

BEST WAYS TO EXPLORE

BIRD-WATCHING

With more than 350 species recorded here, Carara is on every bird-watcher's must-visit list. It's an especially good place to see elusive ground birds, such as antpittas (a small ground-dwelling bird that eats ants), early in the morning and late in the afternoon. Around the lake and in the marshy areas, you may also spot roseate spoonbills, northern jacanas, and stately boat-billed herons. The park's most famous fliers are the scarlet macaws. Once almost absent from the area, a decades-long conservation program has revitalized the local population.

HIKING

The best and really only way to explore this park is on foot. Rubber boots or waterproof shoes are essential in the rainy season, and still a good idea, even in the drier months. Trails are well marked and maintained but the ground is often muddy—this is rain forest, after all. The shortest—and most popular—loop trail can be done in only 15 minutes. But if you venture farther afield, you'll quickly be on your own, except for the wildlife you're bound to encounter. The longer trail that connects with the Quebrada Bonita loop takes about 90 minutes to hike. There is also a short wheelchair-accessible route that starts at the main entrance. It goes deep enough into the forest to give visitors a sense of its drama and diversity.

WILDLIFE WATCHING

Carara is famous for an amazing variety of wildlife, given its relatively small area. Keep alert (and quiet) while walking and you'll have a good chance of spotting big and small lizards, coatimundis (a member of the raccoon family), and sloths. You're almost guaranteed to see white-faced monkeys and, with luck, howler and spider monkeys, too. You may even surprise a nine-banded armadillo snuffling along the ground, or a northern tamandua (anteater) patrolling low branches.

TOP REASONS TO GO

BIRDS

With a varied habitat that attracts both forest and water birds, Carara is a treasure trove for birders. Even if you're not a birder, you'll get a thrill hearing the raucous crowing of beautiful scarlet macaws as they soar over the forest canopy.

THE JUNGLE

The forest here is simply magnificent. Even if you don't spot a single bird or animal, you will experience the true meaning of jungle. Carara has one of the most diverse collections of trees in the country. Breathe deeply, be alert to the symphony of forest sounds, and bask in a totally natural world.

WILDLIFE

For most visitors, wildlife is the park's main attraction. You can count on seeing monkeys and lots of lizards as you walk the trails. Although they are a little harder to spot, look for anteaters, sloths, and armadillos.

7

MANUEL ANTONIO NATIONAL PARK

At only 7 square km (3 square miles), Manuel Antonio National Park—Costa Rica's smallest park—has an impressive collection of natural attractions: wildlife, rain forest, white-sand beaches, and rocky coves with abundant marine life.

The forest is dominated by massive gumbo-limbo trees, recognizable by their peeling bark. It's home to both two- and three-toed sloths, green and black iguanas, agoutis (similar to the guinea pig, but with longer legs), three species of monkeys, and more than 350 species of birds.

Trails are short, well maintained—and heavily traveled. Make no mistake about it: this is no undiscovered wilderness. In fact, Manuel Antonio is Costa Rica's second-most-visited attraction. There are 5 km (3 miles) of coastline, and it's one of the few parks where you can combine nature walks with swimming off idyllic beaches. There's absolutely no commercial beach development, so the beaches are picture-perfect pristine. *(See page 405 for more information.)*

BEST TIME TO GO

Visit any day but Monday, when the park is closed, and any month but September or October, when it's very wet. Come early, ideally between 7 and 8 am, because park rangers allow only 800 people at a time inside.

FUN FACT

The park's territory is too small to support all of its monkeys, so forested corridors and suspended bridges have been built to allow the monkeys to come and go.

BEST WAYS TO EXPLORE

HIKING

Don your hiking shoes and set off on the main trail from the ranger station. You'll immediately find yourself in rain forest and then emerge onto sparkling Playa Espadilla Sur. Another trail leads to Playa Manuel Antonio, which has a good coral reef for snorkeling. These two beaches lie on either side of a *tombolo*, a sandy strip that connects the mainland to rocky Punta Catedral, which used to be an island. Farther east, where fewer visitors venture, Playa Escondido is rocky and secluded. Trails from the entrance to Punta Catedral and Playa Escondido are in good shape. Trails farther east are progressively rougher going. Sturdy walking sandals are good enough for most of the trails, but light hiking boots or closed shoes will help you avoid nasty encounters with biting ants.

WILDLIFE WATCHING

Manuel Antonio is famous for its monkeys, especially the noisy white-faced monkeys that pester tourists at the beach. A troop of rarer squirrel monkeys also lives here, one of the few places in the country where you can still find them. These tiny monkeys—*mono tití* in Spanish—are an endangered species. Catching sight of them is a real wildlife coup. The smallest of Costa Rica's four monkey species, these little guys have squirrel-like bushy tails but they only use them for balance—they can't swing from them.

Watch, too, for less-active creatures, such as the more-or-less stationary sloth, especially along the park's Sloth Trail. They sleep much of the day, curled up high in the trees. Look for clumps of green and brown and watch carefully to see if they move.

You'll see many more animals and birds with a guide than without one. You can hire an official guide at the park entrance. If you're interested in seeing birds, be sure to hire a guide carrying a scope, so you can get close-up views of faraway birds.

TOP REASONS TO GO

BEACHES

Gorgeous beaches without any commercial clutter or noise are one of the best reasons to visit Manuel Antonio. Bring your own snorkeling gear, snacks, and drinks because there's nowhere to buy them. There are basic toilet facilities and cold-water, open-air showers.

MONKEYS

Along with the ubiquitous white-faced monkeys performing for visitors on the beaches, you'll also find howler monkeys (*congos*) draped over tree branches in the forest, and more rarely, the endangered, diminutive squirrel monkey.

PELICANS

Just off Playa Espadilla, you can swim out to some rocks and tread water while pelicans dive for fish, oblivious to visitors who bob quietly in the water.

VIEWS

For a fabulous coastal view, take the steep path that leads up to Punta Catedral's rocky hill, draped with thick jungle. You'll pass a lookout point from which you can gaze out at the Pacific and the park's islets.

7

ECO-LODGES IN THE CENTRAL PACIFIC

The Central Pacific is more renowned for its hedonistic Pacific beaches and resort nightlife than for wildlife or ecotourism. But there are some small pockets of original forest and habitat, and a couple of greener lodging choices.

An ecological transition zone between the dry forests of the North Pacific and the rain forests of the South Pacific, the Central Pacific is home to animals and plants of both regions. It is one of the easiest places to get a good look at the American crocodile, many of which gather near the bridge over the Tárcoles River. It's also easy to spot scarlet macaws in and around nearby Carara National Park, which protects the largest expanse of forest left in the region. Nearby Rainmaker Reserve is another good place to experience wildlife. At Manuel Antonio Park farther down the Pacific coast, you can see wildlife and enjoy an ocean swim at the same time. Over on the Nicoya Peninsula, the smaller Curú National Wildlife Reserve and Cabo Blanco Absolute Nature Reserve (its name says it all) are farther off the beaten path but worth a visit if wild is what you seek.

GOOD PRACTICES

No matter how many warning signs are posted, visitors still feel compelled to feed the animals. At Manuel Antonio National Park, the white-faced monkeys have become a nuisance down at the beach, begging for food and even stealing backpacks and ripping food packages open. They are very cute, but they can also be quite mean and deliver nasty bites to the hands that feed them.

It's not only animal behavior, but also animal health that has been compromised. The white-faced monkeys in Manuel Antonio show elevated levels of cholesterol from all the fried chips they have been fed over decades.

TOP ECO-LODGES IN THE CENTRAL PACIFIC

ARENAS DEL MAR BEACH AND NATURE RESORT

One of the newest hotels in the Central Pacific, this luxury hotel has an impressive eco-pedigree. It is the brainchild of Teri and Glenn Jampol, owners of Finca Rosa Blanca in the Central Valley, one of the first lodges in the country to achieve five-leaf sustainability status. Their goal here was to create a five-star luxury resort that is also a five-leaf sustainable hotel. The first most obvious eco-aspect guests encounter is the reception center in a forest clearing, where you leave your car behind and ride an electric golf cart to the main open-air lobby. You may also not be able to see your room for the trees. For 20 years, the Jampols reforested and allowed these formerly farmed slopes to regenerate before they began building, often wrapping terraces around established trees. The result is a totally natural landscape, home to lots of wildlife. *(Full hotel review on page 411.)*

HOTEL SÍ COMO NO

From its meticulous recycling policy and energetic reduction of waste and energy consumption to its innovative conservation programs, Sí Como No has led the way in sustainable tourism. Perched on a hillside in the center of developed Manual Antonio, this luxury hotel is not a classic eco-lodge. But owner Jim Damalas has worked hard to minimize the hotel's environmental impact. Guests may notice another more ephemeral but no less important policy here: good-natured hospitality. By creating a harmonious workplace, the hotel has retained well-trained, happy staff, who in turn do their best to make guests happy, too.

The hotel's most notable contribution to local ecotourism is the nearby Butterfly Garden and a 30-acre wildlife refuge. Sí Como No also promotes local culture in Quepos and its surrounding farm villages. The hotel is a member of the Green Hotels of Costa Rica and has attained the country's highest sustainability award: Five Green Leaves. *(Full hotel review on page 412.)*

FROM OUR WRITER

"Conserving natural habitat is not only a good idea, ecologically speaking, but also makes for potentially unpredictable and memorable wildlife sightings. On a visit to Arenas del Mar Beach and Nature Resort, in Manuel Antonio, I was relaxing by one of the hotel's two swimming pools, watching white-faced monkeys scrambling among branches over the nearby restaurant roof, throwing down half-eaten fruits and the occasional partially vivisected grasshopper (headless but still squirming).

Suddenly, my peripheral vision caught sight of a coatimundi emerging from the forest at the far side of the pool. He dove into the pool, dog-paddled diagonally across, climbed out, and made a beeline into the forest. It was a surprise to me to learn that coatis could even swim. This one was obviously so at home here that he thought nothing of using the hotel pool as a cool shortcut."

—Dorothy MacKinnon

7

Updated
by Jeffrey
Van Fleet
and Dorothy
MacKinnon

The Central Pacific region of Costa Rica is a long swath of gorgeous land, from sublime coastline dotted with national parks and palm-lined beaches to inland stretches of ranches, coffee plantations, small villages, and forested mountains. There's a reason this is a popular place to visit: the region has a lot of "Pura Vida" to offer.

If you're a first-timer to Costa Rica, this region is all about Manuel Antonio and the acclaimed national park of the same name. (Manuel Antonio and the Arenal Volcano in the Northern Plains make the classic "get your feet wet" visit to Costa Rica.) For Costa Ricans, the Central Pacific means Jacó, the closest beach town to San José, and an odd mix of burgeoning condo development and surf shacks. But you need not limit yourself to these two anchors: Playas Hermosa, Herradura, and Bejuco along this stretch of coast, as well as Tambor, Montezuma, Malpaís, and Santa Teresa at the tip of the Nicoya Peninsula offer a little more solitude, although development is slowly creeping up here, too.

The region has become more accessible than ever, thanks to the opening of the spiffy San José–Caldera Highway, more than 30 years on the drawing board—"Only in Costa Rica" old-timers shake their heads—but finally completed in 2010 *and now putting all the destinations in this chapter an easy one to four hours from the capital.*

PLANNING

WHEN TO GO
HIGH SEASON: DECEMBER TO APRIL
Dry season means high season here. Your payback for braving the crowds is nearly ideal weather. Expect warm, sunny days and pleasant evenings, though if you're not big on heat, March and April may feel stiflingly hot. Lots of visitors push hotel prices up and crowd the beaches, especially on dry-season weekends. Weekdays offer a slight respite from the crowds. During Holy Week and the last week of December, rooms

are even harder to come by. If you're in the area during the high season and want to visit one of the parks, especially Manuel Antonio, get an early start and arrive by 7 am.

LOW SEASON: SEPTEMBER TO NOVEMBER

This is the wettest of the rainy season, when showers become frequent and prolonged. The land mass and wind patterns that cause hurricane activity off the Caribbean coast creates significant rain in the Central Pacific. Nature-theme activities usually go on rain or shine, but beach-lazing plans may well go awry.

SHOULDER SEASON: MAY TO AUGUST

The rains begin in mid-May, but the first half of the wet season sees warm, mostly sunny days with lighter afternoon showers. It's easy to plan around them, and the precipitation keeps everything lush and green. Mid-year school vacations fall in early July, with Costa Rican families flocking to the beach, especially Jacó and Manuel Antonio.

GETTING HERE AND AROUND

Highway 27 connects San José to the Pacific port of Caldera, near Puntarenas. The 77-km (46-mile) tollway varies from four to three to two lanes, but eliminates the former tortuous, winding drive through the mountains, and puts the coast just one hour from the capital. Costa Ricans, who never refer to route numbers, call the modern road the *Carretera a Caldera* (Caldera Highway). Before the coast, an exit to the two-lane coastal highway, or *Costanera*, leads southeast to Tárcoles, Herradura, Jacó, Hermosa, Bejuco, and Quepos. It is well marked and paved. An asphalt road winds its way over the hill between Quepos and Manuel Antonio National Park—plan on about 1½ hours to drive to Jacó and 2½ to Quepos. If you're headed to the southern Nicoya peninsula (Curú, Tambor, Montezuma, Malpaís, or Santa Teresa), the ferry ride from Puntarenas to Paquera across the Gulf of Nicoya has great views of the mountainous coast and the islands. Public buses to and within this entire region are timely and economical, but if you prefer an air-conditioned ride, shuttles leave from San José and can drop you off at your hotel's doorstep.

The 20-minute flight between San José and Quepos, on Nature Air or SANSA, can save you the three-hour drive or bus trip. Flights from San José to Tambor, on Nature Air or SANSA, take 30 minutes—a fraction of the time it takes to drive to Puntarenas and ferry over, and from here it's a reasonable taxi trip to Montezuma and Malpaís.

RECOMMENDED TOUR OPERATORS

Costa Rica 4u (☎ *2508–5000, 888/236–4447 in North America* ⊕ *www.costarica4u.com*) has a variety of Central Pacific tours, plus car rentals, private drivers, shuttle vans, and a 4WD off-the-beaten-path "adventure" transfer between San José and Manuel Antonio.

King Tours (☎ *2643–2441, 800/213–7091* ⊕ *www.kingtours.com*) arranges trips to the top Central Pacific attractions, including Manuel Antonio National Park and Carara National Park.

Ríos Tropicales (☎ 2233–6455, 866/722–8273 ⊕ *www.riostropicales. com*), a high-quality adventure tour company, runs white-water rafting trips on rivers near Manuel Antonio cost $70 to $99.

BIRD-WATCHING GUIDES

Costa Rica Gateway. Since 1993, expert birders (and brothers) Kevin and Steven Easley have been exclusively organizing comprehensive and customized bird-watching tours. They know where the birding hotspots are, as well as all the best birding places to stay and how to capture the birds on film. ⊠ *Alajuela* ☎ *2433–8278, 888/246–8513* ⊕ *www. costaricagateway.com.*

Costa Rica Living and Birding. Guide Patrick O'Donnell is not only knowledgeable but also particularly good at helping new birders actually see the birds. For up-to-date birding news, check out his informative blog. ⊠ *Santa Barbara de Heredia* ☎ *8318–3329, 716/778–2091* ⊕ *birdingcraft.com/wordpress.*

TIMING

A week gives you enough time to visit several beaches on the central coast or get a good grasp of the tip of Nicoya. Most visitors take in one or the other, but not both.

RESTAURANTS

You'll find the liveliest dining mix in the country outside San José here, especially in Manuel Antonio. The crowd of international visitors has brought about a crowd of international cuisines, but, as you'd expect in a coastal region, seafood still reigns here.

Prices in the reviews are the average cost of a main course at dinner or, if dinner is not served, at lunch.

HOTELS

The Central Pacific has a good mix of high-quality hotels, nature lodges, and *cabinas* (low-cost Tico-run hotels, often laid out like motels), including some of the country's priciest lodgings. As a rule, prices drop 20% to 30% during the rainy season. Reserve as far in advance as possible during the busy dry season, especially on weekends. Near Manuel Antonio National Park, Manuel Antonio is the more activity-rich, attractive, and expensive place to stay (though we've culled the best budget options).

Prices in the reviews are the lowest cost of a standard double room in high season.

ESSENTIALS

Bus Contacts Gray Line ☎ 2220–2126, 2643–3231 ⊕ www.graylinecostarica. com. **Interbus** ☎ 2283–5573 ⊕ www.interbusonline.com.

CLOSE UP

Cruising to the Pacific Coast of Costa Rica

This area of the Pacific coast has two large cruise ship ports of call and a few smaller ones. Puntarenas, the country's original Pacific port, hosts ships from Celebrity, Cunard, Norwegian, Princess, Regent Seven Seas, and Royal Caribbean cruises on select Panama Canal and around-the-world itineraries. Farther south along the coast, the newer port of Caldera receives ships from Carnival, Crystal, Holland America, Seabourn, Silversea, and Windstar lines. With the atmosphere of an old-fashioned cruise port—some say "faded elegance"—Puntarenas is more interesting than Caldera itself.

That said, most passengers arriving at either port head out on shore excursions—Manuel Antonio National Park, the Poás volcano, the market town of Sarchí, La Paz Waterfall Gardens, and San José are the most popular ways to spend the day.

Seabourn's smaller ships and Windstar's yachts also call at Quepos. Windstar offers several Costa Rica–only cruises that dock at Curú and Tortuga Island. On its nature-theme excursions, Lindblad Expeditions' smaller vessels call at Quepos and Playa Herradura, along with other Costa Rican destinations farther north and south.

THE SOUTHERN NICOYA PENINSULA

7

The southern tip of the Nicoya Peninsula is one of Costa Rica's less-developed regions, where some of the country's most gorgeous beaches, rain forests, waterfalls, and tidal pools lie at the end of some of its worst roads. Within the region are quiet, well-preserved parks where you can explore pristine forests or travel by boat or sea kayak to idyllic islands for bird-watching or snorkeling. Other outdoor options include horseback riding, gliding through the treetops on a canopy tour, or surfing on some of the country's most consistent waves. In the laid-back beach towns of Montezuma, Santa Teresa, and Malpaís, an international cast of surfers, nature lovers, and expatriate massage therapists live out their dreams in paradise.

PUNTARENAS

82 km/50 miles west of San José.

A launching pad for ferries heading southeast to the coast of the Nicoya Peninsula, Puntarenas could easily be relegated to what you see from your car as you roll through town. Unless you're waiting to catch the ferry, there's really no reason to stay in Puntarenas. Parts of its urban beach look almost like a Dumpster, although residents are making a valiant effort to clean things up. Nonetheless, it's a city with a past as an affluent port town and principal vacation spot for San José's wealthy, who arrived by train in the last century. Once the port was moved and roads opened to other beaches, Puntarenas's economy crashed. Recent attempts by politicians and hotel owners to create tourism-boosting diversions have been only marginally successful thus far. But if you have some downtime here, head for the Paseo de los Turistas, a beachfront promenade lined with concrete benches. From this narrow spit of sand—*punta de arenas* literally means "point of sand"—which protrudes into the Gulf of Nicoya, you get impressive sunsets and vistas of the Nicoya Peninsula.

GETTING HERE AND AROUND

The drive from San José to Puntarenas takes just over one hour. From San José, take the new Highway 27 to the port of Caldera, then swing north toward Puntarenas. From here it's another 15 minutes to the ferry dock. Buses run every 40 minutes between San José (Avda. 12, C. 16) and Puntarenas. If you travel to Puntarenas by public bus, take a taxi to the ferry dock.

Ferries shuttle passengers between Puntarenas and Paquera on the Nicoya Peninsula, where they are met by buses bound for Cóbano, Montezuma, and Malpaís/Santa Teresa.

Coonatramar. The ferries of Coonatramar ply the route four times daily between Puntarenas and Playa Naranjo, farther north than the Tambor port on the peninsula side of the Gulf of Nicoya. Boats depart Puntarenas at 6:30 and 10 am and 2:30 and 7:30 pm; departures are at 8 am and 12:30, 5:30, and 9 pm from Playa Naranjo. Passengers pay $1.75 for the crossing. Standard vehicles are charged $18. ☎2661–1069 ⊕ *www.coontramar.com.*

Naviera Tambor. The passenger and car ferries run by Naviera Tambor depart both Puntarenas and Paquera at 9 and 11 am, and 2 and 5 pm. Additional departures take place from Puntarenas at 5 am and 8:30 pm, and from Paquera at 6 am and 8 pm. The trip takes about 60 minutes. Passengers pay $2 for the crossing; vehicles are charged $20–$30 depending on size. ☎2661–2084 ⊕ *www.navieratambor.com.*

ESSENTIALS

Bank/ATM Banco de Costa Rica (*BCR*). ⊠ *100 m north of municipal market.* **Banco Nacional** ⊠ *200 m west of municipal market* ☎ *2661-0233.*

Hospital Hospital Monseñor Sanabria ⊠ *8 km/5 miles east of Puntarenas* ☎ *2663–0033.*

Internet Millennium Cyber Café ⊠ *Paseo de Los Turistas, east of Hotel Tioga* ☎ *2661-4759.*

Pharmacy Farmacia Andrea ⊠ *75 m east of Victoria Park* ☎ *2661-2866.*

Post Office Correos ⊠ *Avda. 3 near Parque Victoria.*

Tourist Information Cámara de Turismo ⊠ *Plaza de las Artesanías, in front of Muelle de Cruceros* ☎ *2661–2980* ⊙ *Weekdays 8–12:30 and 1:30–4, weekends when cruise ships are in port.* **Oficina de Información Turística** ⊠ *Near car ferry terminal* ☎ *2661-9011* ⊙ *Daily 8-5.*

WHERE TO EAT AND STAY

For expanded hotel reviews, visit Fodors.com.

$ ✕ **Gugas.** Simple but elegant, Gugas receives high praise from locals for
ECLECTIC its fine dining alfresco. "Chicken of the Sea" (fish stuffed with shrimp and spices), pasta dishes, vegetarian options, seafood, and meat plates are all on the menu of this German-owned restaurant. $ *Average main:*

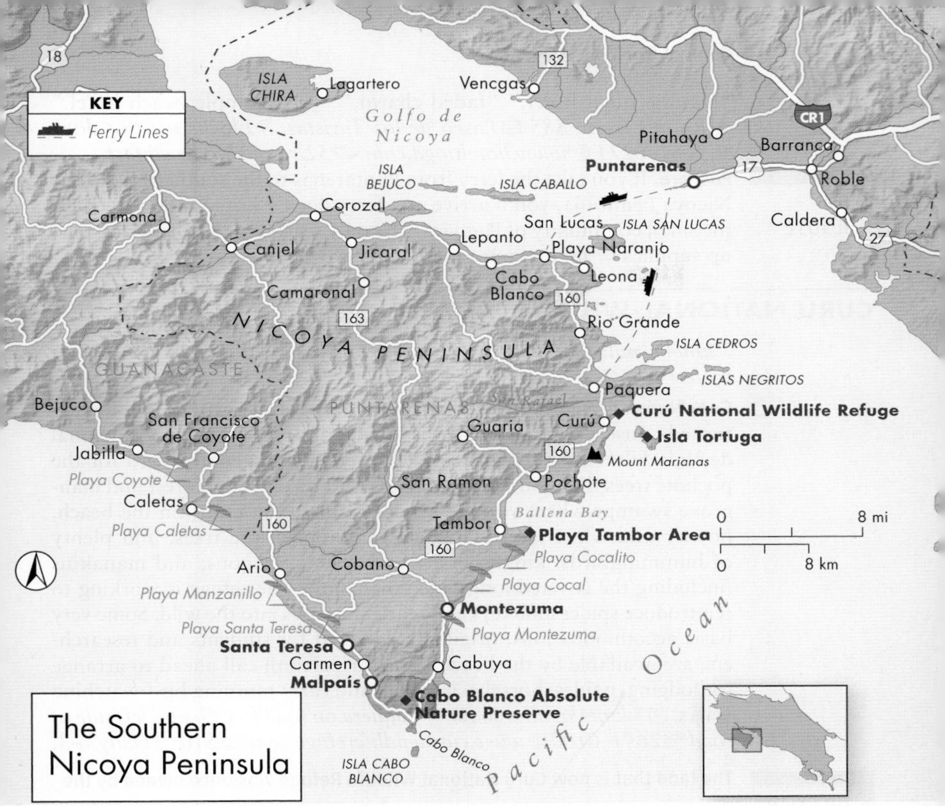

The Southern Nicoya Peninsula

$11 ✉ 100 m north of the cruise-ship port or 100 m from the bus terminal, across from the fishing pier ☎ 2661–4231.

$ COSTA RICAN 🍴 **Restaurante La Yunta.** In a 1928 wooden building that originally served as a vacation home for San José's upper class, this old-fashioned steak house is presided over by mounted ox heads (*yunta* means "a yoked pair of oxen"). Seating is on a large veranda with a view of the ocean and of passersby strolling down the Paseo de los Turistas. The specialty is *churrasco* (tenderloin), but the diverse menu includes seafood dishes like lobster and sea bass cooked 10 different ways. The liquor list is impressively long. [$] *Average main: $10 ✉ West end of Paseo de los Turistas, east of Hotel Tioga ☎ 2661–3216.*

$$ HOTEL 🏨 **Hotel Las Brisas.** Close to the ferry docks, this white, three-story motel-style building wraps around its pool, where the views of the sun setting over the Nicoya Peninsula are terrific. **Pros:** ocean views; decent restaurant. **Cons:** expensive, considering location. **TripAdvisor:** "very hospitable," "family oriented," "keeps getting better." [$] *Rooms from: $95 ✉ West end of Paseo de los Turistas ☎ 2661–4040 🌐 www.lasbrisashotelcr.com ⇆ 27 rooms 🍽 Breakfast.*

$$ HOTEL 🏨 **Hotel Tioga.** This grande dame of Puntarenas hotels is showing a bit of age, but it still evokes a bygone era when Puntarenas was the destination on the Central Pacific coast. **Pros:** good value; across street from beach. **Cons:** timeworn; a bit cramped; busy on weekends. **TripAdvisor:**

"historic quiet hotel," "faded charm," "great simple beach hotel." [$] *Rooms from: $85* ✉ *Paseo de los Turistas, 8 blocks west of dock* ☎ *2661–0271* 🌐 *www.hoteltioga.com* 🛏 *52 rooms* 🍴 *Breakfast.*

EN ROUTE

Paquera. If you take the ferry from Puntarenas to the southern tip of the Nicoya Peninsula, you'll arrive at a ferry dock 5 km (3 miles) north of the small community of Paquera. The only reason to stop here is to pick up supplies or fill up your tank on the way to the beach.

CURÚ NATIONAL WILDLIFE REFUGE

7 km/4½ miles south of Paquera, 1½ to 2 hrs southwest of Puntarenas by ferry.

👍 **Curú National Wildlife Refuge.** Established by former farmer and logger-turned-conservationist Frederico Schutt in 1933, Refugio Nacional de Vida Silvestre Curú was named after the indigenous word for the pochote trees that flourish here. Trails lead through the forest and mangrove swamps where you see hordes of phantom crabs on the beach, howler and white-faced capuchin monkeys in the trees, and plenty of hummingbirds, kingfishers, woodpeckers, trogons, and manakins (including the coveted long-tailed manakin). The refuge is working to reintroduce spider monkeys and scarlet macaws into the wild. Some very basic accommodations, originally designed for students and researchers, are available by the beach ($15 per person); call ahead to arrange for lodging, guides, horseback riding, and early-morning bird-watching walks. ✉ *7 km/4½ miles south of Paquera on road to Cóbano, left side of road* ☎ *2641–0100* 🌐 *www.curuwildliferefuge.com* 🎫 *$10* 🕒 *Daily 7–3.*

DID YOU KNOW?

The land that is now Curú National Wildlife Refuge was once owned by the Pacific Lumber Company, which logged the area's rosewood, cedar, and mahogany trees. Thanks to its protected status, the area is now home to more than 230 species of birds, 78 species of mammals, and 500 species of plants.

GETTING HERE AND AROUND

From the town of Paquera it's a short drive to Curú National Wildlife Refuge. You can also take a bus bound for Cóbano, asking the driver to drop you off at the refugio.

OUTDOOR ACTIVITIES

Turismo Curú. Turismo Curú gives horseback tours of the refuge ($10 per hour plus $10 admission to refuge). You can take a 90-minute guided nature walk ($15) as well. The company also offers inexpensive kayaking trips ($26) and tours to Isla Tortuga ($20). ✉ *Main road, across from Esso station* ☎ *2641–0004* 🌐 *www.curutourism.com.*

EN ROUTE

Cóbano. Paquera is the closest city to Tambor, but if you're headed to Montezuma or Malpaís, you'll pass through Cóbano, 12 km (7½ miles) southwest of Tambor. The town has a supermarket, gas station, and Banco Nacional with the area's only consitently reliable ATM. Although Montezuma and Malpaís/Santa Teresa now have cash machines, those frequently run out of money. Cóbano's ATM may need to be your backup. ✉ *Cóbano.*

PLAYA TAMBOR AREA

27 km/17 miles south of Paquera.

Known for massive, all-inclusive hotels and housing developments, Playa Tambor runs along the large half-moon Bahía Ballena, whose waters are more placid than those of other beaches on Nicoya's southern tip. Playa Tambor is one of the country's least attractive beaches, although there are two small but lovely ones to the south. The tiny fishing village hasn't developed as much as Montezuma or Malpaís, which makes it a better destination for those who want to get away from the crowds. It can serve as a convenient base for fishing excursions, horseback-riding trips, and day trips to Curú National Wildlife Refuge and Isla Tortuga.

HABLA INGLÉS?

Although some Central Pacific areas like Jacó and Manuel Antonio are very touristy, don't assume everyone speaks English. Taxi and bus drivers often won't understand your directions in English. To make traveling smoother, write down the name of the place you're headed to or ask someone at your hotel's reception desk to write out directions in Spanish, which you can pass on with a smile to your driver. This is good advice for any destination in Costa Rica.

GETTING HERE AND AROUND

You can fly directly to Tambor (TMU) from San José on SANSA and Nature Air. Taxis meet every flight and can take you to a nearby hotel ($10 to $15), to Montezuma ($40), or to Malpaís ($40–$50).

ESSENTIALS

Internet Compu-Office del Pacífico ⊠ *In small strip mall on left after Costa Coral Hotel, coming from Paquera* ☎ *2683–0582* ⏲ *Daily 9–7.*

OUTDOOR ACTIVITIES

Unlike other beach towns, Tambor doesn't have tour operators on every corner or rental shops of any kind—not even for a basic bike. The receptionist at your hotel can set up tours of the area's diverse natural attractions.

FISHING

In the open sea off the Gulf of Nicoya, sailfish, marlin, tuna, and wahoo are in abundance from November to March. Local fishermen in small boats are your best guides to finding fish in the gulf, including snapper, sea bass, and jacks, almost year-round. Prices for inshore fishing range from $250 for half-day trips to $500 for full-day excursions.

HIKING

An easy and quick excursion from Tambor is the 1-km (½-mile) hike south of town to the secluded beach of Palo de Jesús. From the town's dock, follow the road south until it becomes a shady trail that winds its way over rocks and sand around Punta Piedra Amarilla. The trees along the way resound with squawks of parakeets and the throaty utterings of male howler monkeys.

Isla Tortuga, just off the coast near Curú National Wildlife Refuge.

HORSEBACK RIDING
The Tango Mar Resort has its own stables and offers a selection of horseback tours that can take you down trails through the rain forest or down to the beach to see an array of wildlife. Set off early in the morning or late in the afternoon, when it is cooler and you are more likely to see birds and animals. Tours range from $40 to $60, depending on the duration.

WHERE TO STAY
For expanded hotel reviews, visit Fodors.com.

$ **Costa Coral del Pacífico.** On the road from Paquera, just outside Tam-
HOTEL bor's entrance, stands this festive blue-and-orange hotel with spacious and tastefully decorated Mexican-theme rooms. **Pros:** wonderful staff; clean. **Cons:** very out of the way; little English spoken. **TripAdvisor:** "old-fashioned rooms," "excellent retreat," "amazing experience." *$ Rooms from: $65* ⊠ *Road to Cóbano, 200 m from Tambor's cemetery, left-hand side* ☎ *2683–0105, 2683–0280* ⊕ *www.costacoral.com* 🍴 *10 rooms* ⦿ *Breakfast.*

$$$ **Tambor Tropical.** You don't come here for the beach—it's not a great
RESORT stretch of sand—but the Tambor Tropical is a convenient base for anyone interested in sportfishing or horseback riding, or for those who simply seek an intimate setting in which to loll by the pool. **Pros:** lovely rooms; tranquil. **Cons:** not on nice beach; no air-conditioning in some rooms. **TripAdvisor:** "incredible place," "unexpected beauty," "beyond our expectations." *$ Rooms from: $160* ⊠ *Main street of Tambor,*

turn left at beach ☎ *2683–0011, 866/890–2537 in U.S.* 🌐 *www.tambortropical.com* 🛏 *12 suites* 🍴 *Breakfast.*

$$$ RESORT 👶 Fodor's Choice ★ 🏨 **Tango Mar Resort.** Colorful villas are scattered across 150-acres that include a small 9-hole golf course, exuberant gardens, tropical forests, and stunning Playa Quitzales, a beach lined with coconut palms and lush foliage. **Pros:** gorgeous setting; friendly; quiet; lots of activity options. **Cons:** not the place for partyers; hard to get to; difficult to find space on weekends. **TripAdvisor:** "lovely views," "posh rooms," "beach is stunning." [$] *Rooms from: $210* ✉ *3 km/2 miles south of Tambor* ☎ *2683–0001, 800/297–4420 in North America* 🌐 *www.tangomar.com* 🛏 *18 rooms, 17 suites, 5 villas* 🍴 *Breakfast.*

ISLA TORTUGA

90 mins by boat from Puntarenas.

👶 **Isla Tortuga.** Soft white sand and casually leaning palms fringe this island of tropical dry forest off the southern coast of the Nicoya Peninsula. Sounds heavenly? It would be if there weren't quite so many people. Tours from Jacó, Herradura, San José, Puntarenas, and Montezuma take boatfuls of visitors to drink from coconuts and snorkel around a large rock. You'll see a good number of colorful fish, though in the company of many tourists. But it does make for an easy day trip out to sea. On the boat ride from Playa Tambor or Montezuma you might spot passing dolphins. A 40-minute hiking trail wanders past monkey ladders, strangler figs, bromeliads, orchids, and the fruit-bearing *guanabana* (soursop) and *marañón* (cashew) trees up to a lookout point with amazing vistas. Though state owned, the island is leased and inhabited by a Costa Rican family. Day trips here cost $20 to $109, depending on the duration and departure point.

GETTING HERE AND AROUND

Every tour operator in Playa Tambor and Montezuma *(⇨ below)* offers trips to Isla Tortuga, one of the area's biggest attractions, or you can kayak from the nearby Curú National Wildlife Refuge. Admission to the island is $7 (included in tour prices).

OUTDOOR ACTIVITIES

KAYAKING

Calypso Cruises Island Tours. Calypso Cruises Island Tours pioneered excursions in the Gulf of Nicoya and takes you to Isla Tortuga from San José, Manuel Antonio, or anywhere in between with bus and boat transportation included ($139). ☎ *2256–2727, 800/887–1969 in North America* 🌐 *www.calypsocruises.com.*

Turismo Curú. Turismo Curú arranges year-round kayak excursions to Isla Tortuga for $20, including entrance fee to the island. Snorkeling equipment is available for an additional fee. ✉ *Main road, across from Esso station* ☎ *2641–0004* 🌐 *www.curutourism.com.*

7

MONTEZUMA

7 km/4½ miles southeast of Cóbano, 45 km/28 miles south of Paquera, 18 km/11 miles south of Tambor.

Beautifully positioned on a sandy bay, Montezuma is hemmed in by a precipitous wooded shoreline that has prevented the overdevelopment that has affected so many other beach towns. Its small, funky town center is a pastel cluster of New Age health-food cafés, trendy beachwear shops, jaunty tour kiosks, noisy open-air bars, and older *sodas* (casual eateries). Most hotels are clustered in or around the town's center, but the best ones are on the coast to the north and south, where the loudest revelers are the howler monkeys in the nearby forest. The beaches north of town, especially Playa Grande, are lovely.

Montezuma has been on the international vagabond circuit for years, attracting backpackers and alternative-lifestyle types. At night, the center of town often fills up with tattooed travelers and artisans who drink in the street and entertain each other and passersby. When college students are on break, the place can be a zoo. Wags used to refer to the town as Monte*fuma*, with *fuma* meaning "smoke" in Spanish—get it?—but, for better or for worse, Montezuma is being tamed. Plenty of grown-up lodging and dining options exist here, too.

North and south of the town center, however, have always been quiet, and the attractions here include swaths of tropical dry forest, waterfalls, and beautiful virgin beaches that stretch across one national park and two nature preserves. One especially good walk (about 2½ hours) or horseback ride leads to a small waterfall called El Chorro that pours into the sea, where there is a small tidal pool at lower tides.

GETTING HERE AND AROUND

Most people get here via the ferry from Puntarenas to Paquera, which is an hour's drive from Montezuma. The quickest way to get here, however, is to fly to nearby Tambor. One of the taxis waiting at the airstrip will take you to Montezuma for $40, about a 1½-hour drive. There are also one-hour water taxis ($40) that travel every morning between Jacó, and Montezuma, departing from Montezuma at 9:30 am, and Jacó at 10:45 am.

ESSENTIALS

ATM Banco Nacional ⊠ *Main road, Cóbano* ☎ *2642–0210.*

Internet Surf the Banana Internet Café ⊠ *Main road, next to El Sano Banano* ☎ *2642–0944.*

OUTDOOR ACTIVITIES

In Montezuma it seems that every other storefront is occupied by a tour operator. In spite of the multitude of signs advertising "Tourist Information," none are officially sanctioned by the Costa Rican tourist office.

Cocozuma Traveller. Montezuma's oldest and most experienced tour company, Cocozuma Traveller, offers horseback riding to a beachfront waterfall ($40), a full-day snorkeling trip to Isla Tortuga with lunch ($50), and various sportfishing options ($170–$750). ⊠ *Main road, next to El Sano Banano* ☎ *2642–0911* ⊕ *www.cocozumacr.com.*

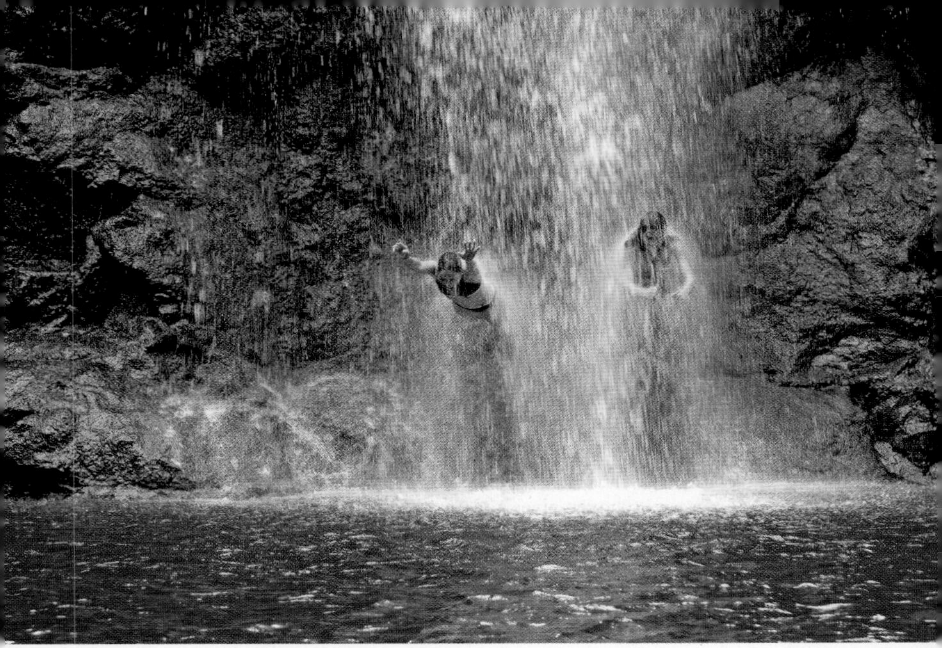
Jumping through one of the two waterfalls in Montezuma.

HIKING

★ Hiking is one of the best ways to explore Montezuma's natural treasures, including beaches, lush coastline, jungles, and waterfalls. There are plenty of options around town or in nearby parks and reserves. Just over a bridge, 10 minutes south of town, a slippery path patrolled by howler monkeys leads upstream to two waterfalls and a fun swimming hole. If you value your life, don't jump or dive from the waterfalls. Guides from any tour operator in town can escort you, but save your money. This one you can do on your own.

El Chorro. To reach the beachfront waterfall called El Chorro, head left from the main beach access and hike about two hours to the north of town along the sand and through the woods behind the rocky points. The trip takes you across seven adjacent beaches, on one of which there is a small store where you can buy soft drinks. Bring water and good sunblock. El Chorro can also be reached on a horseback tour with a local tour operator.

WHERE TO EAT

$$ ECLECTIC 🍴 **Cocolores.** Follow the line of multicolor lanterns to this open-air eatery. The simple wooden tables are on a patio bordered with gardens or, during the drier months, on the beach. The Italian and Argentine owners serve an eclectic menu ranging from shrimp curry to seafood pasta to tenderloin with porcini mushrooms. They also have a good selection of pizzas. [$] *Average main: $11* ✉ *Behind Hotel Pargo Feliz* ☎ *2642–0348* 💳 *No credit cards* 🕒 *Closed Mon. and Oct. No lunch June–Dec.*

$$ ECLECTIC 🍴 **El Sano Banano Restaurant.** Freshly caught seafood, organic chicken, sushi, Thai dishes, and a half-dozen pasta dishes are included on the menu at Montezuma's first natural-food restaurant. Named after the

dried bananas sold by the owners, the eatery serves mostly vegetarian fare, including some excellent salads. On the terrace, which is a popular people-watching spot, you can enjoy a delicious Mocha Chiller, made with frozen yogurt, or a wide variety of coffee drinks. A battalion of ceiling fans keeps the air moving in the spacious, adobe-style dining room. A free movie is shown nightly at 7:30-ish in the dining room, which is a popular diversion, but don't expect a romantic dinner during this time. Rooms to rent on the second floor are a comfortable option if the other hotels are full. $ *Average main: $13* ⊠ *Main road* ☎ *2642–0944* ⊕ *www.elbanano.com.*

$$$ ✕ **Playa de los Artistas.** This open-air restaurant with driftwood tables
ITALIAN scattered along the beach specializes in modern Mediterranean-style
Fodor'sChoice seafood, meat dishes, and pizza. Flickering lanterns combine with crash-
★ ing surf to create a romantic and relaxed dinner experience. Portions are plentiful and dramatically presented on huge platters. The eclectic menu changes daily, and on weekends they fire up a barbecue. An outdoor, coffee-wood oven gives a tropical aroma to pizza, fish, and pork. Meals are accompanied with freshly baked, savory focaccia. $ *Average main: $18* ⊠ *275 m south of town, near Los Mangos Hotel* ☎ *2642–0920* ▭ *No credit cards* ⊘ *Closed Sun., hrs may vary May–Nov.*

$$$ ✕ **Ylang-Ylang Restaurant.** One of Montezuma's best restaurants, Ylang-
ECLECTIC Ylang is nestled between the beach and the jungle. The lunch menu—
★ a selection of sushi, salads, and sandwiches—makes it well worth the 10-minute walk down the beach. The inventive dinner menu ranges from a Thai-style teriyaki tuna steak and stir-fries to penne in a seafood sauce. There are also various vegan and raw live dishes. Whatever you choose, you'll want to save room for one of the scrumptious desserts, such as the tiramisu espresso crepe. At night, they provide free transportation from the Sano Banano, in town. $ *Average main: $18* ⊠ *On beach, ½ km/¼ mile north of town, at Ylang-Ylang Beach Resort* ☎ *2642–0636.*

WHERE TO STAY
For expanded hotel reviews, visit Fodors.com.

$ ⊡ **Horizontes de Montezuma.** Montezuma's only Spanish-language center
B&B/INN is perched on a hill 2 km (1 mile) from town, and rents its rooms to students and travelers. **Pros:** friendly; terrific value; nice respite from the heat of town. **Cons:** outside town; need car to stay here. **TripAdvisor:** "a place of peace and tranquility," "hilltop oasis," "great food." $ *Rooms from: $60* ⊠ *1.8 km (1.1 miles) north of Playa Montezuma* ☎ *2642–0534* ⊕ *www.horizontes-montezuma.com* ⇆ *7 rooms* ⦿*Breakfast.*

$ ⊡ **Hotel Amor de Mar.** About ½ km (¼ mile) south of town, this ruggedly
HOTEL handsome hotel sits across from the entrance to Montezuma's famous waterfall. **Pros:** beautiful property; friendly. **Cons:** most of the rooms are small; can be a little worn. **TripAdvisor:** "kind people," "beautiful grounds," "very relaxing." $ *Rooms from: $60* ⊠ *300 m south of town, past bridge* ☎☎ *2642–0262* ⊕ *www.amordemar.com* ⇆ *11 rooms, 9 with bath; 2 houses* ⦿*No meals.*

$$ ⊡ **Hotel El Jardín.** Spread across a hill several blocks from the beach,
HOTEL this hotel has rooms with ocean, pool, and garden views. **Pros:** central location; good value. **Cons:** a few rooms catch a bit of noise from bars in town. **TripAdvisor:** "nice pool," "open and airy room," "beautiful

Enjoying a snack at Playa De Los Artistas restaurant in Montezuma.

grounds." $ *Rooms from: $85* ⊠ *West end of main road* 🏨 *2642–0074* ⊕ *www.hoteleljardin.com* ⇄ *14 rooms, 2 villas* ⦿ *No meals.*

$ | HOTEL | ★

Hotel Los Mangos. Within sight and sound of the sea, these affordable octagonal wood bungalows are spread across a shady mango grove. **Pros:** great pool; lots of wildlife. **Cons:** noisy; needs updating. **TripAdvisor:** "beautiful little space," "relaxation," "peaceful retreat." $ *Rooms from: $57* ⊠ *Near entrance to waterfall trail, ½ km/¼ mile south of town* 🏨 *2642–0384* ⊕ *www.hotellosmangos.com* ⇄ *10 rooms, 6 with bath; 9 bungalows* ⦿ *No meals.*

$$ | HOTEL

Luz de Mono. About 50 meters from the beach, downtown Montezuma's most elegant hotel has comfortable, tastefully decorated rooms surrounded by large trees and rich vegetation. **Pros:** secluded feel although in center of town; conveniently located. **Cons:** a few blocks from the beach. **TripAdvisor:** "nice staff," "amazing dinner experience," "beautiful gardens." $ *Rooms from: $85* ⊠ *End of the main road, across from beach entrance* 🏨 *2642–0090* ⊕ *www.luzdemono. com* ⇄ *12 rooms, 5 casitas* ⦿ *Breakfast.*

$$ | B&B/INN

Nature Lodge. This 14-acre farm sits at the end of a dirt road high on a hill, just a short ride from town. **Pros:** clean rooms; relaxing ambience. **Cons:** not a great location; no screens on the windows. **TripAdvisor:** "serenity," "beautiful surroundings," "very peaceful." $ *Rooms from: $86* ⊠ *3 km/2 miles north of Montezuma on main road* 🏨 *2642–0124* ⊕ *www. naturelodge.net* ⇄ *12 rooms* ⊘ *Closed May and Oct.* ⦿ *Breakfast.*

$$$ | RESORT | Fodor'sChoice | ★

Ylang-Ylang Beach Resort. Secluded and quiet, this tropical resort with a holistic slant, a 10-minute beach walk from town, nestles between the sea and a lush forest. **Pros:** gorgeous, natural setting; great restaurant; eco-friendly. **Cons:** Ocean View Tent Cabins offer limited privacy; some rooms are small. **TripAdvisor:** "pampering is a given," "a whole lot of magic," "gentle luxury." [$] *Rooms from: $205* ✉ *700 m north of school in Montezuma* ☎ *2642–0636, 888/795–8494 in North America* 🌐 *www.ylangylangresort.com* 🛏 *3 rooms, 3 suites, 8 beachfront bungalows, 6 Ocean View Tent Cabins* 🍴 *Some meals.*

NIGHTLIFE

Montezuma's nightlife is limited to a handful of bars where locals and foreigners mix, a refreshing change from larger beach towns where the clientele tends to be more segregated. Street-side artisans selling their creations often animate the area with drumming and dancing that draws passersby to stop and shake their hips, too.

Chico's Bar. Chico's Bar blasts music from its dark, uninviting entrance, but farther back is a brighter, spacious deck with pool tables and dancing. Directly behind is an open-air beach bar with a more laid-back atmosphere. ✉ *Next to Hotel Moctezuma* ☎ *2642–0526.*

Restaurante Moctezuma. The bar at Restaurante Moctezuma serves the cheapest beers in town. At night, tables in the sand are lighted by candles and moonlight. ✉ *1st fl, Hotel Moctezuma* ☎ *2642–0058.*

SHOPPING

Beachwear, banana paper, wooden crafts, and indigenous pottery are some of what you find in colorful shops in the town's center. During the dry season, traveling artisans from around the world unfold their street-side tables just before the sun begins to set; candles light up the handmade leather-and-seed jewelry, dream catchers, and knit tops.

Librería Topsy. For some intellectual stimulation at the beach, head to Librería Topsy, where you can buy, exchange, or rent a book—one whole room is devoted to a lending library. Some foreign newspapers are available. ✉ *Next door to school* ☎ *2642–0576* 🕒 *Dec.–Apr., weekdays 8–4, Sat. 8–noon; May–Nov., weekdays 8–1.*

CABO BLANCO ABSOLUTE NATURE PRESERVE

10 km/6 miles southwest of Montezuma, about 11 km/7 miles south of Malpaís.

Cabo Blanco Absolute Nature Preserve. Conquistadores named this area Cabo Blanco on account of its white earth and cliffs, but it was a more benevolent pair of foreigners—Nicolas Wessberg and his wife, Karen Mogensen, arriving here from Sweden in the 1950s—who made it a preserve (Reserva Natural Absoluta Cabo Blanco, in Spanish). Appalled by the first clear-cut in the Cabo Blanco area in 1960, the pioneering couple launched an international appeal to save the forest. In time their efforts led not only to the creation of the 12-square-km (4½-square-mile) reserve but also to the founding of Costa Rica's national park service, the National Conservation Areas System (SINAC). Wessberg was murdered on the Osa Peninsula in 1975 while researching the area's potential as a national park. A reserve just outside Montezuma was named in his honor. A reserve has also been created to honor his wife, who dedicated her life to conservation after her husband's death.

Informative natural-history captions dot the trails in the moist evergreen forest of Cabo Blanco. Look for the sapodilla trees, which produce a white latex used to make gum; you can often see V-shaped scars where the trees have been cut to allow the latex to run into containers placed at the base. Wessberg cataloged a full array of animals here: porcupine, hog-nosed skunk, spotted skunk, gray fox, anteater, cougar, and jaguar. Resident birds include brown pelicans, white-throated magpies, toucans, cattle egrets, green herons, parrots, and blue-crowned motmots. A fairly strenuous 4-km (2½-mile) hike, which takes about two hours in each direction, follows a trail from the reserve entrance to **Playa Cabo Blanco.** The beach is magnificent, with hundreds of pelicans flying in formation and paddling in the calm waters offshore—you can wade right in and join them. Off the tip of the cape is the 7,511-square-foot **Isla Cabo Blanco,** with pelicans, frigate birds, brown boobies, and an abandoned lighthouse. As a strict reserve, Cabo Blanco has restrooms and a visitor center but no other tourist facilities, and overnight camping is not permitted. Rangers and volunteers act as guides. ✉ *10 km/6 miles southwest of Montezuma via Cabuya* ☎ *2642–0093* 💲 *$10* ⏱ *Wed.–Sun. 8–4.*

GETTING HERE AND AROUND

Roads to the reserve are usually passable only in the dry season, unless you have a 4WD. From Montezuma or Malpaís, take the road to Cabuya. Taxis can take you to or from Montezuma for $15 one way—that's always the easiest option—but buses toward the park also leave from Montezuma daily at 8 am, 9:50 am, and 2 pm, returning at 9 am, 1 pm, and 4 pm.

MALPAÍS AND SANTA TERESA

12 km/7½ miles southwest of Cóbano, 52 km/33 miles south of Paquera.

This remote fishing area was once frequented only by die-hard surfers in search of some of the country's largest waves and by naturalists en route to the nearby Cabo Blanco Absolute Nature Preserve. But now hotels, restaurants, and shopping centers are springing up at an alarming rate, especially toward the Santa Teresa side. Still, the abundant forest, lovely beaches, and consistent surf make this a great place to spend some time.

Coming from Montezuma, the road hits an intersection, known locally as El Cruce, marked by hotel signs and a strip mall on the right. To the left is the rutted route to tranquil Malpaís, and to the right is the better road to Santa Teresa, with plenty of hotels, restaurants, and shops. Playa Carmen, straight ahead, is the area's best place for surfing, though swimmers will want to be careful of rip currents there. Malpaís and Santa Teresa are so close that locals disagree on where one begins and the other ends. You could travel up the road parallel to the ocean that connects them and not realize you've moved from one town to the other.

GETTING HERE AND AROUND

From Paquera it's a 90-minute drive to Malpaís via Cóbano. After Cóbano, the road quickly deteriorates. It can become quite muddy in the rainy season, so you'll want a 4WD vehicle. There are no direct buses between Paquera and Malpaís; to get here you have to change buses in the southern peninsula's hub town of Cóbano. Taxis waiting at Tambor's airstrip will take up to four people to Malpaís for $40–$50.

Tropical Tours. The trip between Jacó and Malpaís takes about two hours, thanks to the daily boat service from Montezuma. Tropical Tours can set you up with a shuttle to San José ($40). ✉ *50 m north of El Cruce* ☎ *2640–1900* 🌐 *www.tropicaltours-malpais.com.*

ESSENTIALS

ATM Banco Nacional ✉ *Centro Comercial Playa Carmen* ☎ *2640–0640.*

Internet Tropical Tours. Tropical Tours has an Internet café at its office in Santa Teresa. ✉ *50 m north of El Cruce, Santa Teresa* ☎ *2640–1900* 🌐 *www.tropicaltours-malpais.com.*

Pharmacy Farmacia Amiga ✉ *Centro Comercial Playa Carmen* ☎ *2640–0463.*

OUTDOOR ACTIVITIES

Canopy del Pacífico. Here you'll find the only canopy tour in the area ($40 for a two-hour, 11-platform tour). You can walk, glide, or rappel through 64 acres of forest. ✉ *In front of fishermen's village* ☎ *2640–0360* 🌐 *www.canopydelpacifico.com.*

Tropical Tours. Tropical Tours can set you up with a horseback-riding jaunt, or a day trip to Isla Tortuga. ✉ *50 m north of El Cruce* ☎ *2640–1900* 🌐 *www.tropicaltours-malpais.com.*

SURFING

From November to May, the Malpaís area has some of Costa Rica's most consistent surf, as well as clear skies and winds that create idyllic conditions. **Playa Carmen** is the area's most consistent surf spot for all levels, and has dozens of beach breaks scattered along its shores. The sea grows rough and dirty during the May-to-December rainy season, with frequent swells that make it impossible to get out. **Playa Santa Teresa** is a better option when the waves at Playa Carmen are too gnarly. In Malpaís, at **Mar Azul,** more advanced surfers can try the break over a rock platform.

WHERE TO EAT

$$$ SEAFOOD ★ 🍴 **Nectar.** The Florblanca resort's alfresco restaurant by the pool has some tables that provide calming sea views through the tropical foliage. Fresh seafood is the specialty here, with inventive daily specials that focus on the day's catch. Asian and Mediterranean influences shine through in dishes ranging from spicy prawn fettuccine, to succulent pork ribs, to seared tuna with sweet Thai rice and braised bok choy. There's always a pizza of the day and a small sushi menu. [$] *Average main: $23* ✉ *Resort Florblanca, 2 km/1 mile north of soccer field* ☎ *2640–0232* ✍ *Reservations essential.*

$ PIZZA 🍴 **Restaurante Playa Carmen.** This restaurant's location, under the trees on the area's most popular beach, makes it the perfect choice for lunch. It's extremely casual, so you don't even have to put on a shirt. Oven-baked pizza is the house specialty, and these thin-crust pies are big enough for two people, especially if you start with one of the oversize salads. The kitchen also serves shrimp scampi, various pastas, and other dishes. $ *Average main: $9* ✉ *Playa Carmen, east of El Cruce, Santa Teresa* ☎ *2640–0110.*

$$$ SEAFOOD ★ 🍴 **Soma.** This small, tranquil restaurant within the Milarepa hotel serves delicious and creative Asian-inspired plates based on fresh local ingredients. The menu changes each night, but usually has fresh tuna, mahimahi, or other seafood, plus a chicken or beef dish. Any of the dishes can be prepared without meat, so vegetarians can choose from a wide selection. Tables are arranged under an open-air poolside deck a short walk from the beach. The restaurant does not accept credit cards per se, but if you are a guest at the Milarepa hotel, you may pay your dining tab with your hotel bill at checkout. $ *Average main: $17* ✉ *Milarepa hotel, 2 km/1 mile north of soccer field* ☎ *2640–0023, 2640–0663* ✍ *Reservations essential* ▭ *No credit cards* ⏲ *No lunch; closed Oct.*

WHERE TO STAY

For expanded hotel reviews, visit Fodors.com.

$ B&B/INN 🏨 **Blue Jay Eco-Lodge.** Perched along a forested mountainside, these wooden bungalows feel like tree houses; you'll hear howler monkeys and an array of birdsong from your bed. **Pros:** natural setting; good value; nice respite from lowland heat. **Cons:** steep terrain. **TripAdvisor:** "good clean accommodation," "awesome tree house hotel," "amazing views." $ *Rooms from: $69* ✉ *From El Cruce, 800 m south toward Malpaís, Sant Teresa* ☎ *2640–0089* 🌐 *www.bluejaylodgecostarica.com* 🛏 *10 cabins* 🍽 *Breakfast.*

$$$$ RESORT Fodor's Choice ★ 🏨 **Florblanca.** Named for the white flowers of the frangipani trees growing between the restaurant and the beach, this tasteful, friendly resort is dedicated to relaxation and rejuvenation. **Pros:** gorgeous villas and grounds; friendly; great yoga classes. **Cons:** very expensive; on rocky stretch of beach; insects sometimes a problem. **TripAdvisor:** "a special place to relax," "great food," "a true paradise." $ *Rooms from: $300* ✉ *2 km/1 mile north of soccer field, Santa Teresa* ☎ *2640–0232* 🌐 *www.florblanca.com* 🛏 *11 villas* 🍽 *No meals.*

$$ HOTEL 👶 🏨 **Luz de Vida.** This laid-back, beachfront lodge owned by a group of surfers is a good value. **Pros:** beachfront; nice grounds; friendly. **Cons:** service inconsistent; standard rooms too close to road. **TripAdvisor:** "paradise in Costa Rica," "great beach location," "excellent place to stay." $ *Rooms from: $75* ✉ *From El Cruce, 800 m south toward Malpaís, Santa Teresa* ☎ *2640–0320* 🌐 *www.luzdevida-resort.com* 🛏 *6 bungalows, 9 rooms* 🍽 *No meals.*

$$$ RESORT ★ 🏨 **Milarepa.** Named after a Tibetan Buddhist saint who gained enlightenment in just one lifetime, Milarepa is a perfect place for peaceful renewal, whether romantic or spiritual. **Pros:** secluded; small; beachfront; terrific restaurant. **Cons:** loosely managed; insects can be a problem; on rocky section of beach. **TripAdvisor:** "outstanding restaurant with lots of charm," "unforgettable experience," "get away and unwind." $ *Rooms from: $185* ✉ *2 km/1 mile north of school, beside Resort Florblanca, Santa Teresa* ☎ *2640–0023* 🌐 *www.milarepahotel.com* 🛏 *4 bungalows* 🍽 *No meals.*

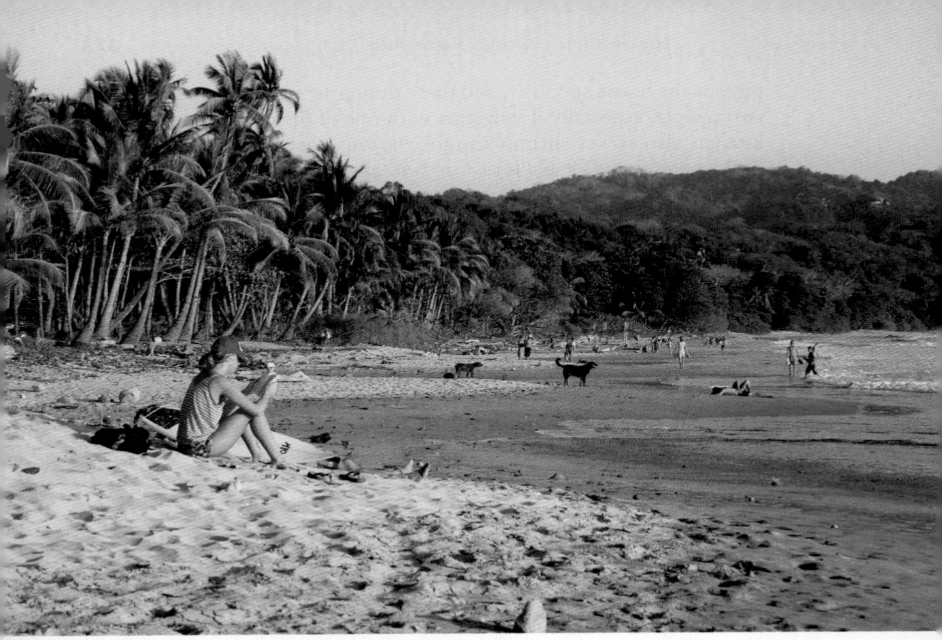

Santa Teresa beach, southern tip of the Nicoya Peninsula.

$ HOTEL ★ **Ritmo Tropical.** Tranquil, comfortable, and nicely priced, this small hotel a short walk from the beach is consistently the best deal in Malpaís. **Pros:** very clean rooms; economical. **Cons:** variety in room type; a bit of a walk to town. **TripAdvisor:** "great pool and restaurant," "lovely grounds," "best service." $ *Rooms from: $70* ✉ *100 m south of El Cruce on road toward Malpaís* ☎ *2640–0174* 🌐 *www.hotelritmotropical.net* 🛏 *9 bungalows* 🍴 *No meals.*

ATENAS AND CARARA NATIONAL PARK

Beaches may be this region's biggest draw, but the countryside holds some splendid scenery, from the steep coffee farms around Atenas to the tropical forests of the lowlands. In the wilderness of Carara National Park and surroundings, you might encounter white-faced capuchin monkeys in the trees or crocodiles lounging on a riverbank. The region is extremely biologically diverse, making it an excellent destination for bird-watchers and other wildlife enthusiasts.

ATENAS

42 km/26 miles west of San José.

Known for its excellent climate—*National Geographic* once dubbed it the world's best—Atenas ("Athens" in Spanish) is a pleasant, friendly town surrounded by a hilly countryside of coffee and cane fields, cattle ranches, and patches of forest. The small city is off the tourist circuit, which means that here, unlike other highly popular destinations, you'll walk alongside more locals than foreigners and get a more authentic idea of the country. Gazing at the tree-covered peaks and exploring the coffee farms are the main activities in this traditional town. Atenas's center has a concrete church, some well-kept wooden and adobe houses, and a park dominated by royal palms.

GETTING HERE

Atenas lies about one hour west on the route between San José and beaches such as Herradura, Jacó, and Manuel Antonio. Take the Pan-American Highway past the airport and turn right at the overpass with the signs for beach resorts and Zoo Ave. Turn left from the exit and stay on the main road. Alternately, Atenas has its own exit on the new Highway 27 that connects San José to Caldera. Buses to Atenas leave hourly throughout the day from the Coca-Cola terminal in San José and arrive near the center of town.

> **BASE CAMP**
>
> Some visitors to Costa Rica prefer using Atenas as their first- and last-night base camp instead of San José, because Atenas is smaller, friendlier, and more tranquil. The international airport is geographically closer to Atenas, but the hilly roads make the ride slightly longer than on San José's express highway.

ESSENTIALS

Bank/ATM Banco de Costa Rica ✉ *200 m west of Catholic church* ☎ *2446–6034.* **Banco Nacional** ✉ *Northern corner of central park* ☎ *2446–5157.*

Hospital Clínica Pública ✉ *150 m south of the fire station* ☎ *2446–5522.*

Pharmacy Farmacia Don Juan ✉ *West corner of Catholic church* ☎ *2446–5055.*

Post Office Correos ✉ *50 m southeast of northeast corner of market.*

WHERE TO EAT AND STAY

For expanded hotel reviews, visit Fodors.com.

$
B&B/INN
El Cafetal Inn. This charming bed-and-breakfast on a hilltop coffee farm feels and looks more like a home than a hotel, since the folks here go out of their way to help with your travel plans. **Pros:** superb food; lovely grounds. **Cons:** not all rooms have views. **TripAdvisor:** "wonderful setting," "amazing place with amazing climate," "fabulous food." $ *Rooms from: $62* ✉ *8 km/5 miles north of Atenas; heading west from San José on hwy. to Puntarenas, turn left (south) just before bridge 5 km/3 miles west of Grecia, Santa Eulalia de Atenas* ☎ *2446–5785* ⊕ *www.cafetal.com* ⤴ *14 rooms, 1 bungalow, 2 houses* ⦿ *Breakfast.*

CARARA NATIONAL PARK

43 km/25 miles southwest of Atenas, 85 km/51 miles southwest of San José.

Carara National Park. On the east side of the road between Puntarenas and Jacó, Parque Nacional Carara protects one of the last remnants of an ecological transition zone between Costa Rica's drier northwest and the more humid southwest. It consequently holds a tremendous collection of plants and animals. Much of the 47-square-km

(18-square-mile) park is covered with primary forest on steep slopes, where the massive trees are laden with vines and epiphytes. The sparse undergrowth makes wildlife easier to see here than in many other parks, but nothing is guaranteed. If you're lucky, you may glimpse armadillos, basilisk lizards, coatis, and any of several monkey species, as well as birds such as blue-crowned motmots, chestnut-mandibled toucans, and trogons.

The first trail on the left shortly after the bridge that spans the Río Tárcoles (a good place to spot crocodiles) leads to a horseshoe-shaped *laguna meandrica* (oxbow lake). The small lagoon covered with water hyacinths is home to turtles, crocodiles, and waterfowl such as the northern jacana, roseate spoonbill, and boat-billed heron. It is a two-to four-hour hike from the trailhead to the lagoon and back, depending on how much bird-watching you do. ■TIP→ **Cars parked at the trailhead have been broken into. If you don't see a ranger on duty at the sendero laguna meandrica trailhead, avoid leaving anything of value in your vehicle. You may be able to leave your belongings at the main ranger station (several miles south of the trailhead), where you can also buy drinks and souvenirs and use the restroom. Otherwise, visit the park as a day trip from a nearby hotel.**

Two trails lead into the forest from the parking lot. The shortest one can be done in 15 minutes, whereas the longer one that connects with the Quebrada Bonita loop takes one to three hours to hike. The latter can be quite muddy during the rainy months, when you may want rubber boots. Carara's proximity to San José and Jacó means that tour buses arrive regularly in high season, scaring some animals deeper into the forest. Come very early or late in the day to avoid crowds. Bird-watchers can call the day before to arrange admission before the park opens. Camping is not permitted. Jacó is the nearest town and the most logical base for trips into the park.

Local travel agencies and tour operators arrange transport to and guides through the park *(⇨ Park Tours, below)*. The park itself has guides, but you must arrange in advance. ⊠ *East of Costanera, just south of bridge over Rio Tárcoles* ☎ *2220–5023* 🔁 *$10* ⊙ *Daily 7–4.*

GETTING HERE

Take the new Highway 27 west of San José beyond Orotina and follow the signs to Jacó and Quepos. The reserve is on the left after you cross Río Tárcoles. From San José, hop on a bus to Jacó, Quepos, or Manuel Antonio, and ask to be dropped off near the park entrance, about a two-hour drive.

PARK TOURS

Horizontes. Horizontes, the country's premier nature-tour operator, can arrange visits to Carara as a day trip from San José or as part of a longer tour. ☎ *2222–2022* ⊕ *www.horizontes.com.*

Jaguar Riders. This Jacó-based tour operator can arrange guided tours through the forests of Carara. ⊠ *Avda. Pastor Díaz, next to Pancho Villa restaurant, Jacó* ☎ *2643–0180.*

FROM TÁCOLES TO MANUEL ANTONIO

Along a short stretch of Costa Rica's Pacific coast from Tárcoles to Manuel Antonio are patches of undeveloped jungle, the popular Manuel Antonio National Park, and some of the country's most accessible beaches. The proximity of these strands to San José leads Costa Ricans and foreigners alike to pop down for quick weekend beach vacations. Surfers have good reason to head for the consistent waves of Playas Jacó and Hermosa, and anglers and golfers should consider Playa Herradura for its golf courses and ocean access. You might find Herradura and Jacó overrated and overdeveloped. Manuel Antonio could be accused of the latter, but nobody can deny its spectacular natural beauty.

TÁRCOLES

90 km/54 miles southwest of San José.

Crocodile boat tours on the Río Tárcoles are this small town's claim to fame. In fact, you don't actually have to drive to Tárcoles to do the tour, because operators can pick you up in Herradura or Jacó. The muddy river has gained a reputation as the country's dirtiest, thanks to San José's inadequate sewage system, but it amazingly remains an impressive refuge for wildlife. A huge diversity of birds results from a combination of transitional forest and the river, which houses crocodiles, herons, storks, spoonbills, and other waterbirds. This is also one of the few areas in the country where you can see scarlet macaws, which you may spot on a boat tour or while hiking in a private reserve nearby.

GETTING HERE

By car, head west from San José on the new Highway 27 to Orotina and follow the signs to Herradura, Jacó, and Quepos. After crossing the bridge over the Río Tárcoles, look for the entrance to the town of Tárcoles on the right. On the left is the dirt road that leads to the Hotel Villa Lapas and the waterfall reserve. Any bus traveling to Jacó can drop you off at the entrance to Tárcoles. Let the driver know in advance.

OUTDOOR ACTIVITIES

BOAT TOURS

On the two-hour riverboat tours through the mangrove forest and Tárcoles River you might see massive crocodiles, Jesus lizards, iguanas, and some of roughly 50 colorful bird species, including the roseate spoonbill and boat-billed heron. Tours reach the river's mouth, providing nice sea views, especially at sunset. ■TIP➔ Around noon is the best time to spot crocs sunbathing; bird enthusiasts prefer afternoon rides to catch scarlet macaws. During the rainy season (May to November), the river may grow too rough for boats in the afternoon.

Crocodile Man Tour. Two brothers run Crocodile Man Tour. The small scars on their hands are the result of the tour's most original (and optional) attraction: feeding fish to the crocs. The boats are small enough to slide up alongside the mangroves for a closer look. Transportation is provided from nearby beaches, but not from San José. ⊠ *Main road into Tárcoles* ☎ *2637–0771* ⊕ *www.crocodilemantour.com.*

CLOSE UP

Diving the Deep at Cocos Island

Rated one of the top diving destinations in the world, Isla del Coco is uninhabited and remote, and its waters are teeming with marine life. It's no place for beginners, but serious divers enjoy 30-meter (100-foot) visibility and the underwater equivalent of a big-game park: scalloped hammerheads, white-tipped reef sharks, Galápagos sharks, bottlenose dolphins, billfish, and manta rays mix with huge schools of brilliantly colored fish.

Encompassing about 22½ square km (14 square miles), Isla del Coco is the largest uninhabited island on earth. Its isolation has led to the evolution of dozens of endemic plant and animal species. The rocky topography is draped in rain forest and cloud forest and includes more than 200 waterfalls. Because of Isla del Coco's distance from shore (484 km/300 miles) and its craggy topography, few visitors to Costa Rica—and even fewer Costa Ricans—have set foot on the island.

Costa Rica annexed Coco in 1869, and it became a national park in 1978.

Today only extremely high-priced specialty-cruise ships, park rangers and volunteers, and scientists visit this place. The dry season (November to May) brings calmer seas and is the best time to see silky sharks. During the rainy season large schools of hammerheads can be seen, but the ocean is rougher.

Two companies offer regular 10- to 13-day dive cruises to Isla del Coco that include three days of travel time on the open ocean and cost roughly $4,545 to $6,485, depending on the boat and dates.

Okeanos Aggressor. The *Okeanos Aggressor* offers 8- and 10-day dive safaris to Cocos Island year-round. ☎ 2289–2261, 800/348–2628 in U.S. ⊕ www.aggressor.com.

Undersea Hunter. Undersea Hunter runs 10-day dive trips to Cocos Island year-round on its boats *Argo, Sea Hunter, DeepSee,* and *Undersea Hunter.* ☎ 2228–6613 in San José, 800/203–2120 in North America ⊕ www.underseahunter.com.

CANOPY TOUR

Hotel Villa Lapas. Hotel Villa Lapas manages a suspension-bridge nature walk and a zip-line tour. **Sky Way** consists of five suspension bridges spread out over a 2½-km (1½-mile) old-growth-forest nature trail. You can do the trail with a guide ($20). A shuttle picks you up at the Hotel Villa Lapas. **Villa Lapas Canopy** has zip lines through primary forest ($30). ⊠ *Off Costanera, after bridge over Río Tárcoles* ☎ 2637–0232, 2203–3553 in San José ⊕ www.villalapas.com.

WHERE TO STAY

For expanded hotel reviews, visit Fodors.com.

$$
RESORT
☾

Hotel Villa Lapas. Within a tranquil rain-forest preserve, far from other hotels (and the beach), Villa Lapas is a great escape for nature lovers, but also has on-site entertainment to keep you busy, such as a large-screen television, a pool table, and foosball. **Pros:** surrounded by forest; lots of activities; birds; kid-friendly. **Cons:** rooms sometimes musty; air-conditioners old; mediocre buffets. **TripAdvisor:** "great staff," "very good grounds," "nice relaxing place." [$] *Rooms from: $120* ✉ *Off Costanera, 3 km/2 miles after bridge over Rio Tárcoles, turn left on dirt road, up 600 m* ☎ *2637–0232, 2203–3553 in San José* 🌐 *www.villalapas.com* 🛏 *56 rooms* 🍴 *Breakfast.*

EN ROUTE

Even if you choose to bypass Tárcoles and its crocodile tours, you can still get a peek at the huge reptiles as they lounge on the riverbanks: on the Costanera, pull over just after crossing the Río Tárcoles bridge and walk back onto it. Bring binoculars if you have them. ■ **TIP→ Be sure to lock your car—vehicles have been broken into here.**

BETWEEN TÁRCOLES AND PLAYA HERRADURA

Past Tárcoles, the first sizable beach town of the Central Pacific coast is Playa Herradura. In between, you'll pass two exclusive hotels, hidden from view at the end of long winding roads.

Playa La Pita. About a kilometer (½ mile) south after the entrance to Tárcoles, the Costanera passes a small beach called Playa La Pita, which provides your first glimpse of the Pacific if you're coming down from San José or the Central Valley. The beach is rocky, and its proximity to the Rio Tárcoles makes the water murky and unfit for swimming, but it's a nice spot to stop and admire the ocean. From here the road heads inland again, and you'll come across the entrance to Punta Leona, a vast hotel and residential complex. The road then winds its way up a steep hill, atop which is the entrance to the luxury hotel Villa Caletas. On the other side of that ridge is the bay and beach of Herradura.

WHERE TO EAT AND STAY

For expanded hotel reviews, visit Fodors.com.

$$$ ECLECTIC 🍴 **El Mirador Restaurant.** White tablecloths, glass walls, and yellow-and-blue-checked curtains contribute to the sophisticated but not overly stuffy atmosphere of this restaurant at Villa Caletas. Expensive prix-fixe meals include your choice of appetizer, main dish, and dessert. Appetizers range from the traditional escargots to a shrimp and lobster bisque. The entrées include beef tenderloin with a red wine and espresso sauce, jumbo shrimp sautéed with coconut and vanilla, and a combination of a veal chop and roast duck. A covered terrace below the restaurant is popular for sunset viewing over a cocktail, and the tapas menu is much less expensive than the main restaurant. [$] *Average main: $21* ✉ *Villa Caletas hotel, off coastal hwy., 3 km/1½ miles south of Punta Leona* ☎ *2637–0505.*

$$ RESORT 🏨 **Punta Leona Hotel & Club.** This 740-acre private reserve and resort community is an odd and sometimes overwhelming mix of nature, residential development, and vacation spot. **Pros:** ample beachfront; lots of variety in activities. **Cons:** far from town; spotty service; not a good option if you crave seclusion. **TripAdvisor:** "very nice property," "beautiful beach," "good food." [$] *Rooms from: $121* ✉ *15 km/9 miles south of Tárcoles on west side of road to Jacó* ☎ *2630–1000, 2231–3131 in San José, 888/301–9473 in North America* 🌐 *www.hotelpuntaleona.com* 🛏 *108 rooms, 13 suites, 27 apartments* 🍴 *Breakfast.*

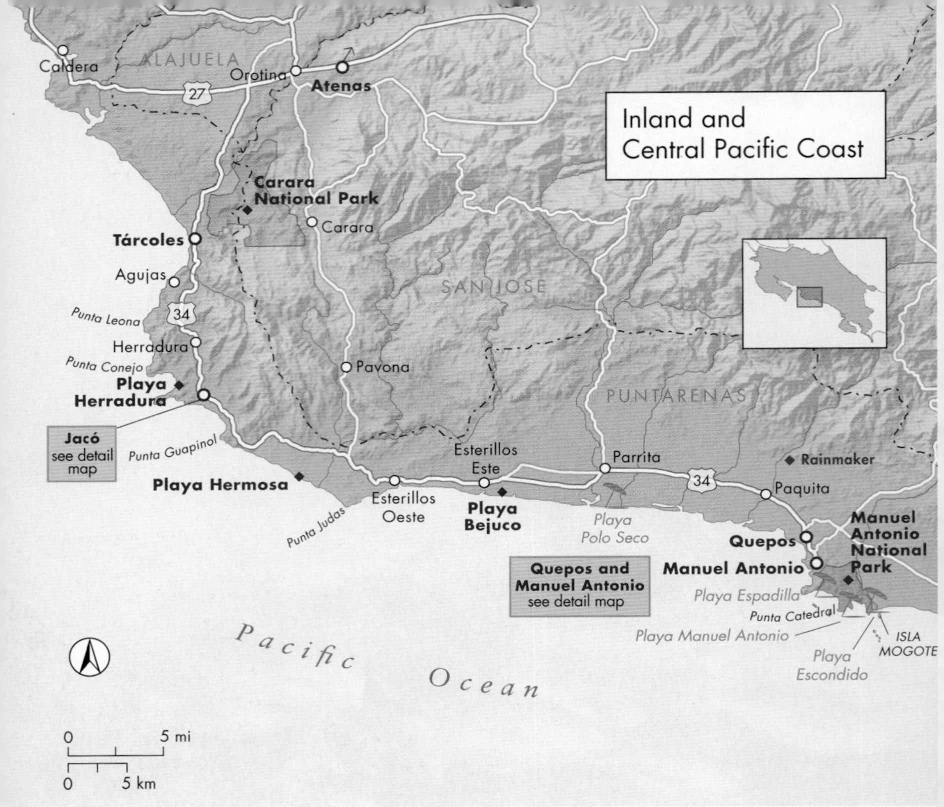

Inland and
Central Pacific Coast
Caldera
ALAJUELA
Orotina
Atenas
27
Carara
National Park
Carara
Tárcoles
Agujas
SAN JOSE
Punta Leona
34
Herradura
Punta Conejo
Pavona
Playa
Herradura
PUNTARENAS
Jacó
see detail
map
Punta Guapinol
Esterillos
Este
Parrita
Rainmaker
Playa Hermosa
Esterillos
Oeste
34
Paquita
Playa
Bejuco
Punta Judas
Playa
Polo Seco
Quepos
Manuel
Antonio
National
Park
Quepos and
Manuel Antonio
see detail map
Manuel Antonio
Playa Espadilla
Punta Catedral
Playa Manuel Antonio
ISLA
MOGOTE
Pacific
Ocean
Playa
Escondido
0
5 mi
0
5 km

$$$ [🏨] **Villa Caletas.** Perched 1,200 feet above the sea on a promontory south of Punta Leona, this collection of elegant rooms sequestered in the jungle has jaw-dropping views of the surrounding foliage and sea below. **Pros:** gorgeous views, forest, and sunsets; good food. **Cons:** abundant insects; lots of stairs; not a good choice if you're looking for action. **TripAdvisor:** "wonderful escape," "private and peaceful," "rooms are incredible." [$] *Rooms from: $185* ✉ *Off coastal hwy., 3 km/1½ miles south of Punta Leona, on right* ☎ *2637–0505, 2257–3653 in San José* 🌐 *www.hotelvillacaletas.com* 🛏 *10 rooms, 13 villas, 7 junior suites, 13 suites* 🍴 *No meals.*

RESORT
★

PLAYA HERRADURA

20 km/12 miles south of Tárcoles.

Playa Herradura. If sportfishing and golf are your priorities, Playa Herradura is a good option. If you're looking for nature, seclusion, a beautiful beach, or a bargain, keep driving. Rocky Playa Herradura, a poor representative of Costa Rica's breathtaking beaches, gets its name from the Spanish word for "horseshoe," referring to the shape of the deep bay in which it lies. Its tranquil waters make it considerably safer for swimming than most central and southern Pacific beaches, and that, coupled with its proximity to San José, has turned it into a popular weekend getaway for *Josefinos*, who compete for shade beneath the sparse palms and Indian almond trees that line the beach. On the north end of the beach is Los Sueños development, which includes a large marina, shopping center, hundreds of condos, a golf course, and a massive Marriott hotel.

THE HAUNTED CART

If you're out late one night and hear a slow scraping of wheels against the road, it just might be the *carreta sin bueyes* (cart without oxen) of ghostly legend. Its owner reputedly stole building materials from a church, and was condemned to perpetually traverse the country's highways and byways in the cart he used to transport his stolen goods. (The oxen were blameless for their role and escaped the curse.)

GETTING HERE

By car, head 20 minutes straight down the Pacific highway. The town's entrance is on the right-hand side, where a long paved road leads to the beach. Follow the signs to the Marriott.

OUTDOOR ACTIVITIES

Few activities are available directly in Playa Herradura, but that doesn't mean you have to settle for less. Most of the area's diverse outfitters can pick you up at your hotel for activities near Jacó and Playa Hermosa. Your hotel's reception desk is often a good source of information.

Costa Rica Dreams. Costa Rica Dreams is one of the area's oldest and most reputable sportfishing outfitters. ✉ *Los Sueños Marina* ☎ *2637–8942, 337/205–0665 in North America* 🌐 *www.costaricadreams.com.*

King Tours. King Tours arranges trips to renowned attractions like Manuel Antonio National Park and Carara National Park, as well as crocodile boat tours, deep-sea and coastal fishing trips, horseback rides, and canopy tours. The company can also book tours to destinations elsewhere in the country, such as Poás and Arenal volcanoes, Monteverde Cloud Forest, and Isla Tortuga. ✉ *Main road into Playa Herradura, in front of Los Sueños* ☎ *2643–2441, 800/213–7091 in North America* 🌐 *www.kingtours.com.*

WHERE TO EAT AND STAY

For expanded hotel reviews, visit Fodors.com.

$$$ LATIN AMERICAN 🍴 **Nuevo Latino.** The most formal restaurant at the Los Sueños Resort (though dress is still Costa Rica casual), softly lighted Nuevo Latino has large arched windows facing cascading water on one wall and large still-lifes of fruits on the other. As the name implies, the menu uses basic Latin American ingredients, like yuca, sweet potato, corn, and beans, in creative ways, fusing them with flavors from other parts of the world. The menu includes pork chops with mint pesto and sea bass with curry and coconut. [$] *Average main: $24* ✉ *Marriott Los Sueos Resort* ☎ *2630–9000* ⌚ *No lunch.*

$$ SEAFOOD 🍴 **Restaurante El Pelícano.** It may not look like much at first glance, but this open-air restaurant across the street from the beach serves some dishes you'd be hard-pressed to find in other casual beach-town places. The decor is limited to green-tile floors, thin wooden columns, lime tablecloths, and soft candlelight. Starters include fish croquettes in a lemon sauce, green pepper stuffed with shrimp and mushrooms, or

7

clams *au gratin.* Grilled tuna in a mango sauce, sea bass in a heart-of-palm sauce, lobster, and tenderloin are a few of the main dishes. [$] *Average main: $13* ✉ *Turn left at end of main road into Playa Herradura* ☎ *2637–8910.*

$$$$ RESORT **Los Sueños Marriott Ocean and Golf Resort.** This mammoth multimillion-dollar resort in a palatial colonial-style building has a gorgeous view of Herradura Bay and combines modern amenities with traditional Central American decorative motifs, such as barrel-tile roofing and hand-painted tiles. **Pros:** impeccable grounds; great service; memorable. **Cons:** expensive, so-so service; beach can be dirty. **TripAdvisor:** "terrific," "great family vacation," "best service." [$] *Rooms from: $289* ✉ *800 m west of road to Jacó from San José, follow signs at entrance of road to Playa Herradura* ☎ *2630–9000, 888/236–2427 in North America, 2298–0000 in San José* 🌐 *www.marriott.com* 🛏 *191 rooms, 10 suites* 🍴 *Breakfast.*

JACÓ

2 km/1 mile south of Playa Herradura, 114 km/70 miles southwest of San José.

Its proximity to San José has made Jacó the most developed beach town in Costa Rica. Nature lovers and solitude seekers should skip this place, which is known mostly for its nightlife, surf scene, and prostitution. More than 80 hotels and cabinas back its long, gray-sand beach, and the mix of restaurants, shops, and bars lining Avenida Pastor Díaz (the town's main drag) give it a cluttered appearance devoid of any greenery. Any real Costa Rican–ness evaporated years ago; U.S. chain hotels and restaurants have invaded, and you can pretty much find anything you need, from law offices and dental clinics to DVD-rental shops and appliance stores. It does have a bit of everything in terms of tours and outdoor activities, and makes a convenient hub for exploring neighboring beaches and attractions. Theft can be a problem here; watch your things like a hawk.

GETTING HERE AND AROUND

The drive from San José takes less than two hours; take the new Highway 27 west of San José beyond Orotina, and then take the exit to Jacó and Quepos. The exit, on the right after Herradura, is well marked. Buses leave from San José's Coca-Cola station seven times daily, with an extra run on weekends.

Pacific Travel & Tours. Pacific Travel & Tours brings passengers across the Gulf of Nicoya between Jacó or Herradura to Montezuma. ☎ *2643–2520, 800/397–5716 in North America* 🌐 *www.pacifictravelcr.com.*

ESSENTIALS

Bank/ATM BAC San José ✉ *Centro Comericial Il Galeone* ☎ *2295–9797.*
Banco Nacional ✉ *Avda. Pastor Díaz* ☎ *2643–3621.*

Hospital Clínica Pública ✉ *In front of Plaza de Deportes* ☎ *2643–1767.*

Internet Jacó Café ✉ *Next to Hotel Canciones del Mar* ☎ *2643–2601.*

Pharmacy Farmacia Jacó ⊠ *Diagonally across from Mas X Menos supermarket* ☎ *2643–3205.*

Post Office Correos ⊠ *Avda. Pastor Diaz.*

Rental Cars Alamo ⊠ *Avda. Pastor Díaz* ☎ *2643–1752* ⊕ *www.alamocostarica. com.* **Budget** ⊠ *Avda. Pastor Díaz* ☎ *2643–2665* ⊕ *www.budget.co.cr.* **Economy** ⊠ *Avda. Pastor Díaz* ☎ *2643–1098* ⊕ *www.economyrentacar.com.*

Taxis Taxi services ☎ *2643–2020, 2643–2121, 2643–3030.*

Tourist Information Pacific Travel & Tours ⊠ *Centro Comercial Las Casonas* ☎ *2643–2520, 800/397–5716 in North America* ⊕ *www.pacifictravelcr.com.*

EXPLORING

Playa Jacó. Long, palm-lined Playa Jacó, west of town, is a pleasant enough spot in the morning but can burn the soles of your feet on a sunny afternoon. Though the gray sand and beachside construction make it less attractive than most other Costa Rican beaches, it's a good place to soak up the sun or enjoy a sunset. The beach is popular with surfers for the consistency of its waves, but when the surf is up, swimmers should beware of dangerous rip currents. During the rainy months the ocean here is not very clean.

OUTDOOR ACTIVITIES

You don't have to physically step into any tour office, because everyone from a reception desk attendant to a boutique salesperson can book you a local adventure. Almost every tour can pick you up at your hotel's doorstep. ■TIP→ Keep in mind that part of your price tag includes the salesperson's commission, so if you hear higher or lower prices from two different people, it's likely a reflection of a shift in the commission. You can try negotiating a better deal directly from the outfitter.

Gray Line Costa Rica. Dealing primarily with large groups, this tour company arranges day trips from Jacó to Arenal and Poás volcanoes, Manuel Antonio National Park, Sarchí, Isla Tortuga, and raft trips on the Savegre River. ⊠ *Best Western Jacó Beach Resort* ☎ *2643–2231, 2220–2126 in San José* ⊕ *www.graylinecostarica.com.*

Jaguar Riders. Jaguar Riders specializes in ATV tours of the mountains east of town and trips to Carara National Park but can arrange all kinds of personalized excursions. ⊠ *Avda. Pastor Díaz, next to Pancho Villa restaurant* ☎ *2643–0180* ⊕ *www.jaguariders.com.*

Pacific Travel & Tours. Pacific Travel & Tours sells an array of tours in and around Jacó. ⊠ *Centro comercial Las Casonas* ☎ *2643–2520, 800/397–5716 in North America* ⊕ *www.pacifictravelcr.com.*

ATV TOURS

Because ATV tours are fairly new here, the vehicles are in good condition. But they're not exactly the most eco-friendly way to see the area's rain forest and wildlife, and rollovers always pose a risk to you. Some operators will ask you to put up a credit card voucher of roughly $500.

Adventure Tours. Adventure Tours is considered by locals to be the best ATV tour with the longest routes. They offer various options: a two-hour sunset tour ($69), a four-hour Carara Park and nearby river tour ($89), and full-day trips ($175). ✉ *In the center of Playa Jacó, behind Subway* ☎ *2643–5720, 877/561–7263 in North America* ⊕ *www.adventurtourscostarica.com.*

BUNGEE JUMPING

Pacific Bungee. Want to plummet from a 39-meter (130-foot) tower? Pacific Bungee offers a bungee jump (into a pool if you like) for $50. For another $50, the facility's Rocket Launcher catapults you into the air, with bungeelike recoils to follow. The Big Swing ($50), the third activity here, takes you on a 25-meter-high (85-foot-high), 180-degree arc through the air. You can mix and match activities, or do them all for $100. ✉ *100 m south of Red Cross* ☎ *2643–6682* ⊕ *www.pacificbungee.com.*

CANOPY TOURS

Rain Forest Adventures. A modified ski lift offers easy access to the rain-forest canopy, with six-seat gondolas that float through the treetops at the Rain Forest Adventures. This tram, a branch of the Rainforest Adventures' aerial-tram complex near Braulio Carrillo National Park north of San José, lies within a 222-acre private reserve 3 km (2 miles) west of Jacó. The company offers guidead tours that explain a bit of the local ecology ($55), as well as early-morning bird-watching tours (six-person minimum; $83 per person). There is also a small serpentarium and medicinal plant garden ($10). A $70 "Tranopy" tour combines the tram with a 10-cable zip-line tour. ✉ *3 km/2 miles west of Jacó* ☎ *2257–5961, 866/759–8726 in North America* ⊕ *www.rainforestadventure.com.*

HANG GLIDING

Hang Glide Costa Rica. Hang gliding gives you the chance to see not just Jacó, but a huge expanse of Pacific coastline. With Hang Glide Costa Rica you can take a tandem hang-gliding flight or fly in a three-seat, open cockpit ultralight plane. You are picked up in Jacó and taken to the airstrip 6 km (4 miles) south of Playa Hermosa. Prices start at $69 per person. ☎ *2643–4200* ⊕ *www.hangglidecr.com.*

HORSEBACK RIDING

Discovery Horseback Tours. Discovery Horseback Tours is owned by a British couple who run 2½-hour trail rides on healthy horses. You'll spend some time in the rain forest and also stop at a small waterfall where you can take a dip. Another tour takes you on a sunset ride on the beach. Either runs $65. An alternate tour ($110) runs 4½ hours and takes in a small village and butterfly farm. ☎ *8830–7550* ⊕ *www.horseridecostarica.com.*

KAYAKING AND CANOEING

Kayak Jacó. Looking for waters calmer than those at Jacó Beach? Kayak Jacó takes you to Playa Agujas for sea-kayaking tours and Hawaiian-style outrigger canoe trips ($60). The half-day tours include snorkeling (conditions permitting) at secluded beaches. ✉ *Playa Agujas* ☎ *2643–1233* 🌐 *www.kayakjaco.com.*

SURFING

Jacó has several beach breaks, all of which are best around high tide. Surfboard-toting tourists abound in Jacó, but you don't need to be an expert to enjoy the waves—the swell is often small enough for beginners, especially around low tide. Abundant surf shops rent boards and give lessons. Prices range from $30 to $50 an hour and usually include a board and transportation. If you plan to spend more than a week surfing, it might be cheaper to buy a used board and sell it before you leave (⇨ *Shopping, below)*. If you don't have much experience, don't go out when the waves are really big—Jacó sometimes gets very powerful swells, which result in dangerous rip currents. During the rainy season, waves are more consistent than in the dry months, when Jacó sometimes lacks surf.

SWIMMING

The big waves and dangerous rip currents that make surfing so popular here can make swimming dangerous. Lifeguards are on duty only at specific spots, and only sporadically. If the ocean is rough, stay on the beach—dozens of swimmers have drowned here over the years.

When the ocean is calm, especially around low tide, you can swim just about anywhere along Jacó Beach. The sea is always calmer near the beach's northern and southern ends, but the ocean bottom is littered with rocks there, as it is in front of the small rivers that flow into the sea near the middle of this beach.

WHERE TO STAY

For expanded hotel reviews, visit Fodors.com.

$$$ HOTEL 🏨 **Amapola.** Several blocks from the beach, near the more tranquil southern end, Amapola is a smaller, slightly tackier version of a resort hotel. **Pros:** quieter than many hotels in Jacó. **Cons:** dated furnishings, several blocks form beach. **TripAdvisor:** "very enjoyable stay," "nice grounds," "lovely hotel." $ *Rooms from: $170* ✉ *200 m east of the Townhouse of Garabito* ☎ *2643–2255, 888/790–5264 in U.S.* 🌐 *www.hotelamapola.com* 🛏 *60 room, 7 junior suites, 3 villas* 🍴 *Breakfast.*

$$ HOTEL 👶 ★ 🏨 **Apartotel Flamboyant.** Though nothing special, this small beachfront hotel is a good deal, especially if you take advantage of the cooking facilities. **Pros:** beachfront; good value; quiet; centrally located. **Cons:** very simple rooms; looks a little worn. **TripAdvisor:** "my favorite hotel in Costa Rica," "near the action," "clean." $ *Rooms from: $90* ✉ *100 m west of Centro Comercial Il Galeone* ☎ *2643–3146* 🌐 *www.apartotelflamboyant.com* 🛏 *18 rooms, 4 apartments* 🍴 *No meals.*

$$$ HOTEL 👶 🏨 **Apartotel Girasol.** A great option for families, or for a small groups of friends looking for comfort and quiet, Girasol is a quiet beachfront hotel with a neighborly feel. **Pros:** beachfront; quiet grounds; big apartments. **Cons:** far from town center; often full. $ *Rooms from:*

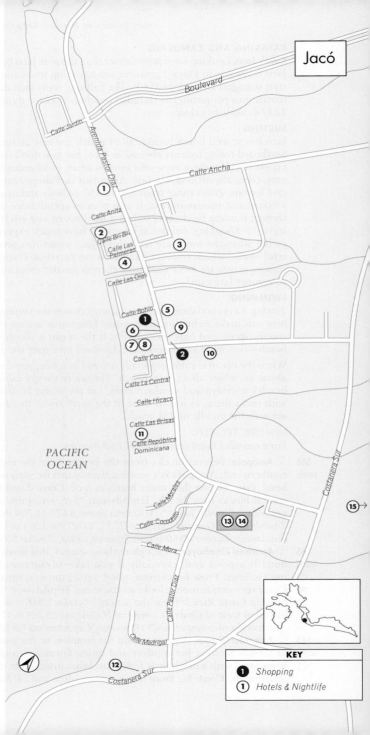

Jacó

PACIFIC
OCEAN

KEY

❶ *Shopping*

① *Hotels & Nightlife*

$162 ✉ 100 m west of Motoshop, end of C. República Dominicana ☎ 2643–1591, 800/923–2779 in North America 🌐 www.girasol.com 🛏 16 apartments 🍴 No meals.

$$ RESORT 🏨 **Best Western Jacó Beach Resort.** Here's a reliable member of the Best Western chain, perhaps not what you came to Costa Rica to see, but we recommend this place as a decent backup. **Pros:** reassuring chain name, many services. **Cons:** sameness of a chain hotel, rooms facing pool can be noisy. **TripAdvisor:** "solid three-star hotel," "great locale," "safe but not quiet." [$] *Rooms from: $125 ✉ Avda. Pastor Díaz, toward northern end, in front of Banco de Costa Rica ☎ 2643–1000, 800/528–1234 in U.S. and Canada 🌐 www.bestwestern.com 🛏 126 rooms 🍴 Breakfast.*

$ HOTEL 🏨 **Cabinas Las Orquídeas.** Just far enough from the beach and main tourist beat to be a bargain, but close enough to be convenient, this pleasant little hotel provides cleanliness and comfort at reasonable rates. **Pros:** good location; clean. **Cons:** no frills; no beachfront. **TripAdvisor:** "cozy lodge with fantastic views," "cute little place," "comfortable rooms." [$] *Rooms from: $51 ✉ East of Frutástica supermarket ☎ 2643–4056 🌐 www.cabinas-las-orquideas.com 🛏 10 rooms, 2 dorm-style rooms with shared bath 🍴 No meals.*

$$$ RESORT Fodor's Choice ★ 🏨 **Club del Mar.** Secluded at the beach's southern end, far from Jacó's crowds, Club del Mar is the area's priciest, and nicest, lodging option. **Pros:** beachfront; tranquil; friendly; lush grounds; tasteful decor. **Cons:** some highway noise reaches back to condos; some insects. **TripAdvisor:** "excellent location," "very enjoyable stay," "a truly memorable place." [$] *Rooms from: $160 ✉ Costanera, 275 m south of gas station ☎ 2643–3194, 866/978–5669 in North America 🌐 www.clubdelmarcostarica.com 🛏 9 rooms, 22 condos, 2 suites 🍴 No meals.*

$$$ HOTEL 🏨 **Docelunas.** Most of Jacó's hotels and visitors huddle around the beach, but "Twelve Moons" sits a couple of miles from the sea and sand, with a mountainous green backdrop, spreading out across 5 acres of lawns shaded by tropical trees and luxuriant gardens. **Pros:** more secluded than other Jacó lodgings; terrific restaurant. **Cons:** far from beach. **TripAdvisor:** "amazingly serene," "a beautiful getaway," "the good life." [$] *Rooms from: $150 ✉ On coastal hwy. from San José, pass the 1st entrance to Jacó; take dirt road on left with signs for Docelunas ☎ 2643–2211 🌐 www.docelunas.com 🛏 10 rooms, 10 suites 🍴 Breakfast.*

$$ RESORT 👶 Fodor's Choice ★ 🏨 **Hotel Canciones del Mar.** The poetically named "Songs of the Sea" is a tranquil, intimate, and charming hotel with rooms that are among the closest to the ocean of any hotel in the area. **Pros:** close to ocean; rooms have kitchens. **Cons:** too close to Jacó; rooms feel worn. **TripAdvisor:** "perfect getaway," "wonderful stay," "fantastic location." [$] *Rooms from: $115 ✉ End of C. Bri Bri ☎ 2643–3273, 888/260–1523 in U.S. 🌐 www.cancionesdelmar.com 🛏 15 suites 🍴 Breakfast.*

$$ RESORT 👶 🏨 **Hotel Tangerí.** One of Jacó's original hotels, the Tangerí has an excellent beachfront location and ample grounds shaded by coconut palms with a mix ranging from spacious rooms by the sea to villas big enough for a large family. **Pros:** beachfront; spacious rooms; centrally located. **Cons:** rooms a bit timeworn; musty. **TripAdvisor:** "nice

"I caught this beautiful heron just outside our beachfront hotel at Jacó." —Photo by Leethal33, Fodors.com member

hotel and staff," "great beachfront family hotel," "great location." ⑤ *Rooms from: $138* ⊠ *Avda. Pastor Díaz, north of river* ☎ *2643–3001, 2222–2924 in San José* ⊕ *www.hoteltangeri.com* ⌑ *14 rooms, 11 villas* ⦿ *Multiple meal plans.*

$$
B&B/INN
Ⓒ

Mar de Luz. It may be a few blocks from the beach, and it doesn't look like much from the street, but Mar de Luz is a surprisingly pleasant place full of flowering plants and shady, bird-attracting trees. **Pros:** attentive owner; plenty to do. **Cons:** rooms a bit dark; service can be spotty. **TripAdvisor:** "a quiet place," "wonderful and relaxing," "nice folks." ⑤ *Rooms from: $100* ⊠ *East of Avda. Pastor Díaz, behind Jungle bar* ☎ *2643–3000, 2224–4704 in San José* ⊕ *www.mardeluz.com* ⌑ *27 rooms, 2 suites* ⦿ *Breakfast.*

$
HOTEL

Tropical Garden Hotel. As its name suggests, this hotel's special charm comes from the impressive lush gardens that fill almost every inch of its property, making it one of the most verdant places in Jacó. **Pros:** pleasant grounds; economical. **Cons:** timeworn; simple. ⑤ *Rooms from: $70* ⊠ *50 m west of Il Galeone mall, toward the beach* ☎ *2643–3003* ⊕ *www.tropicalgardenhotel.com* ⌑ *12 studios, 1 suite* ⦿ *No meals.*

NIGHTLIFE AND THE ARTS
Whereas other beach towns may have a bar or two, Jacó has an avenue full of them, with enough variety for many different tastes. After-dinner spots range from restaurants perfect for a quiet drink to loud bars with pool tables to dance clubs or casinos.

BARS

Restaurante El Colonial. For a laid-back cocktail, people-watching, and a tropical feel, head to Restaurante El Colonial on the main drag, which has a large circular bar in the center and lots of wicker chairs and tables in the front. Occasionally you'll hear live music. ⊠ *Avda. Pastor Díaz, across from Il Galeone mall* ☎ *2643–3326.*

Tabacón. The restaurant Tabacón is a nice place for a cocktail, after-dinner drinks, or a late-night meal. It has a big bar in back, pool tables, and live music on weekends. ⊠ *Avda. Pastor Díaz, north of Il Galeone mall* ☎ *2643–3097* ⊕ *www.restaurantetabacon.com.*

CASINOS

Jazz Casino. Jacó's very own casino has rummy, slot machines, and craps. There's also a roomy bar area. ⊠ *Hotel Amapola, 130 m east of the Municipalidad government building, southern end of town* ☎ *2643–2316.*

SHOPPING

Souvenir shops with mostly the same mass-produced merchandise are crowded one after the other along the main street in the center of town. Most of the goods, like wooden crafts and seed jewelry, are run-of-the-mill souvenir fare, but a few shops have more unusual items.

Cocobolo. The two neighboring shops at Cocobolo are jam-packed with merchandise hanging from the ceiling, walls, and shelves. It's much of what you find in other stores, but with more tasteful items and a richer variety. ⊠ *Avda. Pastor Díaz, next to Banana Café* ☎ *2643–3486.*

Guacamole. Guacamole sells beautiful and comfortable batik clothing produced locally, along with Brazilian bathing suits, Costa Rican leather sandals and purses, and different styles of jewelry. ⊠ *Centro Comercial Costa Brava, south of Il Galeone mall* ☎ *2643–1120.*

SURFBOARDS AND GEAR

Jass. Jass has a good variety of surf gear at decent prices. It sells new and used boards. ■TIP➔ Most shops that sell boards also buy used boards. ⊠ *Centro Comercial Ureña* ☎ *2643–3850* ⊕ *www.jasssurfshop.com.*

PLAYA HERMOSA

5 km/3 miles south of Jacó, 113 km/70 miles southwest of San José.

Playa Hermosa. On the other side of the rocky ridge that forms the southern edge of Jacó Beach is Playa Hermosa, a swath of gray sand and driftwood stretching southeast as far as the eye can see. Despite its name—Spanish for "Beautiful Beach"—Playa Hermosa is hardly spectacular. The southern half of the wide beach lacks palm trees or other shade-providing greenery; its sand is scorching hot in the afternoon; and frequent rip currents make it unsafe to swim when there are waves. But board riders find beauty in its consistent surf breaks. The beach's northern end is popular because it often has waves when other spots are flat, and the ocean is cleaner than at Jacó. There is also plenty of forest covering the hills, and scarlet macaws sometimes gather in the Indian almond trees near the end of the beach. For nonsurfers, outdoor options include horseback and canopy tours in the nearby, forested hills or ultralight and hang-gliding flights over the coast. But all of these can be done from other beaches. As for the town itself, there's really not much, which is part of the attraction for travelers who want to escape Jacó's crowds and concrete towers. Most of the restaurants, bars, and hotels have cropped up one after the other on a thin stretch separating the highway and the beach. From June to December, olive ridley turtles nest on the beach at night, especially when there's not much moonlight.

> ### NOT THAT PLAYA HERMOSA
>
> "¡Ojo!" as they say. Watch out: Costa Rica has two Playa Hermosas. Don't confuse this one with the larger, more developed beach of the same name on the North Pacific coast. Each has it fans, but the Central Pacific's Playa Hermosa is better known to Costa Ricans and to surfers.

GETTING HERE
If you have a car, take the coastal highway 5 km (3 miles) past Jacó. You'll see the cluster of businesses on the right. If you don't, take a taxi from Jacó or a local bus toward Quepos.

ESSENTIALS
Internet Goola Café and Internet ⊠ *Costanera, north of soccer field* ☎ *2643–3696.*

OUTDOOR ACTIVITIES
You can arrange activities throughout the Central Pacific from Playa Hermosa. Most tour operators and outfitters include transportation in their prices. *For more options than we list here, see Outdoor Activities in Jacó, above, or consult your hotel's reception.*

Playa Hermosa Turtle Tours. Raúl Fernández of Playa Hermosa Turtle Tours takes small groups to look for nesting sea turtles on Playa Hermosa between July and December ($40), as part of a project to collect the eggs and raise them in a hatchery. Tour times vary depending on the tide; he can provide transportation from hotels in Jacó. ☎ *8817–0385.*

CANOPY TOUR
Chiclets Canopy Tour. Chiclets Canopy Tour runs four guided tours daily (7 and 9 am and 1 and 3:30 pm) that take you through the rain-forest canopy ($60). Cables strung between platforms perched high in a dozen trees have views of tropical foliage, wildlife, and the nearby coast. ⊠ *West of Costanera, ½ km/¼ mile north of Hermosa* ☎ *2643–3271* ⊕ *www.jacowave.com.*

SURFING
Most people who bed down at Playa Hermosa are here for the same reason—the waves that break just a shell's toss away. There are a half-dozen breaks scattered along the beach's northern end, and the surf is always best around high tide. Because it is a beach break, though, the waves here often close out, especially when the surf is big. If you don't have much experience, don't go out when the waves are really big—Hermosa sometimes gets very powerful swells, which result in dangerous rip currents. If you're a beginner, don't go out at all. Surf instructors in Hermosa take their students to Jacó, an easier place to learn the sport.

Waves Costa Rica. Andrea Díaz, a professional surfer with Waves Costa Rica, takes surf students to calmer Playa Jacó for two-hour lessons ($55 per person for group sessions; $80 for a private surf package). She also offers an All Girls surf-camp packages, which include room and board and yoga. ✉ *Next to the Backyard hotel* ☎ *2643–7025, 800/536–3241 in North America* 🌐 *www.wavescr.com.*

WHERE TO EAT AND STAY

For expanded hotel reviews, visit Fodors.com.

$$ ECLECTIC 🍴 **The Backyard.** Playa Hermosa's original nightlife spot, the North American–style Backyard has two seating areas, each with its own bar. Television sets on the wraparound bar in the front room show sports matches and surf videos. A wooden deck in back overlooking the beach is great for lunch and sunset, mostly because of the pleasant sea breezes and view. The usual bar food—Tex-Mex standards and burgers—is complemented by fresh seafood, including ceviche, grilled tuna, lobster, and jumbo shrimp. It's popular especially on Friday and Saturday, when there's live music. [$] *Average main: $11* ✉ *Costanera, southern end of town next to The Backyard hotel* ☎ *2643–7011* 🌐 *www.backyardhotel.com.*

$$ HOTEL 🏨 **The Backyard.** Surfers—but not the budget backpacking kind—are the main clientele at this small, cream-color hotel on the beach. **Pros:** steps from the surf; nice views from second floor; friendly. **Cons:** expensive; bar next door noisy on weekends. **TripAdvisor:** "endless beaches," "nice room," "amazing view." [$] *Rooms from: $120* ✉ *Costanera, southern end of town* ☎ *2643–7011* 🌐 *www.backyardhotel.com* 🛏 *6 rooms, 2 suites* 🍽 *Breakfast.*

$$ HOTEL 👶 🏨 **Cabinas Vista Hermosa.** Playa Hermosa's original hotel sits at the edge of a pleasant grove of coconut palms and almond trees. **Pros:** economical; lots of activities. **Cons:** very simple; hard to find. [$] *Rooms from: $78* ✉ *Costanera, 150 m south of soccer field* ☎ *2643–7022* 🌐 *www.vistahermosa.20m.com* 🛏 *10 rooms* 🍽 *Breakfast.*

PLAYA BEJUCO

27 km/16 miles south of Playa Hermosa, 32 km/19 miles south of Jacó.

Playa Bejuco. Surfers wanting to escape the crowds at Jacó and Playa Hermosa, or anyone simply seeking to stray from the beaten path, need only drive 20 minutes south to Playa Bejuco's relatively deserted palm-lined beach. One could stroll for an hour along the light gray swath of sand and hardly encounter a soul. Several vacation homes and two small hotels sit behind the first part of the beach, and behind them is a large mangrove forest where you might see macaws or white-faced monkeys. The surf is as big and consistent as at Playa Hermosa, but with a fraction of the surfers. Like Hermosa, it can develop dangerous rip currents, so swimmers should go in no deeper than their waist when the waves are big. Aside from surfing and beachcombing, there is little to do here, which makes it a good place for people wanting to do nothing at all. The mosquitoes can be quite fearsome during the rainy months.

Continued on page 399

SURFING
COSTA RICA

Costa Rica's big surfing community, consistent waves, and not-too-crowded beaches make surfing accessible to anyone who is curious enough to give it a whirl; surf schools, board rentals, and beachside lessons are plentiful. At the most popular beaches, surf tourism is a regular part of the scene. Many instructors are able to bridge generational divides, giving lessons tailored for anyone from tots to retirees. First-timers would be wise to start at a beginner beach and take some lessons.

by Leland Baxter-Neal

Costa Ricans are known for their laid-back attitude, and this usually translates into a welcoming vibe in the water. Of course, as the waves get more intense, and the surfers more serious, the unspoken rules get stricter, so beginners are advised to stay close to the shore. A good instructor should help keep you out of the way anywhere you go, and if you're on your own, just steer clear of the hot shots until you know the

COSTA RICA'S SURF FINDER

THE PACIFIC COAST

For those new to surfing, destinations on the Pacific coast are more welcoming in a number of ways. There are more beaches, hotels, bars, and surf schools than in the Caribbean, and the waves are friendlier. Access to the Northern and Central Pacific coast is also made easy by (sometimes) paved and well-marked roads. As you head southward down the coast, the route becomes untamed. The remoteness of the Osa Peninsula has guarded a couple of world-class breaks surrounded by some of the country's most untouched jungle.

WHEN TO GO: Waves are most consistent from December through April. As you move southward down the coast, the breaks are best from May to November.

THE CARIBBEAN

Costa Rica's truncated Caribbean has comparatively few beaches and they draw only the most dedicated surf seekers. The laid-back culture of that coast seems a perfect match for the surfer vibe. Among the Caribbean waves is perhaps Costa Rica's most famous: Puerto Viejo's Salsa Brava.

WHEN TO GO: Best conditions January through April.

TYPES OF BREAKS

BEACH BREAK: The best type for beginners. Waves break over sandbars and the seafloor. Jacó, Hermosa, and Sámara are all beach breaks.

POINT BREAK: Created as waves hit a point jutting into the ocean. With the right conditions, this can create very consistent waves. Pavones is a point break.

REEF BREAK: Waves break as they hit reef. It can create great (but dangerous) surf. There's a good chance of getting smashed and scraped over extremely sharp coral or rocks. Salsa Brava, in Puerto Viejo, is a reef break.

PACIFIC

❶ Tamarindo: Very popular with all levels of surfers. Beach breaks are great to learn on; nice waves are formed at a rock outcropping called Pico Pequeño and at the river mouth at the beach's north end. Neighboring Playa Grande is a big, fast beach break for advanced riders.

❷ Playa Guiones: If not the best surf in the vicinity of Nosara, it's the best for beginners and longboarders, second only to Sámara. Lots of long, fun beach breaks.

❸ Sámara: Protected, mellow beach breaks where the greatest danger is that the waves are too small. Great for beginners and close to lots of breaks for more advanced surfers.

❹ Malpaís: A variety of beach breaks plus a point break that's good when waves get big. Good for beginners and advanced surfers.

❺ Jacó: Unless the surf gets too big, the consistent beach breaks produce forgiving waves that are good to begin and advance on. The south end is best for beginners. Avoid water pollution problems and the occasional crocodile by staying clear of river mouths.

Tamarindo

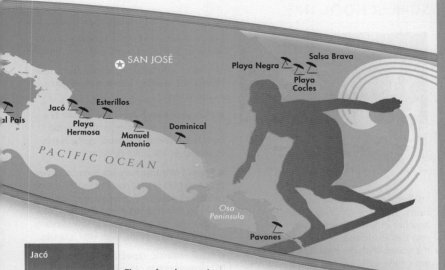

Map labels: SAN JOSÉ, Playa Negra, Salsa Brava, Playa Cocles, Esteríllos, Jacó, al País, Playa Hermosa, Manuel Antonio, Dominical, PACIFIC OCEAN, Osa Peninsula, Pavones

Jacó

6 Playa Hermosa:
A steep beach break just south of Jacó with some of the country's best waves and surfers. Waves can get big, mean, and thunderously heavy; beginners should enjoy the show from the shore. Rip currents make swimming much too dangerous.

7 Esteríllos:
Divided into three beaches, going north to south: Oeste, Centro, and Este. A beautiful stretch of coast, uncrowded to the point of desolation.

The surf and currents can be tough for beginners, and Este and Centro have waves much like Hermosa. Oeste has a variety of beach breaks with softer, friendlier waves.

8 Manuel Antonio:
Just outside the national park you'll find a variety of beach breaks. Playitas, at the park's north end, is perhaps the most consistent.

9 Dominical: At the foot of beautiful, forested coastal mountains. A long set of beach breaks that are fun and great for all levels. When waves do get big, beginners should head south to Dominicalito. Rip cur-

Manuel Antonio

rents make Dominical too dangerous for swimming.

10 Pavones: Legendary, remote, and surrounded by rain forest, Pavones is said to be the world's longest, or second-longest, left-breaking wave, with a perfect ride lasting nearly three minutes. But with fickle conditions and a tough drive to get here, it's best for the very experienced and dedicated.

CARIBBEAN

11 Playa Negra:
A largely undiscovered but quality beach break for all skill levels.

12 Salsa Brava:
When the conditions are right, this is arguably Costa Rica's best and most powerful wave; it's placed right over a shallow coral reef. For advanced surfers only.

13 Playa Cocles:
Plenty of beach breaks to pick from, good for all levels. But beware the currents or you'll drift out to sea.

SURF SCHOOL TIPS

Surf lesson

Surfing is for the young and the young of heart. At many of Costa Rica's top surf beaches, a wide range of ages and skill sets can be found bobbing together in the water. With the right board and some good instructions, just about anybody can stand up and have some fun in the waves. We strongly recommend taking a lesson or two, but be sure to take them from an actual surf school (there's one on just about every beach) rather than the eager kid who approaches you with a board. Trained instructors will be much better at adapting their lesson plans to different skill levels, ages, and body types.

If you're a first-timer, there are a few things you need to know before getting in the water.

- **Pick your beach carefully.** Sámara is a good choice, as is Jacó or Tamarindo. You want beach breaks and small, gentle waves. Make sure to ask about rip tides.

- **Expect introductory lessons to cover the basics.** You'll learn how to lie on the board, paddle out, duck the incoming waves, and how to pop up onto your surf stance. If you're a natural, you'll be able to hop up and stay standing in the white wash of the wave after it breaks.

- **Have realistic expectations.** Even if you have experience in other board sports, like snowboarding or skateboarding, don't expect to be surfing on the face of the wave or tucking into barrels on your first day.

- **Choose the right gear.** If you're a beginner, start on a longboard. Be sure to wear a T-shirt or a wet suit to help protect your chest and stomach from getting scraped.

SURF SLANG (or, how not to sound like a dork)

Barrel: The area created when a wave breaks onto itself in a curl, creating a surfable tube that's the surfer's nirvana. Also called the green room.

Drop in: To stand up and drop down the face of a wave. Also used when one surfer cuts another off: "Hey, don't drop in on that guy!"

Duck dive: A maneuver where the surfer first pushes his or her board underwater and then dives with it, ducking under waves that have already broken or are about to break. It's difficult with a longboard (see Turtle roll).

Goofy foot: Having a right-foot-forward stance on the surfboard. The opposite is known as natural.

Close out: When a wave or a section of a wave breaks all at once, rather than breaking steadily in one direction. A frustrating situation for surfers, giving them nowhere to go as the wave comes crashing down.

Ding: A hole, dent, crack, or other damage to a board.

Funboard: A little longer than a shortboard with a broad, round nose and tail. Good for beginners looking for some-

thing more maneuverable than a longboard.

Outside: The area farther out from where waves are most regularly breaking. Surfers line up here to catch waves.

Shortboard: Usually 6 to 7 feet long with a pointed nose. A tough board to learn on.

Stick: A surfboard.

Turtle roll: A maneuver where the surfer rolls over on the surfboard, going underwater and holding the board upside down. Used by longboarders and beginners to keep from being swept back toward shore by breaking waves.

GETTING HERE

If you have a car, take the coastal highway 27 km (16 miles) south past Playa Hermosa to the turnoff for Playa Bejuco, which is 1 km (½ mile) west of the highway. If you don't, take a taxi from Jacó, or local bus toward Quepos.

OUTDOOR ACTIVITIES

SURFING

There are various high-tide beach breaks scattered along Playa Bejuco. Waves tend to close out here when the swell is big, but then you can try the mouth of the estuary, 1 km (½ mile) south of the hotels. Bejuco is a do-it-yourself beach, with neither surf schools nor board rental nearby, and because the waves break so close to shore, it's not a good spot for beginners.

WHERE TO STAY

For expanded hotel reviews, visit Fodors.com.

$$ HOTEL **Delfín Beach Front Resort.** Every room in this tastefully decorated two-story hotel has an ocean view, and the surf breaks right in front of it. **Pros:** beachfront; clean rooms. **Cons:** limited selection at restaurant; so-so management. **TripAdvisor:** "beautiful beachfront hotel," "a secluded quiet alternative," "quiet and relaxing." [$] *Rooms from: $110* ✉ *On beach, Playa Bejuco* ☎ *2779–4245* 🌐 *www.delfinbeachfront.com* 🛏 *14 rooms* 🍴 *Breakfast.*

$$ HOTEL 👍 **Hotel Playa Bejuco.** In exchange for being 50 meters away from the beach, you get spacious, well equipped rooms with views of the pool and gardens rather than surf and sand. **Pros:** big pool; decent restaurant. **Cons:** lacks ocean view. **TripAdvisor:** "comfortable and relaxing," "extremely accommodating staff," "beautiful hotel with excellent service." [$] *Rooms from: $106* ✉ *Road to Playa Bejuco, on left* ☎ *2779–2000* 🌐 *www.hotelplayabejuco.com* 🛏 *20 rooms* 🍴 *Breakfast.*

7

QUEPOS

23 km/14 miles south of Parrita, 174 km/108 miles southwest of San José.

This hot and dusty town serves as a gateway to Manuel Antonio, and also serves as the area's hub for banks, supermarkets, and other services. Because nearby Manuel Antonio is so much more attractive, there is little reason to stay here, but many people stop for dinner, for a night on the town, or to go sportfishing. Quepos's name stems from the indigenous tribe that inhabited the area until the Spanish conquest wiped them out. For centuries the town of Quepos barely existed, until the 1930s, when the United Fruit Company built a banana port and populated the area with workers from other parts of Central America. The town thrived for nearly two decades, until Panama Disease decimated the banana plantations in the late 1940s. The fruit company then switched to less lucrative African oil palms, and the area declined. Only since the 1980s have tourism revenues lifted the town out of its slump, a renaissance owed to the beauty of the nearby beaches and nature reserves. Forests around Quepos were destroyed nearly a century ago, but the massive Talamanca Mountain Range, some 10 km (6 miles) to the east, holds one of the largest expanses of wilderness in Central America.

GETTING HERE

It's an under-three-hour drive from San José to Quepos; follow the directions for Jacó and continue south another 40 minutes. Buses from San José's Tracopa bus station (Avda. 5 and C. 14/16) drop you off in downtown Quepos. SANSA and Nature Air run multiple flights per day, 20 minutes one way, between San José and Quepos (XQP), as well as direct flights between Quepos and Palmar Sur in the Southern Pacific and La Fortuna in the Northern Plains.

ESSENTIALS

Bank/ATM BAC San José ✉ *Avda. Central.* **Banco Nacional** ✉ *50 m west and 100 m north of bus station* ☎ *2777–0113.*

Hospital Ambulance ☎ *911.* **Hospital de Quepos** ✉ *4 km/2½ miles on road to Dominical* ☎ *2777–0020.*

Pharmacy Farmacia Fischel ✉ *Near bus station, in front of municipal market* ☎ *2777–0816.*

Post Office Correos ✉ *C. Central.*

Rental Cars Alamo ✉ *Downtown, 50 m south of Korean school* ☎ *2777–3344, 800/462–5266 in U.S.*

Taxis Taxi services ☎ *2777–0425, 2777–1693, 2777–1068.*

Tourist Information **Instituto Costarricense de Turismo** ✉ *25 m east of docks* ☎ *2777–4217* ⊕ *www.visitcostarica.com* ⊗ *Weekdays 8–noon and 1–4.*

Travel Agency Lynch Travel ✉ *Downtown, behind bus terminal* ☎ *2777–1170* ⊕ *www.lynchtravel.com.*

EXPLORING

Rainmaker. Spread over Fila Chota, a lower ridge of the Talamanca Range 22 km (13 miles) northeast of Quepos, Rainmaker is a private nature reserve that protects more than 1,500 acres of lush and precipitous forest. The lower part of the reserve can be visited on guided tours from Manuel Antonio, or as a stop on your way to or from Quepos. The best value is a half-day package ($70) that includes transport from Manuel Antonio or Quepos, a guided tour, a river swim, and breakfast and lunch. If you get here on your own, the guided river-walk and canopy-bridge tour runs $35. The park also offers an early-morning bird-watching tour ($90) and a night reptiles and amphibians hike ($60). The reserve is home to many of Costa Rica's endangered species, and you may spot birds here that you won't find in Manuel Antonio. It isn't as good a place to see animals as the national park, but Rainmaker's forest is different from the park's—lusher and more precipitous—and the view from its bridges is impressive. It's best to visit Rainmaker in the morning, since—true to its name—it often pours in the afternoon. ✉ *22 km/13 miles northeast of Quepos* ☎ *2777–3565, 540/349–9848 in North America* ⊕ *www.rainmakercostarica.org* 🖃 *$35–$90 for guided tours* ⊗ *Mon.–Sat. 7:30–4.*

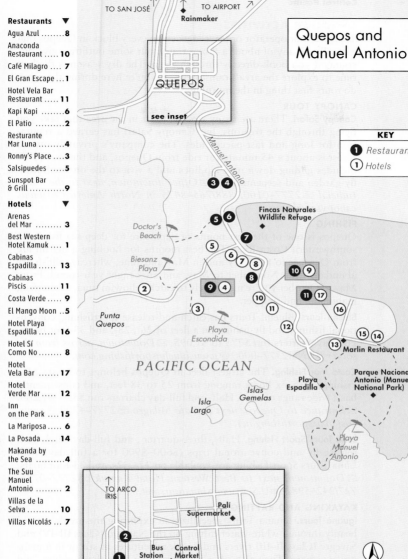

Quepos and Manuel Antonio

Restaurants ▼

Agua Azul **8**
Anaconda Restaurant **10**
Café Milagro **7**
El Gran Escape ...**1**
Hotel Vela Bar Restaurant **11**
Kapi Kapi **6**
El Patio **2**
Resturante Mar Luna **4**
Ronny's Place **3**
Salsipuedes **5**
Sunspot Bar & Grill **9**

Hotels ▼

Arenas del Mar **3**
Best Western Hotel Kamuk **1**
Cabinas Espadilla **13**
Cabinas Piscis **11**
Costa Verde **9**
El Mango Moon ..**5**
Hotel Playa Espadilla **16**
Hotel Sí Como No **8**
Hotel Vela Bar **17**
Hotel Verde Mar **12**
Inn on the Park **15**
La Mariposa **6**
La Posada **14**
Makanda by the Sea **4**
The Suu Manuel Antonio **2**
Villas de la Selva **10**
Villas Nicolás ...**7**

TO SAN JOSÉ TO AIRPORT
Rainmaker

QUEPOS
see inset

Manuel Antonio

KEY
❶ Restaurants
① Hotels

Fincas Naturales Wildlife Refuge

Doctor's Beach

Biesanz Playa

Punta Quepos

Playa Escondida

PACIFIC OCEAN

Islas Gemelas

Isla Largo

Playa Espadilla

Marlin Restaurant

Parque Nacional Manuel Antonio (Manuel Antonio National Park)

Playa Manuel Antonio

TO ARCO IRIS

Palí Supermarket

Bus Station
Control Market

Post Office

Super Mas Market
Soccer Field

Nature Air Office

Dos Locos Restaurante

SANSA Office

OUTDOOR ACTIVITIES

There's a tour operator or travel agency on every block in Quepos that can sell you any of about a dozen tours, but some outfitters give discounts if you book directly through them. The dry season is the best time to explore the area's rain forests. If you're here during the rains, do tours first thing in the morning.

CANOPY TOUR

Canopy Safari. There are many zip-line tours in the area that take you flying through the treetops, but Canopy Safari has earned a reputation for long and fast-paced rides. The company's privately owned forest is about a 45-minute car ride from Quepos, and the tour ($75) includes gliding down nine zip lines and a visit to the on-site butterfly garden and serpentarium. ⊠ *Office downtown, next to the Poder Judicial* ☎ *2777–0100, 888/765–8475 in North America* ⊕ *www. canopysafari.com.*

FISHING

Quepos is one of the best points of departure for deep-sea fishing in southwestern Costa Rica. The best months for hooking a marlin are from October to February and in May and June, whereas sailfish are abundant from November to May, and are caught year-round. From May to October you're more likely to catch yellowfin tuna, roosterfish, mahimahi, and snapper.

Bluefin Tours. Bluefin Tours has catch-and-release sportfishing, conventional fishing, and fly-fishing on a fleet of 26-, 28-, and 33-foot boats. Full-day charters run $775 to $1,095. ⊠ *Downtown, across from the soccer field* ☎ *2777–0000* ⊕ *www.bluefinsportfishing.com.*

Costa Mar Fishing. The largest fleet in Quepos belongs to Costa Mar Fishing, with six boats ranging from 25 to 38 feet, and consequently has a wide range of rates. Half- and full-day charters run $550–$1,200. ⊠ *Entrance to Quepos, next to Café Milagro* ☎ *2777–4700* ⊕ *www. costamarsportfishing.net.*

Luna Tours Sport Fishing. Half-, three-quarter-, and full-day catch-and-release fly and conventional trips ($600–$900 for a full day) with Luna Tours Sport Fishing are available on 27-, 32-, and 33-foot boats. ⊠ *Downtown, next to Best Western Hotel Kamuk* ☎ *2777–0725, 727/242–5982 in U.S.* ⊕ *www.lunatours.net.*

KAYAKING AND RAFTING

Iguana Tours. Iguana Tours specializes in exploring the area's natural beauty through white-water rafting on the Naranjo (Class III–IV) and Savegre (Class II–III) rivers and kayak adventures at sea or in a mangrove estuary. They also offer bird-watching, horseback riding, and canopy tours. ⊠ *Downtown Quepos, across from soccer field* ☎ *2777–2052* ⊕ *www.iguanatours.com.*

MOUNTAIN BIKING

The area's green mountains are great for biking, but in the dry season it's very, very hot. The rainy season is slightly cooler, but be prepared to get muddy.

"I was in complete awe as my fantastic local Quepos guide led me along a delightful path up in the hills outside of Quepos." —Photo by Colleen George, Fodors.com member

Estrella Tour. Estrella Tour has an array of bike tours for intermediate and expert riders ranging from a couple of hours to a full day ($45 to $95). They also offer two- and three-day trips ($140 to $310) that include meals and lodging in mountain cabins. ✉ *Downtown, across the street from Restaurante El Pueblo* ☎ *2777–1286.*

WHERE TO EAT

$$ SEAFOOD ★ 🍴 **El Gran Escape.** A favorite with sportfishermen ("You hook 'em, we cook 'em"), the Great Escape is the town's best place for seafood. The menu is dominated by seafood entrées, from shrimp scampi to fresh tuna with mushrooms to bouillabaisse and paella. You can also get hearty burgers, or a handful of Mexican dishes, and there's a kids' menu. You won't find any billfish, like marlin or swordfish, on the menu, owing to their conservation policy, but the back wall is covered with pictures of them (and their proud reelers). Weathered fishing caps hang from the bar's ceiling. [$] *Average main: $14* ✉ *150 m north of Best Western Hotel Kamuk* ☎ *2777–0395* 🌐 *www.elgranescape.net* ⏲ *Closed Tues.*

$$ LATIN AMERICAN ★ 🍴 **El Patio.** It would be easy to miss this small restaurant squeezed between a couple of shops south of the bridge into town, but don't. The nouveau Latin American cuisine includes some delectable innovations on traditional Central American and Caribbean flavors. Start with some chicken tamales, ceviche, or a mango and *chayote* (green squash) salad, then sink your teeth into a slice of pork loin in a *creole mojo* (spicy tomato sauce), shrimp in a rum coconut sauce, or mahimahi cooked in a banana leaf with a smoked tomato mojo and a squash puree. The lunch menu has a good selection of salads, sandwiches, and wraps. The

nicest tables are in back, around a lush garden and fountain. *$ Average main: $14 ✉ 250 m north of Best Western Hotel Kamuk ☎ 2777–4982.*

$ HOTEL **Best Western Hotel Kamuk.** On Quepos's oceanfront street, this local Best Western affiliate offers the town's priciest accommodations with all the perks of a chain hotel. **Pros:** reassurance of chain name; terrific value; good service. **Cons:** sameness of chain hotel; far from beach. **TripAdvisor:** "it's not fancy but it works," "clean and affordable," "average Best Western." *$ Rooms from: $75 ✉ Downtown, 100 m after last bridge into Quepos ☎ 2777–0811, 800/780–7234 in North America 🌐 www.bestwestern.com 44 rooms No meals.*

NIGHTLIFE

Dos Locos Restaurante. Older American expats often congregate at Tex-Mex Dos Locos Restaurante day and night to people-watch or, on Wednesday and Friday nights, to listen to live music. *✉ Avda. Central at C. Central, near bus station ☎ 2777–1526 ⏲ Mon.–Sat. 7 am–11 pm, Sun. 11–7.*

MANUEL ANTONIO

Fodor's Choice ★

3 km/2 miles south of Quepos, 179 km/111 miles southwest of San José.

You need merely reach the top of the forested ridge on which many of Manuel Antonio's hotels are perched to understand why it is one of Costa Rica's most popular destinations. That sweeping view of beaches, jungle, and shimmering Pacific dotted with rocky islets confirms its reputation. And unlike the tropical forests in other parts of the country, Manuel Antonio's humid tropical forest remains green year-round. The town itself is spread out across a hilly and curving 5-km (3-mile) road that originates in Quepos and dead-ends at the entrance to Manuel Antonio National Park. Along this main road, near the top of the hill or on its southern slope, are the area's most luxurious hotels and fine-dining restaurants, surrounded by rain forest with amazing views of the beaches and offshore islands. The only problem with staying in one of those hotels is that you'll need to drive or take public transportation to and from the main beach and national park, about 10 minutes away. More hotel and restaurant options are available at the bottom of the hill, within walking distance of the beach, but they lack the sweeping view.

Manuel Antonio is a gay-friendly town. Many hotels and bars cater to gay travelers, and all of them offer a warm welcome to anyone walking in the door. The area doesn't especially cater to budget travelers, but there are a few cheap places near the end of the road, and various midrange lodging options.

GETTING HERE

Manuel Antonio is a 15-minute drive over the hill from Quepos and 25 minutes from the Quepos airport. Between SANSA and NatureAir, there are eight flights per day linking San José and Quepos (XQP)—flying time is 20 minutes—as well as direct flights between Quepos and La Fortuna in the Northern Plains and Palmar Sur in the Southern Pacific. Buses depart from San José's Tracopa bus station (Avda. 5, C. 14/16) for Manuel Antonio three times a day, at 6 am, noon, and 6 and 7:30

pm, traveling the opposite direction at 6 and 9:30 am, noon, and 5 pm; they pick up and drop off passengers in front of hotels on the main Quepos–Manuel Antonio road. Shuttle services Gray Line and Interbus offer hotel-to-hotel service to and from San José, Jacó, Monteverde, Arenal, and major North Pacific beaches. The trip from San José takes about 2½ hours by car or 3½ *hours by* bus. A local public bus makes the 20-minute trip from Quepos to Manuel Antonio every half hour from 7 to 7, then hourly until 10 pm.

ESSENTIALS

Bank/ATM Banco Promérica ⊠ *Main road, next to Economy Rent a Car.*

Internet Cantina Internet ⊠ *Main road, across from Costa Verde* ☎ *2777–0548.*

Pharmacy Farmacia La Económica ⊠ *Main road, across from soccer field* ☎ *2777–2130.* **Farmacia Manuel Antonio** ⊠ *Main road, across from Marlin Restaurant* ☎ *2777–5370.*

Rental Cars Economy ⊠ *Next to Banca Proamérica* ☎ *2777–5353.*

Taxis Taxi services ☎ *2777–0425, 2777–0734, 2777–1693.*

EXPLORING

Fincas Naturales Wildlife Refuge. Fincas Naturales Wildlife Refuge, a former teak plantation, has been reforested to allow native trees to spring back among the not-so-native ones. A footpath winds through part of the 30-acre tropical forest, and naturalist guides do a good job of explaining the local ecology and identifying birds. The reserve is home to three kinds of monkeys, as well as iguanas, motmots, toucans, tanagers, and seed-chomping rodents called agoutis. Guided walks are given throughout the day: the first starts at 6:30 am for bird-watching, then at 9 am and 1 pm, plus a nighttime jungle trek that departs at 5:30 pm. The quickest and least expensive tour is an hourly walk through displays on butterflies, reptiles, and amphibians. Unfortunately, you can't explore the reserve at your own pace. ⊠ *Entrance across from Sí Como No Hotel* ☎ *2777–0850* ⊕ *www.wildliferefugecr.com* ⬚ *$15–$45, depending on tour* ☉ *Daily 8–4.*

Parque Nacional Manuel Antonio (Manuel Antonio National Park). Parque

Fodor's Choice
★

Nacional Manuel Antonio (Manuel Antonio National Park) proves that good things come in small packages. Costa Rica's smallest park packs in an impressive collection of natural attractions: lots of wildlife, rain forest, white-sand beaches, and rocky coves with abundant marine life. Trails are short, well maintained, and easy to walk. The forest is dominated by massive ficus and gumbo-limbo trees, and is home to two- and three-toed sloths, green and black iguanas, agoutis, four species of monkeys, and more than 350 species of birds.

Despite being Costa Rica's smallest national park, this is its second most visited, after Volcán Poás. Why? Maybe because it is one of two places in Costa Rica to see adorable squirrel monkeys. It's also one of the best places in Costa Rica to see white-faced capuchin monkeys and three-toed sloths. Make no mistake about it: Manuel Antonio is no undiscovered wilderness. It's one of Costa Rica's most-visited attractions, so if you're looking for an undisturbed natural oasis, this is not it. But what Manuel Antonio does have is great diversity of wildlife, all easily spotted from the well-marked trails. And because animals are so used to humans, this is one of the best places to see them up close.

From the ranger station a trail leads through the rain forest behind Playa Espadilla Sur, the park's longest beach. It's also the least crowded because the water can be rough. The coral reefs and submerged volcanic rocks of white-sand Playa Manuel Antonio make for good snorkeling. The 1-km-long (½-mile-long) beach, tucked into a deep cove, is safe for swimming. At low tide you can see the remains of a Quepos Indian turtle trap on the right—the Quepos stuck poles in the semicircular rock formation, which trapped turtles as the tide receded. Olive ridley and green turtles come ashore on this beach May through November. Espadilla and Manuel Antonio beaches lie on opposite sides of a tombolo, or a sandy strip that connects the mainland to Punta Catedral (Cathedral Point), which used to be an island. The steep path that leads up Punta Catedral's rocky hill draped with thick jungle passes a lookout point from which you can gaze over the Pacific at the park's islands.

Farther east, Playa Escondido (Hidden Beach) is rocky and secluded, but it's also more difficult to access. Before you head out to Escondido, find out when the tides come in so you're not stranded. It's quiet and secluded. Kayaking trips might take you down to Punta Serrucho near the southern border of the park, whose jagged peaks explain its name. (*Serrucho* means "saw.")

A few tips: Hire a guide—you'll walk away with a better understanding of the flora and fauna and see things you probably would have missed otherwise. Get here as early as possible—between 7 and 8 am is ideal. Rangers permit only 800 people inside at a time, and during peak season visitors line up to enter. Early morning is also the best time to see animals (and it's cooler, too.) Beware of manzanillo trees (indicated by warning signs)—their leaves, bark, and applelike fruit secrete a gooey substance that irritates the skin. ⊠ *Manuel Antonio* ☎ 2777–5185 ⫷ $10 ⊗ *Tues.–Sun. 7–4.*

DID YOU KNOW?

More than 100 species of mammals and nearly 200 species of birds call Manuel Antonio home. Superstars include squirrel monkeys, white-nosed coatimundis, snakes, bats, iguanas, dolphins, woodpeckers, motmots, mantled howler monkeys, and sloths.

Playa Espadilla. As the road approaches the national park, it skirts the lovely, forest-lined beach of Playa Espadilla, which stretches for more than 2 km (1 mile) north from the rocky crag that marks the park's border to the base of the ridge that holds most of the hotels. One of the most popular beaches in Costa Rica, Playa Espadilla fills up with sunbathers, surfers, volleyball players, strand strollers, and sand-castle architects on dry-season weekends and holidays, but for most of the year it is surprisingly quiet. Even on the busiest days it is long enough to provide an escape from the crowd, which tends to gather around the restaurants and lounge chairs near its southern end. Though it is often safe for swimming, beware of rough seas, which create deadly rip currents.

OUTDOOR ACTIVITIES

Manuel Antonio's list of outdoor activities is almost endless. Tours generally range from $40 to $100 per person and can be booked through your hotel's reception desk or directly through the outfitter. During the rainy season, some outdoor options might lose their appeal, but clouds usually let loose in the afternoon, so take advantage of sunny mornings. Most nature-themed activities go on rain or shine.

IN THE THICK OF IT

There's more rain forest on private land than in Manuel Antonio National Park, which means it's not unusual to see many of the animals the park is famous for from the balcony of your hotel room or from your breakfast table. It also means that local landowners play an important role in conserving the area's flora and fauna.

Manuel Antonio Tours. A small company run by friendly young locals with a good grasp of the area's activities, Manuel Antonio Tours can arrange any kind of activity in the area, from surf lessons to sunset sails. ⊠ *Next to Musmanni bakery* ☎ *2777–5334.*

CANOPY TOURS

★ **Tití Canopy Tour.** You'll find a relatively slow-paced zip-line tour ($60) here, a rarity in Costa Rica, through a forest reserve that is contiguous with the national park. A night tour runs $70. Guides go above and beyond to make you feel comfortable and safe and will help you spot animals. ☎ *2777–3130* ⊕ *www.titicanopytour.com.*

HIKING

Highly visited Manuel Antonio National Park is the obvious place to go, but in private reserves like Fincas Naturales *(⇨ above)* and Rainmaker *(⇨ Quepos, above)* you can also gain a rich appreciation of the local forests' greenery and wildlife. ■TIP➡ Bring binoculars!

HORSEBACK RIDING

Brisas del Nara. Brisas del Nara takes riders of all ages and levels through the protected Cerro Nara mountain zone, 32 km (20 miles) from Manuel Antonio, and ends with a swim in a natural pool at the foot of a 107-meter (350-foot) waterfall. Full-day tours ($65) include three hours on horseback, with breakfast and lunch included; the ride on the half-day tour ($50) lasts two hours, and there's no lunch. ☎ *2779–1235* ⊕ *www.horsebacktour.com.*

Finca Valmy Tours. Finca Valmy Tours is known for its attentive service and healthy horses. Its six-hour horseback tours take you through the forested mountains above Villa Nueva, east of Manuel Antonio ($65). Lunch and swimming in a pool below a small waterfall on their property are included. ☎ *2779–1118* ⊕ *www.valmytours.com.*

Rancho Savegre. Beach riding is the specialty of Rancho Savegre. Trips set out from a cattle ranch about 15 minutes south of Manuel Antonio and include a stop at a waterfall for swimming or trail walking. The morning tour (7:30) kicks off with breakfast; the afternoon tour (1:30) finishes up with dinner. ☎ *2779–4430, 8834–8687* ⊕ *www. costaricahorsevacation.com.*

7

KAYAKING

Iguana Tours. Iguana Tours runs half-day sea-kayaking trips ($65) to the islands of Manuel Antonio National Park—which require some experience when the seas are high—and a mellower paddle through the mangrove estuary of Isla Damas ($65), where you might see monkeys, crocodiles, and various birds. ☎ 2777–2052 ⊕ *www. iguanatours.com.*

SNORKELING AND DIVING

The islands that dot the sea in front of Manuel Antonio are surrounded by volcanic rock reefs with small coral formations and attract schools of snapper, jacks, barracudas, rays, sea turtles, moray eels, and other marine life.

Oceans Unlimited. Oceans Unlimited offers various offshore sites, an all-day diving excursion to Caño Island ($189), PADI certification courses, and snorkeling. Several tour operators in town can put you on an organized snorkel excursion to the calm waters of Biesanz Beach. ☎ 2777–3171 ⊕ *www.oceansunlimitedcr.com.*

SWIMMING

When the surf is up, riptides are a dangerous problem on Playa Espadilla, Manuel Antonio's main beach, which runs parallel to the road to the park's entrance.

Playa Biesanz. For a less-turbulent swim and smaller crowds, head to Playa Biesanz, which lies within a sheltered cove and also has good snorkeling. ✉ *Near Hotel Parador.*

Playa Manuel Antonio. Manuel Antonio's safest swimming area is sheltered Playa Manuel Antonio, the second beach in the national park. Its white sand makes it attractive for lounging around, and it's also a good place for snorkeling.

■ TIP→ Never leave your valuables unattended while you're swimming.

WHITE-WATER RAFTING

The three white-water rivers in this area have limited seasons. The rains from August to October raise the rivers to their perfect peak.

Adventure Manuel Antonio. Manuel Antonio's original rafting outfitter, Adventure Manuel Antonio, leads half-day trips down the Naranjo river ($69) and full-day tours down the Savegre river ($98). Naranjo tours can be combined with kayaking in the nearby estuary. ☎ 2777–1084 ⊕ *www.adventuremanuelantonio.com.*

H2O Adventures. This is the Manuel Antonio franchise for Ríos Tropicales, the biggest rafting outfitter in the country, and runs kayaking excursions and rafting trips on the Naranjo river ($80). ☎ 2777–4092, 888/532–3298 *in U.S.* ⊕ *www.h2ocr.com.*

Río Naranjo. Río Naranjo (Class III to IV) has a short but exciting run that requires some experience and can be done only from April to December.

Río Parrita. Río Parrita (Class II to III) is a relatively mellow white-water route, and in the dry season it can be navigated only in two-person, inflatable duckies.

Río Savegre. Río Savegre, which flows past patches of rain forest, has two navigable stretches: the lower section (Class II to III), which is a mellow trip perfect for neophytes, and the more rambunctious upper section (Class III to IV). It is usually navigable all year long.

WHERE TO EAT

$$ SEAFOOD ★ 🍴 **Agua Azul.** This simple second-floor restaurant with a small kitchen in one corner offers a breathtaking view by day and a deliciously inventive selection of seafood at night. The lunch menu is strong on salads and sandwiches, but the dinner options include some of the best entrées in town. In addition to nightly fish and pasta specials, they offer such inventive delicacies as seared tuna over a tequila-and-lime cucumber salad, calamari sautéed with capers and olives, and coconut-crusted mahimahi. [$] *Average main: $13* ✉ *Main road, above the Villas del Parque office* ☎ *2777–5280* ⏲ *Closed Wed. and Oct.*

$$ ECLECTIC 🍴 **Anaconda Restaurant.** Named for the humongous snake whose skin is mounted on the wall behind the bar, this open-air restaurant is hidden in the rain forest. You won't see any anacondas (they are found in South America), but you may spot iguanas, squirrel monkeys, or various species of birds from one of the restaurant's oversize chairs. You are sure to enjoy the view of the coast. The eclectic menu ranges from Japanese-style tuna to Tuscan mahimahi. They also serve excellent pastas and salads. The restaurant is a short drive from the beach, making it an excellent option for a quiet lunch. [$] *Average main: $13* ✉ *Costa Verde Hotel* ☎ *2777–1973.*

$ CAFÉ 🍴 **Café Milagro.** The only place in town that serves its own fresh-roasted coffee, Café Milagro is a colorful, cozy choice for breakfast food any time of the day, or to satisfy a chocolate-chip-cookie craving. The North American menu includes bagels, breakfast burritos, baked goods like brownies and muffins, an inventive selection of sandwiches, and a fruit plate with granola. Tables on the front porch overlook the road, but there's also seating in the back garden. [$] *Average main: $8* ✉ *Main road to park, across from La Mariposa* ☎ *2777–0794* 🌐 *www.cafemilagro.com.*

$$ ECLECTIC 🍴 **Hotel Vela Bar Restaurant.** This small, open-air restaurant retains an intimate atmosphere behind a hedge of tropical foliage and beneath a conical thatch roof. They serve a variety of dishes in generous proportions, including mahimahi with an array of sauces, shrimp with ginger, and pork chops in pineapple sauce. There are vegetarian options as well. Service can be slow when it gets busy. [$] *Average main: $13* ✉ *Up road from Marlin Restaurant* ☎ *2777–0413* 🌐 *www.vealbar.com.*

$$$ ECLECTIC ★ 🍴 **Kapi Kapi.** This elegant restaurant at the edge of the forest offers Manuel Antonio's best ambience for dinner, with low lighting, ocher walls, dark hardwoods, and potted palms. The name is a greeting in the indigenous Maleku language, but the menu is the cosmopolitan invention of a Californian chef. It includes such un–Costa Rican starters as a lemongrass, chicken, and coconut soup, and "seafood cigars"—a mix of fresh tuna, shrimp, and mahimahi deep-fried in an egg-roll wrapper and served on a cabbage salad. The main courses include such Asian-inspired dishes as prawns with a tamarindo-coconut-rum glaze and macadamia-encrusted mahimahi with a plum chili sauce. Only in dessert does the chef reveal his nationality, with the chocolate s'more

7

Espadilla Beach, not far from Quepos, is one of the few beaches in Costa Rica with lifeguards.

cake. [$] *Average main: $24* ✉ *East side of main road, across from Pacífico Colonial condos* ☎ *2777–5049* 🌐 *www.restaurantekapikapi.com* ✍ *Reservations essential* 🕘 *No lunch.*

$$$ SEAFOOD 🍴 **Restaurante Mar Luna.** Easy to overlook, this simple blue wooden restaurant propped on the hillside is often packed. The decor is limited to illuminated plastic fish, ceramic mobiles, potted palms, and colorful tablecloths, but the restaurant has a pleasant view of treetops and the sea below. The fresh seafood, caught each morning by one of the cooks, is what draws the crowd. You might start with sashimi or seafood soup, and move on to one of the popular entrées: grilled tuna with peppers and onions, lobster in a brandy sauce, the humongous *mariscada*—a sautéed seafood platter for two—or one of the surf-and-turf options. They have live Latin music Thursday to Saturday, and a small bamboo bar in front. [$] *Average main: $23* ✉ *East side of road, 100 m north of Manuel Antonio Elementary School* ☎ *2777–5107* 🕘 *No lunch.*

$$ COSTA RICAN 🍴 **Ronny's Place.** A spectacular sunset view and friendly, attentive service are this simple, open-air restaurant's best qualities. The small menu includes such typical Tico dishes as *sopa negra* (black-bean soup), ceviche, shrimp and fish on a skewer, and filet mignon wrapped with bacon and topped with a mushroom sauce. Ronny's is somewhat secluded down a long dirt road that crosses a green valley on a narrow ridge in front of the sea. [$] *Average main: $12* ✉ *1 km/½ mile west of main road, down dirt road across from Amigos del Río* ☎ *2777–5120* 🌐 *www.ronnysplace.com.*

$ ECLECTIC 🍴 **Salsipuedes.** This colorful, friendly tapas bar nestled behind a rock formation at the edge of the forest has one of the best sunset views in town, making it a great cocktail and appetizer option. The tapas are fun to share, three to five per couple, depending on how hungry you are. They range from sashimi and grilled tuna or mahimahi to fajitas. Such Costa Rican favorites as *frijolitos blancos* (white beans stewed with chicken) and *chicharrones con yuca* (fried pork and cassava root) are also available. They offer half a dozen full dinners, including larger cuts of fish, and some rice and pasta dishes, plus they're willing to turn any of the tapas dishes into a full meal. At the other end of the day, this is one of the few restaurants around here that serve breakfasts, and you can expect hearty offerings to get you throught the morning. $ *Average main: $8* ✉ *Main road, across from Banco Proamérica* ☎ *2777–5019* ☽ *Closed Tues.*

$$$
ECLECTIC
★

✕ **Sunspot Bar and Grill.** The open-air, poolside restaurant of the exclusive Makanda by the Sea hotel has tables beneath purple cloth tents overlooking the sea and surrounding jungle. Its kitchen, cleverly hidden beneath the bar, serves up such succulent treats as jumbo shrimp in a ginger sauce and grilled beef tenderloin with a choice of sauces. The menu also includes poultry, lamb, and pasta dishes, along with nightly specials. At lunch they offer great pizzas, salads, and sandwiches. You'll want to put on insect repellent at night. $ *Average main: $23* ✉ *Makanda by the Sea hotel, 1 km/½ mile west of La Mariposa* ☎ *2777–0442* ⊕ *www.makanda.com* ⌦ *Reservations essential* ☽ *Closed Mon. May–Nov.*

WHERE TO STAY

For expanded hotel reviews, visit Fodors.com.

$$$$
RESORT
Fodor's Choice
★

▦ **Arenas del Mar Beach and Nature Resort.** What you don't see is what you get at this new eco-luxury hotel: no cars, no crowds, no clutter, but what you do get are the hotel's seven sage-and-beige modern buildings camouflaged on reforested hillsides sloping down to two pristine, almost deserted beaches (although you can hardly see them). **Pros:** best of both worlds: luxury and eco-consciousness; best beach access in Manuel Antonio; wonderful bird-watching and wildlife viewing. **Cons:** very steep paths and stairs, although electric carts constantly transport guests. **TripAdvisor:** "first-class hotel and staff," "comfort in the rainforest," "relaxing." $ *Rooms from: $330* ✉ *Far west end of Playa Espadilla, down El Parador road, in Manuel Antonio* ☎ *2777–2777* ⊕ *www.arenasdelmar.com* ⌦ *38 rooms* ⌦ *No smoking* ⦿ *Multiple meal plans.*

$$
HOTEL
☺

▦ **Cabinas Espadilla.** Owned by the same family that runs the nearby Hotel Playa Espadilla, these quiet cabinas close to the beach are more affordable but have fewer amenities. **Pros:** good value; short walk from beach and national park; nice grounds. **Cons:** mediocre rooms. **TripAdvisor:** "great customer service," "terrific pool," "cute." $ *Rooms from: $100* ✉ *On road beside Marlin Restaurant* ☎ *2777–2113* ⊕ *www.espadilla.com* ⌦ *16 cabinas* ⦿ *No meals.*

$
HOTEL

▦ **Cabinas Piscis.** A short walk through the woods from the beach, this tranquil hotel shaded by tall trees is one of the area's best options for budget travelers. **Pros:** forested property on the beach; inexpensive. **Cons:** spartan rooms; soft beds; no email or web to contact. **TripAdvisor:** "nice cabin," "simple but pleasant," "good location." $ *Rooms from: $52* ✉ *Road to park, past Hotel Karahe* ☎ *2777–0046* ⌦ *9 rooms, 1 casita, 1 cabin* ⦿ *No meals.*

7

The Pacific Coast is backed by mangrove, rain, transitional, and tropical dry forests.

$$ RESORT ★ 🏨 **Costa Verde.** You're likely to see monkeys, iguanas, and all kinds of birds on the forest trails surrounding this extensive hotel's buildings, which are scattered on both sides of the main road. **Pros:** great ocean views; wildlife; restaurants; studios and Building D efficiencies a good value. **Cons:** most efficiencies suffer road noise; no beach access; service inconsistent. **TripAdvisor:** "exquisite views," "still magical," "sloth central." [$] *Rooms from: $115* ✉ *Road to park, south side of hill, on left* ☎ *2777–0584, 866/854–7958 in North America* 🌐 *www.costaverde.com* 🛏 *29 rooms* 🍴 *No meals.*

$$ B&B/INN 🏨 **El Mango Moon.** This bed-and-breakfast's intimate atmosphere and hospitable staff make you feel as if you're staying with a friend rather than at a hotel. **Pros:** nice view; tranquil area; friendly. **Cons:** far from main beaches; not much privacy; some rooms dark; relatively expensive. **TripAdvisor:** "a very special place," "fun staff," "great service." [$] *Rooms from: $150* ✉ *Between La Mariposa and Makanda* ☎ *2777–5323* 🌐 *www.mangomoon.net* 🛏 *10 rooms* 🚭 *No smoking* 🍴 *Breakfast.*

$$$ HOTEL 👶 🏨 **Hotel Playa Espadilla.** A short walk from the beach, this friendly hotel spreads across grounds bordered on two sides by the tall trees of Manuel Antonio National Park, and it has a trail through an area of the park that few people visit. **Pros:** surrounded by forest; close to beach and park. **Cons:** service inconsistent; very small pool. **TripAdvisor:** "very close to the beach," "fantastic restaurant," "comfortable." [$] *Rooms from: $160* ✉ *150 m up side road from Marlin Restaurant, 1st left* ☎ *2777–0903* 🌐 *www.espadilla.com* 🛏 *16 rooms* 🍴 *Breakfast.*

$$$ RESORT 👶 🏨 **Hotel Sí Como No.** This luxury resort, one of Costa Rica's most famous, goes to great lengths to be eco-friendly, and is also quite family-friendly, with a separate kids' pool, complete with waterslide, and an in-house

cinema. **Pros:** friendly; nice views; environmentally sustainab` restaurants. **Cons:** 3 km (2 miles) from beach; standards overpriced few suites too close to road. **TripAdvisor:** "perfect place," "great views of the ocean," "beautiful facility." $ *Rooms from: $230* ✉ *Road to park, just after Villas Nicolás, right-hand side* ☎ *2777–0777, 888/742–6667 in North America* ⊕ *www.sicomono.com* ⮌ *38 rooms, 20 suites* ❙❍❙ *Breakfast.*

$ ⬚ **Hotel Vela Bar.** Abutting the jungle not far from Playa Espadilla, this
HOTEL low-key, eclectic hotel has small but attractive rooms and very competi-
★ tive rates. **Pros:** very affordable; laid-back. **Cons:** basic rooms; spotty service. **TripAdvisor:** "a home away from home," "cool spot," "beautiful." $ *Rooms from: $57* ✉ *Up road from Marlin Restaurant, on left* ☎ *2777–0413* ⊕ *www.velabar.com* ⮌ *13 rooms* ❙❍❙ *No meals.*

$$ ⬚ **Hotel Verde Mar.** This whimsical little hotel and its helpful staff are in
HOTEL the rain forest, with direct access to the beach and minutes away from the park. **Pros:** good value; mere steps from beach; in forest; friendly. **Cons:** rooms smallish; very basic. **TripAdvisor:** "surprisingly friendly," "nice staff," "right on the beach." $ *Rooms from: $90* ✉ *½ km/¼ mile north of park* ☎ *2777–2122, 877/872–0459 in North America* ⊕ *www. verdemar.com* ⮌ *29 rooms* ❙❍❙ *No meals.*

$$ ⬚ **Inn on the Park.** This family-friendly inn is somewhat basic, but it
B&B/INN has a quiet location near the beach and national park. **Pros:** good for
☺ families; lovely locale. **Cons:** no frills; rooms can be dingy. **TripAdvisor:** "wonderful property," "great service," "quiet." $ *Rooms from: $100* ✉ *200 m up side road from Marlin Restaurant* ☎ *2777–3791* ⊕ *www. innontheparkhotel.com* ⮌ *6 rooms* ❙❍❙ *Breakfast.*

$$$ ⬚ **La Mariposa.** The best view in town—a sweeping panorama of verdant
RESORT hills, the aquamarine ocean, and offshore islands—is Mariposa's claim
Fodor'sChoice to fame. **Pros:** gorgeous views; decent restaurant; central location. **Cons:**
★ 4 km (2½ miles) from beach; ocean-view balconies separated by cane barriers, lots of stairs to reach some rooms. **TripAdvisor:** "gorgeous views," "great staff," "so relaxing." $ *Rooms from: $215* ✉ *West of main road, right after Barba Roja* ☎ *2777–0355, 800/572–6440 in U.S.* ⊕ *www.lamariposa.com* ⮌ *57 rooms* ❙❍❙ *Breakfast.*

$$ ⬚ **La Posada Private Jungle Bungalows.** This cluster of distinctive bunga-
RESORT lows is nestled on the edge of the national park and is also just a short
Fodor'sChoice walk from the beach. **Pros:** good value; near beach and park; wildlife;
★ friendly. **Cons:** a bit isolated; small pool. **TripAdvisor:** "relaxing," "comfortable and friendly," "relaxed atmosphere." $ *Rooms from: $100* ✉ *250 m up side road from Marlin Restaurant* ☎☎ *2777–1446* ⊕ *www. laposadajungle.com* ⮌ *4 bungalows, 2 apartments, 1 villa* ❙❍❙ *Breakfast.*

$$$$ ⬚ **Makanda by the Sea.** The bright, spacious, white-and-cream villas
RESORT are among the country's most tasteful (and expensive) accommoda-
Fodor'sChoice tion, and the hypnotic views of the jungle-framed Pacific Ocean make
★ this secluded rain-forest retreat worth it. **Pros:** secluded; tranquil; surrounded by nature; ocean views. **Cons:** far from beach; a few studios need updating. **TripAdvisor:** "luxurious," "awesome views," "relaxing." $ *Rooms from: $265* ✉ *1 km/½ mile west of La Mariposa* ☎ *2777–0442, 888/625–2632 in North America* ⊕ *www.makanda. com* ⮌ *6 villas, 5 studios* ❙❍❙ *Breakfast.*

7

$$$$ RESORT [🏨] **The Suu Manuel Antonio.** One of the newest members of the Manuel Antonio lodging scene proffers gracious luxury that might seem over-the-top if you just want a quiet beach vacation. **Pros:** sumptuous luxury; attentive service; relaxing spa. **Cons:** service might seem *too* attentive if you're not accustomed to it. **TripAdvisor:** "very modern," "excellent service," "gorgeous décor." [$] *Rooms from: $274* ✉ *Road to Quepos, 300 m downhill from La Mansión Inn* ☎ *877/252–0988 in North America* 🌐 *www.thesuuhotels.com* 🛏 *28 rooms* 🍴 *Multiple meal plans.*

$$ B&B/INN [🏨] **Villas de la Selva.** Hidden from the main road behind a mural of monkeys, this unique hillside hotel has comfortable accommodations and great views of the ocean. **Pros:** nice views; beach access; good value. **Cons:** not much privacy. **TripAdvisor:** "relaxation," "great location," "a special place with a heavenly view." [$] *Rooms from: $85* ✉ *Road to park, past Costa Verde and La Arboleda hotels* ☎ *2777–1137, 2253–4890 in San José* 🌐 *www.villasdelaselva.com* 🛏 *7 rooms* 🍴 *No meals.*

$$ RESORT Fodor's Choice ★ [🏨] **Villas Nicolás.** On a hillside about 3 km (2 miles) from the beach, terraced Mediterranean-style privately owned (and rented) villas have impressive views. **Pros:** great location; most rooms have great views. **Cons:** some units need updating; inconsistent service. **TripAdvisor:** "great personal touches," "perfect room," "quiet retreat with a view." [$] *Rooms from: $115* ✉ *Road to park, across from Hotel Byblos* ☎ *2777–0481* 🌐 *www.villasnicolas.com* 🛏 *18 rooms* 🚭 *No smoking* 🍴 *No meals.*

NIGHTLIFE

BARS

Billfish Bar. With large-screen TVs and pool tables, Manuel Antonio's consummate sports bar fills up on game nights. Monday is Ladies' Night. ✉ *Main road, across from Barba Roja* ☎ *2777–0411.*

★ **Salsipuedes.** Salsipuedes, a colorful tapas bar hidden behind tropical foliage, is a great sunset venue. It's one of the few places you can enjoy a quiet drink. ✉ *Main road, north of Barba Roja* ☎ *2777–5019* 🕒 *Wed.–Mon. 7 am–10 pm.*

DANCE CLUB

Barba Roja. Barba Roja has a popular sunset happy hour. The bar becomes a dance club on Saturday night. ✉ *Main road, across from Hotel Divisamar* ☎ *2777–0331* 🕒 *Daily 11 am–10 pm.*

Restaurante Victoria. Part *típico* restaurant, part popular night spot, Restaurante Victoria plays a mix of Latin rhythms most evenings. ✉ *Main road, above La Hacienda Restaurant* ☎ *2777–5143* 🕒 *Daily 4–11.*

SHOPPING

There's no shortage of shopping in this town. The beach near the entrance to the park is lined with a sea of vendors who sell T-shirts, hats, and colorful beach wraps. More-authentic handicrafts are sold at night by artisans positioned along the sidewalk in central Manuel Antonio.

Regalame. Regalame is primarily an art gallery, with paintings, drawings, pottery, and jewelry by several area artists. ✉ *Next to Sí Como No Hotel* ☎ *2777–0777.*

South Pacific

WORD OF MOUTH

"This was taken at sunset on Dominical Beach. The tide goes way out and the sand stays wet. We found this to be one of the most picturesque beaches in Costa Rica."

—Photo by Chad Clark, Fodors.com member

WELCOME TO SOUTH PACIFIC

TOP REASONS TO GO

★ **Bird-watching:** Yields such beauties as scarlet macaws and the resplendent quetzal.

★ **Enormous Corcovado National Park:** The last refuge of such endangered species as jaguars and tapirs.

★ **Kayaking:** Head to the Golfo Dulce or along the jungly channels of the Sierpe or Colorado rivers.

★ **Mountain hikes:** Hikes that range from easy daytime treks around luxurious lodges to Costa Rica's toughest: 3,810-meter (12,500-foot) Cerro Chirripó.

★ **Wild places to stay:** Relax in the country's top eco-lodges, rustic thatch-roof beach bungalows, and cozy mountain cabins.

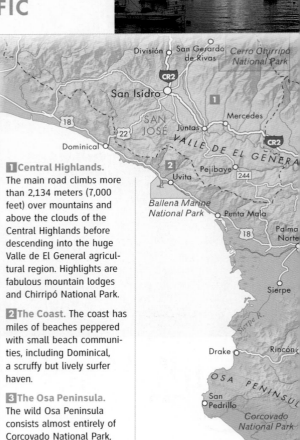

1 Central Highlands. The main road climbs more than 2,134 meters (7,000 feet) over mountains and above the clouds of the Central Highlands before descending into the huge Valle de El General agricultural region. Highlights are fabulous mountain lodges and Chirripó National Park.

2 The Coast. The coast has miles of beaches peppered with small beach communities, including Dominical, a scruffy but lively surfer haven.

3 The Osa Peninsula. The wild Osa Peninsula consists almost entirely of Corcovado National Park, 1,156 square km (445 square miles) of primary and secondary rain forest straight out of a David Attenborough nature documentary.

4 Golfo Dulce. The eastern Golfo Dulce draws anglers and kayakers to Golfito, beachcombers to slow-paced Zancudo, and serious surfers to Pavones.

GETTING ORIENTED

The most remote part of Costa Rica, the South Pacific encompasses the southern half of Puntarenas Province and La Amistad International Biosphere. The region descends from mountainous forests just an hour south of San José to the humid Golfo Dulce and the richly forested Osa Peninsula, 8 to 10 hours from the capital by car.

8

0 ——— 10 mi
0 ——— 10 km

CORDILLERA DE TALAMANCA

LIMÓN

La Amistad National Park

Cabagra

Buenos Aires

Brujo
Terraba

Helechalles

Paso Real

Alturas

Jabillo

237

PUNTARENAS

Union

San Vito

Chacarita

16   **PANAMA**

245

Piedras Blancas National Park

CR2   Río Claro

Ciudad Neily

4   Golfito

Golfo Dulce

14

Zancudo

Paso Canoas

245

Puerto Jiménez

Laurel

Conte

3

Madrigal

El Higo

Carate

Pavones

Cabo Matapolo

Punto Banco

Banco

Pacific Ocean

CHIRRIPÓ NATIONAL PARK

Chirripó National Park is all about hiking. The ascent up Mt. Chirripó, the highest mountain in Costa Rica, is the most popular and challenging hike in the country. It's also the most exclusive, limited to 40 hikers per day.

From the trailhead to the peak, you gain more than 2,438 meters (8,000 feet) of elevation, climbing through shaded highland forest, then out into the wide-open, windswept wilds of the *páramo*, scrubby moorland similar to the high Andes. It's a 48-km (30-mile) round-trip, and you need at least three days to climb to the hostel base, explore the summits, and descend. The modern but chilly stone hostel is the only available accommodation, with small rooms of four bunks each, shared cold-water bathrooms, and a cooking area. A new generator and solar panels provide some electricity, but the hostel is still bare-bones rustic, although improvements are afoot at this writing. Trails from the hostel lead to the top of Chirripó—the highest point in Costa Rica—and the nearby peak of Terbi, as well as half a dozen other peaks and glacier lakes. *(See page 440 for more information.)*

■ TIP➔ **Pack plenty of warm clothes.**

BEST TIME TO GO

Between sometimes freezing temperatures and more than 381 centimeters (150 inches) of rain a year, timing is of the essence here. The best months are in the dry season, January to May. The park is closed the last two weeks in May, all of October and often in November and December as well, if the trails are too wet and slippery for safety.

FUN FACT

A climb up Chirripó is a rite of passage for many young Costa Ricans, who celebrate their graduation from high school or college with a group expedition.

BEST WAYS TO EXPLORE

HIKING
There's no getting around it: the only way to explore this park is on foot. And the only way is up. It's a tough climb to Mt. Chirripó's base camp—6 to 10 hours from the official park entrance, depending on your physical condition—so most hikers head out of San Gerardo de Rivas before the first light of day. You can hire porters to lug your gear up and down for you, so at least you can travel relatively light.

People who live in Costa Rica train seriously for this hike, so be sure you are in good enough shape to make the climb. Smart hikers also factor in a couple of days in the San Gerardo de Rivas area to acclimate to the high altitude before setting out. The hike down is no picnic, either: your knees and ankles will be stretched to their limits. But it's an adventure every step of the way—and the bragging rights are worth it.

MOUNTAIN HIGHS
The base-camp hostel at Los Crestones is at 11,152 feet above sea level, so you still have some hiking ahead of you if you want to summit the surrounding peaks. Take your pick: Chirripó at 12,532 feet; Ventisqueros at 12,467 feet; Cerro Terbi at 12,336; and, for the fainter of heart, Mt. Uran at a measly 11,811 feet. Mountain hikers who collect "peaks" can add all four mountaintops to their list.

BIRD-WATCHING
Although your eyes will mostly be on the scenery, there are some highland species of birds that thrive in this chilly mountain air. Watch for the volcano junco, a sparrowlike bird with a pink beak and a yellow eye ring. Only two hummingbirds venture up this high—the fiery-throated, which lives up to its name; and the volcano hummingbird, which is the country's smallest bird. If you see a raptor soaring above, chances are it's a red-tailed hawk.

TOP REASONS TO GO

DID IT!
The sheer sense of accomplishing this tough hike is the number one reason hikers take on this challenge. You don't have to be a mountain climber but you do need to be in very good shape.

OCEAN VIEWS
On rare, perfectly clear days, the top of Chirripó is one of the few places in the country where you can see both the Pacific and Atlantic oceans.

TOP OF THE WORLD
The exhilaration of sitting on top of the world, with only sky, mountain peaks, and heath as far as the eye can see, motivates most visitors to withstand the physical challenges and the spartan conditions in the hostel.

UNIQUE ENVIRONMENT
A climb up Chirripó gives visitors a unique chance to experience extreme changes in habitat, from pastureland through rain forest and oak forest to bleak, scrubby páramo (a high-elevation ecosystem). As the habitat changes, so does the endemic wildlife, which thins out near the top, along with the air.

8

CORCOVADO NATIONAL PARK

For those who crave untamed wilderness, Corcovado National Park is the experience of a lifetime. Covering one-third of the Osa Peninsula, the park is blanketed primarily by virgin rain forest and holds Central America's largest remaining tract of lowland Pacific rain forest.

The remoteness of Corcovado and the difficult access to its interior make it one of the most pristine parks in the country—barely disturbed by human presence—where massive, vine-tangled primary-forest trees tower over the trails, and birds and wildlife abound. Your chances of spotting endangered species are better here than anywhere else in the country, although it still takes a combination of determination and luck. The rarest and most sought-after sightings are the jaguar and Baird's tapir. Corcovado also has the largest population of scarlet macaws in the country. Bordering the park are some of Costa Rica's most luxurious jungle lodges and retreats, all of which are contributing to the effort to save Corcovado's wildlife. *(See page 486 for more information.)*

BEST TIME TO GO

Dry season, January to May, is the best time to visit, but it's also the most popular. With so little accommodation available, it's crucial to reserve well in advance. June through August will be wetter, but may also be a little cooler. The long-distance trails are virtually impassable from September to December, when most visitors arrive in boats.

FUN FACT

Warning signs to stay on the trails should be heeded: in 2007, the Minister of Tourism got lost and wandered around in a daze for three days after following a baby tapir off the trail and being attacked by its mother.

BEST WAYS TO EXPLORE

BIRD-WATCHING AND WILDLIFE

The holy grail of wildlife spotting here is a jaguar or a Baird's tapir. You may be one of the lucky few to see one of these rare, elusive animals. In the meantime, you can content yourself with coatis, peccaries, and agoutis on the ground and, in the trees, some endemic species of birds you will only see in this part of the country: Baird's trogon, riverside wren, and black-cheeked ant-tanager, to name a few.

GETTING HERE AND AROUND

The easiest way to visit the park is on a day trip by boat, organized by a lodge or tour company in Drake Bay, Sierpe, or Uvita. The well-heeled can fly in on an expensive charter plane to the Sirena airfield. But no matter how you get there, the only way to explore is on foot. There are no roads, only hiking trails. If you have a backpack, strong legs, and a reservation for a tent site or a ranger station bunk, you can enter the park on foot at three staffed ranger stations and spend up to five days deep in the wilds.

HIKING

There are two main hiking routes to Corcovado. When you're planning your itinerary, keep in mind that the hike between any two ranger stations takes at least a day. The hike from La Leona to Sirena is about 16 km (10 miles) and requires crossing a wide river mouth and a stretch of beach best crossed at low tide. Some people plan this hike before dawn to avoid the blistering sun. The 17.4-km (10.8-mile) trail from Los Patos to Sirena is the coolest trail, through forest all the way.

TOP REASONS TO GO

FLORA AND FAUNA

The sheer diversity of flora and fauna and the chance to see wildlife completely in the wild are the main draws here. The number of catalogued species, to date, includes 500 trees (49 of them in peril of extinction), 150 orchids, 375 birds, 124 mammals (11 on the endangered list), 123 butterflies, 116 amphibians, and more than 8,000 insects.

OFF THE BEATEN TRACK

Day visitors get to taste the thrill of being completely off the beaten track, in an untamed natural world. But for campers and guests at the park's main lodge, La Sirena, the chance to spend days roaming miles of trails without hearing a single man-made sound is a rare treat.

TEST YOUR LIMITS

The physical challenges of hiking in high humidity and living very basically, along with the psychological challenge of being completely out of touch with "the real world," appeal to the kind of people who like to test their limits.

8

BALLENA NATIONAL MARINE PARK

Great snorkeling, whale-watching, and beach-combing draw visitors and locals to Parque Nacional Marino Ballena (Whale Marine National Park), which protects four relatively tranquil beaches stretching for about 10 km (6 miles), as well as a mangrove estuary, a recovering coral reef, and a vast swath of ocean.

Playa Uvita, fronting the small town of Bahía Ballena, is the longest and most visited beach, and the embarkation point for snorkeling, fishing, and whale-watching tours. Restaurants line the nearby main street of the town. Playa Colonia, the most easily accessed beach by car, has a safe swimming beach with a view of rocky islands. Playa Ballena, south of Playa Colonia, is a lovely strand backed by lush vegetation. Finally, tiny Playa Piñuela is the prettiest of the park beaches, in a deep cove that serves as the local port. Along with the tropical fish you'll see while snorkeling, you may be lucky enough to see humpback whales and dolphins. *(See page 453 for more information.)*

BEST TIME TO GO

December to April is the best time for guaranteed sunny beach weather, as well as for sightings of humpback whales with their young. The whales also roam these waters in late July through late October. Bottlenose dolphins abound in March and April. Avoid weekends in December to February, and Easter Week, if you want the beach to yourself.

FUN FACT

Playa Uvita features a *tombolo*, a long swath of sand connecting a former island to the coast. At low tide, the exposed brown sandbar resembles a whale's tail, in keeping with the bay's name: Bahía Ballena (Whale Bay).

BEST WAYS TO EXPLORE

BEACHCOMBING

The park's beaches are ideal to explore on foot, especially the Blue Flag–designated Playa Uvita, which has the longest and widest stretch of beach. Visitors and locals flock here in the late afternoon to catch spectacular sunsets. Don't forget your camera! At low tide, you can walk out onto the Whale's Tail sandbar. During the day, you'll see moving shells every-where—hermit crabs of every size are constantly scuttling around. Although it all looks idyllic—and it mostly is—don't leave valuables unattended on the beach.

CAMPING

If you brought a tent, pitch it here. Camping on the beach is allowed at Playas Ballena, Colonia, and Piñuela. You can't beat the price, as camping is included in the park admission. Costa Ricans are avid—and often noisy—campers, so try to avoid busy weekends and *Semana Santa* (Easter Week).

IN, ON, AND OVER THE WATER

Swimming here is relatively safe, but check with the park ranger or your hotel about the best swimming spots. Or just watch where the locals are frolicking in the water. Get a little farther out in the water on a fishing charter and try your hand at reeling in mahimahi, tuna, and mackerel. Whale- and dolphin-watching excursions are also a fun option—bottle-nose dolphins are most often spotted, but humpback whales, especially mothers with babes, are the stars of the show. If you want to be the captain of your boat, sea kayaks are a popular way to explore the park's mangroves and river estuar-ies. Playa Ventanas, just south of the park's official border, has tidal rock caves you can kayak through. You can also paddle out to close-in islets and look for brown boobies, the tropical seabirds that nest here. For the ultimate bird's-eye view, take an ultralight flight over the park.

TOP REASONS TO GO

ALONE TIME

If solitude is what you're after, the park's beaches are relatively uncrowded, except on weekends and school holidays when locals come to relax. Neither Playa Colonia nor Playa Piñuela sees a lot of traffic, so you can have them virtually to yourself almost anytime.

BEACHES

Miles of wide, sandy beach backed by palm trees and distant green mountain ridges make this one of the most scenic and accessible coastlines in the country. Playa Uvita and Playa Ballena, with their warm, swimmable waters and soft sand, attract the most beachgoers.

WHALES AND DOLPHINS

Catching sight of a humpback whale with her youngster swimming alongside is a thrill you won't forget. And watching dolphins cavorting around your excursion boat is the best entertainment on water.

8

ECO-LODGES IN THE SOUTH PACIFIC

The South Pacific Zone is Costa Rica's last frontier, with a wealth of protected biodiversity. It's also the cradle of the country's ecotourism, including some of the world's best eco-lodges.

Costa Rica's wildest corner has vast expanses of wilderness ranging from the majestic cloud forests and high-altitude páramo of the Talamanca highlands to the steamy, lowland rain forest of Corcovado National Park. Quetzals and other high-elevation birds abound in the oak forests of the San Gerardo de Dota Valley, and scarlet macaws congregate in beach almond trees lining the shores of the Osa Peninsula. The Southern Zone has some of the country's most impressive, though least accessible, national parks—towering Chirripó and mountain-studded La Amistad; and Corcovado, where peccaries, tapirs, and, more rarely, jaguars still roam. Stunning marine wonders can be found in the Golfo Dulce, the dive and snorkeling spots around Caño Island Biological Reserve, and Ballena Marine National Park, famous for seasonal whale migrations. The lodges around Drake Bay, together with the off-the-grid lodges of Carate and Cabo Matapalo, provide unequaled immersion in tropical nature.

GOOD PRACTICES

The signage you'll often see in natural areas sums up ecotourism's principal tenets: Leave nothing but footprints; take away nothing but memories.

A few more tips:

Walk softly on forest trails and keep as quiet as you can. You'll spot more wildlife and maintain the natural atmosphere of the forest for other visitors, too.

Stay on marked trails and never approach animals; use your zoom lens to capture close-ups.

Ecotourism is also about getting to know the locals and their culture. Visit a local farm, an artisan's co-op, or a village school.

TOP ECO-LODGES IN THE SOUTH PACIFIC

CASA CORCOVADO

This jungle lodge, bordering Corcovado National Park, gets top eco-marks for its energy-saving solar and microhydroelectric systems, and its recycling and waste-management leadership in the area. The lodge financed the building of a recycling center in Sierpe, and all the area's glass and aluminum is now recycled. Guests receive a refillable bottle to use throughout their stay. Owner Steve Lill is cofounder and president of the Corcovado Foundation, a major supporter of local initiatives to preserve wildlife on the Osa Peninsula. *(Full hotel review on page 494.)*

LAPA RÍOS

Lapa Ríos is the premier eco-lodge in Costa Rica. Along with providing top-notch, sustainable hospitality, the lodge's mission is to protect the 1,000 acres of forest in its private preserve edging Corcovado National Park. Its main weapon is education, through local school programs and community involvement. The lodge owners spearheaded the building of the local school and provide direct employment to more than 45 area families. Lapa Ríos was the first area lodge to offer a free sustainability tour, highlighting innovative eco-friendly practices, including feeding organic waste to pigs to produce methane fuel. *(Full hotel review on page 490.)*

PLAYA NICUESA RAINFOREST LODGE

From its initial construction to its daily operations, this Golfo Dulce lodge, accessible only by boat, has been committed to sustainability. The main lodge and guest cabins were built with fallen wood and recycled materials. Solar power, an organic septic system, composting, and a chemical-free garden also attest to the owners' eco-credentials. The kitchen uses local produce and cooks up fish caught in the gulf. Lodge owners Donna and Michael Butler match guests' donations to the Osa Campaign, a cooperative conservation program. *(Full hotel review on page 464.)*

AFTER DARK

The first night in a remote Southern Zone eco-lodge can be unnerving. You may have looked forward to falling asleep to the sounds of nature, but you may not be prepared for the onslaught of night noises: the chirping of geckos as they hunt for insects in the thatch roof, the thwack of flying insects colliding against window screens, and the spine-tingling calls of owls and nightjars. Add in the chorus of croaking frogs and you may have trouble falling asleep. Once you realize that you're safe under your mosquito net, you can start to enjoy the nocturnal symphony. And after the first day of waking up at dawn to the roars of howler monkeys and the chatter of songbirds, you'll be more than ready to crash early the next night. Most guests are asleep by 8 pm and rise at 5 am, the best time to spot birds and wildlife as they start their day, too. For nighttime visits to the bathroom, be sure to keep a flashlight handy and something to put on your feet if you want to avoid creepy-crawlies.

8

By Dorothy MacKinnon

The South Pacific encompasses everything south of San José, down to the border with Panama, and all the territory west of the Talamanca Mountains, sloping down to the Pacific coast. World-class mountain hikes and bird-watching abound in the highlands, just south of the capital.

The beaches attract surfers, fishers, whale-watchers, and beachcombers. But the jewels in the South Pacific crown are the idyllic Golfo Dulce and the wild Osa Peninsula, brimming with wildlife and natural adventures. Visitors go south to heed the call of the wild. On land, hiking, bird-watching, horseback riding, and wildlife viewing are the main activities, along with some thrilling tree-climbing, zip-line, and waterfall-rappelling opportunities. On the water, there's surfing, snorkeling, diving, fishing, sea-kayaking, and whale- and dolphin-watching, as well as swimming and beachcombing. There's even a sky option, flying in a two-seater ultralight plane.

What makes many of these activities special in the Southern Zone is that, given the wildness of the locations, the focus is more on nature than on entertainment. No matter what you're doing, you'll come across interesting flora and fauna and natural phenomena. Another key to what sets the Southern Zone apart is the large number of trained naturalist guides. Most eco-lodges have resident guides who know not only where to find the birds and wildlife, but also how to interpret the hidden workings of the natural world around you.

PLANNING

WHEN TO GO
PEAK SEASON: JANUARY TO APRIL
The dry season has the most reliably sunny weather. But be aware that the climate swings wildly in the south, from bracing mountain air to steamy coastal humidity. In the mountains it's normally around 24°C (75°F) during the day and 10°C (50°F) at night, though it can fall close to freezing on the upper slopes of Cerro de la Muerte, so be sure to pack a sweater. Temperatures in coastal areas are usually 24°C–32°C (76°F–90°F), but it's the humidity that does you in.

OFF SEASON: SEPTEMBER TO DECEMBER

Rainy season can be very wet indeed, especially September through November. The rainy season is longest in the Osa Peninsula, where showers usually last through January. Roads sometimes flood and many lodges close in the rainiest months (October and November). Elsewhere during the long rainy season, mornings tend to be brilliant and sunny, with refreshing rain starting in mid-afternoon, and many lodges offer discounted "green season" rates. Often, there is a two-or three-week period of dry weather with brilliant sunshine in late June into July, a mini-summer called *il veranillo.*

SHOULDER SEASON: EARLY DECEMBER AND APRIL TO MAY

Early December, when the landscape is lush and green after months of rain and crowds of tourists have yet to arrive, can be delightful in most of the Southern Zone. April into May is another good time to visit, when crowds have thinned out and the rains are just starting to freshen up the landscape

GETTING HERE AND AROUND

SANSA and Nature Air have direct flights to Drake Bay, Palmar Sur, and Puerto Jiménez. SANSA has the most flights to Golfito and the only flights to Coto 47 (for San Vito). *For more information about air travel to the South Pacific from San José, see Air Travel in Travel Smart Costa Rica.*

Alfa Romeo Aero Taxi, at the Puerto Jiménez airport (really more of an airstrip), flies small charter planes to Carate, Tiskita, and Corcovado National Park's airstrip at La Sirena. The one-way price is $390 ($351 cash) for up to five people.

Owing to the dismal state of the roads and hazardous driving conditions—flooded rivers and potholes—we don't recommend driving to the South Pacific, especially in rainy season. If you decide to drive, make sure your vehicle has 4WD, high clearance, and a spare tire. Give yourself lots of daylight time to get to where you are going. You can also fly to Golfito or the Osa Peninsula and rent a 4WD vehicle locally.

Bus fares from San José average about $10, depending on distance and number of stops. The best way to get around the region's roads is by bus—let someone else do the driving. Bus fares are cheap, and you'll meet the locals. But the going is generally slow, buses often leave very early in the morning, and schedules change frequently, so check the day before you want to travel.

Based in Dominical, Easy Ride has three daily shuttle-van services in each direction between San José and the Dominical/Uvita/Ojochal area for $45 to $60 per person, as well as shuttles to Puerto Jiménez or Golfito for $75.

ESSENTIALS

Bus Contacts Easy Ride ☎ 2253–4444, 8812–4012 *[24 hrs]*
⊕ *www.easyridecr.com.*

HEALTH AND SAFETY

You are more likely to suffer from dehydration than any other health issue. Carry plenty of water wherever you go, wear a hat and use sturdy hiking boots and long pants when hiking trails where biting insects may strike or the occasional snake might be sleeping in the sun. Do not leave any valuables in your car or your room—always put them in the safe place provided by hotels and lodges.

MONEY MATTERS

ATMs are sprouting up everywhere in the Southern Zone. The places you won't find a bank are remote communities, for example the beaches south of Golfito on the mainland, or in Drake Bay and lodges south of Puerto Jiménez.

RESTAURANTS

Count on finding lots of fresh fish and tropical fruits on the menu, whether at a roadside *soda* (casual eatery) serving *comida tipica* (typical food) or a sophisticated restaurant in Dominical or Ojochal. Up in the mountains, don't miss out on eating fresh, farmed trout. The food at most remote eco-lodges is excellent.

Prices in the reviews are the average cost of a main course at dinner or, if dinner is not served, at lunch.

HOTELS

Expect reasonable comfort in unbelievably wild settings. Most accommodations are in small hotels, cabins, and lodges run by hands-on owners, many of them foreigners who fell in love with the place on a visit and stayed. Generally speaking, the farther south and more remote the lodge, the more expensive it is. Bad roads (causing supply problems) and lack of electricity and communications make hotel-keeping costly, especially in the Osa Peninsula and Golfo Dulce, where a fresh egg can cost up to a dollar. When you look at the per-person prices, take into account that most of these places include meals, transport, guides, and unique locations.

The country's premier eco-lodges are almost all in the Southern Zone, ranging from simple tents to sophisticated lodges. But keep in mind that if you yearn to be close to nature, you have to be prepared for encounters of the natural kind in your shower or bedroom. Keep a flashlight handy for nighttime trips to the bathroom and always wear sandals.

Prices in the reviews are the lowest cost of a standard double room in high season.

VISITOR INFORMATION

There aren't many official tourist offices in the south. The excellent Uvita Information Center is one of the rare exceptions. Your best bet is to ask for recommendations from your hosts. Lodge and hotel owners know their turf and they want happy guests, so they are unlikely to steer you astray.

TIMING

You need at least a week to truly experience any part of the Osa Peninsula. Even if you fly, transfers to lodges are slow, so plan two days for travel alone. Choose one home base and take day trips. In three weeks, though, you can experience the entire Southern Zone: mountains, beaches, and the Osa Peninsula.

If you are driving south, keep in mind that Cerro de la Muerte is often covered with fog in the afternoon, so plan to cross the mountains in the morning. Don't try to cover too much ground on a set schedule. It is simply impossible to estimate how long it takes to drive the roads or make transportation connections in this part of the country, especially during rainy season when flooding and landslides can close roads and bad weather can delay flights. But remember, getting there is part of the adventure.

TOURS

Costa Rica Expeditions (☎ *2257–0766* ⊕ *www.costaricaexpeditions.com*) is the original ecotourist outfit in Costa Rica, specializing in country-wide nature tours with local naturalist guides.

Horizontes Nature Tours (☎ *2222–2022* ⊕ *www.horizontes.com*) is an expert ecotourist company that arranges custom tours with naturalist guides and ornithologists.

TRAVELING WITH KIDS

The Southern Zone is like Outward Bound for families, where kids and parents can face challenges—such as no TV or video games!—and have adventures together. Plunge the family into real-life adventures with added natural-history educational value. You might inspire a future herpetologist or marine biologist among your progeny.

Go horseback riding to waterfalls and swimming holes. Steal into the night with infrared flashlights to scout out frogs and other fascinating, nocturnal creepy-crawlies. Enjoy kayaking in a calm gulf where dolphins play. Rappel down a waterfall, climb inside a hollow tree, or zip-line through the trees.

The more remote areas of the south are ideal for kids ages seven and up. Babies and all their paraphernalia are hard to handle here, and toddlers are tough to keep off the ground where biting insects and snakes live.

8

THE CENTRAL HIGHLANDS

Famous for spectacular mountain vistas, high-altitude coffee farms, cloud-forest eco-lodges, and challenging mountain hikes, the Central Highlands of Cerro de la Muerte are less than an hour south of San José, climbing up the Pan-American Highway.

ZONA DE LOS SANTOS

Santa María de Dota is 65 km/40 miles south of San José. The Route of the Saints is 24 km/15 miles long.

Empalme, at Km 51 of the Pan-American Highway, marks the turnoff for Santa María de Dota, the first of the picturesque coffee-growing towns named after saints that dot this mountainous area known as the Zona de Los Santos (Zone of the Saints).

★ **La Ruta de Los Santos** (*Route of the Saints*). The scenic road that winds through the high-altitude valley from Empalme to San Pablo de León is appropriately called La Ruta de Los Santos. It's well paved to facilitate shipping the coffee produced in the region. On the 30-minute (24-km/15-mile) drive from Empalme to San Pablo de León Cortés, you travel through misty valleys ringed by precipitous mountain slopes terraced with lush, green coffee plants. The route also captures the essence of a traditional

> **THE FINAL FRONTIER**
>
> The Southern Zone was the very last part of Costa Rica to be settled. The first road, from San José to San Isidro, wasn't begun until the 1950s.

Tico way of life built around coffee growing. Stately churches anchor bustling towns full of prosperous, neat houses with pretty gardens and vintage 1970s Toyota Land Cruisers in a rainbow of colors parked in the driveway.

GETTING HERE

From San José, drive southeast on the paved Pan-American Highway, heading toward Cartago, then follow the signs south for San Isidro de El General. The two-lane road climbs steeply and there are almost no safe places to pass heavy trucks and slow vehicles. Make an early start, because the road is often enveloped in mist and rain in the afternoon. It typically takes about an hour and a half to reach Km 51, where you turn right at Empalme to reach Santa María de Dota, 14 km (8½ miles) along a wide, curving, paved road.

WHERE TO EAT AND STAY

For expanded hotel reviews, visit Fodors.com.

$

CAFÉ

✕ **Café de Los Santos.** This pretty café, within sight of the majestic, domed San Marcos church, showcases the area's high-altitude *arabica* Tarrazú coffee, the "celestial drink" for which this zone is famous. There are more than 30 specialty coffee drinks, plus homemade sweet and savory pastries, and light lunches. It's open weekdays 8 to 6, Saturday 2 to 5:30. $ *Average main: $3 ⊠ 200 m east of church, 6 km/4 miles west of Santa María de Dota, San Marcos de Tarrazú* ☎ 2546–7881 ▭ *No credit cards.*

$

B&B/INN

▦ **El Toucanet Lodge.** For serenity and mountain greenery, you can't beat this family-run lodge with plenty of pastoral scenery and close-up views of hummingbirds from the glassed-in dining room. **Pros:** fresh mountain air; tranquillity; low-key; affordable. **Cons:** simple furnishings; limited menu. **TripAdvisor:** "great hosts," "cozy cabin," "excellent accommodations in a beautiful setting." $ *Rooms from: $66 ⊠ 7 km/4½ miles east of Santa María de Dota along steep, winding paved road to Copey; or from Km 58 of the Pan-American Hwy., turn right at sign for Copey and follow dirt road 8 km/5 miles* ☎ 2541–3045 ⊕ *www.eltoucanet. com* ➘ *6 rooms, 2 junior suites* ⊗ *Closed Sept.* ⏐◯⏐ *Breakfast.*

SHOPPING

Coopedota Santa María. The best place to buy local coffee is where the farmers themselves bring their raw coffee beans to be roasted and packed into jute bags, the Coopedota Santa Maria, the first carbon-neutral coffee producer in the world. You can buy export-quality coffee at their new coffee shop for about $12 per kilo (2.2 pounds). Choose between *en grano* (whole bean) or *molido* (ground), and between light

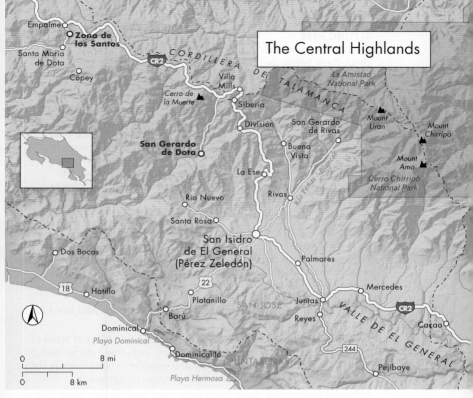

or dark roast. The shop also serves 36 coffee confections. It's open Monday to Saturday 8 to 6, Sunday 1 to 6. You can also reserve a two-hour tour ($18) of the coffee co-op, from bean to bag, including insights into their innovative recycling systems, by calling ahead. ⊠ *Main road, just after bridge as you enter Santa María de Dota* ☎ *2541–2828.*

SAN GERARDO DE DOTA

89 km/55 miles southeast of San José, 52 km/32 miles south of Santa María de Dota.

Cloud forests, invigorating, cool mountain air, well-kept hiking trails, and excellent bird-watching make San Gerardo de Dota one of Costa Rica's premier nature destinations. The tiny hamlet is in the narrow Savegre River valley, 9 km (5½ miles) down a twisting, partially asphalted track that descends abruptly to the west from the Pan-American Highway. The peaceful surroundings look more like the Rocky Mountains than Central America, but hike down the waterfall trail and the vegetation quickly turns tropical again. Beyond hiking and bird-watching, activities include horseback riding and trout fly-fishing.

GETTING HERE

The drive from San José takes about three hours, and from Santa María de Dota about one hour. At Km 80 on the Pan-American Highway, turn down the dirt road signed "San Gerardo de Dota." It's a harrowing, twisting road for most of the 9 km (5½ miles), with signs warning drivers to gear down and go slow. Some newly paved sections help to ease the steepest curves. Tourist vans often stop along the road when the guides spot birds; grab your binoculars and join them!

OUTDOOR ACTIVITIES

BIRD-WATCHING

★ This area is a must for bird-watchers, who flock here with small package tours (⇨ *Tours in Travel Smart Costa Rica).* Individual birders can choose from a roster of expert local guides; check with your hotel for recommendations.

> **THE RESPLENDENT QUETZAL**
>
> The damp, epiphyte-laden oak-tree forest around San Gerardo de Dota is renowned for resplendent quetzals, considered by many to be the most beautiful bird in the Western world. Male quetzals in full breeding plumage are more spectacular than females, with metallic green feathers, crimson stomachs, helmetlike crests, and extravagantly long tail feathers. Ask guides or hotel staff about common quetzal hangouts; early morning during the March-to-May nesting season is the best time to spot them.

Savegre Hotel, Natural Reserve & Spa. Savegre Hotel, Natural Reserve & Spa has the best bird guides in the area, including veteran birder Marino Chacon ($75 for a half day), and organizes hiking tours in the surrounding mountains. ☎ 2740–1028 ⊕ *www.savegre.co.cr.*

Although you can see many birds from your cabin porch, most bird-watching requires hiking, some of it along steep paths made extra challenging by the high altitude (from 7,000 to 10,000 feet above sea level). Come fit and armed with binoculars and layers of warm clothing. The early mornings are brisk up here, but you'll warm up quickly with the sun and the exertion of walking.

HIKING

Some of the best hiking in the country is in this valley.

Cerro de la Muerte. Savegre Hotel (⇨ *below)* runs a daylong natural-history hike (about $150 for up to nine people, including transportation and a packed lunch) that starts with a drive up to the *páramo* (high-altitude, shrubby ecosystem) of Cerro de la Muerte. The trail begins at the cluster of communication towers, near Km 89, and descends through the forest into the valley. Miles of prime bird-watching/hiking trails wind through the forest reserve belonging to the Chacóns. ■ TIP→ Night temperatures on the slopes of Cerro de la Muerte can approach freezing—it's called the Mountain of Death for the very simple reason that long-ago travelers attempting to cross it on foot often froze to death during the night. Pack accordingly.

★ **Río Savegre.** The most scenic and interesting trail in the area is the one that begins at the Savegre Hotel and follows the Río Savegre to a spectacular waterfall. To get to the trailhead, follow the main road past

Savegre Hotel to a fork, where you veer left, cross a bridge, and head over the hill to a pasture that narrows to a footpath. Although it is only 2 km (1¼ miles) each way and there are some new steps built into the steep parts, the hike can be slippery, especially near the bottom, and takes about two hours. Do not attempt to swim in the pool below the waterfall. The current is very swift and dangerous.

WHERE TO STAY

For expanded hotel reviews, visit Fodors.com.

$
B&B/INN
🏨 **Albergue de Montaña Paraíso del Quetzal.** Nestled in a cloud forest just minutes off the main highway, this rustic lodge is, indeed, a paradise for resplendent quetzals and for the visitors who want to see this most beautiful and sought-after bird in Costa Rica. **Pros:** scenic views; pristine cloud forest; amazing bird-watching and hikes. **Cons:** very simple lodging and food; steep paths to some cabins; very cold nights. **TripAdvisor:** "the place to see quetzals," "great view," "friendly family." ⑨ *Rooms from: $62* ✉ *Km 70, Pan-American Hwy., Cerro de la Muerte* 🕾 *2200–0241, 8810–0234* ⊕ *www.paraisodelquetzal.com* ↪ *10 cabins* ¶◎¶ *Some meals.*

$
B&B/INN
🏨 **Cabañas y Senderos Las Cataratas.** One of the best deals—and fresh-trout meals—in the valley is at this family-run, rustic restaurant and bed-and-breakfast, set beside a scenic trout pond. **Pros:** excellent fresh trout; authentic Tico culture. **Cons:** rustic, simple; call ahead on a weekday to make sure someone is there. ⑨ *Rooms from: $52* ✉ *3 km/2 miles down steep road to San Gerardo de Dota* 🕾 *2740–1064, 2740–1065* ⊕ *www.cataratas.tk* ↪ *4 cabins* ¶◎¶ *Breakfast.*

$$$
B&B/INN
🏨 **Dantica Lodge and Gallery.** High style at high altitude, this avant-garde lodge clinging to the side of a mountain has unbeatable valley views, great bird-watching, and luxury accommodation. **Pros:** stylish, comfortable casitas; gorgeous natural setting; 5 km (3 miles) of trails. **Cons:** steep access to forest casitas along narrow trails; some casitas close to road. **TripAdvisor:** "heavenly," "lovely place in the mountains," "wonderful views." ⑨ *Rooms from: $159* ✉ *Road to San Gerardo de Dota, 4 km/2 miles west of Pan-American Hwy.* 🕾 *2740–1067* ⊕ *www.dantica.com* ↪ *6 casitas, 1 suite, 2 houses* ¶◎¶ *Breakfast.*

$$
B&B/INN
Fodor's Choice
★
🏨 **Savegre Hotel, Natural Reserve & Spa.** Famous for its miles of bird-watching trails and expert guides, this once-rustic lodge has been upgraded to luxury, including new cabins with handsome wood furniture, fireplaces, and deep bathtubs—and a new, full-service, riverside spa. **Pros:** great trails; amazing birdlife; excellent guides. **Cons:** buffet-style meals when hotel has lots of groups; older cabins are very simple and lack privacy; be prepared for very cold nights. **TripAdvisor:** "quaint beautiful spot," "bird watcher's paradise," "luxury in the mountains." ⑨ *Rooms from: $95* ✉ *Turn right at sign to San Gerardo de Dota on Pan-American Hwy., about 80 km/50 miles southeast of San José, and travel 9 km/5½ miles down very steep gravel road* 🕾 *2740–1028* ⊕ *www.savegre.co.cr* ↪ *21 cabinas, 20 cabin-suites* ¶◎¶ *Breakfast.*

$$
B&B/INN
🏨 **Trogón Lodge.** Overlooking the same cloud forest and boulder-strewn river as Savegre Hotel, Trogón Lodge, encircling a pond and set in a fantasy garden filled with fuchsias, hydrangeas, and hummingbirds,

8

A male white-throated mountain-gem hummingbird in a defense posture. Río Savegre, San Gerardo de Dota.

is more a relaxing hideaway than a hiking-heavy destination. **Pros:** pretty, lush garden; pleasant, convivial public area; small but excellent gift shop. **Cons:** steep, short trails that end at road; little privacy except in honeymoon suite. **TripAdvisor:** "great birding site," "attractive retreat," "a beautiful and peaceful spot." $ *Rooms from: $83* ✉ *Turn right at sign to San Gerardo de Dota on Pan-American Hwy., about 80 km/50 miles southeast of San José, and follow signs; lodge is 7½ km/4½ miles down a dirt road* ☎ *2740–1051, 2293–8181 in San José* ⊕ *www.grupomawamba.com* ⇆ *22 rooms, 1 suite* ⦿⦿ *Breakfast.*

VALLE DE EL GENERAL REGION

The Valle de El General (The General's Valley) area encompasses vast expanses of highland wilderness on the upper slopes of the Cordillera de Talamanca and the high-altitude páramo of Chirripó National Park, as well as prosperous agricultural communities amid vast, sunbaked fields of pineapple and sugarcane. It is bounded to the north and west by the central highlands of the massive Cordillera de Talamanca and to the south by La Amistad International Park, above San Vito. The valley is named for the Río de El General, one of the many rivers that rise in the Talamancas and run down through the valley, making it ideal for farming.

SAN ISIDRO DE EL GENERAL

54 km/34 miles south of San Gerardo de Dota.

Although San Isidro de El General has no major attractions, the bustling market town is a good place to have lunch, get cash at one of the many ATMs (most accept Visa/Plus cards), or fill your tank—the main highway into town is lined with service stations, some operating 24 hours. Advice to map readers: There are other San Isidros in Costa Rica, but this is the only San Isidro de El General. Just to confuse matters more, this town also goes by the name Peréz Zeledón.

GETTING HERE AND AROUND

The Pan-American Highway takes you straight into San Isidro. It's 129 km (80 miles) south of San José and about 1½ hours' drive south of the San Gerardo de Dota highway exit. Truck traffic can be heavy and painfully slow. Buses to Dominical leave San Isidro from the San Isidro bus terminal, 100 meters (328 feet) south and 200 meters (656 feet) east of the cathedral, near the main highway. Buses to San Gerardo de Rivas, the starting point of the trail into Chirripó National Park, depart from San Isidro at 5:30 am from the central park and at 2 pm from a stop at the central market.

ESSENTIALS

Banks/ATM ATH Coopealianza ⊠ *South side of central park, beside Hotel Chirripó* ☞ *ATM only.* **Banco Nacional** ⊠ *North side of park* 🕾 *2771–3287.*

Hospital Hospital Escalante Pradilla ⊠ *North end of town* 🕾 *2771–3122.*

Internet Internet El Balcón ⊠ *150 m east of Central Market, near Banco de Costa Rica* 🕾 *2771–6300.*

Pharmacy Farmacia Santa Marta ⊠ *Across from cultural center* 🕾 *2771–4506.*

Post Office Correo ⊠ *200 m south of City Hall, south side of park.*

Visitor Information Camara de Comercio de la Region Brunca ⊠ *Beside the Hotel Thunderbird, near the MUSOC bus station where San José buses arrive* 🕾 *2771–6096.* **Selva Mar** ⊠ *50 m south of central park* 🕾 *2771–4582* ⊕ *www.selvamar.com.*

EXPLORING

Las Quebradas Biological Center. In a lush valley 7 km (4½ miles) northeast of San Isidro, community-managed Las Quebradas Biological Center is a *centro biológico* (nature reserve) that protects 1,853 acres of dense forest in which elegant tree ferns grow in the shadows of massive trees, and colorful tanagers and euphonias flit about the foliage. A 3-km (2-mile) trail winds uphill through the forest and along the Río Quebradas, which supplies water to San Isidro and surrounding communities. There's also an easily accessible sensory garden, with plants to smell and taste, and a butterfly garden. On Sunday local cooks will serve home-cooked meals if you make arrangements in advance. ⊠ *At bottom of mountain as you approach San Isidro, take sharp left off Pan-American Hwy. at sign for Las Quebradas, go 7 km/4½ miles northeast; center is 2 km/1 mile north of town, along unpaved road* 🕾 *2771–4131* 🖅 *$4* ☉ *Tues.–Sun. 8–3.*

8

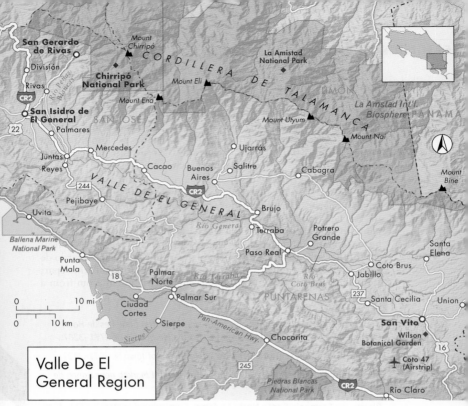

Los Cusingos Bird Sanctuary. Los Cusingos Bird Sanctuary combines bird-ing trails with a museum dedicated to the late Dr. Alexander Skutch, Central America's preeminent ornithologist/naturalist and a coauthor of *A Guide to the Birds of Costa Rica*, the birders' bible. His 190-acre estate, an island of forest amid a sea of new farms and housing devel-opments, is now run by the nonprofit Tropical Science Center, which has improved the trails and restored the simple house where Dr. Skutch lived—without electricity—from 1941 until his death in 2004, just a week shy of his 100th birthday. Bird species you might see include fiery-billed araçaris—colorful, small members of the toucan family—and mixed tanager flocks. ⊠ *12 km/7½ miles southeast of San Isidro, Quizarrá* ☎ *2738–2070* ✉ *cusingosreservation@cct.or.cr* ⊕ *www.cct. or.cr* 🎫 *$10, $5 children* ⊘ *Mon.–Sat. 7–4, Sun. 7–1, preferably by e-mail reservation.*

National Parks Service. The National Parks Service has an office in town where you can get some information on Chirripó National Park, but the main Chirripó office is in San Gerardo de Rivas. ⊠ *Across from Cámara de Cañeros* ☎ *2771–3155.*

OUTDOOR ACTIVITIES

Selva Mar. Selva Mar is the most experienced Southern Zone tour opera-tor. ⊠ *Half a block south of the cathedral* ☎ *2771–4582.*

BIRD-WATCHING

Sunny Travel/Tropical Feathers. Sunny Travel/Tropical Feathers, run by expert birder Noel Urena, has multiday bird-watching packages and arranges customized tours in the San Isidro and Dominical area and points south. ☎ *2771–9686* 🌐 *www.costaricabirdingtours.com.*

HIKING

The major tourist draw is climbing Mt. Chirripó (the highest peak is 3,820 meters or about 12,530 feet high) in Chirripó National Park.

Costa Rica Trekking Adventures. Costa Rica Trekking Adventures, run by Selva Mar, can arrange everything you need to climb the mountain, including transportation, guide, porters to carry your gear, meals, snacks, and beverages. But you still have to make the tough climb yourself, about eight hours uphill to the park lodge, and five hours to come down. The two-night, three-day packages are $477 per person, with at least two people. It's much cheaper to do it on your own, but you have to make all the advance arrangements yourself. ☎ *2771–4582* 🌐 *www.chirripo.com.*

HITTING THE TRAILS

The hiking in the south is simply spectacular, so don't leave home without your boots. The most challenging hike in the country is Chirripó Mountain, a 6- to 10-hour haul up to the national-park hostel, a base camp for exploring surrounding peaks. Dramatic but less-challenging hikes include the well-maintained, wide trails in the cool high-altitude forests of the Savegre Valley; the narrow Coastal Path south of Drake; and forest trails to waterfalls and swimming holes in the Golfo Dulce, Osa Peninsula, and around Dominical.

8

WHERE TO EAT AND STAY

For expanded hotel reviews, visit Fodors.com.

$ COSTA RICAN 🍴 **El Trapiche de Nayo.** This rustic open-air restaurant with a panoramic valley view serves the kind of food Ticos eat at *turnos* (village fund-raising festivals), including hard-to-find *sopa de mondongo* (tripe soup). Easier to stomach are the *gallos* (do-it-yourself filled tortillas), which come stuffed with hearts of palm, other root vegetables, and wood-fire-cooked chicken. On Saturday, raw sugarcane is pressed in an antique mill and boiled in huge iron cauldrons to make smooth *sobado,* a molasses-flavored fudge. Service is leisurely, to say the least, but there is lots of birdlife to watch in the surrounding trees while you wait. The restrooms have been recently upgraded, so it's a decent pit stop, too. It's open 6 am to 6 pm daily. [$] *Average main: $8* ✉ *Pan-American Hwy. 6 km/4 miles north of San Isidro* ☎ *2771–7267.*

$ COSTA RICAN 🍴 **Restaurante Bazooka's.** Their slogan is "American as Apple Pie," and there is indeed apple pie, as well as all-day breakfast and a multipage menu of burgers, triple-decker sandwiches, and meal-size salads in this popular roadside diner in a cheerfully updated wooden hacienda. Pancakes, waffles, and ice-cream sundaes will satisfy any sweet tooth. Hungrier eaters can chow down on hearty servings of BBQ ribs or steak. There are Tico touches, too, with casados, fajitas, local fish and shrimp with rice, and Tres Leches cake, the classic Tico dessert. The lunch specials for $5 are excellent value. The dining area is spread

CLOSE UP

A Mosaic of Forests

Though the rain forest is the most famous region in Costa Rica, there are other types of forests here equally rich in life and well worth exploring. The **tropical dry forests** of the northwestern lowlands are similar to rain forests during the rainy season, but once the weather turns dry, most trees lose their leaves, and some burst simultaneously into full flower, notably the yellow-blossom buttercup tree and the pink tabebuia. Cacti, coyotes, and diamondback rattlesnakes can be found, in addition to typical rain-forest flora and fauna.

The **cloud forests** on the upper reaches of many Costa Rican mountains and volcanoes are so deeply lush that it can be hard to find the bark on a tree for all the growth on its trunk and branches. Vines, orchids, ferns, aroids, and bromeliads are everywhere. More light reaching the ground means plenty of undergrowth,

too. Cloud forests are home to a multitude of animals, ranging from delicate glass frogs, whose undersides are so transparent that you can see many of their internal organs, to the legendary resplendent quetzal. The foliage and mist can make it hard to see wildlife.

Along both coasts are extensive **mangrove forests,** extremely productive ecosystems that play an important role as estuaries. Mangroves attract animals that feed on marine life, especially fish-eating birds such as cormorants, herons, pelicans, and ospreys. The forests that line Costa Rica's northeastern coast are dominated by the water-resistant *jolillo* palm or *palma real.* Mangroves are home to many of the same animals found in the rain forest—monkeys, parrots, iguanas—as well as river dwellers such as turtles and crocodiles.

out in different rooms of the original house, all of them pleasant with lots of natural light. If you're in a hurry, everything is available "to go." An added attraction is the location—right on the main highway so you don't have to negotiate San Isidro's sometimes confusing one-way streets. Just look for the big pink Bazooka's sign at the northern entrance to town. It's open 8 to 10. $ *Average main: $5* ⊠ *Next door to Beto Solis gas station, on east side of main highway as you enter town from north side* ☎ *2771–2050.*

$ **Hotel Los Crestones.** Flowering hedges give this pleasant and afford-
HOTEL able two-story, motel-style building a homey feel, even though it's between the sometimes-noisy local stadium and a sedate funeral home. **Pros:** affordable, pleasant rooms; secure parking for car. **Cons:** avoid rooms at the front, which can be noisy; a few rooms lack air-conditioning. $ *Rooms from: $55* ⊠ *Southwest side of stadium, on road to Dominical* ☎ *2770–1200* ⊕ *www.hotelloscrestones.com* ⟿ *27 rooms* ⏶ *No meals.*

$ **Hotel Zima.** Close to the main bus station and especially popular with
HOTEL backpackers heading up to Chirripó, this hotel's pleasant rooms are in bungalows arranged in a nicely landscaped row, reminiscent of a 1950s motel, complete with swimming pool. **Pros:** handy to bus station and

restaurants in town. **Cons:** not a scenic location, just off main highway; smallish rooms. [$] *Rooms from: $40* ✉ *Half a block east of main highway into San Isidro, across from MUSOC bus terminal* ☎ *2770–1114* 🛏 *28 rooms* 🍴 *No meals.*

SAN GERARDO DE RIVAS

20 km/12½ miles northeast of San Isidro.

Chirripó National Park is the main reason to venture to San Gerardo de Rivas, but if you aren't up for this physically challenging adventure it's still a wildly scenic place, reminiscent of the Himalayas, to spend a day or two. Spread over steep terrain at the end of the narrow valley of the boulder-strewn Río Chirripó, San Gerardo de Rivas has cool mountain air, excellent bird-watching, spectacular views, and an outdoor menu that includes waterfall hikes and hot springs.

GETTING HERE

More than half the one-hour drive from San Isidro is on a very rocky, very hilly, dirt road; 4WD is strongly recommended. There is a bus three times a day from San Isidro, and it is a slow, dusty ride up the mountain.

EXPLORING

👍 **Cloudbridge Private Nature Reserve.** Cloudbridge Private Nature Reserve, a private nature reserve staffed by volunteers, has an easy trail to a waterfall, plus almost 20 km (12 miles) of river and ridge trails bordering Chirripó National Park. It's a pleasant alternative for hikers who aren't up to the challenge of Chirripó. ✉ *2 km/1 mile northeast of San Gerardo de Rivas* 🌐 *www.cloudbridge.org* 🎫 *By donation* 🕒 *Daily, sunrise–sunset.*

👍 **Gevi Hot Springs.** The Gevi Hot Springs (*Aguas Termales Gevi*), on a farm above the road to Herradura, is a favorite tourist stop. To get here, you must cross a raging river on a high bridge, then manage a steep climb on foot or by 4WD vehicle to a combination of natural rock and concrete pools in a forested area. It's nothing fancy and can be crowded with locals on weekends, so aim for a weekday soak. ✉ *Above road to Herradura, about 1½ km/1 mile past the ranger station, north of town* ☎ *2742–5210* 🎫 *$5* 🕒 *Daily 7–5.*

OUTDOOR ACTIVITIES

HIKING

Ruta Urán. Really fit hikers can undertake a guided five-day hike up alternative routes to Chirripó led by experienced local guides. The hike eventually arrives at the Chirripó National Park hostel, and then descends by the usual national park route. Price is about $500 for two hikers, including lodging, meals, guide, and park fees. ☎ *2742–5073* ✉ *denisguiauran@hotmail.com.*

Selva Mar. Selva Mar *(⇨ San Isidro, above)* also runs tours around San Gerardo de Rivas.

8

WHERE TO STAY

For expanded hotel reviews, visit Fodors.com.

$
B&B/INN
🏨 **Hotel de Montaña El Pelícano.** On a precipitous ridge south of town, this budget lodge is popular with hikers and named for a chunk of wood that resembles a pelican—one of dozens of idiosyncratic wooden sculptures carved out of tree roots by owner Rafael Elizondo. **Pros:** proximity to Chirripó and a free ride to the trailhead; very cheap. **Cons:** shared bath; very tiny rooms, but most visitors are only here to sleep before setting off early to climb Chirripó. **TripAdvisor:** "a relaxing stay," "excellent location," "best of the best." 💲 *Rooms from: $50* ✉ *260 m south of national park office* ☎ *2742–5050* ⊕ *www.hotelpelicano.net* 🛏 *6 rooms with shared bath, 2 with private bath, 4 cabins* 🍴 *Breakfast.*

$$$$
B&B/INN
★
🏨 **Monte Azul.** Sleek and chic, this luxury hotel and excellent restaurant, set in a scenic private nature reserve bordering the rushing Chirripó River, is an artistic triumph, both inside and out. **Pros:** gorgeous natural setting; stunning design aesthetics throughout; excellent food. **Cons:** a little pricey. **TripAdvisor:** "incredible essence," "unforgettable," "tranquility and beauty." 💲 *Rooms from: $259* ⊹ *5 km/3 miles south of San Gerardo de Rivas* ☎ *2742–5222* ⊕ *www.monteazulcr.com* 🛏 *4 bungalows* 🌣 *Closed Oct.* 🍴 *Breakfast.*

CHIRRIPÓ NATIONAL PARK

The park entrance is a 4-km/2-mile hike uphill from San Gerardo de Rivas.

Chirripó National Park. The main attraction of this national park is Mt. Chirripó, the highest mountain in Costa Rica and a mecca for both hikers and serious peak summiteers. If you want to take up the challenge, be sure to make arrangements well in advance. The number of hikers in the park each day is limited to 40. Twenty-five reservations can be booked by telephone often months ahead, and those places are usually snapped up by locals and tour companies, leaving only 15 potential spaces (5 of which are held until the last minute for official use) for hikers who show up at the park. Without reservations, you can try your luck and check in at the San Gerardo ranger station, which grants entrance on a first-come, first-served basis. Maximum stay is three days, two nights ($10 per person per night, plus $15 each day you are in the park).

DID YOU KNOW?

Although it takes the fittest hikers at least four hours to get to the base camp of Chirripó, hundreds of competitors from around the world converge on tiny San Gerardo de Rivas every February to run a 34-km (22-mile) race up and down Chirripó. A local family of hardy brothers shares the record time: three hours and 15 minutes!

GETTING HERE
San Gerardo de Rivas National Parks Service. You are required to report to the San Gerardo de Rivas National Parks Service, for a reservation before you start, usually the day before your climb since you need to start

hiking long before the office opens at 6:30 am. The office is open 8 am to noon and 1 to 4 pm Monday through Friday. Park admission is $15 per day, plus $10 per day for hostel lodging; ask for trail maps at the office. Don't try to sneak in: a park ranger will stop you at a checkpoint on the trail and ask to see your reservation voucher. You can reserve lodgings over the phone (maximum four people per reservation); ask for a copy of the wonderfully informative visitor's guide to be sent to you via email (✍ *reservacioneschirripo@gmail.com.*) ✉ *Main street* ☎ *2742–5083.*

OUTDOOR ACTIVITIES

Hikes and other activities in the park are arranged by **Selva Mar** (⇨ *San Isidro, above*) and by the **Guides and Porters Association of San Gerardo** (☎ *2742–5073* ✍ *denisguiauran@hotmail.com*), who provide guides, porters, and provisions for Chirripó hikes, as well as an alternative hike up the Ruta Urán. There is also a new tourism cooperative, **CATURCOCHI**, with an excellent, informative Web site (⊕ *www.aguaseternas.com*) about Chirripó and San Gerardo de Rivas.

SAN VITO

110 km/68 miles southeast of San Isidro, 61 km/38 miles northeast of Golfito.

Except for the tropical greenery, the rolling hills around the bustling hilltop town of San Vito could be mistaken for a Tuscan landscape. The town actually owes its 1952 founding to 200 Italian families who converted forest into coffee, fruit, and cattle farms. A remnant of the Italian flavor lingers on in the statue dedicated to the *pioneros* standing proudly in the middle of town. But San Vito today is a bustling, agricultural market town, the center of the Coto Brus coffee region. Many coffee pickers are from the Guaymí tribe, who live in a large reserve nearby and also over the border in Panama. They're easy to recognize by the women's colorfully embroidered, long cotton dresses.

GETTING HERE AND AROUND

If you are driving south from San Isidro, your best route is along the wide, smooth Pan-American Highway via Buenos Aires to Paso Real, about 70 km (43 miles). Then take the scenic high road to San Vito, 40 km (25 miles) farther along. This road has some bad patches but it's the most direct and prettiest route. Another route, which many buses take, is via Ciudad Neily, about 35 km (22 miles) northeast of Golfito, and then 24 km (15 miles) of winding steep road up to San Vito, at almost 1,000 meters (3,280 feet) above sea level. At this writing, the road is potholed and in *mal estato* (bad shape). There are direct buses from San José four times a day, and buses from San Isidro two times a day. You can also fly to Coto 47 and take a taxi to San Vito.

ESSENTIALS

Most of the banks in town have cash machines that accept foreign cards.

Banks/ATM ATH Coopealianza ✉ *Center of town, north of hospital.*
Banco Nacional ✉ *Across from south side of central park* ☎ *2773-3601.*

Hospital Hospital San Vito ✉ *South end of town on road to Wilson Botanical Garden* ☎ *2773-3103.*

8

A ginger flower at the Wilson Botanical Garden in San Vito.

Pharmacy Farmacia Assisi ⊠ *Center of town across from La Flor pastry shop* ☎ *2773–3281.*

Post Office Correo ⊠ *Far north end of town, beside police station.*

Taxis Taxi service ⊠ *Taxi stand beside park at center of town* ☎ *2773–3939.*

EXPLORING

Wilson Botanical Garden. The compelling tourist draw here is the world-renowned Wilson Botanical Garden, a must-see for gardeners and bird-watchers and enchanting even for those who are neither. Paths through the extensive grounds are lined with exotic plants and shaded by avenues of palm trees and 50-foot-high bamboo stalks. In 1961 U.S. landscapers Robert and Catherine Wilson bought 30 acres of coffee plantation and started planting tropical species, including palms, orchids, bromeliads, and heliconias. Today the property extends over 635 acres, and the gardens hold around 2,000 native and more than 3,000 exotic species. The palm collection—more than 700 species—is the second largest in the world. Fantastically shaped and colored bromeliads, which usu-ally live in the tops of trees, have been brought down to the ground in impressive mass plantings, providing one of many photo opportunities. The property was transferred to the Organization for Tropical Studies in 1973, and in 1983 it became part of Amistad Biosphere Reserve. Under the name **Las Cruces Biological Station,** Wilson functions mainly as a research and educational center, so there is a constant supply of expert botanists and biologists to take visitors on natural-history tours in the garden and the adjoining forest trails. If you spend a night at the gar-den lodge, you have the garden all to yourself in the late afternoon and early morning, when wildlife is most active. ✉ *6 km/4 miles south of San Vito on road to Ciudad Neily* ☎ *2773–4004* 🌐 *www.esintro.co.cr* 🎟 *$8* 🕒 *Weekdays 7–5, weekends 8–5.*

OUTDOOR ACTIVITIES

BIRD-WATCHING

Wilson Botanical Garden. In addition to its plants, Wilson Botanical Garden *(⇨ Exploring, above)* is renowned for its birds. There are about 250 species of birds in the garden alone, including half of the country's hummingbird species, and 410 species total in the immediate area. Competing with the birds for your attention are more than 800 butterflies. Naturalist guides lead visitors on birding and natural-history tours through the garden ($24 per person). The Río Java trail, open only to overnight guests of Wilson, is also a great place to see birds.

WILDLIFE WATCHING

Wilson Botanical Garden. If you are an overnight guest at Wilson Botanical Garden *(⇨ Exploring, above)*, you can walk the Río Java trail, through a forest thick with wildlife, particularly monkeys.

WHERE TO EAT AND STAY

For expanded hotel reviews, visit Fodors.com.

$ ITALIAN ★ 🍴 **Pizzería Liliana.** Follow the locals' lead and treat yourself to authentic pizza at the classiest restaurant in town or dig into the macaroni *sanviteña*-style: with white sauce, ham, and mushrooms. The classics are here as well, and they're all homemade—lasagna, cannelloni, and ravioli. The authentically Italian vinaigrette salad dressing is a welcome change from more acidic Tico dressings. In true Italian fashion, the friendly, family-run restaurant can be noisy, but it's a happy buzz. For a more romantic dinner, ask for a table on the pretty garden terrace. [$] *Average main: $8* ✉ *150 m west of central square* ☎ *2773–3080.*

$ B&B/INN 🏨 **Casa Botania B&B.** Book a comfortable room with a sweeping view of forest and mountains at this delightful new bed-and-breakfast, perched on a hilltop halfway between San Vito and Wilson Botanical Garden, and owned by a charming young Belgian-Colombia couple. **Pros:** affordable; great views; aimiable hosts. **Cons:** close to road but not much traffic noise at night; friendly, outside dog. **TripAdvisor:** "beautiful setting," "great food," "very accommodating and knowledgeable." [$] *Rooms from: $65* ✉ *Off main road, between Wilson Botanical Garden and San Vito, 5 km/3 miles south of San Vito, Linda Vista* ☎ *2773–4217, 8711–3008* 🌐 *www.casabotania.com* 🛏 *1 guest room, 1 bunglow for two, 1 bungalow with 2 bedrooms* 💳 *No credit cards* 🍽 *Breakfast.*

$ HOTEL 🏨 **Hotel El Ceibo.** The best deal in town, El Ceibo is tucked in a quiet cul-de-sac behind the main street, an Italian-style oasis with graceful arcades and decorative balustrades overlooking potted palms. **Pros:** central location; good price; relative quiet. **Cons:** rooms are quite small; furnishings are nothing special. [$] *Rooms from: $43* ✉ *140 m east of San Vito's central park, behind Municipalidad* ☎ *2773–3025* 🛏 *40 rooms* 🍽 *No meals.*

$$ B&B/INN 🏨 **Morphose Mountain Retreat.** An American-French couple presents excellent French fare with flair at this new Balinese-inspired teak-and-glass B&B with a panoramic view. **Pros:** fabulous views; supercomfortable

rooms; excellent food. **Cons:** clouds sometimes obscure the view. **TripAdvisor:** "very comfortable accommodation," "a birder's dream in the clouds," "relaxing at its best." [$] *Rooms from: $95* ✉ *From the main street in Ciudad Neilly, take paved road toward San Vito for 5½ miles, Ciudad Neilly* ☎ *8704–5346* 🌐 *www.morphosecr.com* 🛏 *2 suites* 🍴 *Breakfast.*

$$ B&B/INN ★ **Wilson Botanical Garden.** A highlight of any Costa Rican visit, this magical botanical garden has comfortable rooms in two modern buildings built of glass, steel, and wood, with private balconies overlooking a forested hillside. **Pros:** unparalleled setting with 24-hour access to garden and nature trails; excellent birding and wildlife viewing. **Cons:** rooms are slowly being refurbished; family-style meals are served strictly on schedule so be ready to sit at the table when the dinner bell rings. [$] *Rooms from: $92* ✉ *6 km/4 miles south of San Vito on road to Ciudad Neily* ☎ *2524–0628 San José office, 2773–4004 lodge* 🌐 *www.esintro.co.cr* 🛏 *12 rooms* 🍴 *All meals.*

SHOPPING

Finca Cántaros. In an old farmhouse on the east side of the road between San Vito and the botanical garden, Finca Cántaros sells crafts by indigenous artisans from near and far, including calabash gourds charmingly painted by Maleku artists, and *molas* (colorful appliqué work) made by Kuna women from the San Blas Islands in Panama. You can also find a great selection of colorful, high-glaze ceramics from San José artists. Profits help support the adjacent children's library. **■ TIP→ Along with shopping, you can walk bird-filled nature trails around a lake behind the shop and explore an indigenous archaeological site.** ✉ *Road to Ciudad Neily, 3 km/2 miles south of San Vito* ☎ *2773–3760.*

EN ROUTE

San Vito to Ciudad Neily. The 33-km (21-mile) road from San Vito to Ciudad Neily is twisting and spectacular, with views over the Coto Colorado plain to the Golfo Dulce and Osa Peninsula beyond. You can stop halfway to admire the view at **Mirador La Torre** to enjoy excellent fruit *naturales* and views from their counter stools. Watch out for some tricky spots where the road has fallen away.

San Vito to Paso Real. The road from San Vito to Paso Real is equally scenic, traveling along a high ridge with sweeping valley views on either side. As you descend, the wide valley of El General River opens up before you, planted with miles of spiky pineapples and tall sugarcane. The road is constantly falling into disrepair, so drivers do need to keep watch for potholes.

DOMINICAL AND BALLENA MARINE PARK

On the other side of a mountain ridge, just a scenic hour-long drive west of San Isidro, you reach the sunny southern Pacific coast, with its miles of beaches for surfing, strolling, kayaking, and snorkeling. Ballena National Marine Park alone encompasses almost 10 km (6 miles) of protected beaches. Scattered along the coast are small communities with increasing numbers of international residents and interesting restaurants and lodging options.

DOMINICAL

34 km/21 miles southwest of San Isidro, 40 km/25 miles south of Quepos.

Sleepy fishing village–turned–surfer town, Dominical is changing again as luxury villas pop up all over the hillsides above the beaches, bringing new wealth that is boosting the local economy. It's still a major surfing destination, attracting surfers of all ages, with a lively restaurant and nightlife scene. Bars and restaurants come and go with the waves of itinerant foreigners, so don't hesitate to try something new. Dominical's real magic lies beyond the somewhat scruffy town, in the surrounding terrestrial and marine wonders: the rain forest grows right up to the beach in some places, and the ocean offers world-class surfing.

MAKING OUT

Kissing in public, among heterosexual couples at least, is rarely frowned upon, with parks a favorite venue. But a growing number of locally patronized restaurants have posted signs: "Escenas amorosas prohibidas," literally "Amorous scenes prohibited."

GETTING HERE AND AROUND

The road west over the mountains and down to Dominical is scenic at its best and fog-shrouded and potholed at its worst. It has recently been repaved, but there are lots of curves and dicey landslide areas, and potholes pop up unexpectedly, so take your time and enjoy the scenery along the hour-long drive from San Isidro. From Quepos, the last section of the Costanera has finally been paved and it's now an easy half-hour drive to Dominical. Buses from San Isidro leave four times a day, two times daily from Quepos. If you want to avoid driving altogether, Easy Ride *(⇨ above)* has air-conditioned minibuses with room for six to eight passengers that make two trips to and from San José daily ($45).

ESSENTIALS

Bank/ATM Banco de Costa Rica ✉ *Plaza Pacífica* ☎ *2787–0381.*

Hospital There is no doctor's office or clinic in Dominical now. The nearest pharmacy, doctor, and dentist are in Uvita.

Internet Dominical Internet Cafe ✉ *Above San Clemente Bar, main street* ☎ *2787–0191.*

Post Office San Clemente Bar ✉ *Main street at bus stop; mail and DHL drop-off only.*

Rental Cars Solid Car Rental ✉ *Hotel Villas Río Mar* ☎ *2787–0052* ⊕ *www.solidcarrental.com.*

Visitor Information Dominical Surf Adventures ✉ *Main Street, across from church* ☎ *8897–9540, 2787–0431.* **Southern Expeditions** ✉ *On main street across from San Clemente Bar* ☎ *2787–0100.*

8

CLOSE UP

La Amistad National Park

La Amistad National Park. By far the largest park in Costa Rica, at more than 1,980 square km (765 square miles), La Amistad is a mere portion of the vast La Amistad Biosphere Reserve that stretches into western Panama. Altitudes range from 1,000 meters (3,280 feet) to 3,500 meters (11,480 feet). There are miles of rugged, densely forested trails and plenty of wildlife (two-thirds of the country's vertebrate species live here), but because access is extremely difficult, it's not worth visiting the park unless you plan to spend several days, making this a trip only for experienced hikers. Unless you're comfortable being lost in the wilderness, hire a local guide for $30 a day from ASOPROLA (☎ 2743–1184 ⊕ www.actuarcostarica.com), the local guide association, which also organizes strenuous three-day guided trips, with two overnights at a mountain refuge ($146 per person with all meals). ASOPROLA also operates El Albergue La Amistad, at the Altamira park entrance, with both private and dormitory rooms with hot-water showers ($12), as well as an organic restaurant run by a local women's cooperative. The alternative is rustic campsites (bring your own tent) for $6 per person at the Potrero Grande park entrance. Reserve space about a week in advance. To get to the park entrance (4WD essential), drive 31 km (20 miles) west from San Vito along the road to Paso Real. Turn right at the park sign at Guacimo, near two small roadside restaurants. Then drive about 20 km (13 miles) uphill on a rough road. The last couple of kilometers are on foot. ☎ 2200–5355 ⌨ $10 per day ☉ Daily, sunrise–sunset.

EXPLORING

☺ ★ **Hacienda Barú.** Hacienda Barú nature reserve is a leader in both ecotourism and conservation, with spectacular bird-watching and excellent naturalist guides, along with a turtle-protection project and nature-education program in the local school. You can stay at the cabins and poolside rooms or on platform tents on the beach; or just come for the day to walk the forest and mangrove trails, zip through the canopy on cables, climb a tree, or stake out birds on an observation platform. ✉ 3 km/2 miles north of bridge into Dominical ☎ 2787–0003 ⊕ www.haciendabaru.com ⌨ $6, tours $20–$100 ☉ Daily 7 am–dusk.

☺ **Nauyaca Waterfalls.** Nauyaca Waterfalls (*Cataratas de Nauyaca*), a massive double cascade tumbling down 45 meters (150 feet) and 20 meters (65 feet), are one of the most spectacular sights in Costa Rica. The waterfalls—also known as Barú River Falls—are on private property, so the only way to reach them is to take a hiking or horseback tour (⇨ *Outdoor Activities, below*).

☺ **Parque Reptilandia.** Five years in the making, Parque Reptilandia is an impressive reptile exhibit with more than 300 specimens of snakes, lizards, frogs, turtles, and other creatures in terrariums and large enclosures. You can see a Komodo dragon, Gila monsters, and a 150-pound, African spur-thighed tortoise that likes to be petted. Kids love the maternity ward showcasing newborn snakes. More-mature snakes live under

The South Pacific Coast

0 ——— 8 mi
0 ——— 8 km

a retractable roof that lets in sun and rain. Although snakes are generally more active in sunlight, this is still a great rainy-day-at-the-beach
alternative activity. Guided night tours ($20) can also be arranged to
watch nocturnal animals at work. If you're not squeamish, feeding
day is Friday. Kids under 12 years old pay $5. ✉ *11 km/7 miles east of
Dominical on road to San Isidro* ☎ *2787–0343* ⊕ *www.crreptiles.com*
💲 *$10* 🕙 *Daily 9–4:30.*

Playa Dominical. Playa Dominical is long and flat, rarely crowded, and
good for beachcombing among all the flotsam and jetsam that the surf
washes up onto the brown sand. It's a designated Blue Flag beach,
meaning the water is clean and garbage is properly taken care of. Swimmers should beware of fatally dangerous rip currents. In high season,
flags mark off a relatively safe area for swimming, under the watchful
gaze of a professional lifeguard.

Playa Dominicalito. Playa Dominicalito, just 1 km (½ mile) south of Playa
Dominical, is usually calmer and more suited to boogie boarding. There
are hidden rocks near the shore, so the best time to swim is beyond the
rocks at low tide.

🐾 **Pozo Azul.** A considerably smaller waterfall than Nauyaca Waterfalls,
Pozo Azul is in the jungle about 5 km (3 miles) south of town. Off the
main highway, head up the road toward Bella Vista lodge and take the

"Nauyaca waterfall is a three-tiered waterfall. Well worth the visit." —Photo by Richard Bueno, Fodors.com member

first road to the right, past the new school and through a stream; follow the road straight uphill for about 300 meters (1,000 feet) to where the road widens. You can park here and climb down the steps to the river on the right, where there is a lovely swimming hole and waterfall, often populated by local kids when school is out. There sometimes is a guard on duty in the parking lot (tip him about 350 colones per hour), but be sure not to leave anything of value in your parked car.

OUTDOOR ACTIVITIES

Much of the lush forest that covers the steep hillsides above the beaches is protected within private nature reserves. Several of these reserves, such as Hacienda Barú and La Merced (⇨ *Ballena Marine National Park, below)*, are financing a biological corridor and preservation of the rain forest.

FISHING

Angling options range from expensive sportfishing charters to a trip in a small boat to catch red snapper and snook for supper. The five most common fish species here, in the order in which you are likely to catch them, are sailfish, dorado, yellowfin tuna, wahoo, and marlin.

Capt. Isidro. Go fishing for wahoo and roosterfish the Tico way in a *panga*, a locally made, roofed-over boat. Casual fishers can try their luck in-shore for $60 an hour; more serious fishers can go farther off-shore, around Caño Island, and try for tuna and dorado, for $530 per day. ⊠ *Dominical* ☎ *2787–0341.*

HORSEBACK RIDING

Don Lulo. Don operates tours to Nauyaca Waterfalls that depart Monday to Saturday at 8 am from the stables behind the ticket office on the road to San Isidro, 10 km (6 miles) northeast of Dominical. The tour is $60 (cash preferred) and includes breakfast and lunch at Don Lulo's family homestead near the falls, ending at 2 pm. You can swim in the cool pool beneath the falls, so bring a bathing suit. There is a river to cross, but otherwise the ride is easy; horses proceed at a walk. Be sure to reserve a day in advance. ☎ *2787–0541, 2787–0542* 🌐 *www.nauyacawaterfallscostarica.com.*

PACK YOUR BOARD

The surfing is great in Dominical, thanks to the runoff from the Barú River mouth, which constantly changes the ocean bottom and creates well-shaped waves big enough to keep intermediate and advanced surfers challenged. The best surfing is near the river mouth, and the best time is two hours before or after high tide, to avoid the notorious riptides.

SURFING

Green Iguana Surf Camp. Come here for two-hour individual lessons for $50 or $40 per person for small groups of two or more. They also have weeklong packages that include lodging at upscale Villas Rio Mar, board rental, lessons, transport to whichever nearby beach has the best waves each day, and visits to local nature spots (from $945 per person, double occupancy). These packages include transportation to and from San José and other locations. ☎ *8825–1381* 🌐 *www.greeniguanasurfcamp.com.*

8

WHERE TO EAT

$$ THAI 🍴 **Coconut Spice.** If you like rice with spice, you've come to the right place. This sophisticated restaurant, one of Dominical's most durable and popular eating spots, has authentic Southeast Asian flavor in both food and furnishings. Try the hot-and-sour *tom yan goong* soup, tart with lemongrass and lime and heated up with chilies. The jumbo shrimp vary in price and can get quite expensive, but they're worth it: buttery, sweet, and cooked in spicy coconut sauce. There are also satays, curries, and other Indian standards. The open-air restaurant overlooks the river, so bring along repellent. It's open daily from 1 pm. [$] *Average main: $12* ✉ *Pueblo del Río at entrance to Dominical* ☎ *2787–0073.*

$$$ COSTA RICAN 🍴 **La Parcela.** Picture a dream location: a high headland jutting out into the sea with vistas up and down the coast. Throw in a breeze-swept terrace, polished service, and some fine seaside cuisine. This restaurant has had its ups and downs, often relying on its unmatched location. But the fish dishes, if pricey, are topped with some interesting sauces, including a standout roasted red pepper sauce with almonds. Less expensive is the grilled fish sandwich. Desserts here are rich—mud pie and a delectable chocolate cake—and substantial enough to share. If you're just passing through Dominical, this is a good place for a cold beer or a *naturale,* a tall glass of freshly whipped fruit juice. Sunsets here are spectacular. There is some controversy about this restaurant's eco-sensitive location, so call ahead to make sure it's still up and running. [$] *Average main: $15* ✉ *4 km/2½ miles south of Dominical* ☎ *2787–0016.*

$$ ✕ Maracatù. Who says vegetarian food has to be boring? From spicy
VEGETARIAN   pad Thai with tofu or shrimp, to tasty tuna teriyaki to crunchy falafels
served with brown rice and organic salad, this sophisticated restaurant
can make vegetarians ecstatic and even the most committed carnivore
happy. The fish tacos are delicious and priced to fit even the most bud-
get-conscious beachgoer. The eclectic decor reflects the global reach of
the kitchen, with Moroccan stained-glass lamps, cushions covered in
East Indian fabrics, and bamboo furniture. There are even tablecloths
and cloth napkins—a rarity at the beach. It's definitely the most roman-
tic restaurant in Dominical. $ *Average main: $8* ⊠ *Main street across
from soccer field* ☎ *2787–0091.*

$ ✕ Restaurant Su Raza. Among the handful of sodas in town serving typi-
COSTA RICAN   cal Costa Rican food, this one is notable for its whole fish and hearty
portions of seafood served on a breezy veranda. Stick to the *desayuno
típico* for breakfast, with traditional rice and beans and eggs, starting
at 7 am. The omelets are great, but they come with limp frozen french
fries, the bane of Tico restaurants. $ *Average main: $6* ⊠ *Main road,
across from San Clemente Grill* ☎ *2787–0105.*

$ ✕ San Clemente Mexican-American Bar & Grill. Signs you're in the local
SOUTHWESTERN   surfer hangout: a real Volkswagen van, balanced atop a pole at the
entrance, with life-size, loony caricatures (including Elvis) spilling out
of the windows; broken surfboards affixed to the ceiling; and photos of
the sport's early years adorning the walls. Fresh seafood, sandwiches,
and such Tex-Mex standards as burritos and nachos make up the menu,
which you can enjoy at inside tables or picnic tables on a terrace. Owner
Mike McGinnis is famous for making a blistering hot sauce and for
being a super source of information about the area. They also serve
breakfast during high season. $ *Average main: $7* ⊠ *Middle of main
road* ☎ *2787–0055.*

$ ✕ Tortilla Flats. Another perennially popular surfer hangout, this casual
MEXICAN   place has the advantage of being right across from the beach, although
the surrounding buildings make the neighborhood pretty shabby. Fresh-
baked baguette sandwiches are stuffed with interesting combinations;
the grilled chicken, avocado, tomato, and mozzarella California sand-
wich is the most popular. Light eaters can buy half a sandwich. Fresh-
fish specials, notably the popular fish tacos, and typical Mexican fare
round out the casual menu. The margaritas are excellent, along with
flavored daiquiris. $ *Average main: $7* ⊠ *On beach* ☎ *2787–0033.*

WHERE TO STAY

For expanded hotel reviews, visit Fodors.com.

Lodgings in the lowlands of Dominical and the area a little to the north
tend to be hot and muggy and not as comfortable as the more luxuri-
ous, private, and breezy places up in the hills above Dominicalito, to
the south.

$ ⊞ Coconut Grove Oceanfront Cottages. Right on the beach, this well-
RENTAL   maintained cluster of cabins and beach houses, set in a gorgeous gar-
den with magnificent trees, is ideal for couples or families who want to
fend for themselves. **Pros:** best location in town: right on beach; close
to cool ocean breezes; communal barbecue; friendly owner/hosts. **Cons:**

LIVING OFF THE GRID

Many hotels in the more remote areas of the South Pacific generate their own electricity, so don't count on air-conditioning, using a hair dryer, calling home, checking your email, or paying with a credit card (unless it's arranged in advance). Some lodges do have radio contact with the outside world and satellite phone systems you can use in emergencies, but bad weather can often block the satellite signal. On the positive side, you really can get away from it all in the Southern Zone. Pack as though you are a castaway from modern civilization. Be sure to bring the following:

■ Flashlight with extra batteries, or better still, one of the new kinetic flashlights that need no batteries

■ Insect repellent (lots of it)

■ Sunscreen (ditto)

■ After-sun lotion

■ All toiletries and medications you could conceivably need in small travel containers

■ Sturdy, breathable hiking shoes and lots of socks (your feet will get wet)

■ Waterproof walking sandals

■ Binoculars

■ Sun hat

■ Refillable water bottle

■ Portable, battery-operated reading light

■ Zip-style baggies of all sizes to keep cameras, snacks, etc., dry and bug-free

furnishings are simple, not fancy; guests must love animals **TripAdvisor:** "Pacific Coast paradise," "friendly hosts," "idyllic setting." $\boxed{\$}$ *Rooms from: $65 ⊠ Turn off main highway at Km 147, 3 km/2 miles south of Dominical* ☎ *2787–0130* ⊕ *www.coconutgrovecr.com* ⇗ *3 cabins, 2 beach houses* ▬ *No credit cards* ⬤ *No meals.*

$$
B&B/INN

⬚ **Cuna del Angel Hotel and Spa.** Decorative angels abound at this made-in-heaven fantasyland for grown-ups, a perfect spot for those who like to indulge themselves. **Pros:** delightful decor; excellent food; friendly service in hotel and spa, which is small and intimate. **Cons:** room balconies and terraces are quite close together, so not a lot of privacy; rooms that face the pool can be noisy if children are playing; steep steps to new Jungle Rooms. **TripAdvisor:** "very charming," "a gem of a hotel and restaurant," "excellent customer service." $\boxed{\$}$ *Rooms from: $103 ⊠ Puertocito, 9 km/5 miles south of Dominical* ☎ *2787–8012* ⊕ *www. cunadelangel.com* ⇗ *25 rooms* ⬤ *Breakfast.*

$
B&B/INN
☾
Fodor's Choice
★

⬚ **Hacienda Barú National Wildlife Refuge and Ecolodge.** Base yourself in this comfortable, model eco-lodge to explore vast tracts of surrounding forest, mangroves, and a Blue Flag beach with nesting turtles. **Pros:** prime wildlife viewing; excellent guides; trails and outdoor activities; spacious cabins with kitchens; comfortable new guest rooms; perfect for groups. **Cons:** older cabins are not fancy and have small, basic bathrooms. **TripAdvisor:** "wonderful staff," "rustic but beautiful surroundings," "fabulous for wildlife." $\boxed{\$}$ *Rooms from: $65 ⊠ 3 km/2 miles north of bridge into Dominical* ☎ *2787–0003* ⊕ *www.haciendabaru. com* ⇗ *6 cabinas, 6 guest rooms* ⬤ *Breakfast.*

8

$ **Pacific Edge.** Private, spacious wood cabinas—one sleeps six, others
B&B/INN sleep four—have kitchenettes, tiled bathrooms, hammocks strung on
★ wide porches, and comfortable orthopedic mattresses covered with
colorful Guatemalan bedspreads. **Pros:** fabulous views; bargain prices;
serene setting; can make your own breakfast and simple snacks. **Cons:**
very steep road that requires 4WD to get back and forth to town
restaurants and beaches; must love dogs. **TripAdvisor:** "drink in the
views," "spectacular," "tops for relaxation." $ *Rooms from: $52*
✉ *Drive 4 km/2½ miles south of Dominical to Km 148, then turn up
a rough road 1.2 km/1 mile* ☎ 2787–8010 ⊕ *www.pacificedge.info*
🛏 *4 cabinas* ⦿ *No meals.*

$$$ **Río Magnolia Nature Lodge.** Hidden away in a spectacular mountain
B&B/INN valley, this luxury, jungle eco-lodge has the best of everything: a huge
stone fireplace inside and an infinity pool outside, with distant ocean
views from wraparound decks. **Pros:** seclusion, magnificent views, excel-
lent food, lots of books and field guides. **Cons:** very difficult access over
rough, 4X4-only roads; must love dogs; be prepared for cool mountain
nights. **TripAdvisor:** "beautiful lodge," "perfection is hard to top,"
"great food and even greater hosts." $ *Rooms from: $200* ✉ *6 km
off the main highway between San Isidro and Dominical, Tinamaste*
☎ 8307–1036 ⊕ *www.riomagnolia.com* ⦿ *Breakfast.*

$$ **Roca Verde.** Small and friendly, this hotel has the best beach access
B&B/INN in the area, with sunny, stylish rooms, decorated with swirling flower
murals. **Pros:** right on the beach; friendly bar; reasonably priced. **Cons:**
can be very noisy Saturday night if you don't join the party; restaurant is
just average and a little gloomy. **TripAdvisor:** "taste of old Costa Rica,"
"this place is just perfect," "excellent service." $ *Rooms from: $75*
✉ *1 km/½ mile south of Dominical* ☎ 2787–0036 ⊕ *www.rocaverde.
net* 🛏 *9 rooms* ⦿ *No meals.*

$$ **Villas Río Mar.** Upriver from the beach on exquisitely landscaped
HOTEL grounds, this upscale hotel is awash in clouds of terrestrial orchids and
☾ aflame with bright bougainvillea and hibiscus. **Pros:** huge pool; lovely
★ grounds; good restaurant. **Cons:** some rooms have no air-conditioning,
and it can get hot here; there are small beaches along the river, but it's
a 15-minute walk along an alternately dusty/muddy road to town and
the ocean beach. **TripAdvisor:** "beautiful landscaping," "nice place to
stay," "you'll need a car." $ *Rooms from: $85* ✉ *1 km/½ mile west of
Dominical; turn right off highway into town and then right again under
bridge and follow bumpy river road* ☎ 2787–0052 ⊕ *www.villasriomar.
com* 🛏 *40 rooms, 12 junior suites* ⦿ *Breakfast.*

NIGHTLIFE

During the high season, Dominical hops at night, and when the surfers
have fled to find bigger waves, there are enough locals around to keep
some fun events afloat.

Maracatù World Music Bar. The crowd is young and edgy here, with an
open mike on Tuesday, Latin music on Wednesday, which is also free-
shots-for-ladies' night, and reggae on Thursday, with an all-you-can-eat
Rasta Pasta buffet. On Sunday there's an open jam. ✉ *Main street across
from San Clemente* ☎ 2787–0091.

Roca Verde. Saturday night the dance action is at the Roca Verde, with a mixed crowd that doesn't usually get warmed up until 11 pm; $4 cover charge for nonguests. There's also live music some Friday nights, featuring local jazz and rock bands. ⊠ *1 km/½ mile south of Dominical* ☎ *2787–0036.*

San Clemente Bar. Friday night in high season there's sometimes live music and dancing here, on top of the usual high-decibel music tracks. ⊠ *On main road* ☎ *2787–0055.*

Tortilla Flats. This lively restaurant *(⇨ above)* also has a stage for live bands and DJ music, so check out their program when you are in town. ⊠ *Dominical* ☎ *2787–0033.*

SHOPPING

Banana Bay Gallery & Gifts. Banana Bay Gallery & Gifts is not only air-conditioned, but also stocked with an always-intriguing and -amusing mix of arts and crafts and unusual items, along with indigenous crafts such as tropical masks and lots of insect-themed toys for kids of all ages. ⊠ *Plaza Pacífica shopping center, highway just above Dominical* ☎ *2787–0106* ⊙ *Mon.–Sat.*

Mama Kiya Art Gallery. This is the showplace for local artists and artisans, with canvasses spilling out onto the sidewalk in front of the colorful shop, brimming with oil paintings, sculpture, textiles, and indigenous crafts. Owner Pedro Monzón always has a smile for passersby. If he can't help you find a one-of-a-kind souvenir here, you won't find it anywhere. ⊠ *Centro Comercial Pueblo del Rio* ☎ *2787–0215.*

BALLENA MARINE NATIONAL PARK

20 km/12 miles southeast of Dominical.

Ballena Marine National Park. Parque Nacional Marino Ballena (Whale Marine National Park) has four separate beaches, stretching for about 10 km (6 miles), and encompasses a mangrove estuary, a remnant coral reef, and more than 12,350 acres of ocean, home to tropical fish, dolphins, and humpback whales who use it as a nursery. ⊠ *Park begins at Playa Uvita, about 20 km/20 miles south of Dominical* ☎ *2743–8236* 🎫 *$6* ⊙ *Daily 6–6.*

GETTING HERE AND AROUND

The park area includes the communities of Uvita, Bahía Ballena, and Ojochal, all easily accessible off the Costanera, a wide, paved highway. As soon as you get off the highway, however, the roads are bumpy and dusty. Alternatively, take a taxi or bus from Dominical. Buses leave Dominical at 10:30 am and 5:30 pm daily, and there are longer-haul buses that pass along the Costanera and can drop you off in Uvita. Each of the park's four sectors has a small ranger station where you pay your $10 admission.

ESSENTIALS

Hospital Pacific Medical Clinic. This is the closest doctor's office to Dominical and Ojochal. ⊠ *Beside highway in Uvita, upstairs above Farmacia Bahía, next door to BM Supermarket.* ☎ *2743–8743, 8637–0746.*

Wildlife-Watching Tips

If you're accustomed to nature programs on TV, with visions of wildebeest and zebra swarming across African savanna, your first visit to a tropical forest can be a bewildering experience. If these forests are so diverse, where are all the animals? Websites, brochures, and books are plastered with lovely descriptions and close-up images of wildlife that give travelers high hopes. Reality is much different but no less fascinating. Here are some tips to make your experience more enjoyable.

■ Don't expect to see rarely sighted animals. It might happen; it might not. Cats (especially jaguars), harpy eagles, and tapirs are a few rare sightings.

■ Monkeys can be the easiest animals to spot, but although they are as reliable as the tides in some locations, in others they are rare indeed.

■ Remember that nearly all animals spend most of their time avoiding detection.

■ Be quiet! Nothing is more unsettling to a wary animal than 20 Homo sapiens conversing as they hike. It's best to treat the forest like a house of worship—quiet reverence is in order.

■ Listen closely. Many visitors are surprised when a flock of parrots overhead is pointed out to them, despite the incredible volume of noise they produce. That low-pitched growl you hear is a howler monkey call, which is obvious if nearby, but easily missed over the din of conversation. Try stopping for a moment and closing your eyes.

■ Slowly observe different levels of the forest. An enormous caterpillar or an exquisitely camouflaged moth may be only a few inches from your face, and the silhouettes in the tree 100 meters (330 feet) away may be howler monkeys. Scan trunks and branches where a sleeping sloth or anteater might curl up. A quick glance farther down the trail may reveal an agouti or peccary crossing your path.

■ In any open area such as a clearing or river, use your binoculars and scan in the distance; scarlet macaws and toucans may be cruising above the treetops.

■ Cultivate some level of interest in the less charismatic denizens of the forest—the plants, insects, and spiders. On a good day in the forest you may see a resplendent quetzal or spider monkey, but should they fail to appear, focus on an intricate spiderweb, a column of marching army ants, mammal footprints in the mud, or colorful seeds and flowers fallen from high in the canopy.

Pharmacy Farmacia Bahía ⊠ *Next to BM Supermarket in Uvita, across from Banco Nacional.* ☎ *2743–8583.*

Visitor Information Uvita Information Center. The best place in the area to get information on tours and hotels. And it's air-conditioned inside. ⊠ *In shopping center across from BM Supermarket in Uvita* ☎ *8843–7142, 2743–8889* ⊕ *www.uvita.info.*

EXPLORING

🕐 **Rancho La Merced National Wildlife Refuge.** At this 1,250-acre property combining forest, pasture, and beach, you can ride the range or beach on horseback, explore the forest on a nature hike, or go bird-watching with an excellent guide. Riding tours include a guide and begin at the pleasant reception center, where you can also freshen up in clean, modern restrooms; the full-day tour includes fruit juice and cookies. For $6 you can explore the 10 km (6 miles) of hiking trails on your own with a trail map that includes a wildlife picture guide. ⊠ *Reception center at Km 159 on Costanera, north of Uvita* ☎ *2743–8032* ⊕ *www. rancholamerced.com* 🖅 *$35–$50* ⊙ *By reservation only.*

Oro Verde Private Nature Reserve. You'll also find excellent bird-watching and hiking a little farther up the hill in the Oro Verde Private Nature Reserve, which offers daily three-hour birding tours ($30), as well as guided hikes through their primary forest reserve ($35) and a three- to four-hour morning horseback tour to a waterfall, including lunch ($35). ⊠ *3 km/2 miles uphill from Rancho La Merced, north of Uvita* ☎ *2743–8889, 8843–8833* ⊙ *By reservation only.*

Playa Ventanas. Playa Ventanas, just 1½ km (1 mile) south of Ballena Marine Park, is a beautiful beach that's popular for sea-kayaking, with some interesting tidal caves. The mountains that rise up behind these beaches hold rain forests, waterfalls, and wildlife. Sometimes there is guarded, private parking here for 350 colones (about 75¢) an hour, but whether or not there is a guard, do not leave anything of value in your car.

Uvita Market. Saturday, from 8 am to noon, the place to be is at this combination farmers' market and weekly gathering place for locals. More than 20 vendors sell organic produce, homemade cheeses, fresh fish, baked goods, jams and pickles, and frozen gourmet dinners and soups to take home. You can also feast on ready-to-eat breakfast burritos, tamales, cakes, and cookies. As well as food, there are artisan stalls with painted masks, colorful textiles, plus used books and beautiful photographs of birds by a local photographer. Every third Saturday there's a garage-sale table, too. This is a great place to meet English-speaking locals as they meet and greet. Some weeks, there's live music, too, by local bands. ⊠ *50 m west of Banco de Costa Rica, Rincón de Uvita, Uvita* ☎ *None.*

OUTDOOR ACTIVITIES

Outfitters in Dominical *(⇨ above)* run tours to the park and surrounding beaches. **La Merced National Wildlife Refuge** *(⇨ above)* has birding, forest hikes, and horseback riding. For local bookings and information, contact the Uvita Information Center *(⇨ above)*.

DIVING AND SNORKELING

Bahía Aventuras. This new outfit with bilingual guides runs a recommended half-day tour in covered boats that combines whale- and dolphin-watching with snorkeling, for $85. They also offer a tour of the Terraba Sierpe Mangrove, $85. ⊠ *Bahía Ballena* ☎ *2743–8362, 8846–6576* ⊕ *www.bahiaaventuras.com.*

Mystic Dive Center. Mystic Dive Center specializes in dive and snorkel trips to Caño Island, about 50 km (31 miles), taking a minimum of four divers or eight snorkelers ($95 full-day snorkeling; $145 full-day diving, including equipment, lunch, park fees, and guide); the tour leaves at 6:30 am and returns around 3 pm. Or you can dive or snorkel closer in, only a 15-minute boat ride from Playa Ventanas, morning or afternoon, with a minimum of three ($65 for snorkelers, $95 for divers), including breakfast or lunch, equipment, and guide. ☎ *2786–5217* 🌐 *www.mysticdivecenter.com* 🕒 *Open only during dry season, Dec.–Aug.*

The best spot for snorkeling in the park is at the north end of Playa Ballena, near the whale's tail.

Dolphin Tours of Bahía Ballena. With an office very close to the beach, this tried-and-true tour company takes a minimum of two people on four-hour boat tours that combine dolphin-and whale-watching, with snorkeling and a visit to a rocky island bird sanctuary. Kids 4 to 9 only pay $35. ☎ *2743–8013, 8825–4031* 🌐 *www.dolphintourcostarica.com* 🎫 *$65.*

FISHING

Bahía Aventuras. Go fishing from a 23-foot locally designed and built boat with one of Bahía Aventuras bilingual captain, setting out from the beach at Bahía Ballena. ✉ *Bahía Ballena* ☎ *2743–8362* 🎫 *Half-day $650; full day $800.*

Dolphin Tours of Bahía Ballena. *(⇨ Diving and Snorkeling, above.)* The operators here offer half-day, inshore fishing trips for snook and red snapper that cost $500 for up to four anglers; $650 for a full day offshore.

ULTRALIGHT FLIGHTS

👶 **Ultra Light Tour.** For a thrilling bird's-eye view of Bahía Ballena and the park, take off in a two-seater ultralight flying machine with aeronautical engineer Georg Kiechle on an Ultra Light Tour. Tours cost $140 for 30-minute trips; negotiable for. longer flights. ✉ *PapaKilo airstrip, 450 m north of Costanera entrance to Colonia Beach* ☎ *2743–8037, 8816–6901* 🌐 *www.ultralighttour.com.*

WHERE TO EAT

$$$ ECLECTIC ★ 🍴 **Citrus Restaurant.** This eclectic and exotic restaurant in a Moroccan-inspired palace lives up to its name: it's tangy, tart, and refreshing. The intriguing menu offers sophisticated world cuisine, ranging from a Moroccan-style hamburger served with spicy harissa mayonnaise, to fish and seafood with Asian accents of ginger, Szechuan pepper, curry, and Thai spices. There's a *soupçon* of French flavor, too, with garlicky escargots and steak frites (steak with french fries). Desserts are among the best in the country; if you like chocolate, don't pass up the divine Choco-Choco flourless chocolate cake with vanilla ice cream. Choose from elegant inside tables, or romantic, torch-lighted terrace and riverside garden tables. Service can be slow, so allow lots of time for lunch or dinner, from 11 am to 10 pm. Lunch specials are great value and are available until 5 pm. On Tuesday morning Citrus hosts a small *feria*, a market of local produce, baked goods, and crafts. ⚠ **Menu prices do not include tax and service, so add an extra 23 percent.** [$] *Average main: $15* ✉ *First left turn off main road into Ojochal, 15 km/9 miles south of Uvita* ☎ *2786–5175* 🕒 *Closed Sun.*

"Strolling across Playa Uvita, I saw this iguana; I think it was as interested in me as I was in him." —Photo by Justin Hubbell, Fodors.com member

$$$
FRENCH
★

✕**Exotica Restaurant.** Set in the tiny French-Canadian enclave of Ojochal, this intimate, 10-table thatch-roof restaurant has been serving superb tropical, French-inspired fare for more than a decade. You'll be warmly welcomed by Lucy, the restaurant's chic and charming owner. For starters, there's a tangy refreshing avocado, pineapple, lime, and cilantro appetizer or an intriguing Tahitian fish carpaccio with bananas. Don't miss out on a hearty serving of fish or shrimp in a spicy banana-curry sauce or a spicy Vietnamese chicken soup. French favorites include cognac liver pâté, and a pricey but excellent duck breast with an orange or Port sauce. Presentation is artistic, with garnishes of flowers and sprigs of exotic greenery. Desserts are all homemade, luscious, and reasonably priced. Chocoholics won't want to miss the chocolate chiffon cake with chocolate sauce and an accompanying shot glass of cocoa liqueur. $ *Average main: $15* ⊠ *Main road into Ojochal, 15 km/9 miles south of Uvita* ☎ *2786–5050* ⬧ *Reservations essential* ⊗ *Closed Sun.*

$
FRENCH

✕**Pancito Café.** Besides baguettes, buttery croissants, and divine pastries to go, this French-owned bakery at the entrance to Ojochal serves hearty breakfast omelets, and does a booming lunch business with crepes, quiches, meal-size salads, soup of the day, pizza, and sandwiches on French bread. Customers perch on high stools at tables and counters in this casual, thatch-roofed alfresco café, many with their laptops open, taking advantage of the free Wi-Fi. Get here early on Tuesday for the popular weekly *plat du jour*. $ *Average main: $6* ⊠ *Plaza de Los Delfines, entrance road to Ojochal, 25 m off Costanera, Ojochal* ⊟ *No credit cards* ⊗ *No dinner.*

$$ ✗ **Piccola Italia.** More than 25 versions of pizza, plus homemade pastas
ITALIAN   with your choice of 17 sauces, from Arrabiata to Verdure, are the main-
stays of this new, casual Italian eatery with rustic wooden furniture,
conveniently just off the highway in Uvita, in a quiet garden overlook-
ing a swimming pool. Chef Marcelo Sauda prides himself on using only
authentic Italian ingredients. Don't miss his specialty Rossellinos, round
pasta pillows filled with ricotta cheese and ham and sitting on a salsa of
fresh tomatoes, with a Gorgonzola cheese sauce on top. Marcelo also
has daily specials, depending on what's freshest, for example, *corvina*
(sea bass) with tagliatelle on the side. The home-baked rolls here are
addictive—crusty on the outside; soft and salty on the inside. You can
choose from eight Italian wines by the bottle or drink the Chilean house
wine by the glass. Free Wi-Fi. $ *Average main: $10 ⊠ 300 m north of
Servicentro gas station, Bahia Uvita* ☎ 8769–1663.

$ ✗ **Tilapias El Pavón.** To enjoy an authentically Tico day in the country, fol-
COSTA RICAN   low a winding river road up to this family-run tilapia fish farm. You can
work up an appetite on a short hike to a spectacular, nearby waterfall
with a swimming hole (bring your suit and binoculars for bird-watching),
then catch your own tilapia. The cooks at the open-air wooden restaurant
overlooking the tidily kept fishponds will fry up your fish in 10 minutes,
and present it whole or filleted, with rice, salad, yuca, and excellent *pata-
cones* (fried, mashed plantains), plus a pitcher of refreshing fruit *naturale*,
a feast for only $8. They also serve wine and beer. It's open 9 am to 6 pm
weekdays, until 8 pm on weekends, so it's a good spot for lunch or an
early dinner. $ *Average main: $8 ⊠ Just before bridge in Punta Mala
(2 km/1 mile south of Ojochal), follow a dirt road 4 km/2½ miles uphill
to hamlet of Vergel* ☎ 8311–8213 ▬ No credit cards ☿ Closed Mon.

WHERE TO STAY
For expanded hotel reviews, visit Fodors.com.

$$$ ⛉ **Cristal Ballena Hotel Resort.** High on a hillside with spectacular ocean
B&B/INN   views, this Austrian-owned hotel is the most luxurious base for explor-
♺   ing the area, with a 400-square-meter (4,400-square-foot) swimming
★   pool that commands both mountain and sea views. **Pros:** wonderful
swimming pool for serious swimmers and loungers; great ocean, mountain, and sky views; luxurious rooms. **Cons:** restaurant service can be
slow; steep walk to beach. **TripAdvisor:** "beautiful," "gracious hosts,"
"luxurious and peaceful." $ *Rooms from: $189 ⊠ 7 km/4 miles south
of Uvita on the Costanera* ☎ 2786–5354 ⊕ *www.cristal-ballena.com*
↶ *18 suites* ⼀⦿⼀ *Breakfast.*

$$ ⛉ **Diquis del Sur Botanical Garden & Inn.** At this ideal—and affordable—
RENTAL   tropical retreat for the winter-weary, five bungalows are sprinkled
around lush grounds with views of both mountains and ocean. **Pros:**
reasonable daily rates and weekly bargains; great breakfasts; lots of
privacy in well-spaced bungalows. **Cons:** some bungalows have no air-
conditioning; spare but adequate furnishings; rough road up from main
highway. **TripAdvisor:** "beautiful and comfortable," "lovely grounds,"
"welcome to paradise." $ *Rooms from: $85 ⊠ 1 km/½ mile up dirt
road signed "Calle Papagayo," off Ojochal main road* ☎ 2786–5013
⊕ *www.diquiscostarica.com* ↶ *5 bungalows (10 rooms), 1 cabin with
kitchen* ⼀⦿⼀ *Breakfast.*

$$ B&B/INN **La Cusinga.** Along with one of the best sunset views along the coast, this comfortable eco-lodge on a high cliff bordering Ballena Marine National Park has spacious, airy cabins and a forest trail to a pristine beach. **Pros:** comfortable cabins; forest and beach access. **Cons:** steep path between cabins and lodge; uncomfortable concrete benches on private terraces. **TripAdvisor:** "simply beautiful," "small secluded paradise," "top scenery and hospitality." [$] *Rooms from: $149* ✉ *Between Km 166 and 167 on the Costanera south of Dominical, Bahía Ballena* ☎ *2770–2549* 🌐 *www.lacusingalodge.com* 🍴 *Breakfast.*

$ **Rio Tico Safari Lodge.** You'll feel as though you're on a luxury safari when you step inside one of these spacious South African–made tents. **Pros:** gorgeous, natural setting; dry and airy tents; helpful hosts. **Cons:** some steps to climb up and down from main lodge to tents. **TripAdvisor:** "wonderful luxurious safari tent," "secluded," "an unequalled experience." [$] *Rooms from: $55* ✉ *Just before bridge in Punta Mala (2 km/1 mile) south of Ojochal, follow a dirt road 4 km/2½ miles uphill to hamlet of Vergel, Vergel de Punta Mala* ☎ *8996–7935* 🌐 *www.riotico.com* 🛏 *9 rooms* 🍴 *No meals.*

$$ B&B/INN **Tiki Villas Rainforest Lodge.** Just off the Costanera Highway, these spacious, upscale, Indonesian-style bungalows are cantilevered over a hillside garden, each with a private deck looking onto mature trees and ocean views. **Pros:** comfortable bungalows; excellent breakfasts; close to road. **Cons:** short but steep, 4X4 only access road; steps to climb to bungalows; close to road and truck noise. **TripAdvisor:** "beautifully tranquil spot," "stunning Zen-like surroundings," "helpful staff and hosts." [$] *Rooms from: $130* ✉ *Between Km 155 and 156 on Costanera, 12 km/7 miles south of Dominical; 6 km/4 miles north of Ballena Marine Park, Uvita* 🌐 *www.tikivillas.com* 🛏 *5 bungalows* 💳 *No credit cards* 🍴 *Breakfast.*

8

$$ B&B/INN **Villas Gaia.** Conveniently just off the highway, these spacious, tasteful villas owned by a sophisticated Dutch couple are hidden behind a ridge overlooking forest ravines leading to Playa Tortuga. **Pros:** easy access, right off the highway; serene setting; proximity to beaches and Ballena Park. **Cons:** you must climb some stairs to get to the villas; pool is small; beach is down a steep path; no air-conditioning in four rooms. **TripAdvisor:** "wonderful experience and food," "total relaxation," "rustic feel." [$] *Rooms from: $75* ✉ *15 km/9 miles south of Uvita on coastal highway, Playa Tortuga* ☎ *2786–5044, 2244–0316 in San José* 🌐 *www.villasgaia.com* 🛏 *14 cabinas, 1 house* 🍴 *Breakfast.*

SHOPPING

★ **Green Leaf Arts & Artesania.** Next door to Mystic Dive Center is Green Leaf Arts & Artesania, with a great selection of high-quality local art, indigenous crafts, and eclectic home accessories, plus a wide selection of field guides and jewelry. Next door at the **Licorera Feliz** (same owner), you can pick up imported snacks, cheeses, and treats for a beach picnic, as well as imported beer and wine from the best selection available in the area. Both stores are open daily from 9 to 6. Brand-new **Super Comida** (☎ *2786–5123*), also next door, stocks local and international groceries and has a used-book exchange, open daily 7 to 6. ✉ *Centro Comercial Ventanas, near Km 174, 1 km/½ mile north of Ojochal* ☎ *2786–5313.*

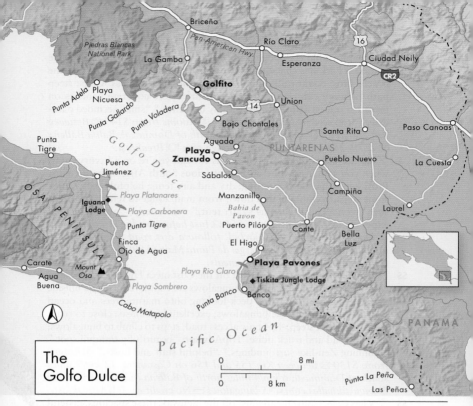

The Golfo Dulce

THE GOLFO DULCE

One of only three tropical fjords in the world, the Golfo Dulce has 180-meter-deep (600-foot-deep) waters in the center of a usually placid gulf where visitors can get out on boats or kayaks to watch dolphins swim and humpback whales feed. At Chacarita, 33 km (20 miles) south of Palmar Sur, the southern coast assumes a split personality. Heading west, you reach the Osa Peninsula and, eventually, the Pacific Ocean and the wildest region of Costa Rica. Continuing due south brings you to the Golfo Dulce, which means "Sweet Gulf," reflecting the usually tranquil waters. This gulf creates two shorelines: an eastern shore that is accessible only by boat above Golfito, and a western shore, which is the eastern side of the Osa Peninsula. South of Golfito the coast fronts the Pacific Ocean once again (rather than the calm gulf), with wilder beaches that beckon surfers and nature lovers.

GOLFITO

339 km/212 miles southeast of San José.

Overlooking a small gulf (hence its name) and hemmed in by a steep bank of forest, Golfito has a great location. Lodges run world-class sportfishing trips and supply kayaks for paddling the gulf's warm, salty, and crystal clear waters. When the sun sets behind the rolling silhouette of the Osa Peninsula, you can sometimes spot phosphorescent fish jumping. Golfito was a thriving banana port for several decades—United Fruit arrived in 1938—with elegant housing and lush landscaping for its plantation managers. After United Fruit pulled out in 1985, Golfito slipped into a state of poverty and neglect. The town itself consists of a pleasant, lushly landscaped older residential section and a long strip of scruffy commercial buildings. Visiting U.S. Coast Guard ships dock here, and small cruise ships moor in the harbor. The Costa Rica Coast Guard Academy is also here.

NAVIGATING GOLFITO Taxis and boats take you wherever you need to go in and around Golfito. You can hire taxi boats at the city dock in Golfito (about $80 round-trip often negotiable to go to area lodges or across to Puerto Jiménez. The only way to reach the remote Golfo Dulce lodges above Golfito is by boat. Early morning is the best time, when the water in the gulf is at its calmest. Most lodges include the boat transport in their rates.

GETTING HERE

From San José the trip is a long and often grueling eight-hour drive along paved roads crossing over often-foggy mountains. Your best bet, especially if you are visiting a lodge on the gulf, is to fly to Golfito, which takes only about an hour. Direct buses from San José leave twice daily, at 7 am and 3 pm.

ESSENTIALS

Banks/ATM ATH Coopealianza ⊠ *Across from hospital, north end of town.* **Banco Nacional** ⊠ *South of hospital* ☎ *2775–1101.*

Hospital Regional Hospital. This is the main hospital for the Southern Zone, including Puerto Jiménez and the Osa Peninsula. This is where you go—by boat, ambulance, or charter plane—if you need anti-venom for a serious snake bite. ⊠ *American Zone, near Deposito* ☎ *2775–7800.*

Internet CSI Internet. Wi-Fi is now widely available if you have your own laptop. Locals use computers here at CSI Internet. ⊠ *150 m south of Banco Nacional near ship dock* ☎ *2775–0718.*

Pharmacy Farmacia Golfito ⊠ *Main street across from city park* ☎ *2775–2442.*

Post Office Correo ⊠ *Across from soccer field; climb flight of stairs off the main road, south of central park.*

Taxis Taxi service. You can call for a taxi, or hail one of the *colectivo* taxis that pick up and drop off multiple passengers along the main road. Be prepared to squeeze in with the locals. ☎ *2775–2020.*

Visitor Information Land Sea Services. Land Sea Services offers tours and tourist information. They also sell SANSA tickets for domestic flights. ⊠ *Next to Banana Bay Marina on left as you enter town* ☎ *2775–1614.*

8

EXPLORING

American Zone. The northwestern end of town is the so-called American Zone, full of handsome wooden houses, some on stilts, where the expatriate managers of United Fruit lived amid flowering trees imported from all over the world. Many of these vintage houses, built of durable Honduran hardwoods, are now being spruced up along with eccentric garden features, such as a restored railway car, so it's worth a stroll in the neighborhood. If you're on foot, there's also excellent birding in and around the gardens here.

★ **Casa Orquideas.** A Garden of Eden with mass plantings of ornamental palms, bromeliads, heliconias, cycads, orchids, flowering gingers, and spice trees, Casa Orquideas has been tended with care for more than 25 years by American owners Ron and Trudy MacAllister. The 2½-hour tour, available Sunday and Thursday at 8:30 am, includes touching, tasting, and smelling, plus spotting toucans and hummingbirds. Trudy is also a font of information on local lore and medicinal plants. Guided tours, given for a minimum of three people, are $8 per person. Self-guided visits cost $5. The garden is accessible only by boat; a water taxi from Golfito to the garden (about $80 round-trip for four or more people) is a tour in itself. ⊠ *North of Golfito on the Golfo Dulce* ☎ *8829–1247* 🖃 *$5–$8* ☉ *Tours Thurs. and Sun. only at 8:30 am; drop-ins any day except closed Fri.*

Piedras Blancas National Park. Piedras Blancas National Park has some great birding. The park is verdant forest, home to many species of endemic plants and animals. It's also an important wildlife corridor because it connects to Corcovado National Park. Follow the main road northwest through the old American Zone, past the airstrip and a housing project: the place where a dirt road heads into the rain forest is ground zero for bird-watchers. There are no marked trails; the best birding is along the road. ⊠ *Adjacent to Golfito National Wildlife Refuge* ☎ *No phone* 🖃 *Free* ☉ *Daily dawn–dusk.*

Playa Cacao. Golfito doesn't have a beach of its own, but Playa Cacao is a mere five-minute boat ride across the bay from town. Hire a boat at the city dock or from a mooring opposite the larger cruise-ship dock, north of Golfito's center. Playa Cacao has two casual restaurants and one collection of basic cabinas, but it makes a cooler, quieter option when the heat and noise in Golfito get unbearable, and it is a good putting-in spot for kayaks.

OUTDOOR ACTIVITIES

FISHING

The open ocean holds plenty of sailfish, marlin, and roosterfish during the dry months, as well as mahimahi, tuna, and wahoo during the rainy season; there's excellent bottom fishing any time of year. Captains are in constant radio contact with one another and tend to share fish finds.

Banana Bay Marina. Banana Bay Marina has a fleet of five boats skippered by world-record-holding captains. A day's fishing for up to four averages $1,300. ☎ *2775–0838, 2775–1111* ⊕ *www.bananabaymarina.com.*

Land Sea. These folks can hook you up with independent captains in the area. ✉ *Waterfront next to Banana Bay Marina* ☎ *2775–1614* 🌐 *www.golfitocostarica.com.*

WHERE TO EAT

$$ AMERICAN 🍴 **Banana Bay.** For consistently good American-style food, you can't beat this breezy marina restaurant with a view of expensive yachts and fishing boats. Locals complain that the prices are high, but portions are hefty, and include generous salads, popular hamburgers, excellent chicken fajitas wrapped in tortillas, and a delicious grilled dorado fish sandwich with a mountain of fries—a deal at $7. It's open for breakfast, too. Try the Eggs in Hell specialty of two poached eggs smothered in hot sauce or the McBilge breakfast sandwich. **■TIP→ Destructive trawling methods by commercial shrimp boats have caused massive damage to the Golfo Dulce fishery, so this restaurant makes a point of having no shrimp on the menu.** Eco-conscious restaurant-goers might want to eschew shrimp as well. While you're waiting for your order, take advantage of the free Wi-Fi. [$] *Average main: $10* ✉ *Golfito main street south of town dock* ☎ *2775–0838.*

$$ COSTA RICAN 🍴 **Restaurante Mar y Luna.** This casual, affordable terrace restaurant jutting out into Golfito Harbor has the best harbor view in Golfito, along with jaunty nautical decor and cool breezes. The seafood-heavy lineup includes grilled whole fish Cajun-style. Mixed chicken and beef fajitas are also on the menu, along with a few vegetarian dishes. The quality varies, depending on who's in the kitchen, but during a recent visit the kitchen was in top form. The bar here is a great place to hang out, with a large flat-screen TV and brightly painted fish frolicking on the varnished bar top. New suites with the same view are available for rent here. [$] *Average main: $10* ✉ *South end of Golfito main street just north of Hotel Las Gaviotas* ☎ *2775–0192* 🌐 *www.hotelmarylunaandsuites.com.*

$$$ COSTA RICAN 🍴 **Restaurante Vitrales.** Dining here is both an aesthetic and gastronomic experience, in a spectacular, oval dining room reminiscent of a 1930s ocean liner, with dark-wood wood paneling; two monumental, fish-theme wall murals, and a stained-glass ceiling (the *vitrales* in the restaurant's name). Happily, the food—sophisticated, modern Costa Rican—is as beautifully presented and prepared as the outstanding decor. The *pejibaye* (peach palm fruit) soup is a taste and textural sensation—nutty and creamy, flavored with avocado and apples, and studded with crispy croutons. Their spinach salad is a meal in itself, loaded with cheddar cheese, chunks of red pepper, real bacon, and bathed in apple-flavored dressing. Main dishes include fish, beef, and chicken with interesting Tico touches. Not to be missed is the coffee-flavored dark chocolate cake, floating on a cream and *mora* (blackberry) sauce. Service here is polished and pleasant. For a special occasion, this is the place to go in Golfito. [$] *Average main: $16* ✉ *Casa Roland Marina Resort, American Zone* ☎ *2775–0180.*

WHERE TO STAY

For expanded hotel reviews, visit Fodors.com.

The atmosphere of the in-town hotels differs dramatically from that of the lodges in the delightfully remote east coast of the Golfo Dulce. The latter is a world of jungle and blue water, birds and fish, and desert-island beaches, with lodges accessible only by boat from either Golfito or Puerto Jiménez.

$$ RESORT **Casa Roland Marina Resort.** Everything at this luxury resort, designed like an art-deco ocean-liner incongruously dry-docked in Golfito's American Zone, is first-class. **Pros:** style and luxury; excellent service; resort facilities for bargain price **Cons:** dark hallways and low ceilings on lower floor. **TripAdvisor:** "a nice surprise," "great hotel and fishing," "beyond expectation." [$] *Rooms from: $115* ✉ *American Zone* ☎ *2775–3405* 🌐 *www.casaroland.com* 🛏 *22 rooms, 4 master and 2 junior suites* 🍴 *Breakfast.*

$$ B&B/INN **Esquinas Rainforest Lodge.** This well-managed eco-lodge is a model conservation project run by Austrians who have tried to instill a sense of Teutonic order. **Pros:** excellent trails and wildlife-viewing opportunities in unique natural setting; hearty meals. **Cons:** no air-conditioning and it can get hot here; some trails are challenging and you need to be steady on your feet; lodge is geared to nature lovers who aren't looking for luxury. **TripAdvisor:** "great atmosphere," "outstanding natural setting," "rustic luxury in the rainforest." [$] *Rooms from: $120* ✉ *Near La Gamba, 5 km/3 miles west of Villa Briceño turnoff* ☎ *2741–8001* 🌐 *www.esquinaslodge.com* 🛏 *14 rooms in 7 bungalows, 1 villa* 🍴 *All meals.*

$$ B&B/INN **Hotel Las Gaviotas.** Just south of town on the water's edge, this recently remodelled hotel has wonderful views over the inner gulf. **Pros:** great location and large pool; safe parking. **Cons:** a little pricey; close to road. **TripAdvisor:** "charming," "right on the ocean," "feels like home." [$] *Rooms from: $86* ✉ *3 km/2 miles south of Golfito town center* ☎ *2775–0062* 🌐 *www.lasgaviotasmarinaresort.com/* 🛏 *18 rooms, 3 cabinas* 🍴 *Breakfast.*

$$ B&B/INN **Hotel Samoa del Sur.** Nautical kitsch at its corniest, this dockside hotel has a ship-shape restaurant ($$), complete with a billowy sail, a mermaid figurehead, and a collection of U.S. Coast Guard caps donated by visiting personnel at the Costa Rican Coast Guard Academy in Golfito. **Pros:** affordable and fun; lively restaurant. **Cons:** can be lots of rambunctious kids in pool; noisy bar in evenings; guard dogs at night may frighten some guests. **TripAdvisor:** "staff is very nice," "excellent food," "exceptional owners." [$] *Rooms from: $75* ✉ *Main street, 1 block north of town dock* ☎ *2775–0233* 🌐 *www.samoadelsur.com* 🛏 *14 rooms* 🍴 *Breakfast.*

$$$ RESORT ALL-INCLUSIVE Fodor's Choice ★ **Playa Nicuesa Rainforest Lodge.** Hands down, this is the best eco-lodge on the gulf, combining comfortable, upscale accommodations and great food with an emphasis on adventure on both land and sea. **Pros:** everything you need to have an active vacation; excellent food and service; idyllic setting; friendly, intelligent owners who interact with guests. **Cons:** no air-conditioning; cabins are fairly open to nature, so there

"Taken on the road to Puerto Jiménez. It was such a beautiful view of Gulfo Dulce." —Photo by jamie722, Fodors.com member

will be some insects outside the mosquito netting at night. **TripAdvisor:** "novel experience," "a magical world," "luxury." $ Rooms from: $195 ✉ Golfo Dulce north of Golfito; accessible only by boat from Golfito or Puerto Jiménez, included in per-person rate ☎ 2258–8250, 2222–0704 in San José, 866/504–8116 in U.S. ⊕ www.nicuesalodge.com ➹ 5 cabins, 4 rooms, 1 house ⊙ Closed Oct. 1–Nov. 15 ⊙ All-inclusive.

SHOPPING

Depósito Libre. Ticos are drawn to Golfito's duty-free bargains on such imported items as TV sets, appliances, stereos, and tires but it's a good place for visitors to stock up on wine and liquor. To shop at the Depósito Libre you have to register in the afternoon with your passport to shop the next morning; this means spending the night in Golfito. Shopping is sheer madness in December. ⊙ Tues.–Sun.

Mercado Artesania. In a class all its own, the Mercado Artesania is filled with every imaginable—and unimaginable—souvenir. Large paintings by local artists, huge painted fans from Thailand, hammocks, beach clothes, and life-size snake carvings are just a few of the offerings here. Even if you don't buy a thing, it's fun to look. ✉ Hotel Samoa Sur, main street, 1 block north of town dock.

Tierra Mar. Tierra Mar has a small but excellent selection of painted wood masks made by the Boruca indigenous group. It also has one-of-a-kind local crafts, such as woven straw hats, cloth dolls, cotton purses, painted gourds, and local paintings. ✉ Waterfront next to Banana Bay Marina.

NIGHTLIFE

Banana Bay Marina. The bar at Banana Bay Marina is usually hopping in the evenings, with a smattering of English-speaking fishermen, boat-owners, and local ex-pats. ✉ *Main street south of town dock.*

Casa Roland Marine Resort. There's music for dancing and karaoke some Thursday nights beside the hotel's huge pool. Friday night there's live music by a small jazz combo or acoustic performances by solo instrumentalists in the hotel's elegant main bar. ✉ *250 m east of old ICE office, American Zone* ☏ *2775–0180.*

Samoa del Sur. The bar at Samoa del Sur has a mix of Ticos and foreigners, mostly of the hard-drinking, fishermen type, who gather for the loud music until 11 pm. Some nights there is also karaoke. ✉ *1 block north of town dock.*

TO FLUSH OR NOT TO FLUSH?

Costa Rican toilets *do* flush, but in most of Costa Rica, septic systems weren't designed to accommodate toilet tissue (the pipes are too narrow). If you don't want to be the gringo who clogs up the works, watch for signs asking you not to put anything in the toilet. A wastebasket (*basurero*) is almost always provided to hold used tissue. Even upscale resorts and other places with modern septic systems have the basket, since the habit has been ingrained in locals.

PLAYA ZANCUDO

51 km/32 miles south of Golfito.

Playa Zancudo. For laid-back beaching involving hammocks strung between palms and nothing more demanding than watching the sun set, you can't beat breezy Playa Zancudo, with its miles of wide, flat beach and romantic views of the Osa Peninsula. It isn't picture-perfect: the 10 km (6 miles) of dark brown sand is often strewn with flotsam and jetsam. But there's a constant breeze and a thick cushion of palm and almond trees between the beach and the dirt road running parallel. The standout feature is the magnificent view across the gulf to the tip of the Osa Peninsula. The beach runs almost due north–south, so you have center-stage seats for sunsets, too. Away from the beach breezes, be prepared for biting *zancudos* (no-see-ums).

Canadians and Americans have built substantial beachfront homes and most hotels and restaurants are within sight of the beach. Life here is laid-back and casual, centering on walking the beach, fishing, kayaking, swimming, and hanging out at the local bars and restaurants. Zancudo has a good surf break at the south end of the beach, but it's nothing compared with Playa Pavones a little to the south. Swimming is good two hours before or after high tide, especially at the calmer north end of the beach. If you get tired of playing in the surf and sand, you can arrange a boat trip to the nearby mangrove estuary to see birds and crocodiles. Zancudo is also home to one of the area's best sportfishing operations, headquartered at the Zancudo Lodge. Oceano Bar and Restaurant has free Wi-Fi at the bar, as does Cabinas Sol y Mar.

GETTING HERE AND AROUND

The road from Golfito is paved for the first 11 km (7 miles), but after the turnoff at El Rodeo the trip entails almost two hours of bone-shaking, rough road. A bridge has finally replaced the ancient cable ferry, making the trip a little shorter, but no less rough. Instead of driving, you can hire a boat at the municipal dock in Golfito for the 25-minute ride ($30–$40 for two) or take a $6 *collectivo* (communal) boat that leaves Golfito's Samoa del Sur Hotel at noon; returning from Zancudo, the boat leaves around 7:30 am Monday to Saturday. (In low season, the shuttle usually runs Monday, Wednesday, and Friday only.) A taxi ride from Golfito to Zancudo costs about $90, so the boat is a bargain.

Cabinas Los Cocos. Cabinas Los Cocos has water-taxi service to Golfito ($15 per person; minimum $50) and service to Puerto Jiménez ($15 per person; minimum $60).

Getting around Playa Zancudo doesn't take much, since there's really only one long, dusty road parallel to the beach. You can rent a bike at Cabinas Sol y Mar or Tres Amigos Supermercado, both on the main road in Zancudo, for about $10 per day. ⊠ *Beach road* ☎ *2776–0012.*

OUTDOOR ACTIVITIES

FISHING

If you've got your own gear, you can do some good shore fishing from the beach or the mouth of the mangrove estuary, or hire a local boat to take you out into the gulf. The main edible catches are yellowfin tuna, snapper, and snook; catch-and-release fish include marlin, roosterfish, and swordfish.

Captain Ronny. Born and raised in Golfito, Captain Ronny has experience working at all the area fishing lodges. His daily rate is an all-inclusive $800 for a maximum of four fishers. ☎ *2776–0201* ✎ *golfitocr@yahoo.com.*

Zancudo Lodge. The Zancudo Lodge runs the biggest charter operation in the area, with 15 boats ranging in length from 28 feet to 36 feet. A day's fishing includes gear, food, and drinks (about $750–$850 for two fishers), and you can arrange to be picked up in Golfito or Puerto Jiménez. ⊠ *North end of town on main road* ☎ *2776–0008* ⊕ *www. zancudolodge.com.*

KAYAKING

The kayaking is great at the beach and along the nearby Río Coto Colorado, lined with mangroves.

Cabinas Los Cocos. Cabinas Los Cocos has a popular tour ($50 per person, minimum two people) that takes you for a 1½-hour motorboat ride up the Coto Colorado River, then a magical two-hour kayak tour along a jungly mangrove channel and a relaxing paddle, moving downstream with the current, back to the river mouth. Capt. Susan can identify the birds you'll see along the way. The company also rents user-friendly sit-on-top kayaks with backrests for $5 per hour. ⊠ *Beach road* ☎ *2776–0012.*

WHERE TO EAT

$ ✕ **Coloso del Mar Restaurant.** Fabulous fish cakes, tasty fish burritos, and
SEAFOOD   savory filet of seabass with a smoky jalapeño cream sauce are a few
of the delights awaiting diners at this screened-in porch restaurant in
a bright-yellow clapboard cottage right on the beach. Chicken or fish
curries here are also popular with the locals. Attention is paid to sides,
too, including creamy mashed potatoes, cheese-topped toasted garlic
bread, and perfectly cooked vegetables. Beer and wine by the glass
or bottle are available. Service here is with a smile, and everything
is cooked to order, so relax: Remember—you're at the beach. If you
want to try their banana pancakes at breakfast, you'll have to stay at
one of their four beachfront cabins. $ *Average main: $9 ⊠ Main road,
100 m north of Soda Tranquillo* ☎ 2776–0050 ⊕ *www.colosodelmar.
com* ☾ *No lunch.*

$ ✕ **Oceano Bar & Restaurant.** This beachfront restaurant has a wide-
ECLECTIC   ranging menu that's popular with locals. Choose from seafood, steaks,
and chicken dishes, all with an Italian accent—think lots of pesto
and hot Italian bread. Fish sandwiches are also popular, along with
enormous hamburgers served on homemade buns and topped with
bacon, mushrooms, peppers, and cheese. Bring your laptop and surf
on their Wi-Fi connection. $ *Average main: $8 ⊠ Beach road, 50 m
south of Supermercado Bellavista* ☎ 2776–0921 ☾ *Closed Oct., sometimes Sept.*

$$ ✕ **Restaurant Sol y Mar.** On a breezy porch with a palm-fringed beach
ECLECTIC   view, this thatch-roofed restaurant has the most ambitious food in Zan-
cudo, with an eclectic menu of spicy Mexican-style quesadillas and
superstuffed burritos, continental chicken in a brandy cream sauce,
and fresh fish with an array of exotic sauces. There's a touch of Thai
here, too; one of the most popular dishes is mahimahi in a coconut-
curry sauce. The hearty bar food includes typical rings and wings, and
more interesting spicy Bangkok tacos: pork and rice wrapped in cab-
bage leaves. There are BBQ specials on Monday and Friday nights in
high season. Desserts are decadent and delicious, including a standout
carrot cake. Breakfasts here are huge and hearty, ranging from healthy
granola to giant breakfast burritos. ⚠ Like many menus catering to tour-
ists, prices here do not include tax and service, so be sure to factor in an
extra 23% to the bill. $ *Average main: $9 ⊠ Cabinas Sol y Mar, main
road* ☎ 2776–0014.

WHERE TO STAY

For expanded hotel reviews, visit Fodors.com.

$ ⌂ **Cabinas Los Cocos.** This secluded cluster of castaway-island, self-cater-
RENTAL   ing cabins is designed for people who want to kick back and enjoy the
beach. **Pros:** like having your own beach house on a practically deserted,
idyllic beach, with everything you need to live well; friendly, funny hosts
who help you get the most out of your stay. **Cons:** no air-conditioning,
but there are ceiling fans and ocean breezes; no phone in rooms. **Trip-
Advisor:** "a magical place," "relax on the beach," "fantastic private
house." $ *Rooms from: $65 ⊠ Beach road about 200 m north of Sol
y Mar* ☎ 2776–0012 ⊕ *www.loscocos.com* ⇱ *4 cabins* ⊟ *No credit
cards* �ⅼ⊙ⅼ *No meals.*

$
B&B/INN
Cabinas Sol y Mar. As the name implies, Cabinas Sol y Mar has plenty of sun and sea, a beach fringed by coconut palms, and peach-painted wooden cabinas with porches furnished with Adirondack chairs—perfect for taking in the spectacular views of the Osa Peninsula. **Pros:** beach location; bargain price; lively restaurant and bar. **Cons:** no air-conditioning; bare-bones furniture in cabins; no-frills bathrooms. **TripAdvisor:** "beautiful," "a peaceful stay," "the perfect place." $ *Rooms from: $41 ⊠ Main road south of Cabinas Los Cocos ☎ 2776–0014 ⊕ www. zancudo.com* ⤴ *5 cabinas, 1 house* ⎮◎⎮ *No meals.*

$$$
The Zancudo Lodge. Many guests staying here are anglers on all-inclusive, sportfishing packages but new, young owners have completely overhauled this beachfront property, turning it into a luxury resort to be enjoyed by wives of fishermen, as well as guests who have never caught anything but a cold. **Pros:** fishers' delight with excellent boats and captains; most luxurious hotel in Zancudo, with air-conditioning, a rarity in these parts. **Cons:** pricey for this area; must like listening to fishermen's stories. **TripAdvisor:** "top notch," "beautiful lodge," "unexplored exuberance." $ *Rooms from: $150 ⊠ Main road north end of town, 200 m past police post ☎ 2776–0008, 800/854–8791 in U.S. ⊕ www.zancudolodge.com* ⤴ *12 rooms, 2 junior suites, 2 master suites* ⎮◎⎮ *No meals.*

PLAYA PAVONES

53 km/33 miles south of Golfito.

Playa Pavones. Driving along remote Playa Pavones, one of the most scenic beaches in Costa Rica, you catch glimpses through the palms of brilliant blue water, white surf crashing against black rocks, and the soft silhouette of the Osa Peninsula across the gulf. This area at the southern edge of the mouth of the Golfo Dulce attracts serious surfer purists, but also has pristine black-sand beaches and virgin rain forest. The coast is very rocky, so it's important to ask locals which beach to try surfing or swimming. One of the best places to swim is in the Río Claro, under the bridge or at the river mouth (dry season only). The town of Pavones itself is a helter-skelter collection of *pensiones* (guest houses) and sodas clustered around a soccer field.

GETTING HERE

There's no avoiding the bumpy road from Golfito to Conte, where the road forks north to Zancudo and south to Pavones. But the dirt road to Pavones is usually well graded. A public bus leaves from Golfito very early in the morning, and the drive takes about 2½ hours. A taxi from the airstrip in Golfito costs upward of $90.

OUTDOOR ACTIVITIES

SURFING

Pavones is famous for one of the longest waves in the world, thanks to the mouth of the Río Claro, which creates ideal sandbanks and well-shaped waves. The ocean bottom is cobblestone where the surfing waves break. The most consistent waves are from April to September, and that's when the surfing crowd heads down here from the Central Pacific coast beaches. But even at the crest of its surfing season Pavones is

8

tranquillity central compared with the surfing hot spots farther north.

Clear River Sports & Adventures. Down by the beach, about 100 meters north of the soccer field, you can rent surfboards here for $20 for 24 hours; bicycles are $10 the first day, then $5 each following day. There are also a couple of computer terminals to use, with Wi-Fi. ☎ *2776–2016.*

La Ponderosa *(⇨ Where to Stay, below)* rents surfboards ($20–$40) as well as bicycles ($15).

Sea Kings Surf Shop. Most surfers here are serious about their sport and bring their own boards. You can buy top-of-the-line surfboards and other surfing gear here, along with the latest in heavy-duty sun screens, or sign up for a 1½-hour lesson ($55 including use of a soft lesson board). ✉ *In town by soccer field, close to Cafe de la Suerte* ☎ *2776–2015, 2776–2107* 🌐 *www.surfpavones.com.*

> **CAUTION**
>
> In the unlikely event that you are bitten by a snake, stay calm, move slowly, and try to remember what the snake looked like, to tell the clinic staff. Allow antivenom to be administered only by a trained person, in case of side effects. Five hours is the window before any tissue loss. To avoid snakebites, stay on trails and wear long, loose pants; in some areas high rubber boots are recommended.

WHERE TO EAT

$ VEGETARIAN 🍴 **Café de la Suerte.** Fortunately for food lovers, the "Good Luck Café" serves truly astonishing vegetarian food from 7:30 to 5 that even a carnivore could love, along with intriguing exotic juice combinations and thick fruit smoothies. The homemade yogurt is a revelation: light, almost fluffy, and full of flavor, served over a cornucopia of exotic fruits, sprinkled with their own granola, and mixed into refreshing fruit-flavor *lassis* (a yogurt-base drink from India). Healthful sandwiches are heavy on excellent hummus, and hot daily specials might include curried hearts of palm or a creamy vegetable quiche loaded with cheese. Don't leave without buying a fudgy brownie or a brown-sugar oatmeal square for the road. Bring your laptop and use their Wi-Fi—the fee of $1 an hour is donated to the local school. The original Israeli owners have leased out the café and so far the new managers are doing an excellent job. [$] *Average main: $8* ✉ *Next to soccer field* ☎ *2776–2388* 🌐 *www.cafedelasuerte.com* 💳 *No credit cards* 🕒 *Closed Sun. and Oct. No dinner Nov.*

$ ITALIAN 🍴 **Ristorante Italiano La Bruschetta.** Come to this casually chic spot within earshot of the surf for the savory bruschetta and 16 varieties of crispy, thin-crusted pizza, best in the area, made with flair by Rosella, a glamorous native of Naples whom everyone here calls Lella. Her four seasons pizza is a triumph of thin, spicy pepperoni; flavorful ham, olives, eggplant, peppers, onion, and zucchini. Save room for the knock-out gnocchi, handmade pillow-soft dumplings made with potatoes and cheese, and bathed in olive oil and rosemary. There are also tortelloni in cream sauce, and filet mignon served with a side of gnocchi. Tiramisu and key lime pie do dessert duty. Japanese lanterns add a romantic touch to the wooden tables and chairs painted in sherbet colors and placed in intimate nooks. $ *Average main: $12* ⊠ *50 meters north of La Ponderosa, look for La Piña sign, Playa Pavones* ☎ *2776–2174.*

WHERE TO STAY

For expanded hotel reviews, visit Fodors.com.

$$
B&B/INN
☺

⌂ **Casa Siempre Domingo.** High on a breezy hill, this spacious bed-and-breakfast has the town's best view of the Golfo Dulce. **Pros:** the view, the view, the view; spacious, well-appointed rooms; great breakfasts; kids welcome. **Cons:** a very steep drive uphill; a thigh-cramping walk up and down to the beach. $ *Rooms from: $85* ⊠ *2 km/1 mile south of town; follow signs after Río Claro Bridge* ☎ *8820–4709, 2776–2185* ⊕ *www.casa-domingo.com* ⇨ *4 rooms* ▤ *No credit cards* ¶O¶ *Breakfast.*

$$
B&B/INN

⌂ **La Ponderosa Beach and Jungle Resort.** The world-famous Playa Pavones surfing break is just a 10-minute walk from this surfer-owned hotel, the only beach resort in the area and a cut above the usual surfer place. **Pros:** a surfer's haven, with gear for rent and lots of local knowledge, courtesy of surfing owners and other guests; affordable; close to beach and town; meal packages available for $30 per person. **Cons:** tends to attract a younger crowd; mosquitoes love the garden when there's no breeze. **TripAdvisor:** "this place is magic," "very unique and remarkable," "awesome location with spectacular grounds." $ *Rooms from: $105* ⊠ *On the beach* ☎ *2776–2076, 954/771–9166 in U.S.* ⊕ *www.laponderosapavones.com* ⇨ *2 rooms, 3 suites, 2 houses* ▤ *No credit cards* ¶O¶ *No meals.*

$$$
B&B/INN
ALL-INCLUSIVE
Fodor's Choice
★

⌂ **Tiskita Jungle Lodge.** This last-outpost lodge is one of the premier eco-lodges in the Southern Zone, attracting nature lovers, bird-watchers, and people who want to get away from it all in comfort. **Pros:** unrivaled wildlife viewing and birding; splendid natural isolation; opportunity to get to know the friendly, knowledgeable owners. **Cons:** some steep walks to cabins in forest; no air-conditioning; expect some insect visitors in rustic cabins; not a lot of privacy in joined double and triple cabins, which share verandas. **TripAdvisor:** "remote and rustic," "wonderfully peaceful," "a nature lover's paradise." $ *Rooms from: $250* ⊠ *6 km/4 miles south of Playa Pavones* ☎ *2296–8125* ⊕ *www.tiskita.com* ⇨ *17 rooms arranged in 4 single cabins, 3 doubles, 1 triple* ⊗ *Closed Aug. to Nov.* ¶O¶ *All-inclusive.*

NIGHTLIFE

La Manta. This is where the action is at night; surfers can watch their own filmed surf sessions projected onto a huge screen, while refueling with classic bar food, burgers, burritos, and lots of beer and cocktails. ⊠ *Just north of town, Playa Pavones* ☎ *No phone* ⊕ *www.la-manta.com.*

8

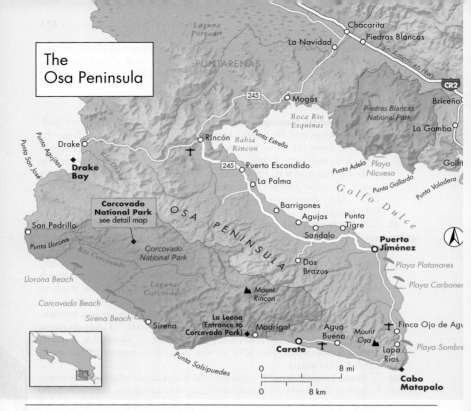

THE OSA PENINSULA

If you came to Costa Rica seeking wilderness and adventure, this is it. You'll find the country's most breathtaking scenery and most abundant wildlife on the Osa Peninsula, a third of which is protected by Corcovado National Park. You can hike into the park, take a boat, or fly in on a charter plane. Corcovado also works for day trips from nearby luxury nature lodges, most of which lie within private preserves that are home for much of the same wildlife you might see in the park. And complementing the peninsula's lush forests and pristine beaches is the surrounding sea, with great fishing and some surfing.

There are two sides to the Osa: the gentler Golfo Dulce side, much of it accessible by car, albeit along rocky roads; and the much wilder and dramatic Pacific side, which is accessible only by boat, by charter plane, or by hiking a sublimely beautiful coastal trail.

PUERTO JIMÉNEZ

130 km/86 miles west of Golfito, 364 km/226 miles from San José.

You might not guess it from the rickety bicycles and ancient pickup trucks parked on the main street, but Puerto Jiménez is the largest town on the Osa Peninsula. This one-iguana town has a certain frontier charm, though. New restaurants, hotels, and "green" newcomers lend an interesting, funky edge. It's also the last civilized outpost on the peninsula. Heading south, you fall off the grid. That means no public electricity or telephones. So make your phone calls, send your email, get cash, and stock up on supplies here. Be prepared for the humidity and mosquitoes—Puerto Jiménez has plenty of both. If you need a refreshing dip, head southeast of the airport to Playa Platanares, where there is a long stretch of beach with swimmable, warm water.

The main reason to come to Puerto Jiménez is to spend a night before or after visiting Corcovado National Park, since the town has the best access to the park's two main trailheads and an airport with flights from San José. It's also the base for the *colectivo* (public transport via pickup truck) to Carate.

GETTING HERE AND AROUND

Most visitors fly to the recently upgraded Puerto Jiménez airfield from San José, since the drive is grueling and long. Driving from Golfito is a little easier these days thanks to new bridges and the newly paved road all the way from Rincón to Puerto Jiménez, though the road between Chacarita and Rincón is still full of potholes and slow going. A better option from Golfito is the motorboat launch. A rickety old passenger launch ($3 each way) leaves Golfito at 11:30 am every day and takes 1½ hours. Faster motorboat launches ($4) make the trip in 45 minutes, leaving Golfito five times a day starting at 7 am, then 10 am, 1, 3:15, and 3:30 pm. Going the opposite direction, the fast launches to Golfito leave Puerto Jiménez at 6 am, 11:30 am, and 2 pm. The schedule changes depending on demand, so check before you head to the dock. You can also hire private taxi boats at the city dock. Prices are $70 to $80 between Golfito and Puerto Jiménez. Water taxis can also take you to beachfront lodges.

A colectivo ($8) taxi—actually an open truck with bench seats—leaves Puerto Jiménez twice daily for Cabo Matapalo and Carate. It's the cheapest way to travel, but the trip is along a bumpy road—not recommended in rainy season (May through December). This group truck-taxi leaves from a stop 200 meters west of the Super 96 at 6 am and 1:30 pm.

Once you get to the main street in town, you can get around on foot or by bicycle. Rent mountain bikes from Ciclo Mi Puerto (35 meters west of Hotel Oro Verde ☎ 2735–5297) for $1.50 an hour (closed Sunday).

ESSENTIALS

Bank/ATM Banco Nacional ⊠ *500 m south of Super 96, directly across from church* ☎ *2735–5020.*

Hospital Public Clinic and First Aid Station ⊠ *25 m west of post office* ☎ *2735–5063.*

Internet Café Internet Osa Corcovado. Café Internet Osa Corcovado has a more reliable high-speed connection, plus laptop data ports and, best of all, really strong air-conditioning. ⊠ *1 block north and 1 block east of Cabinas Marcelina* ☎ *2735–5230.* **CaféNet El Sol** ⊠ *Main street, on corner, 100 m south of soccer field* ☎ *2735–5719* ⊗ *Daily 7 am–10 pm.*

Continued on page 480

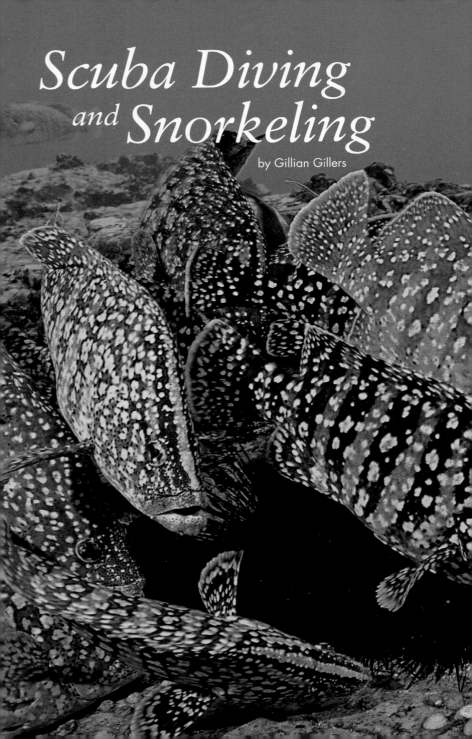

Scuba Diving
and Snorkeling

by Gillian Gillers

For snorkelers and scuba divers, Costa Rica is synonymous with swarms of fish and stretches of coral that hug the country's 910 miles of coastline. Submerge yourself in crystalline waters and enter another world, with bull sharks, brain coral, and toothy green eels. The variety and abundance of marine life are awe-inspiring.

WHEN AND WHERE TO GO

Swimming with the
turtles on Cocos Island

The Pacific tends to be clearer than the Caribbean, and the fish are bigger and more abundant. Northern waters are generally best May through July, after winds die down and the water turns bluer and warmer. The southern Osa Peninsula is popular during the dry season, from January to April.

The Caribbean, known for its diverse coral and small fish, is good for beginners because it has less surge. The best months are September and October, when the ocean is as calm and flat as a swimming pool. April and May also offer decent conditions, but steer clear during the rest of the year, when rain and strong waves cloud the water.

CAHUITA Mounds of coral and a barrier reef (dubbed Long Shoal) run from Cahuita to Punta Mona, along 25 kilometers of Caribbean coastline. Arches, tunnels, and canyons in the reef form a playground for small fish, crabs, and lobsters. Even though sediment and waste water have damaged much of the coral, the healthy sections are dense, colorful, and delightfully shaped. Gentle pools right off the beach allow for some of the country's best snorkeling.

ISLA DEL COCO (Cocos Island) Some 295 nautical miles and a 36-hour sail from Puntarenas, Cocos Island is one of the world's premier sites for advanced divers. Visibility is good all year, and hammerhead and white-tipped reef sharks are the main attractions.

ISLA DEL CAÑO (Caño Island) With clear water, big schools of fish, and healthy coral, this biological reserve is the second-best dive spot after Cocos. Stronger currents make Caño better suited for advanced divers, but novice snorkelers can frolic in the Garden, a shallow area to the north.

ISLA SANTA CATALINA (Santa Catalina Island) Known for sightings of golden cownose rays and giant mantas, these big rocks near Playa Flamingo have spots for beginner and advanced divers. Snorkelers should head to shallower waters near the beach.

GOLFO DE PAPAGAYO (Papagayo Gulf) This northern gulf has Costa Rica's highest concentration of snorkel and dive shops. Calm, protected waters make it the best place for beginner divers on the Pacific.

ISLA MURCIÉLAGO (Bat Island) Located inside Santa Rosa National Park, this cluster of rocks is good for advanced divers and famous for its fearsome bull sharks.

DIVING SCHOOLS

The beach towns on both coasts are riddled with diving schools and equipment rentals shops. If you're a first-timer and plan to go diving just once, taking a basic half-day class isn't difficult, and it will allow you to dive up to 40 feet with an instructor. A three- or four-day certification course gets you a lifetime license and allows you to dive up to 130 feet and without a guide. Outfitters can point snorkelers towards pristine spots. We list only the most reputable schools under the Outdoor Activity section throughout every chapter; look for the ones that are PADI (Professional Association of Diving Instructors) trained or give PADI certifications.

IN CASE OF AN EMERGENCY
DAN (Divers Alert Network) is an organization that provides emergency medical advice and assistance for underwater diving injuries. Doctors, emergency medical technicians, and nurses are available 24 hours a day to answer questions. If you would like to discuss a potential diving-related health problem, contact the non-emergency DAN switchboard (☎ 800/446–2671) or check out their website (⊕ www. diversalertnetwork.org). Their emergency telephone line is 919/684–9111 for international calls.

8

SNORKELING TIPS

Sea Star in Catalina Islands

■ Never turn your back on the ocean, especially if the waves are big.

■ Ask about rip tides before you go in.

■ Enter and exit from a sandy beach area.

■ Avoid snorkeling at dusk and never go in the water after dark.

■ Wear lots of sunscreen, especially on your back and butt cheeks.

■ Don't snorkel too close to the reef. You could get scratched if a wave pushes you.

■ Be mindful of boats.

DIVING TIPS

■ Make sure your instructor is certified by a known diving agency, such as PADI.

■ Stick to the instructor's guidelines on depth and timing.

■ Never hold your breath.

■ Never dive or snorkel (or swim or surf) alone. Also, never touch the coral or the fish—this is for your own good and the good of the marine life.

■ Don't drink alcohol before diving.

■ Never dive while taking medicine unless your doctor tells you it's safe.

■ Diving can be dangerous if you have certain medical problems. Ask your doctor how diving may affect your health.

■ If you don't feel good or if you are in pain after diving, go to the nearest emergency room immediately.

■ Don't fly for 12 hours after a no-decompression dive, even in a pressurized airplane.

CREATURES OF THE SEA

Underwater exploration is as close to visiting another world as you can come. Here you'll encounter some of the most bizarre creatures on this planet.

SEAHORSE
These magical little creatures are hard to spot because they are often camouflaged within black coral trees, with their tails curled around the branches. They are bottom feeders and usually found in 10-meter deep water.

FIREWORM
Look but don't touch! These stunning, slow-moving worms have poisonous bristles that flare out when disturbed. Getting stung is no fun; it will burn and itch for hours afterwards. Try taking the bristles out with adhesive tape and dabbing the infected area with alcohol.

GREEN EEL
Eels have a reputation for being vicious and ill-tempered, but they're really shy and secretive. Eels will only attack humans in self-defense. Though they may accidentally bite the hand that feeds them, it's just because they can't see or hear very well.

Pillar Coral

SPONGES
Common in the Caribbean, these strange animals don't have nervous, digestive, or circulatory systems. Instead, they rely on a constant water flow for food and oxygen, and to remove wastes. To reproduce, some sponges release both sperm and eggs into the water and hope the two collide.

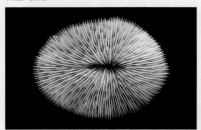

Calcareous skeleton of the coral

CORAL
Coral tends to cluster in colonies of identical individuals. The most diverse coral (at least 31 types) in Costa Rica can be found on the Caribbean coast, near Puerto Viejo. Like other plant-looking sea animals, many types of coral reproduce by spawning.

Orange sponge

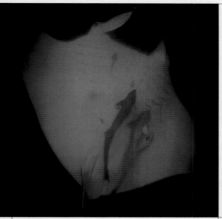

GIANT MANTA RAY

Commonly spotted near Isla Santa Catalina, mantas often hang out at reef-side "cleaning stations" where small fish (like wrasses and angelfish) congregate. These cleaner fish feed in the manta's gills and over its skin, simultaneously scrubbing it free of parasites and dead skin.

HAMMERHEAD SHARK

These sharks are distinctive not only for their strangely shaped, mallet-like head but also because they're one of the few creatures in the animal kingdom (besides humans and pigs) that can tan. If they spend too much time in shallow waters, they'll become noticeably darker. In 2007, scientists also discovered that hammerheads can reproduce asexually through a rare process called parthenogenesis: female hammerheads can actually develop an embryo without ever having been fertilized.

BOTTLENOSE DOLPHIN

Everybody loves dolphins. In some parts of the world they work with local fishermen, driving schools of fish into the nets and then eating the fish that escape. They've also been known to help injured divers to the surface.

BARRACUDA

Barracudas are not aggressive towards humans, but are vicious predators. Their diet consists of all sorts of fish. Large barracudas, when gorged, will even try to herd a school of fish into shallow water so that they can guard over them and eat them off when they're hungry again.

PARROTFISH

Parrotfish are named for their external set of tightly packed teeth that look just like a parrot's beak. These strange looking teeth are used to rasp the algae off of coral and rock, thus feeding themselves and keeping the coral clean and healthy.

Pharmacy Farmacia Hidalgo ✉ *Main street, 25 m north of Cabinas Marcellina* ☎ *2735–5564* ⏱ *Mon.–Sat. 8–8.*

Post Office Correo ✉ *West side of soccer field.*

Rental Cars Solid Car Rental ✉ *150 m north of airport* ☎ *2735–5777* ⊕ *www.solidcarrental.com.*

Visitor Information National Parks Service Headquarters. The National

WORD OF MOUTH

"We woke up in the morning to the sounds of howler monkeys and had a 6:00 am breakfast, at which we saw scarlet macaws flying by. What a way to start our first morning in the Osa."

—RAC

Parks Service Headquarters has a new tourism office with information about hiking trails in Corcovado National Park. The office is open weekdays 8 to 4. ✉ *Next to airport* ☎ *2735–5036.* **Osa Tropical** ✉ *Across from Banco Nacional, about 50 m south, on main street* ☎ *2735–5062* ✉ *osatropical@ice.co.cr.*

OUTDOOR ACTIVITIES

Osa Tropical. Isabel Esquivel at Osa Tropical runs the best general tour operation on the peninsula. Whatever travel question you ask the locals, they will usually say, "Ask Isabel." Along with arranging flights, ground transport, hotel bookings, tours, and car rentals, Osa Tropical is the radio communications center for many of the off-the-grid Osa lodges and tour operators. ✉ *Main road across from Banco Nacional, about 50 m south* ☎ *2735–5062.*

BIRD-WATCHING

The birding around the Osa Peninsula is world renowned, with more than 400 species. Endemic species include Baird's trogon, yellow-billed cotinga, whistling wren, black-cheeked ant tanager, and the glorious turquoise cotinga. There have even been sightings of the very rare harpy eagle in the last couple of years.

★ **Bosque del Río Tigre Lodge.** The best English-speaking birding guides are Liz Jones and Abraham Gallo, who run Bosque del Río Tigre Lodge. They lead birding trips all around the peninsula, including visits to Corcovado National Park. ✉ *Dos Brazos del Tigre, 12 km/7½ miles northwest of Puerto Jiménez* ⊕ *www.osaadventures.com.*

Rincón. One of the best spots on the peninsula to find a yellow-billed cotinga or a white-crested coquette is beside the bridge over the river at Rincón, if you get there before 7 am. ✉ *40 km/25 miles north of Puerto Jiménez.*

FISHING

Along with Golfito across the water, Puerto Jiménez is a major fishing destination, with plenty of billfish and tuna, snapper and snook, almost all year, with the exception of June and July, when things slow down. The best offshore fishing is between December and April. Charter captains follow the fish up and down the Pacific coast, so ask at your hotel for their recommendation of the best fishing boats currently in town.

If you want to fish the old-fashioned way, Aventuras Tropicales *(⊳ below)* also offers four to five-hour fishing tours from kayaks for $65.

Beach views at Drake Bay on the Osa Peninsula.

HIKING

★ **Osa Aventura.** Osa Aventura specializes in multiday Corcovado hiking adventures led by Mike Boston, an ebullient tropical biologist who sounds like Sean Connery and looks like Crocodile Dundee. Hikers stay in way-off-the-beaten-track rustic lodges en route, and camp or stay in basic cabins in Corcovado. Mike also employs bilingual biologists to lead hikes and conduct scientific research projects, in which visitors can sometimes participate. ☎ 2735–5758 ⊕ *www.osaaventura.com.*

Tigre Sector. If you have 4WD, it's just a 30-minute ride west to the village of Dos Brazos and the Tigre Sector of Corcovado Park. There is a new park office on the road to Dos Brazos, where you can check with rangers on trail conditions. Few hikers come to this pristine part of the park because it's difficult to access, which means you'll likely have it to yourself. You can take a taxi to Dos Brazos and hike from here or use Bosque del Río Tigre Lodge as a base.

HORSEBACK RIDING

🕙 **Río Nuevo Lodge.** The most popular horse trails in the area are at this remote lodge, about 12 bumpy km (7½ miles) west of town. Rides along the river and up onto scenic forested ridges last from three to seven hours and include transportation there and back and snacks and drinks for $70 per person. Most hotels and tour agencies can make the reservations for you. ✉ *12 km/7½ miles west of Puerto Jiménez* ☎ 2735–5095.

KAYAKING

🕙 Puerto Jiménez is a good base for sea-kayaking trips on the calm Golfo Dulce and for exploring the nearby mangrove rivers and estuaries.

Aventuras Tropicales Golfo Dulce. Alberto Robleto, an enterprising local, has amassed an impressive fleet of kayaks with excellent safety equipment at Aventuras Tropicales Golfo Dulce. Tours include snorkeling, dolphin-watching, and bird-watching. The most popular is the three-hour mangrove tour ($40). A three- to five-day kayaking tour ($140 per day, four-person minimum) teaches survival skills in the tropical forest. Outrigger canoe trips ($20 for three hours, minimum six paddlers) are also offered at sunset when dolphins are often jumping. A five-hour bike tour takes you through a local village, over hills, and across rivers ($50). All tours longer than three hours include a picnic lunch. ⊠ *South of airport on road to Playa Platanares* ☎ *2735–5195* ⊕ *www.aventurastropicales.com.*

La Sirena Adventure Boat Tour. If you just want to get out onto the water, La Sirena Adventure Boat Tour, provides 4½- to 5-hour tours on a covered boat—explore the gulf, look for dolphins, do some snorkeling, or try plane-boarding. Lunch and snacks are included ($50 per person, minimum six people). For $25 extra, you can visit the Osa Wildlife Sanctuary, a refuge for orphaned and injured wildlife. The boat sails at 8 am. ☎ *2735–5090* ⊕ *www.cabinasjimenez.com.*

TOURS

Finca Köbö Chocolate Tour. Finca Köbö Chocolate Tour takes you right to the source to see how cacao grows and becomes chocolate at this organic cacao plantation. The two-hour tour includes a naturalist-guided walk around the roughly 50-acre property, which includes gardens, orchards, and both primary and secondary forest. The highlight of the tour is the tasting—dipping an array of tropical fruits grown on-site into a pot of homemade chocolate fondue. ⊠ *18 km/11 miles west of Puerto Jiménez, near La Palma* ☎ *8398–7604* ⊕ *www.fincakobo.com* 🎫 *$32* ☉ *Tours 9 am and 2 pm; closed Sept.–Nov.*

Tropic Fins Adventures. Head out onto the Golfo Dulce or the open ocean on a sportfishing adventure aboard a custom-built 27-foot Ocean Runner, equipped with all the latest fishing equipment. Capt. Cory, a transplanted Canadian, has been fishing these waters for 10 years. The boat comfortably accommodates four fishers. Half-day, in-shore excursions, including refreshments and snacks, set off at 7 am ($650); a full-day of offshore fishing includes lunch and refreshements and can last up to 9 hours, depending on how the fish are biting. ⊠ *Playa Platanares* ☎ *8834–6079* ⊕ *www.tropicfins.com.*

WHERE TO EAT

$ ✕ **Corcovado Marisquería, Restaurante y Bar.** If you're hungry for a bargain
SEAFOOD and want to enjoy a little local atmosphere, join the fishermen, local families, and young backpackers at this tiny restaurant that has spilled over into a large waterfront garden. Customers happily sit at wooden tables, nattily covered with blue and white tablecloths and shaded by palm trees. The menu is vast, with more than 40 *bocas* (small bites) and *platos fuertes* (main courses) that run the gamut from seafood rice to whole lobster (about $25). You can make a meal of one or two bocas—say, clams in garlic butter and a cup of tangy ceviche or a shrimp omelet with salad—and walk away for less than $5. Wash it down

CLOSE UP

Where Have All the Forests Gone?

The world gives high marks to Costa Rica for its environmental awareness, but accolades don't always match reality. In the last half century more than two-thirds of Costa Rica's original forests have been destroyed. Forests have traditionally been considered unproductive land, and their destruction was for a long time synonymous with development. In the 1970s and 1980s, international and domestic development policies fueled the destruction of large tracts of wilderness. Fortunately, in the 1970s alarmed Costa Rican conservationists began creating what is now the best national park system in Central America. The government has since made progress in curbing deforestation outside the national parks, too.

As you travel through Costa Rica, you see that its predominant landscapes are not cloud and rain forests but the coffee, banana, and pineapple plantations and cattle ranches that have replaced them. Deforestation not only spells disaster for endangered animals like the jaguar and the harpy eagle, but can also have grave consequences for human beings. Forests absorb rain and release water slowly, playing an important role in regulating the flow of rivers—which is why severely deforested regions often suffer twin plagues of floods during the rainy season and drought during the dry months. Tree covers also prevent topsoil erosion, thus keeping the land fertile and productive; in many parts of the country erosion has left once-productive farmland almost worthless.

with local or imported beer and sit as long as you like, looking out on the Golfo Dulce. It's open from 10 am to 11 pm daily and there's free Wi-Fi. [$] *Average main: $8* ✉ *100 m east of city dock, on the waterfront* ☎ *2735–5659, 8898–2656.*

$$ ITALIAN 🍴 **Il Giardino.** Northern Italian cooking, in the form of tasty homemade pastas and excellent salads, is alive and well at this popular garden restaurant. Fresh fish and sushi round out the menu. Sadly, wood-oven pizzas are not the restaurant's forte, and service can be painfully slow. The owner is also a master carpenter, so the curvy blond-wood bar and hand-carved detailing in the casual restaurant are handsome indeed. Choose a table in the back garden if you're in the mood for a leisurely, romantic dinner. [$] *Average main: $11* ✉ *25 m south of La Carolina, then 25 m west, Downtown* ☎ *2735–5129* 💳 *No credit cards* 🕒 *No lunch.*

$ ITALIAN 🍴 **Mail It Pizza.** Pizza at this cheerful, family-run terrace café comes with an authentic Italian pedigree: The Colovattis are from Trieste and their pizza is simply the best in the Southern Zone. The crust is toasty crisp on the outside and chewy inside, topped with sauce made fresh every day and high-quality fixings. Calzones and homemade pastas are also on the menu, but pizza reigns here. The fresh blue-and-white decor is reminiscent of the owners' hometown on the Adriatic Sea. The restaurant's rather odd name refers to the fact that this building used to be the post office. Restrooms here are notably clean. You can also order pizzas by phone and pick them up to take back to your hotel. [$] *Average main: $9* ✉ *Across from soccer field at entrance to town* ☎ *2735–5483* 💳 *No credit cards* 🕒 *No lunch.*

$ **✕ Restaurante Carolina.** This simple
COSTA RICAN alfresco restaurant in the heart of
Puerto Jiménez is the central meeting place for locals and every foreigner in town, ergo a good place
to pick up information. They also
serve decent comida típica and
reliably fresh seafood. $ *Average
main: $5 ✉ Main road, center of
town ☎ 2735–5185.*

WHERE TO STAY

*For expanded hotel reviews, visit
Fodors.com.*

Playa Platanares is only about 6 km
(4 miles) outside of Puerto Jiménez,
but lodgings there have a different
feeling from those in town because
they are on a lovely and quiet

beach. Bosque del Río Tigre is also outside of town, but inland, in a
forested area beside a river.

$$$ 🛏 **Bosque del Río Tigre Lodge.** You can't get any closer to nature than this
B&B/INN off-the-grid lodge, famous for its excellent birding guides and trails,
★ wedged between forest and the banks of the Río Tigre. **Pros:** a birder's
paradise; great hiking trails; fabulous food. **Cons:** shared bathroom
(except in one separate cabin) and outdoor showers; limited electricity;
must love living very close to nature. **TripAdvisor:** "unique and wonderful," "exquisite tropical birding adventure," "amazing gem." $ *Rooms
from: $340 ✉ Dos Brazos del Tigre, 12 km/7 miles west of Puerto
Jiménez ☎ 8705–3729 leave messages only ⊕ www.bosquedelriotigre.
com ✎ 4 rooms with shared bath, 1 cabin ⊗ Closed Sept. and Oct.
❏ All meals.*

$ 🛏 **Cabinas Jiménez.** Overlooking the harbor, these creatively renovated
B&B/INN rooms and bungalows set in a lush garden are the most comfortable
★ lodging in town and have the best water views. **Pros:** watery views;
air-conditioning; bungalows have pleasant, private terrace with hammock. **Cons:** rooms are on the small side; no food service; some rooms
have no TV. **TripAdvisor:** "friendly owner," "central with nice views,"
"comfortable." $ *Rooms from: $65 ✉ 200 m west of town dock
☎ 2735–5090 ⊕ www.cabinasjimenez.com ✎ 7 rooms, 3 bungalows
❏ No meals.*

$ 🛏 **Cabinas Marcelina.** Two elderly Italian sisters run the best bargain
B&B/INN hotel in town. **Pros:** very affordable; some rooms have air-conditioning;
pleasant garden oasis in middle of town. **Cons:** rooms are quite small;
fan-only rooms are very cheap but can be hot and sticky. **TripAdvisor:** "nice staff," "very clean," "comfortable and friendly." $ *Rooms
from: $47 ✉ Main street, north side of Catholic church ☎ 2735–5007,
2735–5286 ✉ cabmarce@hotmail.com ✎ 8 rooms ▭ No credit cards
❏ No meals.*

"Sweet Pea, a spider monkey, quickly found refuge from the rain underneath Alex's rain poncho!" —Photo by hipvirgochick, Fodors.com member

$$ B&B/INN 👶

🏨 **Danta Corcovado Lodge.** Within hiking distance of the western edge of Corcovado National Park, this artistically rustic lodge is reminiscent of an Adirondacks camp, with creatively designed twig chairs and headboards, twisted-branch windows, and furniture made of leftover tree stumps. **Pros:** proximity to Corcovado National Park; comfortable rusticity; affordable. **Cons:** no air-conditioning; close encounters of the insect kind in cabins. **TripAdvisor:** "an inspiring jungle oasis," "amazing place of friendliness and creativity," "rustic beauty." [$] *Rooms from: $92* ✉ *Guadalupe, 3 km/2 miles northwest of La Palma* ☎ *2735–1111* 🌐 *www.dantalodge.com* ⇨ *3 rooms, 1 suite, 5 cabins sleeping 3–8 people* 🍴 *Breakfast.*

$$$ B&B/INN Fodor's Choice ★

🏨 **Iguana Lodge.** If a long stretch of deserted beach is your idea of heaven, this luxury lodge with breezy, screened-in, two-story cabins set among mature trees is for you. **Pros:** top-of-the-line accommodation and food in tranquil tropical setting; complimentary kayaks; interesting turtle conservation program; breakfast and dinner included in casita rooms. **Cons:** no air-conditioning, so can be hot; club rooms are small and can be noisy; leave your hair dryer at home and be prepared to get friendly with an insect or two. **TripAdvisor:** "encounter nature and total relaxation," "location and service can't be beat," "magical." [$] *Rooms from: $165* ✉ *Playa Platanares, 5 km/3 miles south of Puerto Jiménez airport* ☎ *8848–0752* 🌐 *www.iguanalodge.com* ⇨ *2 duplex cabins with 2 rooms each, 2 family cabins, 8 rooms in hotel, 1 house with 3 bedrooms* 🍴 *Some meals.*

NIGHTLIFE

Pearl of the Osa. With live salsa music, this beachfront bar and restaurant attracts a big crowd Friday nights. There's a mix of ages, and the music is loud and a lot of fun. ⊠ *Next door to Iguana Lodge on Playa Platanares* ☎ *8848–0752.*

SHOPPING

★ **Jagua Arts & Crafts.** Jewelry maker Karen Herrera has collected the finest arts and crafts in the area and displayed them in an impressive shop. Jagua Arts & Crafts has some rare items, including colorful cotton dresses and woven Panama hats made by the Guaymí indigenous group. Other interesting items are exquisitely detailed bird carvings made by a family in Rincón; stained-glass mosaic boxes, mirrors, and trivets made by a San José artist; local paintings; and serious art ceramics. Both Karen and her husband Tom are expert glass artists, producing delicate blown-glass vases and exquisite glass-bead jewelry. There's also an excellent selection of natural-history field guides and books. ⊠ *Beside airport.*

CORCOVADO NATIONAL PARK

GETTING HERE AND AROUND

The easiest way to visit remote Corcovado is on a day trip via boat from a Drake Bay lodge or on foot from Carate. The 20-minute boat trip from Drake Bay gets you to the San Pedrillo entrance. The boat trip from Drake to Sirena takes 45 minutes to one hour. From Carate airfield, where the collective taxi from Puerto Jiménez stops, it's about a 45-minute walk along the beach to La Leona park entrance.

For getting to Corcovado from elsewhere, the most expensive option—but also the easiest way to get right to the heart of the park—is flying in on a small charter plane ($390 or $351 cash) to tiny La Sirena airstrip in the park. **Alfa Romeo Aero Taxi** (⊠ *Puerto Jiménez airport* ☎ *735–5178*).

Less expensive is hiring a taxi in Puerto Jiménez ($90) to Los Patos trailhead, or at least to the first crossing of the Río Rincón (from which you hike a few miles upriver to the trailhead). The cheapest, and least convenient, option is to take a morning bus for less than $1 from Puerto Jiménez at 8 am to La Palma and then hike; or you can take a taxi 14 km (9 miles) ($60) to Los Patos entrance.

ESSENTIALS

Contacts National Parks Service in Puerto Jiménez. The park office in Puerto Jiménez, where you can get information about Corcovado National Park, is right by the airport. ☎ *2735–5036* ✉ *pncorcovado@gmail.com* 🖅 *$10 per day* ☉ *Daily 8–4.*

Fodor's Choice **Corcovado National Park.** Corcovado National Park is the last and largest outpost of virgin lowland rain forest in Central America and teeming with wildlife. Visitors who tread softly along the park's trails may glimpse howler, spider, and squirrel monkeys, peccaries (wild pigs), poison-dart frogs, scarlet macaws, and, very rarely, jaguars and tapirs.

Most first-time visitors to Corcovado come on a daylong boat tour from Drake Bay or hike in from Carate. But to get to the most pristine,

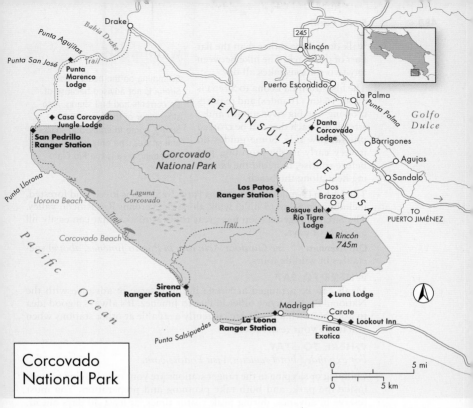

Corcovado
National Park

| 0 | | 5 mi |
| 0 | | 5 km |

wildlife-rich areas, you need to walk, and that means a minimum of three days: one day to walk in, one day to walk out, and one day inside.

Hours of Operation Ranger stations are officially open from 8 am to 4 pm daily, but you can walk in almost any time as long as you pay in advance.

OUTDOOR ACTIVITIES

If your reason for coming to the Osa is Corcovado, choose a lodge that has resident naturalist guides. On the Drake Bay and gulf sides of the park, all the lodges arrange guided tr ips into Corcovado, most with their own guides, but some with freelance guides. Tour operators in Puerto Jiménez and Drake Bay also run guided trips in the park.

HIKING

There are two main hiking routes to Corcovado. One begins near La Palma, at Los Patos entrance. There is one beach trail to the park, an easy 45-minute beach walk from Carate to La Leona entrance. The former beach trail from San Pedrillo to La Sirena has been closed for safety reasons. You can still enter the park at the San Pedrillo station, though, and hike the trails there.

Hiking is always tough in the tropical heat, but the forest route (Los Patos) is cooler than the beach hike to La Leona. Although it is possible to hike La Leona at high tide, it's more difficult because you have to walk on a slope rather than the flat part of the beach. The hike between any two stations takes all day.

The hike from La Leona to Sirena is about 16 km (10 miles) and requires crossing one big river mouth and a stretch of beach that can be crossed only at low tide. Some guides do it very early in the morning, just before sunrise, to avoid the blistering heat along the beach.

The 14-km (9-mile) trail from Los Patos to Sirena is lovely and forested, including an 8-km (5-mile) walk along the verdant Río Rincón valley. The Sirena ranger station has great trails around it that can easily fill a couple of days.

Osa Aventura (⇨ *see Outdoor Activities in Puerto Jiménez, above*) specializes in wildlife tours.

WHERE TO EAT

Meals can be arranged at Sirena if you reserve in advance with the National Parks Service office in Puerto Jiménez. It's always a good idea to ask about what meals are currently available at other stations when you make your reservation.

WHERE TO STAY

For expanded hotel reviews, visit Fodors.com.

Camping or sleeping in the ranger stations are your only lodging options inside the park, and both take planning and preparation. You must reserve in advance, during peak visitor times, at least 30 days ahead. Bunks at the Sirena ranger station (very basic accommodation) are limited to 26 people a day, as are meals, which are decent but relatively expensive (breakfast $20, lunch or dinner $25). Bring your own sheets, a pillow, and a good mosquito net. Campers planning to camp at La Leona, San Pedrillo, Los Patos, or La Sirena need to bring their own tents, gear, and food (although meals are sometimes available at La Leona). There is a maximum stay of four nights and five days. To make reservations you must fill out a request via email or in person at the park office in Puerto Jiménez, then make a deposit in the park's Banco Nacional account, then email, fax, or present the receipt in person to the park office. Lodging is $8 per night, not including meals; camping costs $4 per person per night.

DID YOU KNOW?

Corcovado has 13 ecosystems within its boundaries, ranging from mangroves and swamps to lowland rain forest. The park also has more forest giants—trees that stand 50 to 80 meters (165 to 264 feet) high—than anywhere in Central America.

CABO MATAPALO

21 km/14 miles south of Puerto Jiménez.

Cabo Matapalo. The southern tip of the Osa Peninsula, where virgin rain forest meets the sea at a rocky point, retains the kind of natural beauty that people travel halfway across the world to experience. From its ridges you can look out on the blue Golfo Dulce and the Pacific Ocean, sometimes spotting whales in the distance. The forest is tall and dense, with the highest and most diverse tree species in the country, usually draped with thick lianas. The name Matapalo refers to the strangler fig, which germinates in the branches of other trees and extends its roots downward, eventually smothering the supporting tree by blocking the sunlight. Flocks of brilliant scarlet macaws and troops of monkeys are the other draws here.

GETTING HERE AND AROUND

If you drive one hour south from Puerto Jiménez, be prepared for a bumpy ride and a lot of river crossings. In rainy season cars are sometimes washed out along rivers to the ocean. Most hotels arrange transportation in 4WD taxis or their own trucks. The cheapest—and the roughest—way to travel is by colectivo ($8), which leaves Puerto Jiménez twice a day (at 6 am and 1:30 pm). Buses do not serve Cabo Matapalo.

OUTDOOR ACTIVITIES

Outfitters in Puerto Jiménez run tours in this area. Each of the lodges listed has resident guides who can take guests on nature hikes.

Everyday Adventures. For extreme forest sports, this experienced outfitter takes you on not-so-everyday, adrenaline-pumping adventures: rappelling down waterfalls ($85), climbing up a 70-foot strangler fig tree ($55), and rain-forest hiking ($45). Or you can go all out with a combination rappelling/climbing tour for $120. ⊠ *Cabo Matapalo* 🖷 *8353–8619* ⊕ *www.psychotours.com.*

SURFING

On the eastern side of Cabo Matapalo, waves break over a platform that creates a perfect right, drawing surfers from far and wide, especially beginners. Local surf expert Oldemar (aka Pollo) Fernandez offers daily lessons at Pan Dulce Beach at his Pollo Surf School (🖷 *8366–6559* ⊕ *www.pollosurfschool.com*) for $55 per person in a group lesson; $110 for private lessons.

WHERE TO STAY

For expanded hotel reviews, visit Fodors.com.

$$$$
B&B/INN
Fodor's Choice
★

Bosque del Cabo. Atop a cliff at the tip of Cabo Matapalo, this lodge has unparalleled views of the Golfo Dulce merging with the endless blue of the Pacific, along with hundreds of acres of wildlife-rich primary forest, and the most beautiful landscaping on the peninsula. **Pros:** luxurious, artistic bungalows; fabulous trails and guides; congenial atmosphere among guests at cocktail hour and dinner. **Cons:** steep trail to beach and back; very small pool; limited electricity supply. **TripAdvisor:** "great wildlife viewing," "very impressive," "relaxing rainforest experience." Ⓢ *Rooms from: $210* ⊠ *22 km/14 miles south of Puerto*

8

"This is the view from the deck of the Toucan cabina at Bosque del Cabo." —Photo by Monica Richards, Fodors.com member

Jiménez on road to Carate, Cabo Matapalo ☎ *2735–5206, 8389–2846 at lodge* 🌐 *www.bosquedelcabo.com* 🛏 *10 ocean-view cabins, 2 garden cabins, 3 houses* 🍴 *All meals.*

$$$ B&B/INN ★ 🏨 **El Remanso.** You'll find tranquillity and elegant simplicity at this quiet, sophisticated retreat in a forest brimming with birds and wildlife, 122 meters (400 feet) above a beach studded with tide pools. **Pros:** gorgeous natural setting; privacy in cabins; jungle views; access to beach. **Cons:** no air-conditioning but good ceiling fans; no hair dryers; steep drive down to lodge. **TripAdvisor:** "amazing experience," "friendly staff," "perfect." [$] *Rooms from: $155* ✉ *22 km/14 miles south of Puerto Jiménez on road to Carate* ☎ *2735–5569 office, 8814–5775* 🌐 *www.elremanso.com* 🛏 *4 rooms, 2 suites, 5 cabinas* 🍴 *All meals.*

$$$$ RESORT ALL-INCLUSIVE Fodor's Choice ★ 🏨 **Lapa Ríos.** Hands down the most spectacular eco-resort in Costa Rica, Lapa Ríos has won numerous awards for its mix of conservation and comfort in a huge private nature reserve that brims with wildlife. **Pros:** excellent, professional service; Tico-flavor atmosphere with local employees; delicious typical and international dishes. **Cons:** many steps to climb to farther cabins; steep trail to beach, but there is a shuttle service; no phone or Internet. **TripAdvisor:** "just about perfect," "a very special place," "truly memorable." [$] *Rooms from: $360* ✉ *20 km/12 miles south of Puerto Jiménez* ☎ *2735–5130* 🌐 *www.laparios.com* 🛏 *16 cabinas* 🍴 *All-inclusive.*

CARATE

60 km/37 miles west of Puerto Jiménez.

Carate is literally the end of the road. The black volcanic-sand beach stretches for more than 3 km (2 miles), with surf that's perfect for boogie boarding and body surfing but not for serious board surfing or safe swimming. The main entertainment at the beach is watching the noisy but magnificent scarlet macaws feasting on almonds in the beach almond trees that edge the shore. Carate has no phone service; a couple of lodges have satellite phones and iffy Wi-Fi and cell-phone connections.

GETTING HERE AND AROUND

The road from Matapalo to Carate covers 40 suspension-testing km (25 miles); at this writing, there is a new bridge over the Agua Buena River and the road is graded and relatively smooth, but that can all change with one drenching wet season. You're better off taking the colectivo from Puerto Jiménez (⇨ *Getting Here and Around in Puerto Jiménez, above*). Or give yourself a break and fly via charter plane to Carate's small airport, which has been upgraded recently; arrange flights through your lodge. From here it's 3 km (2 miles), roughly a 40-minute walk along the beach to La Leona ranger station entrance to Corcovado National Park. In rainy season (May to December) it is sometimes impossible to cross the raging Río Carate that separates the landing strip from the beach path to the park, and you may end up stranded on either side. Parking at the store in Carate is $5 per day.

OUTDOOR ACTIVITIES

Activities here revolve around Corcovado National Park and its environs. Hiking, horseback riding, canopy tours, and other adventures must be organized through your hotel.

WHERE TO STAY

For expanded hotel reviews, visit Fodors.com.

$$
B&B/INN
Finca Exotica. A garden paradise that lives up to its name, this combination organic farm, botanical garden, and sophisticated eco-lodge is an otherworldly experience. **Pros:** gorgeous gardens; exotically delicious food; charming hosts. **Cons:** no air-conditioning; must enjoy being in a totally natural setting. **TripAdvisor:** "your little private piece of paradise," "relaxing," "unique and inspiring." $ *Rooms from: $80* ⊠ *50 m east of Carate airstrip* ☏ *2735–5164 in Puerto Jiménez, 416/628–9855 satellite phone at lodge* ⊕ *www.fincaexotica.com* ⇌ *5 cabins, 7 tents, 1 house* ☾ *Closed Sept. and Oct.* ⦿❘ *All meals.*

$$$
B&B/INN
Lookout Inn. The only hotel on Carate's beach, this barefoot inn—shoes come off at the bottom step—is set on a precipitous hillside (steep stairs are plentiful here, including a 500-step "Stairway to Heaven" up to a lofty lookout). **Pros:** proximity to beach and access on foot to Corcovado Park; excellent food; party atmosphere; guaranteed scarlet macaw sightings (or your money back!). **Cons:** very steep drive/stair climb up to lodge and down to beach; very limited communication with outside world; cabins have more privacy than main-lodge rooms. **TripAdvisor:** "slice of paradise," "great concept," "personal touch."

8

One of Punta Marenco Lodge's boat excursions.

$ *Rooms from: $150* ✉ *300 m east of Carate landing strip* ☎ *2735–5431, 757/644–5967 in U.S.* ⊕ *www.lookout-inn.com* ⟿ *3 rooms, 4 cabins, 2 tiki cabins with shared bath* ⦿| *All meals.*

$$$
B&B/INN
★

⌂ **Luna Lodge.** Luna Lodge's ultimate charm, especially for yoga and nature lovers from around the world, is its remoteness and tranquillity, perched on a sublime mountaintop overlooking rain forest and ocean. **Pros:** scenic setting for peace, yoga, and therapeutic massage; comfortable lodging and healthful food; excellent birding. **Cons:** extremely steep road up to lodge; beach is quite a hike back down (and up!); leave your laptop at home—there is satellite Wi-Fi but it is unreliable and costs $15 an hour. **TripAdvisor:** "immersed in nature," "inspiring," "a fantastic experience." $ *Rooms from: $100* ✉ *2 km/1 mile up a steep, partially paved road from Carate* ☎ *2206–5859, 2206–5860, 888/762–4069 in U.S.* ⊕ *www.lunalodge.com* ⟿ *8 bungalows, 3 rooms, 5 tents* ⦿| *All meals.*

DRAKE BAY

18 km/11 miles north of Corcovado, 40 km/25 miles southwest of Palmar Sur, 310 km/193 miles south of San José.

This is castaway country, a real tropical adventure, with plenty of hiking and some rough but thrilling boat rides to get here. The rugged coast that stretches south from the mouth of the Río Sierpe to Corcovado probably doesn't look much different from what it did in Sir Francis Drake's day (1540–96), when, as legend has it, the British explorer anchored here. Small, picture-perfect beaches with surf crashing against dark volcanic rocks are backed by steaming, thick jungle. Nature lodges scattered along the coast are hemmed in by the rain forest, which is home to troops of monkeys, sloths, scarlet macaws, and hundreds of other bird species.

GETTING HERE AND AROUND

The fastest way to get to Drake Bay is to fly directly to the airstrip. You can also fly to Palmar Sur and take a taxi to Sierpe and then a thrilling, if bumpy boat ride to Drake Bay. From the airport, it's a 25-minute taxi ride to Sierpe; small, open boats leave at low tide, usually 11 to 11:30 am for the one-hour trip to Drake. There is also a late-afternoon boat service. Captains will often stop along the way to view wildlife in the river mangroves. Many lodges arrange boat transportation from Drake Bay or Sierpe. From Rincón you can drive to Drake on a 30-km (19-mile) (sometimes) graded dirt road, but only in dry season when the rivers are low enough to cross. Buses leave Puerto Jiménez for La Palma about every two hours from 6 am to 8 pm, connecting in La Palma with buses to Drake Bay at 10:30 am and 4 pm. Buses leave Drake at 4 am and 1 pm for La Palma, to connect with buses to either Puerto Jiménez or San José. The drive from San José to Drake is scenic, but an exhausting seven hours long.

ESSENTIALS

Drake got electricity back in 2004, but there are still very few services.

Drake. The cheapest accommodations in the area can be found in the town of Drake, which is spread out along the bay. A trio of upscale nature lodges—Drake Bay Wilderness Resort, Aguila de Osa Inn, and La Paloma Lodge—are also clumped near the Río Agujitas on the bay's southern end. They all offer comprehensive packages, including trips to Corcovado and Caño Island. Lodges farther south, such as Punta Marenco Lodge and Casa Corcovado, run excursions from even wilder settings. During the dry season you can reach the town of Drake via a graded dirt road from Rincón, but only if you have a high-clearance 4WD vehicle and aren't afraid to ford some fast-flowing rivers.

8

OUTDOOR ACTIVITIES

Blue Water Pelagic. Local marine conservationist and dive master Shawn Larkin offers eco-sensitive tours doing just about anything you can think of in or above the water, including dive trips, underwater photography, snorkeling, sea-kayaking, whale- and dolphin-watching, and yacht services. He can also arrange an aerial photo tour for up to four passengers ($800 for 1 hour), flying in a Cessna with the door open, over the ocean in search of whales and other bird's-eye photo opportunities. ⊠ *Drake Bay* ☎ *8702–1248 text messages* ⊕ *www. costacetacea.com.*

Jinetes de Osa. Jinetes de Osa has diving ($110 for a two-tank dive plus $20 for gear), snorkeling ($75), and dolphin-watching tours ($105), as well as a canopy tour ($55) with some interesting bridge, ladder, and rope transitions between platforms. ⊠ *Drake village, west side of bay* ☎ *2231–5806* ⊕ *www.costaricadiving.com.*

CLOSE UP

Snorkelers' Paradise

Most of uninhabited 2½-square-km (1-square-mile) **Caño Island Biological Reserve** is covered in evergreen forest that includes fig, locust, and rubber trees. Coastal Indians used it as a burial ground, and the numerous bits and pieces unearthed here have prompted archaeologists to speculate about pre-Columbian long-distance maritime trade. Occasionally, mysterious stones that have been carved into perfect spheres of varying sizes are discovered. The uninhabited island's main attraction now is the ocean around it, superb for scuba diving and snorkeling. The snorkeling is best around the rocky points flanking the island's main beach; if you're a certified diver, you'll probably want to explore Bajo del Diablo and Paraíso, where you're guaranteed to encounter thousands of good-size fish, including white-tip, nurse, and trigger sharks.

The only way to get to the island, 19 km (12 miles) due west of the Osa Peninsula, is by boat arranged by your lodge or a tour company. Lodges and the Blue Water Pelagic and Jinetes de Osa tour companies in Drake Bay run day trips here, as do tour companies in Dominical, Uvita, and Sierpe.

WHERE TO STAY

For expanded hotel reviews, visit Fodors.com.

$$$
B&B/INN

🖼 **Aguila de Osa Inn.** A sportfisher's dream lodge, Aguila de Osa has spacious rooms with hardwood interiors, oversize bamboo beds, and luxurious tile-and-glass-brick bathrooms. **Pros:** great for fishing enthusiasts; elegant lodge and rooms; convivial, communal dining, early-morning coffee delivered. **Cons:** no ocean views or breezes, and heat and humidity can be stifling; steep climb to some rooms, on sometimes slippery stone stairs; some rooms have little privacy, notably No. 10. **TripAdvisor:** "beautiful setting," "loved the communal dining," "breathtaking location." $ *Rooms from: $380* ⊠ *South end of Drake at mouth of Río Agujitas* ☎ *2296–2190 in San José, 8840–2929 lodge, 866/924–8452 in U.S.* ⊕ *www.aguiladeosa.com* ⤢ *11 rooms, 2 suites* ⦿ *All meals.*

$$$$
B&B/INN
ALL-INCLUSIVE
★

🖼 **Casa Corcovado Jungle Lodge.** This hilltop, jungle lodge has it all: the closest location to Corcovado National Park, luxurious bungalows with private gardens, and first-class service. **Pros:** unrivaled location adjoining national park and close to Caño Island; excellent tours, service, and facilities. **Cons:** an adventure to get here: be prepared for a thrilling, wet landing; no air-conditioning; expensive but worth it. **TripAdvisor:** "beautiful location," "unique base for exploring," "staffed by wonderful people." $ *Rooms from: $381* ⊠ *Northern border of Corcovado* ☎ *2256–3181, 888/896–6097 in U.S.* ⊕ *www.casacorcovado.com* ⤢ *14 bungalows* ⊗ *Closed mid-Sept.–mid-Nov.* ⦿ *All-inclusive.*

$$
B&B/INN
☾

🖼 **Drake Bay Wilderness Resort.** On a grassy point between Río Agujitas and the ocean, this breezy resort has the best views of Drake Bay and the most kid-friendly grounds, with lots of open space for romping, a saltwater swimming pool, and rocky tidal pools to explore. **Pros:** great location; family-friendly and affordable; good food; free laundry

CLOSE UP

Understanding Costa Rica's Climate

Although you may associate the tropics with rain, precipitation in Costa Rica varies considerably, depending on where you are and when you're here. This is a result of the mountainous terrain and regional weather patterns. A phenomenon called rain shadow—when one side of a mountain range receives much more than the other—plays an important ecological role in Costa Rica. Four mountain ranges combine to create a continental divide that separates the country into Atlantic and Pacific slopes; because of the trade winds, the Atlantic slope receives much more rain than the Pacific. The trade winds steadily pump moisture-laden clouds southwest over the isthmus, where they encounter warm air or mountains, which make them rise. As the clouds rise, they cool, lose their ability to hold moisture, and eventually dump most of their liquid luggage on the Caribbean side.

During the rainy season—mid-May to December—the role of the trade winds is diminished, as regular storms roll off the Pacific Ocean and soak the western side of the isthmus. Though it rains all over Costa Rica during these months, it often rains more on the Pacific side of the mountains than on the Atlantic. Come December, the trade winds take over again, and while the Caribbean prepares for its wettest time of the year, hardly a drop falls on the western side until May.

Climate variation within the country results in a mosaic of forests. The combination of humidity and temperature helps determine what grows where; but whereas some species have restricted ranges, others seem to thrive just about anywhere. Plants such as strangler figs and bromeliads grow all over Costa Rica, and animals such as the collared peccary and coati—a long-nose cousin of the raccoon—can pretty much live wherever human beings let them. Other species have extremely limited ranges, such as the mangrove hummingbird, restricted to the mangrove forests of the Pacific coast, and the volcano junco, a gray sparrow that lives only around the highest peaks of the Cordillera de Talamanca.

service and free kayaks. **Cons:** not a lot of privacy in lined-up cabins. **TripAdvisor:** "wonderfully memorable," "nice accommodation," "welcoming staff." [$] *Rooms from: $130* ✉ *On peninsula at mouth of Río Agujitas, on southern end of bay* ☎ *2775–1716* 🌐 *www.drakebay.com* 🛏 *19 rooms, 3 tents* 🍴 *All meals.*

$ B&B/INN **Jinetes de Osa.** The most comfortable and reasonably priced place to stay right in the village of Drake, this small bay-side hotel with a casual open-air restaurant has simple rooms with tile floors and hot-water showers. **Pros:** convenient location; affordable; adventuresome, active clientele. **Cons:** standard rooms are smallish, so opt for the larger deluxe room if you can; no air-conditioning; access is on foot, since the tide washes right up to the lodge steps. **TripAdvisor:** "great hospitality," "adventure central," "funky but fun." [$] *Rooms from: $140* ✉ *Drake village, west side of bay* ☎ *2231–5806 in San José, 2775–3232 lodge* 🌐 *www.jinetesdeosa.com* 🛏 *9 rooms* 🍴 *All meals.*

$$$$
B&B/INN
★

La Paloma Lodge. Sweeping ocean views, impeccably appointed accommodations, and lots of tropical-foliage privacy make this lodge the area's most romantic. **Pros:** idyllic setting with ocean views and easy access to Coastal Footpath and beach; great service; interesting guests from all over the world. **Cons:** expensive; no air-conditioning; open cabins mean you will have to contend with some insect visitors. **TripAdvisor:** "nature at its finest," "absolutely fabulous," "a very special place." $ *Rooms from: $1230* ✉ *Drake Bay, 300 m past Drake Bay Wilderness Resort* ☎ *2293–7502 office in San José, 2775–1684 lodge* ⊕ *www.lapalomalodge.com* ⤴ *4 rooms, 5 villas, 2 Sunset Ranchos* ⊘ *Closed mid-Sept.–mid-Nov.* ⦿| *All meals.*

$$
B&B/INN
ALL-INCLUSIVE

Punta Marenco Lodge. This rustic lodge has the best location on the Pacific side of the Osa, with South Seas island–style, thatch-roof cabins perched on the spine of a ridge overlooking the sea. **Pros:** castaway-island remoteness; trails are as good as those in Corcovado National Park; reasonable, all-inclusive price. **Cons:** very rustic; steep climb uphill to lodge after thrilling wet landing on beach; limited electricity and contact with outside world. ⚠ The lodge's website has been pirated, so go only to the official website listed below. **TripAdvisor:** "intense nature experience," "a very good lodge," "one of the most beautiful places." $ *Rooms from: $70* ✉ *Beachfront directly east of Caño Island, 6 km south of Drake village* ☎ *2292–2775 for reservations, 2294–8947* ⊕ *www.corcovadozone.com* ⤴ *19 cabinas* ⦿| *All-inclusive.*

NIGHTLIFE

☾
★

Night Tour. When you're on the Osa Peninsula, the wildest nightlife is outdoors. Join entomologist Tracie Stice, also known as the Bug Lady, and herpetologist Gianfranco Gomez, on the Night Tour of insects, bats, reptiles, and anything else creeping or crawling around at night. Tracie is a wealth of bug lore, with riveting stories from around the world. Top-of-the-line Petzl headlamps help you see in the dark. Tours are $35 per person. Book ahead because these nightly tours, at 5:30 and 7:30 pm, are popular. ☎ *8701–7356, 8701–7462* ⊕ *www.thenighttour.com.*

Caribbean

WORD OF MOUTH

"Be prepared for the potential for lots of rain in July in Tortuguero, but it's also the beginning of turtle time. We went in July and had some pretty heavy downpours; they didn't last all day though. It's easiest to do a package with one of the lodges there."

—volcanogirl

WELCOME TO CARIBBEAN

TOP REASONS TO GO

★ **Dolphin-watching:** Bottlenose, tucuxi, and Atlantic spotted dolphins ply the southern Caribbean coast.

★ **Food and flavors:** Leave *gallo pinto* (rice and beans) behind in favor of mouthwatering *rondón* (meat or fish stew), or *caribeno* (Caribbean) rice and beans, stewed in coconut milk.

★ **Music:** Mix reggae and calypso with your salsa. Rhythms waft in from the far-off Caribbean islands; and homegrown musicians are making names for themselves, too.

★ **Sportfishing:** World-class tarpon and snook attract serious anglers to the shores off Barra del Colorado and Tortuguero national parks.

★ **Turtles:** People from around the world flock to the northern Caribbean for the annual nesting of four species.

1 Northern Lowlands. The Northern Lowlands have little to offer tourists in their own right, but are close to Braulio Carrillo Park and rafting-trip put-in points. The region can be done as a long day trip from San José as well.

2 Northern Caribbean Coast. The northern Caribbean coast encompasses the coastal jungles and canals of Tortuguero National Park and Barra del Colorado Wildlife Refuge. Boat and air travel are the only ways to reach this roadless region.

3 Southern Caribbean Coast. The southern Caribbean coast stretches south from port-of-call Limón to Panama. Towns along the coast have an Afro-Caribbean vibe—some are more backpackerish than others. Beaches are fringed with forest, and waters are rough. Surfers make the trip for Salsa Brava.

GETTING ORIENTED

Costa Rica's Caribbean coast is sometimes called its Atlantic coast, so as not to confuse tourists looking for the white sand and clear blue waters of the Caribbean Islands. This Caribbean is different, with sands in shades of brown and black, waters that are rough and murky (ideal for surfing), dense jungle, heavy and frequent rain, and a less-sophisticated, laid-back approach to tourism. It is beautiful and fascinating in its own way, but it's definitely not St. Barths.

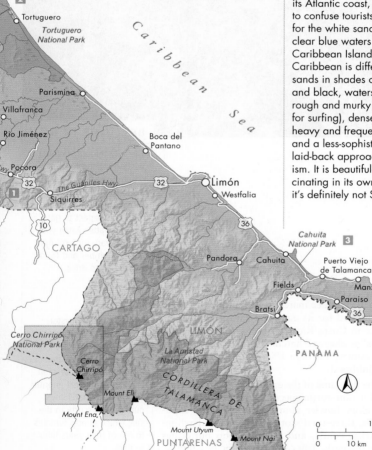

TORTUGUERO NATIONAL PARK

At various times of the year, four species of sea turtles—green, hawksbill, loggerhead, and giant leatherback—lumber up the 35 km (22 miles) of beach to deposit their eggs for safekeeping.

In 1975 the Costa Rican government established Tortuguero National Park to protect the sea turtle population, which had been decimated after centuries of being aggressively hunted for its eggs and carapaces. This is the best place in Costa Rica to observe these magnificent creatures' nesting and hatching rituals. Still, despite preservation efforts, less than 1% of the hatchlings will make it to adulthood.

Turtles may be the name of the game here, but keep your eyes peeled for non–turtle species, too: tapirs, jaguars, anteaters, ocelots, howler monkeys, white-faced capuchin monkeys, three-toed sloths, collared and white-lipped peccaries, coatis, and blue morpho butterflies also populate the park. You can wander the beach independently when the turtles aren't nesting, but riptides make swimming dangerous, and shark rumors persist. *(See page 515 for more information.)*

BEST TIME TO GO

The July-through-October nesting season for the green turtle is Tortuguero's most popular time to visit. It rains here (a lot!) year-round, so expect to get wet no matter when you go. February through April and September and October are a tad drier.

FUN FACT

One of nature's mysteries is how turtles find their way back to the same beach years later. It's thought that the sand leaves a biological imprint on the turtle hatchlings during their scurry to the sea, which directs females to return here years later to nest.

BEST WAY TO EXPLORE

BIRD-WATCHING AND WILDLIFE

This is a birder's dream destination. Some of the rarer species you'll find here include the snowy cotinga, palm warbler, and yellow-tailed oriole. Waterbirds and herons abound. On a recent foray, members of the Birding Club of Costa Rica were treated to a close-up view of a wide-eyed rufescent tiger-heron chick sitting in his nest, squawking impatiently for food. You'll also see iguanas, caimans, and sloths. Bird-watching and wildlife spotting sometimes collide: while watching two beautiful agami herons feeding on a muddy bank, birders were shaken up by the sudden splash of a crocodile attacking the herons. Happily, the herons were quicker off the mark than the birders were!

BOAT RIDES

It's not quite *The African Queen,* but a boat ride along the narrow vine-draped canals here is close. Once you're off the main canal, the specially designed, narrow tour boats glide relatively quietly—using mandated electric motors— and slowly, which makes for better wildlife spotting and less waves that erode the lagoon banks. Another alternative is to rent a kayak and go at your own speed along the canals.

TOURS

Most visitors opt for a fully escorted tour with one of the big lodges, because you're looked after from the moment you're picked up at your San José hotel until you're dropped off a day or two or seven later. All include a couple of standard tours of the park in their package prices. It's entirely possible to stay at a smaller in-town place and make à la carte arrangements yourself. No matter which way you go, your park tour will be on foot or by boat. Remember: You'll find no four-wheeled vehicles up here.

TOP REASONS TO GO

LUXURY IN THE JUNGLE

Don't let tales of Tortuguero's isolation dissuade you from making a trip. No question: The place is remote. But the lodges up here package everything (overnight lodging, meals, tours, and, best of all, guided round-trip transport) into one price in true "leave the driving to them" fashion. You won't lift a finger.

PLANE OR BOAT ONLY

Whoever coined the old adage "Getting there is half the fun" might have had Tortuguero in mind. Plane and boat are the only ways to get to this no-road sector of Costa Rica. If you have the time, the fully escorted boat trips to and from the jungle give you a real Indiana Jones experience.

TURTLES

Tortuguero takes its name from the Spanish word for turtle (*tortuga*), and here you'll get the chance to observe the nesting and hatching of four species of sea turtle, and to ponder one of nature's amazing rituals.

9

CAHUITA NATIONAL PARK

In a land known for its dark-sand beaches, the coral-based white sand of Cahuita National Park (Parque Nacional Cahuita) is a real standout.

The only Costa Rican park jointly administered by the National Parks Service and a community, it starts at the southern edge of the village of Cahuita and runs pristine mile after pristine mile southward. Whereas most of the country's protected areas tender only land-based activities, this park entices you offshore as well.

Roughly parallel to the coastline, a 7-km (4-mile) trail passes through the forest to Cahuita Point. A hike of a few hours along the trail—always easiest in the dry season—lets you spot howler and white-faced capuchin monkeys, coatimundis, armadillos, and raccoons. The coastline is encircled by a 2½-square-km (1-square-mile) coral reef, protection of which was the reason for the park's creation. You'll find superb snorkeling off Cahuita Point, but sadly, the coral reef is slowly being killed by sediment, intensified by deforestation and the erosive effects of the 1991 earthquake that hit the coast. *(See page 536 for more information.)*

BEST TIME TO GO

As is the case on this coast, you can expect rain here no matter what the time of year. February through April and September and October are drier months, and offer the best visibility for snorkeling. (Those are the least desirable months if you're here to surf.)

FUN FACT

When Costa Rica began charging admission to national parks, residents successfully requested an exemption, fearing that such charges would harm the local economy. Your admission fee to this park is voluntary at the town entrance.

BEST WAY TO EXPLORE

BEACHING IT

The waves here are fabulous for bodysurfing along the section of beach at the Puerto Vargas entrance. This wide swath of shoreline is also great for strolling, jogging, or just basking in the Caribbean sun—be careful of riptides along this stretch of coast. The safest swimming is in front of the camping area.

CYCLING

Cycling makes a pleasant way to see the park in the dry season. Seemingly everybody in Cahuita and Puerto Viejo de Talamanca rents bicycles. (The southern entrance to the park is close enough to Puerto Viejo that it could be your starting point, too.) The park trail gets muddy at times, and you run into logs, river estuaries, and other obstacles.

HIKING

A serious 7-km (4-mile) hiking trail runs from the park entrance at Kelly Creek all the way to Puerto Vargas. Take a bus or catch a ride to Puerto Vargas and hike back around the point in the course of a day. Remember to bring plenty of water, food, and sunscreen.

SNORKELING

Tour operators in Cahuita will bring you to a selection of prime snorkeling spots offshore. If you want to swim out on your own, the best snorkeling spot is off Punta Vargas at the south end of the park. Along with the chance to see some of the 500 or so species of tropical fish that live here, you'll see some amazing coral formations, including impressive elk horn, majestic blue stag horn, and eerie yellow brain corals. When the water is clear and warm, the snorkeling is great. But that warm water also appeals to jellyfish—if you start to feel a tingling sensation on your arms or legs, make a beeline for the shore. Each little sting doesn't hurt much, but accumulated stings can result in a major allergic reaction in some people.

TOP REASONS TO GO

EASY ACCESS

With one of its two entrances sitting in "downtown" Cahuita, access to the park is a snap. But ease of access does not mean the place is overrun with visitors. Fortunately, this is no Manuel Antonio.

LOTS OF LODGING

Closeness to Cahuita and Puerto Viejo de Talamanca and their spectrum of lodging options means you'll have no trouble finding a place to stay that fits your budget. You can even camp in the park if you're up to roughing it.

SNORKELING

Costa Rica's largest living coral reef just offshore means the snorkeling is phenomenal here. Watch for blue parrot fish and angelfish as they weave their way among equally colorful species of coral, sponges, and seaweeds. Visit during the Caribbean coast's two mini–dry seasons for the best visibility.

9

ECO-LODGES IN THE CARIBBEAN

Year-round rainfall begets year-round greenery on the Caribbean coast. You can count on lushness here when the rest of Costa Rica's landscape turns dusty during its dry season.

Not only does Costa Rica's Caribbean region host a different culture than the rest of the country, but its landscape is entirely different, too. Things are verdant all year, and that gives the eastern portion of the country a more tropical feel than the rest of Costa Rica. Development has been slow to come to the coast—anyone over the age of 20 well remembers the days of few roads, no phones, and no television. For you, that means far fewer visitors than along north and central Pacific coasts and a far more authentic experience since the environment is better preserved and the local culture respected. *Small* is the watchword for tourism around here—always has been and always will be. Developers do float occasional trial balloons about international megatourism projects in this region, but they get shot down quickly by the folks here who do not want their Caribbean coast to turn into the Pacific coast, thank you very much.

GOOD PRACTICES

Stay at locally owned lodgings. That's easy in the Caribbean, since the international chains are nowhere to be found here. Smaller lodgings that support the local economy are the universal norm. A stay here means that you are supporting those communities, too.

Consider taking public or semipublic transportation when visiting the Caribbean. Cahuita and Puerto Viejo de Talamanca have good bus and shuttle service; your own two feet, bicycles, and taxis make it easy to get around once you arrive. Of course, a Tortuguero visit means you leave the transportation to someone else. There's no other choice.

TOP ECO-LODGES IN THE CARIBBEAN

ALMONDS & CORALS, GANDOCA-MANZANILLO WILDLIFE REFUGE

Almonds & Corals scatters its comfortable platformed bungalows unobtrusively throughout its forest property along the coast and connects them with each other and to its restaurant, reception, and the beach by softly lighted paths. That and the myriad environmentally themed activities conducted by local guides really do give that "get away from it all" experience with a bit of rustic luxury. *(Full hotel review on page 550.)*

CASA MARBELLA, TORTUGUERO

Most visitors to Tortuguero opt for a stay at one of the big all-inclusive lodges lining the canals outside the village. Yet our favorite in-town lodging provides a far more intimate Tortuguero experience with one-on-one nature tours, rather than big groups, for just a fraction of the cost. Canadian owner and naturalist Daryl Loth is a knowledgeable and well-respected figure in the area. Though onetime outsiders, the folks at Casa Marbella have become arguably the town's biggest boosters, working closely with people here to develop sustainable, non-intrusive tourism that will benefit the entire community. We like and appreciate this "transplanted foreigner" model. *(Full hotel review on page 519.)*

RAIN FOREST ADVENTURES BRAULIO CARRILLO NATIONAL PARK

Although the site is best known for its famous aerial tram, there is accommodation here. The park is one of the Caribbean region's premier attractions, and staying here lets you enjoy the place after the day-trippers have left. The nine unobtrusive cabins are so inconspicuously tucked away that few people even know they exist. In an effort to minimize impact, food is locally grown, and electricity shuts off after 9 pm. Of course, the rates include the full complement of the site's eco-theme activities. *(Full hotel review on page 510.)*

BIOGEM

In 2009, the nonprofit Natural Resources Defense Council (NRDC) named the entire country one of its BioGems, a designation the New York–based environmental crusader usually reserves for a single site or species. In doing so, NRDC recognizes the country's wealth of biodiversity and its fragile status. The organization has pledged to work with the Costa Rican government in areas of reforestation and development of renewable energy technology. (With approximately 99% of Costa Rica's energy coming from hydroelectric and wind power, the country already does an impressive job in that latter regard.) Caribbean residents know NRDC well. The organization worked closely with people in the region at the grassroots level to block attempts to turn the southern Caribbean coast over to offshore oil exploration. Such drilling would have damaged the coast's fragile mangroves, sand beaches, and coral reefs. After many years, the oil companies' proposals have, thankfully, been put to rest for good.

9

By Jeffrey Van Fleet

The tourist brochures tout the country's Caribbean coast as "the other Costa Rica." Everything about this part of Costa Rica seems different: different culture, different history, different climate, and different activities. This region was long ago discovered by European adventure seekers—you're quite likely to hear Dutch and German spoken by the visitors here—but is much less known in North American circles.

The ethnic mix differs markedly here, as it does all along the Caribbean coast of Central America. The region was first settled by the British, and then throughout the 19th century, by the descendants of Afro-Caribbean slaves who came to work on the banana plantations and construct the Atlantic railroad. That makes the Caribbean coast the best place in the country to find English speakers, although even traditional English is disappearing as Spanish takes over.

It is rainier here than in other parts of Costa Rica, and the rain is distributed pretty evenly year-round without a distinct dry season. The region will never draw the typical fun-in-the-sun crowd that frequents the drier Pacific coast. Paradoxically, October, when the rest of Costa Rica is getting deluged with rain, is the driest month of the year here.

Never fear though: you'll find a year-round forested lushness and just as many activities at a more reasonable price, and, other than the peak weeks of Christmas and Easter, you can probably show up here without advance hotel reservations.

PLANNING

WHEN TO GO
HIGH SEASON: FEBRUARY TO APRIL
Climate is the Caribbean's bugaboo and will forever prevent it from becoming the same high-powered tourist destination that the northern Pacific coast is. (Frankly, we consider that to be a blessing.) The Caribbean lacks a true dry season, though February to April could be called a "drier" season, with many sunny days and intermittent showers. Yet,

despite weather patterns that differ from the rest of Costa Rica, places here charge high-season rates from December to April, just as they do elsewhere in the country. Prices skew a bit lower in the Caribbean, though, than elsewhere in Costa Rica.

LOW SEASON: MAY TO AUGUST AND DECEMBER TO JANUARY

The heaviest rains (and periodic road closures) come in December and January, high season elsewhere in Costa Rica. During the rainiest months visitors are fewer. May through August sees rain, too, although not quite as much. The popularity of this part of the country among European travelers means that July and August become price-based, if not weather-based, mini–high seasons here during this prime vacation for visitors from across the Atlantic. Tortuguero sets its own high season, with higher prices the norm during prime turtle-watching months of July through September.

SHOULDER SEASON: SEPTEMBER TO NOVEMBER

Want in on a little secret? When the rest of Costa Rica settles into the soggiest time of year, the sun comes out and the weather begins to dry up in this part of the country. The Caribbean coast makes the perfect refuge from the insufferably wet months of September and October elsewhere.

GETTING HERE AND AROUND

This region is one of the country's most accessible. The southern coast is a three- to four-hour drive from San José, over mostly decent roads (by Costa Rican standards), and public transportation is frequent and reliable. Gas stations are plentiful between Guápiles and Limón, but their numbers dwindle to one between Limón and Puerto Viejo de Talamanca. The northern Caribbean coast is another story: the total absence of roads means you have to arrive by plane or boat. Most travelers go with a tour booked through one of the large Tortuguero lodges.

If you're driving here, remember that fog often covers the mountains in Braulio Carrillo National Park, north of San José, by early afternoon. Cross this area in the morning if you can. Always exercise utmost caution on the portion of highway that twists and turns through the park. Check road conditions before you set out; occasional landslide closures through Braulio Carrillo necessitate leaving San José from the southeast, passing through Cartago, Paraíso, and Turrialba, then rejoining the Caribbean highway at Siquirres, a route that adds another 90 minutes onto your trip.

You can fly daily from San José to the airstrip in Tortuguero (TTQ) via Nature Air. Nature Air also flies Thursday and Saturday to the small airport in Bocas del Toro, Panama (BOC).

Autotransportes MEPE, which has a lock on bus service to the south Caribbean coast, has a reputation for being lackadaisical, but is really quite dependable. Drivers and ticket sellers are accustomed to dealing with foreigners; even if their English is limited, they'll figure out what you want. Bus fares to this region are reasonable. From San José, expect to pay $3 to Guápiles, $5.50 to Limón, $8.50 to Cahuita, $9.50 to Puerto Viejo de Talamanca, and $12 to Sixaola and the Panamanian border.

If you prefer a more private form of travel, consider taking a shuttle. Gray Line Tourist Bus has daily service that departs from many San José hotels for Cahuita and Puerto Viejo de Talamanca. Tickets are $44 and must be reserved at least a day in advance. Comfortable air-conditioned Interbus vans depart from San José hotels daily for Cahuita and Puerto Viejo de Talamanca. Reserve tickets ($45) a day in advance.

HOTELS

The high-rise, glitzy resorts of the Pacific coast are nowhere to be found in the Caribbean. The norm here is small, independent lodgings, usually family owned and operated. Fewer visitors in this region mean plenty of decent lodging at affordable prices most of the year. But tourism *is* growing, so it's risky to show up without reservations. Surprisingly few places here have air-conditioning, but sea breezes and ceiling fans usually provide sufficient ventilation. Smaller places frequently don't take credit cards; those that do may give discounts if you pay with cash.

Prices in the reviews are the lowest cost of a standard double room in high season.

RESTAURANTS

The many open-air dining spots out here provide you with that ultimate tropical dining experience, with Puerto Viejo de Talamanca offering one of Costa Rica's most varied dining scenes. Think seafood, chicken, coconut, and fruits in the Caribbean. Restaurateurs take advantage of the bounty of the land and sea in this part of the country.

Prices in the reviews are the average cost of a main course at dinner or, if dinner is not served, at lunch.

THE COMPLETE PACKAGE

One of Costa Rica's most remote regions is also one of its prime tourist destinations. No roads lead to Tortuguero on the northeast coast, so plane or boat is your only option. If you don't want to bother with logistics, consider booking a package tour with one of the lodges we list. It will include all transport from San José, overnights, meals, and guided tours. Prices look high at first, but considering all you get, they are quite reasonable. Other types of regional tours are also available: **Horizontes** (☎ 2222–2022 ⊕ *www.horizontes.com*) tours include naturalist guides and transport by 4WD vehicle.

TIMING

Attractions near Guápiles and Siquirres lend themselves to long day trips from San José. Tour operators also have whirlwind daylong Tortuguero trips from San José. We recommend you avoid these—the area really deserves two or, ideally, three days. Choose a single Caribbean destination and stay put if you have just a few days. (Cahuita and Puerto Viejo de Talamanca are ideal for that purpose.) If you have a week, you can tackle the north and south coasts.

ESSENTIALS

Bus Contacts Gray Line Tourist Bus ☎ 2220–2126 ⊕ www.graylinecostarica.com.**Interbus** ☎ 2283–5573 ⊕ www.interbusonline.com.

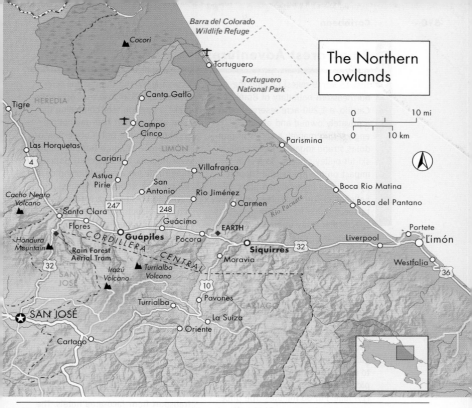

THE NORTHERN LOWLANDS

The lowlands begin about an hour north of San José, and, for most visitors, are a tract of land merely to get through on the way to the coast. The Caribbean does beckon, after all, but a couple of lesser sights here may tempt you to stop. If you stay on the well-maintained main Guápiles Highway, you head southeast toward Limón and the Caribbean coast. The highway passes through sultry agricultural lowlands, home to large banana and cacao plantations, but bypasses the region's three main communities: burgeoning Guápiles and the smaller towns of Guácimo and Siquirres.

GUÁPILES

60 km/38 miles northeast of San José.

The hub towns of Guápiles and Guácimo aren't destinations in their own right, but rather the nucleus for a few on-the-way-to-the-Caribbean activities. Guápiles, one of the country's fastest-growing cities, is the hub of northeastern Costa Rica, and with all the facilities in town, residents of the region barely need to trek to San José anymore. The smaller town of Guácimo lies 12 km (7 miles) east on the Guápiles Highway.

Rain Forest Adventures

Just 15 km (9 miles) beyond the northeastern boundary of Braulio Carrillo, a 1,200-acre reserve houses a privately owned and operated engineering marvel: a series of gondolas strung together in a modified ski-lift pulley system. (To lessen the impact on the jungle, the support pylons were lowered into place by helicopter.) The tram gives you a way to see the rain-forest canopy and its spectacular array of epiphyte plant life and birds from above, a feat you could otherwise accomplish only by climbing the trees yourself. Purists complain that it treats the rain forest like an amusement park, but it's an entertaining way to learn the value and beauty of rain-forest ecology.

The 21 gondolas hold five people each, plus a bilingual biologist-guide equipped with a walkie-talkie to request brief stops for snapping pictures. The ride covers 2½ km (1½ miles) in 80 minutes. The price includes a biologist-guided walk through the area for ground-level orientation before or after the tram ride. Several add-ons are possible, too, with frog, snake, and butterfly exhibits, a medicinal-plant garden, and a zip-line canopy tour on-site ($45), as well as a half-day birding tour ($83). You can arrange a personal pickup in San José for a fee; alternatively, there are public buses (on the Guápiles line) every half hour from the Gran Terminal del Caribe in San José.

Drivers know the tram as the *teleférico*. Many San José tour operators make a daylong tour combining the tram with another half-day option; combos with the Britt Coffee Tour or INBioparque in Santo Domingo, both near Heredia, are especially popular. Nine rustic (no air-conditioning or TV) but cozy *cabinas* (cottages) are available on-site (reservations are required). Electricity shuts off after 9 pm. Cabin rates include meals, tram tours, and guided walks. A café is open to all for breakfast, lunch, and dinner. If you're traveling the Central Pacific coast, you'll find similar installations near the town of Jacó (⇨ *Chapter 7*), 3 km (2 miles) north of Supermercado Maxi Bodega, although without the accommodation, and a restaurant open for breakfast and lunch only. The admission price at the Pacific facility includes the tram ride, nature walk, snake exhibit, heliconia and medicinal-plant gardens, and transport from Jacó-area hotels. The company also operates trams in the Caribbean-island nations of Jamaica, Dominica, and St. Lucia, all outside the scope of this book.

✉ *Teleférico del Bosque Lluvioso, Avda. 7 and C. 7, San José* ☎ *2257–5961, 866/759–8726 in North America* ⊕ *www.rainforestadventures.com* 🖃 *$55; $104 includes all attractions* ⊙ *Tours: Mon. 9–4, Tues.–Sun. 6:30–4. Call for reservations 6 am–9:30 pm.*

GETTING HERE AND AROUND

Guápiles lies just north of Braulio Carrillo National Park and straddles the highway to the Caribbean. It's an easy one-hour drive from San José just 60 km (38 miles) to the southwest, or Limón 84 km (50 miles) to the east. Empresarios Guapileños buses connect San José's Gran Terminal del Caribe with Guápiles every hour from early morning until late evening, and provide service seven times daily to Guácimo. San

Rain-forest trams are a great way to experience the Braulio Carrillo National Park.

José's bus terminals are in sketchy neighborhoods so take care if this is your mode of transport.

ESSENTIALS

Bank/ATM BAC San José ⊠ *Across from AyA* ☎ *2710–7434.*
Banco Nacional ⊠ *400 m east of Palí supermarket* ☎ *2713–2000.*

Hospital Hospital de Guápiles ⊠ *90 m south of fire station* ☎ *2710–6801.*

Pharmacy Farmacia San Martín ⊠ *Across from Palí* ☎ *2710–1115.*
Farmacia Santa Marta ⊠ *Across from Banco Nacional* ☎ *2710–6253.*

Post Office Correos ⊠ *North of MUCAP.*

Tourist Information Instituto Costarricense de Turismo ⊠ *Next to Ban-crédito* ☎ *2710–7516* ⊕ *www.visitcostarica.com* ⊙ *Weekdays 8–noon and 1–4.*

EXPLORING

EARTH. The nonprofit university called EARTH (Escuela de Agricultura de la Región Tropical Húmeda, or Agricultural School of the Humid Tropical Region) researches the production of less pesticide–dependent bananas and other forms of sustainable tropical agriculture, as well as medicinal plants. The university graduates some 100 students from Latin America and Africa each year. EARTH's elegant stationery, cal-endars, and other paper products are made from banana stems, tobacco leaves, and coffee leaves and grounds, and are sold at the on-site Oro-péndola store and in many tourist shops around the country. The prop-erty encompasses a banana plantation and a forest reserve with nature trails. Half-day tours are $15; full-day, $25; and lunch is $12 for day visitors. Though priority is given to researchers and conference groups, you're welcome to stay in the school's 50-person lodging facility, with private bathrooms, hot water, and ceiling fans, for $65 a night, which includes the use of a swimming pool and exercise equipment. The site is a bird-watchers' favorite; some 250 species have been spotted here. Reservations are required. ✉ *Pocora de Guácimo, 15 km/9 miles east of Guápiles on Guápiles Hwy.* ☎ *2713–0000, 404/995–1230 in North America* ⊕ *www.earth.ac.cr.*

SIQUIRRES

28 km/17 miles east of Guápiles.

Siquirres anchors a fertile banana- and pineapple-growing region, and marks the transition point between the agricultural lowlands and the tropical, palm-laden coast. The odd name is a corruption of the words *Si quieres* (if you want), fittingly impassive for this lackluster town. Siquirres has the unfortunate historical distinction of having once been the westernmost point to which Afro-Caribbean people could migrate. Costa Rica implemented the law in the late 1880s—when large numbers of Afro-Caribbeans immigrated (mainly from Jamaica) to construct the Atlantic Railroad—but abolished it in the 1949 constitution.

GETTING HERE

Siquirres lies just off the main highway and is easily accessible from the east, west, or south (if you're arriving from Turrialba). Autotransportes Caribeños buses connect San José's Gran Terminal del Caribe with Siquirres several times daily.

ESSENTIALS

Bank/ATM Banco Nacional ✉ *50 m south of Acon gas station* ☎ *2768–8128.*

Medical Clinic Centro de Salud de Siquirres ✉ *East side of soccer field* ☎ *2768–6138.*

Pharmacy Farmacia Santa Lucía ✉ *50 m west of fire station* ☎ *2768–9304.*

Post Office Correos ✉ *Next to Guardia Rural.*

EXPLORING

Agri Tours Pineapple Tour. Pineapples don't get the same attention in world circles as Costa Rican coffee and bananas, but the Agri Tours Pineapple Tour, affiliated with Del Monte Foods, can acquaint you with the life and times of this lesser-known crop, from cultivation to drying and packing at a farm just east of town. The two-hour tour is $20, samples included. Call to make a reservation. ✉ *On hwy., 7 km/4 miles east of Siquirres* ☎ *2765–8189, 2282–1316 in San José* ⊕ *www. agritourscr.com.*

OUTDOOR ACTIVITIES

RAFTING

★ Siquirres's proximity to the put-in sites of several classic rafting excursions makes it an ideal place to begin a trip.

Ríos Tropicales. Old standby Ríos Tropicales has tours on a Class III to IV section of the Pacuare River between Siquirres and San Martín, as well as the equally difficult section between Tres Equis and Siquirres.

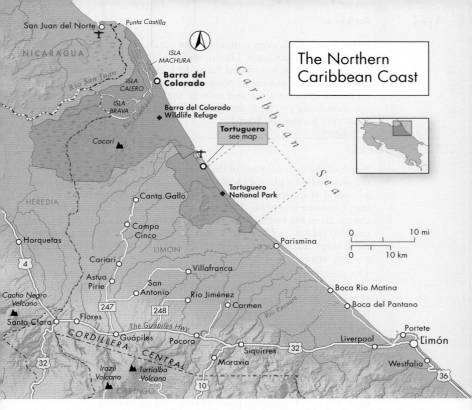

The Northern Caribbean Coast

NICARAGUA

San Juan del Norte · Punta Castilla

ISLA MACHURA

Barra del Colorado

Rio San Juan

ISLA CALERO

ISLA BRAVA

Rio Colorado

Barra del Colorado Wildlife Refuge

Tortuguero
see map

Cocori

Tortuguero National Park

Caribbean Sea

HEREDIA

Canta Gallo

Campo Cinco

Horquetas

LIMÓN

Parismina

4

Cariari

Villafranca

Astua Pirie

San Antonio

Rio Jiménez

Boca Rio Matina

Cacho Negro Volcano

247

248

Carmen

Rio Pacuare

Boca del Pantano

Santa Clara

Flores

The Guápiles Hwy.

Portete

Guápiles

Pocora

Liverpool

Limón

CORDILLERA CENTRAL

Siquirres

32

32

Irazú Volcano

Turrialba Volcano

Moravia

Westfalia

CARTAGO

10

36

0   10 mi
0   10 km

Not quite so wild, but still with Class III rapids, is the nearby Florida section of the Reventazón. Day excursions normally begin in San José, but if you're out in this part of the country, you can kick off your excursion here at the company's operations center in Siquirres. ⊠ *On the hwy. in Siquirres* ☎ *2233–6455, 866/722–8273 in North America* ⊕ *www.riostropicales.com.*

TORTUGUERO AND BARRA DEL COLORADO

Some compare these dense layers of green set off by brilliantly colored flowers—a vision doubled by the jungle's reflection in mirror-smooth canals—to the Amazon. That might be stretching it, but there's still an Indiana Jones mystique to the journey up here, especially when you get off the main canals and into the narrower lagoons. The region remains one of those Costa Rican anomalies: roadless and remote, it's nevertheless one of the country's most-visited places. The tourism seasons here are defined not by the rains or lack thereof (it's wet most of the year) but by the months of prime turtle hatching in Tortuguero, or by what's biting in sportfishing paradise Barra del Colorado.

In 1970 a system of canals running parallel to the shoreline was constructed to provide safer access to the region than the dangerous journey up the seacoast. You can continue up the canals, natural and man-made, that begin in Moín, near Limón, and run all the way to Tortuguero and beyond to the less-visited Barra del Colorado Wildlife Refuge. Or you can embark at various points north of Guápiles and Siquirres, as do public transportation and most of the package tours. (The lodges' minivans bring you from San José to the put-in point, where you continue your journey by boat.)

TORTUGUERO

Fodor's Choice
★

North of the national park of the same name, the hamlet of Tortuguero is a pleasant little place with 600 inhabitants, two churches, three bars, a handful of souvenir shops, and a small selection of inexpensive lodgings. (And one more plus: There are no motor vehicles here, a refreshing change from the traffic woes that plague the rest of Costa Rica.) You can also take a stroll on the 32-km (20-mile) beach, but avoid swimming here because of strong riptides and large numbers of bull sharks and barracuda.

The stretch of beach between the Colorado and Matina rivers was first mentioned as a nesting ground for sea turtles in a 1592 Dutch chronicle. Nearly a century earlier, Christopher Columbus compared traversing the north Caribbean coast and its swimming turtles to navigating through rocks. Because the area is so isolated—there's no road here to this day—the turtles nested undisturbed for centuries. By the mid-1900s, however, the harvesting of eggs and poaching of turtles had reached such a level that these creatures faced extinction. In 1963 an executive decree regulated the hunting of turtles and the gathering of eggs, and in 1970 the government established Tortuguero National Park; modern Tortuguero bases its economy on tourism.

GETTING HERE AND AROUND
It's easier than you'd think to get to remote Tortuguero. Flying is the quickest (and most expensive) option. Nature Air provides early-morning flights to and from San José.

If you're staying at one of the lodges, its boat will meet you at the airstrip.

The big lodges all have packages that include transportation to and from San José along with lodging, meals, and tours. Guide-staffed minivans pick you up at your San José hotel and drive you to the put-in site, usually somewhere north of Siquirres, where you board a covered boat for the final leg on the canals to Tortuguero. The trip up entails sightseeing and animal viewing. The trip back to San José stops only for a lunch break. This is the classic "leave the driving to them" way to get to Tortuguero.

A boat from the port of Moín, near Limón, is the traditional budget method of getting to Tortuguero if you are already on the Caribbean coast. Arrive at the docks before 10 am and you should be able to find someone to take you there. The going price is $35 per person each way, and travel time is about three hours.

If you arrive in Moín in your own vehicle, JAPDEVA, Costa Rica's Atlantic port authority, operates a secure, guarded parking facility for your car while you are in Tortuguero.

It's entirely possible to make the trip independently from San José, a good option if you are staying in the village rather than at a lodge. A direct bus departs from San José's Gran Terminal del Caribe to Cariari, north of Guápiles, at 9 am. At Cariari, disembark and walk five blocks to the local terminal, where you can board a noon bus for the small crossroads of La Pavona. From here, boats leave at 1:30 pm to take you to Tortuguero, arriving around 3 pm. La Pavona has secure parking facilities. The charge is $10 per night.

NICARAGUA CANAL?

During the 1840s California gold rush, the Río San Juan became an important crossroads allowing miners and gold to move between New York and San Francisco some 70 years before the Panama Canal opened. Cornelius Vanderbilt financed the dredging of the waterway to allow ships to pass up the river to Lake Nicaragua. From here a rail line connected to the Pacific Ocean. As the Panama Canal ages, there is again talk of resurrecting this "wet-dry" canal. With the canal undergoing expansion, plans remain on the drawing board, and probably will for the near future.

■TIP→ If you can, avoid Rubén Bananero, a company that provides bus-boat transport from Cariari. Its aggressive agents begin to hustle you the minute you get off the bus in Cariari. (Bananero even maintains an information booth at the Gran Terminal del Caribe bus station in San José.) They'll pressure you into buying a round-trip ticket, limiting your return options, and do everything they can to steer you toward hotels that pay them a commission. Others will also try to take you to their own dedicated "information dock" in the village, steering you toward their own guides. If you've made advance reservations for guides or hotels, stand your ground and say, *"No, gracias."*

Cariari–La Pavona–Tortuguero. The Cariari–La Pavona–Tortuguero bus-boat service is provided by **COOPETRACA** (☎ 2767–7137) or **Viajes Clic-Clic** (☎ 2709–8155, 8844–0463, or 8308–2006) for $10 one way. Clic-Clic is consistently more reliable.

Water taxis provide transport from multiple points in the village to the lodges. Expect to pay about $3 to $5 per trip.

ESSENTIALS

Visitor Information Kiosk. This unstaffed booth with free brochures offers information on the town's history, the park, turtles, and other wildlife. ⊠ *Town center.* **Tortuguero Information Center** ⊠ *Across from Catholic church* ☎ 2709–8011, 8833–0827 ⊕ www.tortuguerovillage.com.

EXPLORING

☺ **Tortuguero National Park.** The name Tortuguero means "turtle region," and what better place to see sea turtles and observe the age-old cycle of these magnificent animals nesting, hatching, and scurrying to the ocean? ☎ 2710–2929 ▱ $10 ☼ Daily 6–6.

Fodor's Choice
★

9

Northern Caribbean Coast and Tortuguero

DID YOU KNOW?

Some people still believe turtle eggs to be an aphrodisiacal delicacy, and some bars around Costa Rica (illegally) serve them as snacks. It's a big part of the human contribution to turtles' disappearance.

CAUTION

Wear mosquito repellent in low-lying coastal areas, where a few cases of dengue have been reported.

Sea Turtle Conservancy. Florida's Sea Turtle Conservancy runs a visitor center and a museum with excellent animal photos, a video narrating local and natural history, and detailed discussions of the latest ecological goings-on and what you can do to help. There's a souvenir shop next door. For the committed ecotourist, the **John H. Phipps Biological Field Station,** affiliated with the organization, has camping areas and dorm-style quarters with a communal kitchen. If you want to get involved in the life of the turtles, helping researchers to track turtle migration (current research, using satellite technology, has tracked turtles as far as the Florida Keys) or helping to catalog the population of neotropical migrant birds, arrange a stay in advance through the center. ⊠ *From beach at north end of village, walk north along path and watch for sign* ☎ *2709–8091, 800/678–7853 in North America* ⊕ *www. conserveturtles.org* ⏱ *$1* ⊙ *Mon.–Sat. 8–4, Sun. 9–5.*

OUTDOOR ACTIVITIES

Tortuguero is one of those "everybody's a guide" places. Quality varies, but most guides are quite knowledgeable. If you stay at one of the lodges, guided tours are *usually* included in your package price (check when you book). If you hire a private guide, $10–$20 per person per hour is the going rate depending on excursion, with most lasting three hours.

TOUR GUIDES AND OPERATORS

Sea Turtle Conservancy. Call or stop by the visitor center at the Sea Turtle Conservancy to get a recommendation for good local guides. ☎ *2709– 8091, 2297–5510 in San José* ⊕ *www.conserveturtles.org.*

★ **Daryl Loth.** Daryl Loth has a wealth of information about the area and conducts boat excursions on the canals and responsible turtle-watching tours in season with advance notice. ☎ *8833–0827, 2709– 8011* ✉ *safari@racsa.co.cr.*

Victor Barrantes. Local guide and area expert Victor Barrantes conducts hiking tours to Cerro Tortuguero and around the area. ☎ *2709–8055, 8928–1169* ✉ *tortuguero_info@racsa.co.cr.*

FISHING

You have your choice of mackerel, tarpon, snook, and snapper if you fish in the ocean; snook and calba if you fish in the canals. If you opt for the latter, the National Parks Service levies a $30 license fee (you are fishing in the confines of Tortuguero National Park), good for one month. Operators add the fee to your price.

Eddie Brown. Longtime area fishing expert Eddie Brown and his brother Roberto are based out of Tortuga Lodge and have daylong fishing packages for $600. ☎ *2710–8016.*

Elvin Gutiérrez. Elvin Gutiérrez, known as "Primo" to everyone in town, takes two passengers out for two hours or more, at $75 per hour, or for a full nine-hour day ($500). Prices include boat, motor, guide, and refreshments. ☎ 2709–8115 ⊕ *www.tortuguerosportsfish.com.*

TURTLE-WATCHING

If you want to watch the *deshove* (egg laying), contact your hotel or the parks office to hire a certified local guide, required on turtle-watching excursions. The Turtle Scout Program, affiliated with the Sea Turtle Conservancy, maintains a network of knowledgeable guides and has cut out a route of less-obtrusive trails that minimize long walks on the beach, all to the benefit of the turtles themselves. Note that you won't be allowed to use a camera—flash or nonflash—on the beach, and only your guide is permitted to use a flashlight (and that must be covered with red plastic), because lights can deter the turtles from nesting. Wear dark clothing if you can and avoid loud talking. Smoking is prohibited on the tours. ■ TIP→ **A few unscrupulous locals will offer to take you on a turtle-watching tour outside the allowed February-through-November season, disturbing sensitive nesting sites in the process. If it's not the season, don't go on a turtle excursion. As the signs around town admonish: "Don't become another predator."**

WHERE TO EAT

If you stay at one of the big lodges up here, your meals will be included in your package price, both in Tortuguero and on your way to and from. Usually *not* included in package prices are alcoholic beverages, soda, and bottled water. Ask to be sure.

If you're staying in town, you have a few simple, but filling restaurant, options to choose from.

$ ✕ **Budda Café.** Pizza, crepes, pastas, and fresh fish are on the menu at
ITALIAN this small, canal-side café in the center of town. Lattice wood over the windows, a thatched roof, and, of course, a Buddha statue make up the furnishings. Jazzy cha-cha or a Dean Martin ballad might be playing in the background. $ *Average main: $6* ⊠ *Next to police station, Tortuguero village* ☎ 2709–8084.

$ ✕ **The Vine Bakery.** Pastas, pizzas, and sandwiches are on the menu, but
CAFÉ this small bakery and coffee shop is also a great place to stop for breads made with banana, carrot, and *natilla* (cream), for example. $ *Average main: $5* ⊠ *25 m north of Catholic church, Tortuguero village* ☎ 2709–8132 ⊟ No credit cards ☾ No dinner.

WHERE TO STAY

For expanded hotel reviews, visit Fodors.com.

$ ⌂ **Casa Marbella.** This bed-and-breakfast, the best of the in-town lodg-
B&B/INN ings, is a real find, and the owner is a virtual encyclopedia of all things
Fodor'sChoice Tortuguero. **Pros:** knowledgeable owner; immaculate rooms. **Cons:**
★ some street noise; no access to lodge-package amenities of big lodges. **TripAdvisor:** "picturesque," "nice bed and breakfast," "stunning jungle river views." $ *Rooms from: $40* ⊠ *Across from Catholic church, Tortuguero village* ☎ 2709–8011 ⊕ casamarbella.tripod.com ⇗ 11 rooms ⊟ *No credit cards* ⦿ *Breakfast.*

9

PACKAGE DEALS

The big lodges here offer one- or two-night excursion packages. (Given the choreography it takes to get up here, opt for a more leisurely two-night stay if you can.) Rates are expensive, but prices include everything from guides, tours, meals, and snacks to minivan and boat transport, and in some cases air transport to and from San José. (The $10 entrance fee to Tortuguero National Park may or may not be included in the package price. Ask to be sure.) If you stop and calculate what you get, the price is actually quite reasonable, and the tours are undeniably great fun. Few of the lodges have phones, although all have radio contact with the outside world. All reservations must be made with their offices in San José. Be sure to travel light; you get a baggage allowance of 25 pounds, strictly enforced. There's simply no space in the boats for you to bring more.

$$$$
RESORT
ALL-INCLUSIVE
Fodor'sChoice
★

Evergreen Lodge. The Evergreen offers an entirely different (and intimate) concept in Tortuguero lodging: whereas other lodges have cabins arranged around a clearing, at Evergreen they penetrate deep into the forest. **Pros:** seclusion from other lodges; lush wooded setting. **Cons:** rustic rooms; farther from town than other lodges. **TripAdvisor:** "great jungle retreat," "eco lodge in paradise," "a rustic place to explore." *$ Rooms from: $418 ⊠2 km/1 mile from Tortuguero village on Canal Penitencia ☎2257–7742 in San José, 800/644–7438 in North America in San José ⊕ www.evergreentortuguero.com ⇝ 55 rooms ⏐⊙⏐ All-inclusive.*

$$$$
RESORT
ALL-INCLUSIVE

Hotel Flor de Tortuguero. A location on the inland side of the second canal in from the ocean gives this place plenty of room to spread out, and indeed, a network of hiking trails on the lodge's grounds is one of the attractions here. **Pros:** seclusion from other lodges; ample grounds; network of hiking trails. **Cons:** rustic rooms; farther from town than other lodges. **TripAdvisor:** "a relaxing stay," "beautiful and peaceful place," "remote and rustic." *$ Rooms from: $426 ⊠2 km/1 mile from Tortuguero village on Canal Penitencia ☎2222–3927 in San José ⊕ www.hotelflordetortuguero.com ⏐⊙⏐ All-inclusive.*

$$$$
RESORT
ALL-INCLUSIVE

Laguna Lodge. Laguna is the largest of the Tortuguero lodges, and it hums with activity as befits its size. **Pros:** many activities; unique architecture. **Cons:** large numbers of guests; not for those who crave anonymity. **TripAdvisor:** "luxury in the rainforest," "unique," "birdwatching haven." *$ Rooms from: $472 ☎2709–8082, 2272–4943 in San José, 888/259–5615 in North America ⊕ www.lagunatortuguero. com ⇝ 100 rooms ⏐⊙⏐ All-inclusive.*

$$$$
RESORT
ALL-INCLUSIVE

Manatus Hotel. Amenities such as air-conditioning, massage, and television are simply not found up here, but Tortuguero's most luxurious hotel has them all. **Pros:** intimate surroundings; numerous creature comforts; packages begin at $391 per person. **Cons:** fills up quickly in high season; degree of luxury may feel out of place in Tortuguero. **TripAdvisor:** "charming and unforgettable," "very nice location," "family atmosphere." *$ Rooms from: $782 ⊠Across river, about 1 km/½ mile north of Tortuguero ☎2709–8197, 2239–4854 in San José ⊕ www. manatuscostarica.com ⇝ 12 rooms ⏐⊙⏐ All-inclusive.*

"Cruising down the canal in Tortuguero Park, we discovered this emerald baselisk, a magnificient looking creature." —Photo by Liz Stuart, Fodors.com member

$$$$ RESORT ALL-INCLUSIVE ★ **Mawamba Lodge.** Nestled between the river and the ocean, Mawamba is the perfect place to kick back and relax, and it is also the only jungle lodge within walking distance (about 10 minutes) of town. **Pros:** many activities; walking distance to village. **Cons:** rustic rooms; not for those who crave anonymity. **TripAdvisor:** "wildlife on doorstep," "simply breathtaking," "a unique place." [$] *Rooms from: $410* ✉ *½ km/¼ mile north of Tortuguero on ocean side of canal* ☎ *2709–8181, 2293–8181 in San José* 🌐 *www.grupomawamba.com* 🛏 *58 cabinas* 🚭 *Non-smoking* 🍴 *All-inclusive.*

9

$$$$ RESORT ALL-INCLUSIVE Fodor's Choice ★ **Pachira Lodge.** This is the prettiest of Tortuguero's lodges, but not the costliest—the owners here market competitively and keep prices reasonable. **Pros:** many activities; good value. **Cons:** large numbers of guests; can be difficult to find space; not for those who crave anonymity. **TripAdvisor:** "beautiful surroundings," "great rainforest experience," "amazing." [$] *Rooms from: $418* ✉ *Across river from Mawamba Lodge* ☎ *2257–4242 in San José, 800/644–7438 in North America* 🌐 *www.pachiralodge.com* 🛏 *88 rooms* 🍴 *All-inclusive.*

$$$$ RESORT ALL-INCLUSIVE ★ **Tortuga Lodge.** Lush lawns, orchids, and tropical trees surround this thatched riverside lodge owned by Costa Rica Expeditions and renowned for its nature packages and top-notch, personalized service. **Pros:** many activities; seclusion from other lodges; close to airstrip. **Cons:** rustic rooms; farther from park than most lodges here. **TripAdvisor:** "a taste of paradise," "good facilities," "first class." [$] *Rooms from: $756* ✉ *Across the river from airstrip, 2 km/1 mile from Tortuguero* ☎ *2710–8016, 2257–0766 in San José* 🌐 *www.costaricaexpeditions.com/tortuga-lodge* 🛏 *26 rooms* 🍴 *All-inclusive.*

BARRA DEL COLORADO

25 km/16 miles northwest of Tortuguero.

Up the coast from Tortuguero is the ramshackle hamlet of Barra del Colorado, a popular sportfishing hub characterized by plain stilted wooden houses, dirt paths, and a complete absence of motorized land vehicles (though some locals have added motors to their hand-hewn canoes).

GETTING HERE AND AROUND

You're likely staying at a fishing lodge if you come this far. Ask about transportation logistics. No scheduled air service presently operates to the airstrip in Barra del Colorado. The lodges up here can arrange charter flights or can arrange for a representative to meet your flight in Tortuguero, a short distance south.

EXPLORING

Barra del Colorado Wildlife Refuge (*Refugio Nacional de Vida Silvestre Barra del Colorado*). Bordered to the north by the Río San Juan and the frontier with Nicaragua is the vast, 905-square-km (350-square-mile) Barra del Colorado Wildlife Refuge, Costa Rica's largest reserve, and really the only local attraction for nonanglers. Most people arrange trips here through one of the fishing lodges. Transportation once you get here is almost exclusively waterborne, as there are virtually no paths in this swampy terrain. The list of species that you're likely to see from your boat is almost the same as that for Tortuguero; the main difference here is the feeling of being farther off the beaten track. You can realistically get as far as the 640,000-acre **Río Indio-Maíz Biological Reserve** when crossing the border here. The reserve is a continuation of the Barra del Colorado Wildlife Refuge, but in Nicaraguan territory. ⊠ *30 km/18 miles north of Tortuguero* 🕾 *No phone* 💲 *Free* 🕒 *24 hrs.*

LIMÓN TO PUERTO VIEJO DE TALAMANCO

The landscape along the Guápiles Highway changes from farmland to tropics as you approach the port city of Limón. Place names change, too. You'll see signs to towns called Bristol, Stratford, and Liverpool, reflecting the region's British Caribbean heritage. European backpackers discovered tourist towns par excellence Cahuita and Puerto Viejo de Talamanca; now visitors of all nationalities and budgets flock there.

LIMÓN

100 km/62 miles southeast of Guápiles, 160 km/100 miles north and east of San José.

The colorful Afro-Caribbean flavor of one of Costa Rica's most important ports (population 90,000) is the first sign of life for seafaring visitors to Costa Rica's east coast. Limón (sometimes called "Puerto Limón") is a lively, if shabby, town with a 24-hour street life. Most travelers do not stop here, heading immediately to Cahuita and Puerto Viejo de Talamanca farther south. The wooden houses are brightly painted, but the grid-plan streets look rather worn, partly because of

Continued on page 527

"It was so awesome to see this huge dorado (mahi-mahi) my husband boated with help from a great first mate." —janenicole, Fodors.com member

SPORTFISHING

by Elizabeth Goodwin

Adventurous anglers flock to Costa Rica to test their will—and patience—against an assortment of feisty fresh- and saltwater fish. Just remember: catch-and-release is sometimes expected, so the pleasure's all in the pursuit.

With so many options the hardest decision is where to go. Inshore fishing in the country's rivers and lakes yields roosterfish, snapper, barracuda, jacks, and snook. Fly-fishing afficiondos love the extra-large tarpon and snook because of their sheer size and fight. The country's coasts swarm with a multitude of bigger game, including the majestic billfish that Hemingway made famous—the marlin and the sailfish.

There are a multitude of top-notch fishing outfitters up and down both coasts and around rivers and lakes, so planning a fishing trip is easy. We list our favorites throughout the book under Outdoor Activities. Charter boats range from 22 feet to 60 feet in length. With a good captain, a boat in the 22- to 26-foot range for up to three anglers can cost from $500 to $750 a day. A 28- to 32-foot boat fits four and costs from $800 to $1,200 per day. A boat for six people costs $1,400 to $1,800 and measures between 36 and 47 feet. A 60-foot boat for up to ten anglers costs about $3,000 a day. A good charter boat company employs experienced captains and offers good equipment, bait, and food and beverages.

CHOOSING A DESTINATION

Costa Rica teems with a constant supply of *pescado* (fish), some of which might seem unique to North Americans. Below are some local catches and where you'll find them.

A local fisherman in Puerto Viejo.
xelas, fodors.com member.

Barra del Colorado (*See Chapter 9*) is a popular sportfishing hub and a great departure point for freshwater fishing on the Caribbean side of the country. Fly fishers looking for the ultimate chal-

lenge head to **San Juan River** for its legendary tarpon. The **Colorado River** lures anglers with jack, tuna, snook, tarpon, and dorado. Transportation and tours can be arranged by the hotels listed in **Puerto Viejo de Sarapiquí** and **Las Horquetas** (*See Chapter 4*).

Lake Arenal and **Caño Negro Lagoon** are also great freshwater spots to snag extra-large tarpon, snook, and the ugly-but-fascinating guapote bass. Start your fishing journey in nearby **La Fortuna** (*See Chapter 5*).

On the Pacific side, **Tamarindo** is the main departure point for anglers looking to find big game, including tuna, roosterfish, and marlin. Boats also leave

from **Playas del Coco, Ocotal, Tambor,** and **Flamingo Beach,** which are best fished May through August. All are close to the well-stocked northern Papagayo Gulf. If you're hunting sailfish and marlin between December and April, head to the Central Pacific coast around **Los Sueños** and **Quepos,** where up to 10 sailfish are caught per boat *(See Chapters 6 and 7).* The southern Pacific towns, like **Puerto Jimenez, Golfito,** and **Zancudo,** are less developed than the other Pacific regions and are famous for their excellent inshore fishing for snapper and roosterfish, though offshore big game is also good in the area, especially November through January *(See Chapter 8).*

FISHING LICENSE

Costa Rica requires that all anglers have a valid Costa Rica fishing license. You can usually pick one up at the dock entrance on the morning of your first day of fishing for $25 (cash only). It's good for one year from the date of purchase. Most charters do not fold this into their costs because license enforcement is lax and it is occasionally difficult to track down people who sell fishing licenses. Ask about this before you head out.

(top) Osa Peninsula, (bottom left) *Plat de jour* is Wahoo, (bottom right) School of Tarpon

THE FISH YOU'LL FIND

By law billfish are catch-and-release only.

GASPAR (alligator gar), found in Barra del Colorado River and Lake Arenal, look like a holdover from prehistoric times and have long narrow snouts full of sharp teeth; they make great sport on light tackle. Gar meat is firm and sweet (some say shrimplike), but the eggs are toxic to humans.

Snook

MARLIN AND SAILFISH migrate northward through the year, beginning about November, when they are plentiful in the Golfito region. From December into April they spread north to Quepos, which has some of the country's best deep-sea fishing, and are present in large numbers along the Nicoya Peninsula at Carrillo and Sámara from February to April, and near Tamarindo and Flamingo from May to September. Pacific sailfish average more than 45 kilos (100 pounds), and are usually fought on a 15-pound line or less. Costa Rican laws require that all sails be released and bans sportsfishers from bringing them on board for photo ops.

Sailfish

GUAPOTE (rainbow bass) make their home in Lake Arenal. It's a hard-hitting catch: 5- to 6-pounders are common. Taxonomically, guapote are not related to bass, but are caught similarly, by casting or flipping plugs or spinner bait. Streams near the Cerro de la Muerte, off the Pan-American Highway leading south from San José, are stocked with guapote. The fish tend to be small, but the scenery makes a day here worthwhile.

TARPON AND SNOOK fishing are big on the Caribbean coast, centered at the mouth of the Barra del Colorado River. The acrobatic tarpon, which averages about 38 kilos (85 pounds) here, is able to swim freely between salt water and freshwater and is considered by many to be the most exciting catch on earth. Tarpon sometimes strike like a rocket, hurtling 5 meters (16 feet) into the air, flipping, and twisting left and right. Anglers say the success rate of experts is to land about 1 out of every 10 tarpon hooked. In the Colorado, schools of up to 100 tarpon following and feeding on schools of titi (small, sardinelike fish) travel for more than 160 km (100 mi) to Lake Nicaragua. The long-standing International Game Fishing Association all-tackle record was taken in this area.

WHEN TO GO

In Costa Rica, you're guaranteed a few good catches no matter what the season, as demonstrated by the cadre of sportsmen who circle the coasts year-round chasing that perfect catch. If your heart is set on an area or a type of fish, do your research ahead of time and plan accordingly.

CLOSE UP

The Nicas

Immigration issues generate intense debate in the United States and Western Europe. Who would guess that it has become a contentious matter here in Costa Rica, too? Over the past four decades, war, poverty, dictatorship, revolution, earthquakes, and hurricanes have beset Nicaragua, Costa Rica's northern neighbor. Each new calamity has brought a wave of refugees fleeing south. Approximations vary—no one can know for sure—but high-end estimates guess that 20% of Costa Rica's population today is Nicaraguan. Speaking with a faster, more clipped accent than Costa Ricans, they do not fade into the scenery.

The refrain among Ticos is a familiar one: "They're taking our jobs!" Yet, truth be told, Nicaraguans are performing the low-end labor that Costa Ricans just won't do anymore: your hotel chambermaid may likely be Nicaraguan; the glitzy resort where you're staying was probably built with the sweat of many Nicaraguan construction workers; and the beans that went into that delicious morning cup of Costa Rican java were likely harvested by migrant Nicaraguan coffee pickers.

Relations between Costa Rica and Nicaragua went way south in 2011 with Nicaragua's occupation of the 58-square-mile Isla Calero, a Costa Rican island in the San Juan River, which forms the border between the two countries (Nicaragua based its decision to invade on a mistaken designation by Google Maps that Calero was its sovereign territory. Google Maps corrected the error, issuing a statement that its site should not be the arbiter of international boundary disputes.) The standoff continued for months, until a ruling by the International Court of Justice that the island does indeed belong to Costa Rica. Although relations between Costa Rica and its northern neighbor still remain chilly at this writing, the dispute need not concern you as a visitor.

9

the damage caused by a 1991 earthquake. Street crime, including pickpocketing and nighttime mugging, is not uncommon here. Long charged with neglecting the city, the national government continually promises to turn new attention to Limón, although the results never match residents' expectations.

Limón receives thousands of visitors every year, owing in large part to its newest incarnation as a port of call. Carnival, Celebrity, Holland America, Princess, and Royal Caribbean cruise ships all dock here on certain of their Panama Canal or western Caribbean itineraries. The downtown Terminal de Cruceros hums with activity between October and May, with one or two boats each day December through March, but many fewer outside those peak months. This is the place to find telephones, Internet cafés, manicurists (they do quite a brisk business), a tourist-information booth, and tour-operator stands, too. Downtown shopkeepers have all learned how to convert their colón prices to dollars, and post the day's exchange rate. St. Thomas or Puerto Vallarta it is not—perhaps someday, residents hope—but Limón has a small, but growing, tourist vibe these days that the city has never

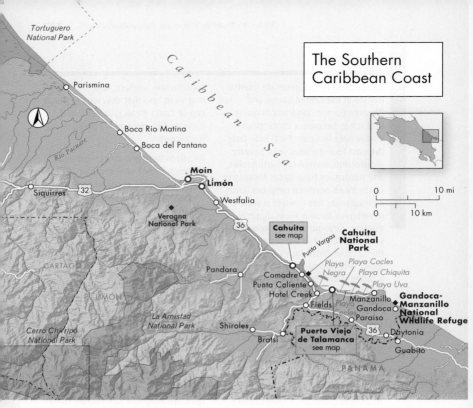

before experienced. The terminal contains souvenir stands staffed by low-key vendors who invite you to look, but don't pester you if your answer is *"No, gracias."*

NAVIGATING LIMÓN

Avenidas (avenues) run east and west, and *calles* (streets) north and south, but Limón's street-numbering system differs from that of other Costa Rican cities. "Number one" of each avenue and calle begins at the water and numbers increase sequentially as you move inland, unlike the evens-on-one-side, odds-on-the-other scheme used in San José. But the scarcity of street signs means everyone uses landmarks anyway. Official red taxis ply the streets, or wait at designated taxi stands near Parque Vargas, the Mercado Municipal, and, of course, the cruise-ship terminal.

GETTING HERE AND AROUND

If you're coming to the Caribbean coast, you'll pass through Limón. The Guápiles Highway that began in San José ends here at the ocean but bypasses the heart of downtown by a couple of blocks. Budget about 3½ hours for the trip. Just after the sign to "Sixaola" and the coastal highway south to Cahuita and Puerto Viejo de Talamanca is the city center. The main bus terminal lies at Avenida 2 and Calle 8, across from the soccer stadium, and serves routes from San José, Guápiles, and Siquirres, with buses arriving several times daily from each.

Opt for the *directo* (express) service from San José rather than the *corriente* buses, which make many stops along the route. Buses to Cahuita and Puerto Viejo de Talamanca and all points on the south coast arrive and depart from a stop across from Radio Casino on Avenida 4 between Calles 3 and 4.

ESSENTIALS
Bank/ATM BAC San José ⊠ *Avda. 3, Cs. 2–3* ☎ *2798–0155.* **Banco Nacional** ⊠ *Avda. 2, Cs. 3–4* ☎ *2758–0094.* **Scotiabank** ⊠ *Avda. 3 and C. 2* ☎ *2798–0009.*

Hospital Hospital Dr. Tony Facio ⊠ *Hwy. to Portete* ☎ *2758–2222.*

Internet Café Internet ⊠ *Gran Terminal del Caribe, Avda. 2 and C. 8, across from the soccer stadium* ☎ *2798–0128.* **Internet Cinco Estrellas** ⊠ *50 m north of Terminal de Cruceros* ☎ *2758–5752.*

Pharmacy Farmacia Buenos Aires ⊠ *25 m east of Mercado Municipal* ☎ *2798–4732.* **Farmacia Limonense** ⊠ *1st fl., Radio Casino* ☎ *2758–0654.*

Post Office Correos ⊠ *Avda. 2 and C. 4.* **DHL** ⊠ *Across from Terminal de Cruceros* ☎ *2758–1256.*

Visitor Information Instituto Costarricense de Turismo ⊠ *300 m north of cathedral* ☎ *2758–0983* ⊕ *www.visitcostarica.com* ☯ *Weekdays 8–noon and 1–4.* **JAPDEVA** (*Atlantic Port Authority*). ⊠ *Terminal de Cruceros* ☞ *Accessible to cruise-ship passengers only.*

> ### SHIP AHOY!
>
> If you arrive in Limón on a cruise ship, a day in the Caribbean is yours for the taking. The Tortuguero canals, the beaches at Puerto Viejo de Talamanca, the sloth rescue center at Aviarios Sloth Sanctuary near Cahuita, or the Veragua Rainforest Adventure Park, just a few miles away, are four popular excursions. A few hardy souls venture as far away as the Rain Forest Aerial Tram or San José. A legion of taxi drivers waits at the terminal exit if you have not arranged an organized shore excursion through your cruise company.

EXPLORING
Cemetery. On the left side of the highway as you enter Limón is a large cemetery. Notice the "colonia china" ("Chinese colony") and corresponding sign in Chinese on the hill in the cemetery: Chinese workers made up a large part of the 1880s railroad-construction team that worked here. Thousands died of malaria and yellow fever.

Municipal Market (*Mercado Municipal*). A couple of blocks west of the north side of Parque Vargas is the lively enclosed Municipal Market, where you can buy fruit for the road ahead and experience the sights, sounds, and smells of a Central American market. ⚠ **The hustle and bustle always means a risk of pickpockets. Watch your things.** ⊠ *Pedestrian mall, Avda. 2, Cs. 3–4.*

Parque Vargas. The aquamarine wooden port building faces the cruise terminal, and just to the east lies the city's palm-lined central park, Parque Vargas. From the promenade facing the ocean you can see the raised dead coral left stranded by the 1991 earthquake. Nine or so Hoffman's two-toed sloths live in the trees of Parque Vargas; ask a passerby to point them out, as spotting them requires a trained eye.

A carnival in Limón.

OUTDOOR ACTIVITIES

Limón's growing crop of tour operators serves cruise-ship passengers almost exclusively.

Laura Tropical Tours. Laura Tropical Tours has excursions to banana plantations, Tortuguero, and Cahuita National Park. ⊠ *Terminal de Cruceros* ☎ *2795–2410* ⊕ *www.viajestropicaleslaura.net.*

Mambo Tour. These folks can take you on three- to eight-hour excursions around the region, and even on an all-day trip to the Rain Forest Aerial Tram or San José. ⊠ *Terminal de Cruceros* ☎ *2798–1542* ⊕ *www.mambotour.com.*

♻ **Veragua Rainforest Adventure Park.** Limon's newest attraction, Veragua Rainforest Adventure Park, is a 4,000-acre nature theme park, about 30 minutes west of the city. It's popular with cruise-ship passengers in port for the day, but if you're in the area, it's well worth a stop. Veragua's great strength is its small army of enthusiastic, superinformed guides who take you through a network of nature trails and exhibits of hummingbirds, snakes, frogs, and butterflies and other insects. A gondola ride overlooks the complex and transports you through the rain-forest canopy. A branch of the Original Canopy Tour, with nine platforms rising 46 meters (150 feet) above the forest floor, is here. The tour is not included in the basic admission to the park but is priced as an add-on. ⊠ *Veragua de Liverpool, 15 km/9 miles west of Limón* ☎ *2296–5056 in San José* ⊕ *www.veraguarainforest.com* 🎟 *Full-day tour $55; full-day tour with canopy $89; full-day tour with transportation (does not include canopy tour) from San José, $119* ☉ *Tues.–Sun. 8–4.*

WHERE TO STAY

For expanded hotel reviews, visit Fodors.com.

$$
RESORT ▢ **Hotel Maribú Caribe.** Perched on a cliff overlooking the Caribbean Sea between Limón and Portete, these white conical thatch huts have great views, but you're a long way from the ocean itself. **Pros:** good moderate value; secluded location, terrific views. **Cons:** no access to beach; far from center of town. **TripAdvisor:** "beautiful," "close to the beach," "wonderful stay." $ *Rooms from: $78* ⊠ *4 km/2½ miles north on road to Portete* ☎ *2795–4010* ⊕ *www.maribu-caribe.com* ⤶ *56 rooms* ⦿ *Breakfast.*

$
HOTEL ▢ **Park Hotel.** The prices at this modern, pastel-and-pink business-class hotel in central Limón can't be beat. **Pros:** good budget value; great ocean views. **Cons:** small rooms; air-conditioning too icy at times. **TripAdvisor:** "great location," "as good as it gets," "probably your best bet in Limon." $ *Rooms from: $72* ⊠ *Avda. 3, Cs. 2–3* ☎ *2798–0555* ⊕ *www.parkhotelcostarica.com* ⤶ *32 rooms* ⦿ *Breakfast.*

> ### RECYCLE!
>
> Unfortunately it's difficult to recycle in most places in Costa Rica, but Cahuita and Puerto Viejo de Talamanca have made it a breeze. Deposit your aluminum cans and glass and plastic beverage bottles in the *Recicaribe* barrels you'll see in either community.

SHOPPING

The cruise-ship terminal contains an orderly maze of souvenir stands. Vendors are friendly; there's no pressure to buy. Many shops populate the restored port building across the street as well.

MOÍN

5 km/3 miles north of Limón.

The docks at Moín are a logical next stop after visiting neighboring Limón, especially if you want to take a boat north to explore the Caribbean coast.

GETTING HERE

Moín is a quick taxi ride from the center of Limón. You'll probably be able to negotiate a waterway and national-park tour with a local guide, and if you call in advance, you can arrange a tour with the man considered the best guide on the Caribbean coast:

★ **Modesto Watson.** Local indigenous Miskito guide Modesto Watson is legendary for his bird- and animal-spotting skills as well as his howler monkey imitations. The family's *Riverboat Francesca* can take you up the canals for two-day–one-night excursions to Tortuguero for $200 to $220 per person, depending on the lodge used. ☎ *2226–0986, 810/433–1410 in North America* ⊕ *www.tortuguerocanals.com.*

9

CLOSE UP

The Old Atlantic Railroad

Christopher Columbus became the Caribbean's (and the country's) first tourist when he landed at Uvita Island near Limón during his fourth voyage to the New World in 1502. But the region was already home to thriving, if small, communities of Kekoldi, Bribrí, and Cabécar indigenous peoples. If Costa Rica was an isolated backwater, its Caribbean coastal region remained even more remote from colonial times through most of the 19th century.

New York industrialist Minor Keith changed all that in 1871 with his plan to launch the British-funded Atlantic Railroad, a mode of transportation that would permit easier export of coffee and bananas to Europe. Such a project required a massive labor force, and thousands of West Indians, Asians, and Italians were brought to Costa Rica to construct the 522-km (335-mile) railroad from Limón to San José. Thousands are reputed to have died of yellow fever, malaria, and snakebite during construction of the project. Those who survived were paid relatively well, however, and by the 1930s many Afro-Caribbean residents owned their own small plots of land. When the price of cacao rose in the 1950s, they emerged as comfortable

landowners. Not that they had much choice about going elsewhere: until the Civil War of 1948, black Costa Ricans were forbidden from crossing into the Central Valley lest they upset the country's racial balance, and they were thus prevented from moving when United Fruit abandoned many of its blight-ridden northern Caribbean plantations in the 1930s for green-field sites on the Pacific plain.

Costly upkeep of rail service, construction of the Braulio Carrillo Highway to the coast, declining banana production, and an earthquake that rocked the region in 1991 all sounded the death knell for the railroad. The earthquake was also a wake-up call for many here. The long lag time for aid to reach stricken areas symbolized the central government's historic neglect of the region. Development has been slow to reach this part of the country. As elsewhere in the country, communities now look to tourism to put colones in the coffers. San José has resurrected commuter-rail service within the metro area, and a few folks out here hold out faint hopes that Caribbean train service will start up once again, but that's likely a long way off.

CAHUITA

44 km/26 miles southeast of Limón.

Dusty Cahuita, its main dirt street flanked by wooden-slat cabins, is a backpackers' vacation town—a hippie hangout with a dash of Afro-Caribbean spice tossed in. Tucked in among the backpackers' digs are a few surprisingly nice get-away-from-it-all lodgings, and restaurants with some tasty cuisine at decent prices. After years of negative crime-related publicity, Cahuita has beefed up security—this is one of the few places in the country where you will be conscious of a visible and reassuring, though not oppressive, police presence—and has made a well-deserved comeback on the tourist circuit. No question that nearby Puerto Viejo de Talamanca has overtaken Cahuita and become the

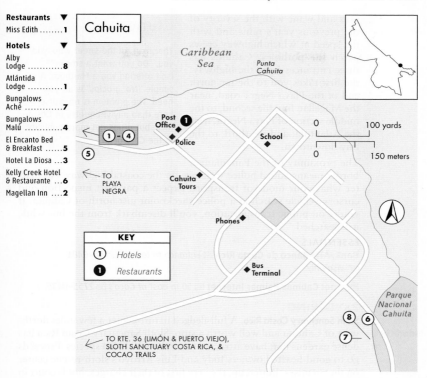

hottest spot on the southern Caribbean coast. But as Puerto Viejo grows exponentially, Cahuita's appeal is that it remains small and manageable. It's well worth a look.

NAVIGATING CAHUITA
Cahuita's tiny center is quite walkable, if dusty in the dry season and muddy in the wet season. It's about a 30-minute walk to the end of the Playa Negra road to Hotel La Diosa. Take a taxi to or from Playa Negra after dark. Cahuita has no officially licensed red taxis; transportation is provided informally by private individuals. To be on the safe side, have your hotel or restaurant call a driver for you.

Bicycles are a popular means of utilitarian transport in Cahuita. Seemingly everyone rents basic touring bikes for $10 per day, but quality varies widely.

Cabinas Brigitte. Here you can rent good bikes for $6 per day. ✉ *Playa Negra road, 1½ km/1 mile from town* ☎ *2755–0053.*

Cahuita Tours. These folks *(⇨ below)* also rent bikes.

GETTING HERE AND AROUND
Autotransportes MEPE buses travel from San José four times a day, and approximately hourly throughout the day from Limón and Puerto Viejo de Talamanca. Car travel is straightforward: watch for signs in Limón and head 45 minutes south on the coastal highway. Road conditions

wax and wane with the severity of the previous year's rains and with the speed at which highway crews patch the potholes. Cahuita has three entrances from the highway: the first takes you to the far north end of the Playa Negra road, near the Magellan Inn; the second, to the middle section of Playa Negra, near the Atlántida; and the third, to the tiny downtown.

> **CAUTION**
>
> That man on the street who asks you, "Do you want a smoke?" isn't offering you a Marlboro. A simple "*No, gracias*" is all you need. The problem is no worse here than anywhere else in Costa Rica, but drugs get more publicity in the Caribbean.

The proximity of the Panamanian border means added police vigilance on the coastal highway. No matter what your mode of transport, expect a passport inspection and cursory vehicle search at a police checkpoint just north of Cahuita. If you're on public transportation, you'll disembark from the bus while it is searched.

ESSENTIALS

Bank/ATM Banco de Costa Rica ✉ *Entrance to town* ☎ 2755–0401 ☞ *Visa only.*

Internet Cabinas Palmer Internet ✉ *50 m east of Coco's* ☎ *2755–0435.*

EXPLORING

⟳ **Sloth Sanctuary Costa Rica.** A full-fledged nature center a few miles north-
Fodor's Choice west of Cahuita and well worth a stop, Sloth Sanctuary Costa Rica has
★ dense gardens that have attracted more than 300 bird species. Proceeds go to good-hearted owners Judy and Luis Arroyo's sloth-rescue center on the premises. Buttercup, the very first of their charges, holds court in the nature-focused gift shop, and you can tour the sloth nursery. Many of the sloths who live on the premises are here because of illness or injury, though, and are not on display to the public. In any case, a visit is a chance to learn about these little-known animals. Your admission includes a two-hour tour. ✉ *9 km/5 miles northwest of Cahuita, follow signs on Río Estrella delta* ☎2750–0775 ⊕ *www.slothsanctuary.com* 🛒 *$25 for tours, free for ages 4 and under* ☉ *Daily 8–2:30.*

OUTDOOR ACTIVITIES

Cahuita is small enough that its tour operators don't focus simply on the town and nearby national park, but instead line up excursions around the region, even as far away as the Tortuguero canals to the north and Bocas del Toro, Panama, to the south.

Cahuita Tours. This is the town's largest and most established tour operator. The folks here can set you up with any of a variety of adventures, including river rafting, kayaking, and visiting indigenous reserves (for a glimpse into traditional life). They can also reconfirm flights and make lodging reservations. We recommend them over their competitors. ✉ *Main street, 180 m north of Coco's* ☎2755–0000 ⊕*www.cahuitatours.com.*

WHERE TO EAT

$ **✕ Miss Edith.** Miss Edith is revered
CARIBBEAN for her flavorful Caribbean cooking, vegetarian meals, and herbal
teas for whatever ails you. Back
in the old days, she served on her
own front porch; she's since moved
to more-ample surroundings on an
easy-to-miss side street at the north
end of town. A bit of the mystique
disappeared with the move, but
her made-to-order dishes—*rondón*
(stew of vegetables and beef or fish)
and spicy jerk chicken—are good
no matter where they are served. You can get breakfast here (except
on Sunday). $ *Average main: $8* ✉ *East of police station* ☎ *2755–0248*
🚫 *No credit cards.*

> **A TOWN THAT WON'T
> LET YOU DOWN**
>
> Cahuita's first tourist of note was
> Costa Rican president Alfredo
> González, whose boat ship-
> wrecked on this stretch of coast
> in 1915. The president was so
> grateful for the aid settlers gave
> him that he purchased a tract of
> land here and donated it to them
> to construct a town.

WHERE TO STAY

For expanded hotel reviews, visit Fodors.com.

$ 🏠 **Alby Lodge.** You're right in town, but you'd never know it at this
B&B/INN friendly lodging. **Pros:** central location; friendly staff. **Cons:** sometimes a
bit noisy; spartan rooms. **TripAdvisor:** "quiet and peaceful," "ultimate
chill out," "very clean cabins and beautiful grounds." $ *Rooms from:
$50* ✉ *180 m west of national park entrance* ☎ *2755–0031* ⊕ *www.
albylodge.com* ⤳ *4 cabins* 🚫 *No credit cards* ⦿ *No meals.*

$ 🏠 **Atlántida Lodge.** Attractively landscaped grounds, the beach across
HOTEL the road, and a large pool are Atlántida's main assets. **Pros:** good
value; decent pool. **Cons:** some dark rooms; lackluster staff. **TripAdvisor:** "chill out at this rustic lodge," "magic place," "nice staff."
$ *Rooms from: $60* ✉ *Next to soccer field at Playa Negra* ☎ *2755–
0115* ✍ *atlantis@racsa.co.cr* ⤳ *32 rooms, 2 suites* 🚫 *No credit cards*
⦿ *No meals.*

$ 🏠 **Bungalows Aché.** Like Alby Lodge next door, Aché scatters wooden
B&B/INN bungalows—three octagonal structures in this case—around wooded
grounds that make the close-by town center seem far away. **Pros:** central location; friendly staff. **Cons:** small rooms; spartan rooms. **Trip-
Advisor:** "beautiful bungalows," "peaceful retreat," "private oasis."
$ *Rooms from: $45* ✉ *180 m west of national park entrance* ☎ *2755–
0119* ⊕ *www.bungalowsache.com* ⤳ *3 bungalows* 🚫 *No credit cards*
⦿ *No meals.*

$ 🏠 **Bungalows Malú.** This is one of the rare places with air-conditioning
RESORT on the coast, but it really doesn't need it: the octagonal stone-and-wood
bungalows spread out on the grounds here get plenty of cool breezes
from the beach across the road. **Pros:** good value; air-conditioning.
Cons: far from sights; bungalows are dark inside. **TripAdvisor:** "very
relaxed," "nice bungalows near the beach," "very good service."
$ *Rooms from: $55* ✉ *Playa Negra road, 2 km/1 mile north of Cahuita*
☎ *2755–0114* ✍ *bungalowmalu@gmail.com* ⤳ *8 bungalows* 🚫 *No
credit cards* ⦿ *Breakfast.*

9

$$ B&B/INN Fodor's Choice ★ 🏨 **El Encanto Bed & Breakfast Inn.** Cahuita doesn't get more serene than these bungalows scattered around a garden with an extensive bromeliad collection and Buddha figures. **Pros:** friendly owners; good value; central location. **Cons:** not for young travelers looking for a scene. **TripAdvisor:** "wonderful and magic place," "best lodging in Cahuita," "peaceful and comfortable." [$] *Rooms from: $76* ✉ *200 m west of police station on Playa Negra road* ☎ *2755–0113* 🌐 *www.elencantocahuita.com* 🛏 *9 rooms* 🍴 *Breakfast.*

$ HOTEL 🏨 **Hotel La Diosa.** The owners' interest in Eastern religions is evidenced in the hotel's name (*La Diosa* means "goddess") and by the sign depicting a Hindu goddess, but all are welcome here at this place on the far north end of Playa Negra. **Pros:** seclusion; air-conditioning available. **Cons:** far from sights; small rooms. **TripAdvisor:** "exquisite natural setting," "the perfect place to relax," "pure magic with gracious and loving hosts." [$] *Rooms from: $70* ✉ *2 km/1 mile north of town at end of Playa Negra road* ☎ *2755–0055, 800/854–7761 in North America* 🌐 *www.hotelladiosa.net* 🛏 *10 cabins* 🍴 *Breakfast.*

$ 🏨 **Kelly Creek Hotel & Restaurante.** Here's a wonderful budget option in a handsome wooden hotel with a terrific Spanish restaurant on the creek bank across a short pedestrian bridge from the park entrance. **Pros:** good value; terrific Spanish restaurant; friendly owners. **Cons:** dark rooms; occasional, but rare, street noise. **TripAdvisor:** "very rustic," "Pura Vida with European twist," "the best hosts in Cahuita." [$] *Rooms from: $55* ✉ *Next to park entrance* ☎ *2755–0007* 🌐 *www.hotelkellycreek.com* 🛏 *4 rooms* 🍴 *No meals.*

$$ B&B/INN ★ 🏨 **Magellan Inn.** Arguably Cahuita's most elegant lodging, this group of bungalows is graced with tile-floor terraces facing a pool and gardens growing on an ancient coral reef. **Pros:** seclusion; good value; scrumptious dinners. **Cons:** far from sights; staff can be too businesslike. **TripAdvisor:** "affordable luxury on Cahuita's quiet side," "beautiful gardens," "perfect piece of paradise." [$] *Rooms from: $75* ✉ *2 km/1 mile north of town at end of Playa Negra road* ☎📠 *2755–0035* 🌐 *www.magellaninn.com* 🛏 *6 rooms* 🍴 *Breakfast.*

NIGHTLIFE

Aside from a local bar or two, Cahuita's nightlife centers on restaurants, all pleasant places to linger over dinner for the evening.

Coco's Bar. Lively reggae, soca, and samba blast weekend evenings from the turquoise Coco's Bar. The assemblage of dogs dozing on its veranda illustrates the rhythm of local life. ✉ *Main road* ☎ *No phone* 🌐 *www.cocosbarcahuita.com* ⏲ *Daily 6–11 pm.*

CAHUITA NATIONAL PARK

Just south of Cahuita.

Cahuita National Park. Parque Nacional Cahuita begins at the southern edge of the town of the same name. Its rain forest extends right to the edge of its curving, utterly undeveloped 3-km (2-mile) white-sand beach. ☎ *2755–0461 Cahuita entrance, 2755–0302 Puerto Vargas entrance* 🎟 *By donation at Cahuita entrance, $10 at Puerto Vargas entrance* ⏲ *Daily 6–5 Cahuita entrance, daily 7–4 Puerto Vargas entrance.*

Wildlife watching in Cahuita National Park.

GETTING HERE AND AROUND

Choose from two park entrances: one is at the southern end of the village of Cahuita; the other is at Puerto Vargas, just off the main road, 5 km (3 miles) south of town. If you don't have a car, you can get here easily via bike or taxi.

OUTDOOR ACTIVITIES

Operators in Cahuita or Puerto Viejo de Talamanca can hook you up with excursions to and in the park, or you can go on your own, especially if you use the entrance at the south edge of the village.

SNORKELING

Cahuita's reefs are just one of several high-quality snorkeling spots in the region. Rent snorkeling gear in Cahuita or Puerto Viejo de Talamanca or through your hotel; most hotels also organize trips. It's wise to work with a guide, as the number of good snorkeling spots is limited and they're not always easily accessible. Cahuita established a community lifeguard team in 2002, unusual in Costa Rica. ■ TIP→ As elsewhere up and down the Caribbean coast, the undertow poses risks for even experienced swimmers. Use extreme caution and never swim alone.

PUERTO VIEJO DE TALAMANCA

16 km/10 miles south of Cahuita.

This muddy, colorful little town is one of the hottest spots on the international budget-travel circuit, and swarms with surfers, New Age hippies, beaded and spangled punks, would-be Rastafarians of all colors and descriptions, and wheelers and dealers—both pleasant and otherwise. Time was when most kids came here with only one thing on their mind: surfing. Today many seem to be looking for a party, with or without the surf.

But if alternative lifestyles aren't your bag, there are plenty of more "grown-up" offerings on the road heading southeast and northwest out of town. At last count, some 50 nationalities were represented in this tiny community, and most are united in concern for the environment and orderly development of tourism. (Few want to see the place become just another Costa Rican resort community.) Some locals bemoan the loss of their town's innocence, as drugs and other evils have surfaced, but this is still a fun town to visit, with a great variety of hotels, cabinas, and restaurants in

BE GENEROUS

Cahuita National Park is the only such facility in Costa Rica with an optional entrance fee. When the government began charging admission to its national parks, residents here expressed concern that the measure would harm tourism. They were granted dispensation from collecting the fee at the in-town park entrance across from the Kelly Creek Hotel. Since Costa Rica's national-park system is largely a perpetually underfunded labor of love, we recommend paying the voluntary entrance fee if you visit the park from the Cahuita-town side. Your $10 will go to a good cause.

every price range. Unlike some other parts of Costa Rica, no one has been priced out of the market here.

Locals use "Puerto Viejo" to refer to the village. They drop the "de Talamanca" part; we use the complete name to avoid confusion with the other Puerto Viejo: Puerto Viejo de Sarapiquí in the Northern Plains. You have access to the beach right in town, and the Salsa Brava, famed in surfers' circles for its pounding waves, is here off the coast, too. The best strands of Caribbean sand are outside the village: Playa Cocles, Playa Chiquita (technically a series of beaches), and Punta Uva, all dark-sand beaches, line the road heading southeast from town. Playa Negra—not the Playa Negra near Cahuita—is the black-sand beach northwest of town. Punta Uva, with fewer hotels and the farthest from the village, sees fewer crowds and more tranquility. Playa Negra shares that distinction, too—for now—but developers have eyed the beach as the next area for expansion.

NAVIGATING PUERTO VIEJO DE TALAMANCA

You can manage the town center quite easily on foot, though it is dusty in the dry season and muddy when it rains. (The main street is, thankfully, paved.) Everyone gets around by bike here, and seemingly everyone has one for rent. Quality varies widely. Expect to pay $10 per day for a good bike.

Cabinas Grant. Here you'll find the best selection of quality bikes in town. ⊠ *100 m south of bus stop* ☎ *2750–0292.*

Casa Verde Lodge. Priority is given to guests at Casa Verde Lodge, but they usually have extra bikes you can rent for a half or full day even if you don't stay here. ⊠ *200 m south and 200 m east of bus stop* ☎ *2750–0015.*

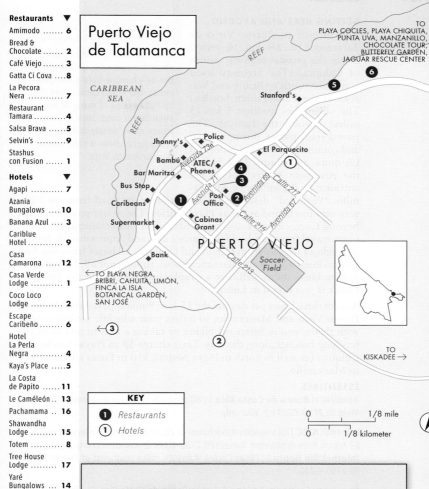

Puerto Viejo de Talamanca

TO
PLAYA COCLES, PLAYA CHIQUITA,
PUNTA UVA, MANZANILLO,
CHOCOLATE TOUR,
BUTTERFLY GARDEN,
JAGUAR RESCUE CENTER →

REEF

CARIBBEAN
SEA

REEF

Stanford's

Jhonny's   Police

Bambú   El Parquecito

Bar Maritza   ATEC/
Phones

Bus Stop

Caribeans   Post
Office

Supermarket   Cabinas
Grant

PUERTO VIEJO

Bank

Soccer
Field

← TO PLAYA NEGRA,
BRIBRI, CAHUITA, LIMÓN,
FINCA LA ISLA
BOTANICAL GARDEN,
SAN JOSÉ

TO
KISKADEE →

KEY

❶ *Restaurants*

① *Hotels*

0   1/8 mile
0   1/8 kilometer

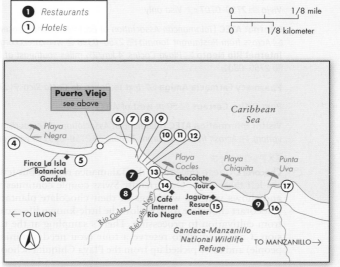

Puerto Viejo
see above

Caribbean
Sea

Playa
Negra

Finca La Isla
Botanical
Garden

Playa
Cocles

Playa
Chiquita

Punta
Uva

Chocolate
Tour

← TO LIMON

Café
Internet
Rio Negro

Rio Cocles

Rio Caño Negro

Jaguar
Resue
Center

Gandaca-Manzanillo
National Wildlife
Refuge

TO MANZANILLO →

GETTING HERE AND AROUND

The turnoff to Puerto Viejo de Talamanca is 10 km (6 miles) down the coastal highway south of Cahuita. (The highway itself continues south to Bribrí and Sixaola at the Panamanian border.) The village lies another 5 km (3 miles) beyond the turnoff. The paved road passes through town and continues to Playas Cocles and Chiquita and Punta Uva before the pavement peters out at the entrance to the village of Manza-

nillo. "Potholed" describes the condition of the road from the highway into town, and as far as Playa Cocles. The newer paved sections beyond Cocles haven't disintegrated . . . yet. Autotransportes MEPE buses travel from San José four times a day, and approximately hourly throughout the day from Limón and Cahuita. All buses from San José go into Puerto Viejo de Talamanca; most, though not all, Limón-originating buses do as well, but a couple drop you off on the highway. Check if you board in Limón.

A scant three buses per day ply the 15-km (9-miles) paved road between Puerto Viejo and Manzanillo, so unless your schedule meshes exactly with theirs, you're better off biking or taking a taxi to and from the far-flung beaches along the way. Taxis charge $8 to Playas Cocles and Chiquita (as well as north to Playa Negra), $10 to Punta Uva, and $15 to Manzanillo.

ESSENTIALS

Bank/ATM Banco de Costa Rica ✉ *50 m south of bridge at entrance to Puerto Viejo* ☎ *2750–0707* ✆ *Visa only.*

Internet ATEC (*Talamancan Association of Ecotourism and Conservation*). ✉ *Across from Restaurant Tamara* ☎ *2750–0398* ⊕ *www.ateccr.org.* **Café Internet Río Negro** ✉ *Playa Cocles, 4 km/2½ miles southeast of Puerto Viejo* ☎ *2750–0801.*

Pharmacy Farmacia Amiga ✉ *Next to Banco de Costa Rica* ☎ *2750–0698.*

Post Office Correos ✉ *50 m west of ATEC.*

Visitor Information ATEC (*Talamancan Association of Ecotourism and Conservation*). ✉ *Across from Restaurant Tamara* ☎ *2750–0191* ⊕ *www.ateccr.org.*

EXPLORING

Chocorart. Cacao once ruled the Talamanca region, but few plantations are left these days. One friendly Swiss couple continues the tradition and shows you the workings of their chocolate plantation on their Chocorart chocolate tour. Follow the little-known life cycle of this crop from cultivation to processing. There's sampling at the tour's conclusion. Call or email to reserve a tour (you need a minimum of four people) and to be picked up from the Playa Chiquita School. Since these

CLOSE UP

Reefs at Risk

One of the most complex organisms in the marine world, a coral reef is an extraordinary and extraordinarily delicate habitat. Coral reefs are the result of the symbiotic relationship between single-cell organisms called zooxanthellae and coral polyps. The zooxanthellae grow inside the cells of the polyps, producing oxygen and nutrients that are released into the coral tissues. Corals secrete calcium carbonate (limestone) that, over time, forms the vast coral reef "superstructure." Zooxanthellae require exposure to sunlight to thrive. The healthiest coral reefs are in clear, clean, tropical seawater at a temperature of 20°C to 25°C (70°F to 80°F). Healthy coral reefs are biologically rich gardens occupied by a diverse selection of life forms, from microscopic unicellular algae and phytoplankton to a wide range of fish.

Unfortunately, coral reefs in Costa Rica are in danger. Dirt and sediment from banana plantations and logging areas, as well as runoff from pesticide use, are killing them. The dirty runoff literally clogs the pores of the zooxanthellae and smothers them. In the southern Pacific coast's Golfo Dulce, 98% of one of the oldest reefs in Costa Rica has been destroyed by this sedimentation. Many of the once-enormous reefs of Cahuita are almost entirely gone.

Human visitors, including careless snorkelers, have also damaged reefs. Simply touching a reef damages it. When exploring a coral reef, look but don't touch, and snorkel only on its outer side, preferably in calm weather. Can the reefs be saved? With commitment and time, yes. Coral is resilient, and will grow back—if the Costa Rican government makes it a priority.

---

folks are Swiss, they can tailor the commentary in German, French, or Italian, in addition to English or Spanish. ⊠ *6 km/4 miles southeast of Puerto Viejo at Playa Chiquita* ☎ *2750–0075* ✐ *chocorart@racsa.co.cr* ⌨ *$15 per person* ⊗ *By appointment.*

Finca la Isla Botanical Garden. At the Finca la Isla Botanical Garden, you can explore a working tropical-fruit, spice, and ornamental-plant farm. Sloths abound, and you might see a few poison dart frogs. A $10 guided tour lasts two hours and includes admission and a glass of the farm's homemade fruit juice. (A shorter, one-hour guided tour runs $8.) You get the fruit juice if you wander around on your own, too—a $1 self-guided-tour book is available in English, Spanish, French, or German. Watch the demonstration showing how cacao beans are turned into chocolate, and sample some of the product at the end of the tour. ⊠ *½ km/¼ mile west of Puerto Viejo at Playa Negra* ☎ *2750–0046* ⊕ *www.costaricacaribbean.com* ⌨ *$5, guided tour $10* ⊗ *Fri.–Mon. 10–4.*

Ⓒ **Jaguar Rescue Center** (*Jaguar Centro de Rescate*). Many regard a visit to the Jaguar Rescue Center as the highlight of their trip to Puerto Viejo. The name is a bit misleading. The original rescued animal here was an orphaned, injured jaguar cub that ultimately did not survive. His memory lives on in the facility's name, even if there are no other jaguars on-site. Primarily howler monkeys, sloths, and lots of snakes

9

make up the charges of the good folks here. The goal, of course, is to return the animals to the wild, although, for some their fragile condition means this will end up being their permanent home. Your admission fee for the 90-minute tour helps fund the work here, and it's a good cause. ⊠ *3 km/2 miles southeast of Puerto Viejo at Playa Chiquita* ☎ *2750–0710* ⊕ *www.jaguarrescue.com* 💲 *$15* 🕑 *Mon.–Sat. tours at 9:30 and 11:30.*

WORD OF MOUTH

"I've taken my daughter, now 15, to Puerto Viejo 3 times over the past few years. We love it there and it's one of our favorite areas in CR. Personally, I wouldn't be out walking alone after dark (but this would apply everywhere) and use taxis instead. Bicycles for during the day. We always walked or biked and never had any trouble, but you will see a decent variety of people there which is part of what makes it interesting."

—hipvirgochick

OUTDOOR ACTIVITIES

As in Cahuita, tour operators and outfitters here can set up tours and activities anywhere on the south Caribbean coast.

ATEC (*Talamancan Association of Ecotourism and Conservation*). Tours with ATEC have an environmental or cultural bent, such as Afro-Caribbean or indigenous-culture walks—tours to the nearby Kekoldi indigenous reserve are especially popular—rain-forest hikes, coral-reef snorkeling trips, fishing trips, bird-watching tours, night walks, and adventure treks. Local organizations and wildlife refuges receive 15% to 20% of ATEC's proceeds. ⊠ *Across from Restaurant Tamara* ☎ *2750–0191* ⊕ *www.ateccr.org.*

Terraventuras. Well-established operator Terraventuras can lead you around Puerto Viejo de Talamanca and Cahuita, or take you on excursions to Tortuguero, the Gandoca-Manzanillo Wildlife Refuge, and Bocas del Toro in Panama. It also rents good-quality surfboards, bicycles, boogie boards, and snorkeling gear. ⊠ *100 m south of bus stop* ☎ *2750–0750* ⊕ *www.terraventuras.com.*

RAFTING

★ **Exploradores Outdoors.** Rafting excursions lie about two hours away, but one San José–based outfitter has an office here. Exploradores Outdoors is highly regarded and has one- or two-day excursions on the Pacuare River, with a pickup point here or in San José, and the option to start in one place and be dropped off at the other. The outfitter also offers sea-kayaking excursions off the coast of the Gandoca-Manzanillo Wildlife Refuge. ⊠ *Across from ATEC* ☎ *2750–2020, 2222–6262 in San José, 646/205–0828 in North America* ⊕ *www.exploradoresoutdoors.com.*

SURFING

Surfing is the name of the game in Puerto Viejo, for everyone from newbies to Kelly Slaters. The best conditions are late December through March, but there's action all year. Longtime surfers compare the south Caribbean to Hawaii, but without the "who-do-you-think-you-are?" attitude. There are a number of breaks here, most famously **Salsa Brava,** which translates to "wild sauce." It breaks fairly far offshore and requires maneuvering past some tricky currents and a shallow reef. Hollow and primarily right breaking, Salsa Brava is one gnarly wave when it gets big. If it gets *too* big, or not big enough, check out the breaks at Punta Uva, Punta Cocles, or Playa Chiquita. Boogie boarders and bodysurfers can also dig the beach-break waves at various points along this tantalizingly beautiful coast.

CAUTION

The conditions that make the Caribbean so popular among surfers spell danger for swimmers. A few drownings occur each year. Strong riptides can pull you out to sea, even in waist-deep water, before you realize what's happening. Never swim alone in these parts—good advice anywhere.

Aventuras Bravas. If you're, say, over 30, but have always wanted to try surfing, consider the friendly, two-hour $50 surf school at Aventuras Bravas. You start out with a small wave near the bus stop, and get a money-back guarantee that you'll be standing by the end of the lesson. (A two-hour private lesson will run you $60.) You can also rent equipment here. ✉ *Across from Stanford's* ☎ *8849–7600* 🌐 *www.braveadventure.net.*

WHERE TO EAT

$$ ITALIAN ★ 🍴 **Amimodo.** The name translates to "my way," and the exuberant Italian owners really do it their way, combining the cuisine of their native northern Italy with Caribbean flavors. Your antipasto might be classic bruschetta or *jamón de tiburón* (shark ham with avocado dressing), and your ravioli might be stuffed with tropical shrimp, pineapple, and curry, with avocado sauce on the side. The tropical veranda with gingerbread trim spills over onto the beach with abundant greenery, and the restaurant is a popular gathering place for Puerto Viejo's Italian community. [$] *Average main: $13* ✉ *200 m east of Stanford's* ☎ *2750–0257* 🕓 *Closed Thurs.*

$ COSTA RICAN ★ 🍴 **Bread & Chocolate.** The takeaway line for brownies forms at the gate before this place opens at 6:30 am, but stick around and fortify yourself with a hearty breakfast of cinnamon-oatmeal pancakes, French toast, or creamy scrambled eggs, washed down with a cup of French-press coffee. Lunch brings jerk chicken, roasted red peppers, and chocolate truffles. Everything is homemade, right down to the mayonnaise. Make your dinner early; the place closes at 6:30 pm. This is one of several bakery-slash-breakfast-and-lunch cafés open in town; the friendly owner gives this place the edge. [$] *Average main: $5* ✉ *50 m south of post office* ☎ *2750–0723* 💳 *No credit cards* 🕓 *No dinner. Closed Mon.*

$ ITALIAN 🍴 **Café Viejo.** This is the hot place to see and be seen on Puerto Viejo's main drag. The owners, four brothers who learned to cook at the knee of their Italian grandmother back in Rimini, have concocted a menu, several pages long, of pizzas and handmade pastas. Recorded reggae and mambo music bops in the background. [$] *Average main: $8* ✉ *Across from ATEC* ☎ *2750–0817* 🕓 *Closed Tues. No lunch.*

$$ ITALIAN 🍴 **Gatta Ci Cova.** Chef-owner Ilario Giannoni strolls the 100 meters (328 feet) over from his La Pecora Nera restaurant to watch over his new baby these days. The restaurant, whose name comes from an Italian expression meaning "things kept secret," provides a less-formal, less-expensive alternative to the original, but still has all the flair and all the fun. Lunch

offerings focus on the $10 *plato del día*, a bargain with appetizer, salad, a rotating selection of pastas, dessert, and a glass of wine. $ *Average main: $13 ⊠ 3 km/2 miles southeast of town at Playa Cocles ☎ 2750–0730 ⊗ Closed Mon.*

$$$ ✕ **La Pecora Nera.** Though the name

ITALIAN means "black sheep" in Italian,

Fodor'sChoice there's nothing shameful about this

★ thatch-roof roadside restaurant. There's always a lot more to choose from than you'll see on the sparse-looking menu. Wait for owner/chef Ilario Giannoni to come out of the kitchen and triumphantly announce—with flair worthy of an Italian opera—which additional light Tuscan entrées, appetizers, and desserts they've concocted that day. Be prepared for a long, leisurely dining experience with attentive service. It's worth the wait; this is one of the country's top Italian restaurants. $ *Average main: $21 ⊠ 3 km/2 miles southeast of town at Playa Cocles ☎ 2750–0490 ⊗ Closed Mon. No lunch.*

$ ✕ **Restaurant Tamara.** Once upon a time, this unpretentious two-story

CARIBBEAN place was the only restaurant in town. The Caribbean food is tasty and authentic: you can't lose with the chicken in Caribbean sauce or virtually any of the fresh fish dishes. In the nondescript indoor seating area you're cooled by a fan and entertained by TV; the outdoor seating area has a palpable Jamaican motif and is a great place for people watching. $ *Average main: $6 ⊠ Across from ATEC ☎ 2750–0148 ▭ No credit cards ⊗ Closed Tues. May–Nov.*

$ ✕ **Salsa Brava.** The restaurant overlooking the Salsa Brava break—with

SEAFOOD sublime surf vistas—has taken the name of this famed surfing spot. Opt for casual counter service or grab a seat at one of the colorful roadside tables. Lunch and dinner center on grilled fish and meat, with red snapper prepared in olive oil, garlic, and cayenne pepper a specialty. $ *Average main: $8 ⊠ 100 m east of Stanford's ☎ 2750–0241 ▭ No credit cards ⊗ Closed Mon. and Tues.*

$ ✕ **Selvin's.** An old standby at Punta Uva, Selvin's keeps limited hours,

CARIBBEAN especially in the off-season, so head out here if you're fortunate enough to be in town when it's open. The owner, known to everyone in town as "Blanca," cooks up a menu of rondón, rice and beans, lobster, shrimp, and chicken with sweet mole sauce. This is one of the few places around that accepts traveler's checks as payment. $ *Average main: $7 ⊠ 7 km/4½ miles southeast of town at Punta Uva ☎ 2750–0664 ▭ No credit cards ⊗ Closed Mon. and Tues.*

$ ✕ **Stashus con Fusion.** This restaurant epitomizes Puerto Viejo: lively,

ECLECTIC organic, all the rage, but confident enough not to seek trendiness. Order-

Fodor'sChoice ing is by sauces: Thai peanut, Indonesian-Caribbean curry, Mexican

★ chipotle, Jamaican jerk-style, or Malaysian-guayaba curry. Then select vegetables, chicken, shrimp, or fish (marlin or tuna). Live music gets going late on Sunday evenings. $ *Average main: $9 ⊠ 200 m south of Stanford's ☎ 2750–0530 ▭ No credit cards ⊗ Closed Wed. No lunch.*

WHERE TO STAY

For expanded hotel reviews, visit Fodors.com.

$ | **Agapi.** Agapi means "love" in Greek, and Costa Rican–Greek owners
HOTEL | Cecilia and Tasso lovingly watch over their guests with some of the most attentive service around. **Pros:** kitchens; central location. **Cons:** not for travelers who want anonymity; first-floor rooms are dark. **TripAdvisor:** "a fantastic beachfront location," "perfect setting," "so friendly." $ *Rooms from: $69* ✉ *1 km/½ mile southeast of Stanford's* ☎ *2750–0446* ⊕ *www.agapisite.com* ⤶ *5 rooms, 12 apartments* ❯❮ *No meals.*

$$ | **Azania Bungalows.** Eight thatch-roof, A-frame bungalows spread
B&B/INN | around Azania's ample gardens, and sleep four. **Pros:** good value; good Argentine restaurant. **Cons:** difficult to make reservations; bungalows are dark inside. **TripAdvisor:** "lovely stay," "perfect," "laid-back Costa Rica." $ *Rooms from: $90* ✉ *1½ km/1 mile southeast of town at Playa Cocles* ☎ *2750–0540* ⊕ *www.azania-costarica.com* ⤶ *10 bungalows* ❯❮ *Breakfast.*

$$ | **Banana Azul.** Hardwood furnishings are abundant at this gay-friendly
RESORT | (but by no means exclusive) hotel at the secluded far end of Playa Negra. **Pros:** friendly management and staff; seclusion set away from hubbub of town; great ocean views. **Cons:** no kids, so not an option for families. **TripAdvisor:** "wonderful people," "very relaxing," "hidden paradise." $ *Rooms from: $79* ✉ *1½ km/1 mile north of Puerto Viejo at end of Playa Negra* ☎ *2750–2035, 877/284–5116 in North America* ⊕ *www.bananaazul.com* ⤶ *12 rooms* ❯❮ *Breakfast.*

$$ | **Cariblue Hotel.** The youthful Italian owners who came here to surf
HOTEL | years ago stayed on and built a lodging that combines refinement with
Fodor'sChoice | that hip Puerto Viejo vibe in exactly the right proportions. **Pros:** friendly
★ | owners; good restaurant. **Cons:** need a car to stay here. **TripAdvisor:** "great location," "perfect mix of jungle and beach," "very nice place." $ *Rooms from: $95* ✉ *2 km/1 mile southeast of town at Playa Cocles* ☎ *2750–0035* ⊕ *www.cariblue.com* ⤶ *23 bungalows* ❯❮ *Breakfast.*

$ | **Casa Camarona.** Though half the rooms have air-conditioning at this
B&B/INN | secluded lodging, you hardly need it. **Pros:** good value; air-conditioning. **Cons:** need a car to stay here; some dark rooms. **TripAdvisor:** "great place on a budget," "beautiful beaches," "nice place and atmosphere." $ *Rooms from: $73* ✉ *3 km/2 miles south of town at Playa Cocles* ☎ *2750–0151, 2283–6711 in San José* ⊕ *www.casacamarona.co.cr* ⤶ *18 rooms* ❯❮ *Breakfast.*

$ | **Casa Verde Lodge.** If you've graduated from your backpacker days and
HOTEL | are a bit more flush with cash but still want to be near the action, this
Fodor'sChoice | old standby on a quiet street a couple of blocks from the center of town
★ | is ideal. **Pros:** good value; immaculate. **Cons:** difficult to find space; businesslike staff. **TripAdvisor:** "tranquility in the center of town," "clean," "awesome staff." $ *Rooms from: $50* ✉ *200 m south and 200 m east of bus stop* ☎ *2750–0015* ⊕ *www.cabinascasaverde.com* ⤶ *17 rooms, 9 with bath; 2 apartments* ❯❮ *No meals.*

$ | **Coco Loco Lodge.** The cool, forested grounds here lie close to the cen-
B&B/INN | ter of town but seem far away. **Pros:** good budget value; central location. **Cons:** rustic rooms; dark road at night. **TripAdvisor:** "lovely quiet spot," "best staff ever," "comfortable and cozy." $ *Rooms from: $54*

9

Calm waters over the reef just off Punta Uva Beach near Puerto Viejo de Talamanca.

✉ *180 m south of bridge at entrance to town* ☎ *2750–0281* ⊕ *www. cocolocolodge.com* ⇱ *10 cabins, 2 houses* ⦿❘ *No meals.*

$

B&B/INN

⊡ **Escape Caribeño.** Wonderfully friendly Italian owners Gloria and Mauro Marchiori are what make this place: they treat you like family. **Pros:** central location; gregarious owners. **Cons:** some small rooms; some spartan rooms. **TripAdvisor:** "quiet getaway," "very relaxing stay," "lovely laid-back cabins." ⓈI *Rooms from: $70* ✉ *400 m southeast of Stanford's* ☎☎ *2750–0103* ⊕ *www.escapecaribeno.com* ⇱ *18 cabins* ⦿❘ *No meals.*

$$

HOTEL

⊡ **Hotel La Perla Negra.** Fine design is evident in the construction of this handsome, two-story dark-wood structure across a tiny dirt road near the end of Playa Negra. **Pros:** secluded; quality construction of buildings. **Cons:** far from sights; situated on lesser-known Playa Negra. **TripAdvisor:** "amazing staff," "tranquil hideaway," "beautiful surroundings." Ⓢ *Rooms from: $90* ✉ *Playa Negra, 1 km/½ mile north of Puerto Viejo* ☎ *2750–0111* ⊕ *www.perlanegra-beachresort.com* ⇱ *24 rooms, 7 houses* ⦿❘ *Breakfast.*

$

HOTEL

⊡ **Kaya's Place.** Rooms range from the upper-level half-dozen rooms with shared cold-water bath to the sumptuous garden-view rooms at the back at this place at Playa Negra just outside town. **Pros:** good value; friendly owner. **Cons:** slightly removed from action. **TripAdvisor:** "great atmosphere," "beautiful place," "comfortable rooms." Ⓢ *Rooms from: $50* ✉ *200 m north of town at Playa Negra* ☎ *2750–0690, 205/389– 8232 in North America* ⊕ *www.kayasplace.com* ⇱ *25 rooms, 19 with bath* ⦿❘ *No meals.*

$$

HOTEL

⊡ **La Costa de Papito.** Papito's raised cabins are deep in the property's wooded grounds and furnished with whimsical bright tropical blue and zebra-stripe prints. **Pros:** good value; friendly owner. **Cons:** need a car to stay here; some noise from bar area. **TripAdvisor:** "beautiful location," "a refuge by the beach," "excellent lodging." $ *Rooms from: $84 ⊠ 2 km/1 mile southeast of town at Playa Cocles ☎ 2750–0080, 516/252–4509 in North America ⊕ www.lacostadepapito.com ⟿ 12 cabins ⎰○⎱ No meals.*

$$$$ ⬚ **Le Caméléon.** The area's newest lodging is decidedly un–Puerto Viejo
HOTEL in its sumptuous luxury, but if you're in the mood for a splurge here on the coast, why not? **Pros:** stylish luxury; attentive staff; many amenities. **Cons:** luxury might seem out of place in Puerto Viejo. **TripAdvisor:** "comfort and luxury," "beautiful architecture in the jungle," "great service." $ *Rooms from: $295 ⊠ Playa Cocles, 200 m east of soccer field ☎ 2750–0501, 2291–7750 in San José ⊕ www.lecameleonhotel. com ⟿ 12 rooms, 1 suite ⬦ No smoking ⎰○⎱ Breakfast.*

$ ⬚ **Pachamama.** So cool and shady is this place set within the confines of
B&B/INN the Gandoca-Manzanillo Wildlife Refuge that the owners took out the ceiling fans. **Pros:** wonderful seclusion; friendly owners. **Cons:** far from sights; need a car to stay here. **TripAdvisor:** "beautiful setting and awesome hospitality," "top-notch service," "great host." $ *Rooms from: $55 ⊠ 9 km/5½ miles southeast of town at Punta Uva ☎ 2759–9196 ⊕ www.pachamamacaribe.com ⟿ 2 bungalows, 2 houses ⎰○⎱ Multiple meal plans.*

$$ ⬚ **Shawandha Lodge.** The service is personalized and friendly at Shawa-
RESORT ndha, whose spacious, beautifully designed bungalows are well back
★ from the road at Playa Chiquita. **Pros:** elegant bungalows; sumptuous restaurant. **Cons:** far from sights; easiest to stay here with a car. **TripAdvisor:** "tranquil jungle lodge," "stunning," "quirky rooms and brilliant staff." $ *Rooms from: $120 ⊠ 6 km/4 miles southeast of town at Playa Chiquita ☎ 2750–0018 ⊕ www.shawandhalodge.com ⟿ 13 bungalows ⎰○⎱ Breakfast.*

$$ ⬚ **Totem.** Each of the tropical blue units here contains a living room and
HOTEL bedroom with bamboo furnishings, a queen bed, and bunks. **Pros:** good value; terrific restaurant. **Cons:** need a car to stay here; some reports of lackluster staff. **TripAdvisor:** "great times," "helpful and proactive," "friendly staff." $ *Rooms from: $80 ⊠ 1½ km/1 mile southeast of town at Playa Cocles ☎ 2750–0758 ⊕ www.totemsite.com ⟿ 12 rooms, 8 suites ⎰○⎱ Breakfast.*

$$$$ ⬚ **Tree House Lodge.** They're not exactly the tree house you had as a
HOTEL kid—no ladders are necessary here. **Pros:** attention to style in furnishings; romantic seclusion. **Cons:** far from sights. **TripAdvisor:** "unique experience," "very pleasant and exotic," "secluded jungle paradise." $ *Rooms from: $280 ⊠ Punta Uva ☎ 2750–0706, 323/245–8739 in North America ⊕ www.costaricatreehouse.com ⟿ 4 houses ⊟ No credit cards ⎰○⎱ Breakfast.*

$ ⬚ **Yaré Bungalows.** The sound of the jungle is overpowering, especially
HOTEL at night, as you relax in your brightly pastel-painted Yaré cabina. **Pros:** good value; whimsical bungalows. **Cons:** sound travels far; far from sights. $ *Rooms from: $69 ⊠ 3½ km/2 miles southeast of town at Playa Cocles ☎ 2750–0106, 888/250–6472 in North America ⊕ www. bungalowsyare.com ⟿ 22 rooms ⎰○⎱ Breakfast.*

NEED A BREAK?

Caribeans. At first glance, this small café could use a spelling lesson, but since Caribeans deals in coffee, the play on words is apt. Treat yourself to a latté, mocha, or coconut cappuccino, all made from organic, fair-trade coffee from the Turrialba region in the far-eastern Central Valley, and roasted here. The place is open daily except Tuesday. ✉ *50 m west of bus stop* ☎ *8836–8930.*

NIGHTLIFE

The distinction between dining spot and nightspot blurs as the evening progresses, as many restaurants become pleasant places to linger over dinner. Bars each have their special nights for live music. The town's main drag between El Loco Natural and Salsa Brava is packed with pedestrians, bicycles, and a few cars most evenings, the block between Café Viejo and El Parquecito getting the most action. Wander around; something is bound to entice you in. ■TIP→ **When out after dark, ask a staff member at the restaurant, bar, or club to call you a taxi at the end of the night.**

A BAD RAP

The Caribbean has a reputation among Costa Ricans for being crime-ridden, mainly because of a few high-profile cases here years ago, the nearness of the Panamanian border, and the fact that this is an impoverished region compared with other parts of the country. In actuality, the problem is no better or worse here than elsewhere. Take the standard precautions you would when you travel anywhere and do stick to well-traveled tourist paths.

BARS

Bar Maritza. This spot is frequented by locals and has live music on Sunday night. ✉ *50 m east of bus stop.*

El Dorado. Grab a beer, and chow down on pizza or sandwiches at El Dorado, a much quieter alternative to the noisier bars. ✉ *Across from ATEC.*

DANCE CLUBS

Café Mango. A lively mix of expats and tourists holds court of Café Mango each evening. ✉ *20 m south of bus stop* ☎ *8691–0756* ☉ *Daily noon–2 am.*

Stanford's. Stanford's is the place to merengue or salsa the weekend nights away. Partake of light meals on the new second-floor patio dining room if dancing isn't your thing. ✉ *100 m from the town center on the road to Manzanillo.*

Tasty Waves Cantina. Tuesday is $2 Taco Night at the lively Tasty Waves Cantina. Movies get underway at 7:30 pm on Monday evening and several other nights a week as well. ✉ *Playa Cocles, 1 km (½ mile) southeast of town* ☎ *2750–0507* ☉ *Thurs.–Tues. noon–midnight.*

LIVE MUSIC

Stashus con Fusion. Organic-food restaurant Stashus con Fusion has live music Sunday evenings. ✉ *150 m west of ATEC* ☎ *2750–0263* ☉ *Thurs.–Tues. 6–11.*

El Parquecito. Caribbean restaurant El Parquecito pulls live-music duty Tuesday, Friday, and Saturday evenings. You're bound to hear "No Woman No Cry" and all the other reggae anthems. ⊠ *50 m east of ATEC.*

SHOPPING

Vendors set up stands at night on the beach road near El Parquecito, jewelry being the prime fare. But the town counts a few honest-to-goodness souvenir stores, too.

Color Caribe. Buy your semiofficial Puerto Viejo T-shirt at Color Caribe, and check out the huge selection of Rastafarian clothing, plus hammocks, wood carvings, and whimsical mobiles. ⊠ *100 m south of bus stop* ☎ *2750–0263.*

★ **Luluberlu.** Puerto Viejo's best shop sells a wonderful selection of local indigenous carvings—balsa and *chonta* wood are especially popular—and jewelry, paintings, and ceramics by 30 artists from the region. ⊠ *200 m south and 50 m east of bus stop* ☎ *2750–0394* ⊙ *Daily 9–9.*

GANDOCA-MANZANILLO NATIONAL WILDLIFE REFUGE

15 km/9 miles southeast of Puerto Viejo.

GETTING HERE

The paved road from Puerto Viejo de Talamanca ends at the entrance to the village of Manzanillo. Just three buses each day—morning, midday, and late afternoon—connect the two. Taxis are a much easier proposition. Drivers in Puerto Viejo charge $15 for the trip here.

EXPLORING

Gandoca-Manzanillo National Wildlife Refuge. The Refugio Nacional de Vida Silvestre Gandoca-Manzanillo stretches along the southeastern coast beginning southeast of Puerto Viejo de Talamanca to the town of Manzanillo and on to the Panamanian border. Its limits are not clearly defined. Because of weak laws governing the conservation of refuges and the rising value of coastal land in this area, Gandoca-Manzanillo is less pristine than Cahuita National Park and continues to be developed. However, the refuge still has plenty of rain forest, *orey* (a dark tropical wood) and jolillo swamps, 10 km (6 miles) of beach where four species of turtles lay their eggs, and almost 3 square km (1 square mile) of *cativo* (a tropical hardwood) forest and coral reef. The Gandoca estuary is a nursery for tarpon and a wallowing spot for crocodiles and caimans.

The easiest way to explore the refuge is to hike along the coast south of Manzanillo. You can hike back out the way you came in or arrange (in Puerto Viejo de Talamanca) to have a boat pick you up at Punta Mono (Monkey Point), a three- to four-hour walk from Manzanillo, where you find secluded beaches hidden by tall cliffs of fossilized coral. The mangroves of Gandoca, with abundant caimans, iguanas, and waterfowl, lie six to eight hours away. Park administrators can tell you more and recommend a local guide; inquire when you enter Manzanillo village and the locals will point you toward them. ⊠ *15 km/9 miles southeast of Puerto Viejo de Talamanca* ☎ *2750–0398 for ATEC* 🎫 *Free* ⊙ *Daily 7–4.*

9

Manzanillo. The nearby village of Manzanillo maintains that "end-of-the-world" feel. Tourism is still in its infancy this far down the coast, though with the road paved all the way here, the town is now a popular destination among people in Limón for weekend day trips. The rest of the week, you'll likely have the place to yourself.

OUTDOOR ACTIVITIES

A guide can help you get the most out of this relatively unexplored corner of the country.

DIVING AND SNORKELING

Aquamor Talamanca Adventures. The friendly staff at Aquamor Talamanca Adventures specializes in land- and ocean-focused tours of the Gandoca-Manzanillo Wildlife Refuge, and can tend to all your water-sporting needs in these parts, with guided kayaking, snorkeling, and scuba-diving tours, as well as equipment rental. They also offer the complete sequence of PADI-certified diving courses. ✉ *Main road, Manzanillo* ☎ *2759–9012* 🌐 *www.greencoast.com/aquamor.htm.*

Companies in Puerto Viejo de Talamanca *(⇨ above)* can arrange boat trips to dive spots and beaches in the refuge as well.

DOLPHIN-WATCHING

Talamanca Dolphin Foundation (*Asociación Pro Delfines de Talamanca*). The Talamanca Dolphin Foundation has 2½-hour dolphin observation tours—excellent opportunities to see bottlenose, *tucuxi* (gray), and Atlantic spotted dolphins swimming this section of the coast. ✉ *Main road, Manzanillo* ☎ *2759–9118, 406/586–5084 in North America* 🌐 *www.dolphinlink.org.*

WHERE TO EAT AND STAY

$ SEAFOOD 🍴 **Restaurant Maxi's.** Cooled by sea breezes and shaded by tall, stately palms, this two-story, brightly painted wooden building offers weary travelers cold beer, potent cocktails, and great seafood at unbeatable prices after a day's hike in the refuge. Locals and expatriates alike—and even chefs from Puerto Viejo's fancier restaurants—come here for their lobster fix, and the fresh fish is wonderful, too. At one time, perhaps before tourism became big in this area, Costa Ricans made Maxi's into an entire day trip. Now that the road is paved all the way to Manzanillo, the weekend crowds are getting ever larger. Locals tend to congregate in the rowdy but pleasant downstairs bar, where reggae beats into the wee hours. [$] *Average main: $8* ✉ *Main road, Manzanillo* ☎ *2759–9073* 💳 *No credit cards.*

$$$$ RESORT 🏨 **Almonds & Corals.** Buried in a dark, densely atmospheric beachfront jungle within the Gandoca-Manzanillo Wildlife Refuge, Almonds & Corals scatters bungalows throughout its site on freestanding platforms raised on stilts and linked by boardwalks lighted by kerosene lamps. **Pros:** rustic comfort; lots of activities. **Cons:** far from sights; need a car to stay here. **TripAdvisor:** "an amazing experience," "fantastic natural lovely beach," "you must go." [$] *Rooms from: $300* ✉ *Near end of road to Manzanillo* ☎ *2759–9056, 2271–3000 in San José* 🌐 *www.almondsandcorals.com* 🛏 *24 bungalows* 🍽 *Some meals.*

$ B&B/INN 🏨 **Cabinas Something Different.** On a quiet street, these shiny, spic-and-span motel-style cabinas are the nicest option in the village of Manzanillo. **Pros:** good budget value; television; in a remote locale.

"We found Playa Manzanillo while visiting the Caribbean side of Costa Rica. A beautiful beach and very laid-back atmosphere." —Photo by dgray, Fodors.com member

Cons: small, spartan rooms. $ *Rooms from: $50* ⊠ *180 m south of Aquamor, Manzanillo* ☎ *2759–9014* ⤴ *18 cabinas* ⊟ *No credit cards* ⦿ *No meals.*

CROSSING INTO PANAMA VIA SIXAOLA

Costa Rica's sleepy border post at Sixaola fronts Guabito, Panama's equally quiet border crossing, 44 km (26 miles) south of the turnoff to Puerto Viejo de Talamanca. Both are merely collections of banana-plantation stilt houses and a few stores and bars; neither has any lodging or dining options, but this is a much more low-key crossing into Panama than the busy border post at Paso Canoas on the Pan-American Highway near the Pacific coast. If you've come this far, you're likely headed to **Bocas del Toro**, the real attraction in the northwestern part of Panama. This archipelago of 68 islands continues the Afro-Caribbean and indigenous themes seen on Costa Rica's Atlantic coast, and offers diving, snorkeling, swimming, and wildlife viewing. The larger islands are home to a growing selection of hotels and restaurants, everything from funky to fabulous. "Bocas" has acquired a cult following among long-term foreign visitors to Costa Rica, who find it a convenient place to travel when their permitted three-month status as a tourist has expired, since a quick 72-hour jaunt out of the country gets you another 90 days in Costa Rica.

■ **TIP →** Whatever your destination in Panama, come armed with dollars. Panama uses U.S. currency, but refers to the dollar as the *balboa*. (It does mint its own coins, all the same size as their U.S. counterparts.) No one anywhere will accept or exchange your Costa Rican colones.

Costa Rican rental vehicles may not leave the country, so crossing into Panama as a tourist is an option only via public transportation. The public bus route from San José to Cahuita and Puerto Viejo de Talamanca terminates here at the border approximately six hours after leaving the capital. Taxis in Puerto Viejo de Talamanca charge about $75 for the jaunt to the border, a much quicker and reasonable option if you can split the fare among a group. Disembark and head for the Costa Rican immigration office (☎ 2754–2044) down a flight of stairs from the west end of a former railroad bridge. Officials place an exit stamp in your passport, after which you walk across the bridge and present your passport to Panamanian immigration. The bridge looks rickety, but is safe for walking. Plans to construct a larger, more modern bridge are underway at this writing. U.S. visitors must also purchase a $5 tourist card for entry into the country. ■ TIP→ Although some local residents here make the crossing without going through border formalities, you cannot. Make sure you exit and enter Costa Rica and Panama properly in either direction.

ANOTHER GOOD BOOK

If you're headed to Panama, we'd be remiss in not recommending that you pick up a copy of *Fodor's Panama* for far more detail about Bocas del Toro and the rest of the country than we can provide here.

Consulate of Panama. The Consulate of Panama in San José can provide more information. ☎ 2280–1570.

The border crossings are open 7 am to 5 pm (8 am to 6 pm Panamanian time) daily. Set your watch one hour ahead when you enter Panama.

Taxis wait on the Panamanian side to transport you to the small city of Changuinola, the first community of any size inside the country, from which there are bus and air connections for travel farther into Panama. Taxis can also take you to Almirante, where you'll find boat launches to Bocas del Toro.

UNDERSTANDING COSTA RICA

COSTA RICA AT A GLANCE

WILDLIFE AND
PLANT GLOSSARY

MENU GUIDE

VOCABULARY

COSTA RICA AT A GLANCE

FAST FACTS

Capital: San José

Type of government: Democratic republic

Independence: September 15, 1821 (from Spain)

Population: 4,563,539

Population density: 89 persons per square km (221 persons per square mi)

Literacy: 95%

Language: Spanish (official); English spoken by most in the tourism industry

Ethnic groups: White (including mestizo) 94%, black 3%, Amerindian 1%, Asian 1%, other 1%

Religion: Roman Catholic 76%, Evangelical Protestant 14%, other 7%, none 3%

GEOGRAPHY AND ENVIRONMENT

Land area: 51,100 square km (19,730 square mi); slightly smaller than the U.S. state of West Virginia

Coastline: 1,290 km (802 mi)

Terrain: Rugged central range with 112 volcanic craters that separates the eastern and western coastal plains

Natural resources: Hydroelectric power, forest products, fisheries products

Natural hazards: Droughts, flash floods, thunderstorms, earthquakes, hurricanes, active volcanoes, landslides

Flora: 9,000 species, including 1,200 orchid species and 800 fern species; tidal mangrove swamps, tropical rain forest, subalpine forest

Fauna: 36,518 species, including 34,000 species of insects and 2,000 species of butterflies

Environmental issues: Deforestation, rapid industrialization and urbanization, air and water pollution, soil degradation, plastic waste, fisheries protection

ECONOMY

Currency: Colón, (*pl.*) colones

GDP: $51.17 billion

Per capita income: $11,300

Unemployment: 7.3%

Major industries: Microprocessors, tourism, food processing, textiles and clothing, construction materials, fertilizer, plastic products

Agricultural products: Bananas, coffee, pineapples, sugarcane, corn, rice, beans, potatoes, beef

Exports: $9.4 billion

Major export products: Bananas, coffee, pineapples, electronic components, fertilizers, sugar, textiles, electricity

Export partners: (in order of volume) U.S., China, Netherlands, United Kingdom

Imports: $12.95 billion

Major import products: Chemicals, consumer goods, electronic components, machinery, petroleum products, vehicles

Import partners: U.S. (40%), Mexico (6.6%), Japan (5.6%), China (5.3%)

DID YOU KNOW?

■ Tourism earns more foreign exchange than bananas and coffee combined.

■ Costa Rica did away with its military in 1949.

■ Five percent of the world's identified plant and animal species are found in this country.

■ Costa Rica is the home of five active volcanoes—including Volcán Arenal, the second-largest active volcano in the world.

WILDLIFE AND PLANT GLOSSARY

Here is a rundown of some of the most common and attention-grabbing mammals, birds, reptiles, amphibians, plants, and even a few insects that you might encounter. We give the common Costa Rican names, so you can understand the local lingo, followed by the latest scientific terms.

Fauna

Agouti (*guatusa; Dasyprocta punctata*): A 20-inch, tail-less rodent with small ears and a large muzzle, the agouti is reddish brown on the Pacific side, more of a tawny orange on the Caribbean slope. It sits on its haunches to eat large seeds and fruit and resembles a large rabbit without the long ears.

Anteater (*oso hormiguero*): Three species of anteater inhabit Costa Rica—the very rare giant (*Myrmecophaga tridactyla*), the nocturnal silky (*Cyclopes didactylus*), and the collared, or vested (*Tamandua mexicana*). Only the last is commonly seen, and too often as roadkill. This medium-size anteater, 30 inches long with an 18-inch tail, laps up ants and termites with its long, sticky tongue and has long, sharp claws for ripping into insect nests.

Armadillo (*cusuco; Dasypus novemcinctus*): The nine-banded armadillo is widespread in Costa Rica and also found in the southern United States. This nocturnal and solitary edentate roots in soil with a long muzzle for a varied diet of insects, small animals, and plant material.

Baird's Tapir (*danta; Tapirus bairdii*): The largest land mammal in Costa Rica (to 6½ feet), Baird's tapir is something like a small rhinoceros without armor. Adapted to a wide range of habitats, it's nocturnal, seldom seen, but said to defecate and sometimes sleep in water. Tapirs are herbivorous and use their prehensile snouts to harvest vegetation. The best opportunities for viewing wild tapirs are in Corcovado National Park.

Bat (*murciélago*): With more than 100 species, Costa Rica's bats can be found eating fruit, insects, fish, small vertebrates, nectar, and even blood, in the case of the infamous vampire bat (*vampiro, Desmodus rotundus*), which far prefers cattle blood to that of any tourist. As a group, bats are extremely important ecologically, and are essential to seed dispersal, pollination, and controlling insect populations.

Butterfly (*mariposa*): Estimates of the number of butterfly species in Costa Rica vary, but all range in the thousands. The growing number of butterfly gardens popping up around the country is testament to their popularity among visitors. Three Costa Rican morpho species—spectacular, large butterflies—have a brilliant blue upper-wing surface, giving them their local nickname of *pedazos de ciel* (pieces of sky). The blue morpho (*Morpho peleides*), arguably the most distinctive, is common in moister areas and has an intense ultraviolet upper surface. Adults feed on fermenting fruit; they never visit flowers.

Caiman (*caimán*): The spectacled caiman (*Caiman crocodilus*) is a small crocodilian (to 7 feet) inhabiting freshwater, subsisting mainly on fish. Most active at night (it has bright red eye shine), it basks by day. It is distinguished from the American crocodile by a sloping brow and smooth back scales.

Coati (*pizote; Nasua narica*): This is a long-nose relative of the raccoon, its long tail often held straight up. Lone males or groups of females with young are active during the day, on the ground, or in trees. Omnivorous coatis feed on fruit, invertebrates, and small vertebrates. Unfortunately, many have learned to beg from tourists, especially in Monteverde and on the roads around Arenal.

Cougar (*puma; Felis concolor*): Mountain lions are the largest unspotted cats (to 8 feet, including the tail) in Costa Rica. Widespread but rare, they live in essentially all-wild habitats and feed on vertebrates ranging from snakes to deer.

Crocodile (*lagarto; Crocodylus acutus*): The American crocodile, up to 16 feet in length, is found in most major river systems, particularly the Tempisque and Tárcoles estuaries. It seldom attacks humans, preferring fish and birds. It's distinguished from the caiman by size, a flat head, narrow snout, and spiky scales.

Ctenosaur (*garrobo*; *Ctenosaura similis*): Also known as the black, or spiny-tailed, iguana, this is a large (up to 18 inches long with an 18-inch tail) tan lizard with four dark bands on its body and a tail ringed with sharp, curved spines, reminiscent of a dinosaur. Terrestrial and arboreal, it sleeps in burrows or tree hollows. It lives along the coast in the dry northwest and in wetter areas farther south. The fastest known reptile (clocked on land), the ctenosaur has been recorded moving at 21.7 mi per hour.

Dolphin (*delfín*): Several species, including bottlenose dolphins (*Tursiops truncatus*), frolic in Costa Rican waters. Often seen off Pacific shores are spotted dolphins (*Stenella attenuata*), which are small (up to 6 feet), with pale spots on the posterior half of the body; they commonly travel in groups of 20 or more and play around vessels and in bow wakes. Tucuxi dolphins (*Sotalia fluviatilis*) have also been spotted in small groups off the southern Caribbean coast, frequently with bottlenose dolphins.

Frog and Toad (*rana,* frog; *sapo,* toad): Some 120 species of frog exist in Costa Rica; many are nocturnal. The most colorful daytime amphibians are the tiny strawberry poison dart frog (*Dendrobates pumilio*) and green-and-black poison dart frog. The bright coloration of these two species, either red with blue or green hind legs or charcoal black with fluorescent green markings, warns potential predators of their toxicity. The red-eyed leaf frog (*Agalychnis callidryas*) is among the showiest of nocturnal species. The large, brown marine toad (*Bufo marinus*), also called cane toad or giant toad, comes out at night.

Howler Monkey (*mono congo*; *Alouatta palliata*): These dark, chunky-bodied monkeys (to 22 inches long with a 24-inch tail) with black faces travel in troops of up to 20. Lethargic mammals, they eat leaves, fruits, and flowers. The males' deep, resounding howls sound like lions roaring, but actually serve as communication among and between troops.

Hummingbird (colibrí, *Trochilidae*): Weighing just a fraction of an ounce, hummingbirds are nonetheless some of the most notable residents of tropical forests. At least 50 varieties can be found in Costa Rica, visiting typically red tubular flowers in their seemingly endless search for energy-rich nectar. Because of their assortment of iridescent colors and bizarre bills and tail shapes, watching them can be a spectator sport. Best bets are hummingbird feeders and anywhere with great numbers of flowers.

Iguana (*iguana*): Mostly arboreal but good at swimming, the iguana is Costa Rica's largest lizard: males can grow to 10 feet, including tail. Only young green iguanas (*Iguana iguana*) are bright green; adults are much duller, females dark grayish, and males olive (with orangish heads in breeding season). All have round cheek scales and smooth tails.

Jaguar (*tigre*; *Panthera onca*): The largest New World feline (to 6 feet, with a 2-foot tail), this top-of-the-line predator is exceedingly rare but lives in a wide variety of habitats, from dry forest to cloud forest. It's most common in the vast Amistad Biosphere Reserve, but it is almost never seen in the wild.

Jesus Christ Lizard (*gallego*): Flaps of skin on long toes enable this spectacular lizard to run across water. Costa Rica has three species of this lizard, which is more properly called the basilisk: lineated (*Basiliscus basiliscus*) on the Pacific side is brown with pale lateral stripes; in the Caribbean, emerald (*Basiliscus plumifrons*) is marked with turquoise and black on a green body; and striped (*Basiliscus vittatus*), also on the Caribbean side, resembling the lineated basilisk. Adult males grow to 3 feet (mostly tail), with crests on the head, back, and base of the tail.

Leaf-Cutter Ant (*zompopas*; *Atta* spp.): Found in all lowland habitats, these are the most commonly noticed neotropical ants, and one of the country's most fascinating animal phenomena. Columns of ants carrying bits of leaves twice their size sometimes extend for several hundred yards from an underground nest to plants being harvested. The ants don't eat the leaves; their food is a fungus they cultivate on the leaves.

Macaw (*lapas*): Costa Rica's two species are the scarlet macaw (*Ara macao*), on the Pacific side (Osa Peninsula and Carara Biological Reserve), and the severely threatened great green macaw (*Ara ambigua*), on the Caribbean side. These are huge, raucous parrots with long tails; their immense bills are used to rip fruit apart to reach the seeds. They nest in hollow trees and are victimized by pet-trade poachers and deforestation.

Magnificent Frigatebird (*tijereta del mar*; *Fregata magnificens*): A large, black soaring bird with slender wings and forked tail, this is one of the most effortless and agile flyers in the avian world. More common on the Pacific coast, it doesn't dive or swim but swoops to pluck its food, often from the mouths of other birds.

Manatee (*manatí*; *Trichechus manatus*): Although endangered throughout its range, the West Indian manatee can be spotted in Tortuguero, meandering along in shallow water, browsing on submerged vegetation. The moniker "sea cow" is apt, as they spend nearly all their time resting or feeding. Their large, somewhat amorphous bodies won't win any beauty contests, but they do appear quite graceful.

Margay (*caucel*; *Felis wiedii*): Fairly small, this spotted nocturnal cat (22 inches long, with an 18-inch tail) is similar to the ocelot but has a longer tail and is far more arboreal: mobile ankle joints allow it to climb down trunks head first. It eats small vertebrates.

Motmot (*pájaro bobo*): These handsome, turquoise-and-rufous birds of the understory have racket-shaped tails. Nesting in burrows, they sit patiently while scanning for large insect prey or small vertebrates. Costa Rica has six species.

Northern Jacana (*gallito de agua*; *Jacana spinosa*): These birds are sometimes called "lily trotters" because their long toes allow them to walk on floating vegetation. Feeding on aquatic organisms and plants, they're found in almost any body of water. They expose yellow wing feathers in flight. Sex roles are reversed; "liberated" females are larger and compete for mates (often more than one), whereas the males tend to the nest and care for the young.

Ocelot (*manigordo*; *Felis pardalis*): Mostly terrestrial, this medium-size spotted cat (33 inches long, with a 16-inch tail) is active night and day, and feeds on rodents and other vertebrates. Forepaws are rather large in relation to the body, hence the local name, *manigordo,* which means "fat hand."

Opossum (*zorro pelón*; *Didelphis marsupialis*): Like the kangaroo, the common opossum belongs to that rare breed of mammal known as marsupials, distinguished by their brief gestation period and completion of development and nourishment following birth in the mother's pouch. The Costa Rican incarnation does not "play possum," and will bite if cornered rather than pretend to be dead.

Oropendola (*oropéndola*; *Psarocolius* spp.): These crow-size birds in the oriole family have a bright-yellow tail and nest in colonies, in pendulous nests (up to 6 feet long) built by females in isolated trees. The Montezuma species has an orange beak and blue cheeks, the chestnut-headed has a yellow beak. Males make an unmistakable, loud, gurgling liquid call. The bird is far more numerous on the Caribbean side.

Parakeet and Parrot (*pericos,* parakeets; *loros,* parrots): There are 15 species in Costa Rica (plus two macaws), all clad in green, most with a splash of a primary color or two on the head or wings. They travel in boisterous flocks, prey on immature seeds, and nest in cavities.

Peccary: Piglike animals with thin legs and thick necks, peccaries travel in small groups (larger where the population is still numerous); root in soil for fruit, seeds, and small creatures; and have a strong musk odor. You'll usually smell them before you see them. Costa Rica has two species: the collared peccary (*saíno, Tayassu tajacu*) and the white-lipped peccary (*chancho de monte, Tayassu pecari*). The latter is now nearly extinct.

Pelican (*pelícano*): Large size, a big bill, and a throat pouch make the brown pelican (*Pelecanus occidentalis*) unmistakable in coastal areas (it's far more abundant on the Pacific side). Pelicans often fly in V formations and dive for fish.

Quetzal (*Pharomachrus mocinno*): One of the world's most exquisite birds, the resplendent quetzal was revered by the Maya. Glittering green plumage and the male's long tail coverts draw thousands of people to highland cloud forests for sightings from February to April.

Roseate Spoonbill (*garza rosada*; *Ajaja ajaja*): Pink plumage and a spatulate bill set this wader apart from all other wetland birds; it feeds by swishing its bill back and forth in water while using its feet to stir up bottom-dwelling creatures. Spoonbills are most common around Palo Verde and Caño Negro.

Sloth (*perezoso*): Costa Rica is home to the brown-throated, three-toed sloth (*Bradypus variegatus*) and Hoffmann's two-toed sloth (*Choloepus hoffmanni*). Both grow to 2 feet, but two-toed (check forelegs) sloths often look bigger because of longer fur and are the only species in the highlands. Sloths are herbivorous, accustomed to a low-energy diet, and well camouflaged.

Snake (*culebra*): Costa Rica's serpents can be found in trees, above and below ground, and even in the sea on the Pacific coast. Most of the more than 125 species are harmless, but are best appreciated from a distance. Notable members of this group include Costa Rica's largest snake, the boa constrictor (*Boa constrictor*), reaching up to 15 feet, and the fer-de-lance (*terciopelo, Bothrops asper*), which is a much smaller (up to 6 feet) but far more dangerous viper.

Spider Monkey (*mono colorado, mono araña*): Lanky and long-tailed, the black-handed spider monkey (*Ateles geoffroyi*) is the largest monkey in Costa Rica (to 24 inches, with a 32-inch tail). Moving in groups of two to four, they eat ripe fruit, leaves, and flowers. Incredible aerialists, they can swing effortlessly through branches using long arms and legs and prehensile tails. They are quite aggressive and will challenge onlookers and often throw down branches. Caribbean and southern Pacific populations are dark reddish brown; northwesterners are blond.

Squirrel Monkey (*mono titi*): The smallest of four Costa Rican monkeys (11 inches, with a 15-inch tail), the red-backed squirrel monkey (*Saimiri oerstedii*) has a distinctive facial pattern (black cap and muzzle, white mask) and gold-orange coloration on its back. It is the only Costa Rican monkey without a prehensile tail. The species travels in noisy, active groups of 20 or more, feeding on fruit and insects. Numbers of this endangered species have been estimated between 2,000 and 4,000 individuals. Most squirrel monkeys in Costa Rica are found in Manuel Antonio National Park, in parts of the Osa Peninsula, and around the Golfo Dulce.

Three-Wattled Bellbird (*pájaro campana*; *Procnias tricarunculata*): Although endangered, the bellbird can be readily identified in cloud forests (around Monteverde, for example), where it breeds by its extraordinary call, a bold and aggressive "bonk," unlike any other creature in the forest. If you spot a male calling, look for the three pendulous wattles at the base of its beak.

Toucan (*tucán, tucancillo*): The keel-billed toucan (*Ramphastos sulfuratus*) with the rainbow-colored beak is familiar to anyone who's seen a box of Froot Loops cereal. Chestnut-mandibled toucans (*Ramphastos swainsonii*) are the largest (18 inches and 22 inches); as the name implies, their lower beaks are brown. The smaller, stouter emerald toucanet (*Aulacorhynchus prasinus*) and yellow-eared toucanet (*Selenidera spectabilis*) are aptly named. Aracaris (*Pteroglossus Spp.*) are similar to toucans, but colored orange-and-yellow with the trademark toucan bill.

Turtles (*tortuga*): Observing the nesting rituals of the five species of marine turtles here is one of those truly memorable Costa Rican experiences. Each species has its own nesting season and locale. The olive ridley (*lora; Lepidochelys olivacea*) is the smallest of the sea turtles (average carapace, or hardback shell, is 21–29 inches) and the least shy. Thousands engage in nighttime group nesting rituals on the North Pacific's Ostional. At the other extreme, but only slightly farther north on Playa Grande, nests the leatherback (*baula; Dermochelys coriacea*) with its five-foot-long shell. On the north Caribbean coast, Tortuguero hosts four of them: the leatherback, the hawksbill (*carey; Eretmochelys imbricata*), the loggerhead (*caguama; Caretta caretta*), and the green (*tortuga verde; Chelonia mydas*), with its long nesting season (June–October) that draws the most visitors and researchers.

Whales (*ballena*): Humpback whales (*Megaptera novaeanglia*) appear off the Pacific coast between November and February; they migrate from California and as far as Hawaii. You can also spot Sey whales, Bryde's whales, and farther out to sea, blue whales and sperm whales. On the Caribbean side, there are smaller (12 to 14 feet) Koiga whales.

White-Faced Capuchin Monkey (*mono cara blanca; Cebus capuchinus*): Medium-size and omnivorous, this monkey (to 18 inches, with a 20-inch tail) has black fur and a pink face surrounded by a whitish bib. Extremely active foragers, they move singly or in groups of up to 20, examining the environment closely and even coming to the ground. It's the most commonly seen monkey in Costa Rica. It's also the most often fed by visitors, to the point where some monkey populations now have elevated cholesterol levels.

White-Tailed Deer (*venado; Odocoileus virginianus*): Bambi would feel at home in Costa Rica, although his counterparts here are slightly smaller. As befits the name, these animals possess the distinctive white underside to their tail (and to their bellies). They are seen in drier parts of the country, especially in the northwest province of Guanacaste.

White-Throated Magpie-jay (*urraca; Calocitta formosa*): This southern relative of the blue jay, with a long tail and distinctive topknot (crest of forward-curved feathers), is found in the dry northwest. Bold and inquisitive, with amazingly varied vocalizations, these birds travel in noisy groups of four or more.

Flora

Ant-acacia (*acacia; Acacia spp.*): If you'll be in the tropical dry forest of Guanacaste, learn to avoid this plant. As if its sharp thorns weren't enough, acacias exhibit an intense symbiosis with various ant species (*Pseudomyrmex spp.*) that will attack anything—herbivores, other plants, and unaware human visitors that come in contact with the tree. The ants and the acacias have an intriguing relationship, though, so do look, but don't touch.

Bromeliad (*piña silvestre*): Members of the family Bromeliaceae are *epiphytes,* living on the trunk and branches of trees. They are not parasitic, however, and so have adapted to acquire all the necessary water and nutrients from what falls into the central "tank" formed by the leaf structure. Amphibians and insects also use the water held in bromeliads to reproduce, forming small aquatic communities perched atop tree branches. In especially wet areas, small bromeliads can even be found on power lines. Their spectacular, colorful efflorescences make popular—and expensive—houseplants in northern climes.

Heliconia (*heliconia; Heliconia* spp.): It's hard to miss these stunning plants, many of which have huge inflorescences of red, orange, and yellow, sometimes shaped like lobster claws, and leaves very much the size and shape of a banana plant. With luck, you'll catch a visiting hummingbird with a beak specially designed to delve into a heliconia flower—truly a visual treat.

Mangroves (*manglares*): Taken together, this handful of salt-tolerant trees with tangled, above-ground roots make up their own distinct ecosystem. Buttressing the land against the sea, they serve as nurseries for countless species of fish, crabs, and other marine animals and provide roosting habitat for marine birds. Mangroves are found on the coast in protected areas such as bays and estuaries.

Naked Indian Tree (*indio desnudo; Bursera simaruba*): This tree can be found in forests throughout Costa Rica, often forming living fences, and is instantly identifiable by its orange bark that continually sloughs off, giving rise to another common name, the sunburnt tourist tree. One theory suggests that the shedding of its bark aids in removing parasites from the tree's exterior.

Orchid (*orquídea*): The huge Orchidaceae family has more than 1,200 representatives in Costa Rica alone, with nearly 90% percent living as epiphytes on other plants. The great diversity of the group includes not only examples of great beauty but exquisite adaptations between flowers and their insect pollinators. With a combination of rewards (nectar) and trickery (visual and chemical cues), orchids exhibit myriad ways of enticing insects to cooperate.

Strangler Fig (*Matapalo; Ficus* spp.): Starting as seedlings high in the canopy, these aggressive plants grow both up toward the light, and down to the soil, slowly taking over the host tree. Eventually they encircle and appear to "strangle" the host, actually killing it by hogging all the available sunlight, leaving a ring of fig trunk around an empty interior. Figs with ripe fruit are excellent places for wildlife spotting, as they attract monkeys, birds, and an assortment of other creatures.

VOCABULARY

Rice and beans are the heart of Costa Rica's *comida típica* (typical food). It's possible to order everything from sushi to crepes in and around San José, but most Ticos have a simple diet built around rice, beans, and the myriad fruits and vegetables that flourish here. Costa Rican food isn't spicy, and many dishes are seasoned with the same five ingredients—onion, salt, garlic, cilantro, and red bell pepper.

SPANISH	ENGLISH
GENERAL DINING	
Almuerzo	Lunch
Bocas	Appetizers or snacks (literally "mouthfuls") served with drinks in the tradition of Spanish tapas
Casado	Heaping plate of rice, beans, fried plantains, cabbage salad, tomatoes, macarrones (noodles), and fish, chicken, or meat—or any variation thereof; casado and plato del día are often used interchangeably.
Cena	Dinner
Desayuno	Breakfast
Plato del día	Plate of the day
Soda	An inexpensive café; casados are always found at sodas.
ESPECIALIDADES (SPECIALTIES)	
Arreglados	Sandwiches or meat and vegetable puff pastry
Arroz con mariscos	Fried rice with fish, shrimp, octopus, and clams, or whatever's fresh that day
Arroz con pollo	Chicken with rice
Camarones	Shrimp
Ceviche	Chilled, raw seafood marinated in lime juice, served with chopped onion and garlic
Chilaquiles	Meat-stuffed tortillas
Chorreados	Corn pancakes, served with natilla (sour cream)
Corvina	Sea bass
Empanadas	Savory or sweet pastry turnover filled with fruit or meat and vegetables
Empanaditas	Small empanadas

SPANISH	ENGLISH
Gallo pinto	Rice sautéed with black beans (literally, "spotted rooster"), often served for breakfast
Langosta	Lobster
Langostino	Prawns
Olla de carne	Soup of beef, chayote squash, corn, yuca (a tuber), and potatoes
Palmitos	Hearts of palm, served in salads or as a side dish
Pejibaye	A nutty, orange-color palm fruit eaten in salads, soups, and as a snack
Pescado ahumado	Smoked marlin
Picadillo	Chayote squash, potatoes, carrots, or other vegetables chopped into small cubes and combined with onions, garlic, and ground beef
Pozol	Corn soup
Salsa caribeño	A combination of tomatoes, onions, and spices that accompanies most fish dishes on the Caribbean coast

POSTRES (DESSERTS) AND DULCES (SWEETS)

Cajeta de coco	Fudge made with coconut and orange peel
Cajeta	Molasses-flavored fudge
Dulce de leche	Thick syrup of boiled milk and sugar
Flan	Caramel-topped egg custard
Mazamorra	Cornstarch pudding
Pan de maíz	Sweet corn bread
Torta chilena	Flaky, multilayer cake with dulce de leche filling
Tres leches cake	"Three milks" cake, made with condensed and evaporated milk and cream

FRUTAS (FRUITS)

Aguacate	Avocado
Anón	Sugar apple; sweet white flesh; resembles an artichoke with a thick rind
Banano	Banana
Bilimbí	Looks like a miniature cucumber crossed with a star fruit; ground into a savory relish
Fresa	Strawberry

SPANISH	ENGLISH
Cas	A smaller guava
Granadilla	Passion fruit
Guanábana	Soursop; large, spiky yellow fruit with white flesh and a musky taste
Guayaba	Guava
Mamon chino	Rambutan; red spiky ball protecting a white fruit similar to a lychee
Mango	Many varieties, from sour green to succulently sweet oro (golden); March is the height of mango season
Manzana de agua	Water apple, shaped like a pear; juicy but not very sweet
Marañón	Cashew fruit; used in juices
Melón	Cantaloupe
Mora	Blackberry
Palmito	Heart of palm
Piña	Pineapple
Papaya	One of the most popular and ubiquitous fruits
Pipa	Green coconut; sold at roadside stands with ends chopped off and straws stuck inside
Sandía	Watermelon
Carambola	Star fruit

BEBIDAS (BEVERAGES)

Agua dulce	Hot water sweetened with raw sugarcane
Batido	Fruit shake made with milk (con leche) or water (con agua)
Café con leche	Coffee with hot milk
Café negro	Black coffee
Fresco natural	Fresh-squeezed juice
Guaro	Harsh, clear spirit distilled from fermented sugarcane
Horchata	Cinnamon-flavor rice drink
Refrescos	Tropical fruit smoothie with ice and sugar

ENGLISH	SPANISH	PRONUNCIATION

BASIC PHRASES

ENGLISH	SPANISH	PRONUNCIATION
Yes/no	Sí/no	see/no
OK.	De acuerdo.	de a-**kwer**-doe
Please.	Por favor.	pore fah-**vore**
May I?	¿Me permite?	may pair-**mee**-tay
Thank you (very much).	(Muchas) gracias.	(**moo**-chas) **grah**-see-as
You're welcome.	Con mucho gusto.	con **moo**-cho **goose**-toe
Excuse me.	Con permiso.	con pair-**mee**-so
Pardon me.	¿Perdón?	pair-**dohn**
Could you tell me?	¿Podría decirme?	po-dree-ah deh-**seer**-meh
I'm sorry.	Disculpe.	dee-**skool**-peh
Good morning!	¡Buenos días!	**bway**-nohs **dee**-ahs
Good afternoon!	¡Buenas tardes!	**bway**-nahs **tar**-dess
Good evening!	¡Buenas noches!	**bway**-nahs **no**-chess
Goodbye!	¡Adiós!/¡Hasta luego!	ah-dee-**ohss**/**ah**-stah-lwe-go
Mr./Mrs.	Señor/Señora	sen-**yor**/sen-**yohr**-ah
Miss	Señorita	sen-yo-**ree**-tah
Pleased to meet you.	Mucho gusto.	**moo**-cho **goose**-toe
How are you?	¿Cómo está usted?	**ko**-mo es-**tah** oo-**sted**
Very well, thank you.	Muy bien, gracias.	**moo**-ee bee-**en**, **grah**-see-as
And you?	¿Y usted?	ee oos-**ted**

DAYS OF THE WEEK

Sunday	domingo	doe-**meen**-goh
Monday	lunes	**loo**-ness
Tuesday	martes	**mahr**-tess
Wednesday	miércoles	me-**air**-koh-less
Thursday	jueves	hoo-**ev**-ess
Friday	viernes	vee-**air**-ness
Saturday	sábado	**sah**-bah-doh

ENGLISH	SPANISH	PRONUNCIATION

MONTHS

January	enero	eh-**neh**-roh
February	febrero	feh-**breh**-roh
March	marzo	**mahr**-soh
April	abril	ah-**breel**
May	mayo	**my**-oh
June	junio	**hoo**-nee-oh
July	julio	**hoo**-lee-yoh
August	agosto	ah-**ghost**-toh
September	septiembre	sep-tee-**em**-breh
October	octubre	oak-**too**-breh
November	noviembre	no-vee-**em**-breh
December	diciembre	dee-see-**em**-breh

USEFUL PHRASES

Do you speak English?	¿Habla usted inglés?	**ah**-blah oos-**ted** in-**glehs**
I don't speak Spanish.	No hablo español.	no **ah**-bloh es-pahn-**yol**
I don't understand (you).	No entiendo.	no en-tee-**en**-doh
I understand (you).	Entiendo.	en-tee-**en**-doh
I don't know.	No sé.	no seh
I am American/ British.	Soy americano (americana) / inglés(a).	soy ah-meh-ree-**kah**-no (ah-meh-ree-**kah**-nah)/ in-**glehs (ah)**
What's your name?	¿Cómo se llama usted?	koh-mo seh **yah**-mah **oos**-ted
My name is . . .	Me llamo . . .	may **yah**-moh
What time is it?	¿Qué hora es?	keh **o**-rah es
It is one, two, three . . . o'clock.	Es la una. . . . Son las dos, tres.	es la **oo**-nah/sohn lahs dohs, tress
How?	¿Cómo?	**koh**-mo
When?	¿Cuándo?	**kwahn**-doh

ENGLISH	SPANISH	PRONUNCIATION
This/Next week	Esta semana / la semana que entra	**es**-teh seh-**mah**-nah/lah seh-**mah**-nah keh **en**-trah
This/Next month	Este mes/el próximo mes	**es**-teh mehs/el **proke**-see-mo mehs
This/Next year	Este año/el año que viene	**es**-teh **ahn**-yo/el **ahn**-yo keh vee-**yen**-ay
Yesterday/today/tomorrow	Ayer/hoy/mañana	ah-**yehr**/oy/mahn- **yah**-nah
This morning/afternoon	Esta mañana/tarde	**es**-tah mahn-**yah**-nah/**tar**-deh
Tonight	Esta noche	**es**-tah **no**-cheh
What?	¿Qué?	keh
What is it?	¿Qué es esto?	keh es **es**-toh
Why?	¿Por qué?	pore **keh**
Who?	¿Quién?	kee-**yen**
Where is . . . ?	¿Dónde está . . . ?	**dohn**-deh es-**tah**
the bus stop?	la parada del autobus?	la pah-**rah**-dah del oh-toh-**boos**
the post office?	la oficina de correos?	la oh-fee-**see**-nah deh koh-**reh**-os
the museum?	el museo?	el moo-**seh**-oh
the hospital?	el hospital?	el ohss-pee-**tal**
the bathroom?	el baño?	el **bahn**-yoh
Here/there	Aquí/allá	ah-**key**/ah-**yah**
Open/closed	Abierto/cerrado	ah-bee-**er**-toh/ ser-**ah**-doh
Left/right	Izquierda/derecha	iss-key-**er**-dah/ dare-**eh**-chah
Straight ahead	Derecho	dare-**eh**-choh
Is it near/far?	¿Está cerca/lejos?	es-**tah** **sehr**-kah/**leh**-hoss
I'd like . . .	Quisiera . . .	kee-see-ehr-ah
a room.	un cuarto/una habitación.	oon **kwahr**-toh/**oo**-nah ah-bee-tah-see-**on**
the key.	la llave.	lah **yah**-veh
a newspaper.	un periódico.	oon pehr-ee-**oh**-dee-koh
a stamp.	la estampilla.	lah es-stahm-**pee**-yah

ENGLISH	SPANISH	PRONUNCIATION
I'd like to buy . . .	Quisiera comprar . . .	kee-see-**ehr**-ah kohm-**prahr**
a dictionary.	un diccionario.	oon deek-see-oh- **nah**-ree-oh
soap.	jabón.	hah-**bohn**
suntan lotion.	loción bronceadora.	loh-see-**ohn** brohn- seh-ah-**do**-rah
a map.	un mapa.	oon **mah**-pah
a magazine.	una revista.	**oon**-ah reh-**veess**-tah
a postcard.	una tarjeta postal.	**oon**-ah tar-**het**-ah post-**ahl**
How much is it?	¿Cuánto cuesta?	**kwahn**-toh **kwes**-tah
Telephone	Teléfono	tel-**ef**-oh-no
Help!	¡Auxilio!	owk-**see**-lee-oh
	¡Ayuda!	ah-**yoo**-dah
	¡Socorro!	soh-**kohr**-roh
Fire!	¡Incendio!	en-**sen**-dee-oo
Caution!/Look out!	¡Cuidado!	kwee-**dah**-doh

SALUD (HEALTH)

I am ill.	Estoy enfermo(a).	es-**toy** en-**fehr**- moh(mah)
Please call a doctor.	Por favor llame a un médico.	pohr fah-**vor ya**-meh ah oon **med**-ee-koh
acetaminophen	acetaminofén	a-say-ta-**mee**-no-fen
ambulance	ambulancia	ahm-boo-**lahn**-see-a
antibiotic	antibiótico	ahn-tee-bee-**oh**-tee-co
aspirin	aspirina	ah-spi-**ree**-na
capsule	cápsula	**cahp**-soo-la
clinic	clínica	**clee**-nee-ca
cold	resfriado	rays-free-**ah**-do
cough	tos	toess
diarrhea	diarrea	dee-ah-**ray**-a
fever	fiebre	fee-**ay**-bray
flu	gripe	**gree**-pay
headache	dolor de cabeza	doh-**lor** day cah- **bay**-sa

ENGLISH	SPANISH	PRONUNCIATION
hospital	hospital	oh-spee-**tahl**
medication	medicamento	meh-dee-cah-**men**-to
pain	dolor	doh-**lor**
pharmacy	farmacia	fahr-**mah**-see-a
physician	médico	**meh**-dee-co
prescription	receta	ray-**say**-ta
stomachache	dolor de estómago	doh-**lor** day eh-**sto**-mah-go

Travel Smart
Costa Rica

WORD OF MOUTH

"Go to Costa Rica—you'll love it! We loved the mix of beach time and adventure time that Manuel Antonio and Arenal offered. There is such a huge variety of activities and sights that it would be impossible to have a less than fantastic time. I mean, seriously, I had a huge pregnant belly and I had a blast! All in all, the people were delightful, the food was foreign but truly delicious and the wildlife added another dimension to scenery that was already breath taking. We would go back in a minute! "

—steviegene

GETTING HERE AND AROUND

■ AIR TRAVEL

If you are visiting several regions of the country, flying into San José, in the center of Costa Rica, is your best option. Flying into Liberia, in northwest Costa Rica, makes sense if you are planning to spend your vacation only in the North Pacific.

Rarely does an international flight get into San José early enough to make a domestic connection, particularly in the rainy season, as the weather is typically unsuitable for flying in the afternoon. So you'll likely end up spending your first night in or near the city, and leave for your domestic destination via air or land the next morning.

Heavy rains in the afternoon and evening during the May-to-November rainy season occasionally cause flights coming into San José to be rerouted to Panama City, where you may be forced to spend the night. October, with its frequent evening fog, tends to be the worst month for reroutes. ■TIP➜ In the rainy season, try to book a flight with the earliest arrival time available.

Once you're in Costa Rica, some airlines recommend that you call the San José office about three days before your return flight to reconfirm; others, such as TACA, explicitly say it's not necessary. It's always a good idea to call the local office or check online the day before you are scheduled to return home to make sure your flight time hasn't changed.

If you arrive in Costa Rica and your baggage doesn't, the first thing you should do is go to the baggage claims counter and file an official report with your specific contact information. Then call your airline to find out if they can track it and how long you have to wait—generally bags are located within two days. Continue on your trip as you can; bags can be sent to you just about anywhere in the country. Don't expect too much from local agents; try to get updates from the airline directly.

If your bag has been searched and contents are missing or damaged, file a claim with the TSA Consumer Response Center as soon as possible. If your bags arrive damaged or fail to arrive at all, file a written report with the airline before leaving the airport.

When you fly out of Costa Rica, you'll have to pay a $28 airport departure tax in colones or dollars or with a Visa credit card. (Paying the tax via credit card means the transaction will be processed as a cash advance and incur additional fees.) You can pay the tax on arrival or departure at the Bancrédito counter in the airport—the counter line may look long but it moves quickly—or at any Bancrédito branch in Costa Rica during your trip. Be warned: Lines at banks are *long*, making this a time-consuming option. A few North Pacific hotels will collect the tax for you if you are flying out of Liberia.

Airline Security Issues Transportation Security Administration ⊕ *www.tsa.gov.*

AIRPORTS

Costa Rica has two international airports. Aeropuerto Internacional Juan Santamaría (SJO) is the country's main airport, about 17 km (10 miles), or 30 minutes by car, northwest of downtown San José, just outside the city of Alajuela. The SANSA terminal for domestic flights is here. The country's other international airport is Aeropuerto Internacional Daniel Oduber Quirós (LIR), a small airport near Liberia, in the North Pacific. The tiny Tobias Bolaños airport (SYQ), in the western San José suburb of Pavas, serves domestic airline Nature Air, domestic charter companies, and a handful of private planes.

Other places where planes land in Costa Rica aren't exactly airports. They're more like a carport with a landing strip, at which an airline representative arrives just minutes before a plane is due to land or take off.

Most North American flights arrive in the evening and depart early in the morning, which are the busiest times. Prepare yourself for long waits at immigration and customs, and for check-in and security checkpoints at both airports. Enhanced security measures took effect in 2010. Liquids and gels (over 3 ounces) and powders are not permitted through security checkpoints or the gates. Carry-on bags are searched again at the gates for flights to the United States. Get to the airport three hours before your flight—Juan Santamaría is a full-service airport with many arrivals and departures each day, so if you miss your flight or have some other unexpected mishap, you're better off here. Fares are usually lower to San José than to Liberia.

Airport Information Aeropuerto Internacional Daniel Oduber Quirós (*LIR*). ✉ *13 km/8 mi west of Liberia* ☎ *2668–1010 in Costa Rica.* **Aeropuerto Internacional Juan Santamaría** (*SJO*). ✉ *17 km/10 mi northwest of downtown San José, just outside Alajuela* ☎ *2437–2400, 2437–2626 in Costa Rica for departure and arrival info* ⊕ *www.aeris.cr.* **Aeropuerto Internacional Tobías Bolaños** (*SYQ*). ✉ *6 km/4 mi west of San José, Pavas, San José* ☎ *2232–2820 in Costa Rica.*

GROUND TRANSPORTATION

At Aeropuerto Internacional Juan Santamaría, you exit the terminal into a fume-filled parking area flanked by hordes of taxis and tour vans. If you're with a tour, you need only look for a representative of your tour company with a sign that bears your name. If you need a taxi, a uniformed agent will ask you as you exit the arrivals area and will pick up a voucher at a counter just to the left, then escort you to one of the orange Taxis Unidos cabs (no other taxis are allowed in the arrivals area). Rates are metered to the various parts of town; most areas of San José are $22 to $30.

FLIGHTS

From the United States to San José: American flies from Miami and Dallas and, from November to April, from New York (JFK); Continental flies from Houston and Newark; Delta flies from Atlanta; US Airways flies from Charlotte; Spirit Air flies from Fort Lauderdale; JetBlue flies from Orlando; Frontier flies from Denver; Central American airline TACA flies from Miami, New York, and Los Angeles. Mexico's AeroMéxico provides connections from several U.S. gateways via its hub in Mexico City; Panama's Copa does the same through its hub in Panama City. From New York, flights to San José are 5½ hours nonstop or 7 to 8 hours via Miami. From Los Angeles, flights are about 5½ hours nonstop or 8½ hours via Houston; from Houston, 3½ hours nonstop; from Miami, 3 hours; from Charlotte, 4 hours. In general, nonstop flights aren't that much more expensive. Median ticket prices from hubs such as New York, Los Angeles, and Seattle hover between $500 and $600, although the range can vary widely up or down.

Six commercial airlines fly to Liberia: American, from Dallas and Miami; Delta, from Atlanta; Continental, from Houston; JetBlue from Orlando; US Airways from Charlotte, North Carolina; and Frontier from Denver, February through August.

TACA connects San José with other Central American countries. Nature Air flies between Bocas del Toro, Panama, and San José, and between Managua and San José.

Given Costa Rica's often-difficult driving conditions, domestic flights are a desirable and practical option. The informality of domestic air service— "airports" other than Liberia and San José usually consist of only an airstrip with no central building at which to buy tickets—means you might want to purchase your domestic airplane tickets in advance (by phone or online), although you can buy them at the San José or Liberia airports or at travel agencies once you're in the country. We recommend grabbing a seat as soon as you know your itinerary.

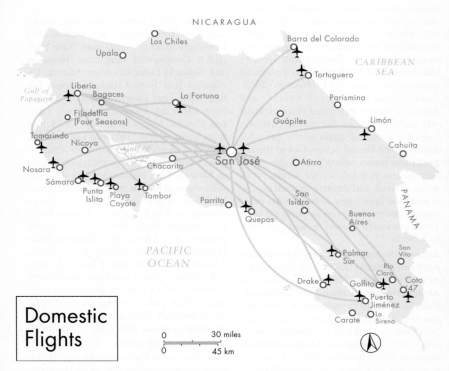

Domestic Flights

0 ————— 30 miles

0 ————— 45 km

There are two major domestic commercial airlines: SANSA and Nature Air. Most Nature Air and SANSA flights leave from the San José area (⇨ *Airports, above*). You can buy SANSA and Nature Air tickets online, over the phone, and at most travel agencies in Costa Rica. The tiny, domestic passenger planes in Costa Rica require that you pack light. A luggage weight limit of 30 pounds is imposed by SANSA; Nature Air allows 15–40 pounds, depending on fare paid. On some flights extra luggage is allowed but is charged about $1 to $3 per pound and will go standby. Heavy packers can leave their surplus for free in a locked area at Nature Air's terminal. SANSA does not store extra baggage.

Charter flights within Costa Rica are not as expensive as you might think, and can be an especially good deal if you are traveling in a group. If a group this size charters a small plane, the price per person will be only slightly more than taking a regularly scheduled domestic flight, and you can set your own departure time. The country has dozens of airstrips that are accessible only by charter planes. Charter planes are most often booked through tour operators, travel agents, or remote lodges. Most charter planes are smaller than domestic commercial planes.

■TIP➔ Don't book a domestic flight for the day you arrive in or leave Costa Rica; connections will be extremely tight, if possible at all, and you'll be at the mercy of temperamental weather and delays.

Airline Contacts American Airlines
☎ 800/433–7300, 2248–2010 in Costa Rica ⊕ www.aa.com. **Continental Airlines**
☎ 800/231–0856 for international reservations, 0800/044–0005 in Costa Rica ⊕ www.

continental.com. **Delta Airlines** ☎ *800/241-4141 for international reservations, 0800/056-2002 in Costa Rica* 🌐 *www.delta.com.* **Frontier Airlines** ☎ *800/432-1359 for international reservations* 🌐 *www.frontierairlines.com.* **JetBlue** ☎ *800/538-2583 for international reservations, 2441-6851 in Costa Rica* 🌐 *www.jetblue.com.* **Spirit Airlines** ☎ *800/772-7117, 0800/011-1103 in Costa Rica* 🌐 *www.spiritair.com.* **TACA** ☎ *800/400-8222 for international reservations, 2299-8222 in Costa Rica* 🌐 *www.taca.com.* **United Airlines** ☎ *800/538-2929 for international reservations, 0800/044-0005 in Costa Rica* 🌐 *www.united.com.* **US Airways** ☎ *800/428-4322 for international reservations, 0800/011-0793 in Costa Rica* 🌐 *www.usairways.com.*

Domestic and Charter Airlines **Aerobell Air Charter** ☎ *888/359-1359 in North America, 2290-0000 in Costa Rica* 🌐 *www.aerobell.com.* **AeroMéxico** ☎ *800/237-6639, 2231-6891* 🌐 *www.aeromexico.com.* **Copa** ☎ *800/359-2672, 2223-2672 in Costa Rica* 🌐 *www.copaair.com.* **Nature Air** ☎ *800/235-9272 in North America, 2299-6000 in Costa Rica* 🌐 *www.natureair.com.* **SANSA** ☎ *2290-4100 in Costa Rica, 877/767-2672 in North America* 🌐 *www.flysansa.com.*

BUS TRAVEL

Tica Bus has daily runs between Costa Rica and Panama or Nicaragua; Transnica has daily service between Costa Rica and Granada and Managua. We recommend choosing Tica Bus if at all possible, but Transnica is acceptable in a pinch. Both companies have comfortable, air-conditioned coaches with videos and onboard toilets, and help with border procedures.

All Costa Rican towns are connected by regular bus service. Bus service in Costa Rica is reliable, comprehensive, and inexpensive. Buses between major cities are modern and sometimes air-conditioned, but once you get into the rural areas, you may get a converted school bus without air-conditioning. The kind of bus you get is the luck of the draw (no upgrades here). Bus travel in Costa Rica is formal, meaning no pigs or chickens inside and no people or luggage on the roof. On longer routes, buses stop midway at modest restaurants. Near the ends of their runs many nonexpress buses turn into large taxis, dropping passengers off one by one at their destinations; to save time, take a *directo* (express) bus, which still might make a few stops. Be prepared for bus-company employees and bus drivers to speak Spanish only.

The main inconvenience of long-distance buses, aside from being much slower than flying, is that you usually have to return to San José to travel between outlying regions. For example, a bus from San José to the Osa Peninsula is nine hours or more, whereas the flight is one hour. Shorter distances reduce the difference—the bus to Quepos is 3½ hours and the flight 30 minutes—and in those cases the huge price difference might be worth the extra hours of travel. There is no main bus station in San José; buses leave from a variety of departure points, depending on the region they serve.

TIP→ Don't put your belongings in the overhead bin unless you have to, and if you do, keep your eye on them. If anyone—even someone who looks like a bus employee—offers to put your luggage on the bus or in the luggage compartment underneath for you, politely decline. If you must put your luggage underneath the bus, get off quickly when you arrive to retrieve it.

Most bus companies don't have printed bus schedules to give out, although departure times may be printed on a sign at the bus company's office and ticket window. Bus-line phones are usually busy or go unanswered. The schedules and prices we list are accurate at this writing, but change frequently. **TIP→ For the most reliable schedule information, go to the bus station a day before your departure.** The ICT tourist office *(⇨ Visitor Information, below)* provides a PDF bus schedule version on its website, but this should be used as only a rough guide, as it is updated infrequently.

Hotel employees can usually give you the information you need.

Buses usually depart and arrive on time; they may even leave a few minutes before the scheduled departure time if full.

Tickets are sold at bus stations and on the buses themselves; reservations aren't accepted, and you must pay in person with cash. If you pay on the bus, be sure to have loose change and small bills handy; avoid paying with a 10,000-colón bill. Buses to popular beach and mountain destinations often sell out on weekends and the days before and after a holiday. It's also difficult to get tickets back to San José on Sunday afternoon. Some companies won't sell you a round-trip ticket from the departure point; especially during the peak season, make sure the first thing you do on arrival in your destination is to buy a return ticket. Sometimes tickets include seat numbers, which are usually printed on the tops of the chairs. Smoking is not permitted on buses.

Two private bus companies, Gray Line and Interbus, travel to the most popular tourist destinations in modern, air-conditioned vans. Interbus vans usually seat 10 to 20 people, and coaches can also be reserved for large groups; Gray Line vans seat 14 to 20 people. Be sure to double-check information that is listed on the website—published prices may not be accurate and routes are not always running. This service costs about $30 to $89 one-way, but can take hours off your trip. Gray Line has a weekly pass ($149) good for unlimited travel for one week; reservations need to be made 24 hours in advance. Interbus offers three- to seven-trip Flexipasses; prices range from $125 to $275 and the passes are good for one month. Hotel-to-hotel service is offered as long as your lodging is on the route; if you're heading off the beaten track, it's a hotel-to-nearest-hotel service. Costa Rica Shuttle offers similar minvan point-to-point transfers, but for your party only. Rates range from $100 to $250 for a group up to five people.

Bus Information Tica Bus ⊠ *200 m north and 100 m west of Torre Mercedes, Paseo Colón, Paseo Colón, San José* ☎ *2221–0006* ⊕ *www.ticabus.com.* **Transnica** ⊠ *C. 22, Avdas. 3–5, San José* ☎ *2223–4242* ⊕ *www.transnica. com.*

Shuttle-Van Services Costa Rica Shuttle ☎ *4000–1040, 800/849–9403 in North America* ⊕ *www.costaricashuttle.com.* **Gray Line** ☎ *2220–2126, 800/719–3905 in North America* ⊕ *www.graylinecostarica.com.* **Interbus** ☎ *2283–5573* ⊕ *www.interbusonline.com.*

▌ CAR TRAVEL

Hiring a car with a driver makes the most sense for sightseeing in and around San José. You can also usually hire a taxi driver to ferry you around; most will stick to the meter, which at this writing will tick at a rate of about $15 per hour for the time the driver is waiting for you. At $100 to $130 per day plus the driver's food, hiring a driver for areas outside the San José area costs almost the same as renting a 4WD, but is more expensive for multiday trips, when you'll also have to pay for the driver's room. Some drivers are also knowledgeable guides; others just drive. Unless they're driving large passenger vans for established companies, it's doubtful that drivers have any special training or licensing. Hotels can usually direct you to trusted drivers; you can also find recommendations on ⊕ *www.fodors.com.* Alternatively, Alamo (⇨ *below*) provides professional car-and-driver services for minimum three-day rentals (available May to November only). You pay $75 on top of the rental fee, plus the driver's food and lodging. Costa Rica Shuttle (⇨ *Bus Travel*) provides drivers on similar terms for $100–$250 per day.

Most rental companies have an office close to Aeropuerto Internacional Juan Santamaría where you can drop off your car (even if you picked up the car at another San José branch) and provide transport to get you to your flight. Leave yourself a half hour for the return time and shuttle.

GASOLINE

There is no self-service gas in Costa Rica; 24-hour stations are generally available only in San José or on the Pan-American Highway. Most other stations are open from about 7 to 7, some until midnight. It is not customary to tip attendants.

Gas prices are fixed by the government, and gas stations around the country are legally bound to stick to the determined prices. Ten-percent-ethanol gas is gradually being introduced. Try to fill your tank in cities—gas is more expensive (and more likely to be dirty) at informal fill-up places in rural areas, where gas stations can be few and far between. Major credit cards are widely accepted. Ask the attendant if you want a *factura* (receipt). Regular unleaded gasoline is called *regular* and high-octane unleaded, required in most modern vehicles, is called *súper*. Gas is sold by the liter.

PARKING

On-street parking is scarce in downtown San José; where you find it, you'll also find *guachimanes* (informal, usually self-appointed guards). They freely admit they don't get paid enough to actually get involved if someone tries something with your car, but it's best to give them a couple of hundred colones per hour anyway. In centers such as San José, Alajuela, and Heredia, you'll find several signs with a large E in a red circle, and the words *con boleto* (with a ticket). These tickets can be bought for ½ hour (250 colones), 1 hour (500 colones), or 2 hours (1,000 colones) at the respective municipal hall. *It's a 4,000-colón fine (about $8) if you're caught in one of these spaces without a ticket.*

Safer and ubiquitous are the public lots (*parqueos*), which average flat rates of approximately $2 per hour. Most are open late, especially near hopping nightspots or theaters, but check beforehand. Never leave anything inside the car. It is illegal to park in the zones marked by yellow curb paint, or in front of garage doors or driveways, usually marked with signs reading *"No Estacionar"* ("No Parking"). Downtown parking laws are strictly enforced; the fine for illegal parking is 5,000 colones (about $10). However, the city center's narrow throughways are often bottlenecked by "waiting" cars and taxis—double-parked with someone in the car. Despite the cacophonic honking, this is largely tolerated. Outside the main hubs of the Central Valley, parking rules are far more lax, and guachimanes, private walled, and guarded hotel or restaurant parking are the rule, with few public lots.

RENTAL CARS

When you reserve a car, ask about cancellation penalties, taxes, drop-off charges (if you're planning to pick up the car in one city and leave it in another), and surcharges (for being under or over a certain age, for additional drivers, or for driving across state or country borders or beyond a specific distance from your point of rental). All these things can add substantially to your costs. Request such extras as car seats and GPS devices when you book.

Rates are sometimes—but not always—better if you book in advance or reserve through a rental agency's website. There are other reasons to book ahead, though: for popular destinations, during busy times of the year, or to ensure that you get certain types of cars (vans, SUVs, exotic sports cars).

■ TIP→ If you're planning to go to only one or two major areas, taking a shuttle van or a domestic flight is usually a better and cheaper option than driving. Renting is a good choice if you're destination hopping, staying at a hotel that's a trek to town, or going well off the beaten path. Car trips to northern Guanacaste from San José can take an entire day, so flying is probably better if you don't have long to spend in the country. Flying is definitely better than driving for visiting the South Pacific.

A standard vehicle is fine for most destinations, but a *doble-tracción* (4WD) is often essential to reach the remoter parts of the country, especially during the rainy season. Even in the dry season, you must have a 4WD vehicle to reach Monteverde and some destinations in Guanacaste. The big 4WD vehicles, such as a Suzuki Grand Vitara, can cost roughly twice as much as an economy car, but compact 4WDs, such as the Daihatsu Terios, are more reasonable, and should be booked well in advance. Most cars in Costa Rica have manual transmissions. ■TIP→ **Specify when making the reservation if you want an automatic transmission; it usually costs about $5 more per day, but some companies, such as Alamo and Hertz, don't charge extra.** Larger, more expensive automatic Montero and Sorento models are also available.

If you plan to rent any kind of vehicle between December 15 and January 3, or during Holy Week (the week leading up to Easter)—when most Costa Ricans are on vacation—reserve several months ahead of time.

Costa Rica has around 30 car-rental firms. Most local firms are affiliated with international car-rental chains and offer the same guarantees and services as their branches abroad; local company Tricolor gets high marks from travelers on our Fodor's Forum. At least a dozen rental offices line San José's Paseo Colón; some large hotels and Aeropuerto Internacional Juan Santamaría have representatives. Renting in or near San José is by far the easiest way to go. It's getting easier to rent outside San José, particularly on the Pacific coast. Several rental companies have set up branches in Liberia, Quepos, Jacó, Tamarindo, and La Fortuna. In most other places across the country, it's either impossible or very difficult and expensive to rent a car.

Car seats are compulsory for children under four years old, and can be rented for about $5 per day; reserve in advance. Rental cars may not be driven across borders to Nicaragua and Panama. For a $50 fee, National and Alamo will let you drop off a Costa Rican rental car at the Nicaragua border and provide you with a Nicaraguan rental on the other side. Seat-belt use

is compulsory for all passengers. Fuel-efficiency measures restrict certain cars from San José's city center during rush hours once a week, according to the final license-plate number (e.g., plates that end in 9 are restricted on Friday). This also applies to rental cars; if you are stopped, do not pay a bribe. To rent a car, you need a driver's license, a valid passport, and a credit card. The minimum renter age varies; agencies such as Economy, Budget, and Alamo rent to anyone over 21; Avis sets the limit at 23, Hertz at 25. Though it's rare, some agencies have a maximum age limit.

High-season rates in San José begin at $45 a day and $180 a week for an economy car with air-conditioning, manual transmission, unlimited mileage, plus obligatory insurance; but rates fluctuate considerably according to demand, season, and company. Rates for a 4WD vehicle during high season are $70 to $90 a day and $450 to $550 per week. Often companies will also require a $1,000 deposit, payable by credit card.

Cars picked up at or returned to Aeropuerto Internacional Juan Santamaría incur a 12% surcharge. Arrangements can be made to pick up cars directly at the Liberia airport, but a range of firms have offices nearby and transport you from the airport free of charge—and with no surcharge for an airport pickup. Check cars thoroughly for damage before you sign the rental contract. Even tough-looking 4WD vehicles should be coddled. ■TIP→ **The charges levied by rental companies for damage—no matter how minor—are outrageous even by U.S. or European standards.** It's very wise to opt for full-coverage insurance. One-way service surcharges are $50 to $150, depending on the drop-off point; National allows travelers free car drop-off at any of its offices with a minimum three-day rental. To avoid a hefty refueling fee, fill the tank just before you turn in the car. It's almost never a deal to buy the tank of gas that's in the car when you rent it; the understanding is that you'll return it empty, but some fuel usually remains.

Additional drivers are about $10 per day if there is any charge at all. Almost all agencies, with the exception of Budget Rent-a-Car, have cell-phone rental; prices range between $3 and $8 per day, with national per-minute costs between 50¢ and $2.

International driving permits (IDPs), which are used only in conjunction with a valid driver's license and translate your license into 10 languages, are not necessary in Costa Rica. Your own driver's license is good for the length of your initial tourist visa. You must carry your passport, or a copy of it with the entry stamp, to prove when you entered the country.

Local Agencies Economy ☎ 877/326-7368 in North America, 2299-2000 in Costa Rica ⊕ www.economyrentacar.com. **Tricolor** ☎ 800/949-0234 in North America, 2440-3333 in Costa Rica ⊕ www.tricolorcarrental. com.

Major Agencies Alamo ☎ 2242-7733 in Costa Rica, 877/222-9075 in North America ⊕ www.alamocostarica.com. **Avis** ☎ 2293-2222 in Costa Rica, 800/331-1084 in North America ⊕ www.avis.co.cr. **Budget** ☎ 2436-2000 in Costa Rica, 800/472-3325 in North America ⊕ www.budget.co.cr. **Dollar** ☎ 877/767-8651 in North America, 866/746-7765 in North America, 2443-2950 in Costa Rica ⊕ www.dollarcostarica.com. **Hertz** ☎ 888/437-8927 in North America, 2221-1818 in Costa Rica ⊕ www.costaricarentacar. net. **National Car Rental** ☎ 877/862-8227 in North America, 2242-7878 in Costa Rica ⊕ www.natcar.com.

ROAD CONDITIONS

Many travelers shy away from renting a car in Costa Rica, if only for fear of the road conditions. Indeed, this is not an ideal place to drive: in San José traffic is bad and car theft is rampant (look for guarded parking lots or hotels with lots); in rural areas roads are often unpaved or potholed—and tires aren't usually covered by the basic insurance. And Ticos are reckless drivers—with one of the highest accident rates in the world. But though

driving can be a challenge, it's a great way to explore certain regions, especially the North Pacific, the Northern Plains, and the Caribbean coast (apart from roadless Tortuguero and Barra del Colorado). Keep in mind that mountains and poor road conditions make most trips longer than you'd normally expect.

San José is terribly congested during weekday morning and afternoon rush hours (7 to 9 am and 4 to 6 pm). Avoid returning to the city on Sunday evening, when traffic to San José from the Pacific coast beaches can back up for hours. The winding Pan-American Highway south of the capital is notorious for long snakes of traffic stuck behind slow-moving trucks. Look out for potholes, even in the smoothest sections of the best roads. Also watch for unmarked speed bumps where you'd least expect them, particularly on rural main thoroughfares. During the rainy season roads are in much worse shape. Check with your destination before setting out; roads, especially in Limón Province, are prone to washouts and landslides.

San José has many one-way streets and traffic circles. Streets in the capital are narrow. Pedestrians are supposed to have the right-of-way but do not in reality, so be alert when walking. The local driving style is erratic and aggressive but not fast, because road conditions don't permit too much speed. Frequent fender benders tie up traffic. Keep your windows rolled up in the center of the city, because thieves may reach into your car at stoplights and snatch your purse, jewelry, and so on.

Signage is notoriously bad, but improving. Watch carefully for "*No Hay Paso*" ("Do Not Enter") signs; one-way streets are common, and it's not unusual for a street to transform from a two-way to a one-way. Streetlights are often out of service and key signs missing or knocked down because of accidents.

Outside San José you'll run into long stretches of unpaved road. Frequent hazards in the countryside are potholes, landslides during the rainy season, and cattle on the roads. Drunk drivers are a hazard throughout the country on weekend nights. Driving at night is not recommended anyway, because roads are poorly lighted and many don't have painted center lines or shoulder lines.

ROADSIDE EMERGENCIES
Costa Rica has no highway emergency service organization. In Costa Rica 911 is the nationwide number for accidents. Traffic police (*tránsitos*) are scattered around the country, but Costa Ricans are very good about stopping for people with car trouble. Whatever happens, don't move the car after an accident, even if a monstrous traffic jam ensues. Call 911 first if the accident is serious (nearly everyone has a cell phone here and it's almost a given that someone will offer to help). Also be sure to call the emergency number your car-rental agency has given you. For fender benders, contact the Traffic Police, who will try to locate a person to assist you in English—but don't count on it. If you don't speak Spanish, you may want to contact the rental agency before trying the police. If your own car is stolen, call the Judicial Investigative Police (OIJ, pronounced oh-ee-hota), which will find an English-speaking representative to assist you.

Emergency Services Ambulance and Police 📞 *911.*

RULES OF THE ROAD
■ TIP→ Obey traffic laws religiously, even if Costa Ricans appear not to. Fines are frightfully high—a speeding ticket could set you back more than $600—and evidence exists that transit police target foreigners for infractions.

Driving is on the right side of the road in Costa Rica. The highway speed limit is usually 90 kph (54 mph), which drops to 60 kph (36 mph) in residential areas. In towns, limits range from 30 to 50 kph (18 to 31 mph). Speed limits are enforced in all regions of the country. Seat belts are required, and an awareness campaign has increased enforcement. "*Alto*" means

"stop" and "*ceda*" means "yield." Right turns on red are permitted except where signs indicate otherwise, but in San José this is usually not possible because of one-way streets and pedestrian crossings.

Local drunk driving laws are strict. You'll also get nailed with a $450 fine if you're caught driving in a "predrunk" state (blood alcohol levels of 0.049% to 0.099%). If your level is higher than that, you'll pay $900, the car will be confiscated, and your license will be taken away. Police officers who stop drivers for speeding and drunk driving are often looking for payment on the spot—essentially a bribe. Whether you're guilty or not, you'll get a ticket if you don't give in. Asking for a ticket instead of paying the bribe discourages corruption and does not compromise your safety. You can generally pay the ticket at your car-rental company, which will remit it on your behalf.

Seat-belt use is mandatory. Car seats are required for children ages four and under, but car-seat laws are not rigorously enforced. Children over 12 are allowed in the front seat. Drivers are prohibited from texting or using handheld cell phones.

▌TAXI TRAVEL

Taxis are cheap and your best bet for getting around San José. Just about every driver is friendly and eager to use a few English words to tell you about a cousin or sister in New Jersey; however, cabbies truly conversant in English are scarce. Most are knowledgeable, but given the haphazard address system, may cheerfully engage passersby or other taxi drivers to find your destination. Tipping is not expected, but a good idea when you've had some extra help, especially with your bags.

Cabs are red, usually with a yellow light on top. To hail one, extend your hand and wave it at about hip height. If it's available, the driver will often flick his headlights before pulling over. Cabs can be scarce when it's raining or during rush hour. The city is dotted with *paradas de taxi,* taxi lineups where you stand the best chance of grabbing one. Your hotel can usually call you a reputable taxi or private car service, and when you're out to dinner or on the town, the restaurant or disco can just as easily call you a cab—it's much easier than trying to hail one on the street in the wee hours, and safer, too.

■ TIP→ **Taxi drivers are infamous for "not having change." If it's just a few hundred colones, you may as well round up. If it's a lot, ask them to drive to a store or gas station where you can make change.** They'll often miraculously come up with the difference, or wait patiently while you get it. To avoid this situation, never use a 10,000-colón bill in a taxi, and avoid paying with 5,000-colón bills unless you've run up almost that much in fares.

Technically this system applies throughout the country, but rural and unofficial cabs often use their odometers to creatively calculate fares. Manuel Antonio drivers are notorious for overcharging. It's illegal, but taxis charge up to double for hotel pickups or fares that take them out of the province (such as San José to Alajuela or vice versa). Ask the manager at your hotel about the going rate for the destination to which you're heading. Drivers have a fairly standard list of off-the-meter illegal fares.

In the capital there's usually no reason to take the risk with an unofficial taxi (*pirata*), but they are often the only option outside main hubs. *See the regional chapters for recommended drivers, or check with your hotel or restaurant for reliable service.*

It's always a good idea to make a note of the cab number (painted in a yellow triangle on the door), and sit in the backseat for safety.

▌ TRAIN TRAVEL

An earthquake in 1991 wreaked havoc on the country's century-old rail links, and service was completely suspended in 1995. An east–west commuter-rail route now plies San José, and another route connects the capital with Heredia, but these are geared to the needs of workaday commuters.

ESSENTIALS

▌ ACCOMMODATIONS

Low-end alternatives are often referred to as *cabinas* whether they offer concrete-block motels or freestanding cottages. Most have private rooms, cold-water concrete showers, fans instead of air-conditioning, and limited—if any—secure parking or storage, and may share bathrooms. Owners tend to be Costa Rican. Often without websites, email, or links to major agencies, these hotels tend to follow a first-come, first-served booking policy. They may have room during peak seasons when mid- or upper-end options are booked solid.

Midrange options include boutique hotels, tasteful bungalows, bed-and-breakfasts, and downtown casino hotels. Those in the hotter beach areas may not have hot-water showers. Many have pools, Internet access, and meal options. They tend to be foreign-owned and, with the exception of the casinos, have personalized service. Because they're generally small, you may have to book one or two months ahead, and up to six months in the high season. Booking through an association or agency can significantly reduce the time you spend scanning the Internet, but you can often get a better deal and negotiate longer-stay or low-season discounts. The Costa Rican Hotel Association has online search and booking capabilities. ICT provides hotel lists searchable by star category.

High-end accommodations can be found almost everywhere. They range from luxury tents to exquisite hotels and villa rentals, and are often more secluded. You'll find all the amenities you expect at such areas, with one notable exception: the roads and routes to even five-star villas can be atrocious. This category is sometimes booked up to a year in advance for Christmas, and during this season you may be able to book only through agents or central reservations offices. Resorts are generally one of two kinds: luxurious

privileged gateways to the best of the country (such as Punta Islita) or generic budget all-inclusives (such as the Barceló) that probably run counter to what you're coming to Costa Rica for. Several chain hotels have franchises in Costa Rica, leaning toward the generic and all-inclusive. The upside is that they are rarely booked solid, so you can always fall back on one in a worst-case scenario, and they often have member discounts.

Nature lodges and hotels in the South Pacific (where restaurants aren't an option) may be less expensive than they initially appear, as the price of a room usually includes three hearty meals a day, and sometimes guided hikes. These, and other remote accommodations, may not have daily Internet access even though they have a website: be patient if you're attempting to book directly. (Email still does not have the urgency in Costa Rica that it does in the United States.) Many of the hotels are remote and have an eco-friendly approach (even to luxury), so air-conditioning, in-room telephones, and TVs are exceptions to the rule. Consider how isolated you want to be; some rural and eco-lodges are miles from neighbors and other services and have few rainy-day diversions.

The ICT's voluntary "green leaf" rating system evaluates establishments in terms of sustainable-tourism criteria; a detailed description of the program and a search function to find lodging by sustainability level can be found at ⊕ *www.turismo-sostenible.co.cr.*

The lodgings we list are Costa Rica's cream of the crop in each price category. We always list the facilities that are available, but we don't specify whether they cost extra; when pricing accommodations, always ask what's included and what costs extra. Properties are assigned price categories based on the range from the least-expensive standard double room at high season (excluding holidays) to the most expensive. Keep in mind that hotel prices we list exclude 16.4% service and tax.

For Costa Rica's popular beach and mountain resorts, be sure to reserve well in advance for the dry season (mid-December to April everywhere except the Caribbean coast, which has a short September to October "dry" season). During the rainy season (May to mid-November except on the Caribbean coast, where it's almost always rainy) most hotels drop their rates considerably, which sometimes sends them into a lower price category than the one we indicate.

■ TIP➔ If you're having trouble finding a hotel that isn't completely booked, consider contacting a tour operator who can arrange your entire trip. Because they reserve blocks of rooms far in advance, you might have better luck.

Most hotels and other lodgings require you to give your credit-card details before they will confirm your reservation. If you don't feel comfortable emailing this information, ask if you can fax it (some places even prefer faxes). However you book, get confirmation in writing and have a copy of it handy when you check in.

Be sure you understand the hotel's cancellation policy. Some places allow you to cancel without any kind of penalty—even if you prepaid to secure a discounted rate—if you cancel at least 24 hours in advance. Others require you to cancel a week in advance or penalize you the cost of one night. Small inns and bed-and-breakfasts are most likely to require you to cancel far in advance. Most hotels allow children under a certain age to stay in their parents' room at no extra charge, but others charge for them as extra adults; find out the cutoff age for discounts.

Lodging Resources Costa Rican Hotels Association (*Cámara Costarricense de Hoteles*). ☎ 2220-0575 in Costa Rica ⊕ www.costaricanhotels.com. **Instituto Costarricense de Turismo** (*ICT*). ☎ 866/267-8274 in North America, 2299-5800 in Costa Rica ⊕ www.visitcostarica.com.

APARTMENT AND HOUSE RENTALS

Rental houses are now common all over Costa Rica, and are particularly popular in the Pacific coast destinations of Manuel Antonio, Tamarindo, Ocotal, and Jacó. Furnished rentals accommodate a crowd or a family, often for less and at a higher comfort level. Generally, properties are owned by individual owners or consortiums, most of them based in the United States, with property managers in Costa Rica. Resort communities with villa-style lodgings are also growing. Nosara Beach Rentals lists apartments and villas on the Nicoya Peninsula; Villas International has an extensive list of properties in Quepos and Tamarindo. For the southern Nicoya Peninsula, check Costa Rica Beach Rentals. The Marina Trading Post, a Century 21 affiliate, arranges houses and condos in the Flamingo and Potrero areas.

Contacts Costa Rica Beach Rentals ☎ 2640-0065 ⊕ www.costarica-beachrentals. com. **Marina Trading Post/Century 21** ☎ 2654-4004 in Costa Rica, 877/661-2060 from U.S. ⊕ www.century21costarica.net. **Nosara Beach Rentals** ☎ 2682-0153 ⊕ www. nosarabeachrentals.com. **Villas & Apartments Abroad** ✉ 183 Madison Ave., Suite 1111, New York, New York, USA ☎ 212/213-6435 in North America ⊕ www.vaanyc.com. **Villas Caribe** ☎ 800/645-7498 ⊕ www.villascaribe. com. **Villas International** ✉ 17 Fox Lane, San Anselmo, California, USA ☎ 415/499-9490 in North America, 800/221-2260 ⊕ www. villasintl.com.

BED-AND-BREAKFASTS

A number of quintessential bed-and-breakfasts—small and homey—are clustered in the Central Valley, generally offering hearty breakfasts and friendly inside information for $50 to $75 per night. You'll also find them scattered through the rest of the country, mixed in with other self-titled bed-and-breakfasts that range from small cabins in the mountains to luxurious boutique hotel–style digs in the North Pacific region.

Reservation Services Bed and Breakfast. com. Bed and Breakfast.com also sends out an online newsletter. ☎ *512/322–2710, 800/462– 2632* ⊕ *www.bedandbreakfast.com.* **Bed and Breakfast Inns Online** *310/280–4363, 800/215–7365* ⊕ *www.bbonline.com.* **Pamela Lanier's Bed and Breakfast Inns** ⊕ *www. lanierbb.com/Costa_Rica.*

HOME EXCHANGES

With a direct home exchange you stay in someone else's home while they stay in yours. Some outfits also deal with vacation homes, so you're not actually staying in someone's full-time residence, just their vacant weekend place.

A handful of home exchanges are available; this involves an initial small registration fee, and you'll have to plan ahead. It's an excellent way to immerse yourself in the true Costa Rica, particularly if you've been here before and aren't relying so heavily on the tourism support that hotels can offer. Drawbacks include restricted options and dates. Many companies list home exchanges, but we've found HomeLink International, which lists a handful of jazzy houses in Costa Rica, and Intervac to be the most reliable.

Exchange Clubs Home Exchange. Home Exchange; $119 for a one-year online listing. *800/877–8723* ⊕ *www.homeexchange.com.*

HOSTELS

Hostels offer bare-bones lodging at low, low prices—often in shared dorm rooms with shared baths—to people of all ages, though the primary market is young travelers, especially students. Most hostels serve breakfast; dinner and/or shared cooking facilities may also be available. In some hostels you aren't allowed to be in your room during the day, and there may be a curfew at night. Nevertheless, hostels provide a sense of community, with public rooms where travelers often gather to share stories. Many hostels are affiliated with Hostelling International (HI), an umbrella group of hostel associations with some 4,500 member properties in more than 70 countries. Other hostels are

completely independent and may be nothing more than a really cheap hotel. Costa Rica has a sprinkling of youth hostels and hotels affiliated with Hostelling International; most are tantamount to inexpensive hotels, appropriate for families.

▌ ADDRESSES

In Costa Rica addresses are usually given in terms of how many meters the place is from a landmark. Street names and building numbers are not commonly used. Churches, stores, even large trees that no longer exist—almost anything can be a landmark, as long as everyone knows where it is, or where it used to be. A typical address in San José is *100 metros este y 100 metros sur del Más X Menos* (100 meters east and 100 meters south from the Más X Menos supermarket). ▌TIP➔ In towns and cities in Costa Rica, each block is assumed to be 100 meters, although some blocks may be much longer and some may be shorter. So if someone tells you to head down the road 500 meters, they mean five blocks. Ticos, as Costa Ricans call themselves, are generally happy to help lost visitors, and they spend a lot of time describing where things are. But be warned—even if they don't know where something is, Ticos will often give uncertain or even wrong information rather than seem unhelpful; triangulated direction-asking is a must. Ask at least two, if not three, people in quick succession to avoid getting hopelessly lost. Key direction terms are *lugar* (place), *calle* (street), *avenida* (avenue), *puente* (bridge), *piso* (floor), *edificio* (building), *cruce* (intersection), *semáforo* (traffic light), *rotonda* (traffic circle), and *cuadra* (block).

■ COMMUNICATIONS

INTERNET

Downtown San José is full of Internet cafés with high-speed connections; prices are usually less than $1 per hour. As you move away from the capital, prices rise to $2 to $4 per hour and connections become slower and more unreliable. Wildly expensive satellite Internet is available at some remote, exclusive hotels. Cafés are generally good places to make international Internet calls, but expect echoes and a mediocre connection. Most major hotels have free wireless access or use of a guest Internet computer. Eateries such as Denny's, Bagelmen's, and a number of upscale cafés are also Wi-Fi–friendly, although a few travelers have been robbed of their laptops in public restaurants. Dial-up access is spotty and frustrating, but if you're desperate and have both a computer and access to a telephone line, you can buy one of RACSA's (the state Internet service provider) prepaid Internet cards in three amounts: 1,800 colones (5 hours), 3,550 colones (10 hours), and 5,300 colones (15 hours). Cards are sold at Kodak stores, Perimercado supermarkets, and some branches of the Banco Nacional. The cards come with the access numbers, and a help line with English-speaking operators.

Contacts Cybercafes. Cybercafes lists more than 4,000 Internet cafés worldwide. ⊕ *www.cybercafes.com.*

PHONES

The good news is that you can now make a direct-dial telephone call from virtually any point on earth. The bad news? You can't always do so cheaply. Calling from a hotel is almost always the most expensive option; hotels usually add huge surcharges to all calls, particularly international ones. In some countries you can phone from call centers or even the post office. Calling cards usually keep costs to a minimum, but only if you purchase them locally. And then there are mobile phones *(⇨ below)*, which are sometimes more prevalent—particularly in the developing world—than landlines; as expensive as mobile phone calls can be, they are still usually a much cheaper option than calling from your hotel.

CALLING WITHIN COSTA RICA

In 2008, all phone numbers in Costa Rica were assigned an extra number. A 2 was tacked onto the front of all landline numbers and a 4, 7, or 8 was added to the front of all mobile phone numbers. In-country 800 numbers were not affected by the change. Many signs and business cards still show the old seven-digit number.

The Costa Rican phone system is very good by the standards of other developing countries. However, phone numbers do change often. There are no area codes in Costa Rica, so you only need dial the eight-digit number, without the 506 country code. Coin-operated phones are disappearing rapidly.

CALLING OUTSIDE COSTA RICA

The country code for the United States is 1.

Internet telephony is by far the cheapest way to call home; it is a viable option in the Central Valley and major tourist hubs. For other regions or for more privacy, a pay phone using an international phone card *(⇨ Calling Cards, below)* is the next step up; you can also call from a pay phone using your own long-distance calling card. Dialing directly from a hotel room is very expensive, as is recruiting an international operator to connect you.

■ TIP→ Watch out for pay phones marked "Call USA/Canada with a credit card." They are *wildly* expensive.

To call overseas directly, dial 00, then the country code (dial 1 for the United

States and Canada), the area code, and the number. You can make international calls from almost any phone with an international calling card purchased in Costa Rica. First dial 1199, then the PIN on the back of your card (revealed after scratching off a protective coating), then dial the phone number as you would a direct long-distance call.

When requesting a calling card from your phone provider, ask specifically about calls from Costa Rica. Most 800-number cards don't work in Costa Rica. Callingcards.com is a great resource for pre-paid international calling cards. At this writing, it lists at least two calling-card companies with rates of 29¢ and 56¢ per minute for calls from Costa Rica to the United States.

You may find the local access number blocked in many hotel rooms. First ask the hotel operator to connect you. If the hotel operator balks, ask for an international operator, or dial the international operator yourself. For service in English, you'll have more luck dialing the international operator (☎ 1175 or 1116). One way to improve your odds of getting connected to your long-distance carrier is to sign up with more than one company: a hotel may block Sprint, for example, but not MCI. If all else fails, call from a pay phone.

AT&T, MCI, and Sprint access codes make calling long distance relatively convenient but can be very expensive.

To make a person-to-person direct-dial call from any phone, dial 09 (instead of 00 for a regular call), the country code for the country you're calling, and then the number. The operator will ask for the name of the person you're contacting, and billing at direct-dial rates begins only once that person comes to the phone.

Direct-dial calls to the United States and Canada are 27¢ per minute.

Phone Resources Callingcards.com
☎ *866/299–3937* ⊕ *www.callingcards.com.*
International information ☎ *1124.* **International operator** ☎ *1175, 1116.*

CALLING CARDS

Most public phones require phone cards (for local or international calls), but phone cards can also be used from any nonrotary telephone in Costa Rica, including residential phones, cell phones, and hotel phones. It's rare to be charged a per-minute rate for the mere use of the phone in a hotel.

Phone cards are sold in an array of shops, including Más X Menos supermarkets, post offices, offices of the Costa Rican Electricity Institute (ICE), and at any business displaying the gold-and-blue "*tarjetas telefónicas*" sign. International cards tend to be easier to find in downtown San José and in tourism areas.

Tarjetas para llamadas nacionales (domestic calling cards) are available in denominations of 500 colones and 1,000 colones. Phone-card rates are standard throughout the country, about 1¢ per minute, half that at night; a 500-colón card provides about 125 minutes of daytime landline calls. This decreases sharply if calling a cell phone; rates vary. *Tarjetas para llamadas internacionales* (international calling cards) are sold in $10, $20, 3,000-colón, and 10,000-colón amounts (denominations are inexplicably split between dollars and colones). It's harder to find the 10,000-colón cards; your best bet is to try a Fischel pharmacy or an ICE office. In busy spots, roaming card-hawkers abound; feel free to take advantage of the convenience—they're legit.

Some public phones accept *tarjetas chip* ("chip" cards), which record what you spend, but ■ TIP➡ avoid buying chip cards: they frequently malfunction, you can use them only at the few-and-far-between chip phones, and they are sold in small denominations that are not sufficient for international calls.

MOBILE PHONES

If you have an unblocked phone (some countries use different frequencies than what's used in the United States) and your service provider uses the world-standard GSM network (as do T-Mobile, Cingular, and Verizon), you can probably use your phone abroad. ■TIP→ If you travel internationally frequently, save one of your old mobile phones or buy a cheap one on the Internet; ask your cell phone company to unlock it for you, and take it with you as a travel phone, buying a new SIM card with pay-as-you-go service in each destination.

If your cell phone company has service to Costa Rica, you theoretically can use it here, but expect reception to be impossibly bad in many areas of this mountainous country. Costa Rica works on a 1,800 MHz system—a tri- or quad-band cell phone is your best bet. Note that roaming fees can be steep.

Most car-rental agencies have good deals on cell phones, often better than the companies that specialize in cell-phone rental. If you're not renting a car, a number of companies will rent TDMA or GSM phones; remember, coverage can be spotty. Although service is evening out, TDMA phones have tended to work best in the Central Valley and Guanacaste; GSM is better for remote areas such as Dominical, Sámara, and Tortuguero. Specify your destination when renting. Rates range from $5 to $15 per day, plus varying rates for local or international coverage and minimum usage charges. Local calls average 70¢ per minute, international $1 to $1.50. You'll need your passport, a credit card, and a deposit, which varies per phone and service but averages $300 to $400; some rent only to those over 21. The deposit drops significantly with companies that can hook you up with a rented local chip for your own phone.

Friendly and professional, Cell Service Costa Rica will get you hooked up and provides door-to-door service; it doesn't rent SIM cards. Cellular Telephone Rentals Costa Rica has higher daily rates but free local calls, and will set you up with a card for your phone.

Contacts Cell Service Costa Rica ☎ 2296–5553 in Costa Rica ⊕ www.cellservicecr.com. **Cellular Telephone Rentals Costa Rica** ☎ 800/769–7137 in North America, 2290–7534 in Costa Rica ⊕ www.cellulartelephonerentals.com.

▌ CUSTOMS AND DUTIES

You're always allowed to bring goods of a certain value back home without having to pay any duty or import tax. But there's a limit on the amount of tobacco and liquor you can bring back duty free, and some countries have separate limits for perfumes; for exact figures, check with your customs department. The values of so-called duty-free goods are included in these amounts. When you shop abroad, save all your receipts, as customs inspectors may ask to see them as well as the items you purchased. If the total value of your goods is more than the duty-free limit, you'll have to pay a tax (most often a flat percentage) on the value of everything beyond that limit.

When shopping in Costa Rica, keep receipts for all purchases. Be ready to show customs (*aduanas*) officials what you've bought. Pack purchases together in an easily accessible place. The Patrimony Protection Department recommends obtaining a letter (free) from its office in the National Museum attesting that high-quality replicas of pre-Columbian artifacts are in fact copies, to avoid customs hassles. In practice, few people request such a letter, and problems with such souvenirs are infrequent. The only orchids you can take home are packaged in a tube and come with an export permit.

If you think a duty is incorrect, appeal the assessment. If you object to the way your clearance was handled, note the inspector's badge number. In either case, first ask to see a supervisor. If the problem isn't resolved, write to the appropriate authorities, beginning with the port director at your point of entry.

It usually takes about 10 to 30 minutes to clear customs when arriving in Costa Rica.

Visitors entering Costa Rica may bring in 500 grams of tobacco, 5 liters of wine or spirits, 2 kilograms of sweets and chocolates, and the equivalent of $500 worth of merchandise. One camera and one video camera, six rolls of film, binoculars, and electrical items for personal use only are also allowed. Make sure you have personalized prescriptions for any medication you are taking. Customs officials at San José's international airport rarely examine tourists' luggage by hand, although all incoming bags are x-rayed. If you enter by land, they'll probably look through your bags. Officers at the airport generally speak English and are usually your best (only, really) option for resolving any problem.

Pets (cats or dogs) with updated health and vaccination certificates are welcome in Costa Rica; no prior authorization is required if bringing a dog or cat that has up-to-date health and vaccination cards. The Servicio Nacional de Salud Animal can provide more info.

Information in Costa Rica Customs (*Dirección General de Aduanas*). ☎ 2522–9000 in Costa Rica ⊕ www.hacienda.go.cr. **Patrimony Protection Office** ☎ 2291–3517 in Costa Rica. **Servicio Nacional de Salud Animal** (*SENASA*). ☎ 2260–8300 in Costa Rica ⊕ www.senasa.go.cr.

U.S. Information U.S. Customs and Border Protection ⊕ www.cbp.gov.

▌ EATING OUT

Dining options around Costa Rica run the spectrum from elegant and formal to beachy and casual. San José and popular tourist centers offer a wide variety of cuisine types. Farther off the beaten track, expect hearty, filling local cuisine. Increasingly common as you move away from San José are the thatched conical roofs of the round, open *rancho* restaurants that serve a combination of traditional staples with simple international fare. Every town has as least one soda—that's Costa Rican Spanish for a small, family-run restaurant.

MEALS AND MEALTIMES

In San José and surrounding cities, sodas are usually open daily 7 am to early evening, though some close Sunday. Other restaurants are usually open 11 am to 9 pm. In rural areas restaurants are usually closed Sunday, except around resorts. In resort areas some restaurants may be open late. Normal dining hours in Costa Rica are noon to 3 and 6 to 9. *Desayuno* (breakfast) is served at most sodas and hotels. The traditional breakfast is gallo pinto, eggs, plantains, and fried cheese; hotel breakfasts vary widely and generally offer fruit and lighter international options in addition to the local stick-to-your-ribs plate. *Almuerzo* (lunch) is the biggest meal of the day for Costa Ricans, and savvy travelers know that lunch specials are the biggest bargain of the day, too. *Cena* (dinner or supper) runs the gamut of just about anything you choose.

Except for those in hotels, many restaurants close between Christmas and New Year's Day and during Holy Week (Palm Sunday to Easter Sunday). Call before heading out. Even if you keep your base in San José, consider venturing to the Central Valley towns for a meal or two.

Unless otherwise noted, the restaurants listed in this guide are open daily for lunch and dinner.

Credit cards are not accepted at many restaurants in rural areas. Always ask before you order to find out if your credit card will be accepted. Visa and MasterCard are the most commonly accepted cards; American Express and Diners Club are less widely accepted. The Discover card is increasingly accepted. ▌TIP→ Remember that 23% is added to all menu prices: 13% for tax and 10% for service. Legally, restaurant menus are required to show after-tax, after-tip prices; in practice, many do not. Because a gratuity (*propina*) is included, there's no need to tip, but if your service is good, it's nice to add a little money to the obligatory 10%.

RESERVATIONS AND DRESS

Costa Ricans generally dress more formally than North Americans. For dinner at an upscale restaurant, long pants and closed-toe shoes are standard for men except for beach locations, and women tend to wear dressy clothes that show off their figures, with high heels. Shorts, flip-flops, and tank tops are not acceptable, except at inexpensive restaurants in beach towns.

VEGETARIAN OPTIONS

Vegetarians sticking to lower-budget establishments won't go hungry, but may develop a love-hate relationship with rice, beans, and fried cheese. A simple *sin carne* (no meat) request is often interpreted as "no beef," and you may get a plate of pork, chicken, or fish, so don't be afraid to sound high-maintenance. Specify *solo vegetales* (only vegetables), and for good measure, *nada de cerdo, pollo o pescado* (no pork, chicken, or fish). More-cosmopolitan restaurants are more conscious of vegetarians—upscale Asian restaurants often offer a vegetarian section on the menu. If your kids balk at the choices on the menu, ask for plain grilled chicken, fish, or beef: *"Pollo/pescado/carne sencillo para niños"* ("Grilled chicken/fish/meat for children"). Most restaurants are willing to accommodate with options and portion size.

WINES, BEER, SPIRITS, AND BEVERAGES

The ubiquitous sodas generally don't have liquor licenses, but getting a drink in any other eatery isn't usually a problem. Don't let Holy Thursday and Good Friday catch you off guard; both are legally dry days. Bars close, and coolers and alcohol shelves in restaurants and stores are sealed off with plastic and police tape. In general, restaurant prices for imported alcohol—which includes just about everything except local beer, rum, and *guaro*, the local sugarcane firewater—may be more than what you'd like to pay.

WORD OF MOUTH

Was the service stellar or not up to snuff? Did the food give you shivers of delight or leave you cold? Did the prices and portions make you happy or sad? Rate restaurants and write your own reviews in Travel Ratings or start a discussion about your favorite places in Travel Talk on ⊕ *www. fodors.com*. Your comments might even appear in our books. Yes, you, too, can be a correspondent!

Water is generally safe to drink (especially around San José), but quality can vary; to be safe, drink bottled water.

▌ ELECTRICITY

North American appliances are compatible with Costa Rica's electrical system (110 volts) and outlets (parallel two-prong). Australian and European appliances require a two-prong adapter and a 220-volt to 110-volt transformer. Never use an outlet that specifically warns against using higher-voltage appliances without a transformer. Dual-voltage appliances (i.e., they operate equally well on 110 and 220 volts) such as most laptops, phone chargers, and hair dryers need only a two-prong adapter, but you should bring a surge protector for your computer.

Consider making a small investment in a universal adapter, which has several types of plugs in one lightweight, compact unit. Always check labels and manufacturer instructions to be sure. Don't use 110-volt outlets marked "for shavers only" for high-wattage appliances such as hair dryers.

Contacts Global Electric & Phone Directory. Global Electric & Phone Directory has information on electrical and telephone plugs around the world. ⊕ *www.kropla.com*. **Walkabout Travel Gear.** Walkabout Travel Gear has a good coverage of electricity under "adapters." ☎ *800/852–7085, 707/385–0299* ⊕ *www.walkabouttravelgear.com*.

■ EMERGENCIES

Dial 911 for an ambulance, the fire department, or the police. Costa Ricans are usually quick to respond to emergencies. In a hotel or restaurant, the staff will usually offer immediate assistance, and in a public area passersby can be counted on to stop and help.

For emergencies ranging from health problems to lost passports, contact your embassy.

General Emergency Contacts Ambulance **(Cruz Roja), Fire, Police** ☎ 911. **Traffic Police** ☎ 2222–9330, 911 for emergencies.

U.S. Embassy United States Embassy (*Embajada de los Estados Unidos*). ✉ *C. 120 and Avda. 0, Pavas, San José* ☎ *2519–2000, 2519–2280 in Costa Rica for after-hrs emergencies* ⊕ *costarica.usembassy.gov* ⊙ *Mon.–Fri. 8–4:30.*

■ HEALTH

Most travelers to Costa Rica do not get any vaccinations or take any special medications. However, according to the U.S. Centers for Disease Control, travel to Costa Rica poses some risk of malaria, hepatitis A and B, dengue fever, typhoid fever, and rabies. The CDC recommends getting vaccines for hepatitis A and B and typhoid fever, especially if you are going to be in remote areas or plan to stay for more than six weeks.

Check with the CDC for detailed health advisories and recommended vaccinations. In areas with malaria and dengue, both of which are carried by mosquitoes, bring mosquito nets, wear clothing that covers your whole body, and apply repellent containing DEET in living and sleeping areas. There are some pockets of malaria near the Nicaraguan border on the Caribbean coast. You probably won't need to take malaria pills before your trip unless you are staying for a prolonged period in the north, camping on northern coasts, or crossing the border into Nicaragua or Panama. You should discuss the

option with your doctor. Children traveling to Central America should have current inoculations against measles, mumps, rubella, and polio.

SPECIFIC ISSUES IN COSTA RICA

Malaria is not a problem in Costa Rica except in some remote northern Caribbean areas near the Nicaraguan border. Poisonous snakes, scorpions, and other pests pose a small (often overrated) threat. The CDC marks Costa Rica as an area infested by the *Aedes aegypti* (dengue-carrier) mosquito, but not as an epidemic region. A few thousand cases in locals are recorded each year; the numbers had been dropping, but dramatic spikes in 2005 and 2007 did spur major eradication efforts. Cases of fatal hemorrhagic dengue are rare. The highest-risk area is the Caribbean, and the rainy season is peak dengue season elsewhere. You're unlikely to be felled by this disease, but you can't take its prevention too seriously: *repelente* (insect repellent spray) and *espirales* (mosquito coils) are sold in supermarkets and small country stores. U.S. insect repellent brands with DEET are sold in pharmacies and supermarkets. Mosquito nets are available in some remote lodges; you can buy them in camping stores in San José.

■ TIP→ Mild insect repellents, like the ones in some skin softeners, are no match for the intense mosquito activity in the hot, humid regions of the Caribbean, Osa Peninsula, and Southern Pacific. Repellents made with DEET or picaridin are the most effective. Perfume, aftershave, and other lotions and potions can actually attract mosquitoes.

It's unlikely that you will contract malaria or dengue, but if you start suffering from high fever, the shakes, or joint pain, make sure you ask to be tested for these diseases when you go to the local clinic. Your embassy can provide you with a list of recommended doctors and dentists.

Costa Rica has experienced cases of H1N1 influenza, the so-called "swine flu." Even its former president was laid low by a week of the illness, to date, the world's only head of state to be affected.

Standard precautions, such as washing hands regularly and getting vaccinated yourself, can minimize the risk.

Government facilities—the so-called Caja hospitals (short for Caja Costarricense de Seguro Social, or Costa Rican Social Security System)—and clinics are of acceptable quality, but notoriously overburdened, a common complaint in socialized-medicine systems anywhere. Private hospitals are more accustomed to serving foreigners. They include Hospital CIMA, Clínica Bíblica, and Clínica Católica, which all have 24-hour pharmacies. Outside San José most major towns have pharmacies that are open until at least 8 or 9 pm, but usually the nearest hospital emergency room is the only after-hours option. The long-established and ubiquitous Fischel pharmacies are great places for your prescription needs, and usually staff a doctor who can help with minor ailments. Antibiotics and psychotropic medications (for sleep, anxiety, or pain) require prescriptions in Costa Rica. Little else does. But plan ahead and bring an adequate supply with you from home; matches may not be exact.

For specific clinic, hospital, and pharmacy listings, see Chapters 3 through 9. Most food and water is sanitary in Costa Rica. In rural areas you run a mild risk of encountering drinking water, fresh fruit, and vegetables contaminated by fecal matter, which in most cases causes a bit of *turista* (traveler's diarrhea) but can cause leptospirosis (which can be treated by antibiotics if detected early). You can stay on the safe side by avoiding uncooked food, unpasteurized milk (including milk products), and ice—ask for drinks *sin hielo* (without ice)—and by drinking bottled water. Mild cases of turista may respond to Imodium (known generically as loperamide) or Pepto-Bismol (not as strong), both of which can be purchased over the counter. Drink plenty of purified water or tea; chamomile (*manzanilla* in Spanish) is a good folk remedy. In severe cases, rehydrate yourself with a salt-sugar solution

(½ teaspoon salt and 4 tablespoons sugar per quart of water).

Ceviche, raw fish cured in lemon juice—a favorite appetizer, especially at seaside resorts—is generally safe to eat. ■TIP→ Buy organic foods whenever possible; chemicals, many of which have been banned elsewhere, are sprayed freely here without regulation.

Heatstroke and dehydration are real dangers, especially for hikers, so drink lots of water. Take at least 1 liter per person for every hour you plan to be on the trail. Sunburn is the most common traveler's health problem. Use sunscreen with SPF 30 or higher. Most pharmacies and supermarkets carry sunscreen in a wide range of SPFs, though it is relatively pricey.

The greatest danger to your person actually lies off Costa Rica's popular beaches—riptides are common wherever there are waves, and tourists run into serious difficulties in them every year. If you see waves, ask the locals where it's safe to swim; and if you're uncertain, don't go in deeper than your waist. If you get caught in a rip current, swim parallel to the beach until you're free of it, and then swim back to shore. ■TIP→ Avoid swimming where a town's main river opens up to the sea. Septic tanks aren't common. Do not fly within 24 hours of scuba diving.

OVER-THE-COUNTER REMEDIES
Farmacia is Spanish for "pharmacy," and the names for common drugs *aspirina,* Tylenol (*acetaminofina*), and *ibúprofen* are basically the same as they are in English. Pepto-Bismol is widely available. Many drugs for which you need a prescription back home are sold over the counter in Costa Rica. Pharmacies throughout the country are generally open from 8 to 8, though it's best to consult with your hotel's staff to be sure. Some pharmacies in San José affiliated with clinics stay open 24 hours.

∎ HOURS OF OPERATION

Like the rest of the world, Costa Rica's business hours have been expanding. Megamalls are usually open seven days a week, opening around 10 am and closing around 9 pm; tourism-based businesses and museums also usually keep a Monday-to-Sunday schedule but open an hour earlier. Many smaller or rural museums are open weekdays. National parks often close one day for maintenance; for example, Manuel Antonio is closed Monday. Restaurants in the city often close Sunday, and sometimes Monday. Eateries in beach towns and other tourism-oriented areas are more likely to open seven days a week. Bars and nightclubs are generally open until 1 or 2 am, at which time night owls flock to places like El Pueblo center in San José to keep partying until 4 am. Last calls vary from place to place.

Some government offices and smaller businesses close for lunch, especially in rural areas, but *jornada continúa* (without the lunch break) is becoming more common in San José and its suburbs, and most commercial establishments follow an 8 am to 5 pm schedule.

Three public holidays (April 11, July 25, and October 12) are bumped to the following Monday when they fall on a weekend or midweek. Government offices and commercial establishments observe all the holidays. The only days the country truly shuts down are Holy Thursday and Good Friday; some buses still run, but no alcohol can be purchased, and most restaurants and all stores are closed.

HOLIDAYS

January 1: New Year (*Año Nuevo*)

April 11: Juan Santamaría Day, a national hero

Easter Week: Thursday and Good Friday, religious activities (*Semana Santa*)

May 1: International Labor Day (*Día del Trabajador*)

July 25: Annexation of Guanacaste Province (*Anexión de Guanacaste*)

August 2: Day of the Virgin of Los Angeles, patron saint of Costa Rica (*Virgen de los Ángeles*)

August 15: Mother's Day (*Día de la Madre*)

September 15: Independence Day (*Día de Independencia*)

October 12: Culture Day (*Día de la Cultura*, or *Día de la Raza*)

December 25: Christmas (*Navidad*)

∎ MAIL

The Spanish word for post office is *correo*. Mail from the United States can take up to two to three weeks to arrive in Costa Rica (occasionally it never arrives at all). Within the country, mail service is even less reliable. Outgoing mail is marginally quicker, with delivery to North America in 5 to 10 days, especially when sent from San José. It's worth registering mail; prices are only slightly higher. All overseas cards and letters will automatically be sent airmail. Mail theft is a chronic problem, so do not mail checks, cash, or anything else of value.

Minimum postage for postcards and letters from Costa Rica to the United States and Canada costs the equivalent of U.S. 65¢.

You can have mail sent *poste restante* (*lista de correos*) to any Costa Rican post office (specify Correo Central to make sure it goes to the main downtown office). In written addresses, *apartado*, abbreviated *apdo.*, indicates a post-office box.

Post offices are generally open weekdays 7:30 to 5:30, and Saturday 8 to noon. Stamps can be purchased at post offices and some hotels and souvenir shops. These vendors will also accept the mail you wish to send; don't bother looking for a mailbox, as only a handful (usually in rural areas with no post office) have been authorized. Always check with your hotel, which may sell stamps and post your letters for you.

SHIPPING PACKAGES

Shipping parcels through the post office is not for those in a hurry, because packages to the United States and Canada can take weeks. Also, packages may be pilfered. However, post-office shipping is the cheapest way to go, with rates at $7 to $15 per kilogram.

Some stores offer shipping, but it is usually quite expensive. If you can, carry your packages home with you.

UPS has offices in San José, Tamarindo, Jacó, Manuel Antonio, Sarchí, Nuevo Arenal, La Fortuna, and Limón. DHL has drop-offs in San José (Rohrmoser, Paseo Colón), Curridabat, Escazú, Heredia, Liberia, Limón, Ciudad Quesada, Jacó, Quepos, and San Isidro de El General. Both have central information numbers with English-speaking staff to direct you to the nearest office. FedEx has offices in San José; it offers package pickup service in San José and other centers, such as Limón; call for availability. Prices are about 10 times what you'd pay at the post office, but packages arrive in a matter of days. ("Overnight" is usually a misnomer—shipments to most North American cities take two business days.)

Express Services Main Offices DHL ✉ *600 m northwest of the Real Cariari Mall, La Aurora, Heredia* ☎ *2209–6000 in Costa Rica* ⊕ *www. dhl.co.cr* ☞ *Call for other locations.* **FedEx** ✉ *Paseo Colón, 100 m east of León Cortés statue, San José* ☎ *800/463–3339 in Costa Rica* ⊕ *www.fedex.com* ☞ *Call for other locations.* **UPS** ✉ *50 m east of Pizza Hut, Pavas, San José* ☎ *2290–2828 in Costa Rica* ☞ *Call for other locations.*

▌ MONEY

In general, Costa Rica is cheaper than North America or Europe, but travelers looking for dirt-cheap developing-nation deals may find it's more expensive than they bargained for—and prices are rising as more foreigners visit and relocate here.

Food in modest restaurants and public transportation are inexpensive. A 2-km (1-mile) taxi ride costs about $1.50.

ATMS AND BANKS

Lines at San José banks would try the patience of a saint; instead, get your spending money at a *cajero automático* (automatic teller machine). If you do use the bank, remember that Monday, Friday, and the first and last days of the month are the busiest days.

Although they are springing up at a healthy rate, don't count on using an ATM outside San José. Though not exhaustive, the A Toda Hora (ATH) company website lists locations of its ATH cash machines, and notes which ones offer colones (usually in increments of 1,000 colones), dollars (in increments of $20), or both; choose your region or city in the box on the homepage called *Búsqueda de Cajeros.*

All ATMs are 24-hour; you'll find them in major grocery stores, some hotels, gas–station convenience stores, and even a few McDonald's, in addition to banks. ATH, Red Total, and Scotiabank machines supposedly accept both Cirrus (a partner with MasterCard) and Plus (a partner with Visa) cards, but sometimes don't. If you'll be spending time away from major tourist centers, particularly in the Caribbean, get most or all the cash you need in San José and carry a few U.S. dollars in case you run out of colones. It's helpful to have both a Visa and a MasterCard—even in San José—as some machines accept only one or the other. Both companies have sites with fairly comprehensive lists of accessible ATMs around the world (⇨ *below*).

ATMs are sometimes out of order and sometimes run out of cash on weekends. ▌TIP➔ **PIN codes with more than four digits are not recognized at Costa Rican ATMs. If you have a five-digit PIN, change it with your bank before you travel.**

The Credomatic office, housed in the BAC San José central offices on Calle Central between Avenidas 3 and 5, is the local representative for most major credit cards; get cash advances here, or at any bank (Banco Nacional and BAC San José are good for both MasterCard and Visa;

LOCAL DO'S AND TABOOS

CUSTOMS OF THE COUNTRY

Ticos tend to use formal Spanish, preferring, for example, *con mucho gusto* (with much pleasure) instead of *de nada* for "you're welcome." Family is important in Costa Rica. It is considered polite to ask about your marital status and family.

Ticos can be disarmingly direct; don't be surprised (or offended) if locals pick up on a physical trait and give you a nickname: *Chino* for anyone of Asian ethnicity, or *Gordita* if you have even an extra ounce around your hips. It's meant affectionately. In almost every other situation, a circumspect approach is advised; North American straightforwardness often comes across as abrupt here. Preceding requests with a bit of small talk (even if it's a hotel employee) goes a long way. Also, be very aware of body language and other cues—Costa Ricans don't like to say no, and will often avoid answering a question or simply say *gracias* when they really mean no.

A large number of Costa Rican men make a habit of ogling or making gratuitous comments when young women pass on the street. Women should take care not to dress in skimpy clothing.

The expression "Tico time" was coined for a reason. Transportation, theaters, government, and major businesses tend to stick to official schedules. Anything else is flexible, and best handled by building in a little buffer time and sliding into the tropical groove.

GREETINGS

Costa Ricans are extremely polite, quick to shake hands (light squeezes are the norm) and place a kiss on the right cheek (meaning you need to bear left when going in for the peck). The formal pronoun *usted* (you) is used almost exclusively; the slangier *vos* is thrown about in informal settings and among close or young friends and relatives.

SIGHTSEEING

As you would anywhere, dress and behave respectfully when visiting churches. In churches men and women should not wear shorts, sleeveless shirts, or sandals; women should wear pants or skirts below the knee. Bathing suits, short shorts, and other skimpy attire are inappropriate city wear, but tend to be the uniform in beach towns; even here, however, cover up for all but the most informal restaurants. Locals tend to dress somewhat formally, with women favoring clothes that show off their curves.

Beggars are not a major problem, but if you're in San José, you'll come across a few. It's always better to give to an established organization, but the safety net for Costa Ricans with disabilities is riddled with holes, so even a couple of hundred colones will be appreciated. Simply keep walking past the addicts—they will almost always just move on to the next person. A couple of savvy panhandlers speak excellent English and will try to draw you into conversation with a sob story about a lost passport. Keep walking.

Banks and other offices allow pregnant women and the elderly to move immediately to the front of the line, and this respect is carried over to other establishments and crowded buses. If you're in a crowd and need to step in front of them, murmur, *"Con permiso"* ("Excuse me").

OUT ON THE TOWN

To catch a waiter's attention, wave discreetly or say, *"Disculpe, señor"* (or *señora* for women); best to leave the finger snapping to the locals. For the bill, ask for *"La cuenta, por favor."* (No one will bring the check to you until you ask.) Pockets of no-smoking sections are growing, especially in the swankier restaurants, but smoking is still tolerated in many public spaces. It's prohibited in government buildings, cinemas, theaters, and public transport. Excessive displays of affection draw frowns, clearly lost on the gaggles of lip-locked couples. Locals tend to dress up to go out, whatever the activity: a snazzy (but not too dressy) outfit will serve you well in San José. If invited to someone's home, bring a gift such as flowers or a bottle of wine or some trinket from your home country. If offered food at someone's home, it's polite to accept it and eat it (even if you aren't hungry).

LANGUAGE

One of the best ways to avoid being an Ugly American is to learn a little of the local language. You need not strive for fluency; even just mastering a few basic words and terms is bound to make chatting with the locals more rewarding.

Spanish is the official language, although many tour guides and locals in heavily touristed areas speak English. You'll have a better time if you learn some basic Spanish before you go and if you bring a phrase book with you. At the very least, learn the rudiments of polite conversation—niceties such as *por favor* (please) and *gracias* (thank you) will be warmly appreciated. *For more words and phrases, see the Spanish glossary in the back of the book.* In the Caribbean province of Limón a Creole English called Mekatelyu is widely spoken by older generations. English is understood by many people in these parts.

An open-ended *"¿Dónde está . . .?"* ("Where is . . .?") may result in a wall of rapid-fire Spanish. Better to avoid language as much as possible when asking for directions. You're going to have to stop often anyway, so it can be helpful to make the journey in segments: in the city, say the name of the place you want to go, and point [adding a questioning *izquierda* (left), *derecha* (right), or *directo* (straight)]; do this frequently, and you'll get there. On longer journeys, keep a good map handy, and use the same strategy, asking for a nearby town on your journey

rather than the final destination—you're more likely to get accurate directions.

And of course, you can't go wrong with an amiable *Pura vida*, which serves as "hello," "good-bye," "thanks," "cool," "how's it going," and all things amiable.

A phrase book and language-tape set can help get you started. *Fodor's Spanish for Travelers* (available at bookstores everywhere) is excellent.

Banco Popular, and Banco de Costa Rica always accept Visa).

State banks have branches with slightly staggered hours; core times are weekdays 9 to 4, and some are open Saturday morning. Several branches of Banco Nacional are open until 6, or occasionally 7. Private banks—Scotiabank and BAC San José—tend to keep longer hours and are usually the best places to change U.S. dollars and traveler's checks; rates may be marginally better in state banks, but the long waits usually cancel out any benefit. Multinational banks Citi, HSBC, and Scotiabank have branches here, but none has any link to your back-home account except via your ATM card. The BAC San José in Aeropuerto Internacional Juan Santamaría is open every day 5 am to 10 pm.

Although it seems counterintuitive, ■TIP→ whenever possible use ATMs only during bank business hours. ATMs here have been known to "eat" cards, and are frequently out of cash. When the bank is open, you can go in to retrieve your card or get cash from a teller. As a safety precaution, look for a machine in a bank with a guard nearby.

Resources A Toda Hora (*ATH*). ⊕ *www.ath. fi.cr.* **MasterCard** ⊕ *www.mastercard.com/cr/.* **Visa** ⊕ *www.visa.com.*

CREDIT CARDS

It's a good idea to inform your credit-card company before you travel, especially if you're going abroad and don't travel internationally very often. Record all your credit-card numbers—as well as the phone numbers to call if your cards are lost or stolen—in a safe place. Both MasterCard and Visa have general numbers you can call (collect if you're abroad) if your card is lost, but you're better off calling the number of your issuing bank, since MasterCard and Visa usually just transfer you to your bank; your bank's number is generally printed on your card.

All major credit cards are accepted at most major hotels and restaurants in this book; establishments affiliated with local credit-card processor Credomatic also accept the Discover card, although many businesses don't know what it is. As the phone system improves and expands, many budget hotels, restaurants, and other properties have begun to accept plastic; but plenty of properties still require payment in cash. Don't necessarily count on using your credit card outside San José. ■TIP→ Carry enough cash to patronize the many businesses without credit-card capability. Note that some hotels, restaurants, tour companies, and other businesses add a surcharge (around 5%) to the bill if you pay with a credit card, or give you a 5% to 10% discount if you pay in cash. It's always a good idea to pay for large purchases with a major credit card if possible, so you can cancel payment or get reimbursed if there's a problem.

CURRENCY AND EXCHANGE

At this writing, the colón is about 500 to the U.S. dollar and 690 to the euro. Coins come in denominations of 5, 10, 25, 50, 100, and 500 colones. Be careful not to mix up the very similar 100- and 500-colón coins. Bills come in denominations of 1,000, 2,000, 5,000, 10,000, 20,000, and 50,000 colones. Bills are undergoing a design change at this writing. Motifs and sizes of old are changing, with new bills being quickly phased in. Avoid using larger-denomination bills in taxis or small stores. Many businesses accept U.S. dollars, although will use a less favorable exchange rate in their calculations.

Costa Rican colones are sold abroad at terrible rates, so you should wait until you arrive in Costa Rica to get local currency. U.S. dollars are still the easiest to exchange, but euros can be exchanged for colones at just about any Banco Nacional branch and San José and Escazú branches of other banks, such as BAC San José. Private banks—Scotiabank and BAC San José—are the best places to change U.S. dollars and traveler's checks. There is a branch of the BAC San José in the check-in area of Juan Santamaría airport (open daily 5 am to 10 pm) where you can exchange money when you arrive—it's a much better deal than the Global Exchange counter. Taxi and van drivers who pick up at the airport accept U.S. dollars.

Outdoor money changers are rarely seen on the street, but avoid them if they approach; you will most certainly get a bad deal, and you risk robbery pulling out wads of cash in such a public place.

■ TIP→ Even if a currency-exchange booth has a sign promising no commission, rest assured that there's some kind of huge, hidden fee. (Oh . . . that's right. The sign didn't say no fee.) And as for rates, you're almost always better off getting foreign currency at an ATM or exchanging money at a bank.

■ PACKING

Travel light, and make sure you can carry your luggage without assistance. Even if you're planning to stay only in luxury resorts, odds are that at least once you'll have to haul your stuff a distance from bus stops, the shuttle drop-off, or the airport. Another incentive to pack light: domestic airlines have tight weight restrictions (at this writing 11.3 to 13 kilograms [25 to 30 pounds], and sometimes less for their discounted fares) and not all buses have luggage compartments. Frameless backpacks and duffel bags can be squeezed into tight spaces and are less conspicuous than fancier luggage.

Bring comfortable, hand-washable clothing. T-shirts and shorts are acceptable near the beach and in tourist areas; long-sleeve shirts and pants protect your skin from ferocious sun and, in some regions, mosquitoes. Leave your jeans behind—they take forever to dry. Pack a waterproof, lightweight jacket and a light sweater for cool nights, early mornings, and trips up volcanoes; you'll need even warmer clothes for trips to Chirripó National Park or Cerro de la Muerte and overnight stays in San Gerardo de Dota or on the slopes of Poás Volcano. Bring at least one good (and wrinkle-free) outfit for going out at night.

Women might have a tough time finding tampons, so bring your own. For almost all toiletries, including contact lens supplies, a pharmacy is your best bet. Don't forget sunblock, and expect to sweat it off and reapply regularly in the high humidity. Definitely bring sufficient batteries, because they're expensive here.

Snorkelers staying at budget hotels should consider bringing their own equipment; otherwise, you can rent gear at most beach resorts.

You have to get down and dirty—well, more like wet and muddy—to see many of the country's natural wonders. This following packing list is not comprehensive; it's a guide to some of the things you might not think to bring. For your main piece of luggage, a sturdy internal-frame backpack is great, but a duffel bag works, too. You can get by with a rolling suitcase, but then bring a smaller backpack as well.

■ PASSPORTS

U.S. citizens need only a passport to enter Costa Rica for stays of up to 90 days. Make sure it's up to date—you'll be refused entry if the passport is due to expire in less than three months. To be on the safe side, make sure it is valid for at least six months. The only way to extend your stay is to spend 72 hours in Nicaragua or Panama—but don't expect to do that undetected more than a couple of times. Customs forms ask how many visits you've made to Costa Rica in the past year.

Costa Rica has one of the highest rates of U.S. passport theft in the world. Travelers in Costa Rica are not required to carry their original documents with them at all times, although you must have easy access to them. Photocopies of the data page and your entry stamp are sufficient; those, at least, must be with you at all times. Although there have been reports from around the world about security problems with in-room safes, if your hotel doesn't have a safe in reception, locking

PACKING LIST FOR COSTA RICA

- Quick-drying synthetic-fiber shirts and socks

- Hiking boots or shoes that can get muddy and wet

- Waterproof sport sandals (especially in the Osa Peninsula, where most transportation is by boat, and often there are no docks)

- Knee-high socks for the rubber boots that are supplied at many lodges

- A pair of lightweight pants (fire ants, mosquitoes, and other pests make covering yourself a necessity on deep-forest hikes)

- Pants for horseback riding (if that's on your itinerary)

- Waterproof, lightweight jacket, windbreaker, or poncho

- Day pack for hikes

- Sweater for cool nights and early mornings

- Swimsuit

- Insect repellent (with DEET, for forested areas and especially on the northern Caribbean coast, where there are pockets of malaria)

- Flashlight or headlamp with spare batteries (for occasional power outages or inadequately lighted walkways at lodges)

- Sunscreen with a minimum of SPF 30 (waterproof sunscreens are best; even if you're not swimming, you might be swimming in perspiration)

- Large, portable water bottle

- Hat and/or bandannas (not only do they provide shade, but they prevent perspiration from dripping down your face)

- Binoculars (with carrying strap)

- Camera (waterproof, or with a waterproof case or dry bag, sold in outdoor-equipment stores)

- Film (film in Costa Rica can be expired and is expensive)

- Imodium and Pepto-Bismol (tablet form is best)

- Swiss Army knife (and remember to pack it in your checked luggage, never your carry-on—even on domestic flights in Costa Rica)

- Zip-style plastic bags (they always come in handy)

- Travel alarm clock or watch with an alarm (don't count on wake-up calls)

- Nonelectric shaving utensils

- Toilet paper (rarely provided in public bathrooms)

---

a passport in a hotel-room safe is better than leaving it in an unlocked hiding place or carrying it with you.

TIP→ For easy retrieval in the event of a lost or stolen passport, before you leave home scan your passport into a portable storage device (like an iPod) that you're carrying with you or email the scanned image to yourself.

If your passport is lost or stolen, first call the police—having the police report can make replacement easier—and then call your embassy (⇨ *Emergencies*). You'll get a temporary Emergency Travel Document

that will need to be replaced once you return home. Fees vary according to how fast you need the passport; in some cases the fee covers your permanent replacement as well. The new document will not have your entry stamps; ask if your embassy takes care of this, or whether it's your responsibility to get the necessary immigration authorization.

GENERAL REQUIREMENTS FOR COSTA RICA	
Passport	Must be valid for 3 months after date of arrival
Visa	Free upon entry for Americans
Vaccinations	None required
Driving	International driver's license not required; CDW is optional on car rentals
Departure Tax	US$28

RESTROOMS

When nature calls, look for signs that say "*servicios sanitarios*" or simply "*sanitarios.*" Toilet paper is not discarded into some toilets in smaller venues in Costa Rica, but rather in a trash bin beside it. Septic systems are delicate and the paper will clog the toilet. At some public restrooms you might have to pay 50¢ or so for a few sheets of toilet paper. At others, there may not be any toilet paper at all. It's always a good idea to have some tissues at the ready. Gas stations generally have facilities, but you may decide not to be a slave to your bladder once you get a look at them. On long trips, watch for parked buses; generally this indicates some sort of better-kept public facilities.

Find a Loo The Bathroom Diaries. The Bathroom Diaries is flush with unsanitized info on restrooms the world over—each one located, reviewed, and rated.
⊕ *www.thebathroomdiaries.com.*

SAFETY

Violent crime is not a serious problem in Costa Rica, but thieves can easily prey on tourists, so be alert. The government has created a Tourism Police unit, whose 250-plus officers can be seen on bikes or motorcycles patrolling areas in Guanacaste, San José, and the Arenal area. Crimes against property are rife in San José. In rural areas theft is on the rise.

For many English-speaking tourists, standing out like a sore thumb can't be avoided. But there are some precautions you can take:

■ Don't bring anything you can't stand to lose.

■ Don't wear expensive jewelry or watches.

■ In cities, don't carry expensive cameras or lots of cash.

■ Carry backpacks on your front; thieves can slit your backpack and run away with its contents before you notice.

■ Don't wear a waist pack, because thieves can cut the strap.

■ Distribute your cash and any valuables (including credit cards and passport) between a deep front pocket, an inside jacket or vest pocket, and a hidden money belt. (If you use a money belt, carry some cash in your purse or wallet so you don't have to reach for the hidden pouch in public.)

■ Keep your hand on your wallet if you are in a crowd or on a crowded bus.

■ Don't let your purse just dangle from your shoulder; always hold on to it with your hand for added security.

■ Keep car windows rolled up and car doors locked at all times in cities.

■ Park in designated parking lots, or if that's not possible, accept the offer of the *guachimán* (a term adopted from English, pronounced "watchie man")—men or boys who watch your car while you're gone. Give them the equivalent of a dollar per hour when you return.

■ Never leave valuables visible in a car, even in an attended parking lot.

■ Padlock your luggage.

■ Talk with locals or your hotel staff about crime in the area. Never walk in a narrow space between a building and a car parked on the street close to it, a prime hiding spot for thieves. Never leave a drink unattended in a club or bar: scams involving date-rape drugs have been reported in the past few years, targeting both men and women.

■ Never leave your belongings unattended anywhere, including at the beach or in a tent.

■ If your hotel room has a safe, use it, even if there's an extra charge. If your room doesn't have one, ask the manager to put your valuables in the hotel safe and ask him or her to sign a list of what you are storing there.

■ If you are involved in an altercation with a mugger, immediately surrender your possessions and walk away quickly.

Scams are common in San José, where a drug addict may tell tales of having recently been robbed, then ask you for donations; a distraction artist might squirt you with something, or spill something on you, then try to clean you off while his partner steals your backpack; and pickpockets and bag slashers work buses and crowds. To top it all off, car theft is rampant. Beware of anyone who seems overly friendly, aggressively helpful, or disrespectful of your personal space. Be particularly vigilant around the Coca-Cola bus terminal, one of the rougher areas but a central tourism hub.

Don't believe taxi drivers when they say the hotel is closed, unless you've personally gotten out and checked it yourself. Many want to take you somewhere else to earn a commission. If a taxi driver says he does not have change and the amount is substantial, ask him to drive to a store or gas station where you can get change. This might be enough to prompt him to suddenly "find" the difference to give you. Avoid paying with large bills to prevent this.

A number of tourists have been hit with the slashed-tire scam: someone punctures the tires of your rental car (often right at the airport, when you arrive) and then comes to your "aid" when you pull off to the side of the road and robs you blind. Forget about the rims: always drive to the nearest open gas station or service center if you get a flat.

Lone women travelers will get a fair amount of attention from men; to avoid hassles, avoid wearing short shorts or skirts. On the bus, try to take a seat next to a woman. Women should not walk alone in San José at night or venture into dangerous areas of the city at all. Ask at your hotel which neighborhoods to avoid. Ignore unwanted comments. If you are being harassed on a bus, at a restaurant, or in some other public place, tell the manager. In taxis, sit in the backseat. If you want to fend off an earnest but decent admirer in a bar, you can politely say, *"Por favor, necesito un tiempo a solas"* (I'd like some time on my own, please). Stronger is *"Por favor, no me moleste"* (Please, stop bothering me), and for real pests the simple *"Váyase!"* (Go away!) is usually effective.

▌ TAXES

The airport departure tax for tourists is $28, payable in cash (dollars or colones) or with Visa. (Paying the tax via credit card means the transaction will be processed as a cash advance and incur additional fees.) All Costa Rican businesses charge a 13% sales tax. Hotels charge a 16.4% fee covering service and tax. Restaurants add 13% tax and 10% service fee to meals. Tourists are not refunded for taxes paid in Costa Rica.

▌ TIME

Costa Rica does not observe daylight saving time, so from November to March it's the equivalent of Central Time in the United States (one hour behind New York). The rest of the year, it is the equivalent of Mountain Time in the United States (two hours behind New York).

Time Zones Timeanddate.com
⊕ www.timeanddate.com/worldclock.

▋ TIPPING

Bellhop	$1–$5 per bag, depending on the level of the hotel
Hotel Concierge	$5 or more, if he or she performs a service for you
Hotel Doorman	$1–$2 if he helps you get a cab
Hotel Maid	$1–$3 a day (either daily or at the end of your stay, in cash)
Hotel Room-Service Waiter	$1–$2 per delivery, even if a service charge has been added
Tour Guide	$10 per day
Waiter	10%–15%, with 15% being the norm at high-end restaurants; nothing additional if a service charge is added to the bill

Restroom attendants in more expensive restaurants expect some small change or $1. Tip coat-check personnel at least $1–$2 per item checked unless there is a fee, then nothing.

Costa Rica doesn't have a tipping culture, but positive reinforcement goes a long way to fostering a culture of good service; good intentions are usually there, but execution can be hit-and-miss. Tip only for good service. ■ TIP➜ Tipping in colones always makes it easier logistically for the recipient; never use U.S. coins to tip, because there is no way for locals to exchange them.

Taxi drivers aren't tipped, but it's common courtesy to leave an extra 200–300 colones if they've helped you navigate a complicated set of directions, or 500 colones if they've helped you with luggage. Chambermaids get 1,000 to 1,500 colones per day; for great service try to leave up to 10% of your room bill. Concierges are usually not tipped. Room-service waiters should be tipped about 500 colones, as should bellhops (more in the most expensive hotels).

Restaurant bills include a 13% tax and 10% service charge—sometimes these

amounts are included in prices on the menu, and sometimes they aren't. If the menu doesn't indicate whether service is included, ask. An additional gratuity is not expected, especially in cheap restaurants, but people often leave something extra when service is good. Leave a tip of about 200 colones per drink for bartenders, too.

At some point on a trip, most visitors to Costa Rica are in the care of a naturalist guide, who can show them the sloths and special hiking trails they'd never find on their own. Give $10 (or 5,000 colones) per day per person to guides if they've transported and guided you individually or in small groups, and about 10% of the rental to a hired driver of a small car. Give less to guides or drivers on bigger tours. For tour guides, it's okay to pay with U.S. dollars.

▋ TOURS

BIKING

Costa Rica is mountainous and rough around the edges. It's a rare bird that attempts a road-biking tour here. But the payoff for the ungroomed, tire-munching terrain is uncrowded, wildly beautiful off-road routes. Most bike-tour operators want to make sure you're in moderately good shape and do some biking at home. Others, such as Coast to Coast Adventures, have easier one- and two-day jaunts. Lava Tours offers great expert- and intermediate-level riding, as well as "gravity-assisted" (cruising down the paved road from Poás Volcano, for example) trips. Bike Arenal has biking packages in the Arenal area for all skill levels, with short and long ride options for each day. Operators generally provide top-notch equipment, including bikes and helmets, but welcome serious bikers who bring their own ride. Leave the hybrids at home—this is mountain-biking territory. Operators usually meet you at the airport and take care of all logistics. All companies can design custom tours for extreme cyclists if requested.

Useful topographical maps (not biking maps per se) are generally provided as part of the tour, and include unpaved roads. If you're striking out on your own, these maps can usually be found at downtown San José's Lehmann bookstore for about $5. Some basic Spanish is highly recommended if you're going to do it yourself.

■ TIP➔ **Check with individual airlines about bike-packing requirements and blackouts.** Cardboard bike boxes can be found at bike shops for about $15; more secure options start at $40. International travelers often can substitute a bike for a piece of checked luggage at no charge (if the box conforms to regular baggage dimensions), but U.S. airlines will sometimes charge a $100 to $200 handling fee each way.

■ TIP➔ **Most airlines accommodate bikes as luggage, provided they're dismantled and boxed.**

Contacts Bike Arenal ☎ 2479–7150, 866/465–4114 in North America ⊕ www.bikearenal.com. **Coast to Coast Adventures** ☎ 2280–8054 in Costa Rica ⊕ www.coasttocoastadventures.com. **Lava Tours** ☎ 2281–2458, 888/862–2424 in North America ⊕ www.lava-tours.com.

BIRD-WATCHING

You will almost definitely get more out of your time in Costa Rica by taking a tour rather than trying to find birds on your own. Bring your own binoculars but don't worry about a spotting scope; if you go with a tour company that specializes in birding tours, your guide will have one. Expect to see about 300 species during a weeklong tour. Many U.S. travel companies that offer bird-watching tours subcontract with the Costa Rican tour operators listed here. By arranging your tour directly with the Costa Rican companies, you avoid the middle person and save money. Selva Mar, a tour agency specializing in the Southern Zone, runs comprehensive tours through Birding Escapes Costa Rica.

Contacts Birding Escapes Costa Rica ☎ 2771–4582 in Costa Rica ⊕ www.birdwatchingcostarica.com. **Costa Rica Expeditions** ☎ 2521–6099 in Costa Rica ⊕ www.costaricaexpeditions.com. **Horizontes Nature Tours** ☎ 2222–2022 in Costa Rica ⊕ www.horizontes.com.

DIVING

Costa Rica's Cocos Island—one of the best dive spots in the world—can be visited only on a 10-day scuba safari with *Aggressor* or *Undersea Hunter*. But Guanacaste, the South Pacific, and to a lesser extent, the Caribbean, offer some respectable underwater adventures. Bill Beard's Costa Rica in the Gulf of Papagayo, Guanacaste, is a diving-tour pioneer and has countrywide options. Diving Safaris, in Playa Hermosa, has trips to dive sites in Guanacaste. In the South Pacific, Costa Rica Adventure Divers in Drake Bay arranges five-night trips. In this same area, Caño Island is a good alternative if you can't afford the money or time for Cocos Island, particularly in the rainy season, when dive sites closer to shore are clouded by river runoff.

Contacts Aggressor ☎ 800/348–2628 in North America ⊕ www.aggressor.com. **Bill Beard's Costa Rica** ☎ 877/853–0538 in North America ⊕ www.billbeardcostarica.com. **Costa Rica Adventure Divers** ☎ 2231–5806, 866/553–7073 in North America ⊕ www.costaricadiving.com. **Costa Rica Diving Safaris** ☎ 2672–1259 in Costa Rica ⊕ www.costaricadiving.net. **Undersea Hunter** ☎ 2228–6613, 800/203–2120 in North America ⊕ www.underseahunter.com.

FISHING

If fishing is your primary objective in Costa Rica, you are better off booking a package. During peak season you may not even be able to find a hotel room in the hot fishing spots, let alone one of the top boats and skippers. If you're less of a planner, some Fodor's readers say they've had good luck hanging out at "fish bars" in popular areas and asking around for recommendations. The major fish populations move along the Pacific coast through the year, and tarpon and snook fishing on the Caribbean is subject to the vagaries of seasonal wind and weather, but viable year-round. San José–based Costa Rica Outdoors has been in business since 1995, arranging fishing packages; it is one of the best bets for full service and honest advice about where to go, and works with the widest range of operators around the country. More than 100 outfits have high-quality, regionally based services. Anglers in the know recommend Kingfisher Sportfishing in Playa Carrillo, Guanacaste; Bluefin Sportfishing and J.P. Sportfishing Tours in Quepos; The Zancudo Lodge near Golfito; and Río Colorado Lodge on the northern Caribbean coast.

Contacts Bluefin Sportfishing ☎ *2777–0000 in Costa Rica* ⊕ *www.bluefinsportfishing. com.* **Costa Rica Outdoors** ☎ *2231–0306, 800/308–3394 in North America* ⊕ *www. costaricaoutdoors.com.* **J.P. Sportfishing Tours** ☎ *2244–6361, 866/620–4188 in U.S.* ⊕ *www.jpsportfishing.com.* **Kingfisher Sportfishing** ☎ *2656–0091 in Costa Rica* ⊕ *www. costaricabillfishing.com.* **Río Colorado Lodge** ☎ *2232–4063, 800/243–9777 in North America* ⊕ *www.riocoloradolodge.com.* **The Zancudo Lodge** ☎ *2776–0008, 800/854–8791 in North America* ⊕ *www.thezancudolodge.com.*

GOLF

Putting on a green against a dramatic Pacific backdrop isn't the first image that springs to mind for Costa Rican vacations, but the increase in luxury resorts and upscale tourism has created a respectable, albeit small, golfing circuit in the Central Valley and along the Pacific coast. Most packages maximize links time with side excursions to explore the country's natural riches. Costa Rica Golf Adventures organizes multiday tours at four- and five-star lodgings.

Contacts Costa Rica Golf Adventures ☎ *888/672–2057 in North America* ⊕ *www.golfcr.com.*

HIKING

Most nature-tour companies include hiking as part of their itineraries, but these hikes may be short and not strenuous enough for serious hikers. Let the tour operator know what you expect from a hike. Ask many questions about hike lengths and difficulty levels before booking the tour or you may be disappointed with the amount of time you get to spend on the trails. The following companies cater to both moderate and serious hikers.

Contacts Gap Adventures ☎ *888/800–4100 in North America* ⊕ *www.gapadventures.com.* **Serendipity Adventures** ☎ *888/226–5050 in North America, 2558–1000 in Costa Rica* ⊕ *www.serendipityadventures.com.*

SURFING

Most Costa Rican travel agencies and tour companies have packages that ferry both veteran and would-be cowboys (and cowgirls) of the ocean to and between the country's famed bicoastal breaks. Local experts at Surf Costa Rica really know their stuff, and offer standard or custom packages. Del Mar Surf Camp on the Pacific specializes in women-only surf lessons and packages. Learn how to surf, camp on the beach, and delve into personal development on Outward Bound Costa Rica's weeklong adult surf journeys.

Contacts Del Mar Surf Camp ☎ *2643–3197 in Costa Rica, 2682–1433 in Costa Rica, 855/833–5627 in North America* ⊕ *www. costaricasurfingchicas.com.* **Outward Bound Costa Rica** ☎ *2278–6062 in Costa Rica, 800/676–2018 in North America* ⊕ *www. crrobs.org.* **Surf Costa Rica** ☎ *866/502–0817 in North America* ⊕ *www.surf-costarica.com.*

SPANISH-LANGUAGE PROGRAMS

Thousands of people travel to Costa Rica every year to study Spanish. Dozens of schools in and around San José offer professional instruction and homestays, and there are several smaller schools outside the capital. Conversa has schools off Paseo Colón, and in Santa Ana, west of the capital, offering hourly classes as well as a "Super Intense" program (5½ hours per day). On the east side of town, ILISA provides cultural immersion in San Pedro. Mesoamérica is a low-cost language school that is part of a non-profit organization devoted to peace and social justice. La Escuela D'Amore is in beautiful Manuel Antonio. Language programs at the Institute for Central American Development Studies include optional academic seminars in English about Central America's political, social, and economic conditions.

Contacts Conversa ☎ 2203–2071, 888/669–1664 in North America ⊕ www.conversa.com. **ILISA** ☎ 2280–0700, 800/454–7248 in North America ⊕ www.ilisa.com. **Institute for Central American Development Studies** (*ICADS*). ☎ 2225–0508 in Costa Rica ⊕ www.icads.org. **La Escuela D'Amore** ☎ 2777–1143, 800/261–3203 in North America ⊕ www.edcostarica. com. **Mesoamérica** ☎ 2253–3195 in Costa Rica ⊕ www.mesoamericaonline.net.

VOLUNTEER PROGRAMS

In recent years more and more Costa Ricans have realized the need to preserve their country's precious biodiversity. Both Ticos and far-flung environmentalists have founded volunteer and educational concerns to this end.

Volunteer opportunities span a range of diverse interests. You can tag sea turtles as part of a research project, build trails in a national park, or volunteer at an orphanage. Many of the organizations require at least rudimentary Spanish. Most of the programs for volunteers who don't speak Spanish charge a daily fee for room and board. The **Sea Turtle Conservancy** is devoted to the preservation of sea turtles. **Earthwatch Institute** leads science-based trips studying monkeys, turtles, or the rain forest. The **Talamancan Association of Ecotourism and Conservation** (ATEC), as well as designing short group and individual outings centered on Costa Rican wildlife and indigenous culture, keeps an updated list of up to 30 local organizations that welcome volunteers.

FODORS.COM CONNECTION

Before your trip, be sure to check out what other travelers are saying in Talk on ⊕ www.fodors.com.

Beach cleanups, recycling, and some wildlife projects don't require proficiency in Spanish. The **Costa Rican Humanitarian Foundation** has volunteer opportunities with indigenous communities, women, community-based clinics, and education centers. They also organize homestays.

The **Institute for Central American Development Studies** (ICADS) is a nonprofit social justice institute that runs a language school and arranges internships and field study (college credit is available); some programs are available only to college students. ICADS can also place students with local social service organizations, environmental groups, and other organizations, depending on interests.

Contacts Costa Rican Humanitarian Foundation (*Fundación Humanitaria*). ☎ 2282–6358 in Costa Rica ⊕ www.crhf.org. **Earthwatch Institute** ☎ 978/461–0081, 800/776–0188 in North America ⊕ www.earthwatch.org. **Institute for Central American Development Studies** (*ICADS*). ☎ 2225–0508 in Costa Rica ⊕ www.icads.org. **Sea Turtle Conservancy** ☎ 800/678–7853, 352/373–6441 in North America ⊕ www.conserveturtles.org. **Talamancan Association of Ecotourism and Conservation** (ATEC) ☎ 2750–0398 in Costa Rica ⊕ www.ateccr.org.

▌ VISITOR INFORMATION

The official tourism board, the Instituto Costarricense de Turismo (ICT), has a small desk in the baggage claim area at Juan Santamaría airport. It contains a few brochures but is staffed only sporadically. Visitor information is provided by the Costa Rica Tourist Board in the United States.

**Contacts Instituto Costarricense de Tur-
ismo** (*ICT*). ☎ *2299–5800, 866/267–8274
in North America* ⊕ *www.visitcostarica.com*
✉ *Aeropuerto Internacional Juan Santamaría*
☎ *2437–2400.*

ONLINE TRAVEL TOOLS

InfoCostaRica has a website with good
cultural info, and chat rooms. **Horizontes** is
a tour operator that offers nature vacations
but also has extensive information on Costa
Rica and sustainable tourism on its website.
The **U.S. Embassy**'s comprehensive site has
health information, travel warnings, lists of
doctors and dentists, and much more. **The
REAL Costa Rica** slips in a bit of attitude with
its information, and is a bit lax on updating,
but scores high marks for overall accuracy.
Scope out detailed maps, driving distances,
and pictorial guides to the locations of hotels
and businesses in some communities at
CostaRicaMap.com. The **Association of
Residents of Costa Rica** online forums are
some of the region's most active and informed,
with topics ranging from business and pleasure
trips to the real-estate market.

**Contacts Association of Residents of Costa
Rica** ⊕ *www.arcr.net.* **Costa Rica.com**
⊕ *www.costarica.com.* **Horizontes**
⊕ *www.horizontes.com.* **InfoCostaRica**
⊕ *www.infocostarica.com.* **The REAL Costa
Rica** ⊕ *www.therealcostarica.com.*

INDEX

PHOTO CREDITS

ABOUT OUR WRITERS

World traveler and seasoned journalist Dorothy MacKinnon arrived in Costa Rica in 1999, promptly fell in love with the country, and took up a post in San José contributing stories to the *Tico Times* on dining out and ecotourism. Along the way, she has learned passable Spanish, and become a passionate birder (she used to be president of the Birding Club of Costa Rica) and enthusiastic nature lover. After seven years of city life in *el puro centro de San José*, she now lives in the cool, peaceful hills above Heredia. In her past life, she was a feature writer and copy editor for the *Financial Post* in Canada and the *Washington Post*. This year Dorothy updated the North Pacific and South Pacific chapters, as well as sections of the Central Valley chapter.

San José–based freelance writer and pharmacist Jeffrey Van Fleet has spent the the better part of the last two decades enjoying Costa Rica's long rainy seasons and Wisconsin's cold winters. (Most people would try to do it the other way around.)

He saw his first resplendent quetzal, that bird-watcher's Holy Grail, while researching this guide. Jeff is a regular contributor to Costa Rica's English-language newspaper, *The Tico Times*, and has written for United Airlines' inflight magazine *Hemispheres*. He has contributed to Fodor's guides to Guatemala, Honduras, Panama, Chile, Argentina, Peru, Los Cabos & Baja, Mexico, and Central and South America. For all the fun and exciting travel around Latin America that the guidebook work offers, he always appreciates coming back home to Costa Rica.

Special thanks to the following writers for their contributions to this edition:

Leland Baxter-Neal contributed to the Biodiversity chapter; Gillian Gillers wrote the Scuba Diving and Snorkeling feature; Liz Goodwin contributed the Sportfishing article; and Holly Sonneland lent her expertise to the Last-Minute Souvenirs piece.